STRUCTURAL ADJUSTMENT AND ECONOMIC PERFORMANCE

ORGANISATION FOR ECONOMIC CO-OPERATION AND DEVELOPMENT

Pursuant to article 1 of the Convention signed in Paris on 14th December, 1960, and which came into force on 30th September, 1961, the Organisation for Economic Co-operation and Development (OECD) shall promote policies designed:

- to achieve the highest sustainable economic growth and employment and a rising standard of living in Member countries, while maintaining financial stability, and thus to contribute to the development of the world economy;
- to contribute to sound economic expansion in Member as well as non-member countries in the process of economic development; and
- to contribute to the expansion of world trade on a multilateral, non-discriminatory basis in accordance with international obligations.

The original Member countries of the OECD are Austria, Belgium, Canada, Denmark, France, the Federal Republic of Germany, Greece, Iceland, Ireland, Italy, Luxembourg, the Netherlands, Norway, Portugal, Spain, Sweden, Switzerland, Turkey, the United Kingdom and the United States. The following countries became Members subsequently through accession at the dates indicated hereafter: Japan (28th April, 1964), Finland (28th January, 1969), Australia (7th June, 1971) and New Zealand (29th May, 1973).

The Socialist Federal Republic of Yugoslavia takes part in some of the work of the OECD (agreement of 28th October, 1961).

Publié en français sous le titre :

AJUSTEMENT STRUCTUREL
ET
PERFORMANCE DE L'ÉCONOMIE

This study has been made available to the public on the responsibility of the Secretary-General of the OECD. The data and analysis presented were prepared for the May, 1987 meeting of the OECD Council at Ministerial level, and the text was finalised in July 1987.

SUMMARY TABLE OF CONTENTS

TABLE OF CONTENTS

SYNTHESIS

INTRODUCTION

TECHNICAL REPORT
I. THE SUPPLY AND ALLOCATION OF FACTORS OF PRODUCTION

II. THE OPERATION OF PRODUCT MARKETS

Chapter 5

AGRICULTURE

Chapter 6

STRUCTURAL ADJUSTMENT IN INDUSTRY

Chapter 7

WORLD TRADE

III. EFFICIENCY AND EFFECTIVENESS IN THE PUBLIC SECTOR

LIST OF TABLES

9

LIST OF GRAPHS

SYNTHESIS

INTRODUCTION

Economic circumstances are in many respects more favourable to strong growth in the OECD area now than at any time in the recent past. The abatement of inflation and the substantial decline in prices of internationally traded energy and raw materials have created renewed room for increasing incomes and creating jobs. Rapid technological progress has made possible a wide range of new products and processes, while a decade of far-reaching structural change in industry has rendered many firms more efficient. Yet the OECD economies' response to these opportunities, though uneven, remains largely sluggish and falls well short of earlier expectations.

The gap between outcomes and expectations

A shortfall of economic performance relative not only to what was desired but also to what had earlier been thought feasible and even likely, has been an enduring feature of the last fifteen years. In the early 1970s, most observers – including the OECD – confidently expected the decade which lay ahead to yield output growth even more rapid and sustained than that which had characterised the 1960s. Again, in 1977, a special study by the OECD concluded that the poor showing of recent years was likely to be only temporary, and that a return to strong growth was possible and indeed probable. Most recently, improvements in the OECD area's terms of trade have only slowly been translated into gains in income and employment.

The gap between outcomes and expectations has partly reflected developments over which policy makers in the OECD area have little control – most obviously the successive oil price increases which precipitated the sharp recessions of 1974-75 and 1980-81. But the importance of the external shocks should not be exaggerated; for while they doubtless worsened and generalised the deterioration in performance, there were earlier signs of a sharp falling off in employment expansion, notably in Europe, and (though the evidence is more mixed in this respect) of a slowing in the rate of growth of productivity. Moreover, developments outside the OECD area cannot account for the persistence of poorer performance, and for the disappointing response when external factors turned broadly favourable. Nor can the external shocks explain the differences in individual OECD economies' response – differences most starkly visible in the behaviour of employment, but also evident in output trends and inflation.

Rather, the sources of the broader deterioration and of the national differences must be sought primarily within the OECD economies: in factors which limited individual capabilities and collective outcomes.

The impact of structural constraints

Though their precise impact is difficult to gauge, it cannot be doubted that macroeconomic policies played an important role. With hindsight, it can be argued that policies in the early 1970s were too expansionary, and in the 1980s possibly contractionary for too long; and inconsistencies between the policies pursued in different countries clearly created imbalances which made good performance harder to sustain. Yet those who had decisions to make did not have the luxury of hindsight to draw on; and the policies put in place reflected perceptions of what could be achieved, and of how rapidly individual economies could grow before running into internal and external constraints. It may be that at times the perceptions were mistaken – or poorly translated

15

into effective policy, especially at an international level; but this does not detract from the fact that the task of macroeconomic policy making would have been considerably easier had economies and indeed electorates been more responsive to changing realities – had wage and price inflation been controllable at a lower cost in foregone output and lost jobs, had firms and workers identified promising activities sooner and moved more readily from those in decline, and had expectations of public action and public action itself (and hence outlays) adjusted more quickly to new constraints.

These factors are eminently structural. They refer to the capacity of economies, institutions and societies in general to adjust to changing circumstances, to create and exploit new opportunities, and on that basis deploy and redeploy resources. It is not possible to put a number on this capacity; and its relation to macroeconomic performance is clearly one of interaction, rather than mechanical causation. Yet it seems reasonable to believe that this capacity was strong and contributed to the rapid growth of the first postwar decades; but then weakened as growth peaked. But why might this capacity have declined? And, even more importantly, how can it be restored?

Reviewing the role of government

These questions are at the centre of this report. Its primary concern is with the structural features of national economies – the supply and allocation of factors of production, the market for goods and services, and the taxing, spending and regulatory functions of the public sector – and with the flows of international trade and investment. Though increasingly recognised, the role of these microeconomic processes in shaping aggregate performance has not been adequately taken into account in the overall framing of economic policy; and analysis of this role and its policy implications is complicated by the almost bewildering range and diversity of issues involved.

This report seeks to pull these threads together. Drawing on the Secretariat's *Technical Report on Structural Adjustment and Economic Performance* (where the supporting analysis and data can be found), it examines broad trends in the structural components of the OECD economies, the effects which microeconomic policies have had on each of these, and the implications for economic performance; and it advances recommendations for policy reform: for how policies could be reoriented to best contribute to the goal of job-creating, non-inflationary growth.

The issues dealt with centre on the policies of governments and their effects on efficiency. The role of government in society needs to be regularly reviewed; it is only natural that the balance between the public and private sector, and indeed the interplay of public action and private initiative, be adapted to changing circumstances. If the public sector has acquired great weight in modern societies it is because the demands to which it responds have been so strong; but this makes all the greater the importance of enhancing the efficiency and effectiveness of public policy – in its conception, administration and implementation.

The changes required will of course vary from country to country, in line with differing traditions and circumstances. Yet these differences, though they make particularly hazardous the generalisations inevitable in a report such as this one, do not detract from the general trend – a trend to review more critically policies long taken for granted or considered too difficult to change; a greater willingness to recognise that public policy is likely to be most effective when it is mindful of the limits to what can be done; an acceptance that even the best intentioned policies may produce perverse outcomes as contexts and aspirations change.

The task of assessing the areas where policy reform is most urgent and desirable can only be manageable if the topics to be covered are clearly set out. This report does not pretend to be encyclopaedic; and two broad issue areas which fall outside its terms of reference are worth special mention.

To begin with, the report, and the studies on which it is based, deal only with the OECD Member countries. Nonetheless, it seems reasonable to suppose that many of the policies advocated in this report have broader applicability.

Secondly, the report concentrates on microeconomic policies. This is not to deny the importance of macroeconomic policy, nor to play down the interactions between the decisions and conduct of individual economic agents and the broader monetary and fiscal framework. But in the day-to-day pressures of economic policy making, there is a constant danger that the longer-term evolution of economic structures will be neglected; and that the very diversity of these structures, and the range of policies which act on them, will hinder the development of a consistent and overall view.

The report begins by examining the microeconomic aspects of postwar economic growth. It concentrates on the factors that contributed to the outstanding performance of the 1950s and 1960s, but that waned in later years, at least partly because of the effects of public policies; and examines the differing ways in which the OECD economies responded to the slowing of growth (Part I). It then sets out a programme for the reform of microeconomic policy across a broad range of areas, with the objective of facilitating sustainable growth (Part II). Finally, it examines the relations between the reform of microeconomic policy and broader social and economic goals (Part III).

I. STRUCTURAL FACTORS AND ECONOMIC GROWTH

From 1950 to the first oil price shock in 1973, real GDP in the OECD area increased by an average of nearly 5 per cent a year, two and a half times more rapidly than in the four preceding decades and approximately twice as rapidly as in the years from the oil price shock to today. A number of microeconomic factors bolstered this performance (*Section A*) – factors which either eventually ceased to operate, or came to operate less fully (*Section B*). The consequent deterioration in economic performance was associated with quite differing patterns of structural change within the OECD area; but each of these patterns contained an important element of unsustainability, increasing the adjustment burden the OECD economies will need to face in coming years (*Section C*).

A. THE MAIN SOURCES OF STRONG GROWTH

Over the longer term, economic growth arises from the interplay of *incentives* and *capabilities*. The capabilities define the best that can be achieved; while the incentives guide the use of the capabilities and, indeed, stimulate their expansion, renewal or disappearance. In the advanced economies, the capabilities refer primarily to the supplies of human capital, of savings and of the existing capital stock, as well as to the technical and organisational skills required for their use; the incentives originate largely in product markets and are then more or less reflected in markets for factor supplies – thereby determining the efficiency with which capabilities are used. Both incentives and capabilities operate within an institutional framework: institutions set rules of the game, as well as directly intervening in the play; they act to alter capabilities and change incentives; and they can modify behaviour by changing attitudes and expectations.

Seen in this schematic perspective, the freeing of market incentives and the strengthening of capabilities were critical factors in the exceptionally strong growth of the first postwar decades. From the standpoint of today's world, it is difficult to realise the extent to which price signals had become distorted in the years between the two world wars; but three factors – which contributed to the poor performance of the 1920s and 1930s,

and the reversal of which was a key element in postwar growth – stand out.

The first – and in many respects the most significant – was the persistence of far-reaching barriers to trade after the end of the First World War, and their further rapid spread in the late 1920s and then 1930s. By the eve of World War II, the ratio of international trade to world output had been halved from its previous peak; and much of the trade which took place occurred under state-to-state arrangements in which market forces played little role.

Secondly, the move to protectionism coincided with and indeed permitted the widespread cartelisation of domestic and international industry. In most European countries and Japan, domestic cartels, frequently mandated by national policy, controlled markets for products ranging from coal to cigarettes; and – though more difficult to organise and maintain – effective international cartels were at work in a wide span of world markets, including coal, steel and for some time rubber among the traditional industries and electrical products and chemicals among the new.

Finally, international capital flows – which had been of enormous significance in earlier years – became subject to a tightening web of private and public controls; so that foreign direct investment – a key vehicle for transferring technology and introducing new competition – declined from some 4-5 per cent of total world investment at the turn of the century, to well under 1 per cent.

Postwar reconstruction swept away many of these barriers. By the mid-1950s, the process of trade liberalisation was well in train, with quantitative restrictions largely removed and tariffs declining by some 10 percentage points on average. The formation of the European Economic Community, which in time became the world's largest common market, provided further impetus to the dynamic of market opening, a dynamic which largely culminated in the Kennedy round of multilateral trade negotiations. Liberalisation also extended to capital movements, and restrictions on foreign direct investment were substantially relaxed. More open trade, together with actual or potential entry of new competitors through foreign investment, heralded the end of domestic and international cartels – a process accelerated by the shift in many countries to more active competition policies.

Not only did these changes bring price signals more closely into line with world market opportunities; they also changed the realities of competition. This was partly because open markets drastically reduced the leeway any producer had to ignore change and postpone adjustment – for delay would bring the loss of market share and the threat of takeover or liquidation. But it was also because liberalisation created powerful new incentives: incentives to build larger, more efficient plants, which could be exploited only through export sales; incentives to shift to more specialised products, justified by being able to serve demand in several countries at once; and incentives to invest in developing new products and processes, because the associated high fixed costs could be spread over the world market as a whole.

The response to these incentives was visible in the spectacular growth of world trade and in its changing composition. *Table S.1* sets out estimates of the ratio of imports to supplies of finished manufactures for thirteen OECD countries over the course of this century. This ratio, which in 1950 stood at less than half its previous

peak, trebled over the subsequent two decades. Much of this growth took place in industries characterised by significant economies of scale, pervasive product differentiation and/or far above average investment in research and development – industries whose combined share in OECD manufactured imports had by 1973 exceeded 60 per cent. At the same time, foreign direct investment was reshaping industrial structures, notably through the transfer to the European market of the technical and (perhaps most importantly) organisational know-how pioneered in the mass market of the United States – and it is worth recalling that throughout the late 1950s and early 1960s, United States firms were establishing subsidiaries in Europe (most frequently through takeover) at a rate exceeding one a day.

The links are difficult to quantify and probably impossible to prove. But it seems plausible to suppose that the need to adjust to international competition, and the high perceived returns from doing so, underpinned what perhaps most distinguished postwar growth from

Table S.1. **Import content of "supplies" of finished manufactures[1]**
1899-1985
Percentages

	Maizels[2]					Batchelor[2]		OECD estimates[3]			
								1971		1985	
	1899	1913	1950	1959	1963	1963	1971	A	B	A	B
United Kingdom[4]	16	17	4	6	7	9	16	12	16	29	36
France	12	13	7	6	12	12	19	17	19	27	34
Germany[5]	16	10	4	7	10	9	17	16	16	26	29[6]
Italy	11	14	8	8	13	13	15	12	16	20	27
United States	3	3	2	3	3	3	8	9	9	24	24
Japan	30	34	3	4	6	4	5	4	5	6	7
Total	9	8	3	4	6	6	11	10	11	21	23
Belgium/Luxembourg	26	24	14	15	24	25	34	43	46	55	62
Netherlands	—	—	33	33	39	35	44	40	46	55	62[6]
Norway	—	35	33	34	34	35	44	50	52	61	61
Sweden	8	14	12	17	17	18	22	37	35	46	47[6]
Canada[4]	20	23	16	20	18	22	32	37	36	45	45
Australia[4]	—	39	25	15	16	20	26	19	22	33	32
Total[7]	—	—	18	21	24	25	33	36	38	47	49
Total industrial[7]	—	10-11	5	6	8	8	14	14	15	25	27

1. "Supplies" are defined as gross value of production of non-food manufactures free of duplication, plus cif value of imports of finished manufactures (goods not normally subject to further processing). The figures of Maizels and Batchelor *et al.* were based on production data (value added) which were inflated by the ratio of net output to gross output (excluding taxation and items sold by one part of the manufacturing sector as inputs to another part), both valued at factor costs. The data on intra-manufacturing purchases and sales which are needed for computing this ratio were available only for a limited number of countries in individual years. Maizels based his calculations partly on the ratios which he had been able to compute for individual countries (mainly relating to the early 1950s) and partly on a "rule of thumb". Batchelor *et al.* used a regression based on the investment/output ratio to calculate gross output. (For a further exposition to the methodologies used, see Batchelor.) The OECD data for production are based on gross domestic product at market prices for total manufacturing, excluding food, beverages and tobacco (for the United Kingdom and Canada, gross domestic product for total manufacturing at factor costs) and are converted into dollars, using purchasing power parities and dollar exchange rates respectively. Import data are based on cif value of imports of "finished manufactures" which is a separate category in the Brussels Nomenclature and were converted to and calculated on the SITC (Rev. 1) basis. The import content ratio is based on current prices because volume data for production and imports of non-food finished manufactures, free of duplication, are not available.
2. 1955 prices.
3. Current prices; first column (A) conversion with purchasing power parities for GDP, and second column (B) conversion with dollar exchange rates.
4. For United Kingdom, Australia and Canada, gross domestic production of total manufactures for OECD estimates.
5. Federal Republic of Germany from 1950 on.
6. For Netherlands, Sweden and Germany, GDP for 1985 is calculated by the ratio non-food manufacturing/total manufacturing of the latest available year, since for 1985 no breakdown was available.
7. Australia is not included in totals for small and industrial in the figures from Maizels and Batchelor.
Source: Maizels, A., *Industrial Growth and World Trade,* Cambridge, Mass., 1963; Batchelor, R.A. *et al., Industrialisation and the Basis for Trade,* Cambridge, Mass., 1980; OECD, *National Accounts;* compatible trade and production data base.

the virtual stagnation of the inter-war years: the trebling in the rate of growth of the non-residential capital stock, with capital accumulation apparently being quickest in the sectors most exposed to world trade. Equally, the evidence (though again incomplete) suggests that it was in the export sectors that the greatest gains in productivity were made – gains which fed and sustained overall productivity growth that on average was more than twice as rapid as in the eight preceding decades. The experience of those OECD countries which retained relatively high levels of trade protection during the first two postwar decades – such as Australia, New Zealand and Spain – highlights these effects: for though their economic fortunes differed in important respects, they shared a uniform tendency for productivity growth to fall short of the area-wide average.

The extent of the response to enhanced incentives reflected partly the confidence that decision-makers in industry and finance could place in the resilience of the new market conditions – particularly in the field of international trade. The rapid spread of trade barriers in the inter-war period – generally on a discriminatory basis – had not only distorted relative prices; it had undermined firms' capacity to plan. Despite occasional setbacks, the continuing focus on liberalisation in the postwar years created a quite different climate for private decision making – a climate sustained by the GATT and the OEEC (subsequently the OECD), and by the phasing out of most quotas and the shift to the binding of tariffs (a move which made it costly for countries to withdraw tariff reductions). This ensured that individual firms' gains in efficiency would go rewarded through larger markets, lower unit costs and higher margins – so that the benefits which could be obtained from new investment would outweigh the risks.

But if investment, output and employment responded so strongly to the signals coming from domestic and international demand it was also because the capabilities – in terms of human, physical and technical capital – were there and could be mobilised through factor markets that were markedly more efficient than in earlier years.

The most obvious cases were technology and organisation. In the early 1950s, the gap between the United States and the other advanced economies in the application of new technologies and organisational methods was large, as were the differences in capital stock. These were reflected in levels of industrial productivity (measured by GDP per manhour) in most countries that were less than half those in the United States. An enormous backlog of innovations existed that could be drawn on through acquisition, imitation or foreign investment as economies grew.

But capital and labour markets had also been reshaped. The efficient mobilisation of savings was facilitated first by the early postwar success in bringing inflation under control; and secondly by the recovery and extension of financial systems which had been weakened by the succession of internal instability, the shift to a war economy and the widespread rationing of credit during reconstruction. But once immediate reconstruction came to an end, the financial reforms of the late 1940s and early 1950s and the easing of credit rationing permitted significant financial innovation – in particular, the expansion of household credit, which helped fuel the rise in demand for consumer durables, notably cars, and in home ownership. And after 1958, currency convertibility rapidly revived international capital markets, which had largely collapsed in the early 1930s.

The changes in labour markets were even greater. Seen from an economic perspective, labour markets carry out both macro and micro functions. Their macroeconomic role consists of maintaining a balance between the average level of wages and economies' "capacity to pay" – in other words, of sustaining a sufficient level of profitability to finance the investment required to support high levels of employment and raise living standards. The microeconomic function involves allocating labour among competing uses and ensuring that it is efficiently utilised where it is employed. These functions are largely exercised through systems of industrial relations – that is, institutionalised procedures by which wages and the conditions of employment are set and work practices determined; and the functioning of these systems depends both on their internal structure and on the broader economic, social and indeed political environment – so that it is these which shape the quality of the outcomes. Overall, a well-functioning labour market, with low levels of unemployment and reasonable internal and external mobility, is conducive to sustained productivity growth and smooth structural change. The circumstances and developments of the first two postwar decades were largely favourable in these respects.

Following initial turbulence, industrial relations moved to a more settled pattern, broadly supportive of moderate wage growth and of improved labour utilisation. Especially in the Nordic countries, depression followed by war had encouraged a rationalisation and centralisation of bargaining structures, sustained by a broad social consensus about national economic and social goals. In other countries – Germany, Austria and Japan – free labour movements adjusted to the responsibilities and opportunities of economies rapidly emerging from a legacy of destruction. In yet others, internal divisions between unions and labour market constraints were the primary factors affecting collective bargaining.

At the same time, and virtually throughout the OECD area, domestic and international migration made labour not only abundant but mobile – facilitating the growth of new firms and industries. Between 1950 and 1973, there was net immigration of nearly 10 million people into Western Europe, compared with a net outflow of 4 million from 1914 to 1949. And meanwhile, the shift out of agriculture alone swelled the urban labour force in the OECD area by more than 15 per cent. Urbanisation not only changed life-styles and aspirations – it made for a labour force exposed to a broader range of employment opportunities, so that it became better able both to compare earnings and working conditions in different activities and to act on that information.

The willingness of workers to change regions, industries and firms not only reflected greater knowledge of what could be obtained – it must also have been shaped by the perception that the risks of change were, on balance, worth taking. The critical factor in this respect was the steady approach to full employment – a situation which, despite cyclical fluctuations, most European countries and Japan achieved by the early 1960s.

In this sense, microeconomic flexibility and macroeconomic performance were self-reinforcing: low unemployment facilitated both the widespread acceptance of technological and organisational change and the redeployment of labour; high levels of demand made investment in new plant and equipment easier to justify and to finance – as did the increases in market size brought by international economic integration. Together, labour mobility and buoyant investment raised productivity – leading to a rapid rise in living standards. This contained inflationary pressures in the labour markets; and these pressures were further eased by the opening of markets to international competition, whereby prices in world trade rose (over the period 1950-1973) at a rate only half that in domestic markets. This in turn made it possible for macroeconomic policy to permit or sustain high levels of demand – creating a climate of confidence which further increased the incentives to invest.

B. THE DETERIORATION IN ECONOMIC PERFORMANCE

Yet, by the end of the 1960s, these "virtuous circle" effects were operating less fully – and after 1973 hardly at all.

In retrospect, it is clear that many of the impediments to continued strong growth had developed during the period when performance was seemingly at its peak. The changes were partly macroeconomic in origin: the belief that aggregate demand policies could and would guarantee full employment may have lulled firms and workers into a false sense of security, slowing the adjustment to changing circumstances and accentuating inflationary wage and price increases. Repeated applications of stabilization policies, giving rise to alternating surges of inflation and episodes – however moderate – of recession, further confounded market signals and made a steady course of wage growth and capital formation yet more difficult to maintain. But governments and observers remained over-optimistic about what policies could achieve long after the first signs of a deterioration in performance; and this created strong pressures for a continued expansion of entitlements, the acceptance of restrictive measures in product and factor markets, and the extension of spending commitments well beyond the margin provided by economic growth. At the same time, complacency in the face of the emerging difficulties was compounded by shifts in attitudes, and in particular, by the belief that economic growth was not an entirely desirable goal of policy.

Yet the constraints on economic performance were becoming increasingly tight. They emerged first and proved most intractable in the wage-setting behaviour of labour markets – and notably in the weakened capacity of collective bargaining to generate wage settlements consistent with economies' aggregate capacity to pay.

This was partly because of exogenous factors reducing aggregate capacity to pay. After two decades of rapid growth, many European economies had largely exhausted the scope for raising productivity through "catching-up" with the United States; and by the mid-1970s, the same could be said of Japan. The room for absorbing wage increases through productivity gains was accordingly smaller; and strong pressures for an abatement of nominal wage growth also came from government concern at the trend rise in inflation. However, wage aspirations remained strong; and a slowing of nominal wage increases in the mid-1960s was followed by a wave of industrial militancy which placed great pressure on industrial relations systems in much of Europe, in Australia and (to a lesser extent) Japan. By the early 1970s, the unrest itself had calmed; but its legacy was a lasting one. This was most obviously so in the United Kingdom, France and Italy, where wages moved decisively out of line with national income. But elsewhere too, policy makers' perceptions had been affected and a perhaps exaggerated weight was given to the social and political risks involved in wage restraint.

The first oil shock came on top of this legacy. The initial reduction in oil supplies itself involved only a minor and temporary physical constraint on growth; but the price effects proved far more durable and substantial. Their direct impacts were to strengthen inflationary tendencies and – in most countries – to precipitate current account difficulties. Both these were manifestations of a loss in countries' real national income as a result of the worsening in their international terms of trade. The fundamental task was to absorb this income loss while maintaining a level of profitability and capital formation sufficient to preserve employment and allow industry to adjust to changed energy market conditions. And it is in this respect that labour market institutions, and notably the wage formation process, proved most wanting – though the difficulties proved far more acute in some countries than in others.

The second oil shock made these constraints more binding. Concern about a further acceleration in the wage-price spiral led monetary policies to a less accommodating stance, which succeeded in controlling inflation and in reducing the gap between the actual evolution of the wage share and the trend warranted by productivity developments; but notably in Europe, wage and price moderation was obtained at a high cost in lost jobs and foregone output.

The extent of these costs partly reflected a decline in the efficiency with which markets could respond to the new circumstances and absorb their consequences. In product markets, this decline was visible in the difficulties firms encountered in adjusting their operations to the new pattern of energy and labour costs and to shifting technological and commercial opportunities. Equally, in the factor markets, it was perhaps especially acute in the deepening segmentation of employment opportunities, though it was more broadly reflected in the lags with which capital and human resources were redeployed between uses. Finally, in the public sector, it was associated with the pursuit of courses of action which, though intended to ease the adjustment process, in fact made adjustment more difficult while imposing major burdens on the economy as a whole.

A loss in the efficiency of markets was partly the inevitable result of adverse macroeconomic trends – and here again the interaction of microeconomic behaviour and the macroeconomic context is worth stressing.

The macroeconomic circumstances of the years subsequent to the first oil shock were certainly not such as to make industry's task easier in responding to changing product market signals. By the early 1970s, firms in the OECD area were used to an environment of relatively steady growth – an environment where excess capacity was rapidly absorbed by the expansion of markets. Adjusting to persistently slower growth required a far-reaching reorientation in corporate planning and strategies; and this inevitably took several years. But macroeconomic policies did not always facilitate this reorientation by providing a stable, medium-term framework against which firms could set their bearings. Rather, in a first period, persistent inflation made changes in relative prices difficult to identify and emptied corporate accounting of much of its meaning. And as inflation abated, inconsistencies in policies internationally came even more to the fore and induced exchange rate movements which distorted patterns of competitiveness and introduced new and pervasive uncertainties.

At the same time, the macroeconomic context reduced the efficiency of factor markets. For much of the 1970s and early 1980s, monetary conditions were such that high inflation was associated with low real returns on financial assets, which distorted financial markets by encouraging the development of instruments whose primary attraction was in hedging against unexpected increases in the price level. Moreover, the provision of finance for private economic activity, and notably for business, was compromised by the growing financing needs of the public sector – needs which

became all the greater as monetary policy shifted to a more restrictive stance while fiscal policy did so more slowly or not at all.

Equally, the rise in unemployment itself altered the behaviour of labour markets. Workers naturally became more reluctant to leave their current job to seek another – so that labour mobility declined and with it the ease with which firms, industries and regions in difficulty could reduce employment. At the same time, high unemployment bred a defensive attitude to change – a greater resistance to adopting and adapting to new ways of doing things, even within the individual firm; a growing demand for action by governments and trade unions to slow the pace of adjustment.

Finally, the changes in macroeconomic trends widened the gap between earlier public sector spending and taxing commitments and what could realistically be achieved. Short of a major review of entitlements, certain public outlays had to rise – most obviously unemployment insurance, though there was also upward momentum in other areas of social expenditure. Given a continuing rise in expenditures, slower growth made some rise in the ratio of taxation to income inevitable (though many countries initially sought to postpone this by increasing public sector borrowing); and the virtually mechanical effect of inflation in systems of progressive income taxation, few of which were indexed, was to raise the marginal rates facing the average taxpayer and to shift the balance of fiscal systems towards a greater reliance on the taxation of personal incomes.

But important as the effects of the macroeconomic context doubtless were, the adverse impacts on the efficiency and responsiveness of markets would have been smaller had the stance of microeconomic policy been different – had microeconomic policy generally facilitated rather than hindered change. A wide range of policy instruments was involved; and the effects of each of these and the options for reform will be examined subsequently. But the broad feature of policies – in product markets, factor markets and the public sector – was to react to short-term problems rather than to contribute to long-term alternatives and to erode if not reverse the features which had made growth so strong in previous years.

To begin with, pervasive interventions in *product markets* both distorted the price signals facing firms and further undermined the predictability of the competitive environment. The changes were most striking in trade policy; for by the early 1970s, the postwar dynamic of trade liberalisation was largely spent. Exceptions to liberal trade had accumulated during the period of rapid growth; and despite some important gains in the Tokyo round, the onset of recession greatly aggravated the trend to protectionism. By 1983, non-tariff barriers affected some 27 per cent of the industrial countries' imports; and not only agriculture, but entire manufacturing sectors – including textiles and clothing, steel, shipbuilding and automobiles – had been largely removed from the ordinary discipline of the GATT.

Table S.2. **Cost of agricultural policy**

Some indicators of the level of cost related to the implementation of agricultural policy

Average 1979-1980-1981

| | Cost (billion ECU) | ECU/ha | ECU/per holding | ECU/per agric. worker | Compared with | | | ECU/total population |
					GDP %	GVA %	FVAP %	
United States	26.2	61.3	10 810	7 453	1.3	42.1	22.1	115
Canada	2.5	35.9	10 248	4 203	1.2	42.6	23.7	103
Australia	0.6	1.3	3 708	1 558	0.5	9.2	6.1	43
New Zealand	0.2	17.0	3 458	1 778	1.4	13.7	8.5	79
Japan	23.8	4 361.5	5 110	4 090	2.9	104.3	57.6	204
Austria	1.4	384.2	4 584	4 786	2.6	60.4	39.9	188
EEC	56.5	613.4	11 437	7 465	2.8	93.2	49.9	208

GDP   =   Gross domestic product at market prices.
GVA   =   Gross value added by agriculture at market prices.
FVAP =   Final value of agricultural production.
Note: The cost of agricultural policies is defined as the *sum* of public budgetary expenditures on agriculture (the "taxpayer costs") and of the subsidies to production financed by consumers (generally referred to as the "consumer costs"). This subsidy has been calculated using the method set out in Chapter 5 of the Technical Report, but in the case of commodities for which a country is less than self-sufficient the tariff or external/internal price differential has been applied to production rather than consumption because in such cases the burden imposed on consumers is greater than the corresponding subsidy given to production.
Source: Secretariat estimates.
Basis statistics   —   OECD, *National Accounts; Labour Force Statistics;* unpublished data on agricultural accounts.
                    —   FAO, *Production Yearbook,* 1983.
                    —   EEC, *The Agricultural Situation in the Community,* 1984.

The distorting effects of these changes in trade policy were compounded by policy measures in domestic markets. The highest points were reached in agriculture where, between 1979-81, the transfers to producers induced by agricultural policies were equivalent to 42 per cent of the sector's value added in the United States, 93 per cent in the EEC and over 100 per cent in Japan *(Table S.2).* Though not of this order of magnitude, industrial subsidies were also significant, as governments responded to pressures to assist firms, sectors and regions in difficulty, and became increasingly involved in promoting new areas of activity, frequently associated with high technology.

The effects of measures which distorted the signals and incentives coming from product markets were aggravated by policies which eroded the capability of *factor markets* to respond.

The trends in this respect were most pervasive in the microeconomic functioning of labour markets – that is, their function of allocating labour among competing uses. The problems were multi-dimensional; and they arose not only from government policies narrowly defined but also from the operations of collective bargaining and, indeed, of secular economic and social trends. However, three facets, primarily of relevance to Europe, are of particular importance.

First, from the early 1970s to the early 1980s, a fairly widespread compression of occupational and industrial wage differentials occurred as a result both of collective bargaining and of government policies. This aggravated the position of the weakest elements of the labour force – the unskilled young, the old, and those who had been without work for some time – in a context which, given rising overall unemployment, was in any case unfavour-able to them. The effects of shrinking wage differentials in terms of youth and long-term unemployment appear to have been quite limited in the countries where labour mobility has traditionally rested on an extensive system of vocational training, buttressed by active manpower policies; but they were acute in the countries where vocational education has a narrow base and large parts of the labour force have few certified skills – so that the wage spread has traditionally served to share the risks employers take in recruiting workers whose skills they cannot judge at the moment of hiring. Though wage differentials reopened somewhat in the early 1980s, significant damage had been done, the job prospects of many having been durably set back by the loss of work experience.

Second, particularly in the mid- to late 1970s, legislative and regulatory restrictions were imposed in a number of countries on retrenchments, notably in larger firms. Though these measures subsequently were eased, their legacy proved longer lasting, for several reasons. To begin with, they frequently served as a basis for clauses restricting redundancies in collective agreements, which typically remained in place even after the legislation had been loosened. Moreover, by the time the controls were relaxed, the financial viability of a number of firms had been so eroded that the scale of the required manpower reductions was much increased. And finally, while engendering an illusory sense of security among those with jobs, they may have contributed to creating a presumption in company management against employment expansion – an excessive caution in recruitment which not only increased the required real wage adjustments overall, but particularly penalised the weaker elements in the labour force.

23

Third, restrictive work practices – common in countries with a tradition of craft unionism, though especially far-reaching in unionised firms in the United States – clashed with a need for greater flexibility and mobility in firms' internal labour markets. In a few countries – for example, Italy – the trend in the 1970s was for restrictions on internal mobility actually to tighten; but even abstracting from a worsening in the restrictive practices themselves, in many countries long-established ways of organising work conflicted with the requirements both of new process and product technologies – which blurred the traditional distinctions between skills – with shortened product life times and with the increased instability of economic circumstances.

In short, changes in the microeconomic features of labour markets tended to segment employment opportunities, increase firms' difficulties in adjusting employment levels – not only downward but upward as well – and make the efficient use of labour within enterprises more costly to achieve.

Finally, further modifications in the efficiency of resource use arose from the growth of the *public sector*, both as an economic agent in its own right and as a pervasive influence on incentives in the economy as a whole. Several aspects of public sector growth were particularly significant.

In the first place, there was a sustained rise in both public provision and finance of social services, notably in the fields of health, education and welfare. As demand for these services grew, and with it their share in societies' total use of resources, the efficiency of their provision became progressively more important. But growth tended to outstrip the management capabilities of the organisations responsible for providing service; and as problems emerged, the institutional framework – the sheer size of the structures contributing – made efficiency increases difficult to obtain and hindered these services' adaptation to changing circumstances. At the same time, there was a tendency to expand entitlements and financial commitments more rapidly than resources – and to resolve the ensuing problems through administrative rationing and tighter budgetary constraints, rather than by reviewing the institutional arrangements involved.

It is difficult to assess whether the policies engendered broader losses by altering incentives to work or to save. The evidence in this respect is mixed, and there is certainly no simple correlation between economic performance and the scale of transfer payments – or indeed any other single indicator of the size of government. Where the incentive effects of transfer payments were most significant, this was a result of their interaction

Table S.3. **Total marginal and average tax rates on labour use at average production worker level**

Percentage of total compensation including payroll taxes

	Single worker				Single-earner married couple with two children			
	Marginal			Average	Marginal			Average
	1979	1981	1983	1983	1979	1981	1983	1983
Australia	44.37	43.49	42.31	35.85	44.37	43.49	42.31	31.01
Austria	60.63	64.14	63.99	42.44	60.63	64.14	63.99	40.64
Belgium	64.61	65.95	66.86	52.83	62.19	62.05	61.65	48.12
Canada	43.32	45.09	42.72	36.83	41.12	42.96	42.72	29.17
Denmark	68.49	69.04	71.24	57.33	68.49	69.04	71.24	53.41
Finland	63.13	63.08	62.48	48.25	63.13	63.08	62.48	44.03
France	66.92	66.67	68.77	51.74	57.47	57.15	59.70	47.57
Germany	61.13	60.53	60.91	41.31	56.81	56.44	57.02	36.62
Ireland	55.51	57.78	70.21	51.68	55.51	57.78	63.80	44.91
Italy	56.28	59.54	62.66	50.25	56.28	59.54	62.66	48.88
Japan	40.50	43.90	43.68	23.73	35.93	39.41	39.93	19.05
Luxembourg	62.36	63.15	67.21	42.70	47.60	48.68	50.61	32.56
Netherlands	66.75	68.97	73.47	39.16	66.75	68.97	73.47	37.51
New Zealand	43.86	54.32	40.31	36.29	43.86	54.32	35.50	31.98
Norway	72.54	70.52	69.47	54.89	65.91	67.01	63.00	50.36
Portugal	44.03	46.75	46.94	37.77	40.08	43.25	44.29	37.05
Spain	43.94	45.38	46.66	38.64	43.94	45.38	46.66	35.52
Sweden	74.42	73.47	73.02	62.85	74.42	73.47	73.02	61.67
Switzerland	44.42	44.15	42.16	27.00	40.48	42.20	40.21	22.61
United Kingdom	51.33	53.44	54.53	42.17	51.53	53.44	54.53	38.97
United States	47.12	52.87	48.63	34.83	40.19	45.20	42.64	28.21
Average (unweighted)								
OECD Europe	59.79	60.78	62.54	46.31	56.95	58.23	59.27	42.53
OECD Non-Europe	43.84	47.93	43.53	33.50	41.10	45.08	44.62	27.88
Total OECD	55.99	57.72	58.01	43.26	53.18	55.10	55.78	39.04

Note: The rates include payroll taxes, employer and employee contributions for social insurance, personal income taxes, and general consumption taxes and excise taxes.
Source: Secretariat estimates.

with the tax system; and it is through the concomitant rise in the burden of taxation that the growth of public spending probably imposed its greatest economic costs.

In particular, marginal and average tax rates in many countries became very high; on average in the OECD area, by 1983, a two-child, single-earner married couple earning the wages of an average production worker, had a tax liability equivalent to 40 per cent of its income, while facing a marginal tax rate of over 55 per cent *(Table S.3)*. As tax rates rose, tax systems became increasingly complex and in many cases discriminated quite arbitrarily between different persons and activities. High marginal tax rates in the labour market encouraged the spread of tax avoidance and tended to reduce the supply of labour, especially among the more highly paid, who faced the highest marginal tax rates, but also among the poor, for whom taxes in combination with decreased social payments often created high effective rates (sometimes known as a "poverty trap"). And the taxation of capital income, by imposing quite different rates on competing investment projects, distorted the allocation of investment resources among alternative uses.

The net result of the rise in taxation/GDP ratios was to increase the real resource cost of tax-funded government spending – that is, to increase the return required from this spending for its benefits to exceed the costs of financing it through the tax system. Few systematic studies of these effects are available and their magnitude is in any case likely to differ significantly from country to country; but estimates suggest that $1 raised through taxes may, at the margin, reduce national income by 10 to 15 cents and possibly considerably more, depending on the tax measures used, while the net overall cost of present tax systems could be in the order of 3 to 5 per cent of GNP. Yet – at least partly because of inflation – the need to monitor more carefully the quality of public outlays did not become apparent until the late 1970s, by which time a significant expansion of government commitments had occurred.

C. PATTERNS OF ECONOMIC, SOCIAL AND INSTITUTIONAL LINKAGES

In short, a broad range of microeconomic policies acted over the last decade in such a way as to reduce the efficiency of individual markets – and slow the recovery from internal and external shocks.

But while the broad tendency to deteriorating performance was strong, the shape it took differed from country to country; and the outcomes diverged too, as varying macroeconomic contexts modified the effects of trends and policies in the microeconomy.

The most striking macroeconomic disparities were in unemployment rates. *Graph S.1* sets out average unemployment rates for individual OECD countries, for 1973 and 1986; the relative volume of the shaded area for each country is proportional to its share of the OECD labour force – and hence to its contribution to the unemployment rate for the OECD area as a whole. It is clear from the data that the deterioration in area-wide employment performance was accompanied by a significant widening in the spread of unemployment rates, with the four larger European economies – Germany, France, the United Kingdom and Italy – accounting for fully 28 per cent of the rise in unemployment overall.

These disparities in macroeconomic outcomes were paralleled by significant differences in the pattern of resource use. *Tables S.4 and S.5*, which are based on national accounts data, present trends over the period 1970-83 in the sectoral distribution of output, employment and total factor productivity (a weighted index of the combined productivity of capital and labour) using two ways of aggregating sectors. The first – set out in *Table S.4* – classifies sectors into the three categories of high, medium or low growth according to their growth rates of value added relative to the average growth rate for all sectors. The second – set out in *Table S.5* – ranks sectors by degree of openness to international trade, the first grouping corresponding to the government sector, the second to market services, the third to the activities largely based on natural resources (such as agriculture or minerals) and the fourth to manufacturing.

The data presented in the bottom part of each table are normalized so as to single out the extent of structural change – that is, the change in the composition of domestic output relative to world output. This is done by expressing the data for each sector as the difference between the actual growth rate of that sector in a country (or group of countries) and the growth rate which could have been expected given that country's overall growth rate of value added and the growth rate of that sector across all countries. In other words, a positive value for a particular sector represents the average annual percentage amount by which that sector grew in a particular country above and beyond the growth warranted by that country's overall growth rate and the OECD-wide growth of the sector.

A general conclusion which emerges from the data is that demand trends did not differ significantly between countries. However, considerable differences occurred on the supply side – in the way individual economies responded to the opportunities arising from demand and technological trends.

The most marked differences were those between Japan, the United States and Europe, with the Nordic countries departing somewhat from the main European pattern. These differing outcomes reflected *interactions* between microeconomic and macroeconomic factors and between markets, institutions and broader economic, social and even cultural contexts. The complexity

Table S.4. Trends in output structure and resource use

Sectors ranked by growth rate of value added of all countries combined

Average annual growth rates for the period 1970 to 1983

	NOR	BEL	DNK	FIN	SWE	FRA	GER	ITA	UK	CAN	AUS	US	JPN	EU5	NORDIC	TOTAL
PERCENTAGE GROWTH RATES OF: VALUE ADDED (VOLUME)																
All sectors	3.03	2.55	2.30	3.48	1.99	2.99	2.30	2.28	1.15	3.21	2.73	2.59	4.66	2.29	2.51	2.82
Sectors with:																
Low growth	2.10	0.32	0.51	2.18	0.17	0.40	-0.05	1.13	-1.30	1.85	1.51	-0.13	1.32	0.23	0.90	0.43
Medium growth	4.16	3.35	4.24	4.35	2.82	2.79	2.45	2.41	1.46	2.42	2.19	2.09	4.10	2.35	3.59	2.54
High growth	2.76	2.87	2.12	3.89	2.10	4.18	2.99	2.86	1.76	4.40	3.34	3.38	6.06	3.06	2.51	3.68
TOTAL FACTOR PRODUCTIVITY																
All sectors	1.12	1.60	0.99	1.87	0.71	1.39	1.37	0.66	0.49	0.29	0.91	0.38	1.52	1.06	1.04	0.75
Sectors with:																
Low growth	1.91	2.48	0.97	2.22	1.37	1.29	1.57	1.61	0.28	0.16	1.57	-0.68	-0.23	1.35	1.60	0.38
Medium growth	1.41	2.34	1.34	1.52	0.18	1.52	1.29	0.70	1.24	-0.28	1.13	0.89	1.17	1.28	0.84	1.04
High growth	0.61	0.78	0.82	1.75	0.76	1.35	1.32	-0.03	0.17	0.77	0.54	0.41	2.26	0.80	0.89	0.85
CAPITAL STOCK																
All sectors	4.02	4.03	2.92	4.08	3.02	4.41	3.42	3.61	2.43	4.73	3.51	2.82	7.84	3.47	3.38	3.68
Sectors with:																
Low growth	4.59	2.25	3.36	3.75	3.52	2.98	1.26	2.95	1.86	4.63	1.88	2.75	6.81	2.27	3.77	3.37
Medium growth	4.36	3.45	2.81	3.98	2.86	3.75	3.22	3.19	1.79	4.61	2.73	2.30	8.30	3.07	3.30	3.30
High growth	3.71	4.69	2.89	4.26	3.05	5.06	3.91	4.00	2.74	4.82	4.35	3.15	7.84	3.90	3.35	3.94
EMPLOYMENT																
All sectors	0.74	-0.07	0.55	0.51	0.60	0.22	-0.44	0.43	-0.37	2.34	1.27	1.58	0.79	-0.07	0.59	0.82
Sectors with:																
Low growth	-1.68	-3.68	-2.97	-1.75	-2.97	-2.45	-2.84	-1.65	-2.85	0.54	-0.84	-0.18	-1.37	-2.41	-2.38	-1.49
Medium growth	2.26	0.80	3.40	2.77	3.01	0.81	0.86	1.76	0.18	2.23	0.39	0.75	0.94	0.79	2.95	0.96
High growth	1.04	1.05	0.20	1.05	0.36	1.55	0.17	1.69	0.13	3.17	2.39	2.36	1.95	0.77	0.56	1.76
Memorandum item																
Labour force	2.04	0.75	1.24	1.25	0.86	0.79	0.22	0.82	0.42	2.89	1.80	2.32	1.03	0.54	1.23	1.37
DIFFERENCE BETWEEN ACTUAL AND CALCULATED GROWTH RATES OF: VALUE ADDED (VOLUME)																
Sectors with:																
Low growth	1.39	0.25	-0.45	0.52	0.41	-0.14	0.08	0.82	0.18	0.75	1.10	-0.05	-0.86	0.25	0.44	—
Medium growth	1.28	0.99	2.26	0.77	1.13	-0.16	0.25	-0.03	0.56	-0.55	-0.28	-0.06	-0.33	0.17	1.33	—
High growth	-1.10	-0.57	-1.14	-0.85	-0.93	0.13	-0.14	-0.37	-0.35	0.04	-0.27	0.03	0.36	-0.17	-1.00	—

TOTAL FACTOR PRODUCTIVITY

Sectors with:															
Low growth	1.24	1.33	0.63	0.47	1.22	0.38	0.92	1.16	0.37	0.01	0.71	-0.48	-1.28	0.77	0.89	—
Medium growth	0.09	0.54	0.21	-0.45	-0.53	-0.16	-0.39	-0.24	0.46	-0.62	-0.29	0.30	-0.59	-0.07	-0.27	—
High growth	-0.57	-0.89	-0.36	-0.12	-0.20	-0.10	-0.16	-0.66	-0.35	0.44	-0.23	-0.02	0.62	-0.31	-0.29	—

CAPITAL STOCK

Sectors with:															
Low growth	0.94	-0.71	0.80	0.28	0.97	-0.52	-1.37	0.07	0.60	0.70	-0.92	0.58	-0.30	-0.40	0.73	—
Medium growth	0.60	-0.35	0.18	-0.05	0.09	-0.35	0.16	-0.16	-0.19	0.01	-0.60	-0.13	0.73	-0.11	0.18	—
High growth	-0.51	0.32	-0.24	-0.06	-0.21	0.27	0.14	0.05	-0.01	-0.17	0.55	0.02	-0.38	0.12	-0.25	—

EMPLOYMENT

Sectors with:															
Low growth	-0.38	-1.51	-1.52	-0.40	-1.64	-0.56	-0.61	-0.34	-0.18	0.65	0.16	0.82	0.04	-0.47	-1.03	—
Medium growth	1.19	0.71	2.59	1.66	2.05	0.14	0.94	0.45	0.44	-0.06	-0.27	-0.74	0.03	0.50	1.98	—
High growth	-0.59	0.16	-1.26	-0.94	-0.96	0.21	-0.20	0.03	-0.21	-0.19	0.01	0.13	-0.03	-0.05	-0.96	—

Source: Secretariat estimates.

27

Table S.5. **Trends in output structure and resource use**

Sectors ranked by openness to foreign competition

Average annual growth rates for the period 1970 to 1983

	NOR	BEL	DNK	FIN	SWE	FRA	GER	ITA	UK	CAN	AUS	US	JPN	EU5	NORDIC	TOTAL
PERCENTAGE GROWTH RATES OF: VALUE ADDED (VOLUME)																
All sectors	3.03	2.55	2.30	3.48	1.99	2.99	2.30	2.28	1.15	3.21	2.73	2.59	4.66	2.29	2.51	2.82
of which:																
Gov & Soc	4.84	3.88	3.92	4.09	3.03	3.08	3.47	2.68	1.89	2.40	3.74	2.17	3.78	2.95	3.66	2.73
Sheltered	3.26	2.03	1.23	3.75	2.04	3.26	2.52	1.94	1.86	4.09	2.93	2.93	4.84	2.49	2.38	3.10
Supply	2.17	1.20	2.90	1.30	0.76	0.97	0.21	1.59	-1.23	1.89	2.56	-0.83	1.30	0.62	1.55	0.43
Open	0.65	2.90	2.66	3.77	0.99	3.16	1.54	2.48	-0.06	2.30	1.15	2.91	6.07	1.83	1.85	2.96
TOTAL FACTOR PRODUCTIVITY																
All sectors	1.12	1.60	0.99	1.87	0.71	1.39	1.37	0.66	0.49	0.29	0.91	0.38	1.55	1.06	1.05	0.75
of which:																
Gov & Soc	1.28	0.86	0.13	0.56	-0.24	0.40	0.57	-1.21	0.87	-1.10	0.30	0.16	-0.87	0.13	0.18	-0.02
Sheltered	1.02	0.75	0.19	1.86	0.86	1.06	1.23	0.50	-0.16	0.60	0.55	-0.18	1.25	0.69	0.89	0.36
Supply	3.15	2.93	3.89	2.37	1.98	2.12	2.17	2.42	0.91	0.72	2.70	-0.62	1.34	2.04	2.64	1.05
Open	0.16	3.72	2.83	2.36	1.01	2.49	1.82	1.98	1.33	0.83	1.43	2.03	3.91	1.95	1.53	2.22
CAPITAL STOCK																
All sectors	4.02	4.03	2.92	4.08	3.02	4.41	3.42	3.61	2.43	4.73	3.51	2.82	7.84	3.47	3.38	3.67
of which:																
Gov & Soc	4.48	3.49	2.63	3.52	2.63	4.26	4.25	5.28	1.79	4.29	2.90	2.27	8.96	3.86	3.09	3.51
Sheltered	3.85	4.46	2.85	4.35	3.05	4.73	3.41	3.36	2.75	5.00	4.13	3.00	7.61	3.57	3.39	3.72
Supply	4.12	2.80	4.21	3.77	3.66	3.17	1.34	3.31	1.92	4.69	1.31	2.81	7.39	2.53	3.89	3.62
Open	4.21	3.48	3.15	3.96	3.20	4.10	2.75	2.65	2.31	4.36	2.28	3.60	7.02	2.92	3.50	3.83
EMPLOYMENT																
All sectors	0.74	-0.07	0.55	0.51	0.60	0.22	-0.44	0.43	-0.37	2.34	1.27	1.58	0.79	-0.07	0.59	0.83
of which:																
Gov & Soc	3.10	2.82	4.19	3.55	3.31	2.09	2.20	2.90	0.70	3.44	3.51	1.72	2.92	1.88	3.52	2.14
Sheltered	1.05	0.10	-0.27	0.69	0.09	0.71	-0.10	0.82	0.96	2.85	1.45	2.57	1.82	0.57	0.30	1.68
Supply	-2.97	-3.34	-2.72	-3.05	-3.01	-2.97	-3.31	-2.51	-3.28	-0.22	-0.64	-0.85	-3.08	-2.97	-3.15	-2.49
Open	-0.95	-2.59	-1.44	0.55	-1.22	-0.77	-1.60	-0.32	-2.85	0.50	-1.13	-0.18	0.01	-1.53	-0.82	-0.70
Memorandum item																
Labour force	2.04	0.75	1.24	1.25	0.86	0.79	0.22	0.82	0.42	2.89	1.80	2.32	1.03	0.54	1.23	1.37
DIFFERENCE BETWEEN ACTUAL AND CALCULATED GROWTH RATES OF: VALUE ADDED (VOLUME)																
Gov & Soc	2.02	1.49	1.83	0.48	1.42	0.20	1.20	-0.03	1.03	-0.50	0.73	-0.09	-1.20	0.61	1.46	—
Sheltered	-0.10	-0.88	-1.29	-0.27	-0.24	-0.12	0.18	-0.26	0.34	0.32	-0.24	0.03	-0.03	-0.02	-0.47	—
Supply	1.59	1.28	2.73	-0.25	1.08	0.45	0.61	1.36	0.45	0.97	2.33	-0.70	-1.01	0.75	0.97	—
Open	-2.67	0.41	0.16	0.28	-1.36	-0.07	-1.13	-0.02	-1.40	-0.66	-1.09	0.13	1.32	-0.66	-0.89	—

28

TOTAL FACTOR PRODUCTIVITY

Gov & Soc	1.04	-0.01	-0.22	-0.53	-0.19	-0.22	0.32	-0.92	1.19	-0.80	0.15	0.55	-1.78	0.01	-0.07
Sheltered	0.27	-0.58	-0.42	0.44	0.69	0.11	0.63	0.32	-0.14	0.59	-0.08	-0.18	0.04	0.17	0.29
Supply	1.93	1.31	2.36	0.20	1.02	0.65	1.07	1.53	0.59	0.06	1.40	-1.18	-0.62	0.97	1.12
Open	-2.33	0.79	0.35	-0.47	-1.11	-0.36	-0.86	-0.11	-0.54	-0.57	-0.59	0.12	1.25	-0.49	-0.85

CAPITAL STOCK

Gov & Soc	0.68	-0.47	0.02	-0.47	-0.13	-0.54	0.70	1.36	-1.38	-0.68	-0.48	-0.27	1.27	0.01	-0.01
Sheltered	-0.29	0.27	-0.22	0.17	-0.06	0.35	-0.08	-0.34	0.44	0.33	0.50	-0.01	-0.43	0.11	-0.10
Supply	0.45	-0.48	1.47	0.04	1.11	-0.55	-1.50	0.10	0.40	0.43	-1.78	0.55	-0.04	-0.44	0.71
Open	0.30	-0.27	0.40	-0.11	0.04	-0.06	-0.45	-0.55	0.21	-0.30	-1.14	0.85	-0.73	-0.22	0.10

EMPLOYMENT

Gov & Soc	1.05	1.63	2.44	1.38	1.61	0.53	1.06	0.59	-0.01	0.21	0.86	-0.69	0.26	0.55	1.68
Sheltered	-0.42	-0.60	-1.63	-0.96	-1.19	-0.46	-0.60	-0.59	0.52	-0.27	-0.52	0.37	0.01	-0.28	-1.11
Supply	-0.50	-0.21	0.08	-0.74	-0.28	-0.12	0.02	-0.19	0.25	1.18	1.64	1.32	-0.79	-0.06	-0.42
Open	-0.47	-0.93	-0.63	0.96	-0.48	0.33	-0.11	0.42	-0.96	-0.09	-0.67	0.11	0.18	-0.15	-0.20

Notes: "Gov & Soc" = Producers of Government and Community services.
"Sheltered" = Market services.
"Supply" = Sectors based primarily on natural resources.
"Open" = Manufacturing minus primary metals (included in "Supply").

Source: Secretariat estimates.

NOTES TO TABLES S.4. AND S.5.

1. *Method:* The data presented in the Tables are normalised for differences in growth rates between countries and in OECD-wide growth rates between sectors. In other words, the data presented in the Tables represent the *difference* between the growth rate of a particular group of sectors in a country or grouping of countries and the growth rate that could have been expected, *given* that country's (or group of countries') overall growth rate and the growth rate of the sector (or group of sectors) on an OECD-wide basis[1]. In this sense, the data reflect structural change in the composition of domestic output *relative to world output,* rather than being the actual growth rates of the sectors involved.

2. *Data:* The data are derived from national accounts sources and are all expressed at constant prices. Eighteen national accounts sectors are used and their ranking in terms of the aggregates is as follows:

Sector	Classified in group high, medium or low by growth of output	Classified according to international exposure
Agriculture	L	Supply
Electricity, gas and water	M	Sheltered
Construction	L	Sheltered
Wholesale and retail trade	H	Sheltered
Transport	H	Sheltered
Financial institutions	H	Sheltered
Real estate	H	Sheltered
Community services	H	Gov & Soc
Government services	M	Gov & Soc
Food and tobacco	M	Open
Textiles and clothing	L	Open
Wood products	L	Open
Paper and allied products	M	Open
Chemicals	M	Open
Glass and allied products	L	Open
Primary metals	L	Supply
Machinery and equipment	H	Open
Miscellaneous manufacturing	M	Open

Ranking by growth of output is done on an OECD-wide basis, with growth rate of value added at constant prices over the period 1970-1983 being the ranking criterion.

As far as exposure to international competition is concerned, the sheltered sectors are the sector of government services and community and social services (Gov & Soc) and the other service sectors (Sheltered). The remaining sectors are divided into the sectors whose development is mostly affected by supply conditions (Supply) or which are most open to foreign competition (Open).

The European countries are grouped together: EU5 includes France, Germany, Italy, United Kingdom and Belgium, and Nordic covers Denmark, Norway, Sweden and Finland.

1. The growth rates that could have been expected are calculated with the RAS method developed by R. Stone (Department of Applied Economics, Cambridge University). *Input-Output Relationships, 1954-1966,* Vol. 3, in: *A Programme for Growth,* Chapman and Hall, London, 1963.

of these interactions makes them difficult if not impossible to model; yet the broad patterns, suggestive of quite differing adjustment paths, can be identified.

Despite *Japan's* far greater dependence on imported energy and raw materials, several factors combined to speed adjustment and sustain macroeconomic outcomes which – while well below performance in the previous period – compared more than favourably with outcomes elsewhere. In particular, Japan was distinguished by a highly efficient process of wage adjustment, as the organisation of unions on an enterprise basis and the competitive nature of wage setting in the largely non-unionised small-firm sector led to a closer and more rapid link between corporate profitability and collective bargaining outcomes than prevailed elsewhere. At the same time, there was intense competition between suppliers in the domestic market, which placed firms under continuing pressure to respond to changing technological and commercial opportunities – a response greatly facilitated by high (and still rising) levels of education in the labour force, considerable labour mobility within large firms and between smaller

firms, and the close links between the banking system and industry. Though expanding, the public sector remained far smaller in Japan than in other countries. As a consequence, levels and rates of taxation were significantly lower, notably on labour use; and this reduced the wedges between market prices and post-tax returns, facilitating the response to market signals.

The interaction of these factors resulted not only in very high relative growth rates (the Japanese capital stock, for example, growing at twice the OECD average), but also in large-scale output redeployments. In particular, a marked transfer occurred from the non-traded to the traded goods sector, the normalized output shift being in the order of 2.2 per cent a year. This shift was paralleled by a transfer of output from the sectors growing less rapidly on an OECD-wide basis towards those expanding most rapidly.

These output shifts largely reflected the pattern of productivity advance in Japan. Thus, while total factor productivity in the Japanese traded goods sector was increasing at twice the OECD average, it remained virtually constant in the services sector, large parts of

Graph S.1. Unemployment rates in 1973 and 1986

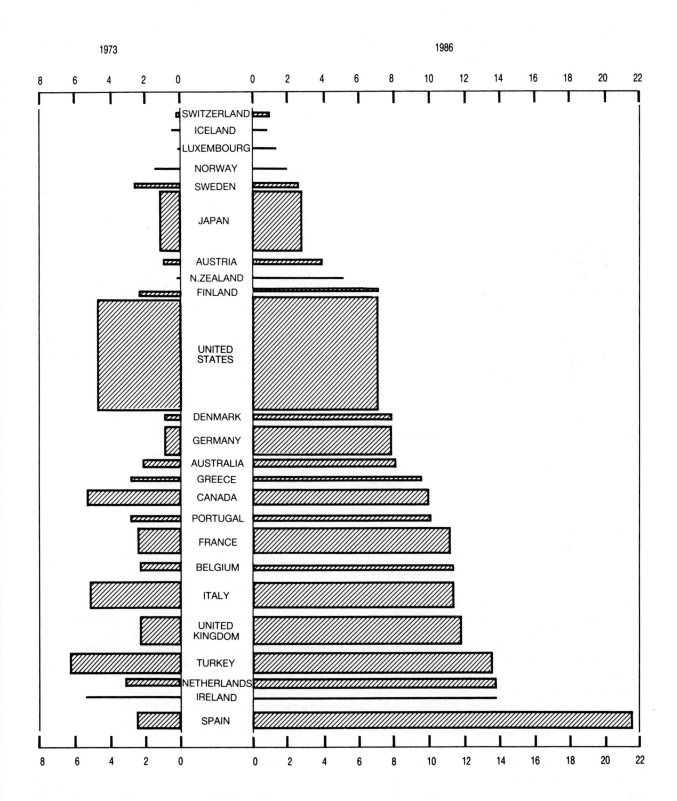

Note: The height of the shaded areas represents the share of the labour force of the respective countries in the labour force of the OECD area in 1986.
Source: OECD.

which (notably distribution and transport) were significantly affected by direct and indirect regulation. At the same time, productivity in the heavily protected agricultural sector was growing far more slowly than in the rest of the OECD area. The traded goods sector was therefore becoming increasingly competitive, both relative to other domestic uses of resources and internationally; and this contributed to the rising dependence of the Japanese economy on the growth of external markets and of Japanese shares in them, in a trend aggravated in the first half of the 1980s by the over-valuation of the dollar and the associated under-valuation of the yen.

As in Japan, wage adjustment in the *United States* occurred relatively rapidly, though at the expense of very large (but short-lived) increases in unemployment rates. The factors underlying wage adjustment were also in certain respects similar to those in Japan: the decentralisation of collective bargaining to the enterprise level and the strength of competition between the union and non-union parts of the economy, the non-union sectors adjusting more rapidly. At the same time, the response of firms and industries to emerging opportunities was facilitated by the continental scale of the United States market and the favourable effects market size had on the intensity of competition; by an abundant supply of highly trained scientific and technological personnel; by the speed with which skills and knowhow diffused through the United States economy; and by the diversity and sophistication of the financial system.

As a result, a rapidly growing labour force was absorbed into employment. Shifts in output between activities were not as great as in a number of other countries, owing in part to the size and diversity of the US economy and to the relatively small share of foreign trade in US economic activity, as well as to the blunting effects of protection in the industries – such as steel and automobiles – where United States competitiveness had declined most severely. But considerable adjustment occurred within (rather than between) sectors, as in many industries new competitors appeared who faced lower wage costs than established firms, often thanks to a shift in location. While employment growth was strong, it combined with relatively small flows of savings into productive investment and a shift of activity to sectors with slow productivity growth, thereby leading to extremely low growth rates of productivity overall – indeed, among the lowest in the OECD area. Given the low ratio of trade to output, the consequent loss of competitiveness was only felt with a considerable lag; but the growth of living standards faltered and, indeed, was kept from slipping further only by a continued decline of household saving and, recently, by extensive foreign borrowing.

The *Nordic* countries illustrate an adjustment process in which wages were sensitive to external competitiveness and to changing internal circumstances, though the extent of adjustment was perhaps not as complete as in the United States and Japan. However, the forces underlying wage adjustment were quite different. In particular, during much of the 1970s, the centralisation of collective bargaining played an important role by encouraging wage setters to take a broad view of their functions and responsibilities and by forcing them to bear the macroeconomic consequences of their actions in mind; and wage outcomes reflected a strongly held attachment to solidaristic principles and to full employment.

A willingness to adjust in labour and product markets appears to have been to some extent predicated on government commitments to support incomes through transfers and through direct employment, as well as through government labour market schemes. Consequently, while high levels of employment were maintained, as were reasonable rates of output growth, much of the growth in output and virtually all of the growth in employment occurred in the public sector, with value added in government expanding at a rate 30 per cent above that for the countries combined. In contrast, growth rates in the activities exposed to international competition fell significantly behind those in other countries, as did growth rates in the activities which were expanding most rapidly on an OECD-wide basis. These shifts in structure entailed moving output and resources from activities with above-average rates of productivity growth to those whose productivity performance was distinctly poorer – a shift which clearly could not be maintained over the longer term without compromising the rise in living standards. These strains and others have resulted in an erosion of the solidaristic foundations and macroeconomic responsiveness of centralised bargaining, as increasingly divisive conflicts have emerged between public and private sector employees, reflecting broader difficulties in operating economies with a very large non-market sector.

Finally, among a number of other *European* countries, the difficulties of adjustment were most visible in rising unemployment – especially but not only in the United Kingdom, France, Italy and Spain. These imbalances reflected persistent problems of the industrial relations system in securing reasonable wage outcomes, averting industrial conflict, and achieving and maintaining efficient work practices. Aggregate wages tended to depart from a course consistent with the evolution of real national incomes, placing considerable pressure on profit shares – even in the face of extremely high unemployment. On average, over the two decades to the mid-1980s, a 1 per cent increase in the unemployment rate reduced semi-annual nominal wage growth by 1.66 per cent in Japan and by 0.60 per cent in the United States; though the figure for Italy was comparable to that for the United States, the moderating effect of unemployment on wage demands was only 0.33 per cent in France, 0.23 per cent in Spain and 0.15 per cent in the United Kingdom – that is, each percentage point increase in unemployment had a moderating effect on wage settlements five times greater in Japan than in these European countries. The effects of wage trends on employment levels were compounded, first, by pervasive regulatory action in labour markets (notably through minimum wage legislation and restrictions on hiring and firing); and second, through distortions to the relative wage structure which priced those with few skills out of jobs and aggravated labour market segmentation.

Paralleling these rigidities in labour markets were industry structures long used to an environment in which competition had been restricted by various means; and firms were hindered in their response to change by lagging education and training of the labour force and by an excessive concentration of technological skills in activities working mainly or solely for government. As adjustment pressures mounted, firms and industries in difficulty often succeeded in obtaining extensive subsidies and trade protection – reducing even further the incentives to adjust. At the same time, public sector expenditure was rising rapidly, and this was reflected in a sharp increase in average and marginal tax rates, and notably in the taxation of labour markets.

Together, these trends contributed to the rise of unemployment, particularly among the young; but also to important shifts in the pattern of resource allocation. In particular, the only sectors to substantially increase their share in resource use (and especially of capital inputs) were the sheltered sectors and the energy sector (expanding rapidly in the United Kingdom). At the same time, there was a decline in the share of manufacturing that was most exposed to international competition, as well as in that of the sectors growing most rapidly on an area-wide basis.

In essence, though the strains bearing on the various countries were broadly similar, the national responses centred on differing adjustment mechanisms; but the process was in no case ideal and in each case tended to postpone an important feature of the problems to the future. Thus, Japan could not indefinitely continue to rely on a demand dynamism driven by exports in order to sustain growth above that of the rest of the world; the United States could not continue to increase or even maintain living standards through low domestic savings and borrowing from abroad; the Nordic countries could not continue to rely on the expansion of the government sector to provide increased jobs and output; and among the larger European countries, inefficiencies arising from factor and product markets, as well as from the growth of the public sector, were leading to significant losses of income and higher rates of unemployment. Other OECD countries too faced unresolved adjustment problems that combined these features in different ways.

The results of these accumulated imbalances are now emerging: in exchange-rate movements which entail sharp shifts in competitiveness; in tighter constraints on the extent to which the public sector can ease the difficulties of individual firms and workers; in mounting concern about the persistence of unemployment. Resolving these imbalances will place yet greater burdens on the adaptability of national economies; and much will depend on the efficiency with which firms and workers respond to relative price changes, domestically and internationally. Enhancing the capabilities to respond and strengthening the incentives for needed adjustments to occur are therefore urgent tasks – both to ease the immediate problems of economic policy and to place economic growth on a surer footing.

II. STRUCTURAL POLICIES: A PROGRAMME FOR CHANGE

Many countries have, in recent years, sought systematically to review microeconomic policies and reduce distortions to the functioning of markets. Yet the progress to date is uneven; and if the prospects for growth are to be durably improved, further action is needed.

This action is best seen in terms of a strategy or a *programme* – a connected set of measures for easing the constraints which impeded better performance in recent years, and for obtaining greater flexibility in the economy as a whole. By achieving a consistent thrust of reform across a wide range of areas, such a programme would be designed to secure the greatest gains from progress on a broad front; it must centre on action to increase competition in product markets, to strengthen the responsiveness of factor markets, and to secure increased efficiency and effectiveness in the public sector.

A. INCREASING COMPETITION IN PRODUCT MARKETS

Competition in product markets not only stimulates an efficient use of existing resources but is essential for rational investment decisions and provides incentives for the development of new products and processes. Yet the full benefits of product market competition will not be reaped without an extensive reassessment of current policies.

1. Agriculture

The *agricultural* policies pursued by the OECD countries are unsustainable. By maintaining returns to farmers at levels inconsistent with market balance, they have encouraged enormous over-production, forcing prices down on the relatively narrow markets open to international competition while accentuating protectionist pressures on others. Yet the policies have hardly met their stated goals: the subsidies they provide have largely been capitalised into land values and almost everywhere have overwhelmingly gone to the largest producers; by increasing the intensity and intermediate input usage of farming they have created a range of

environmental concerns; and far from stabilizing the sector, they have encouraged over-capitalisation and increased vulnerability to market shocks. A growing number of countries have attained food self-sufficiency, but the economic cost has been high – estimates suggesting that current agricultural policies reduce OECD GNP by as much as one percentage point.

There is no economic reason for sheltering agriculture as a whole from the operation of market forces. Far from being an inflexible sector, incapable of responding to changing market trends, modern farming has demonstrated an extraordinary facility to adjust to the incentives of prices and returns. Moreover, it is likely that in a liberalised agricultural market, financial institutions would – in this area as in others – prove resourceful in finding ways of spreading and easing the risks that the sector is often thought to face.

A transition to a more market-oriented agriculture is therefore desirable – and indeed many would view it as unavoidable, if the sector is not to collapse under the weight of its own surpluses. The key in this respect is the fundamental reform of domestic agricultural policies; for it is these policies which are responsible for the present disarray in world food markets. The aim must be to increase the role of international market signals in the sector's decision-making; and this requires price adjustments so as to reduce the incentives which current support levels give for over-production and to bring prices on major markets into line with those prevailing on the markets open to international competition.

At least in the high-income countries, it is unlikely that price reductions would lead to a further significant decline in sectoral employment; rather, they would affect primarily the sector's demand for non-labour inputs. But though it would not necessarily reduce employment, a transition to more competitive agricultural markets would erode the gains larger farms now make from price supports and, most importantly from a social and political point of view, could reduce the often low incomes of smaller producers. It is a matter of judgement and political circumstance whether compensation for these effects is considered desirable or indeed feasible.

There may nonetheless be a case for providing continuing income support to poorer farmers, or for farming in environmentally or strategically significant areas. If the political will can be found to confine income support to marginal farms, the impact of such support on total agricultural output – and hence on market distortions – is likely to be minimal. However, any policy on these lines will need to be formulated bearing in mind that in the past many of the policies which have proved so unsustainable have been advocated in the name of the marginal farmer. All of this suggests that the policies adopted should as far as possible "decouple" the provision of income support from production incentives, so that attempts to ease the transition difficulties reform will undoubtedly create do not unnecessarily impede the sector's return to market balance.

In the lower-income OECD countries, the price reductions needed to achieve market balance could have the most serious effects for large numbers of producers. This would create economic, social and political problems which straightforward income support payments might not entirely resolve. For these countries it will be necessary to find appropriate policies that will enable the necessary adjustment to be achieved without serious repercussions on the social fabric in their rural areas.

The tensions arising from the accumulation of surplus stocks and the widespread recourse to dumping on third markets need to be reduced in a shorter time-frame than that required for the fundamental reform of agricultural policies. Yet it is essential that the measures taken should neither preclude nor prejudice the sector's longer term move to a more sustainable policy setting; but this can hardly occur if markets are further disrupted. A gradual and disciplined reduction in current excess stocks, accompanied by intensified price adjustments, notably in the markets where levels of trade distorting assistance are now highest, would provide the most favourable conditions for initiating the indispensable process of reform.

2. Industrial adjustment

As growth slowed and unemployment mounted, governments came under intense pressure to ease the strain of adjustment both in certain mature industrial sectors – such as textiles, shipbuilding and steel – as well as in sectors which were highly energy-intensive – notably basic chemicals, non-ferrous metals and transport. The difficulties of these sectors were compounded by changes in international competitiveness, and especially by the steady rise in the Newly Industrialising Countries' share of world markets. And they became even more severe with the shift to less accommodating macroeconomic policies following the second oil shock.

In fact, assistance to firms and industries in difficulty comprised a large and – until the early 1980s – rapidly growing part of governments' industrial policy efforts. However, the instruments used varied significantly from country to country, as did the results obtained.

In Europe, policies for industries in difficulty have centred on financial assistance, frequently provided on a targeted basis to individual firms. The subsidies thus provided accounted for much of the rise in government transfers to industry over the period from the early 1970s to the mid-1980s; at constant prices, these more than trebled in France and Italy, doubled in Germany and increased significantly in a number of other countries. In Japan, direct financial transfers have not been a major instrument of government policy; industries in difficulty have been encouraged to reduce capacity rapidly within the context of "concerted actions" which have frequently benefitted from derogations to competition policy. In the United States, subsidies have remained very limited; but several of the sectors facing the most acute adjustment problems have been granted trade protection which, once accorded, has tended to be perpetuated.

At the same time, a number of governments, faced with the inevitable decline of sectors which had traditionally been major employers, have sought to promote new, more promising areas of activity, frequently in industries associated with "high technology". The level of financial assistance provided is difficult to quantify; but to take only one indicator, public funding of R & D for industrial development doubled in real terms over the period 1973-85.

Experience highlights the limits of these policies. Subsidies to firms and industries in difficulty have kept capacity no longer viable in operation; and they have hindered industrial adjustment by confusing the signals which influence corporate decision-making:

- Inconsistencies between policy objectives (for example, rationalisation and the maintenance of employment) have led firms into unsustainable strategic options;
- The availability of government subsidies has made it difficult to obtain labour force approval of painful but ultimately indispensable changes in employment levels and working practices;
- Subsidisation has distorted competition between favoured firms and sectors on the one hand and less politically influential players on the other.

Severe constraints also bear on policies aimed at promoting new, "high-technology" activities. The results have frequently been disappointing – and especially so of policies which have sought to replace market signals and "create" comparative advantage in a broad range of sectors considered strategic. These policies, especially widespread in Europe, have exercised their major influence in sectors dominated by public procurement. But even when they have achieved their proximate technological goal, they have frequently led to an excessive concentration of technical capabilities in activities geared to the public sector, thus adversely affecting the competitiveness of other industries.

Overall, the ease or difficulty with which manufacturing industry in different countries has responded to changing opportunities and constraints has depended less than is often thought on specific industrial policies and more on the characteristics of each country's market environment – on the extent of rivalry between firms and the pressure of competition; the efficiency of capital markets in identifying new activities and sustaining restructuring in old; the flexibility of labour markets not only in terms of the mobility of labour but of the responsiveness to evolving needs for skills; and the effectiveness of the links between firms and the research system – notably that of the universities – in guiding the allocation of research efforts and promoting the diffusion of their results.

The experience of the United States, Japan and Germany confirms the crucial role of competitive forces and of the environment in which industry operates not only in ensuring rationalisation of sectors in difficulty but also in promoting speedy adjustment to technological opportunity. Firms in each of these countries have proved particularly successful in exploiting the potential for innovation, be it in entirely new activities or in more traditional ones; and this is linked to a number of common features in the stance governments in these countries have taken, though individual policies have of course differed.

In each case, the policies have departed from what might have been desirable: in Japan, the policy process has been such as to generate persistent charges of discrimination against foreign firms; in the United States, the large scale transfers provided through defence-related R&D may have "crowded out" civilian innovation efforts; and German policy did not entirely escape the temptation to rely on "national champions" for technological projects considered of particular significance. Yet governments in these three countries have been especially reticent to act as entrepreneurs; and in a context of intense competition on the domestic market, firms have taken primary responsibility for maintaining traditional areas of strength and/or developing new ones. Their efforts in this respect have been sustained by the depth and breadth of national education and training systems and by the efficient functioning of factor and product markets.

By the mid-1980s, governments were to some extent withdrawing from policies of selective subsidy, notably of firms and industries in difficulty – even in the countries where assistance had previously been provided on the greatest scale. At the same time, though to a lesser extent, policies of support for activities considered promising were being reviewed; and horizontal measures, aimed at promoting a broadly-based capacity for developing and diffusing technology, gained importance relative to assistance more narrowly aimed. But to a considerable degree, the shift has reflected concerns about policies' budgetary costs as much as their economic consequences; and in many countries, there has been a strong tendency to at least partially replace visible, on-budget support with the less transparent but no less real subsidies provided by trade protection.

Looking to the future, the objectives, instruments and methods of implementation of industry policies will continue to reflect the specific requirements of each national context. However, experience shows that all the policies that have proved effective have a number of features in common, and that, conversely, there are certain features that make it likely that policies will fail in any national environment.

In particular, the outcomes of industrial policies have frequently been disappointing because the goals set were too broad and the priorities too diluted; and because the policies themselves were inconsistent with government action in other areas. The costs imposed by these more general weaknesses have been compounded when policies have sought to go against the fundamental course of comparative advantage; have provided assistance on a basis which, in practice, is open-ended, despite initial intentions for its progressive phasing-out; have failed to assess carefully the displacement effects which assistance granted to any particular firm or sector has on others; and have been subject to little effective monitoring of outcomes against intentions.

Overall, the changes that have taken place in industry and in its environment – lower overall economic growth, increased uncertainty in the monetary and energy fields, converging patterns of national consumption, internationalisation of production and trade, technological advance – create conditions for government action that are radically different from those under which the broad principles and instruments of industrial policy were devised in the 1950s and 60s. These conditions make narrowly targeted, selective measures increasingly less effective; and they heighten the importance of securing a swift and adequate response from private agents to market pressures. Whether such a response is forthcoming depends first and foremost on the environment in which firms in each country operate; and it is through action to improve this environment that policies can best promote the adjustment of firms to technological advance, as well as to changing patterns of supply and demand more generally.

Policies in a broad range of areas are relevant – including competition policy, education and training, the regulation of capital markets and of course international trade; but action to strengthen *research* capabilities in the advanced economies, and to encourage their more efficient use, have a particularly close bearing on industry's capacity to create and exploit opportunity.

Much of the research effort of the OECD economies is oriented to immediate needs, in particular to the development of new products and processes. The funding and performance of applied research and development is primarily a responsibility of industry – and the evidence suggests that the private and social returns on applied R&D are often greatest when it is left in industry's hands. Yet there is also a significant component of research which is more long-term in its orientation – which aims not at particular commercial outcomes but at advancing understanding of basic scientific properties; and though less easily quantifiable, the economic importance of this type of research is no less real. In numerous areas of current technical advances – for example, microelectronics and biotechnology – the boundaries between basic and applied research have blurred; and, the accelerating pace and changing nature of science and technology confer on some applied research and most basic research a renewed strategic character, making it all the more important that future developments and their efficient exploitation be based upon and nourished by a continuing influx of new fundamental knowledge. The adequacy of the basic research system is consequently of increasing significance to economies' capacity to create and exploit scientific advance.

Governments have an acknowledged responsibility for funding basic research – and indeed they carry the main burden of doing so. But particularly in Europe, the combined effect of changing government priorities and rising costs for research has been to place increasing pressures on the basic research system, and notably on the universities. In fact, universities in the OECD area (with the noticeable exceptions of Japan and the United States) have undergone a gradual erosion of their ability to carry out research using up-to-date equipment and of their capacity to renew their skill base, reflected in an ageing scientific work-force. In their search for new sources of income, universities have turned to external financial support; though desirable in many respects, this has resulted in a general shift away from basic research towards more visible, shorter-term oriented research. In Europe, it did not prevent a real decline over the period 1975-83 in the average resources available per university researcher, a decline only partially reversed in subsequent years.

The extent of the difficulties has differed from country to country; and it has proven especially difficult to reallocate resources among competing projects and institutions in countries where government laboratories account for a large share of all resource use in basic research. This is especially so in Europe and Australia, where government laboratories account for as much as half of all government expenditure on R&D; and these laboratories have generally succeeded in protecting (and in several cases actually increasing) their funding while that of universities was being cut (Table S.6).

Securing greater flexibility in the research system, while maintaining a commitment to the highest quality levels, requires improvements both in the institutional framework and in resource allocation mechanisms – in particular, a review of the role of government laboratories as centres for long-term research; a move towards employment contracts which favour labour mobility; more systematic appraisal of research performance, not only on an *ex ante* basis but also *ex post*; and the encouragement of links with industry. International co-operation in basic research can also make a significant contribution to increasing the efficiency of the science system, by allowing countries to share the high costs of advanced facilities and ensuring the rapid international diffusion of research results.

Ultimately, whether firms respond to the opportunities arising from technological advance, as well as to broader changes in economic circumstances, depends largely on the intensity of competition – and on the incentives this creates for the firms which successfully adjust, and the penalties for those which do not. *Competition policy* has an essential role to play in strengthening these incentives and penalties, domestically and internationally.

A clearly set out legal framework, which establishes a presumption in favour of market rivalry and of the development of new and more efficient sources of supply, contributes to economic and social pluralism and encourages firms to concentrate on achieving greater competitiveness, rather than to dissipate resources in creating artificial barriers to new competition. Moreover, an active competition policy can provide an efficient means of achieving public objectives – and notably that of securing reliable and cost-effective service – in areas which have traditionally been subject to more direct and constraining forms of government intervention, for example, through regulation. In all of

Table S.6. **Level and changes in R&D resources, per researcher, 1983**

In $1 000 and index (1975 = 100, at 1980 prices)

	Business enterprises		Higher education		Government		All sectors	
	Level ($1 000)	Index	Level ($1 000)	Index	Level ($1 000)	Index	Level ($1 000)	Index
United States	119	102	118	100	179	114	123	102
Japan[1]	87	131	40	118	103	131	70	130
EEC[2]	155	105	57	82	133	99	116	98
Other[2]	146	104	74	108	107	108	119	106
Total[2]	119	106	66	99	141	109	106	105

1. Official data. Adjusted to OECD standards, R&D expenditures per researcher would read as follows:
   $118 000 per researcher in the higher education sector;
   $130 000 per researcher for all sectors.
2. *EEC:* excluding the United Kingdom and Greece; *Other:* excluding New Zealand, Turkey and Yugoslavia.
Source: OECD Secretariat estimates.

...he legal framework for competition policy
...se the efficiency of market outcomes
...direct government involvement all the less

...ng these functions requires that competition
poli.... adapt to changing circumstances. It is increasingly recognised that many forms of corporate behaviour once thought unacceptable are rational and indeed desirable responses by firms to opportunities for achieving greater efficiency through horizontal and vertical co-operation. Nonetheless, these responses can create risks for the open functioning of markets – as mergers and co-operation between firms may facilitate collusion, concentrate resources and increase the difficulties a new supplier would have to face. Whether these risks are worth bearing depends to a very great extent on other aspects of policy – and first and foremost on the effective degree of exposure to international competition. In the long run, a policy against restrictive business practices, however vigorous it may be, can do little to promote efficiency in an economy where firms benefit from government interventions which shield them from market realities, domestically and internationally.

3. International trade

The single most effective means of securing responsiveness to changing opportunities is through exposure to *international trade*. The efficiency gains of trade are most visible in product markets: they are the gains which come from access to markets world-wide, from the diversity and variety of goods which only markets on this scale can provide, and from the constant contact with, and pressure to adapt to, new ways of doing things. But openness to international trade is also important in reshaping factor markets – and notably in ensuring that collective bargaining is exposed to market signals which can clearly indicate when outcomes are unsustainable and which can help in guiding bargainers to better solutions. For all of these reasons liberal trade is more than a means of reallocating economic resources – rather, it is the key to securing the consumer interest in an efficient and high-income economy, providing all goods and services on the best terms.

Looking to the future, the scope for improving living standards through international trade is, if anything, likely to increase. At a regional level, there remain large unexploited gains from economic integration – and recent estimates suggest that the gains from achieving a degree of economic integration in Europe equal to that of the United States could be as great as 10 per cent of European GDP, though its effects on non-European countries would also have to be taken into account. The continuing industrialisation of the developing economies also creates new markets for OECD exports – and new sources of supply in a broad range of industries. At the same time, the efficient use of new product and process technologies evidently depends heavily on access to large markets. And in areas such as data processing, new technologies are making an increasing range of services tradable, with the gains from trade in these likely to be no smaller than those reaped in manufacturing.

Action to strengthen and extend the open, multilateral trading system – both by the OECD countries and by the developing countries – is the key to securing those gains; yet even within manufacturing, where the gains from liberalisation have been greatest, a considerable erosion of liberal trade has occurred in recent years. This erosion should be reversed as a matter of urgency.

It is of primary importance to dismantle the protectionist measures which – having been put in place to ease immediate sectoral problems – have become an enduring feature of the industrial landscape. The Multi-Fibre Arrangement (MFA), and the different trade restrictions with which it is associated, stand out. When the current Arrangement expires, fully thirty years will have passed since the first derogations of textiles trade from the ordinary discipline of the GATT – derogations which were intended to be strictly temporary. But prolonged exemptions from liberal trade have also become a feature of other industries, notably steel and automobiles; and more recently, discriminatory measures have spread from industries in serious difficulty to sectors such as semiconductors which have high growth rates and excellent prospects. The net effect has been to severely undermine the principle of non-discrimination, eroding the MFN clause which underpins open trade.

Even removing these measures will not suffice to restore the confidence of traders and investors that reductions in cost and improvements in quality will be rewarded through increases in world market share. This will require an assurance of greater discipline by all trading partners in their future behaviour, including progress as regards forms of protection which at present escape international obligations. The objective of granting foreign competitors a treatment no less favourable than that accorded domestic producers should remain paramount; the manner in which safeguard options in world trade are implemented is of utmost importance in this respect, as is the use more generally made of administrative protection and of anti-dumping action.

However, the need to strengthen the open trading system goes beyond the system's traditional manufacturing focus. Most immediately, the distortions currently affecting agricultural trade not only impose significant economic costs – they breed tensions which threaten open trade as a whole. Though these distortions are largely the products of domestic agricultural policies, a multilateral and multi-commodity approach to improving agricultural markets can play an important role in easing and sustaining the process of change.

This is firstly because an international approach to the problems of the agricultural sector has important economic advantages. Compared with unilateral liberalisation, a co-ordinated and multilateral approach would almost certainly lead to a smaller reduction in domestic prices in the more highly protected markets. The expansion of world trade induced by a co-ordinated strategy would ease adjustment problems, while the multi-commodity nature of the approach would ensure that reduced assistance to one set of products does not compound market problems in others. The overall result would be a firming of prices on world markets, so that the overall shock to the sector would be smaller than a static comparison of current support prices and world prices suggests.

Multilateral trade agreements would also facilitate the political process of agricultural policy reform. The experience of three decades of trade liberalisation shows that these agreements, once entered into, are generally implemented – mainly because they create powerful coalitions between the domestic interests which gain from the opportunities trade liberalisation creates, while the balance of advantages they provide to countries gives them substantial public legitimacy. By committing themselves to such agreements, governments can lend credibility to domestic policy changes which will be phased in only over a period of several years.

Finally, the full benefits of interdependence will not be secured if the world trade regime is not brought into line with the changing character of trade flows. Three areas stand out in this respect. First, the albeit slow increase in the share of science-based products in world trade creates new challenges to trade policy – challenges associated with the importance which technical norms and standards and the protection of intellectual property have in encouraging the rapid diffusion of goods based on new technologies. Second, it is becoming clear that there is great scope for specialisation in services: for example, in telecommunications, where new technologies are broadening the range and diversity of services which can be provided; but exploiting these gains will require an important extension of multilateral trade liberalisation. Third, trade and foreign investment have long been complementary elements of international economic interdependence; and their complementarity may be becoming tighter as high technology goods and services – which require extensive marketing and support – become of greater significance. Ensuring an open international environment for foreign investment is consequently an important component of a strategy for sustaining the trading system.

The Uruguay Round of the GATT provides an essential opportunity to meet these challenges. The outlook for small and large economies alike now depends on access to global markets, access which enhances both microeconomic efficiency and macroeconomic responsiveness. Rapid and sustained progress in a new round of multilateral trade liberalisation would yield immediate economic benefits – and the benefits would become all the greater as firms could with increased confidence plan on open markets in future.

B. IMPROVING THE RESPONSIVENESS OF FACTOR MARKETS

Combined, these measures would preserve and strengthen the role of product markets, domestically and internationally, as the engines of structural change. But adjusting efficiently to the incentives and signals coming from product markets requires a capacity to redeploy resources: to move labour and investment towards new opportunities – and to ensure that they are used effectively where they are employed. This capacity hinges on the efficiency of *factor markets*. Here, too, there is important scope for policy reform.

1. Financial markets

By allocating the economy's savings among competing investment projects, and monitoring the effectiveness with which these resources are used, capital markets have a major role to play in enhancing microeconomic and macroeconomic outcomes. Developments in OECD financial markets over the last decade have made it considerably easier for the financial system to exercise this role. The liberalisation and integration of capital markets, nationally and internationally, as well as greater competition among financial institutions, have led to better resource allocation decisions and strengthened the mechanisms for monitoring efficient resource use.

Significant advances have been made in financing industrial enterprises, with numerous new credit instruments complementing traditional types of borrowing and equity issues. Funding via negotiable instruments, in particular, has made considerable headway. This has permitted a broader spreading of industrial risks, increased firms' access to large-scale capital markets, and narrowed the capital cost differentials which the fragmentation of financial markets previously engendered – in particular at the international level. Though the major initial beneficiaries of these advances were the largest manufacturing and service companies, they are now becoming widely available throughout the industrial system; and in a number of countries, actual or potential constraints on the availability of bank lending to small and medium-sized enterprises have largely disappeared as competition has increased in domestic markets.

The development of the venture capital industry, and the expansion of unlisted and third-tier stock markets, have assisted new business start-ups, especially in the high technology and high-growth service sectors – with considerable longer term consequences in terms of generating jobs and incomes. Here too internationalisation has contributed to efficiency by encouraging the diffusion of venture capital skills and investment from a relatively narrow base to a far broader group of countries.

Lastly, developments in financial markets have facilitated the restructuring of corporate assets and portfolios, the introduction of new management teams, and the funding of large-scale projects. More diversified sources of funds for these operations have become available, with management buy-outs being of particular importance in durably improving the situation and prospects of many firms in decline or on the verge of bankruptcy.

Nonetheless, the process of learning and experimentation inherent in these developments has brought in its train problems and concerns, as investors and borrowers take on new risks. Undoubted though these risks may be, they are a natural component of dynamic economies and are manageable so long as they are being taken with foreknowledge and with an adequate backing in terms of investors' capital. Moreover, certain of the new financial instruments themselves contribute to a more balanced risk spread, domestically and internationally. Seen over the longer term, an increased willingness of investors to bear risk, and an increased capacity of financial systems to diversify it and fund large-scale and/or high-risk projects, can only enhance economic efficiency.

Nonetheless, there may be concern that at present, the ultimate structure and distribution of risk – domestically and internationally – and the extent of its systemic effects are poorly understood and monitored. Prudential supervision policies need to be reviewed to provide better information about the nature and spread of these risks, to see that they are well understood by those who bear them and to ensure that their distribution poses the least threat to the integrity of the financial system.

Similar prudential principles should apply to the extent possible to all financial enterprises, without sharpening the statutory differences that traditionally distinguished various types of institutions – and limited competition among them. A transition from supervision based largely on institutions to one based mainly on functions is a significant factor in policies to enhance competition on a "level playing field" in financial markets.

The reform of prudential policies also has an important international dimension. In an increasingly globalised financial system, safeguards cannot adequately be provided without reinforced international co-operation on prudential matters. At the same time, persistent differences between countries in prudential arrangements can only impede the international openness of financial systems, and distort competition between financial institutions. In this market as in others, integration provides gains in promoting innovation and cost-effectiveness; this makes the efforts now under way in a number of international fora, including the OECD, all the more significant.

2. Labour markets and collective bargaining

Labour markets serve a broad range of economic and social functions, as do the mechanisms through which employers and employees regulate their relationships. These functions reflect a mix of distinct but interrelated objectives: the search for a balance between wage levels and capacity to pay, which is an indispensable basis for maintaining high levels of employment; the need to obtain sufficient flexibility in labour allocation to be able to shift human resources towards the activities with greatest promise; the widely held aspiration for stability and security in employment, and the recognition that longer-term employment relations may contribute to the development and effective use of skills; and last but by no means least, the desire by employees to "have a say" in setting and implementing the conditions of employment and work.

These objectives are not always mutually consistent; both the institutions through which they are pursued and the emphasis they are given in different countries reflect a wide range of economic, social and political factors, many of them rooted in national history and aspirations. As a result, the process of institutional change is particularly complex, constrained, and in some respects, controversial. Yet it must also be recognised that in some countries, notably in Europe, improvements in the way labour market institutions function are essential if unemployment is to return to, and remain at, socially acceptable levels – and if the institutions themselves are to retain their social legitimacy and broader role.

This is not to deny that considerable progress has been made in correcting the wage-profit imbalances (or "wage gaps") which had opened up at the end of the 1960s and continued to widen in the 1970s, as well as in reversing the excessive narrowing of wage differentials which had also occurred in that period. Yet the extent of the improvement, notably in Europe, should not be overestimated. Though the wage gaps have been reduced, this has generally been obtained at an extremely high cost in terms of unemployment; and in the countries where the problems have been greatest, there is little evidence that the underlying pattern of wage formation has changed – so that another adverse external shock would very probably create yet further substantial joblessness. Every postwar recovery has come to an end because of the accumulation of inflationary pressures; and though the dangers appear more remote in present circumstances, the persistence of imbalances in labour market functioning cannot but increase the risks bearing on economic policy making – and make a more expansionary course all the more difficult to justify and implement.

A durable improvement in the wage setting process hinges on the evolution of labour market institutions and in particular, of collective bargaining. Given the range of objectives pursued in labour markets, and the distinct national features of labour markets and of the contexts in which they operate, it is extremely difficult to draw international lessons in this respect; but two quite different approaches to structuring the process of collective bargaining appear to have proved reasonably successful in obtaining economically sensible wage outcomes.

The first involves negotiations which are relatively highly decentralised. In Japan, the enterprise structure of unionism, combined with factors which strengthen the association between employees and their firms, ensures that wage settlements in larger enterprises adjust relatively speedily to companies' changing circumstances – though this occurs in a context of relatively effective national co-ordination of pay bargaining, notably among employers. Wage adjustment is buttressed by a sizeable non-union sector, largely among smaller enterprises, which is probably most responsive to labour market conditions. In the United States, unions are mainly organised on an industry basis; but collective bargaining generally occurs at the enterprise level and is greatly affected by competition between a unionised and non-unionised sector. The unionised sector has tended to adjust only slowly (not only in terms of wages but also of working practices) and over the long term to shrink, so that market forces play an increasingly direct role in pay determination.

A second pattern, typical of the Nordic countries, but also found in Austria and (though to a much lesser extent) Germany, involves a relatively centralised system of wage-setting, hinging on a relatively small number of agreements with broad coverage. It also involves a sharp separation between areas of the employment relations which are subject to *negotiation* between unions and employers – most notably wages – and other areas which though they may be subject to *consultation* are dealt with on a basis which is not generally adversarial. By and large, these systems have proved successful in setting aggregate wages because they confront wage bargainers with the macroeconomic consequences of their actions, thus overcoming some of the "prisoner's dilemma" features inherent in the adjustment of nominal wage demands to changes in economic circumstances. At the same time, the distinction between negotiation and consultation has made it easier for good work practices to be maintained and has encouraged harmonious relations at the place of work. Outcomes in both these respects have also been tempered by a high level of exposure to international competition – and by a recognition that failure to adjust can only increase the costs which must be borne.

However, labour market outcomes have been consistently poorer in those countries – notably the United Kingdom, France, Italy and Belgium – where collective bargaining structures fall between these extremes: where outcomes have been neither subject to the direct constraints of decentralised bargaining and competition in labour markets, nor guided by a wider recognition of economic and social responsibility; where the setting of wages and of the conditions of employment have typically functioned through a multiplicity of overlapping and competing levels, fragmenting employer solidarity and encouraging inflationary spirals of bargaining around long established pay relativities; and where the legal framework for bargaining has been poorly spelt out in terms of the rights and duties of the parties to collective agreements.

There are no easy solutions to these problems. But bargaining structures in these countries are unlikely to evolve towards highly centralised structures – and indeed, centralisation itself seems to be under great pressure even in the Nordic countries where it has prevailed for many years. Rather, a greater degree of decentralisation of collective bargaining to the enterprise level appears to be the most likely outcome and corresponds to a broad OECD-wide trend.

However, decentralisation is not a panacea and indeed, in economies with high levels of unionisation, it may aggravate inflationary pressures. To lead to sustainable wage outcomes it needs to occur within a legal framework which establishes the contractual status of collective agreements and facilitates the resolution of disputes. It must also be underpinned by a recognition of the role which competition plays in steering collective bargaining towards sustainable solutions. This is first and foremost a question of competition in product markets – notably through international trade; but the review of measures which reduce competition in labour markets can also play a significant role in this respect.

Improving the functioning of the labour market requires more than changes in pay determination – it is intimately linked to improvements in the microeconomic processes by which labour is allocated among competing uses and by which the efficiency of labour utilisation is set: that is, to labour market flexibility. It is clear that long-term relations between firms and their employees can make an important contribution to the efficient development and deployment of skills; and that even the most efficient labour market, far from operating on a "hire and fire" basis, will be characterised by mutual commitments between employers and workers as each makes costly and largely sunk investments in competence and understanding. But the experience of the last decade shows that many government-imposed restrictions on and distortions to the flexibility of labour markets do nothing to bring these efficiency gains closer; they merely aggravate segmentation in employment, lulling those with jobs into a false sense of security, while worsening the hardship of those who are out of work.

As these lessons have become clearer, a substantial reversal has occurred of the legislation and regulations which impeded the microeconomic functioning of labour markets in the 1970s, notably in Europe. Statutory minimum wages now play a reduced role, though they remain highly significant in the Netherlands, Spain and France, where (in 1984) they were equivalent to respectively 65 per cent, 41 per cent and 37 per cent of average manufacturing earnings; administrative constraints on recruitment and lay-off decisions have been eased; the fixed element of non-wage labour costs has generally been reduced; and replacement ratios (the ratio of unemployment benefit to the average income of an employed worker) now do not appear to provide significant disincentives to work. Yet restrictive work practices and inefficient labour utilisation remain significant problems in many countries.

This may partly be because certain restrictions on labour utilisation – especially on internal and external labour mobility – are being perpetuated through collective bargaining. These impediments are perpetuated even when not legally imposed because they are in the immediate interests of employers and their present employees – in part because of official policies which limit the extent of competition in product and factor markets. But it needs to be recognised that these immediate interests may be met at the eventual cost of excluding large sectors of the work-force from effective participation in labour markets – that is, of deepening segmentation between the "insiders", who benefit in higher wages and greater job security from the economic rents restrictions on competition create, and the "outsiders" who bear the costs.

There are relatively few specific measures governments can take in this respect, above and beyond supporting improvements in collective bargaining. And even these are unlikely to succeed if they are not underpinned by community understanding – about what labour market institutions can and cannot achieve; about the evolving constraints to which adjustment must occur; and about the opportunities successful adjustment can create. It is these factors which make it so important to develop a broader consensus between and with unions and employers about the desirability of adjusting to change – not only in terms of wage-setting, but in terms of adapting working practices and developing a policy dialogue.

Developing such a consensus is largely in the self-interest of unions and employers, and it is with them that responsibility ultimately must rest. Consultative procedures at the firm and industry level have a clear role to play in ensuring that employees are aware of changing constraints and opportunities, and that the legitimate concerns they may express are taken into account; such procedures can contribute both to greater productivity on the shop floor and to better collective bargaining outcomes.

However, governments too have a responsibility for improving community understanding of economic circumstances and their consequences. The primary role of economic policy in this respect is to set a clear and predictable medium-term framework for the growth of nominal incomes; but as the Japanese experience strikingly demonstrates, a medium-term setting in economic policy need not rule out the continuing search for consensus at the national level with unions and employers' associations, even in collective bargaining structures which are relatively decentralised. Yet experience shows that consultative mechanisms can do little if the incentives and constraints bearing on collective bargaining are not such as to promote recognition of the need for adjustment; so that the search for consensus is an important complement to – and not substitute for – a move towards more rational systems of industrial relations.

Governments can underpin these efforts to achieve realistic outcomes in labour markets through the proper conduct of their own role as employers. Indeed, collective bargaining poses special problems in the public sector – and these problems have become more acute over the longer term as the share of the public sector in total employment has risen; in more recent years, they have been further accentuated by budgetary restrictions on public sector pay. The economic consequences, notably of industrial conflicts, have been magnified by the fact that the public sector is the sole provider of services in many areas; so that disputes may have particularly serious implications for economic activity as a whole and cause grave inconvenience to third parties.

There are inevitably important differences between what can be achieved in the public and private sectors; but the priorities are similar: improving, where necessary, the legal framework for collective bargaining and enhancing incentives and external constraints. Efficient dispute settlement procedures are one key. Ultimately, however, constraints on public sector wages depend on the effectiveness of budget discipline, including acceptance that excessive wage increases will – as in the private sector – lead to employment reductions; and on government willingness to draw on outside suppliers of services if costs are lower. In this sense achieving better wage outcomes in the public sector is closely linked to the review of the public sector's scope – a topic dealt with below.

3. Education and training

Over the longer term, the capacity of individuals and indeed of labour markets as a whole to respond to changing circumstances is greatly affected by the adequacy of national *education and training* systems – because these systems so heavily condition the depth, breadth and flexibility of skills in the labour force, the ability to perceive and exploit emerging opportunities, and – perhaps most importantly – the understanding of the constraints bearing on individual firms and national economies.

Yet education and training systems are under pressure from multiple sources: from labour market conditions which preclude many young people from gainful employment for long periods of time and which have led to the proliferation of training programmes relatively poorly co-ordinated with other components of the education system; from new technologies which alter the desirable type and pattern of education – and which,

Table S.7. **Patterns of post-compulsory youth education around 1984**
Estimated ratios in per cent of total population in relevant age classes
(Countries ranked by total enrolment rate at age 17)

| Country | Enrolment of 17-year-olds: | | | | | Share of age class getting credentials for entry into higher education | | Ratio of the number of entrants into higher education to size of an age class (%) | | Ratio of the number of persons taking post-secondary degrees to size of an age class (%) | |
| | School education | | Apprentice-ship, part-time, etc. | Post-secondary, etc. | Total | Universities in general | of which: Limited choice only | Universities[2] | Other | "Bachelors" | Lower |
	General	Vocational[1]									
Germany	32	18	46	1	97	28	6	17	9	12	8
Japan	63	27	0	0	90	92[8]	:	26	12	24	11
United States	81	0	:.	6	88	73	:	28[3]	34[4]	24[3]	34[5]
Netherlands	35	41	10	0	86	50	:	10	24	6	18
Belgium	78	0	8	0	86	20[3]	:	12	20	15	:
Sweden	32	51[6]	2	0	85	77	50	36	0	15	15[7]
Switzerland	20	7	55	0	82	14	:	:	:	:	:
Austria	14	20	44	0	78	13[3]	:	17	:	16	13
Canada	67	0	:.	9	76	75	:	:	:	23	12
France	25	38	10	2	75	29	:	18	12	13	42[3]
Norway	38	36	1	0	75	70[3]	35	18	:	18[3]	11
Denmark	35	33	6	0	74	25[3]	:	22	13	14	:
Italy	22[3]	25[3]	23[3]	0[3]	70	51	:	27	1	11	6[3]
Australia	37	0	20[9]	9	66	43	:	31	17	16	:
United Kingdom	18	12	35[10]	0	65	37	:	31	0	15	12
Spain	34	15	:.	0	49	25	:	17	12	8	6
New Zealand	34	11	0	1	46	:.	:	15	9	11	4
Portugal	38	0	3	0	41	19	:	12	2	:.	:.

1. Vocational and technical courses, to the extent that they can be distinguished from general ones (not always an official distinction).
2. Including four-year colleges, etc.
3. 1981.
4. 1981 figures covering non-university colleges, excluding non-collegiate schools.
5. 1981 figures covering two-year colleges and non-collegiate post-secondary schools with occupational programmes.
6. Two-year upper-secondary courses.
7. The distinction between "bachelor" and "lower" degrees is not official since 1977. The figures for Sweden in the last two columns are therefore estimates based on the total number of first degrees in 1984 and their distribution in 1976.
8. Including diplomas from three- and four-year high-school programmes, full-time or part-time, regardless of student age at graduation.
9. Mainly part-time technical education.
10. Including further education, private and public part-time study and the Youth Training Scheme.

Note: Comparability of the figures both between countries and within countries is limited as data may come from different sources. By "age class" is meant the total population born in a certain year. The years of reference differ according to the educational patterns typical of each country.

Source: OECD educational data bank and national statistical publications.

together with demographic trends, create a need for greater flexibility in allocating resources within education itself; from the difficulty of monitoring and maintaining quality levels in systems with high levels of enrolments; and – interacting with all the above – from budgetary constraints that limit the scope to absorb strains merely by increasing spending.

The extent of each of these pressures differs from country to country – as must the appropriate response. But three priorities for policy can be identified.

First, in many countries a need remains, according to the case, to either increase retention rates in secondary education to levels comparable to those in the other advanced economies (see *Table S.7*) or to ensure better co-ordination between school education and the wide variety of training programmes which are provided in other settings, including those within enterprises. Furthermore, in most European countries, there is a need to provide wider and more flexible opportunities for access to tertiary studies for both qualified school leavers and adults. And in many cases, the content and structure of studies beyond compulsory schooling and in training need to be reviewed towards a better balance between general education and the teaching of more specific vocational skills.

Second, higher levels of secondary enrolment, and the consequent expansion in the school system, can bring in their train severe problems in maintaining standards and in ensuring flexible adjustment to changing educational needs. An important step in both these respects is to improve the resource allocation process between and within educational sectors, so that it provides incentives for schools and training institutions themselves to enforce standards and adapt to demand trends.

In particular, there is a strong case for more parental choice and diversified opportunities in the education and training system, both within the public sector and between public and private providers. But it is important that a shift towards more diversified provision be accompanied by measures to maintain equity and promote equal opportunity – notably by providing relatively greater resources to schools in disadvantaged areas and for the education of social groups which tend to fail in the school system and then in the labour market.

Third, in virtually all OECD countries there is scope for increasing the adequacy of training and retraining facilities for adults. The need to do so is rendered urgent by present labour market conditions as well as by broader equity considerations; but it is underscored by longer-term demographic trends. Given these trends, the educational system itself – if it is to maintain its claim on resources – will have to expand its role as a provider of recurrent education; and it is particularly important that it do so, because in an economy undergoing rapid structural change, but where the working population is growing very slowly or even declining, additions and retirements from the labour force will no longer provide an effective means of adjusting the supply of skills. However, efficiently discharging this function will require greater openness in the formal educational system to the growing amount of training activity which takes place in other settings.

Desirable improvements in the quantity and quality of education will often involve considerable expenditure. New ways of financing education may have to be investigated, unless significantly increased costs can be covered in present systems. Particularly for higher education, there appears to be scope in many countries for increasing the financial contributions made by students and from other private sources – although it is also essential that there be adequate systems of financial support for students from low-income families as well as student loans available more generally. A greater reliance on private funding may appear to conflict with declared equity goals but the alternative of not making needed increases in educational provision would hardly be more equitable; and the evidence suggests that the benefits of publicly funded higher education do not primarily accrue to students from low-income families. The diffusion of tertiary education would be more effectively stimulated by reducing present inequities in educational attainment and quality at primary and secondary levels while using higher levels of cost-recovery to expand the number of places available in universities and other tertiary institutions.

C. EFFICIENCY AND EFFECTIVENESS IN THE PUBLIC SECTOR

Overall, the interaction of enhanced incentives in product markets and increased responsiveness in factor markets should provide a sound basis for improving performance overall; yet the gains in performance are likely to be considerably greater insofar as they are accompanied by improved efficiency and effectiveness in the public sector.

This is most obviously because the public sector now accounts for so large a share of societies' use of resources – and yet the processes by which these resources are allocated and the efficiency with which they are employed very largely escape the control of market processes. But it is also because the functioning of product and factor markets is so strongly influenced by the conduct of the public sector – not only directly, through the purchasing, spending and taxing functions of government, but also indirectly, as in the linkages between public and private sector collective bargaining.

Many of the problems of the public sector today arise from its previous growth; because the efficient management of resources is far more complicated when it is carried out at the public sector's present size and diversity, than at the scale of even only two decades ago; and because the impacts of public programmes on overall efficiency may alter as spending rises and coverage expands. But the need to reform the public sector also comes from the imperative of adapting to change: of reviewing programmes whose goals have been met or whose underlying premises are no longer valid; of adjusting overall spending and taxing to the altered trend of growth; and of developing new forms of co-operation between the public and private sector.

What is required is a continued search for cost-efficiency in public management: for ways of attaining public objectives at an acceptable resource cost. It is by no means obvious that this requires any sacrifice of social goals; but what it does require is greater emphasis on *incentives* for improving the quality and grade of service, eliminating unnecessary expense, reallocating resources more flexibly, achieving greater transparency and accountability, and for more carefully weighing the costs of a course of action against its benefits. Such an emphasis is important both in the internal conduct of the public sector's affairs and in its relations to the economy more generally.

1. Regulation and the scope of the public sector

A first step is to review the functions carried out by the public sector. These of course vary greatly from country to country; but in all countries the burden on public management could be eased both by more broadly decentralising the implementation process within government to regional and local authorities, and by improving the balance of activities between the public sector and private provision.

The need for review is particularly great in the area of the regulation. There is no blanket case for removing all regulations; indeed, notably in the environmental area, and in the protection of health and safety, public action is essential – though here too it is important that the regulations adopted be such as to achieve their objectives in the most cost-effective manner and while leaving the greatest room for innovation and the working of market forces.

There are, however, strong arguments for reforming the economic regulation of industries and firms – that is, the process by which government issues instructions which alter the resource allocation decisions of private agents. These arguments are partly negative: that is, based on visible inefficiencies in the way regulated industries operate, set prices and decide on investment. But they are also based on the fact that liberalising regulations yields benefits which go well beyond the measurable costs of regulation – benefits in the form of technological and organisational innovation and of enhanced dynamism in the economy as a whole.

Thus in the transport industries, where governments have traditionally exercised far-reaching controls over prices and output, it has become apparent that considerable gains can be obtained through greater exposure to market forces. In effect, far from serving social objec-tives, the net impact of regulatory controls has been frequently to raise costs, distort prices and perpetuate excess capacity; and where industries have been deregulated, prices have come down, the frequency of service has often improved, and demand has generally increased significantly.

Deregulation in these industries has typically not led to a deterioration in service to smaller and rural communities – indeed, organisational innovations and increases in efficiency have usually made it easier to ensure affordable service even to remote areas. Nor has deregulation typically resulted in "destructive competi-tion" – although industry structures have tended to change in the immediate wake of market opening, and continue to shift in line with market circumstances, the broad pattern has been one of workable and effective competition.

The industries which have been traditionally consid-ered as "natural monopolies" – that is, as being most efficiently served by a single supplier – pose more complex regulatory problems. These problems are inherent in technologies which provide incumbent firms with a large cost advantage over potential rivals, and thus undermine the effectiveness of competitive disci-plines. But even in these industries, there is frequently significant scope for competition; and the experience of the telecommunications industry highlights the gains that a shift to competition can generate – so long as the policies through which this shift occurs are mindful of the distinctive characteristics of these industries' tech-nologies, of the need to provide adequate safeguards for new suppliers, and of difficulties which can arise for consumers from abrupt changes in prices and conditions of services.

It is therefore likely that even in a more competitive environment, there will be a need for continuing regu-lation of the industries traditionally considered natural monopolies, both to prevent the abuse of dominant positions and to ease the transition problems a move to competitive provision may create. But regulatory proce-dures should be such as to maximise the incentives for efficient supply; a promising approach in this respect is that of regulating by setting a maximum rate at which the price of the regulated service can increase relative to the retail price index. At the same time, full application to these industries of competition policies can strengthen the safeguards provided to firms seeking to enter the market.

Both in these industries and in others, obtaining the greatest benefits from regulatory reform may require a review of the status and operation of public enter-prises.

Ultimately, the ownership of companies matters far less than the efficiency of their operation; and it is a competitive product market which – by ensuring that the most efficient firms displace their rivals – provides the key conditions in this respect. It is consequently essential to enhance the competitive environment in which public enterprises operate; and this can be accompanied by measures to place public enterprises on a more commercial footing. Enhancing public enterprises' operating autonomy, clarifying the functions and objectives of their boards and strengthening accountability through more transparent financial arrangements are important elements in this respect. The transfer of public enterprises to private ownership may well bring further gains, both by reducing the scope for political interference and by subjecting the firms' operating efficiency to monitoring by equity markets; though there is an undoubted trend in this direction, the experience is too recent to provide a basis for systematic analysis.

2. Social policies

Overall, the reform of regulation does not in general imply the abandonment of long-standing public objectives – it simply involves recognising that these objectives can better be met in a modified framework. This need to adapt the institutional framework most efficiently to meet the objectives of governments also underlies the reform of social policies.

Here too, the strengthening of incentives must play a key role. This is firstly because the services these policies involve are now such large industries in their own right – industries which would be more efficiently run were the incentives for their producers and consumers simpler, clearer and more transparent. But it is also because the present policies are in numerous instances simultaneously incompatible with demographic trends and limited taxable capacity.

Thus, by 1984, the health services alone accounted for over 7 per cent of GNP in the OECD area – and demand for health services will tend to rise further. There are no simple solutions to reconciling the desire for social equity in access to health care with advancing technology and the need to maintain public health expenditures within reasonable budgetary constraints. Though involving a mix of measures, policy in recent years has leaned heavily towards regulation of the supply of services through price and budget controls. Yet there are obvious political and social limits to how far such policies can be pursued. There has also been a trend to increasing user fees for health care, both as a rationing device and as a means of cost-recovery; and there seems to be some room for further shifts in this direction. Ultimately, however, the most promising approach appears to be that of revising the incentives bearing on the supply of health services. A shift to greater competition, in the context of improved information and of increased consumer participation in the financing of health care, would provide suppliers with more direct incentives to contain the costs and improve the quality of service. At the same time, strengthened interaction between insurance organisations – public and private – and the health service suppliers could enhance productivity in terms of the health outcomes. "Health Maintenance Organisations" (HMOs), though in many respects specifically adapted to the institutional context of the United States

health care system, provide valuable lessons in this respect.

Public pension schemes will also face substantial problems as a result of demographic trends. Governments in many countries have committed themselves to providing old-age pensions on a scale which is likely to be incompatible with budgetary constraints and present views of taxable capacity, even were GDP growth rates to increase significantly. The political and economic tensions this will create between pensioners and the active population can be most easily resolved if steps in the direction of reform are taken as of now – rather than having to implement crisis solutions when the situation has become untenable.

Though there is a range of options in this respect, it appears particularly important to increase the funded component of pension schemes. While this can be done in the context of public funded schemes, privately run programmes may prove more effective in developing attractive savings instruments and ensuring efficient placement of the funds collected. But this requires a regulatory context which clearly sets out and enforces responsibilities for operating these programmes and which adequately protects savers. Portability of private pensions is also essential if labour mobility is not to be impeded.

Finally, the major challenges facing unemployment compensation systems arise from the need to cope with continuing high levels and long duration of joblessness. Declines in replacement ratios in recent years have created significant hardship especially for the long-term unemployed and also for new entrants to the labour force. The scope for further such reductions will very likely be limited – though, in many countries, there is room to reduce the disincentive effects of unemployment benefits by making them taxable and tightening up tests of availability for work. At the same time, it appears desirable to accompany recent initiatives for the long-term unemployed with a generally greater emphasis on the provision of training, retraining and work experience for those out of work, especially in the countries where unemployment among the unskilled is high; and, more broadly, on measures to enhance the operation of placement services at least where high vacancies coexist with high unemployment.

3. Taxation

Improving regulation, reducing its scope and reviewing the framework for the provision of social services should significantly increase the effectiveness of government; but some of the most adverse impacts of the public sector on economic efficiency in the private sector come from the structure and level of taxation.

The problems are familiar. They arise from high marginal tax rates, which create incentives for evasion and avoidance, distort the allocation of resources, notably for investment, and reduce the supply of labour, and from tax provisions which discriminate more or less arbitrarily between broadly similar activities.

These costs can to some extent be attenuated by altering the structure of taxation. There are three important elements in this respect. The first is to reduce those marginal tax rates that have high disincentive effects (possibly as a result of their interaction with eligibility rules for social benefits) – because these almost invariably cause damage far in excess of the revenue they raise. Inevitably, concerns about equity are involved; but it is well to consider whether the pattern of marginal rates actually contributes effectively to the desired redistribution – and the income tax system is certainly a less effective tool for achieving an equitable income distribution than are full employment and well-functioning social policies.

The second element is to eliminate differences in tax rates applying to essentially similar transactions. Such differences ultimately lower revenue, and the occasional benefits they bring are typically overwhelmed by the damage they do to economic growth, as well as to the integrity of the tax system.

Finally, in the countries where such a shift has not already occurred, there is a strong case for changing the tax structure towards greater reliance on taxes which have a more neutral impact on economic decisions, in particular through a move from income taxes to taxes on consumption, for example, value added tax.

These goals can typically be brought about with no reduction in revenues. Indeed, elimination of tax-based discrimination among similar activities may raise revenues, providing room for a general lowering of tax rates. But while the reform of tax systems can reduce the damage they currently do, the tax burden ultimately reflects the size of public expenditure. The consequences of this expenditure clearly depend on the specific nature of the policies involved; and the overall economic effects of programmes to broaden the skill base or improve basic research are quite different from those of subsidies to industries no longer viable. Yet against the undoubted benefits certain spending programmes may create must be set the costs of financing these through taxation – costs in terms of eroded incentives and distorted choices. The evidence suggests that these costs are particularly high at the margin – so that the costs of increasing the size of the public sector, as well as the gains from reducing it, are significantly larger than the average economic cost of public sector spending.

This underlines the need to carefully review the quality of public expenditure, to ensure that the benefits obtained from outlays fully justify their costs and to exploit opportunities to reduce public spending relative to national income. Vigorous action in this respect can relatively easily provide both for a selective lowering of extreme tax rates as well as for a more general lowering. It can therefore make tax reform a significantly easier undertaking – but this will require hard economic and political choices about expenditure, and indeed about the appropriate role and responsibilities of government.

III. THE STRATEGY OF REFORM

Reform is therefore needed across a broad range of areas. But the economic desirability of change is hardly sufficient to bring it about; and a decisive shift in the stance of policy inevitably raises concerns and opposition. How can change most effectively be brought about?

There are three imperatives in this respect: drawing on broadly shared values of fairness to advance economic reform; capturing the public imagination through a programme of reform which is broad, bold and sustained; and ensuring that action domestically is reinforced by co-operative action at an international level.

A. ADVANCING FAIRNESS AND EQUITY

Inevitably, many microeconomic policies are first and foremost about *equity* – about attempts to bring market outcomes into line with societies' perceptions of what is just and tolerable. Few would deny that public policies have achieved a great deal in this area – and the review of these policies creates fears that hardship would be increased and burdens unfairly distributed. Yet, far from compromising widely shared goals, the reform of present policies would advance the cause of fairness.

In some cases, this is because inequitable outcomes are inherent in the policies presently pursued – in a manner often quite contrary to their original intentions. Thus, as tax levels have risen, increased complexity of income tax structures has greatly diminished their effective progressivity in many countries, in some instances to the point of actually favouring the best-off. Equally, it would be difficult to justify, on any broader social grounds, the redistributive effects of current agricultural policies: redistribution from poorer households to better-off farmers, from smaller to larger landowners. Yet these transfers are the largely unavoidable result of relying on price support as a means of raising agricultural incomes.

In other cases, inequities arise because the redistributions induced by the policies are not really under policy makers' control. Public utilities, for example, typically impose higher prices (relative to cost) on some services to fund lower prices on others – with the objective of assisting low-income households or those in rural areas; but because the redistributive effect depends on the extent to which different income groups use the various services, the pattern of transfers frequently does not correspond to the stated objectives.

And finally, inequities arise from the way policies have been changed in line with budgetary constraints. This is most striking in the case of social insurance: reductions in eligibility for unemployment compensation have created considerable hardship for the long-term unemployed; the costs of rationing public health care have fallen most heavily on the poorer consumers, at least in systems with both public and private providers of health services; if public schooling is cut back it is those who have no options who suffer most. In short, as policies which sought to do too much have been retrenched, the interests of those in genuine need have not been sufficiently protected.

These inequities can be diminished – by the reform of policies which provide rents to some at the expense of many; by carefully assessing whether purported goals of redistribution are actually being met in tax systems, subsidies and social policies; and by more clearly distinguishing income transfers from the supply of social services – so that more adequate transfers can be targeted at those in need.

Reform is also compatible with greater equity because social progress depends so heavily on growth. The major source of hardship in the OECD countries is almost certainly current high unemployment – and that unemployment is the principal cause of increased inequality in the distribution of income and of social opportunities. Relieving poverty and attaining a fairer distribution of life-chances hinges to a considerable extent on returning the advanced economies to sustainable, job-creating growth – yet this will be more difficult to achieve and maintain without the extensive review of microeconomic policies.

However, the move to a more competitive environment will not be painless, even in a context of improved economic performance – and a continuing process of adjustment involves "losers" as well as "winners". A recognition of social obligations is an important part of democratic values; and it is natural and desirable that help should be available for those who need assistance to obtain and sustain a standard of living judged socially acceptable. Perhaps the greatest help is that which allows individuals to return to a useful and productive life, freer if not free of dependence on the public purse and it is here that much remains to be done, through the more broadly based provision of education, training and retraining, by taking effective measures to assist the long-term unemployed, and by removing "poverty traps" which discourage responsiveness to job opportunities – but also by shifting policies onto a path supportive of overall growth. Economic and social policies therefore have a broadly complementary role in allowing as many people as possible to play an active role in society.

B. A BROAD APPROACH TO ACTION

The case for reform consequently goes beyond considerations of economic efficiency alone. But reform depends on more than convincing arguments; it hinges on the capacity of governments to secure broadly based support for change.

Approaching the reform of microeconomic policy as a whole can facilitate this process. There are clear economic benefits to reform on a broad front – and the mutually reinforcing nature of the measures adopted would make the gains not only greater but more readily visible. At the same time, the broadness of a programme of reform, which tackled the measures favouring narrow sectional interests at the general expense, would mobilise support through its evenhandedness and non-discriminatory nature – as recent experience with tax reform confirms. Finally, a bold approach, promising determined action across a range of areas, is more likely to capture the public imagination and highlight the opportunities change creates.

To be viable, a programme of reform also needs to be sustained – to provide time for the cumulative effects of measures to be felt, to allow for learning and experimentation, and to ensure that initial steps are not subsequently reversed. A commitment to *transparency* – the process of periodic, public and independent policy review – can support the momentum for change over the longer term and facilitate community understanding of needed policy adjustments. At the same time, public discussion and dialogue about policy reform can broaden the base of support and help avert the polarisation of conflicting points of view.

Such an approach can facilitate the task of economic reform; but it cannot make reform easy. Combined, fear of the unknown, the inertia of established procedures, and hostility by the vested interests can provide powerful forces obstructing change. Ultimately, overcoming these forces can only depend upon political leadership – on the willingness of governments and oppositions to make possible what is desirable.

C. THE INTERNATIONAL DI_

Nowhere is political leadership more impo_ in the international arena – for here the diffi_ exercising responsibility and ensuring better ou_ are greatest. But the effective functioning of the _er-national economic system is not only an essential goal of economic reform; it can also bolster efforts domestically to place microeconomic policy on a new course.

International agreements play an essential role in this respect: for they create a framework of rules and obligations which limit the scope for interest group pressures domestically, while increasing the legitimacy of change by visibly sharing its burdens and opportunities. Conversely, a weakening respect for international obligations – as has so markedly occurred over the last decade in the trading system – can only render domestic adjustment more difficult, encouraging rent-seeking and the narrow pursuit of sectional interests, while misleading communities into the belief that change can be postponed or even entirely avoided.

Present circumstances make it all the more important that the gains from co-operative action be exploited. A prospect of continued slow growth cannot be avoided without determined action to create an international environment conducive to expansion. In particular, it is essential that macroeconomic policies be brought into a medium-term, internationally compatible orientation which can reduce current imbalances and prevent the development of new disequilibria. But steps in this direction are not a substitute for the reform of structural policies; and action on the microeconomic front cannot and should not be postponed until all features of economic circumstances are entirely favourable.

This is because securing improved microeconomic behaviour takes time: because the range of areas in which policy reform is needed is so great; because the process of policy reform is slow and complex; and because the lags between the changes in policy and shifts in outcomes are frequently long. Yet, experience has shown time and again that expansions cannot be maintained, and the cost of the ensuing recessions is greatest, when the structural components of economies are functioning poorly: when labour markets respond to stimulus through unsustainable wage outcomes; when firms increase prices rather than output as demand rises; when possibilities for reducing costs, increasing efficiency and introducing new products are passed by; and when taxes and transfers blunt the incentives for growth.

It is for these reasons that the problems of microeconomic policy are crucial – for unless they are resolved, a return to sustainable growth is unlikely; and the gap between what is achieved and what communities could legitimately and realistically expect will remain unacceptably large.

INTRODUCTION

This report examines the economic impact of structural policies in Member countries and advances proposals for policy reform. In introducing the major themes of the report and setting out its structure, this chapter begins by surveying the broad course of OECD economic performance in recent years, concentrating on the deterioration in overall performance (Part I). It then examines the major changes which have occurred in patterns of resource use, highlighting the large adjustment challenges which lie ahead, and the need to place OECD economies on a footing consistent with and supportive of sustainable, job-creating growth (Part II). It subsequently examines the role of microeconomic policy in this respect and lays out the issues addressed in each chapter of the report (Part III). It concludes by discussing briefly some of the methodological problems that beset analysts who attempt to study the nexus between individual policies and aggregate performance, problems which necessarily condition and qualify the other chapters in this report (Part IV).

I. AN HISTORICAL PERSPECTIVE

Since the end of World War II, the OECD economies have gone through two distinct phases of growth which could be characterised as much by what was projected to occur as by what actually happened. In both periods, economic performance for a long time was the opposite of that which had been confidently expected.

The first of these was the long period of surprisingly strong growth from the late 1940s until the early 1970s. At the end of the war, most thoughtful observers expected a return to the conditions of depression, or at least of very low growth, which characterised the decade preceding the war. This forecast was proved false first in the United States, then in the reconstructed countries of Europe and, eventually, in Japan. Indeed, the next two decades – often cited as a "golden age" – saw unprecedentedly high and sustained growth throughout the OECD area. By the late 1960s, buoyant growth seemed the normal state of affairs and was widely expected to continue.

But even in the early 1970s there were signs of developing danger. Some might date this, in Europe at least, to the wage explosion following the events of 1968, others to the breakup of the Bretton Woods system in the early 1970s, but most would agree that it was the oil shock of 1973-74 that marked a definitive turn for the worse. In retrospect, the OECD-wide recession of 1974-75 which followed marked a clear-cut change not only in the quality of the business cycle, but also in the trend of economic performance. Still, even in 1977-78 a special study by the OECD – the McCracken Report – concluded that the poor showing of recent years was likely to be only temporary, and that a return to the growth of the 1960s was possible.

But the McCracken Report, however sober the optimism of its projections, overstated the potential for recovery. Within a year the second oil shock occurred and the weak recovery aborted. A shift to more restrictive monetary policies brought inflation under control but at an extremely high cost in terms of lost jobs and output. And although the recent two years have given cause for optimism, as yet no improvement has been seen in some of the more fundamental economic indicators, while the accumulation of macroeconomic imbalances casts grave uncertainties over the medium-term prospect. Thus, the severity, duration, and universality of the deterioration of economic performance stand out. Indeed, the deterioration seems to have been self-reinforcing.

Graph I.1 puts these developments in historical perspective. The chart shows the long course of economic growth as measured by output per capita for Europe, Japan and the United States over the last century and a half. Two facts are evident from this chart: postwar gains were very good indeed, and the more recent period of stagnation would, in many other periods, have represented a welcome gain. However, this latter fact does not justify a lack of concern over the slowdown in growth, for recent experience has indeed been poor across a wide range of economic indicators.

Table I.1 shows, for recent decades, three broad indicators of different aspects of economic performance: growth, inflation and employment. The table adopts the convention of dating the onset of stagflation from the first oil shock, and, seen in this more myopic view, the magnitude, sharpness and universality of the dislocation remain striking.

The deterioration in performance is even more apparent when the data are corrected for the effects of business cycles. Thus, Graphs I.2, I.3 and I.4 present a decomposition of historical data which show the trends of output, inflation and unemployment both for a

Graph I.1. Productivity growth, 1870-1985

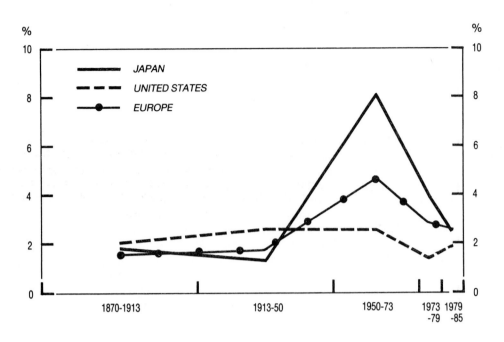

JAPAN

UNITED STATES

EUROPE

Note: Annual average compound growth rate of GDP per man-hour.
Source: Maddison, A., *Phases of Capitalist Development,* Oxford, *1982.*

Table I.1. **Growth in real output, inflation and employment 1965-1985**

Annual average percentage change

	US	Japan	Europe	OECD
Growth in real output				
1965-1973	3.8	9.8	4.7	4.9
1973-1979	2.8	3.7	2.5	2.8
1979-1985	2.1	4.3	1.3	2.1
Inflation				
1965-1973	4.5	6.2	5.3	5.1
1973-1979	7.5	7.9	10.6	9.0
1979-1985	5.9	1.5	11.0	7.7
Employment				
1965-1973	2.3	1.3	0.3	1.1
1973-1979	2.5	0.7	0.3	1.1
1979-1985	1.3	1.0	− 0.2	0.6

Source: OECD.

selection of OECD countries and for several major aggregates. Each chart shows the course of the relevant variable as a solid line and the smoothed trend as a line of dashes, both measured against the left-hand (logarithmic) scale. In addition, the shorter line of dashes shows year-to-year percentage changes of the variable measured against the right-hand scale. Starting dates vary according to the availability of data.

Attention focuses primarily on the line of dashes representing trend. A straight line would represent a constant trend. Examining the variables in turn:

- In each case the trend for real output displayed in Graph I.2 clearly shows deterioration. Furthermore, and perhaps somewhat surprisingly, the beginnings of the slowdown in trend growth generally precede the first oil shock. For the OECD as a whole, the trend begins to decline earlier in the 1970s, for the United States it commences in the latter half of the 1960s, and for Japan the slowdown is evident, beginning as early as 1971-72. In contrast, the slowdown in Europe as a whole does not commence until after the shock;

Graph I.2. **Level, percentage change and trend of GDP (volume)**
(billion $ (PPP) and percentages)

—— LEVEL   —— PERCENTAGE CHANGE   ----- TREND

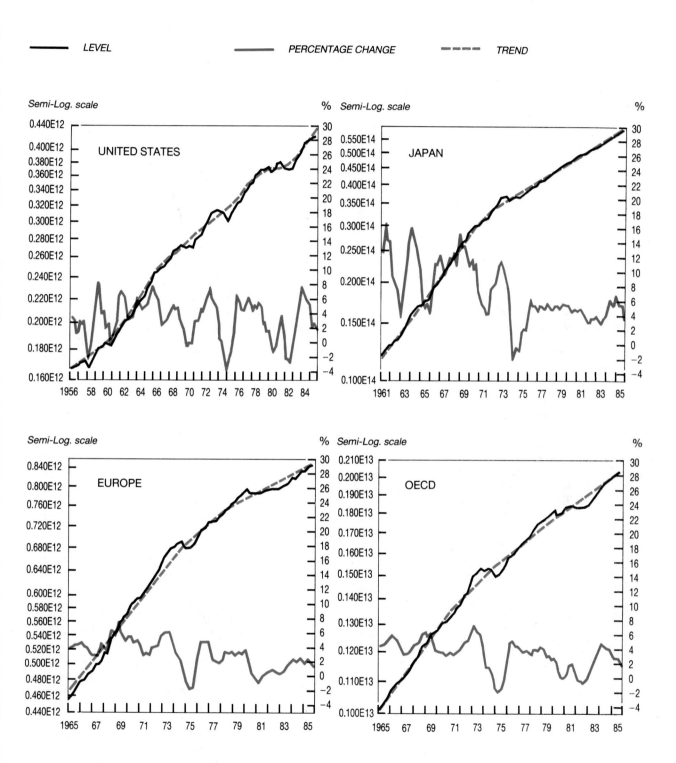

Source: OECD.

Graph I.3. Level, percentage change and trend of inflation
(percentages)

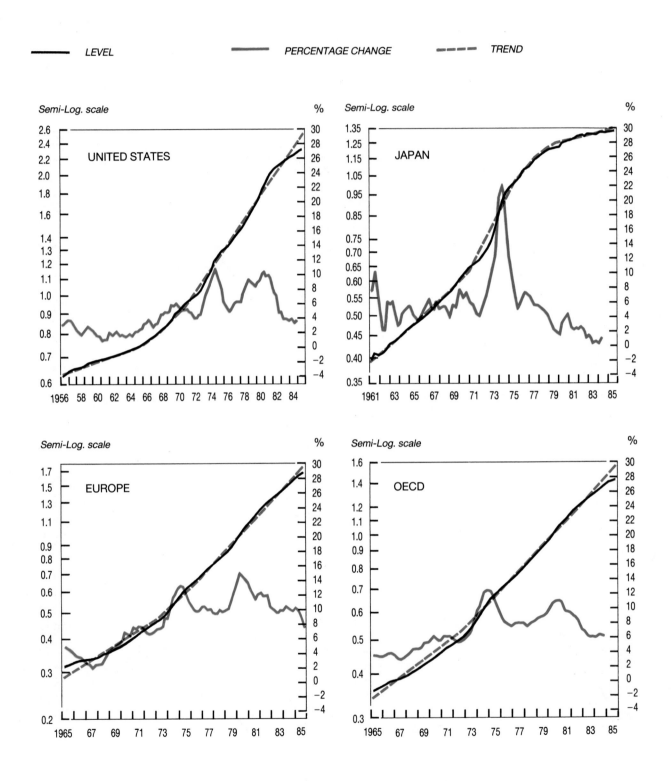

Source: OECD.

Graph I.4. **Level and trend of unemployment**

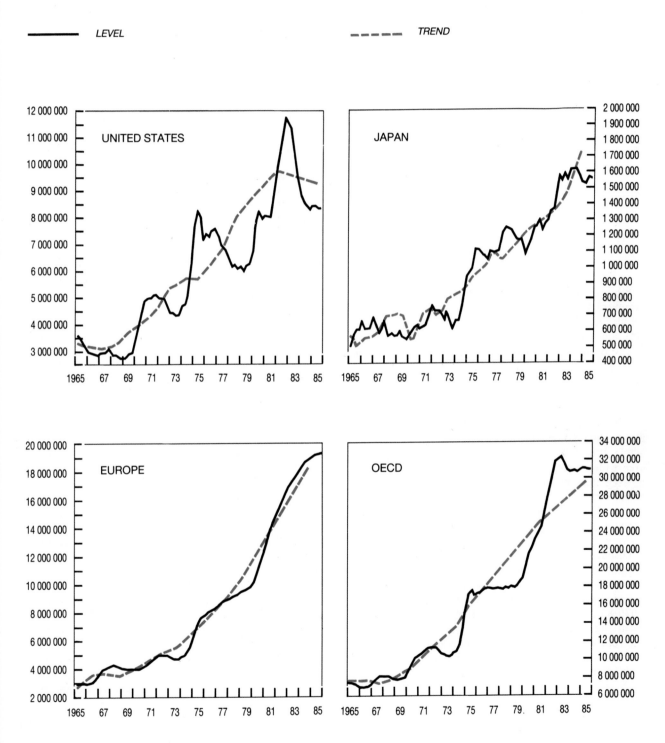

Note: The trend is calculated as the difference between the trend of the labour force and the trend in employment.
Source: OECD.

- Concerning inflation, shown in Graph I.3, for the Member countries taken together there is gradual increase going as far back as data are available and continuing, of course, only until the disinflation of the 1980s. The acceleration in prices is so gradual and continuous that it is not readily apparent from the trend chart but is quite visible from the percentage changes. In the case of the United States the acceleration, beginning in the early 1960s, is quite striking. For Europe the acceleration appears to commence in the late 1960s. By contrast, for Japan, the transitory "trend" acceleration in prices is clearly only a reflection of OPEC-I;
- Again, with unemployment in Graph I.4, the sample of unemployment trends shows virtually steady increases beginning in the middle to late 1960s.

II. THE CHANGING INTERNATIONAL PATTERN

While the overall trend towards deterioration is clear, however, there are also major differences between countries and regions and these differences raise important concerns about the medium-term prospects.

The most striking disparities at the macroeconomic level were in unemployment rates. Graph I.1 sets out average unemployment rates for individual OECD countries for 1973 and 1986; the relative volume of the shaded area for each country is proportional to its share of the OECD labour force – and hence to its contribution to the unemployment rate for the OECD area as a whole. It is clear from the data that the deterioration in area-wide employment performance was accompanied by a significant widening in the spread of unemployment rates, with the four larger European economies – Germany, France, the United Kingdom and Italy – accounting for fully 28 per cent of the rise in overall unemployment.

Disparities in macroeconomic outcomes have been paralleled by significant differences in the pattern of resource use. Tables S.4 and S.5, which are based on national accounts data, present trends over the period 1970-83 in the sectoral distribution of output, employment and total factor productivity (a weighted index of the combined productivity of capital and labour) using two ways of aggregating sectors. The first – set out in Table S.4 – classifies sectors into the three categories of high, medium or low growth according to their growth rates of value added relative to the average growth rate for all sectors. The second – set out in Table S.5 – ranks sectors by degree of openness to international trade, the first grouping corresponding to the public sector, the second to other non-traded services, the third to the activities largely based on natural resources (such as

agriculture or minerals), and the fourth to manufacturing.

The data presented in these tables are normalized so as to single out the extent of structural change – that is, the change in the composition of domestic output relative to world output. This is done by expressing the data for each sector as the *difference* between the *actual* growth rate of that sector in a country (or group of countries) and the growth rate which could have been *expected* given that country's overall growth rate of value added and the growth rate of that sector across all countries. In other words, a positive value for a particular sector represents the average annual percentage amount by which that sector grew in a particular country above and beyond the growth warranted by that country's overall growth rate and the OECD-wide growth of the sector.

A general conclusion which emerges from the data is that demand trends have been relatively uniform. Nonetheless, there are considerable differences on the supply side – in the way individual economies responded to the opportunities arising from demand and technological trends.

What set Japan apart from the other countries in this sample are not only its very high relative growth rates (the Japanese capital stock, for example, growing at over twice the OECD average), but also the extent of output redeployments – that is the extent of the shifts in the composition of economic activity. Thus, to take only one indicator of these shifts, the weighted standard deviation of sectoral growth rates was three times greater in Japan than in France, Germany and Italy, and the disparity was only slightly smaller between Japan and the average for the countries examined.

These output shifts have been associated with a marked transfer from activities oriented to the domestic market to those also working for exports. Thus, while on an OECD-wide basis, value added in the traded goods sector expanded over the period 1973-83 at around 3 per cent a year, in Japan it increased at an annual rate of 5.2 per cent. The shift to the traded goods sector is even more striking when the data are normalized, from which it appears that the "pure" output shift to traded goods was in the order of 2.2 per cent a year. This shift has been paralleled by a transfer of output towards the sectors growing rapidly on an OECD-wide basis from those growing less rapidly.

These output shifts have largely reflected the pattern of productivity advance in Japan. Thus, while total factor productivity in the Japanese traded goods sector was increasing at three times the OECD average, it grew little if at all in the services sector, large parts of which (notably distribution and transport) were significantly affected by direct and indirect regulation. At the same time, productivity in the resource-based sector, and especially in agriculture, was growing far more slowly than in the rest of the OECD area. In the absence of corresponding shifts in the exchange rate, and given continuing high levels of trade protection of important

Graph I.5. Unemployment rates in 1973 and 1986

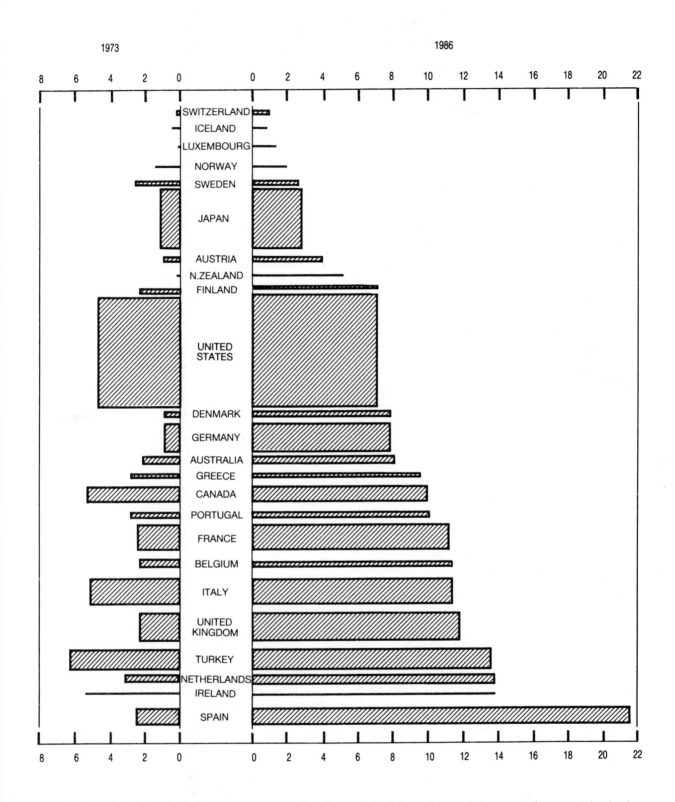

Note: The height of the shaded areas represents the share of the labour force of the respective countries in the labour force of the OECD area in 1986.
Source: OECD.

parts of the resource-based sector, adjustment entailed a net transfer of output to the traded goods sector above and beyond that required to compensate for external terms-of-trade shocks; combined with the demand stimulus coming from US macroeconomic policy, this led to the emergence of a significant current account surplus, which exchange rate movements are only now correcting.

The pattern in the *smaller European countries* is in some respects the polar opposite of that in Japan. In essence, resources and output in these countries have been transferred from the tradable and resource-based sectors to the non-traded sectors, with value added in the latter growing at a rate only slightly more than half that for the economy as a whole. This transfer has occurred despite the fact that productivity growth rates in the traded sector have been considerably higher than those in the non-traded sector; and the driving force in this transfer appears to be the growth of the government sector, which (notably in the Nordic countries) expanded at a growth rate double that for the OECD as a whole. The expansion of employment in the government sector was responsible for virtually all of these countries' employment growth; and it can be argued that the government sector and those activities closely associated with it – notably social services and the public utilities – acted as "employers of last resort", absorbing the increment to the labour force.

The *larger European countries* – the United Kingdom, Germany, France and Italy – also witnessed a shift of value added away from the non-resources traded goods sector. This was accompanied by a shift in output from the sectors growing rapidly on an OECD-wide basis towards those growing more slowly.

A distinctive feature of the pattern of resource and output shifts in these countries is the relatively rapid growth (on a normalized basis) of the agricultural sector, whose actual value added growth rates were nearly three times the OECD average. In contrast to the smaller European countries, there has not been a significant expansion in the output of the government sector; indeed, though transfer payments have increased considerably, value added in government services has expanded less rapidly than in the OECD area as a whole. In this sense these economies have not had (and presumably could not have had) an "employer of last resort"; and given wage formation in the private sector (discussed in Chapter 3 below), this has been associated with negative growth rates of employment and rising levels of joblessness.

Finally, the distinctive features of the evolution of resource use in the *United States* are the very low growth rates of total factor productivity and the high rates of growth of employment, the latter being more than double the OECD average. These trends are fairly uniform across sectors, with the result that the structure of the United States economy has changed relatively little, though the sectoral distribution of the capital stock has changed significantly more than that of

employment or value added. This relative stability has possibly reflected the continental size of the United States economy (which means that offsetting inter-regional changes in specialisation may lead to a relatively stable overall pattern) and sectoral wage adjustments which have allowed the maintenance of high employment levels across a range of sectors. But given low rates of increase in total factor productivity, the growth of consumption in the United States has depended to a considerable extent on the running down of domestic savings and an increase in foreign indebtedness, with a concomitant rise in the current account deficit.

Each of these patterns has an inherent element of unsustainability. Thus, it is difficult to presume that Japan could continue to shift resources to export-oriented activities and maintain growth rates above those of the rest of the world. Equally, low rates of growth of productivity and low levels of domestic savings ultimately must constrain the growth of living standards in the United States. Nor can the Nordic countries indefinitely rely on the expansion of the government sector (with its corollary of growing tax requirements) to sustain employment and output levels. Finally, high and persistent unemployment in the large European countries not only entails a high economic cost but threatens social consensus and legitimacy.

Correcting these unsustainable configurations will impose a further significant burden on the OECD economies – a further need to absorb external shocks, to redeploy resources, to adjust to largely unpredictable patterns of supply and demand. In this sense, the OECD economies face a dual challenge: to deal with the immediate consequences of the winding back of unsustainable situations; and to create the conditions for a return to durable, job-creating growth.

III. THE ROLE OF MICROECONOMIC POLICIES AND THE STRUCTURE OF THIS REPORT

How can the OECD economies meet these challenges? It is obvious that macroeconomic policy has a crucial role to play in this regard; and much will depend on whether monetary and fiscal policies provide a clear, medium-term and sustainable orientation. But the OECD economies' capacity to face immediate difficulties and exploit future opportunities also hinges on the microeconomic context: on whether this context encourages economic actors to respond to or to ignore possibilities for growth; and on whether it reduces or increases the risks involved in maintaining aggregate demand at a high level.

Virtually by definition, the microeconomic context is diffuse, covering a broad range of outcomes and processes, each influenced by a myriad of specific and general government measures. These measures are often outside the control of economic policy makers, and their consequences for overall performance are themselves diffuse and uncertain, frequently depending as much on the interaction between and accretion of policies as on the discrete effects of any particular intervention. As a result, the role of microeconomic factors in shaping overall performance is often not taken adequately into account – and even more importantly, the scope for improving the microeconomic context not fully utilised.

This report examines the manner in which policies can contribute to creating a microeconomic context supportive of sustained growth. The issues involved go beyond the conventional meaning of "structural adjustment".

Structural adjustment is often taken to be synonymous with structural change in the composition of output and notably in industry. But this is likely to be misleading for three reasons. First, there is no reason to assume that responding to new opportunities always involves a shifting of resources – indeed, resource shifts typically account for no more than 30 per cent of aggregate productivity advance. Rather, productivity is increased *both* by shifting resources and by augmenting efficiency in existing uses. Second, some resource shifts may reflect policy distortions in market signals and notably in relative prices – witness the growth of agricultural output in recent years or the trend of steel output in the 1970s; so that it would be dangerous to assume that changes in resource use are always desirable. Third, on a more empirical note, there is no discernible link between the extent of resource shifts in an economy and its overall performance. For example, in terms of the data reviewed above, the two countries with the greatest degree of change in the composition of output are the United Kingdom and Japan – countries whose aggregate performance is quite different. Statistical analysis of this data finds no relation between any indicator of resource shift and growth or employment, casting doubt on the often expressed view that strong output growth "facilitates" change in the composition of resource use.

In short, responding to opportunities means far more than shifting resources among industries. Rather, it entails exposure to *incentives* for efficiency and a *capacity* to respond to these incentives – regardless of whether this involves moving resources around or making better use of them where they are. The focus of this report is consequently on the opportunities for increasing the effectiveness of this process: that is, for enhancing the incentives economic actors face and strengthening their capacity to respond.

In carrying out this task, the report surveys the major policy areas involved, examines the consequences of policies for performance and advances recommendations for how policies could be improved. It seeks, in other words, to overcome the diffuseness of government involvement in the microeconomy by providing a systematic review of a broad range of areas – and identifying a programme of reform which can improve the functioning of incentives in each of these.

The structure of this review follows that of national economies: the report begins by examining the supply and allocation of factors of production – the inputs of labour, capital, skill and scientific knowledge. It then turns to the operation of product markets, which provide the signals by which resources are directed among competing uses. And finally, it analyses the economic impacts of the public sector – which (abstracting from household production) is the major non-market component of national economies, as well as being a component which has grown rapidly in the last fifteen years.

In each of these areas, the report focuses on the major concerns which policy makers have had to face: that is, on the principal factors which have been seen as preventing stronger growth today and which could make good performance more difficult to sustain in future, with particular emphasis on the role of government policies. This section provides a brief overview of the issues addressed.

A. The supply and allocation of productive factors

Thus, starting with factor availability, it is questionable whether shortages either of labour or of capital have constrained growth in the last fifteen years. After all, labour markets have become increasingly slack, and on an area-wide basis, investment shares have actually risen, while capital productivity has tended to fall. However, there are legitimate concerns about whether education and training systems are performing adequately in adapting skills – or "human capital" broadly defined – to changing needs; and the rise in youth joblessness, notably in Europe, underscores the urgency of these concerns, which are dealt with in Chapter 1.

Equally, the prospects for stronger growth over the long term are affected in important but largely unquantifiable ways by society's investment in scientific knowledge; and as far as basic research is concerned, much of this investment is publicly funded and allocated. Both the level of funding and its distribution have been severely affected in recent years by budgetary constraints and by changes in government priorities and these trends have created particular problems for the universities. The scope for raising the productivity of investment in basic research, and notably for improving the institutional framework in which it is carried out, is considered in Chapter 2.

While the physical availability of labour and capital has not been a major constraint on growth, the processes by which these resources – and notably labour – are allocated has constrained performance in many countries. The problems at a macroeconomic level are familiar: they centre on the tendency of nominal wages to grow more rapidly than economies' capacity to pay, creating inflationary pressures and making full employment difficult to achieve and maintain. But these macroeconomic concerns are paralleled by inefficiencies in the microeconomic functioning of labour markets, which segment employment opportunities and impose great costs on the weaker elements of the labour force: the young, those approaching retirement age, and the long-term unemployed. These outcomes are largely the result of labour market institutions and especially of the process of collective bargaining; the mechanisms involved and the possibilities for reform are reviewed in Chapter 3.

Almost every characteristic of labour markets finds its opposite in financial markets. They are especially important because they are the mechanism by which national saving is translated into investment. Financial markets are widely recognised to be very flexible; and increasing financial integration within many national economies and increasing integration internationally have increased this flexibility further. The resulting transformation in the way financial markets operate has enormous consequences for the advanced economies: they allow new efficiencies in the processes by which savings are allocated and the efficiency of their use is monitored; but they also increase the sensitivity of markets to distortions arising domestically and internationally from taxes and subsidies; and they create new concerns about the adequacy and efficiency of the regulatory framework. At the same time, the perceived "asymmetry" between the responsiveness of financial markets and rigidities in factor and product markets creates fears that too much of the burden of adjustment may fall on changes in asset values. These issues are examined in Chapter 4.

B. The operation of product markets

The degree to which an economy makes the best use of its resources hinges on the operation of product markets – on the capacity of markets to ensure that firms concentrate their efforts on those activities which yield the highest return and that opportunities are seized to increase productivity and to introduce new products and processes. The effects microeconomic policies have on the efficiency of product markets are examined in Part II of the report.

Agriculture is in many respects a pathological case of government intervention in the microeconomy. By the early 1980s, subsidies for farming were equivalent to more than half of the sector's value added in the OECD area – leading to growing supply-demand imbalances and widespread trade frictions, as well as imposing a non-negligible cost on the economy as a whole. The mechanisms at work and the options for reform are addressed in Chapter 5.

Many of the most acute problems of coping with structural change have arisen in manufacturing industry, as a result of changes in input prices, in competitiveness and in patterns of demand. In numerous cases, governments have sought to cushion the effects of these changes, usually with adverse implications for the adjustment process. The need for a new view of industry policy, which takes into account the blurring of sectoral boundaries within manufacturing, and the increasing interdependence between manufacturing and services, is argued in Chapter 6.

International trade is the single most effective way of exposing firms to continuing pressures to innovate and increase competitiveness. The liberalisation of international trade in the years following World War II played an essential role in permitting rapid growth – not only by moderating price increases but also by allowing fuller exploitation of the gains from economies of scale, product differentiation and investment in R&D. This had effects well beyond the product markets themselves, for it acted as an important competitive discipline on labour markets and bolstered the confidence of investors. Chapter 7 analyses the processes at work; it also shows that from the start important sectors were excluded from trade liberalisation. Under the impetus of slower growth, the protectionist tendencies have become more dominant, threatening liberal trade itself. Trade liberalisation needs a new start – based on reversing the protectionist measures of recent years, resolving outstanding trade conflicts and extending the open trading system to services and high technology.

C. Efficiency and effectiveness in the public sector

The expansion of the public sector, in both size and scope, has been an outstanding feature of postwar economic development, most markedly in Europe. As the public sector expands, an increasing share of society's resources – in some countries half of GDP – is allocated not through market-based processes but administratively; and administrative processes also have a far-reaching impact on the manner in which factor and product markets work. The potential for increasing the efficiency and effectiveness of the public sector is the subject of Part III.

A first set of issues refers to the scope of the government sector – the extent to which the efficiency of resource use could be enhanced by revising the range of public activities. This reassessment has been particularly significant in the industries which have traditionally been regulated: the transport industries and the public utilities – such as telecommunications and electricity, gas and water. Together, these industries account for some 10 per cent of OECD GDP; and there has been growing awareness in recent years of the potential for increasing efficiency and accelerating innovation by removing, easing or reforming the regulatory framework. Experience in this respect and some directions for policy are surveyed in Chapter 8.

Redistribution of income by governments grew steadily throughout the postwar period. It was achieved directly through tax and transfer systems as well as indirectly through other programmes, be it public investment, defence spending, or industrial support, whose primary aims may not have been redistributional, but in which the choice of ways and means was often conditioned in part on redistributional goals. This redistribution served to maintain social consensus in the face of a radical change in the social and economic environment. And, by the late 1960s, there was evidence that some of these programmes, particularly publicly supported pensions, had sharply reduced the incidence of poverty and want among some of the targeted groups.

However, government commitments generally came to be expressed as a collection of entitlements of private groups to public resources. Such entitlements – to the poor, the unemployed, the aged, the ill, and those affected by special adverse conditions such as industrial change or foreign competition – were manageable only so long as there was little call upon them; that is, so long as economic growth proceeded at a smooth and rapid tempo. But with the slowing of economic growth, the call upon these entitlements exploded even as the resources available to maintain them became subject to tighter constraints. Funding at a higher level seemed to require a greater fiscal commitment than the social consensus in many countries could maintain. Likewise, reducing the level of commitment also strained social consensus. At the same time, critics pointed to the adverse effects, both of the programmes themselves and of the associated tax burdens, on incentives to work and to save. Thus, the recipients of entitlements felt that governments were failing to deliver the promised support, and critics of redistribution felt that, rather than delivering a more desired income distribution, governments were developing and maintaining a large population of chronic dependants. The options for resolving these difficulties in the areas of health, old-age pensions and unemployment insurance are reviewed in Chapter 9.

The concomitant of rising public spending has been growing tax requirements, though in some cases governments have sought to postpone tax increases by accumulating government debt. The consequences for economic growth of the rising financing requirement of the public sector have probably been substantial. They have come about both by reducing the supplies of labour and capital and by channelling available supplies into activities that are tax-favoured rather than productive. Furthermore, the prevalence of high marginal tax rates in many countries has created political pressure for exceptional treatment of many groups and activities, a problem that tends to mount: given the level of tax revenues needed to finance the public sector, the creation of exceptions implies higher tax rates for non-favoured activities, which creates pressure for still greater favouritism and for new exceptions. The proliferation of tax-favoured activities leads to a tax system that is complicated and widely perceived as unfair – as well as being inefficient. The evidence in this respect, and the possibilities for change, are discussed in Chapter 10.

IV. ADDING UP

It would be helpful – and indeed, it would foreclose argument – if, after such a wide-ranging review of the problems of and prospects for microeconomic policy in the developed countries, it were possible to conclude by presenting one comprehensive set of statistics that would summarise the whole. Such a set of statistics would identify each major cause and the degree to which that cause was responsible first for the rapid growth of the 1950s and 1960s, then for slower growth of recent years. And it would pinpoint with undeniable precision the contributions, both positive and negative, of major government policy measures – both micro- and macroeconomic. And this, in turn, would allow Member governments to apply this quantitative knowledge in formulating and improving future policies and especially in setting their priorities for policy reform.

But, of course, no such data exist, nor, at this time, is it possible for economists to produce them. This is not to say that there have not been attempts, and some partial information is most enlightening. Moreover, the range of estimates available has expanded in recent years, as has the range of techniques for analysis. Nevertheless, there are a number of reasons why it is difficult if not impossible to "add up" the effects of microeconomic policies – or indeed the gains that could be made by improving them.

First, quite simply, to measure the effects of policies requires that the policies themselves be measurable. While this may be relatively simple (albeit timeconsuming) for some policies, such as taxes, others, such as many regulations, present nearly insurmountable problems. At the same time, it is important to remember that some of these unmeasurable policies may have the same effect as measurable policies – as non-tariff barriers to trade have effects similar to tariffs. Besides pointing to the essential similarity of the effects of policies which may be formulated in very different ways, this means that measuring only where possible the costs of policies can lead one to conclude that the unmeasurable policies are always better.

A good deal of work has been done to provide quantitative estimates of the costs of some of the policies whose effects are difficult to measure – for example, by converting non-tariff barriers into their notional tariff equivalents. But even if all comparable policies could be measured in a common fashion, it is not possible at this time to integrate these policies into a single model of a whole economy – a model, for example, which would allow one to estimate the total number of jobs lost because of taxes, regulations and inappropriate industry policies.

This is because microeconomic policies are of two kinds, which differ in the way they alter economic performance, and no model exists in which both kinds fit together in an explicit way. The first kind of policy *permanently* alters market prices and quantities and can for many purposes be evaluated *without* respect to the "transitory" effects such policies have on the process of market adjustment. This is the case for policies that induce distortions or alter spillovers – for example a tax on pollution. In contrast, the second kind of policy – one that alters flexibility – acts to delay or to hasten market adjustments toward ultimate longer-run values which are themselves unchanged by the policy. These policies do not, in principle, indefinitely distort economic outcomes, but they may impose or reduce costs as economies adjust to disturbances; and given the potential frequency and importance of shocks, these policies can affect the level of economic performance over long periods. Moreover, through repeated application, these policies can alter the expectations of economic agents, and hence their behaviour over the longer term. Although this classification may appear relatively straightforward, in fact the two sorts of policies typically interact in such a way as ultimately to be indistinguishable in their effects. Thus, a complete model would need to focus on the interaction of their effects, and such a focus must take into account both "static" (permanent) and "dynamic" (adjustment) effects.

Although there is as yet no common model in which these two sorts of effects, static and dynamic, can be weighed quantitatively, there does exist a family of models that is increasingly widely used to evaluate *static* effects alone. These "general equilibrium" models ignore adjustment processes and assume, in a sense, that all markets are ultimately balanced by price and quantity adjustments. But the equilibrium that is attained may be influenced by various distortions, including distortions imposed by policy. These models have been extensively used to evaluate the long-run effects of tax structures and trade policy, and their results are discussed in the relevant chapters. In the tax area, for example, it may be fair to characterise the general tenor of results as follows: actual tax structures do tend to reduce overall economic well-being by a significant amount, perhaps 3 to 5 per cent of GDP in many cases studied. Although this number may not be large in comparison to the costs of some business cycles, a more striking result characteristic of this analysis is that the economic losses are disproportionately larger at the margin than for the total tax structure. In practical terms this suggests that well-designed tax reforms and reductions in public spending which resulted in some reduction of tax distortions would result in relatively large gains in economic performance.

It is less easy to characterise the results for trade. This is partly because in the trade area some of the weaknesses become more apparent. The present generation of models generally rests upon assumptions of constant returns to scale – that doubling an economy's inputs will double its outputs – so that international trade stems primarily from considerations of comparative advantage. However, economists have come to emphasize the importance of "increasing returns" – that doubling inputs will more than double outputs – and specialisation in generating trade patterns. Thus, model-based evaluations of barriers to trade will substantially understate the potential gains from more liberal trade patterns – as some of the results cited in the chapter on trade show.

Beyond this, there remain subject areas where these models could be applied but have not yet been, and areas where such models seem inappropriate. Still, these models themselves remain a topic of research in their own right, so that any results are tentative and experimental. This is basically because the models are grounded on very strong assumptions. In particular, assumptions need to be made about key demand and supply elasticities – most of which cannot be adequately tested against the data; and the further assumption must be made that the elasticities used are globally stable and that even major movements from the reference scenario will not alter the fundamental behavioural features of the model. Finally, in implementing these models, the level of economic activity is often taken as exogenous, so that the effects of policy changes are confined to the pattern rather than intensity of resource use. Nonetheless, these models can provide a valuable basis for policy analysis in situations where a policy change would have a fairly broad horizontal impact on an economy and where the primary concern is with outcomes in the long term, rather than with the path by which these outcomes will be achieved.

In contrast, there exist virtually no well-developed models of adjustment processes which would allow quantification of dynamic effects in an economy-wide framework. The problem is that very little is known about the dynamic context in which individuals make decisions, decisions that are affected by costs encountered in changing behaviour and by the fundamental uncertainty that governs the environment around us. For example, economists, business leaders, and government policy makers are all aware of the importance of expectations, of attitudes towards risk, and of "animal spirits", in the decision to innovate or to invest, but these essentially subjective features of the economic landscape have thus far escaped measurement or agreement as to their determinants. Consequently, work on these and related topics remains at the frontier of economic research.

Yet it may be that some of the most decisive effects of policy are on expectations – both at a macro- and at a microeconomic level. Thus, it has been argued that in the 1950s and 1960s, the climate of confidence engendered by stabilization policy may have played a significant role in promoting microeconomic efficiency. This could be thought to have come about particularly by promoting a willingness to take risks in exploiting new opportunities. But the consequences may have changed in nature with the repeated application of these policies. The process of inflation itself, by raising now one price, now another, confounded market signals and incentives. And alternating surges of inflation and episodes of recession, however moderate, may have tended to increase uncertainty where risky ventures are concerned. But such policies also induced another and rather different kind of certainty: insofar as government was committed to maintaining full employment, the expectation grew, and was in many cases validated, that governments would intervene in individual markets where necessary to protect industries from harm. And as this occurred, market participants may have come to ignore market signals in expectation that government would change the signals.

In short, policies need not only alter outcomes – they may alter the entire dynamics by which outcomes are generated. And the broader the range of policies, the more likely it is that, cumulatively, they will do just that – but these effects cannot be adequately modelled.

In the absence of models that explicitly incorporate these factors, attempts can be made to infer the possible macroeconomic gains from appropriate microeconomic policies quite indirectly. For example, usual macroeconomic models implicitly incorporate existing inflexibilities in the labour markets of the economies being modelled. A comparison of parameters and results from these different models can show the gains to be derived from more flexible markets in the event of shocks by suggesting how performance in country A would improve if its labour market had parameters more like those of better-performing country B. Some work along these lines is discussed in the chapter on labour markets.

But this is really no more than saying that the economy of country A would operate as well as that of country B if it worked the same way. This sort of comparison has two very severe shortcomings. First, it remains to be determined what the actual contribution of policies is to the existing difference and, second, it is

yet another matter to decide whether policies can be designed to change the ill-performing market in the desired direction.

In this sense, the natural starting point for improving the functioning of microeconomic processes is an analysis of individual policy areas and of the prospects for reforming policy in each of these. And this is indeed the approach of this report. But it needs to be emphasized at the outset that the gains from improving policy in any particular area almost always go well beyond that area. The interlinkages between areas, though difficult to model, are nonetheless real – and they are more important in some areas than in others. Competition in product markets is particularly important; for it not only guides an efficient use of resources but exerts pressure for efficiency on factor markets, notably for labour. But more generally, the competitive process needs to be viewed as a whole, and it is impossible to durably insulate any one part of the economy – say agriculture – from market forces without affecting expectations and behaviour elsewhere. Equally, there are pervasive linkages from microeconomic behaviour to macroeconomic policy: for it is clearly less risky to keep aggregate demand at a high level in an economy which responds flexibly to opportunities and constraints than in one with pervasive rigidities in product and factor markets.

These linkages make the gains from improving policy all the greater – even though a number cannot be put on this effect. But each of the reforms advocated in this report can be justified in terms of the specific policy area it addresses. After all, policy in these areas has evolved to meet specific needs; and it is relative to these needs that it must first of all be assessed. The reform of educational systems, for example, will not only help labour markets function better, but will also yield an educational system which is fairer and more efficient; the reform of agricultural policies will not only remove a particularly severe set of distortions to overall efficiency but will also help put the agricultural sector on to a surer and more sustainable medium-term basis; the reform of social policies is necessary if long-standing goals of social equity are to be met. Improvement in each area yields its own rewards – and the fact that markets interact, as do policies, only makes the case for review stronger.

TECHNICAL REPORT

I. THE SUPPLY AND ALLOCATION OF FACTORS OF PRODUCTION

Chapter 1

EDUCATION AND HUMAN CAPITAL

INTRODUCTION

The development of contemporary economies depends crucially on the knowledge, skills and attitudes of their work-forces – in short, on human capital. In many respects, human capital has become even more important in recent years. Technical progress, continual change in productive structures and the growing complexity and internationalisation of markets have made the working lives of large parts of the population more demanding – with unemployment harshly illustrating the consequences of insufficient competitiveness.

In several Member countries there are still too many young people who leave education without completing upper-secondary school. For these countries the expansion of educational attainment remains an important objective; its achievement may in many cases require some restructuring towards providing more of a broad preparation useful both for work and further education. Elsewhere, where average educational attainment is already high, there are often reasons for concern about the quality of the instruction dispensed and its orientation.

The present chapter is motivated by the need to improve educational provision in the face of the challenges posed by economic change. Both general education and vocational training may be in need of improvement; new forms of delivery, administration and financing may have to be introduced.

The relevant policy options are manifold and vary from country to country, each of the latter having its own educational legacy with particular strengths and shortcomings. There is no universal educational model suitable for emulation in all countries. However, much can be drawn from comparison of national experiences. The necessarily sketchy presentation that follows is not meant to serve as a basis for comprehensive analysis of education systems in individual countries, let alone their critical assessment; but it highlights the case for enhancing both the general educational level of OECD work-forces and their vocational skills.

The organisation of the chapter is straightforward. Part I discusses the nature of the challenges and the relevant policy objectives. Part II analyses the operation of educational institutions against the background of these objectives. Part III deals with financing and with the allocation of resources within educational systems. The conclusions are summed up in Part IV.

I. CHALLENGES AND POLICY OBJECTIVES

Although educational policy making is everywhere a concern of government, it must be kept in mind that responsibilities are often shared among various levels of authority as well as with non-profit and private organisations. The existence of private markets and profit-maximising institutions for some kinds of education tends to limit the role for public policy making even more. To be successful, educational policies must be conceived and implemented in ways compatible with this diversity of institutional framework.

Though institutional structures differ, a basic policy goal permeating education in all countries is to increase the productivity of human resources – so as to enable more valuable output of work, and thus allow higher wages and/or profits in the economy as a whole. This objective is closely intertwined with non-economic goals, such as the promotion of culture, equity and social cohesion. Although there is a risk of conflict between these objectives, in practice they have often proved quite consistent – promoting equity, for instance, may also improve the functioning of the economy, since it involves a wider spread of opportunities which may make the work-force more flexible[1].

In recent years, high unemployment has raised acute concerns about the performance of education systems in many countries. The labour market situation has triggered widespread experimentation with new forms of courses facilitating young people's transition from school to work and supporting adults displaced by structural change. Though valuable, recourse to such *ad hoc* activities should not obscure the need for longer term adjustment within the core educational system, i.e. the regular system for youth education and its ramifications for recurrent and adult education.

The labour market challenges that call for long-term adjustment of the educational systems stem from the pressures of international competition, technological change and, more generally, the need for flexibility.

Though individual Member countries all have their own economic, cultural and educational legacies, they now face largely the same market conditions and use more or less the same technologies and sources of information. In this situation, each country's prosperity hinges to a great extent on the skill with which it pursues the activities in which it has a comparative advantage, and on its ability to enhance its competitiveness under what are inherently unpredictable market conditions.

The global character of these competitive challenges does not imply that all countries should necessarily adopt the same educational policies; there may after all be several viable options. But failure to meet the challenges is certain to have grave consequences, a fact which inevitably raises serious concerns for countries whose education systems perform poorly by international standards – be it in terms of quantity, quality or flexibility.

Shortages of workers in certain skill groups, such as computer software specialists, numerically controlled machine-tool operators and multilingual secretaries are a common occurrence, particularly in cyclical upturns. They may impose significant constraints on the economy, although they remain on the whole a largely temporary phenomenon. A more serious, but less easily defined, deficiency may reside in the mediocrity of a work-force's overall level of proficiency – in a firm, an occupational group or a country. This can create a social environment which, over the long term, inhibits the exploitation of new opportunities and efficient management of technological change.

The remedies to these problems must be sought both in the education system and in the labour market. Work in itself contributes to the development of skills, a process which can be strengthened with the help of better organisation. Educational deficiencies can also be attenuated by more substitution between various levels and kinds of skills. In most labour markets the demand for skills adapts to some extent to prevailing supply conditions, a phenomenon which may have important implications both for industrial structures and for the organisation of work within enterprises. The objective is thus not only more and better education, but also an improvement in the labour market's ability to develop and make use of skills.

The present pace of change has reduced the scope for basing educational provisions on forecasts of demand for particular qualifications, and the time horizon over which such forecasts can reliably be made is now quite short. As a result, part of the burden of responding to changes in qualification requirements tends to shift from organisers of youth education to individuals on the job and to providers of adult education in various forms. Young individuals are in the long run best served by a broad education that opens many alternative options for further education or work-related training; excessive specialisation should consequently be avoided in youth education.

Understanding the challenges to education systems is therefore not primarily a matter of specifying particular changes in occupational distributions or technologies, and such specification will not be attempted in the present chapter. Rather, the key aspect of current challenges is flexibility. Workers must be prepared to meet change – in terms of both the nature of work itself and the need for further education or retraining. Recurrent education should be systematically facilitated, for instance by eliminating dead-end tracks in secondary schooling. In many cases, the rules of access and the design of courses may have to be modified in order to make it easier for adults to resume education after years of work.

Education systems also need internal flexibility. Resources may have to be shifted, for instance from primary to secondary and post-secondary education, or between general and vocational courses. Furthermore, curricula and teaching methods need to reflect the continuous changes that occur in technology and economic organisation.

In the economic theory of human capital, it is conventional to distinguish between general skills, which are useful for many jobs, and specific skills, which are typically tied to particular employers. This distinction has little to do with the separation between general education and vocational training, since many vocational skills are perfectly transferable. For policy purposes, it may be better to distinguish between general education (at various levels), training for transferable vocational skills, and training for firm-specific skills. In practice the extent to which skills are specific or transferable depends largely on institutional factors related both to education systems and to the organisation of work in firms. National systems differ greatly in the extent to which they are geared towards producing general education, transferable vocational skills or firm-specific skills. It will be argued in this chapter that government policies should, first, promote a wide diffusion of general education, and, second, ensure that vocational training as far as possible leads to skills which are documented and readily transferable.

The benefits *general education* generates in working life are largely indirect. It facilitates the learning and re-learning of more work-related skills, and it trains the student's abstract and creative thought processes, thus improving his or her ability to respond to changes in the work environment. Many studies have shown that these benefits can be substantial, even under the most varied conditions. Thus, higher average levels of general education, e.g. upper-secondary rather than just compulsory education, tend to be associated both with greater occupational mobility and with easier acceptance of new technologies in manufacturing, agriculture and services[2].

Rapid economic and social change is therefore in itself a factor that increases the need for general education at both compulsory and post-compulsory levels. General education – also above the levels that presently correspond to compulsory schooling – should be dimensioned and designed so as to prepare large parts of the population for flexibility in their working lives, rather than being seen purely as a basis for further academic studies.

Vocational skills are even more closely linked to the functioning of labour markets. The very notion of vocational training can hardly be understood without reference to labour market institutions, which inevitably differ from country to country. Regardless of its organisation, a good education and training system should not simply adjust to prevailing conditions in the world of work. It should also provide labour markets with standardized credentials by which particular skills can be identified and matched efficiently to jobs.

Thus, an important role of education and training is to help employers "sort" (or "screen") individuals. This sorting function has a positive impact on work productivity, despite the fact that it may be unrelated to the quality of the skills actually created. But it may have unfortunate repercussions on the education system itself. This is particularly the case when selection is exercised primarily in general education, with undue emphasis on the rather one-dimensional criterion of academic performance (or, simply, on the social status of education institutions). By contrast, well differentiated systems for certifying skills in particular vocations increase the coverage and transparency of training, and hence promote the efficiency of both the education system and the labour market.

In the following sections, the contribution of education to increasing economic efficiency is discussed in relation to the following operational objectives.

First, in addition to being made familiar with the "three R's" and other basics, everyone should be afforded a secondary education which can serve as a useful preparation both for working life and for further studies. Secondary education should always have sufficient breadth and depth to allow some choice between alternative kinds of further education and adult education.

Secondly, the education system should ensure the development of vocational skills which are in demand and recognised in the labour market. These skills should not be too narrowly defined in terms of the job tasks covered.

Thirdly, opportunities for adult education should be accessible in practice to the majority of the population, including those who missed educational opportunities during their youth, those wishing to upgrade their skills and those who need retraining.

A fourth objective – touched upon only briefly in this chapter – is the provision of scientific and other advanced qualifications. These are discussed in the chapter on long-term research.

II. THE FUNCTIONING OF EDUCATION SYSTEMS

A. The quantity and type of education given to young people

The majority of young people receive general or vocational education until at least the age of 18 in most OECD countries. This implies, in practice, that most of them get some formal education at upper-secondary level. In higher – post-secondary – education, the differences among countries are more striking[3] (see Table 1.1).

There are many definitional problems which call for caution when making international comparisons using these data. They describe the "through-put", i.e. enrolment and graduations, rather than the quality and amount of knowledge dispensed. Compulsory schooling starts at lower ages in some systems than in others, and the curricula may be more or less intensive. In some countries, notably in Europe, many young people continue upper-secondary level studies for one or several years after the "regular" graduation age of 18, while elsewhere this is far less common. Nonetheless, while such particularities must be kept in mind, the following differences among OECD countries seem to be sufficiently robust to be considered relevant.

First, the percentage of 17-year-olds attending educational institutions is highest in Germany and Japan, followed by the United States and some of the smaller European countries.

Second, Japan, the United States and Canada are the only larger countries where a majority obtain the credentials required for entering university. In these countries, even those who take vocational upper-secondary courses can go on to college and university, although in North America some of them may need to start with remedial courses. The number of young people obtaining credentials for university entrance is particularly high in Japan; the United States' high schools have somewhat higher drop-out rates.

Third, the proportion of young people actually studying at post-secondary level is higher in the United States than elsewhere. As indicated by the frequency of post-secondary degrees, Canada, Japan and Norway have also achieved a wider diffusion of post-secondary study than most countries.

Fourth, in Germany, Austria and Switzerland, the majority of upper-secondary students are apprentices who undergo part-time general education in schools for one or two days a week. In these countries the general education system is much more selective than in Japan and North America; thus only a minority has the opportunity to study at university level.

Fifth, in the rest of Europe, upper-secondary education is usually split between general and vocational streams, both mainly located in schools. Apprenticeships often exist, but are less important. On the whole,

Table 1.1. **Patterns of post-compulsory youth education around 1984**

Estimated ratios in per cent of total population in relevant age classes
(Countries ranked by total enrolment rate at age 17)

Country	Enrolment of 17-year-olds:					Share of age class getting credentials for entry into higher education		Ratio of the number of entrants into higher education to size of an age class (%)		Ratio of the number of persons taking post-secondary degrees to size of an age class (%)	
	School education		Apprenticeship, part-time, etc.	Post-secondary, etc.	Total	Universities in general	of which: Limited choice only	Universities[2]	Other	"Bachelors"	Lower
	General	Vocational[1]									
Germany	32	18	46	1	97	28	6	17	9	12	8
Japan	63	27	0	0	90	92[8]		26	12	24	11
United States	81	0	..	6	88	73		28[3]	34[4]	24[3]	34[5]
Netherlands	35	41	10	0	86	50		10	24	6	18
Belgium	78	0	8	0	86	20[3]		12	20	15	..
Sweden	32	51[6]	2	0	85	77	50	36	0	15	15[7]
Switzerland	20	7	55	0	82	14		..	..	..	..
Austria	14	20	44	0	78	13[3]		17	..	16	..
Canada	67	0	..	9	76	75		..	..	23	13
France	25	38	10	2	75	29		18	12	13	12
Norway	38	36	1	0	75	70[3]	35	18	..	18[3]	42[3]
Denmark	35	33	6	0	74	25[3]		22	13	14	11
Italy	22[3]	25[3]	23[3]	0[3]	70	51		27	1	11	1
Australia	37	0	20[9]	9	66	43		31	17	16	6[3]
United Kingdom	18	12	35[10]	0	65	37		31	0	15	12
Spain	34	15	..	0	49	25		17	12	8	6
New Zealand	34	11	0	1	46	..		15	9	11	4
Portugal	38	0	3	0	41	19		12	2	..	..

1. Vocational and technical courses, to the extent that they can be distinguished from general ones (not always an official distinction).
2. Including four-year colleges, etc.
3. 1981.
4. 1981 figures covering non-university colleges, excluding non-collegiate schools.
5. 1981 figures covering two-year colleges and non-collegiate post-secondary schools with occupational programmes.
6. Two-year upper-secondary courses.
7. The distinction between "bachelor" and "lower" degrees is not official since 1977. The figures for Sweden in the last two columns are therefore estimates based on the total number of first degrees in 1984 and their distribution in 1976.
8. Including diplomas from three- and four-year high-school programmes, full-time or part-time, regardless of student age at graduation.
9. Mainly part-time technical education.
10. Including further education, private and public part-time study and the Youth Training Scheme.

Note: The figures are theoretically comparable both between countries and within countries, but some incongruencies are inevitable since the data often come from different kinds of sources. By "age class" is meant the total population born in a certain year. The years of reference differ according to the educational patterns typical of each country.

Source: Educational data bank of the OECD and national statistical publications.

the percentage of young people obtaining credentials that give access to higher education is only slightly higher than in the German-speaking countries, but vocational education is considerably less widespread.

The data in Table 1.1 suggest that the structure of secondary education is a major factor determining the scale of higher education in different countries.

Thus, in most of Europe, the selective nature of general education at secondary level and the great differences in the content of general and vocational courses are outstanding features. Students are separated early according to their abilities – often already in lower-secondary schools, and nowhere in Europe later than at the beginning of the upper-secondary stage. As a result, those young people whose school performance is substandard at low ages tend, in practice, to have fewer opportunities to compensate for this as they grow older, even if some remedial courses are available. (In Norway and Sweden, the borderline between general and vocational secondary education is somewhat less rigid than elsewhere in Europe and a large part of the university system is open to vocational school graduates.)

By contrast, the school systems of Japan and North America give broad general education to large majorities. At upper-secondary level, i.e. in high schools, the stress is on general and civic education. All high schools lead to some kind of diploma which, at least in principle, confers general eligibility for post-secondary studies. There are relatively few vocational high schools and their students receive more general education than is common in European vocational training. In Japan, the vocational element constitutes less than 30 per cent of all lessons given in "vocational" high school classes[4]. As a result of the structure of high schools and their high enrolment rates, vocational preparation in Japan and North America typically occurs at higher ages than it does in Europe. Colleges and universities in these countries offer a wide variety of courses with a more or less marked orientation towards specific occupations. In most cases, however, there is considerable stress on a common core of general subjects even at this level.

Although these differences are conspicuous in themselves, the more crucial questions in this context are how the supply of skills fits demand, and to what extent the interaction of supply and demand actually produces skills and work patterns favourable to economic growth.

A cursory glance at supply and demand for skills in some countries reveals striking contrasts. For example, in the 1970s fears of an "over-supply" of theoretical education – and of ensuing employment difficulties for highly educated people – were most widespread in Europe, where the actual supply of such education was low compared to Japan and North America[5]. On the other hand, the Japanese authorities perceived their experience of vocational and technical teaching in upper-secondary schools as somewhat disappointing. Japanese employers had not been particularly interested in hiring people with vocational education. To some extent, these contrasting experiences resulted in two opposite shifts of resources, i.e. one towards more vocational and technical education in some European countries, such as Belgium, France, Italy, Spain and the United Kingdom, and the other towards even more general education in Japan (see Table 1.2).

Conventional measures of the demand for skills, such as job vacancies, are unreliable as indicators of the relative adequacy of education. Employers' demand for skilled labour is influenced by existing supply conditions. For instance, if certain skills are known to be in

Table 1.2. **Trends in the distribution of enrolments in different types of upper-secondary education**

	1970				1975				Latest available year[1]			
	Vocational	Technical	Vocational and technical	General education[2]	Vocational	Technical	Vocational and technical	General education[2]	Vocational	Technical	Vocational and technical	General education[2]
Austria	66.0	11.1	77.1	22.9	67.7	13.8	81.5	18.5	63.5	19.1	82.6	17.4
Belgium[3]	11.4[4]	31.0[4]	42.4[4]	57.6[4]	18.1	30.3	48.4	51.6	27.7	27.8	55.5	44.5
Denmark	47.4[5]	19.3	66.7	33.3	37.8[5]	22.1	59.9	40.1	21.5[3]	41.0	62.5	37.5
Finland					37.2	15.9	53.1	46.9	39.2	13.9	53.1	46.9
France	49.4[6]	8.8	58.2	41.8	48.7	10.9	59.6	40.4	47.7	12.5	60.2	39.8
Germany	75.5	10.2	85.7	14.3	70.4	12.0	82.4	17.6	68.7	10.8	79.5	20.5
Greece	20.5[7]	1.9[7]	22.4[7]	77.6[7]	19.0	2.5	21.5	78.5	14.0	4.5	18.5	81.5
Ireland	31.5[8]	2.0[8]	33.5[8]	66.5[8]	33.2	0.8	34.0	66.0	32.1	0.6	32.7	67.3
Italy	18.1	40.9	59.0	41.0	19.1	44.5	63.6	36.4	21.6	44.5	66.1	33.9
Japan			41.5	58.5			37.0	63.0			30.3	69.7
Netherlands	37.3	30.9	68.2	31.8	24.9	30.7	55.6	44.4	20.4	38.9	59.3	40.7
New Zealand							26.4	73.6			24.6	75.4
Norway			55.0	45.0			51.7	48.3			56.4	43.6
Portugal												
7-11th year			45.2	54.8			36.3	63.7			9.6	90.4
10-11th year			22.2	77.8			22.9	77.1			27.8	72.2
Spain	8.4	6.4	14.8	85.2	23.0	15.4	38.4	61.6	29.9	15.9	45.8	54.2
Sweden	27.2	47.2	74.4	25.6	19.0	52.9	71.9	28.1	13.9	56.1	70.0	30.0
Switzerland					68.8[9]	6.0[9]	74.8[9]	25.2[9]	66.8	8.3	75.1	24.9
Turkey	11.1	12.7	23.8	76.2	16.3	15.2	31.5	68.5	14.0	13.8	27.8	72.2[10]
United Kingdom[9]			39.5	60.5			31.1[12]	62.9[12]			43.3[13]	56.7[13]
United States			24.0[14]	76.0[14]							24.0	76.0

1. 1979: Greece, Ireland, Portugal; 1980: United States; 1981: Denmark, Finland, Norway, Spain, Turkey, United Kingdom; 1982: Austria, Belgium, France, Germany, Italy, Japan, Netherlands, New Zealand, Sweden; 1983: Switzerland.
2. Including teacher training.
3. French- and German-speaking courses only.
4. 1972.
5. Apprenticeship.
6. Not including apprenticeship.
7. 1973.
8. 1965.
9. 1977.
10. Increase mainly in Moslem teacher training schools.
11. Estimations for students from 16 to 18 years old.
12. 1974.
13. Dates of data collection were changed from 31 December to 31 August.
14. 1971.
Sources: OECD, *Educational Trends in the 1970s,* Paris, 1984; OECD, *Education and Training after Basic Schooling,* Paris, 1985.

short supply, many employers will be deterred from looking for them even though they may be needed. To the extent that it is feasible, employers may organise the necessary training on the job. Furthermore, employers in any labour market have an incentive to organise work so as to reduce the need for particularly scarce or expensive skills – or, in the extreme case, to abandon the critical activities altogether.

The complex interactions between supply and demand for skills have been illustrated in comparative studies of the manufacturing sector in France and Germany[6]. According to these studies, differences between the two countries in the distribution of labour demand between manual and theoretical skills can be explained by differences in the respective education systems – namely, in France, a historically greater supply of persons with academic skills and a relative neglect of generic vocational skills, with the opposite pattern prevailing in Germany. In the absence of adjustments in the supply of skills, enterprises have gradually adjusted their demand through different patterns of work organisation. On average, French firms have relatively high shares of white-collar workers and many levels of management, and are inclined to maintain close supervision of the work done by blue-collar workers; in Germany, the more numerous skilled blue-collar workers tend to be relatively independent, reducing the need for supervision and detailed management.

A conclusion that can be drawn from these and similar studies is that the short-term demand for education and skills may be significantly influenced by traditions and institutions which are more or less independent of current economic trends. However, although these traditions and institutions may seem rigid, the possibility of long-run changes cannot be overlooked – and indeed may represent a major potential for improvement in a country's economic performance. In examining these possibilities, it is useful to look in more detail at some of the issues related to regular education for youth as well as some specific questions regarding vocational training and adult education, respectively.

B. Educational quality and fairness

1. Student performance in different systems

Much of the education debate in recent years has focused on quality. Reports on the performance of students have caused alarm in several OECD countries. There are fears that the pursuit of "excellence" in educational elites has been compromised by the post-war emphasis on equity and mass education at post-compulsory level. But there is also concern about the alleged failure of schools to achieve even the most fundamental goals, such as universal literacy[7].

Since the 1960s, the International Association for the Evaluation of Educational Achievement (IEA) has undertaken a series of studies in various countries on the achievement levels of students at the ages of 10, 14 and 18 years in a number of basic subjects (including mathematics, reading, science, and foreign languages). The organisers of these studies have repeatedly warned against their use as "educational Olympics"[8], arguing that differences in educational objectives preclude direct comparisons of student performance between countries. Nonetheless, the IEA material has on several occasions – in the absence of other evidence better suited to the purpose – been referred to for precisely such comparisons.

In the United States, for instance, the National Commission on Excellence in Education[7] has observed, along with numerous others[9], that the academic performance of high school students compares unfavourably with that in other countries in several of the IEA tests. The IEA researchers have pointed out that this may be due to the fact that American high schools enrol much higher shares of relevant age groups than do the corresponding schools in most other countries. It is probably more difficult to attain high average performance rates in a system that enrols the majority of young people than in a more selective system; but in Japan both enrolment rates and performance levels are well above the international average. (The tests in the United States and Japan cover samples of students from all kinds of high schools, while those in European countries exclude vocational streams.) At the ages of 10 and 14 years, for which school enrolment is almost universal in all industrialised countries, performance differs somewhat less. Some results for the United States[10] also suggest a significant deterioration in the average performance of 18-year-old students in the decade following the mid-1960s – a deterioration that has since been only marginally reversed. This cannot be explained by rising enrolment, since the major expansion took place in previous years.

Regardless of the interpretations that can be given to international differences, few doubt that the quality of student achievement is cause for concern in most OECD countries. There is little consensus, however, on how to tackle the problem. In Europe, the debate has often been related to the issue of unitary ("comprehensive") versus differentiated schools at the lower-secondary level. Perceived quality deficiencies have also been seen in some European countries as a more general warning against excessive enrolment in academically oriented education; in particular it has been argued that not all students are sufficiently gifted to benefit from the academic content of secondary education and that the development of the most able students may be hindered if they have to share classrooms with low performers. On balance, there appears to be little evidence to support these fears[11]. Thus, a large number of studies have shown that post-compulsory general education, in particular the completion of upper-secondary education, tends to be associated with an increase in the subsequent incomes of students in virtually all occupational groups[12]. And some IEA results have also been interpreted as indicating, though not quite unambiguously[13], that the top ten per cent of students achieve more or less equally good results in most countries, despite the fact that some have selective and others comprehensive systems. At the same time, there is some evidence that disadvantaged students can benefit from the presence of more high-performing classmates[14]. The worst results are typically found in classes where students from disadvantaged social backgrounds are in a majority and have little contact with more education-minded social groups.

In the United States and Canada, the unitary character of lower-secondary schools has seldom been seriously questioned, and virtually universal high school enrolment is widely considered as a desirable goal. Young people who do not complete high school are looked upon as drop-outs, and their numbers – 25-30 per cent of an age group – constitute a considerable social problem, since high school diplomas are frequently required for both jobs and vocational training. In the United States, policy responses to the problem of inadequate student performance have not as a rule involved any increase in the differentiation of high school curricula. On the contrary, the National Commission on Excellence in Education[7] has proposed stricter requirements as regards the common core of basic subjects that are to be studied by all high school students, and changes in this direction have already been implemented in many states. Another key proposition advanced by this influential commission is that teachers and students should work harder: the recommendations included longer school days, shorter holidays and more homework.

The long-standing problems associated with *de facto* social and racial segregation due to geographic patterns of habitation remain a major educational issue in the United States. To a somewhat lesser extent, this is also true in several other countries. As will be discussed later, both the patterns of competition within the education system and the ways in which resources are allocated to schools have in several cases created inequalities in educational quality that were not intended when the systems were designed.

In effect, parts of the vast range of post-secondary educational facilities in the United States need to compensate for deficiencies in students' achievements in high school. As indicated earlier, fewer Americans than Europeans continue secondary education after the age of 18 years. In Germany, for instance, many apprenticeships and some other secondary courses normally extend beyond the age of 18. Repetition of school years is also common in many European countries. Furthermore, in several of those countries requirements are such that many students fail altogether, despite the fact that they can often repeat school years. In the United States and in some parts of Europe, such as Scandinavia, stronger emphasis is placed on limiting the number of drop-outs and sticking to the normal duration of time spent in schooling, i.e. on the "through-put". These differences indicate the variety of approaches to the enforcement (or non-enforcement) of quality standards, but they also reflect the fact that the American college system is relatively generous in offering several chances to those who did not perform particularly well in high school. Such relatively easy access, in combination with a sufficient supply of remedial courses, is probably a necessary condition for as wide a diffusion of academic education as has been achieved in the United States.

Many European countries have moved towards greater uniformity in the content of secondary education, though not as far as Japan and North America. Even where education systems have undergone particularly radical changes in the post-war period, as in Finland, Norway and Sweden, a relatively deep split between vocational and university-preparatory streams has been maintained at the upper-secondary level. Nonetheless, a number of university courses have been opened to people without the formal secondary qualifications normally required for university entrance. Thus, in Sweden anybody aged 25 years or over who has been working for five years can study at university. This has created new education opportunities for large numbers of adults, though in practice many have to start with remedial courses.

2. The selective function of education

Several of the problems affecting education are due to its function of selecting individuals. Although this function is primarily related to education itself – i.e. it "screens out" those deemed unable according to education's own criteria – it has a great importance in the labour market as well. Indeed, the educational selection may often be of crucial importance to students in their subsequent working lives, sometimes even regardless of the actual content of education. Thus, intense competition among students tends to occur whenever employers are perceived to attach high value to certain kinds of credentials or to those of particular institutions. Such competition encourages student performance but if carried to extremes, it may also prove detrimental. When this selective function is valued to such an extent as to obscure education's other functions, it may have adverse effects on the priorities established by policy makers and teachers and on students' education choices.

Patterns of selection and competition in educational systems are closely linked to social structures. Historically, educational differentiation has largely been based on the patterns of stratification typical of each society. A fundamental goal behind the introduction of standardized performance ratings, aptitude tests and other screening devices has been to reduce or neutralise the impact of social background factors and, consequently, to increase fairness and efficiency. As these are introduced, previous mechanisms of social stratification connected with the traditions and resources of families have to some extent been replaced by more individual-centred and competitive – "meritocratic" – career models. But experience has shown that higher socio-economic groups are often over-represented in attractive schools even when selection is strictly based on performance. The very fact of differentiation has seemed to produce such a bias, especially when it occurs at low ages. Moves toward more unitary secondary-school systems, as discussed above, have proved the most successful in reducing these disparities. These moves have therefore often been deemed necessary on equity grounds, in addition to pedagogic considerations.

In the United States, longitudinal studies of former high school students have suggested that in the 1950s ability was only slightly more important than social background factors in explaining variations in college attendance; by the early 1970s ability was much more important than social background. Though it is clear that the role of socio-economic factors in education is far from eliminated, it is no longer pervasive[15]. Even higher levels of social mobility were achieved in Japan, where a 1978 survey[16] found that 22 per cent of students in national universities and 18 per cent of students in municipal universities and colleges came from the lowest quintile of the household income distribution (controlling for the age of parents). Thus, enrolment in Japan's public higher education institutions was virtually unaffected by parental income. In private higher education institutions, by contrast, enrolment was influenced by household income, with the lowest income quintile accounting for only 11 per cent of students. On the whole, social factors are probably less important for educational attainment in Japan than in almost any other OECD country. This achievement is widely held to be due to the far-reaching reforms implemented after World War II, including the introduction of a highly unitary school organisation and the virtual eradication of dead-end courses at upper-secondary level. In the social environment thus created, individual careers depend almost entirely on proven ability – a fact which appears to have profound effects on the atmosphere felt by students in Japanese schools, notably in fostering fierce competition.

The highly competitive atmosphere is a key element in the "state of desolation" recently attributed to Japanese schools by the National Council on Educational Reform[17]. Despite the fact that the Japanese school system now leads the world both in terms of high school completion (92 per cent of an age group) and – to the extent that such comparisons can be made – in terms of the scores obtained in cognitive tests such as those of the IEA, the National Council has heavily criticised the system's current performance. It argues that a high price has been paid for the impressive student achievements, a price which includes not only hard work but also a marked bias on measurable cognitive and academic skills. By international standards, Japanese students generally have long school days, few holidays and a great deal of homework[18]. School classes are large, implying some neglect of individual needs. Many students consider it necessary to take additional private lessons after ordinary school hours[19].

There is deep concern in Japan about the negative effects of the competitive school atmosphere – these involve, for instance, nervous breakdowns, too little leisure, and neglect of children's social and emotional development. "Bullying" and other kinds of disturbing behaviour are said to be increasingly widespread among less motivated students. The National Council on Educational Reform has emphatically argued that Japanese schools must pay more attention in the future to the "full development of personality", including "respect for individuality, freedom and self-restraint, responsibility for oneself and the importance of the human mind", rather than to just the cognitive skills[20].

It would seem that some selection among students is inevitable in any education system, and that this selection tends to enhance competition to the extent that it is not determined by socio-economic factors other than student performance. Selection, however, does not require the exclusion of large numbers of students from those kinds of secondary education that can serve as a basis for higher education. Thus, in Japan the "losers" in the educational competition are not usually excluded from higher education – unlike their European counterparts – but their choice of institutions becomes limited. This is also the case in the United States. Both Japan and the United States have large numbers of high schools and colleges which may be formally comparable, but which differ strongly in terms of their reputation for quality and educational style. These differences are enhanced by variations in entrance requirements, forms of ownership, tuition fees and other financial resources.

The entrance requirements of high schools and universities in Japan and the United States are often based on aptitude tests. In the United States, tests are organised independently of the education institutions and subject to special regulations. Each institution may also have its own entrance tests, interviews and other procedures; requirements vary from school to school and then frequently go beyond the mere measurement of academic achievements, attention being paid also to social skills such as ability to work in groups, participation in sports, music, etc. In Japan, a joint achievement test forms the basis of entrance to all public universities; but this test is typically followed by further tests, interviews and other procedures which are particular to each institution.

In Japan, the more prestigious institutions of higher education include national universities, particularly that of Tokyo. Their counterparts in the United States are a handful of private universities and, in the United Kingdom, Oxford and Cambridge. Many of the students attending these institutions come from a relatively small number of upper-secondary schools with equally selective entrance requirements. Degrees from the leading universities are valued highly in the labour market, often virtually regardless of course content. It has been argued, therefore, that the education systems in Japan and the United States – though inspired by egalitarian principles – have in reality developed into two-tier structures, whereby the difference is made up not so much by the quantity or orientation of the education as by the institutions' social status and reputation for quality – and by the selective procedures themselves.

These features can only be understood in relation to the ways in which labour markets function for most middle-grade jobs in Japan and the United States. When recruiting, Japanese and American employers tend to attach more importance to where candidates have graduated from and at what levels than to the subjects studied. College education is often not very specialised (with the exception of professions such as medicine and law), and employers largely content themselves with hiring persons who have a broad enough general education to be able to learn the job at work.

A relatively low degree of occupational specialisation is also typical of large parts of the university systems in the United Kingdom and Australia. By contrast, many continental European countries have strong traditional ties to polytechnics and specialised university education. It has been observed, for instance, that an industrial manager in Germany typically has a degree in the technical speciality in which his firm is operating, while his or her counterpart in the United Kingdom is more likely to have a BA or B.Sc. degree in science or some other academic field[21].

It is possible that the relative absence of specialised labour markets for various occupational sectors has in some cases encouraged an excessively one-dimensional pattern of selection, based on academic performance in general or simply on the social status of education institutions. Indeed, in Japan many large enterprises recruit their skilled workers almost entirely among the graduates of well reputed high schools and universities. This explains the fact that the competitive school atmosphere in Japan extends to almost all students regardless of which kind of work they aim at.

It is interesting to compare the Japanese experience of educational competition with that of the French *grandes écoles*, which form part of a highly selective system for education and career structures. In France, not only the admission rules but also the content of education itself are largely oriented towards selecting and channelling the most gifted young people towards leading posts in the civil service and large enterprises[22].

Thus, the selective functions of education seem to work almost regardless of the actual content of education. In the French school system, the sorting function has a clear impact on educational content – only a minority of an age group is prepared for higher education, a minority which is subject to successive stages of screening, so that only a few receive the instruction required for taking the entrance examinations of the *grandes écoles*. On the other hand, a widespread removal of differences in educational content, as in postwar Japan, has not fundamentally altered the sorting process. A paramount feature in both France and Japan is precisely the above-mentioned use by important employers of uniform and one-dimensional recruitment criteria. In the United States, by contrast, a more heterogeneous labour market may have helped to avoid some of this excessive reliance on one-dimensional rankings of intellectual performance.

A common characteristic of Japanese and American high schools is the relatively strong stress on civic education. In North America, the curricula often include considerable amounts of non-academic activities. Europe's academic upper-secondary streams, by contrast, are still seen mainly as preparation for university and, accordingly, offer less to students who will enter the labour market without any further education. Nonetheless, many young Europeans follow the academically oriented tracks without ever obtaining a post-secondary degree. As a result, "over-education" has become a common concern in European countries, despite the modest diffusion of general education in their school systems compared to those of Japan and North America. This apparent paradox may be explained by the fact that academic upper-secondary education in Europe still has an important sorting function. The alternatives to academic streams are often educational dead-ends – or, at least, avenues that are likely to provide a much more limited range of opportunities and lower social status. In Japan and the United States, the sorting process is intimately linked with the existence of a multi-layered hierarchy of institutions but not, as in Europe, with the very access to academically oriented education.

A good general education, and the opportunities it brings for further education and adult education, can be useful to a much broader range of people than just the academic elite. Therefore the process of selecting elites should not prejudice educational provision for other groups. In other words, the fact that some selection may appear as inevitable should not be allowed to obscure the desirability of a good general education for all.

3. Recommendations concerning education systems in general

A number of tentative policy recommendations can be drawn from the above which apply to the quantity, quality and orientation of formal education provided to young people.

First of all, a wider participation in formal education at post-compulsory levels is desirable in many countries. The need for a theoretical understanding of complex technologies and abstract information, and a capacity for critical reflection in general, is not limited to academic elites. It appears to be increasing across a broad range of occupations, partly because of the very pace of structural change.

Furthermore, excessive specialisation at secondary level should be avoided. The strict differentiation between the educational content of various tracks that occurs at this level in many countries should thus be substantially reduced. International comparisons strongly suggest that such differentiation is a major obstacle to increasing the diffusion of upper-secondary and higher education in Europe and Australia; it is important to remove this obstacle. Where some differentiation is retained, it should not constitute an insurmountable barrier to access to post-secondary education. Cross-overs between educational tracks need to be facilitated.

Upper-secondary education should also be organised so as to be meaningful for all categories of students, i.e. as a preparation for both work and further studies. The organisation of courses and credentials should be sufficiently standardized to fit into a system of recurrent education, where everyone has opportunities for further study.

The quality of education has become a major concern of all OECD countries, not only because of alleged deterioration but also out of the necessity to prepare young people for increasing requirements in the future. Different kinds of measures may be warranted. These include smaller classes and more qualified teachers, extra resources for problem groups and problem areas, a more balanced social composition of classes and stricter enforcement of attendance rules and performance standards. However, the performance of many "problem" students is probably also related to the degree of motivation that a society as a whole can inspire in them. This in turn depends only partly on the education system; it is more closely linked to the range of opportunities that society has to offer. The range of opportunities can often be broadened by increasing the coverage and quality of general education; but some of the major determinants of opportunities are to be found in the labour market and in the arrangements for vocational training.

C. Vocational training

Vocational training has all too often been regarded as a residual choice for the losers in the general-education competition. It is often attributed low social status and sometimes doubtful quality. This problem has affected both apprenticeships and vocational schools. Apprenticeships have frequently been criticised for being used as a source of cheap labour, giving poor theoretical instruction and being oriented towards too narrow occupational sectors. Vocational training in school settings, on the other hand, has in many instances failed to respond to changes in the labour market. Vocational school systems usually have some procedures whereby employers, and sometimes also trade unions, are consulted on questions of curricula; but this has seldom given rise to any really strong ties to the labour market of the kind that might

have helped to offset their poor image of negative student selection[23].

Funding has in some respects been a greater problem for vocational schools than for other educational institutions. Vocational training usually requires more expenditure on equipment than does general education. In education systems that are essentially geared to general education, improvements in vocational training are often difficult to attain, particularly when there are strong pressures to reduce overall public spending. More public funding will, however, be necessary in many countries, unless their systems can be changed so as to increase the scope for financing by industry.

A comparison of the vocational training systems in Europe, Japan and the United States reveals two fundamental differences (see Boxes 1 and 2). First, much of the vocational training in Europe is given at the secondary level, while in Japan and the United States most of it belongs to the post-secondary sphere and tends to start at somewhat higher ages. Secondly, training in Europe is more standardized and integrated into the regular education system. European vocational schools and apprenticeships are mostly subject to detailed curriculum regulations and standardized exams, which are intended to ensure that the skills taught are identifiable and transferable, rather than firm-specific. In Japan and North America vocational training itself tends to be less regulated and private in character, though vocational examinations play some role also in these countries.

In recent decades most OECD countries have increasingly provided training and training-related activities specially designed for unemployed youth. Typically, these activities do not form part of "regular" education systems and they are mostly sponsored by labour market authorities. Often a major rationale is the need to facilitate transition from school to work for certain groups of young people, a need requiring for its effective implementation special concurrence with labour market partners. However, there is hardly any intrinsic advantage in keeping such measures entirely apart from the realm of school authorities. Once established as a more or less permanent element in youth policies, training schemes need to be co-ordinated – if not integrated with regular education. In particular, labour market policies must not give the young incentives to quit education prematurely. Therefore, for example, the British Youth Training Scheme (see Box 1) is currently intended to become a regular skill-training system leading to standardized vocational credentials though it has developed from temporary measures to provide work experience. The Swedish labour market authorities, who earlier provided extensive support measures for jobless teenagers, now do so only for those of age 18 and above, the younger job seekers being referred to programmes organised by school authorities unless they can be placed in ordinary jobs.

As with all kinds of education, policies for vocational training need to be devised in terms of both quantity and

Box 1

EUROPE

SYSTEMS FOR STANDARDIZED VOCATIONAL TRAINING

In most European countries, and particularly in the German-speaking ones, there is a long tradition of vocational training which aims at providing transferable skills that are accepted throughout the labour market. With or without the active co-operation of employers, these systems are intended to give workers a vocational identity more or less independent of the particular job for which the worker is trained.

The German, Austrian and Swiss training systems – with their extensive apprenticeships – have to some extent been looked upon as examples for other European countries. They have also been criticised in many respects. Important changes have been made in all three countries, principally with the aim of improving quality. Employers still provide most of the training, but the public sector's provision of day-release classroom teaching and other forms of assistance has been extended. The credentials awarded are often highly valued in the labour market; they give access to relatively broad ranges of job tasks, and they also provide some opportunities for further training. Thus, despite the selective character of their general education systems, these countries have a relatively wide range of training opportunities that are available and attractive to those young people who do not perform well in the general schools. For example, more than two-thirds of the total labour force in Germany have some credentials of general validity[1]; less than a third have no formal qualification at all.

In certain other European countries, such as the United Kingdom, the situation is the reverse: in the mid-1970s almost two-thirds of the British labour force lacked any generally valid qualifications[2]. A major thrust of recent developments in Britain, France and elsewhere has been to try to reduce the percentage of unqualified workers through new training programmes. The British Youth Training Scheme (YTS), for instance, resembles the German apprenticeship system in many ways, although most of the costs are as yet borne by the government. It is intended that in future the YTS – as distinct from the United Kingdom's traditional apprenticeship system, which is now being largely dismantled – will lead to vocational credentials issued in accordance with nation-wide standards. The number of trainees in YTS has recently been about 350 000 a year attending one-year courses. Courses have now been increased to two years.

1. Mikrozensus 1978, quoted in Prais, "Vocational Qualifications of the Labour Force in Britain and Germany", *National Institute Economic Review*, November 1981, No. 98.
2. See Prais, *ibid*.

quality. Government policies should therefore promote the widest possible diffusion of job-related training. Furthermore, the skills acquired in basic vocational training should have sufficient depth and breadth to allow workers to learn new tasks as work conditions change. Skills should as far as possible also be transferable between firms.

It would seem that the most effective way of achieving this is for governments to set up, or encourage industries to set up, nation-wide standards for vocational training and qualifications, as for instance Austria, Germany and Switzerland have done. Approaches would, by necessity, vary from country to country. In several Member countries, including most of those outside Europe, traditions are largely unfavourable to centralised intervention in this area, and where standards exist they tend to be informal and set by industry rather than government. In most European countries some degree of government involvement in setting such standards has been considered necessary. The labour market partners play a crucial role almost everywhere.

Standards have two functions. First, they provide an instrument for classifying and identifying skills, which is important for both the development of specialised labour markets and the markets for training. The apprenticeship systems in the German-speaking countries currently identify several hundred occupations, while in school-based systems the tracks are usually fewer and more broadly defined – as for instance in Sweden, where upper-secondary schools have about twenty non-academic tracks. This difference may not be as important as it appears, since in Germany many training subjects are

Box 2

JAPAN AND NORTH AMERICA

VOCATIONAL TRAINING AS A PRIVATE SECTOR ACTIVITY

Parts of the post-secondary education system in Japan and North America consist of vocational courses outside the more academically oriented universities and colleges. Of the approximately 2.8 million students completing post-secondary education in the United States in the school year 1981-1982, almost one-third followed "non-collegiate" occupational courses[1]. Likewise, of the almost 800 000 students who graduate annually from Japanese universities, junior colleges, technical colleges and special training colleges, some 200 000 come from the latter category. In addition, there are large numbers of other schools giving adults and young people a wide range of educational opportunities similar to those in formal secondary or post-secondary institutions. Of the approximately 800 000 students per year completing courses in these "miscellaneous" schools, several hundred thousand follow remedial courses for university entry, while much of the rest of the courses are for vocational training[2]. The quality and orientation of these schools vary greatly – as in the American non-collegiate institutions – and they are usually subject to little or no regulation by the authorities.

North America and Japan have no strong traditions as regards vocational training of a general character. The training that occurs on the job in these countries is predominantly informal and limited to the needs of each employer. Although this training can often be organised on the presumption that the workers have a better basis of general non-vocational education than most of their counterparts in other countries, there is nonetheless a risk that the resulting vocational skills are very limited. It would seem that this risk is particularly great in the United States, where the share of youth leaving school without high school diplomas is considerably higher than in Japan.

It is likely, although difficult to prove, that the present situation in North America leads to sub-optimal investment in vocational training by firms. Two factors seem to be at work here. First, there are hardly any institutional provisions for conferring on workers special "trainee" status with lower wages. Unless trainees' wages are substantially lower than unskilled workers' – which is not usually the case – employers will bear a net cost for any training they perform; this net cost is unlikely to represent a profitable investment for the employer. The worker may leave after training; or, if he stays, he will have to be paid the higher wage commanded by transferable skills on the external labour market. The fact that training for transferable skills produces external economies which may benefit those employers who do not invest in training may thus discourage training[3].

Secondly, parts of the American labour market, notably in the manufacturing industry, have long been dominated by a highly formalised and rigid system of elaborate work rules and job descriptions which tends to impede horizontal mobility and discourage training[4]. Wage rises are typically accorded only with promotions along given job ladders, the promotions themselves depending on seniority within each class of related jobs, or "seniority district". On-the-job training is then limited to the often quite narrow range of tasks that constitutes a seniority district. There is presently, however, a trend towards less strict work rules in many American enterprises.

In Japan, mobility between firms is generally lower than in North America, while mobility within firms is much higher. Wage differentials are considerable, but largely based on seniority in the firm. Among the key characteristics of the Japanese labour market – and particularly of its larger employers – are enterprise-centred training and career practices involving the more or less continuous development of skills. Japanese on-the-job training in itself also tends to promote firm-specific norms. It involves more deliberate job rotation within firms than is common in most other countries; and in combination with the relatively high general educational background of most Japanese workers, it equips the labour force with a broad if not always very deep familiarity with a range of tasks. It increases workers' flexibility and acceptance of mobility within the firm, thus reducing the need for mobility between firms.

Both in Japan and the United States there is a tendency among employers to try to "privatise" their skill definitions – as distinct from the European tradition of relying on generally accepted skill definitions, intended to make skills transferable. While in Japan this has been associated with employment patterns stable enough to encourage a considerable amount of in-firm training, the effects on the whole appear to have been more negative in the United States. Although some United States employers do make great training efforts, these tend to be limited to certain groups of workers whose propensity to move is moderate.

1. Data from national education statistics quoted in *Competence and Competition, op. cit.* in Note 4.
2. Source: *Statistical Yearbook of Japan*, 1984.
3. An often quoted example, which may be more extreme than typical, is the American shipyard described by Ryan, P., "Job Training, Employment Practices and the Large Enterprises" in Osterman, *Internal Labour Markets*, MIT Press, Cambridge, Mass., 1984. In this case, the employer made deliberate efforts, involving non-trivial additional costs, with the outspoken purpose of preventing the in-firm training from giving any skills that could be of value to competing firms, lest the workers move.
4. Piore, M.J. and Sabel, C.F., *The Second Industrial Divide: Possibilities for Prosperity*, Basic Books, New York, 1984.

common to several tracks. In Germany, the number of apprenticeship tracks has fallen in recent decades; this trend is likely to continue, since the labour market is not as multi-segmented as the system would seem to imply – there is considerable mobility between skills.

Second, skill standards specify ways of measuring performance. This measurement should be independent of the training process and related only to its outcome – not to numbers of training years or other inputs. Otherwise training may assume a time-serving character and create artificial barriers to access to certain jobs – particularly when the number of trainees is determined by labour market partners, as in most apprenticeship systems. Standardized skill measurement and credentials are potentially useful for both on-the-job and institutional training, as well as for independent providers of courses in private markets[24].

A certain degree of standardization in training for particular occupations is just as desirable at post-secondary as at lower levels. As the need for theoretical understanding increases in many jobs, it will often be necessary to raise the requirements pertaining to the general educational background of trainees in vocational courses.

The extensive in-firm training provided by the large Japanese firms, and also by a minority of employers elsewhere, may be seen as an alternative to formally regulated training. Even in Japan, however, this informal system does not cover the whole labour market. It depends entirely on certain patterns of labour relations, which it may not be possible to emulate elsewhere, and on a permanently low degree of mobility between firms. It is doubtful also whether such a spontaneous system could ever be efficient in promoting training for the needs of smaller firms. It would seem, therefore, that the establishment of generalised training standards would be of considerable advantage in all countries where such standards do not exist already.

D. Recurrent education

In most countries, part of the expansion of formal education in recent decades has been devoted to adult education, including refresher courses, remedial and further education courses and retraining for new occupations. However, there are great variations in the extent to which the adults' regular schooling – which may have occurred long ago – has actually prepared them for further education. Differences among countries in terms of the diffusion of general education and the character of vocational training have profound implications for the ways in which adult education can be provided.

Many adults, particularly in Europe, have not received the amount of general education that is compulsory for today's youth, let alone any upper-secondary or tertiary education. Even among those with some upper-secondary or tertiary education, there are wide variations in ability to pursue further studies. This is inevitably an obstacle to adult education, but it has also contributed to the demand for it. Thus, demand for adult education, and efforts to provide it, have been particularly great in some of those countries where the frequency of upper-secondary education used to be relatively low, for instance in Scandinavia. Much of this education has the character of remedial courses that do not lead to any vocational qualifications unless they are followed by other courses. The total effort required of an adult student is therefore often relatively large and time-consuming.

The most attractive kind of education for many adults consists of courses in an ordinary upper-secondary or higher institution – either special adult courses or the same courses as those in which young people are being trained. A problem in this respect is that regular training schemes – notably apprenticeship systems – often have upper age limits. Even when there are no formal age limits many adults are in effect excluded by other kinds of admission rules, such as requirements referring to educational certificates that did not exist or were uncommon some time ago. Adults also have family responsibilities more often than young students, and in many cases they want to pursue part-time studies while holding jobs. Furthermore, the fact that potential adult students often have jobs makes it less essential for some of them to achieve full degrees; many prefer to take only selected courses provided that this is allowed.

Some countries, including Canada, New Zealand and the United Kingdom, offer special non-university opportunities in higher education for adults, such as the British Open University. Elsewhere, measures have been taken to accommodate more adult and recurrent education into existing institutions by making admission standards more flexible and by permitting part-time and intermittent education. This is the case for instance with the Australian Technical and Further Education (TAFE) System and with junior and community colleges and many private institutions in North America, as well as with the systems for higher education in Nordic countries. In several cases authorities have also taken steps to facilitate distance education for persons who do not live in the neighbourhood of the institutions.

The numbers of adult students in regular education vary considerably, as exemplified in Table 1.3 which refers to tertiary education. In 1983 the share of university students aged 30 or more was over 20 per cent in Australia, Canada, Denmark, Finland and the United States; in Australia and the United States the share was even higher in non-university tertiary education. In Australia and North America the share of students aged 30 or more was also higher than that of students aged 25-29 – a fact which seems to indicate that the practice of recurrent education with intermittent periods of work is relatively common in these countries. In most of Europe the opposite seems to be true. (Note however that the figures given for the United Kingdom exclude the Open University.) It appears that high rates of

Table 1.3. **Percentage of adults in the enrolments of formal tertiary education, 1983**

Country/Year	Type of education	Per cent of total enrolment:	
		Age 25-29 years	Age 30 years or more
Australia	University	14.0	26.3
	Non-university	14.0	29.4
Canada	University	16.5	25.2
Denmark	University	28.4	24.7
	Non-university	22.8	12.3
Finland	University	29.4	20.3
	Non-university	26.3	15.6
France[3]	University	19.3	14.7
	Non-university (IUT)	2.1	0.9
Germany	University	31.2	12.8
Greece[2]	University	9.4	4.1
	Non-university	3.0	1.3
Ireland	University	5.3	3.9
	Non-university	9.1	8.0
Netherlands	University	24.6	14.5
	Non-university	15.8	16.3
New Zealand	University	10.1	13.9
Switzerland	University	21.8	12.4
	Non-university	23.0	16.9
United Kingdom[2]	University	8.6	11.0
United States[2]	University	14.5	20.6
	Non-university	13.2	24.3
Yugoslavia[1]	University	12.2	8.7
	Non-university	18.1	15.9

1. 1980.
2. 1981.
3. 1982.
Source: OECD.

tertiary education in general (Table 1.3) are to some extent connected with large proportions of adult students. In addition, specific policy measures taken in some countries to meet the needs of adults seem to have played a role in creating a framework favourable to recurrent education.

Some European countries have long traditions in further vocational education for skilled workers who do not have the qualifications for regular higher education. This is particularly the case in Germany, where those who have taken a full apprenticeship have the statutory option of further education; this may lead to higher credentials such as those of a *Meister*, and to jobs as supervisors, technicians, etc.[25]. Similar options in other countries are usually less institutionalised and are probably less important[26]. The attractiveness of such courses depends greatly on the system of credentials and the opportunities it offers in specialised labour markets.

The surge of theoretical education among young people that occurred in most countries in the 1960s and rapid technological developments in working life have created a need to re-evaluate most of the older systems of adult education. In Europe, there has been a general trend towards increasing the theoretical content of further education courses for adults, and thus towards reducing the differences between such courses and ordinary post-secondary education. However, these differences – which also pertain to the formal status of the courses – still exist in all European countries.

Finally, relatively large efforts have been undertaken in recent years to retrain displaced workers and others facing particular difficulties in the labour market. Trainees usually receive special allowances, which often correspond to the unemployment benefit. These courses have existed for several decades in Canada, Finland, Germany, Sweden, the United Kingdom and some other countries; in the 1980s they have expanded particularly rapidly in France and Germany. In Germany, for instance, about 450 000 people or 1.7 per cent of the labour force received retraining some time during 1986; some 300 000 of these were unemployed. In Sweden the corresponding annual figure is over 2 per cent of the labour force, with 0.5 to 1 per cent in labour market training at any point in time. The courses are often quite successful: in 1984 between 70 per cent and 83 per cent of trainees in various German courses for unemployed had a job by the end of the quarter following completion of training[27].

Like the measures taken for jobless youth discussed above, retraining has often been organised by special bodies set up outside the mainstream education system. There are several reasons for this. First, labour market authorities may want to have special influence over the delivery of courses to make sure that these can be started and discontinued on short notice in response to changes in labour market conditions and in the composition of unemployment. Secondly, retraining often requires that courses be specially designed for the unemployed – a target group that includes many with poor previous educational achievements as well as the social problems often connected with joblessness. Most unemployed want to return to work as soon as possible, and hence retraining must concentrate more than other vocational courses on what is essential for improving job chances in the short run.

There are, however, some problems connected with maintaining extensive training provisions of this kind. As with the courses for unemployed youth there is no intrinsic advantage in separation from the regular education system; courses should in any case meet established standards whenever these are not incompatible with the special needs of the jobless. It is vital that the certificates issued on completion of courses are well received in the labour market, which often means that they must be comparable, if not identical, with those used in other forms of training. There may also be considerable costs related to upholding high degrees of

82

flexibility in training facilities – as can be exemplified by the Swedish labour market training programme which includes about 100 special training centres. These centres can frequently start new courses on only a few weeks' notice, compared with planning delays of six months to a year commonly occurring in ordinary schools. Such flexibility has been achieved mainly by keeping capacity utilisation low (sometimes as little as 50 per cent). To increase competition and efficiency, the Swedish Government has recently made the training centres independent of labour market authorities and instructed the latter to commission training courses at a lowest-cost basis from any public or private institution willing to enter the market.

In sum, courses designed specially for adults are needed as long as many of them are significantly less well prepared for further education than are most young school-leavers. Such differences between young people and adults are likely to persist in the foreseeable future, particularly in Europe. The most urgent area for provision of special adult courses is the retraining of unemployed and others displaced by structural change. In addition, demand for recurrent education is likely to increase among adults who are not unemployed but nonetheless affected by economic and technological change in working life. In the long run, improvements in regular education should facilitate recurrent participation in regular or privately provided education for everyone. Thus the need for governments to provide special adult courses may eventually become smaller, but this requires sufficient consideration of the situation of adults in the organisation of other courses.

III. FINANCING AND RESOURCE ALLOCATION

A. Financing education

Improving the provision of education has important implications, not only for the level of education expenditure but also for resource allocation processes within the education and training system. These need to be seen in the broader context of the financing of education.

Education accounts for at least 5 per cent of GDP in almost every OECD country. With few exceptions, public expenditure on education varies between roughly 4 per cent and 8 per cent of GDP (see Table 1.4). Education is typically the third or fourth largest public expenditure area after social security, health care and defence, its share in the public sector's total outlays ranging from 9 per cent (as in Germany in 1982 and France in 1981) to 19 per cent (as in Australia in 1981)[28].

The private sector's financial contribution to education – tuition fees, efforts by employers and others – is

Table 1.4. **Public expenditure on education in per cent of gross domestic product (GDP) in current prices**

	1970	1980	1981	1982	1983
Australia	4.3	5.7	5.7	..	..
Austria	4.6	5.5	5.7	5.9	5.9
Canada	8.8	7.2	7.2	7.6	7.5
Denmark	6.7	6.6	..	..	..
Finland	5.9	5.4	5.5	5.5	..
France	..	5.1	5.2	..	..
Germany	3.7	4.7	4.7	4.6	4.4
Greece	2.1	2.2[2]	..	..	..
Ireland	5.0	6.3	6.7	6.2	..
Italy	4.6[1]	5.0	5.5	5.5	..
Japan	3.1	5.5	5.5	5.4	..
Luxembourg	4.6	7.4	7.6	8.3	..
Netherlands	6.8	7.6	7.4	7.3	..
New Zealand	4.8[3]	5.7	5.4	5.3	5.0
Norway	6.0	5.9	6.2	6.3	6.3
Portugal	..	4.1	4.4	4.2	..
Sweden	7.2	9.0	8.4	8.2	7.6
Switzerland	4.1	5.2	5.1	5.2	..
Turkey	2.5	..	..	2.8	3.3
United Kingdom	5.3	5.5	5.4	5.4	5.3
United States	6.4	5.6	..	..	..

1. 1971.
2. 1979.
3. 1972.
Source: OECD and national authorities.

more difficult to measure. It is clear, however, that the extent and character of private financing differs much more between countries than public spending. Two features are particularly important in this respect. First, public spending on education is less in countries with extensive apprenticeship systems. Secondly, in those countries where the quantity of post-secondary education is particularly great, i.e. Japan and the United States, the private sector's financial contributions are relatively greater than in most other countries.

In Austria, Germany and Switzerland, public expenditure represents only a minor part of the total vocational training effort at upper-secondary level. It has been estimated that the German apprenticeship system involves a training effort by employers corresponding to about 1 per cent of GDP, or 2 per cent if apprentices' wages are included; wages seem to roughly match the value of what the apprentices produce. The estimated net "cost" of in-firm training – around 1 per cent of GDP – may overstate the actual outlays, since it includes the imputed cost of the use of regular production facilities. These facilities are in place in any case, but would otherwise have been expensive to acquire[29]. The German federal, state and local governments' expenditure on vocational training activities (other than in their capacity as employers) accounted for about 0.7 per cent of GDP in the early 1980s.

Table 1.5. **Total expenditure of education institutions in the United States by type of funding source**
Billion dollars and per cent

	1970	1979	1982
Total, billion dollars	70.4	152.1	199.8
Of which (%) from			
— Federal government	11	11	10
— State and local government	63	63	64
— Other sources	26	26	27
Public elementary and secondary schools, billion dollars	41.0	87.1	112.4
Of which (%) from			
— Federal government	8	10	9
— State and local government	91	90	91
— Other sources	0	0	0
Private elementary and secondary schools, billion dollars	4.7	10.9	14.3
Public higher education institutions, billion dollars	15.8	36.4	48.8
Of which (%) from			
— Federal government	15	12	12
— State and local government	45	49	49
— Other sources	40	39	39
Private higher education institutions, billion dollars	18.9	17.8	24.3
Of which (%) from			
— Federal government	19	18	19
— State and local government	2	2	2
— Other sources	79	80	79

Source: Statistical Abstract of the United States, 1982-1983.

Tables 1.5, 1.6 and 1.7 show the relative importance of private and public funding at different levels of education in Japan and the United States. Private funding in these two countries is particularly important at the higher education level. Institutions of higher education derive less than half of their combined revenues from public sources, tuition fees alone accounting for more than 20 per cent of total higher education costs. Since the mid-1970s Japan has implemented a series of significant increases in tuition fees in public education at both upper-secondary and university level; in 1984, the fee in public universities was as high as Y 252 000 per year and student. Furthermore, the

earlier trend of rising subsidies to private education in Japan has come to a halt in the 1980s.

The total contribution of private finance to formal education can be estimated at about 1.8 per cent of GDP in the United States and 1.2 per cent of GDP in Japan. In addition to tuition fees, these contributions include donations and funds from enterprises that run the schools. Particularly in the United States, many firms in industry and services have their own facilities for regular post-secondary education.

Comparable data for other countries are not available, but it is clear that the extent of private funding is generally much lower than in Japan and the United States. In most other OECD countries, schools and universities are run predominantly by central or local governments, and student fees seldom play more than a marginal role in their funding. In Europe, most countries have long since abolished fees altogether in public education, and Australia did so in the 1970s[30]. Among the exceptions are France, the Netherlands and the United Kingdom, which charge fees in higher education even though the role of those fees in its financing is much more limited than in Japan or the United States. In the United Kingdom, university fees are mostly paid by local governments.

In most countries, however, some private schools operate and these receive a broad range of subsidies. In the Netherlands and certain regions in Canada, large

Table 1.6. **Total revenues of institutions for higher education in the United States in 1979**

Source	Revenues:	
	Billion dollars	Per cent
Federal government	7.8	13
State and local government	18.4	32
Tuition and other fees	11.9	20
Auxiliary enterprises	6.5	11
Others	13.7	23
Total	58.7	100

Source: Manpower Services Commission, op. cit. in Note 4.

Table 1.7. **Expenditure and revenues in education institutions in Japan**

Type of institution	Expenditure billion yen (1984)	Of which paid for by central and local government per cent[1] (1982)
Primary schools		
— Public	5 318	100
— Private	40	25
Lower secondary		
— Public	3 055	100
— Private	114	24
Upper secondary		
— Public	2 397	92
— Private	889	32
Junior colleges		
— Public	39	86
— Private	332	16
Universities, etc.		
— Public	1 456	89
— Private	1 855	17
Special training schools, etc.		
— Public	62	..
— Private	356	1
Miscellaneous		
— Public	2	..
— Private	218	0

1. For public education institutions: all revenue sources except tuition fees. For private institutions: grants from all levels of government, but excluding tuition fees, donations and loan financing.
Sources: Statistical Yearbook of Japan, 1986, and OECD.

parts of the primary and secondary school systems are run by churches but still mainly tax-funded. Religiously affiliated schools with a more genuinely private character, and higher fees, play a small but not insignificant role at the primary and secondary levels in Australia, Ireland, France and the United States.

There are also markets for private adult courses outside the regular education system, e.g. language courses, art and music instruction, and training for secretaries, technicians and various other trades. Although the size of these markets is not easily determined, their existence is an indication that there is a considerable monetary demand for education in OECD societies, and that this demand includes courses for both work and leisure-related purposes.

Public support for students, i.e. grants and subsidised loans towards tuition and cost of living, was improved in most countries during the 1960s and 1970s. However, during the 1980s there has been a trend among governments to try to contain or reduce expenditure for student support. In this field, too, the role of government (central as well as local) remains much smaller in North America and Japan than elsewhere. In Europe and

Australia, a large share of students in higher education generally receive grants or loans, and sometimes (as in France) subsidised meals and accommodation. In several European countries, support is no longer means-tested against the parents' incomes, i.e. university students are considered as independent households. By contrast, most students in the United States, Canada and Japan generally have to rely substantially on their parents and on work incomes of their own. Student support schemes in the latter countries cover a relatively smaller proportion of students and generally also a smaller part of their expenses – sometimes only tuition fees and not subsistence.

An important question is how desirable improvements in a country's educational effort can realistically be financed. In some countries, more resources will be required for general education, whereas in others there are deficiencies related to vocational training. There is obviously no single solution – both public and private financing, or combinations of the two, are possible. It may, in some cases, become necessary to investigate new avenues which appear unconventional in the respective national contexts. It would be unfortunate and counter-productive if economically sound investments in human capital – and educational goals in general – had to be sacrificed for short-sighted budgetary and institutional reasons.

With respect to general education, a larger increase in the amount of private financing would imply a break with tradition in most European countries. Such a break might appear difficult to reconcile with declared equity goals. But an inadequate education effort is hardly a more equitable alternative. Some of the problems associated with private financing can probably be offset if other measures are taken that enhance equity in the system. First of all, an increase in the number of students obtaining access to upper-secondary and higher education would in itself be a step towards greater equity; so would, in many cases, a reduction in ability-based differentiation of the educational content at secondary level. Moreover, programmes for scholarships and student loans can be designed to help students with limited resources complete higher education. Since higher education in most cases leads to relatively well-paid jobs, the financial support could largely be given in the form of loans rather than grants.

The international experience would seem to indicate that the cost to students is not generally the most important constraint on demand for higher education. In Japan and the United States, relatively high private costs have proved compatible with mass education at this level[31]. In Europe, where post-secondary education is more heavily subsidised, access is limited mainly by the number of students completing academically oriented upper-secondary schooling. In economic terms, the separation of student streams that occurs in European secondary schools has the effect of rationing access to higher education (by limiting the number of people receiving the necessary preparation for it relative to the number who would be willing to pay what it currently costs); this rationing is apparently more important than the price as a determinant of demand. A somewhat higher rate of recovery of public costs in European higher education, e.g. higher fees, would therefore not necessarily be inconsistent with a policy to promote greater enrolment; but this would require a lower degree of differentiation in secondary schooling.

There are several reasons why student families' willingness to pay for further education may increase when secondary school systems are made less differentiated. Most importantly, a wide diffusion of good secondary education increases the number of people who can benefit from further education. In addition, less discrimination in secondary schools may transfer more of education's selective functions to the post-secondary level; this is likely to create excess demand, in particular for courses that lead to the most well-paid jobs – which are also those most easily financed by loans[32]. It may be argued, therefore, that governments facing budgetary constraints should give particular priority to improvements in the quantity and quality of secondary education. Any improvement at the secondary level is likely to increase the spontaneous demand for higher education – even if somewhat more of the costs for the latter have to be borne by the students.

In vocational training the issues are different. The functional links between training and work are strong, and employers or industries often undertake considerable training efforts. Those countries that have extensive school-based vocational training systems have often found it desirable to increase industry's involvement, for instance through various kinds of practical co-operation between schools and employers. The creation of wholly or partly employer-organised alternatives to vocational schools has been encouraged in many countries. However, since the educational image of traditional apprenticeships is not always excellent, it has often been deemed necessary to impose stringent requirements on the quality and content of training in firms. This, in turn, has been difficult to achieve without some public expenditure – either in the form of grants to employers, as in the United Kingdom's Youth Training Scheme, or part-time classroom teaching, as in Germany, or both. For many governments it has been a priority to reduce these outlays for the public. Sometimes costs have been recovered with the help of special levies on employers who do not finance their own training. Elsewhere, where traditions and corporate culture are more generally favourable to training, it has proved possible to persuade employers to provide large enough numbers of training places without such pressure. Increasing employers' and employees' awareness of the need for recurrent education may therefore in itself be an important long-term objective for government action. In any case, even if grants are accorded, government expenditure generally remains much lower when training occurs in firms than when it is located in full-time schools.

In many countries, the least costly way of improving the qualifications of the work-force may therefore be to encourage and standardize vocational training that is provided wholly or partly at the workplace. In the United States and Canada, for instance, where one-quarter or more of each age class now fail to obtain a high school diploma at age 18, this option may well deserve more attention than it receives at present. It may prove to be both cheaper and more feasible than the alternative of raising regular high school attendance closer to one hundred per cent.

B. Resource allocation within the education system

The question to be addressed in this sub-section is how priorities within education systems can be made more responsive to developments in the environment such as demographic change and new demands in the labour market. The size of youth cohorts has historically been subject to considerable variation; they are currently declining in most countries. The rapid pace of change in skill requirements – due to technological, economic and other factors – calls for several kinds of adjustment. In some situations, resources have to be shifted between major educational categories, e.g. from youth to adult education, from production training to preparation for jobs in information and services, or towards more technical rather than manual skills in production. Perhaps even more importantly, the content of existing courses must be continually adjusted to changing requirements; this is usually a gradual but nonetheless difficult process.

The obstacles to change in education systems are partly related to the conditions of teachers' training and employment and to investments already made in buildings and equipment. Such rigidities may to some extent seem unavoidable – given the necessarily multifaceted character of education systems – but they are often worsened by administrative inertia and by the absence of sufficient incentives for adjustment.

Changes in the supply of education may be brought about by three principal means: a) planning by the institutions themselves or by education authorities; b) direct influence exerted by employers; and c) demand as expressed by prospective students and their parents. Much of the problem consists in striking a balance between the need for public control of education and the desirability of decentralisation and competition between institutions. In all countries, some degree of public control is seen as necessary to ensure that policy objectives are met, but too much of it may foster bureaucratisation and reduce incentives for local initiatives.

In Europe, educational planning by governments is generally more comprehensive, and labour market forecasting in connection with educational policy making more common, than in other Member countries. In most countries employer representatives or tripartite bodies at central, regional or local levels have some influence on the planning of public education systems, and particularly on vocational training. Such bodies also exist in Japan and the United States, but they are less important because vocational courses play a smaller role in their public education systems. As a general observation, it can be said that individual high schools and colleges in Japan and the United States are less dependent on public policy making and more dependent on private funding than is common in Europe. To some extent this difference is probably due to a traditional aversion to an unduly strong mercantile influence on cultural institutions in Europe, and a correspondingly strong fear of excessive government planning in the United States.

The size of the private education sector is obviously one factor that reduces the scope of public educational policies in Japan and the United States, particularly at the post-secondary level. There is also considerable variation in the degree of centralisation within public systems. For instance, some European countries have centralised procedures for setting university curricula, while elsewhere this is done locally. The debate on decentralisation has in many countries focused mainly on possible changes within the public education system, while in others the role of private schools has repeatedly been subject to revision.

In any system, the demand for education by the prospective students themselves is necessarily a major determinant of the pattern of supply. At the upper-secondary level, it is an outspoken policy of most OECD countries to encourage as many young people as possible – if not all – to pursue some kind of education. The challenge is then to produce courses which are attractive to various target groups. Even in countries where education planning includes labour market forecasting, the actual wishes of students, as expressed for instance by the numbers of applications, probably play an equally important role.

The educational choices of individuals, however, may in some cases seem hard to reconcile with the interests of society as a whole. Many of the market signals that reach students may be weak or distorted. When education is paid for by the public, student choices are likely to be influenced by the rewards from education rather than by the costs. Signals from the labour market may be misleading or irrational from society's point of view, notably when the labour market attaches more importance to selection procedures than to the content of education. The demand for status symbols may lead to "over-education" in some academic disciplines. University studies may tend to be too general in some countries. Although students may of course have perfectly legitimate reasons, e.g. academic interest, for disregarding labour market implications when they choose their education, it is nonetheless clear that this can create a political problem if it gives rise to large costs for the public.

Policy responses to such problems have often consisted in attempts to reduce the range of choices available to students. Rules of access have sometimes been tightened, particularly in post-secondary institutions. Such changes have often met with strong resistance. In universities, they have been seen as assaults on the traditions of liberal arts faculties. Most countries on the European mainland have therefore retained, in principle, more or less free access to universities for all holders of diplomas from academic upper-secondary schools; nonetheless, this access has been increasingly circumscribed by limitations on specific courses. Non-university institutions for post-secondary education in Europe almost invariably have rules restricting access. In Japan, the United Kingdom, Australia and North America, there is no corresponding tradition of free access to universities, each institution being free to decide whom it wishes to admit; in North America, however, the public non-university colleges are usually open to anybody with a high school diploma[33]. Thus, most countries' higher education systems seem to include at least some sets of institutions with liberal access. The degree of specialisation of these institutions is often relatively low, as is the market value of their degrees.

A question to which no satisfactory answer can be given here is to what extent the costs borne by students actually affect the orientation of their educational choices. It might be hypothesised, for instance, that high university fees make it more important for students to choose courses leading to relatively high-paid jobs. Conversely, they might reduce the affordability (in the long run) of the kind of studies that are pursued mainly for their own sake. Such a hypothesis cannot be easily borne out by statistics on the orientation of studies. Nonetheless, it would seem that the financial stakes for individuals, in combination with the often considerable independence of educational institutions, contribute to educational flexibility and hence to the capacity of the Japanese and North American economies to benefit from relatively large amounts of general education.

As was argued earlier, the recruitment criteria of many employers in Japan and the United States favour general education to the detriment of vocational and other courses ill-fitted to their crediting systems. Changes in the crediting systems might well improve the interaction between education and labour markets in several countries. To the extent that standardized vocational credentials can facilitate the functioning of specialised labour markets for particular occupations, they might also contribute to making specialised education more profitable for the individual.

Some degree of decentralisation and a greater element of competition among education institutions could have advantageous effects in most systems. Decentralised decision structures allow individual institutions to respond directly to changes in demand as expressed by actual and potential students. This reduces the need for central planning. In most cases, decentralised management is also a necessary condition for competition among institutions, which – as in other fields of the economy – would encourage rapid adjustments to changing conditions.

Within publicly funded education systems, competition among institutions can be enhanced to some extent by allowing students to enrol in the schools of other districts. If public money is allocated to schools in proportion to their enrolment, such student choice would create competitive pressure. Each school would have to produce courses acceptable to potential customers, lest their teachers and other resources need to be transferred to other schools.

Broadening individuals' choices may also have to involve a somewhat greater element of private education. In the educational debate[34], it has been suggested that this could be facilitated – notably at primary and secondary levels – by the introduction of a "voucher", which governments would distribute to parents. The "voucher" would be good for payment in any school up to an amount corresponding to the costs of education in the public system. According to its proponents, the voucher would strengthen competition between education institutions, without being inequitable. The purchasing power inherent in the vouchers would be available to members of all social groups alike. Those willing to pay additional fees would be allowed to use the voucher as partial payment in schools that are more expensive than public ones.

There is practically no experience of such systems. The effects on social equity could be both negative and positive, depending on the circumstances. On the one hand, parents of socially disadvantaged children may in some environments tend to show less-than-average interest in education; if this is the case, the possibility to choose might increase the concentration of disadvantaged students in the worst schools. On the other hand, with sufficient information, low-income families could in fact benefit more than others from a broader choice, since they have the smallest possibilities to influence their children's education in current systems: they cannot afford to "vote with their feet", and they often lack the social and political skills to participate in education systems' consultative procedures. More competition between schools accompanied by measures to provide families with the financial means to choose could therefore improve the relative position of children from poorer families.

The most important reasons for introducing competition between education institutions are, however, economic and administrative ones. With competition between institutions, more of the impetus to both quality improvement and adjustment of the quantity and type of education would come to local schools straight from potential customers rather than via remote planning procedures which have often proved to be excessively centralised and detailed. Incentives for individual schools to make their education attractive would help to solve some of the problems of maintaining quality in mass education; market forces could to some extent fulfil the functions of present administrative controls. Competitive pressures would also encourage school managers to find ways of responding more rapidly to changes in the demand for different kinds of education and of adjusting the remuneration offered individual teachers to performance and skill needs. Decentralisation could thus encourage several administrative changes which are likely to make the system as a whole more flexible.

A move towards more competition between institutions and decentralisation in some form may thus appear as an attractive option in many OECD countries – provided that the risks of growing or re-emerging inequities can be controlled. Two kinds of measures would probably be required to contain these risks. First, schools in "problem areas" and, more generally, schools with large numbers of disadvantaged students need relatively more support from government – for instance extra funds, more and better-paid teachers, better equipment and better premises allowing for more small-group teaching. Second, educational objectives and credentials at primary and secondary levels should be largely standardized to ensure that the individual schools' decentralised decision-making remains within the framework of a unitary and transparent education system. Such measures in primary and secondary education would also serve to give more people the chance to benefit from the post-secondary education system, which by necessity remains highly differentiated.

IV. CONCLUSIONS

This chapter has discussed the functioning of education and training systems and how they can be improved to respond to the challenges of structural change. These challenges – such as international competition, technological development and an often rapid and unpredictable pace of change in working life – all have important implications for education.

The need for the more theoretical kinds of education is increasing in large parts of the work-force of industrialised countries. This raises questions of the quality and quantity of education and the rules governing access to it. The measures required to raise the population's general educational level will differ from country to country.

A first set of problems is related to the maintenance and improvement of educational quality – school failures, drop-outs and even functional illiteracy being the more extreme results of poor quality. There are indications that such problems exist especially in certain disadvantaged regions, but also elsewhere. Not least in countries with formally egalitarian systems, such as Japan and the United States, measures are needed to counteract a *de facto* degradation of some schools and to ensure that all institutions at the same educational level can offer instruction of a more comparable quality. Such measures might also help temper the excessively competitive atmosphere that is typical of parts of some education systems.

Moreover, in all but a few countries, there are still considerable numbers of young people who enter the labour market with little or no education beyond the lower-secondary stage. This usually results in mediocre levels of competence in general; in particular, it is indicative of low propensities to manage change in work-life and limited practical possibilities to undertake and succeed in adult education.

There is therefore in most countries a case for gradually increasing post-compulsory enrolment, as well as for revision of the ways in which students are selected for it. Higher participation rates will, in turn, underscore the necessity of making general education curricula more relevant to the realities of working life. Upper-secondary general education should no longer be seen only as a preparation for further academic studies.

It would seem that most of the countries with formally differentiated school systems will have to find ways to improve the general education offered to young people who are not selected for academic streams. Changes in this direction can be achieved through moves towards greater comprehensiveness – integration of vocational and academic streams – or through improvements within the existing streams. Most European countries have taken some such steps in the recent past. Often, however, there is still too deep a split between the minorities that have access to higher education and the majorities that do not.

There is also insufficient provision of vocational training in many OECD countries. Vocational training is by its very nature highly conditioned by the characteristics of each country's labour market, including the patterns of recruitment and work organisation. Despite this interdependence, there are often severe shortcomings precisely in the relations of vocational training to labour markets, notably when the training is organised in schools.

Measures to improve vocational training could in many countries include the setting of standards and the creation of better systems for awarding credentials for skills in particular occupations. Such measures, taken in co-ordination by employers and education authorities, are useful regardless of whether the training is organised by authorities or by industry. If successfully implemented, they are likely to improve the transparency and functioning of specialised labour markets for the occu-

pations concerned. They will give an impetus both to the training itself and to the labour market's demand for it, and thus improve the overall level of vocational skills.

In the area of adult education, the most urgent needs are related to the unemployed and others whose employment prospects are significantly affected by structural change. A wide range of courses may have to be offered, suitable for people with very different educational backgrounds. In institutions for higher education, adults often need opportunities for distance education and for part-time or intermittent studies.

Many adults need remedial courses – either to improve their productivity at work or to gain access to further education – and it is important that such courses be available. In the long run, individuals' readiness for adult education should be systematically improved with changes in the youth education system (as discussed above), so that the adults of the future are better prepared for recurrent educational spells.

If a country's educational effort is to be increased, additional financial resources may need to be found. In the present institutional framework, much of the increase in funding will typically have to be provided by governments. To the extent that the general constraints placed on public expenditure are seen as insuperable barriers to such increases, it may prove more feasible to seek alternatives involving more private funding.

An increase in private financing of education may appear to conflict with the equity goals of education policies. It must be kept in mind, however, that failure to make a desirable increase in a country's educational effort is hardly a more equitable alternative; nor is it economically sound. Measures to encourage private funding of education can be combined with special steps to safeguard social equity, including, for instance, targeted supports to schools with high shares of disadvantaged students.

One way of making the education system more responsive to developments in the economy is to increase its administrative flexibility. Flexibility can be enhanced by delegating to schools the decisions on the dimensioning and orientation of courses within a framework of standardized educational objectives and credentials. Such delegation is facilitated if some degree of competition is established between education institutions, for instance by allowing students to go to schools in neighbouring districts.

There are, in sum, good reasons for many countries to investigate both conventional and unconventional ways of meeting the present challenges to their education systems. In the final analysis, a successful response to these challenges can but promote the basic goals of education.

NOTES AND REFERENCES

1. Another preoccupation of educational policies, which will not be dealt with here, though it has been important in the past decades, is demographic change, *viz.* the postwar baby booms and the ensuing gradual stagnation or decline in the numbers of children.

2. Concerning the influence of different education systems on careers and mobility in labour markets, see for instance, Haller, M., König, W., Krause, P. and Kurz, K., "Patterns of Career Mobility and Structural Positions in Advanced Capitalist Societies: A Comparison of Men in Austria, France and the United States", *American Sociological Review*, October 1985, Vol. 50. As regards the correlation between education and the diffusion of new technologies, a survey of several mainly American studies is to be found in Schultz, T.W., "The Value of the Ability to Deal with Disequilibria", *Journal of Economic Literature*, September 1975, Vol. XIII, No. 3.

3. In Table 1.1, as well as in the text throughout this chapter, the conventional definition is used according to which "secondary" education in normal cases corresponds roughly to the ages 12 through 18. "Lower-secondary" education constitutes the final part of what is in almost all OECD countries the compulsory schooling, while "upper-secondary" education is with few exceptions voluntary. The inclusion of apprenticeships in the figures for upper-secondary education follows the norm in most of the countries where apprenticeships play a significant role, though the educational element may be modest in some cases (notably where there are no provisions for regular day-release classroom teaching).

4. See Manpower Services Commission, *Competence and Competition*, National Economic Development Office, London, 1984.

5. See for instance, OECD, *Universities under Scrutiny*, Paris, 1987, Chapter 7.

6. See Maurice, M., Sellier, F. and Silvestre, J.J., *Politique d'éducation et organisation industrielle en France et en Allemagne : essai d'analyse sociétale*, PUF, Paris, 1982; Lutz, B., "Education and Employment: Contrasting Evidence from France and the Federal Republic of Germany", *European Journal of Education*, 1981, Vol. 16, No. 1.

7. In the United States, the National Commission on Excellence in Education found in its report *A Nation at Risk. The Imperative for Educational Reform*, Washington D.C., 1983, that 23 million American adults and 13 per cent of all 17-year-olds could be considered as functionally illiterate.

8. See Husén, T. (ed.), *International Study of Achievement in Mathematics*, Almqvist and Wiksell, Stockholm, and Wiley, New York, 1967; Walker, D.A., *The IEA Six-Subject Survey: An Empirical Study of Education in Twenty-One Countries*, Wiley, New York, 1976; and Travers, K.J. and McKnight, C.C., "Mathematics Achievement in US Schools: Preliminary Findings From the Second IEA Mathematics Study", *Phi Delta Kappan*, February 1985, Vol. 66, No. 6.

9. See for example, Mincer, J., "Comment: Overeducation or Undereducation?" in Dean, E. (ed.), *Education and Economic Productivity*, Ballinger, Cambridge, Mass., 1984; Lerner, B., "How Are We Doing?", *Public Interest*, Fall 1982, No. 69; Walberg, H.J., "Scientific Literacy and Economic Productivity in International Perspective", *Daedalus*, Spring 1983, Vol. 112, No. 2. According to Lerner, *ibid.*, p. 64, the mean scores of 18-year-olds placed the United States in the bottom half of the countries studied in thirteen of the nineteen tests in which it was represented. Only in six of these tests was the United States among the top half of countries. Japan took part in six tests and surpassed all other countries in three of them. The participating West European countries – Belgium, England, Finland, Germany, Italy, Netherlands, Scotland and Sweden – generally scored between Japan and the United States, while several developing countries showed relatively poor results.

10. See Lerner, *ibid.*, and United States Department of Education, *Elementary and Secondary Education Indicators in Brief*, Washington D.C., 1987, p. 12.

11. See for instance, Hopkins, A., "Able Children and Comprehensives" in Pluckrose, H. and Wilby, P. (ed.), *Education 2000*, Temple Smith, London, 1980, which refers to the British debate on the issue.

12. See Schultz, *art. cit.* in Note 2.

13. See Lerner, *art. cit.* in Note 9, p. 62.

14. See Hopkins, *art. cit.* in Note 11.

15. Results from longitudinal studies of students attending American high school as seniors in 1957 and 1972 were reported in Sewell, William H. & Shah, Vimal, "Socio-Economic Status, Intelligence, and the Attainment of Higher Education", *Sociology of Education*, 1967, No. 40, and in Bailey, J.P. Jr. and Collins, E.F., "Entry into Post-Secondary Education", *Symposium: National Longitudinal Study of the High School Class of 1972: Trends in Post-Secondary Education*, Research Triangle Institute, 1977. These results were compared in Geiger, R.L., *The Limits of Higher Education: A Comparative Analysis of Factors Affecting Enrolment Levels in Belgium, France, Japan and the United States*, Yale Higher Education Research Group, Working Paper No. 41, New Haven, 1980.

    On the basis of Geiger's presentation, *ibid.*, p. 5a, Table 2:3, it can be estimated that the percentage of students subsequently going to college may have increased by some 17 per cent units in the lowest quartile on a scale of socio-economic status (SES), while it may have fallen by some 11 per cent units in the highest SES quartile. By contrast, the share going to college increased almost uniformly in all quartiles emerging from a rating of performance in high school. (Overall, the share of American high school seniors going on to college increased from 50 per cent in 1957 to 58 per cent in 1972.) Differences in college attainment between men and women and between whites and blacks also fell significantly. Still, SES remained an important factor in explaining college attainment in the early 1970s (comparable data from more recent years is not available). Despite the equalising trend, the percentage going to college remained about twice as high in the highest SES quartile within comparable ability groups. But ability was clearly more important than SES: within most SES groups, the share going to college was three to four times greater in the highest ability quartile than in the lowest ability quartile.

16. Japanese Ministry of Education, *Survey Report of Student Living Conditions*, 1978, quoted in Geiger, *ibid.*, p. 34.

17. See for instance, the National Council on Education Reform, *Second Report on Educational Reform*, Tokyo (preliminary summary translated into English, 1986).

18. See for instance, Cummings, *Education and Equality in Japan*, Princeton University Press, 1980.

19. A recent survey by the Japanese Education Ministry (quoted in the *Japan Economic Journal*, 26 April 1986) showed that 47 per cent of all students in the last year before high school attended private instruction outside normal school hours in order to improve their chances of getting accepted in their desired high school.

20. *Second Report on Educational Reform, op. cit.* in Note 17, p. 9.

21. See Sorge, A. and Warner, M., "Manpower Training, Manufacturing Organization and Workplace Relations in Great Britain and West Germany", *British Journal of Industrial Relations*, November 1980, Vol. 18, No. 3; Ahlström, G., *Engineers and Industrial Growth*, Croom Helm, London and Canberra, 1982.

22. See Commission du Bilan, *La France en mai 1981. L'enseignement et le développement scientifique*, Paris, 1981.

23. For shortness, the expression "vocational training" is used here, though it should be understood in the wide sense of "vocational education and training". Clearly, a good vocational preparation must include much of what may more properly be referred to as "education".
    The notion of vocational training as used here covers all kinds of preparation where the main stress is on the work tasks of some particular occupation rather than on general education. The principal arguments in this section refer to such training for any occupation in any sector of the labour market. Although some training systems may have a focus primarily on manual jobs in manufacturing, it should thus be understood that vocational training may be equally important for a host of other job categories, e.g. in offices, construction, health care, transportation and many private services.

24. As regards the role of private markets for relatively short and simple courses, a case in point is the training for driving licences – a credit which can be obtained by anyone who passes the test regardless of how he or she learned to drive. In many OECD countries, the existence of more or less generally accepted skill measurements or examinations has also encouraged considerable markets for courses in skills such as typing, shorthand, plumbing and repair of household appliances.

25. In 1985, the gross expenditure of German employers for further training was about DM 10 billion, or 0.7 per cent of GDP. Over 20 per cent of the German work force take part in such courses each year. Sources: Institut der deutschen Wirtschaft, quoted in *Wirtschaftswoche*, 11 April 1986, and *Report No. 9*, 1986, of the Sonderforschungsbereich 3, University of Frankfurt.

26. See for instance, the comparison between Germany and the United Kingdom in Sorge and Warner, *art. cit.* in Note 21.

27. The higher figure refers to further education, the lower to retraining. Source: *Wirtschaftswoche*, 4 October 1985.

28. *Source:* OECD data.

29. See Noll, I. *et al.*, *Nettokosten der betrieblichen Berufsausbildung*, Bundesinstitut für Berufsbildung, Berlin, 1983. According to Noll, the German employer's gross cost per apprentice, including wages, was about DM 17 000 in 1980. This corresponded to a total cost for all employers of about DM 29 billion that year, or almost 2 per cent of GDP. Of this gross cost, about DM 7 000 per apprentice represented the estimated costs of involving regular plant and staff capacity in the training; the measure assumes that there was no idle capacity to use for the purpose, which may be unrealistic (p. 47). The employers' costs for special training facilities were on the average about DM 2 000 per year per apprentice, while the rest – DM 8 000 – was wages and social security for the apprentices themselves. The value of what an average apprentice produced was estimated at about DM 7 000 per year, making the employer's net cost about DM 10 000 per year.

30. OECD, *Review of Student Support Schemes in Selected OECD Countries*, Paris, 1978.

31. In Japan, the fact that tuition fees are being charged by both private and public colleges seems to have only moderately negative effects – if any – on the demand for enrolment. Along with the fee increases undertaken since 1975, the share of high school graduates seeking entry into Japanese universities fell marginally – *viz.* from 48 per cent of the high school leavers in 1975 to 45 per cent in 1984.

32. In France, for example, the rates of interest and other conditions of student loans currently offered by commercial banks are often significantly more favourable to those studying at *grandes écoles* than to most university students, according to a review in *Le Monde:* Supplément "Campus", 23 October 1986.

33. See OECD, *Policies for Higher Education in the 1980s*, Paris, 1983.

34. For an account of the British debate on this issue, see Seldon, A., *The Riddle of the Voucher*, Institute of Economic Affairs, London, 1986.

Additional references consulted:

Coleman, "International Comparisons of Cognitive Achievement", *Phi Delta Kappan, op. cit.* in Note 8.

Husén, T., *Talent, Equality, and Meritocracy*, The Hague, 1974.

Keeves, J., "Changing Standards of Performance and the Quality of Education. Concepts and Findings Relevant for Policy-Making" (mimeo), paper submitted to the OECD

Directorate for Social Affairs, Manpower and Education, 1986.

Lévy-Garboua, L. and Orivel, F., "Inefficiency in the French System of Higher Education", *European Journal of Education*, 1982, Vol. 17, No. 2.

Peston, "Higher Education: Financial and Economic Aspects", *Royal Bank of Scotland Review*, December 1985, No. 148.

Rüegg, W., "Diversification and Competition in Higher Education", Discussion Paper No. 1 for a conference organised by the OECD Centre for Educational Research and Innovation on 8-10 September 1986.

Smith, M., "Quality in Education: the Vital Role of Teachers. Education Reform in the United States" (mimeo), paper submitted to the OECD Directorate for Social Affairs, Manpower and Education, 1986.

Chapter 2

LONG-TERM RESEARCH

INTRODUCTION

The OECD economies are in the midst of a process in which scientific and technological achievements and their dissemination are having an increasing impact on the restructuring of economic systems and on each nation's competitiveness.

Productive systems are increasingly incorporating new technologies, which not only tend to become more sophisticated but also more generalised by the widespread uses made of them. The recent changes in the nature of science and technology have started to influence everybody's work and life to an unanticipated extent.

The scientific and technological process is not always confined to just one direction, i.e. leading from basic research to new products and processes. It is often characterised by loops where new technologies frequently require further scientific exploration. This has resulted in the emergence of a new and closer, symbiotic relationship between science and technology, which makes the continuous contribution of science to industry all the more vital for fully exploiting further advances. Thus a country with a strong scientific base increases its potential not only to make the best use of existing technologies but also to master future technologies better.

These arguments vindicating the need for basic research have important policy implications. Firstly, they partly help to explain why the frontier between basic research and applied research has become blurred by the gradual involvement of "consumers" in basic research. Furthermore, they point to the inherent long-term character of most of today's basic research and an increasing share of applied research. Although the term "long-term research" is therefore not completely synonymous with basic research, the latter comes closest to its actual meaning and will be used in this chapter as its nearest approximation.

Present circumstances make it all the more important for OECD economies to extend the frontier of innovation by bridging the gap between "basic" and "applied" research. The best way of accomplishing this objective is to carry out not simply more, but also better, basic research with a view to usefully absorbing existing and, if necessary, additional resources so that industrial opportunities in a world of adjusting and changing patterns of competitiveness can be sustained and replenished.

The importance of basic research is, therefore, much greater than statistics imply. Of an estimated total of 225 billion dollars spent in 1985 by OECD countries on research and experimental development (R&D), basic research accounted for only about 35 billion dollars and employed some 250 000 researchers. Although these proportions are now on the increase, it still represents less than one-tenth of OECD GNP and labour force respectively.

Yet it is not easy to assess the current situation of basic research and its outlook. At its simplest, this is because basic research is mainly government funded – and is likely to remain so. Consequently it is highly vulnerable to constraints on government outlays, all the more so because it represents that part of the R&D spectrum where long periods of investigation are often required and results are less visible.

In addition, more than half of national basic research in OECD countries is carried out in the higher education sector which, in contrast to industry and government, is financed primarily from external sources. But there are also endogenous pressures for change stemming from the rising cost of scientific instruments, the consequences of demographic shifts, and from the new patterns of industry-university co-operation. As a result of the combination of these factors, basic research is facing not only new constraints but also significant new opportunities. In many countries, adjusting to these changes will require a reappraisal of how basic research is organised.

This chapter examines these challenges to the research system. It does not, however, review all the major issues confronting governments in the areas of science and technology. Some of these issues are dealt with elsewhere in this report: in particular, the educational system *per se* is the main focus of the Chapter 1 on human capital, and the industrial implications of technological innovation are dealt with in Chapter 6 on structural adjustment and industry. All too frequently there is a temptation to focus attention and policy on immediate needs rather than on preparing the groundwork for future advance, a temptation which is obviously strongest in periods of perceived rapid structural change. It is in this context that a discussion of the more long-term aspects of research policy becomes worthwhile.

The first part of this chapter looks at the changing role of governments in basic research. The second part highlights the importance of institutional structures and funding mechanisms in shaping the efficiency of national basic research systems. Building on the results of these sections, the third part examines priority areas for policy relating to basic research.

I. THE CHANGING ROLE OF GOVERNMENTS IN BASIC RESEARCH

Basic research is a fairly small part of OECD countries' overall R&D efforts (Graph 2.1), efforts which vary greatly from country to country in their extent and nature (Table 2.1). Yet in almost all countries governments play a major, if not dominant, role in funding basic research. Taking the OECD as a whole, governments account for roughly 75 per cent of basic research funding[1], almost twice as high as their share in the funding of R&D as a whole. This heavy government involvement is partly linked to the economic characteristics of basic research, but it also reflects the broader role of basic research.

The economic case for government support of basic research is straightforward[2]. It is a familiar proposition that basic research involves significant externalities – that is, that the benefits it creates for society as a whole are greater than those which the individual scientist (or laboratory) could appropriate through an "ownership right" in scientific advance. At the same time basic research entails high and indivisible risks, most obviously because the outcome is usually technically uncertain despite the large fixed investments needed in human and physical capital for the research to be done in the first place. This combination of substantial externalities and high risks means that private firms acting on their own initiative are likely to under-invest in basic research. Their chosen level of investment in basic research will usually be less than that desirable from the standpoint of the community as a whole, since the community "internalises" the external benefits of basic research and can pool risks across projects and even generations. It follows that the burden for financing basic research must primarily rest with the public sector.

Appealing as these arguments may be, they should not be interpreted too simplistically. To begin with, it is worth noting that industry does invest in basic research although nowhere near as heavily as the non-competitive sectors of the economy (Table 2.2). Moreover, developments in technology are altering the balance between basic and applied research: in particular, "generic" or "core" technologies, which span the spectrum from science to application, are of increasing importance in such areas as electronics (notably in sub-micron structures and in advanced optics, but also,

Graph 2.1. **R&D by type of activity in the OECD area, 1981**

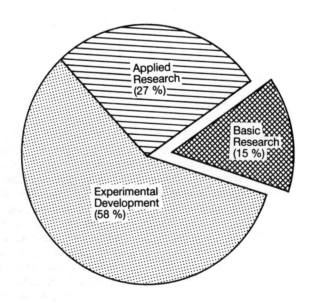

Source: OECD, Science and Technology Indicators, No. 2, 1986.

Table 2.1. **R&D intensity and international dissemination of technology in 1983**

Countries ranked by researchers per 1 000 labour force

(See Note 32 for further explanation)

	Researchers (FTE) per 1000 labour force	R&D per capita in $	Basic research per capita in $	Patent balance[6]	Coverage ratio of technology transfer[8]	Apparent comparative advantage in high R&D intensity industries 1984[9]
United States	6.4	379	47	2.89	32.7	1.56
Japan	5.9[1]	257	32[10]	1.92	0.9	1.47
Germany	4.8	272	49	1.86	0.5	0.82
Norway	4.1	170	24	0.27	..	0.32
France	3.9	223	..	0.90	0.9	0.83
United Kingdom	3.9[2]	218	..	0.78	1.3	1.18
Sweden	3.9	273	54[10]	0.64	2.2	0.67
Finland	3.7	134	..	0.74	0.6	0.30
Netherlands	3.7	206	51	0.53	0.6	0.62
Iceland	3.6	83	23	0.11	..	0.01 (1983)
Australia	3.5[3]	102	35[3]	0.44	..	0.19
Switzerland	3.4[4]	270[3]	21[3]	1.08	..	1.28
Italy	2.7	94	12	0.53[7]	0.3	0.56
Canada	2.7	174	..	0.24	0.5	0.43
Denmark[5]	2.7	114	..	0.60	1.5[3]	0.66
Belgium[4]	2.6	151	..	0.19	..	0.37
Ireland	2.5	45	5	0.15	..	1.59
Austria[3]	2.0[3]	117[3]	..	0.28	0.2	0.63
Spain	1.0	31	5	0.20	0.2	0.34 (1983)
Portugal[5]	0.7	17	..	0.01	0.1	0.49 (1983)
Greece	0.6	10[3]	..	0.06	..	0.13

1. Researchers adjusted to full-time equivalence.
2. OECD estimate.
3. 1981.
4. 1979.
5. 1982.
6. External patent applications divided by foreign patent applications (including international channels through EPC and PCT).
7. 1980.
8. Receipts divided by payments concerning the international transfer of patents, licensing agreements, know-how and technical assistance, etc.
9. Share of high R&D-intensive industries exports in a country's total exports of manufacturing industries divided by the corresponding share of all OECD countries combined.
10. Natural sciences and engineering only.
Note: FTE = Full-time equivalent.
Source: OECD.

Table 2.2. **Sectoral distribution of basic research in 1983 (in percentage of total national basic research)**

Countries ranked according to the importance of non-competitive sectors

In percentages

	Industry	Government	Higher education	Private non-profit	Total non-competitive sectors
	(A)	(B)	(C)	(D)	(B) + (C) + (D)
Switzerland (1979)	0.0	21.9	78.1	0.0	100.0
Iceland	0.2	26.4	63.7	9.7	99.8
Australia (1981)	3.5	39.9	54.7	2.0	96.6
Portugal (1976)	4.1	16.8	64.1	15.0	95.9
Ireland	6.1	16.7	77.5	0.5	94.7
Italy	5.4	30.0	64.5	—	94.6
Norway	6.4	15.5	77.5	0.5	93.5
Sweden[1]	6.8	3.7	89.2	0.3	93.2
France (1979)	8.9	21.7	66.8	2.6	91.1
Spain	11.4	41.8	46.8	—	88.6
United Kingdom (1979)	14.0	24.0	60.0	2.0	86.0
Germany	17.1	23.9	58.4	0.6	82.9
United States	19.7	15.3	56.4	8.6	80.8
Netherlands	23.6	18.8	55.4	2.2	76.4
Japan[1]	29.0	10.0	58.5	2.5	71.0

1. Natural sciences and engineering only.
Source: OECD.

Graph 2.2. Trends in basic research by sector
(in million $ (PPP) at 1980 prices)

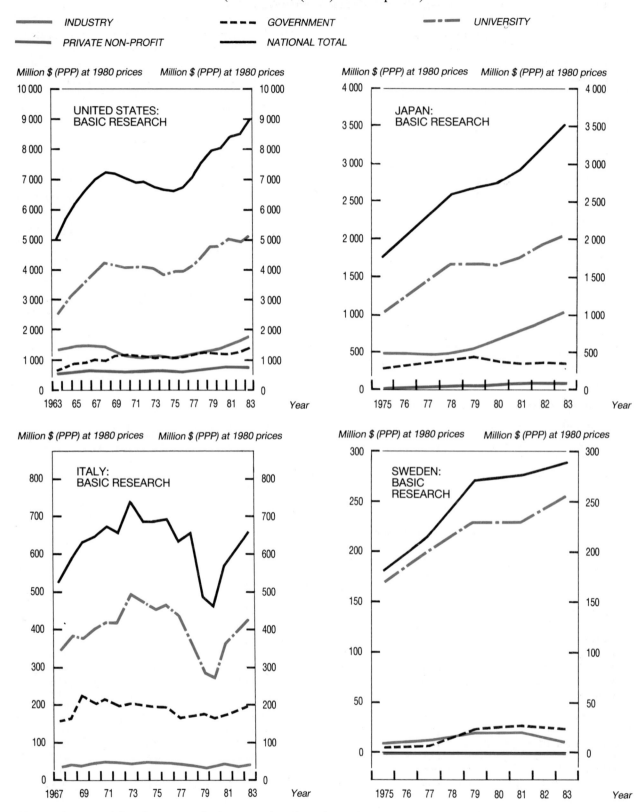

Note: Japan and Sweden: natural sciences and engineering only.
Source: OECD.

for example, in artificial intelligence), materials (especially in ceramics and in the design of new alloys) and of course the life sciences (where the boundaries between the differing stages of research are very blurred)[3]. As a result, there are signs of growing interest on the part of industry in basic research, especially in the United States and Japan (Graph 2.2). In turn, this raises complex issues about property rights in scientific advances, such as the assumption that the benefits of scientific advance at a fundamental level are, and should remain, largely inappropriable by the individual scientist or institution. This and other issues are discussed in more detail below.

These developments qualify the view that the financing of basic research should rest almost entirely with the public sector. But they do not detract from the fact that the public sector has an important responsibility in this area. In practice, the institutional structure through which this responsibility is discharged has largely been shaped by the broader role of basic research in society (see Part II of this chapter).

The growth of basic research has therefore historically been closely associated with the emergence of the university system as a centre for scientific activity. In the context of training for professions (including that of teaching), research work has become an increasingly important part of curricula in higher education. In turn, the funding of this work as part of the broader financing of universities has been seen as an important component of academic freedom[4]. This connection between the sources of finance and the freedom of enquiry, particularly in the social sciences, remains a major consideration underlying government support, especially since the higher education system performs over half of all basic research in OECD countries.

Nonetheless, the greatest impetus ensuring public support for basic research has come from governments' own needs. In the World War II period, the emergence of science-based technologies of strategic significance precipitated a massive rise in government research funding – most obviously in nuclear energy and aerospace and, somewhat later for a broad range of reasons, in medicine[5]. The circumstances of that period made it unlikely that these technologies could have been developed under private funding or initiative, and many of the structures and procedures put in place then remain the backbone of the basic research system in many countries. These structures are usually centred on "national laboratories" – the sizeable, mission-oriented facilities through which governments carry out research considered of particular national significance. The share of government funding for basic research awarded to these institutions (as proxied by government institutions' share in the use of resources for basic research) varies from about 5 per cent in Sweden to about 24 per cent in the United Kingdom and in Germany, and even more in smaller countries.

As a natural result of their role in financing basic research, governments have found themselves vested with a responsibility for allocating resources both between scientific institutions and between projects. However, in practice, the very same factors which discourage private industry's involvement in basic research have made it difficult for the public sector to design an efficient financing mechanism.

For example, indivisibility in many areas of basic research is associated with large equipment size so that there is generally a minimum efficient size, or "critical mass", below which research teams cannot work effectively. This severely limits the scope for funding flexibility, since large facilities and integrated research teams cannot be run on the basis of short-term commitments. Equally, inappropriability entails a lack of market valuations of outcomes, while technical uncertainty is usually associated with long and variable time-lags between outlays and results. This deprives administrators of the possibility of defining, in operational terms, the rate of return to basic research as a tool for evaluation. Hence, strategic decisions as well as the day-to-day planning of basic research are bound to assume a largely subjective character, influenced by an interplay of the perceived needs of society, personal (or group) influence, political pressures and even sometimes scientific fashion.

These difficulties are inherent in the nature of basic research. It can be argued that they generally had less acute effects in the period when overall spending for R&D was rising rapidly – partly under the impetus of the general expansion of higher education outlays and partly as a consequence of the launching of large and ambitious national programmes, notably in space exploration and nuclear energy. However, two developments have made the effectiveness of resource allocation mechanisms in basic research more important in recent years.

The first is the changing pattern of research priorities, as well as the changing priorities of the public for research and development activities as a whole, as indicated in government budgets. So, although government financial support for R&D has continued to rise during the past ten years, albeit at a slower pace than in the preceding decade, a significant shift in the composition of this research has occurred. In the 1970s, growing weight was given to research on energy sources and environmental issues, followed by a fairly widespread move in the early 1980s towards greater emphasis on R&D spending for economic development (which mainly involves subsidising industrial R&D), with the United States (where defence R&D has been the primary growth area in recent years) being the significant exception in this regard[6]. The net outcome of these trends has been an almost universal decline within the OECD area in the share of government R&D spending devoted to the general advancement of knowledge, of which university research is the most important component (Graph 2.3).

At the same time, the cost of basic research has tended to rise more rapidly than price inflation as a

Graph 2.3. Share of the "advancement of knowledge" objective in government R&D outlays

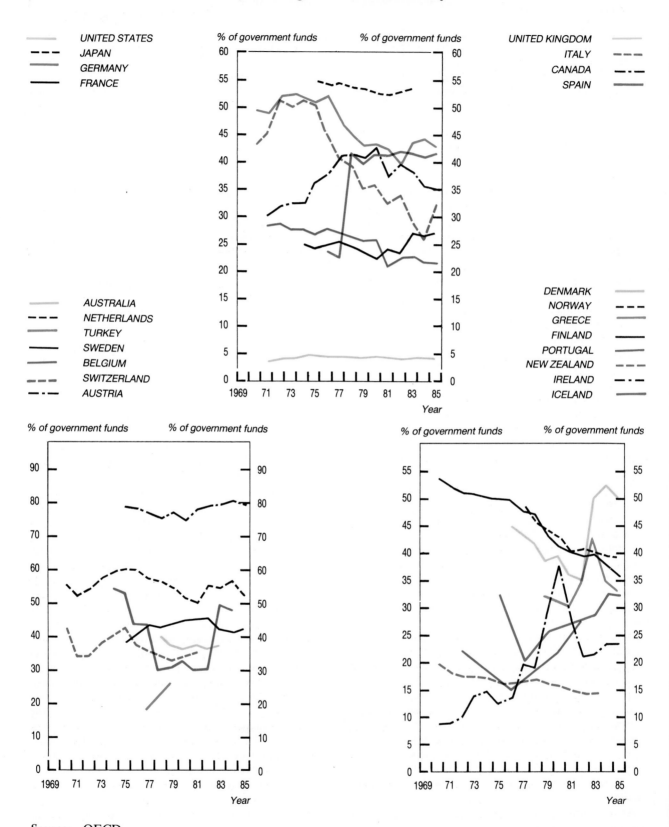

Source: OECD.

Graph 2.4. Trends in R&D capital expenditure per university researcher

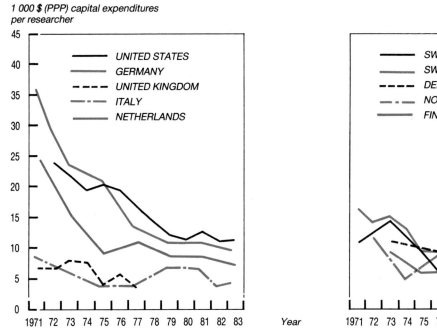

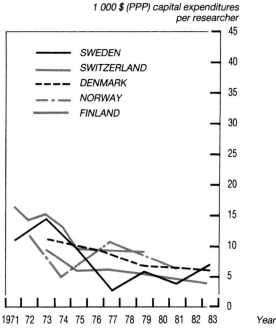

Notes: Natural sciences and engineering only for the United Kingdom, Italy and Sweden. University graduates instead of researchers for Finland.
Source: OECD.

whole. This has partly occurred as a result of the growing sophistication and complexity of scientific instrumentation[7], but is also due to an increasing need for ancillary facilities such as access to data banks and to more stringent security systems. This has contributed to raising the minimum efficient scale of scientific facilities in the context of tighter budgetary constraints on research expenditures[8]. These effects are difficult to quantify, however.

This combination of changing government priorities and rising costs has placed increasing pressures on the basic research system, and in particular on the universities[9]. There has been virtual stagnation from 1975 through 1983 in the financial resources allocated per researcher[10] in the higher education sector in the OECD area, whereas those in the government sector and industry increased. Furthermore, since current expenditures have continued to rise, albeit at a slower rate than in the late 1960s and early 1970s, the brunt of adjustment has occurred through a decline in capital outlays (especially for material and instrumentation) with the share of capital expenditures in university research outlays being cut by around half in a little more than a decade (Graph 2.4 and Table 2.3). These changes may be partially due to the increasing relative cost of capital equipment.

At the same time, the slowing of growth in expenditure (and in some countries actual reductions in expenditure), together with a general deceleration in the expansion of higher education enrolments, has limited job opportunities in basic research. The shift in virtually all OECD countries from a decade of exceptionally rapid expansion in higher education to modest or zero growth has led to a marked skewing in the age structure of academic staff, with a bulge in the age distribution towards the late thirties and forties (Graph 2.5). Given high, and in a few cases even rising, ages of retirement, this means that retirement rates are currently well below prior levels and can be expected to remain so for the next twenty years. Combined with a reduction in mobility induced by the changing age structure (mobility generally declines with increasing age), vacancy rates for new entrants are low and are likely to remain so[11].

The resulting pressures to find new sources of funding – in order to upgrade equipment and to create new posts for younger researchers – have led to a major shift in the financing pattern of research institutions, most notably, once again, in higher education.

The funding of higher education institutions can generally be split into two categories: block grants [also referred to as "General University Funds" (GUF)], which are most often linked to student numbers and

Table 2.3. **Trends in R&D expenditure in the higher education sector and as a percentage of capital expenditure**

In million 1980 $ at purchasing power parities

Natural sciences and engineering only

	1971	1973	1975	1977	1979	1981	1983
United States							
Constant $	7297[1]	7239	7383	7917	8643	9246	9286
% capital expenditure	24[1]	20	21	18	13	13	12
Japan							
Constant $	—	—	—	—	3363	3576	4046
% capital expenditure	—	—	—	—	21	19	19
Germany							
Constant $	—	2096	1960	1895	1930	2030	2016
% capital expenditure	—	24	24	16	14	15	13
United Kingdom							
Constant $	717	795	736	746	—	1156	1219
% capital expenditure	9	11	6	6	—	6	5
Italy							
Constant $	487	559	526	548	489	622	745
% capital expenditure	15	10	8	8	17	16	15
Netherlands							
Constant $	419	389	425	449	463	426	482
% capital expenditure	25	17	10	11	9	9	8
Sweden							
Constant $	269	331	359	336	382	570	656
% capital expenditure	11	14	9	3	5	4	6
Denmark							
Constant $	—	93	100[2]	—	92	—	105[3]
% capital expenditure	—	20	15[2]	—	14	—	12[3]
Norway							
Constant $	107[1]	—	108[4]	147	142	130	131
% capital expenditure	21[1]	—	9[4]	17	15	13	10
Finland							
Constant $	43	51	54	60	61	—	—
% capital expenditure	22	26	21	24	20	—	—

1. 1972. 2. 1976. 3. 1982. 4. 1974.
Source: OECD.

Table 2.4. **Share of project funds in total public funding for higher education research**

In percentages

	1971	1975	1977	1979	1981	1983
United States	74.3[1]	74.6	76.6	80.9	85.0	83.6
Japan	19.3	23.4	27.7	30.0	27.8	25.5
France	58.7	64.8	61.7	62.0	[46.2[2]]	[47.5[2]]
Netherlands	5.2	2.9	7.3	6.8	5.9	6.7
Canada	46.6	42.1	41.8	42.3	55.7	57.7
Norway	13.9[1]	..	13.1	15.3	15.8	17.0
Finland	..	16.9	17.4	19.5	19.5	31.1
Belgium	..	30.0	32.8	29.7	..	..
Denmark	..	9.6[3]	..	12.5	10.9[4]	..
Spain	..	..	..	24.8	18.4	23.3
Sweden[5]	..	40.1	33.4	..	26.1	27.2
Ireland	37.6	28.6	28.1	[17.5[6]]	[18.1[6]]	..

1. 1972.
2. Not comparable with preceding years because of increased research coefficients in block grants.
3. 1976.
4. 1982.
5. Natural sciences and engineering only.
6. Not comparable with preceding years.
Source: OECD.

Graph 2.5.   **Age structure of academic staff**

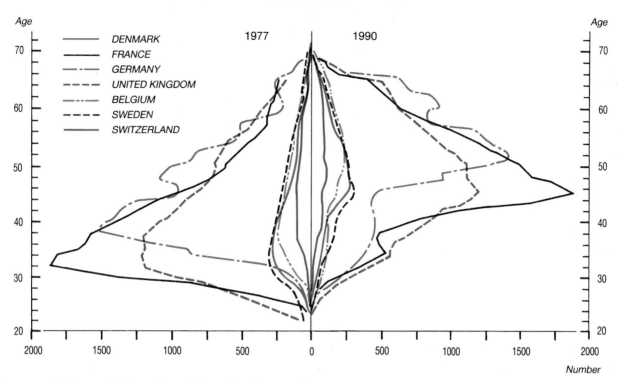

Source: European Science Foundation, *Employment Prospects and Mobility of Scientists in Europe, op. cit.* in Note 11.

which tend to be allocated between functions and departments on a fairly rigid basis; and project funding, which is usually derived from outside sources and is more or less earmarked for specific purposes, providing the principal source of flexibility in university income. As general grants have become more limited, project funding has become progressively more important (Table 2.4), with two significant implications.

Firstly, greater reliance on project funding has increased the pressures on the scientific community to obtain more rapid pay-offs, to augment the visibility of its research efforts and to avoid the risks inherent in the exploration of underlying principles and phenomena. The consequence of these pressures has been a fall in the share of basic research being carried out in relation to the total research effort of higher education institutions, with resources being transferred from basic research to applied research and even to experimental development (Table 2.5)[12].

A second consequence of the shift in funding patterns has been to increase the strain on resource allocation mechanisms in basic research. This has been notable in the process of "peer reviews" – that is, project appraisal by a panel of experts in a particular discipline or set of disciplines. Although this system is clearly a far better regulatory mechanism than straight budgetary allocations, the weaknesses of peer review are familiar[13]. They are generally not a particularly useful mechanism for selecting between disciplines, rather than within them; they have a strong conservative bias, with well-established lobbies generally succeeding in advancing their interests at the expense of newer rivals; and it is rarely possible to use peer reviews as a basis for selecting areas in which funding should be entirely discontinued. These features of peer reviews apply quite universally, but their capacity to cope with the more difficult budgetary circumstances of recent years has also been significantly affected by the institutional structure of each country's research system. How different these structures are is briefly summarised for five major countries, together with an illustration of major flows of resources, in the next part of this chapter.

More specifically, it has proved especially difficult to reallocate resources among competing projects and institutions in countries where government laboratories account for a large share of all resource use in basic research. This is particularly the case in the EEC countries (notably France and the Mediterranean countries) and Australia (Tables 2.2 and 2.6, Graph 2.6).

Table 2.5. **Shifts in higher education R&D by type of activity**

In percentages

	United States			Japan[1]			Italy		
	1971	1975	1983	1975	1981	1983	1971	1975	1983
Basic research	68	62	59	71	49	51	59	60	52
Applied research	21	25	28	22	31	34	39	39	42
Experimental development	11	13	13	7	7	8	2	2	6
Total	100	100	100	100	87[2]	93[2]	100	100	100
	Norway			Austria[1]			Ireland		
	1972	1979	1983	1970	1975	1981	1971	1979	1982
Basic research	59	53	47	47	46	45	64	57	42
Applied research	30	34	37	38	40	42	32	38	44
Experimental development	11	13	16	15	14	13	4	5	14
Total	100	100	100	100	100	100	100	100	100

1. National sciences and engineering only.
2. Japan: total inferior to 100 because no estimates have been made by the national authorities for non-respondents to the survey sample.
Source: OECD.

Table 2.6. **Estimated R&D expenditure by type of activity in the OECD area in 1981**

In percentages

	A. Share of each OECD area in total of OECD by type of activity			B. Share of each OECD area in basic research by sector of performance (in total of OECD)			
	Basic research	Basic and applied research	Experimental development	Business enterprise	Government	Higher education	Total
United States	44	45	56	46	34	44	44
Japan	10	11	13	19	7	9	10
EEC	36	34	24	31	45	36	36
Other countries	10	10	7	4	14	11	10
OECD	100	100	100	100	100	100	100

Source: OECD Science and Technology Indicators: No. 2, Paris, 1986.

Table 2.7. **Level and changes in R&D resources, per researcher, 1983**

In $1 000 and index (1975 = 100, at 1980 prices)

	Business enterprises		Higher education		Government		All sectors	
	Level ($1 000)	Index	Level ($1 000)	Index	Level ($1 000)	Index	Level ($1 000)	Index
United States	119	102	118	100	179	114	123	102
Japan[1]	87	131	40	118	103	131	70	130
EEC[2]	155	105	57	82	133	99	116	98
Other[2]	146	104	74	108	107	108	119	106
Total[2]	119	106	66	99	141	109	106	105

1. Official data. Adjusted to OECD standards, R&D expenditures per researcher would read as follows:
   $118 000 per researcher in the higher education sector;
   $130 000 per researcher for all sectors.
2. *EEC:* excluding the United Kingdom and Greece; *Other:* excluding New Zealand, Turkey, and Yugoslavia.
Source: OECD, Secretariat estimates.

Graph 2.6.   **Basic research by main areas and sector of performance, 1981**

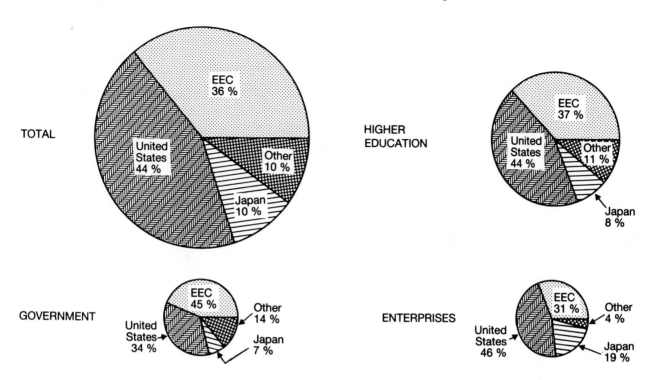

Source: OECD, Science and Technology Indicators, No. 2, 1986.

The difficulties of resource reallocation in these circumstances have been partly due to the political legitimacy and scientific standing of the larger government laboratories, as well as to the large-scale and long-term nature of their capital investments (which means that heavy financial commitments may persist long after interest in their field of activity has waned). However, the rigidities thus created have been exacerbated by the close links which typically exist between the laboratories and the agencies responsible for resource allocation for basic research. Indeed, in some cases – such as the United Kingdom and France – the functions of resource allocation have not generally been clearly separated from those of carrying out research, and notably of managing national laboratories. Faced with tighter budget constraints, such funding agencies have frequently privileged their own facilities in preference to the funding of external work – especially in higher education institutions[14].

A comparison between several OECD countries, set out in Table 2.7, highlights this pattern. Over the period 1975-83, although the resources available per OECD researcher did slightly increase, a look at the intersectoral distribution reveals that only researchers in government and industrial laboratories received net

funding increases per researcher, whereas their counterparts in universities had to live in 1983 with slightly less than in 1975. In EEC countries, expenditure in higher education was cut by 20 per cent on a per researcher basis, while government laboratories were able to maintain the same level of funding per researcher.

In short, there can be little doubt that (with the possible exception of Japan) governments have found it increasingly difficult to effectively discharge their role as the guardian of basic research. Yet the difficulties have been more acute in some institutional contexts than in others; and these examples can provide some lessons for improving science policy in the future.

II.   THE INSTITUTIONAL INFRASTRUCTURE WITHIN WHICH BASIC RESEARCH IS CONDUCTED

Part I presented a brief, across-the-board review of the major funding problems facing basic research in the last decade. The necessary generalisations are valid for several, or almost all, OECD countries; but the exceptions and qualifications are also numerous. The reason

Table 2.8. **Share of non-industrial R&D and of public finance in national R&D**

Countries ranked according to non-industrial R&D share

In percentages

Country	Share of non-industrial R&D in national R&D				Share of public funding in national R&D			
	1971	1975	1981	1983	1971	1975	1981	1983
Iceland	98.9	97.1	90.4	83.0	89.8	84.6	85.6	65.8
Greece	—	—	77.5	—	—	—	84.4	—
Australia	—	76.8[3]	77.6	77.0	—	74.7[3]	75.8	76.7
Portugal	75.3	78.9[3]	71.4[4]	68.8[5]	65.6	71.7[3]	66.8[4]	61.9[5]
Ireland	61.1	69.4	56.4	56.4[5]	53.1	61.0	56.5	56.5[5]
Canada	64.8	63.4	50.9	53.1	62.8	61.9	49.4	52.2
Spain	56.2	43.4	51.2	48.2	54.6	42.7	52.9	49.6
Denmark	55.4[2]	55.8	50.2	48.2[5]	55.0[2]	56.4	53.4	51.5[5]
Netherlands	44.8	46.4	46.7	46.6	44.5	44.9	47.2	47.2
Austria	—	49.2	44.2	—	—	51.6	43.8	—
Norway	56.0[1]	52.0	47.1	44.0	63.6[1]	59.1	57.2	51.5
Finland	45.5	47.9	45.3	43.2	44.3	48.4	46.0	42.3
France	43.8	40.4	41.1	43.2	58.7	54.2	52.8	54.0
Italy	44.1	44.3	43.6	42.9	41.1	43.1	47.2	52.4
United Kingdom	38.7[1]	41.6	38.2	39.0	49.5[1]	54.7	49.0	50.2
Japan	41.6	43.4	39.3	36.5	28.9	29.7	26.9	24.0
Belgium	49.0	35.8	—	—	51.8	—	—	—
Sweden	31.8	31.4	33.4	32.5	41.2	39.1	39.9	36.6
Germany[6]	36.3	37.0	30.5	29.3	46.5	47.4	40.7	39.4
United States	34.3[1]	34.1	29.7	28.7	58.5[1]	54.8	49.3	49.2
Switzerland	21.0	23.3	25.8	25.7	14.2	17.4	—	22.6

1. 1972.
2. 1973.
3. 1976.
4. 1980.
5. 1982.
6. 1981 and 1983 not strictly comparable with preceding years, due to a downward revision of government-funded R&D.
Source: OECD.

for this diversity of national experiences is that in each country the funding of basic research is largely conditioned by the broad institutional framework of the R&D system, which changes only slowly (Table 2.8). In particular, and as illustrated by flow charts in this part, there are major contrasts between countries in the relative importance of government, industry and higher education structures in both the funding and the actual conduct of R&D work.

Additional insight into the findings of the previous part can be gained by studying the specific features of national R&D systems which have a direct bearing on how basic research is run at a national level. This analysis is confined to the five largest OECD countries, and even then in a highly selective manner for reasons of space. It is not intended to give a full description of all national R&D systems; only major features are presented which either have a direct effect on basic research, which are typical of a country, or which distinguish it from other countries.

Since research work is a highly fragmentary activity in every country, with a multitude of actors involved, it is by its very nature difficult to manage. This problem is further complicated by shifts in research policy objectives as well as by emerging new fields of scientific investigation. It therefore matters who is formulating demands for research, who is the "customer", and what kind of links exist between the two. Indeed, the orientation and relevance of scientific efforts is, as already stated by the OECD one and a half decades ago, rather a matter of mechanisms than of objectives[15].

In the *United States*, government accounts for a fairly high share of total research funding. But a very large proportion of these funds is contracted out on a competitive basis to industry and higher education institutions (see Figure 2.A). Only a small fraction of national R&D is carried out by government agencies as part of their overall objectives, and even then only in a decentralised manner.

The predominant sources of federal basic research support in universities and colleges are the National Institute of Health (NIH), followed by the National Science Foundation (NSF) and the Department of Defence (DOD). The National Science Foundation, which is more basic research-oriented than mission-oriented, spends almost all its funds externally, notably

Figure 2.A.

UNITED STATES 1983

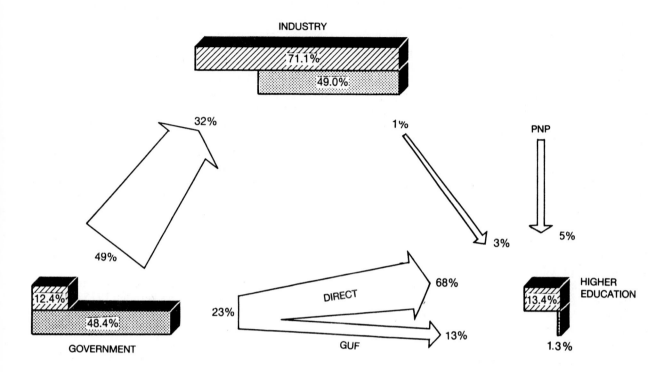

Notes:

Upper box: % of national R&D carried out.
Lower box: % of national R&D funded.
Arrows   :   % of funding sector $\Longrightarrow$ % of performing sector.
All figures are in per cent.
Only relevant flows are shown, highlighting in particular the funding structure of the higher education sector and extra-mural funding of the government sector.
GUF: General University Funds.
PNP :   Private Non-Profit Institutes.

The length of the two bars is proportionate to the share of each sector in the national R&D funding and performance respectively. The origin of the arrows shows the relative importance of the outgoing funding flows for the sector in terms of its own total *funding*. The destination of the arrows, by contrast, shows the importance of the flow relative to the *performance* of the receiving sector. Flows are also calibrated relative to each other.

Thus the figure for the United States can be read as follows:
- Government accounts for 48.4 per cent of research funding, but only for 12.4 per cent of the use of research funds, the remainder being transferred to industry and higher education;
- The massive transfer of government funds to industry, representing 49 per cent of total government funding, explains the large difference between funding and performance of industry, since 32 per cent of industrial R&D is publicly financed;
- For higher education, carrying out 13.4 per cent of national R&D while funding 1.3 per cent, direct public funding accounted for 68 per cent and general university funding for 13 per cent of its total research income. Altogether, 8 per cent of higher education R&D was financed by private sources (5 per cent by private non-profit institutions and 3 per cent by industry).

Source: OECD Secretariat calculations.

in universities. This support function is remarkably similar to that of the German DFG and indeed the NSF is in some ways the United States equivalent of central science agencies found in other countries. In recognition of the crucial importance of basic research, the budget of the NSF is expected to double by 1992 as part of an overall programme by the US Government to restore national competitiveness[16].

The Federally Funded Research and Development Centres (FFRDCs) play an important role in meeting particular government research objectives and in providing major facilities at universities for research and associated training purposes, essentially in the physical sciences. Although these are the functional equivalent of large government laboratories in other countries, they are run on a completely different basis, generally being managed by an industrial forum, a university, or another non-profit institution. About one-third of the R & D funds of the nineteen university-affiliated FFRDCs is directed towards basic research; in 1982 this amount was equivalent to almost one-fifth of university expenditure on basic research.

The integration of large-scale research into the US university system gives the higher education sector a strategic role in American basic research. At the same time, the US system of financing federal research relies largely on funds earmarked for specific purposes[17]. Universities therefore have to find additional sources to finance the "floor" of research activities. This is done largely through their own funds (notably in private universities) and through traditional links with industry and foundations, stimulated by fiscal incentives. As a result, United States universities – and their basic research funding – are somewhat less dependent on public sources of finance than their counterparts in other countries[18].

The diversity of funding without the dominance of a single agency, and the decentralised university system where the orientation of research rests with individuals and small sub-units, provides a fairly high degree of flexibility and adaptability in responding to changing needs.

However, a possible negative spin-off from these positive features is that scientists end up spending a great deal of time seeking what is basically short-term project finance in a very competitive environment. The resulting rather unfocused nature of the United States research system could have detrimental effects on research areas which need concentration of resources in a long-term perspective.

With its pluralism and decentralisation, as well as its breadth and diversity of sources of support, the *German* system (see Figure 2.B) is somewhat similar to that of the United States, although mechanisms differ. Its main characteristic is a "division of labour": the State Governments (Länder) are responsible for the universities and provide the basis of their research funding, with this then being supplemented by Federal funds especially for capital expenditures. Other supplementary sources of finance are private and public foundations. As a result, German universities are less dependent on outside grant support than is generally the case in the United States. Another difference is the relative absence of large-scale research facilities on campus since, as in other European countries, most major research projects in Germany are carried out by parallel government-run systems.

The most important large research facilities are the thirteen "big science" institutions, somewhat similar to the American FFRDCs, financed up to 90 per cent by the Federal government. Although these cover the whole spectrum of R & D, broadly over a third of their funds are directed towards basic research which requires expensive instrumentation.

The "big science" institutions are complemented by the sixty institutes of the Max-Planck Society for the Promotion of Science (Max-Planck Gessellschaft – MPG), an autonomous body which promotes basic research, especially in new areas requiring expensive equipment or otherwise less suitable for university studies[19]. Financed on a shared basis by the federal and state governments, the MPG institutions are "built around" internationally known scientists and may be dissolved in order to free resources for the setting-up of new institutes.

This flexibility is evidenced by the creation of eighteen new research facilities between 1975 and 1985. This perceived "expansion" was offset by the concomitant closure of six institutes and twelve independent science research departments[20].

The principal direct funding source for universities is the German Research Association (Deutsche Forschungsgemeinschaft – DFG), an autonomous body which is jointly financed by the Federal Government and the Länder, and which allocates 90 per cent of its funds to universities. One out of seven university researchers is paid by the DFG through three major channels of finance. The most important system is the so-called "normal procedure" where funds are released for a large number of specific, rather short-term projects. These projects are not specified by the DFG, so the broad scope is left to the initiative and creativity of the researchers and young scientists. The second system is the financing of "special research areas" which focus on interdisciplinary inter-institutional research projects of a more long-term nature, aimed at creating a certain continuity for areas of investigation identified as being important. The last form of funding is the "priority procedure", a programme which is intended to foster intra- and inter-regional co-operation among institutions and which has a time horizon of around five years.

The public financing of research is consequently largely left to autonomous bodies such as the MPG and DFG; notably in the case of the DFG these research funds are allocated more by function, e.g. basic research promotion, across scientific disciplines than to specific missions. This diversity of funding using different mechanisms is further supplemented by project funds to

Figure 2.B.

GERMANY 1983

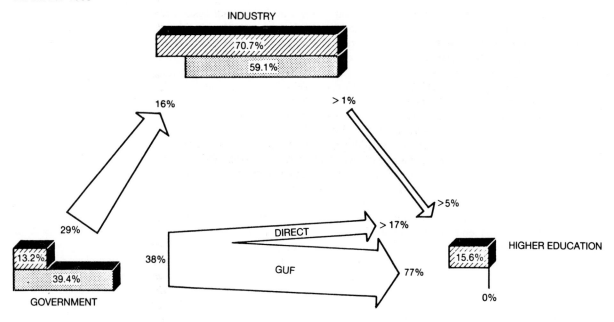

Figure 2.C.

FRANCE 1983

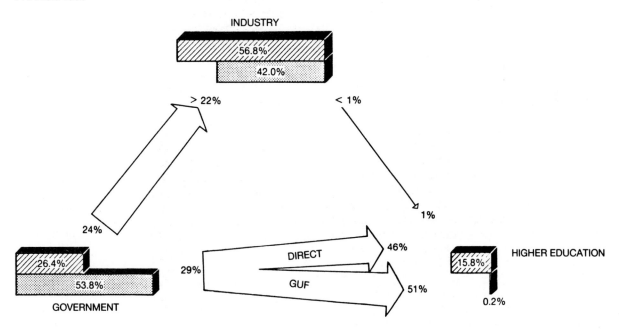

Notes: As for Figure 2A.
Source: OECD Secretariat calculations.

universities and non-university research establishments from the Federal Ministry for Research and Technology (BMFT).

The entire German research system therefore manages to combine fairly stable financing for basic research from diversified sources with a high degree of freedom in the choice and conduct of research. Its drawbacks are a slight loss of quality control for individual research work and less rapidity in exploiting new opportunities. Moreover, the sharing of competence (and funding) between federal and state governments increases the administrative work-load and, more importantly, requires consensus in decision-making. Frictions created by conflicting views can, and to some extent do, impede shifts in resource allocation and institutional change.

The *French* system is highly centralised, with the government assuming an active and directive role. The tradition of prestigious state-funded and controlled research organisations and of direct subsidies for major technology programmes has led to a situation where the French Government finances more than half of all national R&D. This share is only surpassed in a few countries, all of them relatively small (Table 2.8). Approximately half of public funds are spent in government institutions – again, a very high ratio in international terms (see Figure 2.C and Table 2.9). The existence of a multitude of specialised national research centres and agencies for specific missions explains the heavy reliance on "in-house" research. A central role is played by the National Centre for Scientific Research (CNRS), which covers virtually all fields of research.

Employing almost 10 000 researchers, the CNRS devotes about half of its total budget to basic research. It has widespread responsibilities, ranging from research in all scientific disciplines to the application and exploitation of research results and the diffusion of scientific information. Organised into seven scientific departments and two national institutes, the activities and funding of CNRS laboratories generally follow recommendations made by the forty-five disciplinary panels of the National Science Research Council of CNRS.

Many CNRS laboratories are located on university campuses and a significant share of university research is carried out through association with the CNRS. Since this research is not integrated into the university system, university scientists working for the CNRS tend to neglect the close coupling of education and research that is so characteristic of the American university system. As a result, students receive little research training, and this is now considered to be a major reason for weak industry-university links and for industry's lack of interest in basic research[21].

Although roughly one-half of civilian basic research is carried out under the auspices of the CNRS, other large government organisations are also involved, notably the National Institute for Health and Medical Research (INSERM) and the Atomic Energy Commission (CEA).

Centralised decision-making on policy options and mid-term orientations confers a high degree of financial stability and political legitimacy to research undertakings, but weakens incentive and inhibits resource

Table 2.9. **Destination of public R&D funds by sector in 1983**

Countries ranked according to percentage used within government

In percentages

	Government	Business enterprise	Higher education	Other	Total
Greece (1981)	74.7	8.1	18.1	—	100.0
Portugal (1982)	68.0	0.8	31.2	0.0	100.0
Iceland	67.2	1.6	28.9	2.3	100.0
Ireland	60.9	10.2	27.8	1.0	100.0
Spain	60.2	4.2	35.7	—	100.0
Australia (1981)	59.0	2.9	37.3	0.8	100.0
Canada	50.2	11.3	37.5	1.1	100.0
France	46.9	23.7	28.7	0.7	100.0
Italy	43.8	19.7	36.5	—	100.0
Finland	43.3	8.9	47.3	0.5	100.0
Denmark (1982)	40.2	11.5	48.2	0.2	100.0
Japan	39.5	4.5	52.5	3.5	100.0
United Kingdom	36.4	36.8	23.7	3.1	100.0
Netherlands	35.3	9.6	51.5	3.6	100.0
Germany	32.5	29.0	37.5	1.0	100.0
Norway	30.7	21.9	46.5	0.9	100.0
United States	25.1	46.9	23.7	4.2	100.0
Switzerland (1981)	24.7	4.7	70.6	—	100.0
Austria (1981)	18.7	8.8	68.9	3.5	100.5
Sweden[1]	13.2	19.3	67.2	0.2	100.0

1. Natural sciences and engineering only, 1981.
Source: OECD.

reallocation. Recognising this weakness, the government has recently considered moving towards more decentralisation and a more limited government role in the research system as a whole[22].

In the *United Kingdom*, government research and development requirements are defined by individual ministerial departments. Various advisory boards and committees assist in formulating selective priorities, but no strong central co-ordinating body exists. Government research is characterised by mission-oriented agencies (notably for applied research and development) plus five research councils. Some of these councils fulfil a dual function – they operate their own research facilities and provide support for university research, as well as being responsible for the "big science" establishments.

As in the case of France, the UK system is characterised by a fairly high share of government finance in national R&D, a high proportion of government in-house research, large flows of government funding to industry and a comparatively low share of industrial finance in national R&D. Approximately half of government R&D funds are spent on defence research.

University research, which accounts for a modest share of national R&D, faces increasing resource constraints. As set out in the accompanying flow chart (see Figure 2.D), the United Kingdom's university share of government-funded research was, at 18 per cent, the lowest of all five countries considered (and remained at 18 per cent in 1984-85, according to national sources). As increasing costs have not been met by recurrent block grants, universities have become more dependent on finding additional external funds[23]. The research councils, despite similar financial pressures, have increased their grants to universities both in real terms and as a proportion of their budgets. Universities managed to supplement their funds by important contributions from private non-profit institutions and from abroad. The industry share, having declined from its 1971 peak of 7.5 per cent to 3.2 per cent in 1981, is now showing a marked upward trend.

Overall, the United Kingdom system, with its multitude of committees, generates rigidities which limit its ability to shift resources. The tendency to perpetuate existing structures has also meant that budgetary constraints have often been met by spreading resources too thinly.

The *Japanese* Government's share of in-house research as a proportion of national basic research is quite low (about the same amount as in France and half that of Germany) and its share in national basic research is one of the three lowest of all OECD countries (Table 2.2). A large number of government institutes are operated by agencies or ministries and universities, and they, with the exception of universities, have traditionally oriented their activities towards more applied research and development. However, they are now putting more stress on basic research than in the past.

Industry receives very little financial support from the Japanese Government so that the bulk of public funding for research is directed towards universities, other government institutes and public corporations for research (see Figure 2.E). Japan relies mostly on universities for the management and operation of large research facilities, which are run by "national inter-university research institutes" set up from 1971 onwards as the academic equivalent to large industrial research institutes. The emergence of these institutes suggests that the government is now willing to put more emphasis on basic research, having admitted that excessive emphasis was placed on applied research and development in the past. Basic research is carried out mainly by the national universities, owned and operated by central government, with private universities being the next most important performers in this field (public universities operated by local governments play only a very limited role). National universities receive their funds from the Ministry of Education through institutional support, special funds for research equipment or direct grants to researchers on a competitive basis. Other government institutes and public corporations for research are funded by other agencies and ministries.

Despite recent efforts by the authorities to encourage closer industry-university collaboration, private sponsoring of university research is still very limited in Japan. As civil servants, faculty members of national universities have been reluctant to establish close relations with industry. It is felt that the past course of greatly relying on basic research conducted abroad has reached its limits and the national policy for science and technology now seems to put a high priority on basic research. This shift in focus seems to mean that the traditional rigidities resulting from compartmentalisation of research will have to be relinquished. In particular, it acknowledges that new co-operative networks between government, industry and universities and greater emphasis on multidisciplinary research are needed in order to develop leading-edge technologies[24].

Some efforts were made recently to promote and implement co-operative R&D between the Japanese Government, industry and universities. In fact, a law for "Facilitating Governmental Research Co-operation" was enacted in May 1986 to eliminate some bottlenecks in existing laws and to encourage research co-operation between the private sector, universities and research establishments overseas.

These differences, but also similarities, between research structures and funding mechanisms in different countries help to explain why the scope of action and chances of success in achieving more efficient research will be greater in some countries than in others. The extent to which national research systems possess the capacity to implement measures to reap benefits from a continuously changing environment also depends, to a large degree, on the size and operating mode of the national system. Consequently, each country has to assess its possibilities and limitations individually. But there are some broader areas which

Figure 2.D.

UNITED KINGDOM 1981

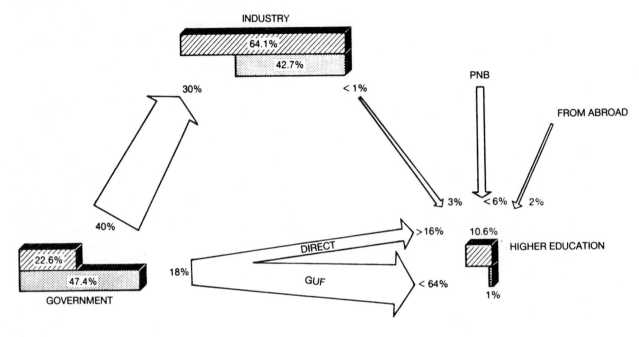

Figure 2.E.

JAPAN 1983

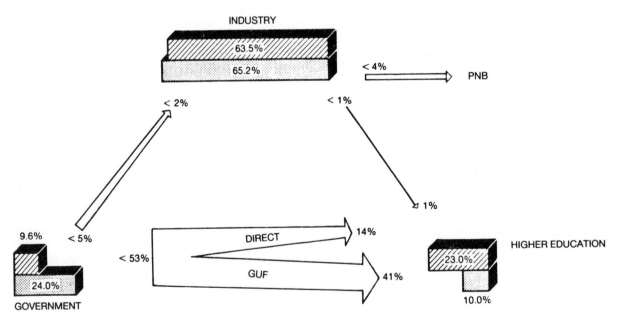

Notes: As for Figure 2A.
Source: OECD Secretariat calculation.

offer scope for improvement, applicable to most – if not all – OECD countries. They will be discussed in the following part.

III. STRENGTHENING THE BASIC RESEARCH SYSTEM

There is no identifiable "optimal" level for the funding of basic research, nor can a single distribution pattern for research resources be identified as preferable to all others. In allocating resources to basic research, governments are inevitably guided by the often conflicting pressures of responsibility for future advancement, perceived scientific opportunities, the immediate needs of society, and – last but not least – the weight of vested interests.

These outcomes will doubtless be imperfect. They can only be improved by a research system which is able to shift resources between changing needs, can efficiently diffuse its results, and which is open to the stimuli coming from applied research and international cooperation.

A. Enhancing flexibility

Securing greater flexibility in the research system while maintaining a commitment to the highest quality levels requires improvements both in the structure of the institutional framework and in resource allocation mechanisms.

As far as structures are concerned, there is a strong case, especially in certain European countries and Australia, for reviewing the far-reaching reliance on government laboratories as centres for long-term research. Problems arise when these laboratories are run in virtual symbiosis with funding agencies, as the scope for conflicts of interest in resource allocation can compromise the efficiency of the system as a whole. At the same time, the civil status of researchers in these institutions (although not necessarily very dissimilar from that of tenured staff in higher education) does not facilitate inter- and intra-sectoral mobility. Of course, there are areas of research where reliance on government laboratories is virtually inevitable. But, in these circumstances, it would be desirable for the legislation or act establishing such a laboratory to contain "sunset" provisions ensuring the periodic review of its mandate – currently a rare practice.

A greater reliance on non-governmental agencies may ease some of the rigidities of the basic research system but cannot solve its manpower problems, which themselves create major obstacles to resource reallocation. These problems are largely due to demographics, but are aggravated by low levels of labour mobility throughout the basic research system and not only in its government segment.

Many governments, aware of the dangers of the present situation, have implemented schemes aimed at lowering entrance barriers by providing young researchers with temporary employment through scholarships and fellowships. Other measures have also been introduced to facilitate greater mobility, especially financial support for transfers within and between sectors. Helpful as these measures may be in the short term, they do not address the real issue: tenured positions with a high degree of job security and civil service status in both government and higher education research establishments tend to prevent mobility. A review of the legal framework of employment contracts, coupled with an examination of more liberal leave opportunities (especially through greater portability of pensions) and of provisions for early retirement, may be the key to alleviate blockages in the long term. Furthermore, unqualified tenure may be a major factor hindering change and flexibility in universities and could be worth being reviewed.

A more flexible structure, both in terms of institutional arrangements and of career patterns, would allow enhanced resource allocation procedures to prove more effective in redirecting research efforts as priorities change[25]. The peer review system, combined with a continued trend towards project funding, is at the centre of these procedures; and it seems desirable to improve it in three respects. Firstly, and as is already being done in a number of countries, greater use should be made of objective performance indicators (such as publication and citation indices) in evaluating projects and research teams[26]. Secondly, peer review panels should, wherever possible, include a number of "outsiders" to the research community being appraised, for example through the periodic inclusion of foreign scholars. Finally, there should be increased reliance on systematic *ex post* evaluation as a complement to the selection of new projects.

Useful as procedures for assessing project funding doubtless are, they cannot and should not replace the longer-term funding needed to obtain state-of-the-art equipment and to build coherent research teams. Given continuing budgetary constraints, the major danger – even in the largest countries – is that resources will be spread too thinly, with the result that no research team is fully capable of meeting world standards. In this context, a greater degree of selectivity appears desirable, with resources being concentrated on "centres of excellence". A number of countries have already implemented measures aimed at protecting high-quality research from under-funding. The increased focus on conditional, project-related university funding in the Netherlands, and the special allocation of finance to ten high-level research centres in Australia, are examples which point in this direction. In some Scandinavian countries, increasing emphasis is being given to the build-up of regional centres of competence (as proposed by the Thulin Commission in Norway) and to restructuring the location of research institutions (Finland).

Although apparently geared towards more decentralisation, these measures seem to combine some broadening of the research base with long-term financial support for high-quality research[27].

Nonetheless, greater selectivity should not lead to the creation of insurmountable entry barriers for new research teams, nor create vested interests capable of resisting future change. At its simplest, this entails subjecting designated "centres of excellence" to particularly stringent periodic review on a public and independent basis. But it is also useful to parallel selectivity with a procedure (along the lines of that implemented by the DFG in Germany) whereby scientists, and especially younger researchers, can obtain funds for more innovative research directions. Moreover, "centres of excellence" should, wherever possible, also have the function of servicing the research community in their discipline as a whole, thus averting the dangers which can arise when access to the most sophisticated instrumentation and facilities is subject to administrative rationing. These issues should be seen in the broader framework of maintaining a high-quality physical infrastructure for research. Indeed, it may well be desirable for certain types of facilities, for example, super-computers, to be provided mainly on a service basis (that is, separate from dedicated research facilities), with their funding being provided only partly through direct grants, the remainder coming on a fee-for-service basis from user institutions.

B. Strengthening links with industry

Reforms in institutions and procedures should make the overall research system more responsive to changing needs. In turn, this should provide a basis for closer co-operation with industry.

It has already been noted that the emergence of "generic technologies" in a number of fields spanning the spectrum from applied to basic research is increasing industry interest and involvement in longer-term research efforts. Even the largest firms recognise that scientific institutions have a comparative advantage in this type of research effort. Together with higher education's search to diversify its funding sources, this is leading to a proliferation of industry-university links mainly, but by no means solely, in applied research[28]. These links are valuable not only as a source of additional finance, but as a means of improving the external stimuli to the research system. Numerous countries have taken measures (notably the easing of restrictions on contract research) to encourage this development.

One example in this respect is the recently launched LINK programme in the United Kingdom aimed at strengthening links between universities and industry. Under the scheme, the British Government supports up to half the cost of collective programmes between industry and universities, with the expectation of funding up to £210 million of research over the next five years, providing that industry contributes matching funds. The objectives are to foster strategic areas of scientific and interdisciplinary research, to stimulate industry's R&D spending, to encourage industry to exploit scientific discoveries and to make scientists more aware of the real needs of industry[29].

Another internationally recognised example of efficient contact between research institutions and industry is the integrated co-operation of the SINTEF (Foundation for Scientific and Industrial Research at the Norwegian Institute of Technology) Group with the Norwegian Institute of Technology (NTH). SINTEF operates as a national centre of expertise and, with more than one thousand researchers, is the largest technological contract research organisation in northern Europe. Sixty per cent industry funded, it fosters and stimulates public and private clients. Its success stems from the symbiotic effects of co-location, where research scientists from NTH participate in research projects of the SINTEF group, whilst SINTEF staff often lecture at NTH. Laboratories and equipment are used jointly. The benefits of this (rather informal) association are mutual – the technical competence level of NTH researchers is raised on the one hand, while the SINTEF scientific staff benefit from teaching in an industry-oriented environment on the other.

Nonetheless, growing industry involvement raises a number of complex issues, especially for higher education institutions. One of these centres on the property rights which may or may not be accorded to those funding the research – with these problems generally most acute in biotechnology and genetic engineering. It can, at its simplest, be argued that the case for allowing firms to protect the results of research carried out in-house should apply equally to research they contract out in specific research institutions. This would mean that the property rights relating to corporate research should also bear on that research done under contract in (for example) universities. But it can also be argued that one of the functions of the public research system – and notably of higher education – is to partly offset the economic costs inherent in providing patent protection to strictly private innovative efforts, and that the case for maintaining research as a "public good" is strongest when the research involved pertains to the underlying properties of matter. There is no easy solution to these issues. It may be that any answers will have to emerge on a case-by-case basis rather than through an overall approach.

But these qualifications do not detract from the fact that changing external circumstances have obliged universities to act, more than in the past, as a catalyst for the improved transfer and diffusion of new knowledge into industry. Progress in science and technology increasingly hinges upon connections between pure science and commercial applications, and universities can play an eminent role in increasing a country's capacity to absorb new knowledge.

C. Reinforcing international co-operation

Even the largest countries now have difficulty in covering the costs of, and fully utilising, the large capital-intensive facilities increasingly needed in many fields of basic science – for example, in particle physics and astronomy. Moreover, co-operation in providing and operating these facilities not only reduces the financial burden of basic research but also raises the potential return on research efforts, especially by encouraging the more rapid dissemination of scientific information and the setting-up of international research teams.

However, careful attention has to be paid to avoid potential disadvantages that could arise from international scientific co-operation. In particular, there are the risks of reduced flexibility, less stringent management and the tendency for facilities to be extended beyond their useful lives. As on national level, these possible costs should be formally considered in appraisal and evaluation of international research efforts and action should be taken to minimise their effects.

These factors are likely to have even greater weight in the coming years. It is sometimes claimed that individual countries can, and in some cases should, take a "free-rider" attitude to basic research, absorbing the results of research overseas at a cost well below that incurred by the countries generating the research. It is dubious whether this argument has ever been valid, for it has generally proved very difficult for countries to sustain a technological capability without an effective scientific infrastructure, if only for training purposes. However, whatever force this argument may have had in the past, it is far less likely to apply in future, especially given the growing importance of generic technologies. As the time span between scientific advance and commercial exploitation diminishes, a growing number of countries will come under pressure to maintain scientific competence across the board. Yet this is hardly conceivable for the smaller countries and, in some areas, not even for the largest.

International co-operation can provide an effective means of reconciling these conflicting forces. Basic science is already becoming increasingly internationalised, a trend evidenced by the growing significance of international research facilities (such as CERN, the European Laboratory for Particle Physics)[30], by the rising number of scientific articles co-authored on an international basis[31], and (further downstream) by the steady increase in the international transfer of technology, as measured by payments for licences and royalties.

European Community countries and other smaller OECD countries already pay, on average, the equivalent of one-sixth of their own industrial R&D for this form of technology import. Altogether they spend over 80 per cent of all OECD payments for technology transfer – which is two and a half times their share in OECD industrial R&D. In countries which are small and/or developing their technology base, the reliance on inward transfers of technology is such that it may exceed in cost terms their industry's expenditures on research.

The advantages of these flows are not very different from those arising from trade in other goods and services. Like other forms of trade, their importance for the smaller countries, and some others, is overwhelming. Again, like other forms of trade, these flows rely on an open trading order in which the scientific community can freely exchange data and information. Yet it is a fact of life that scientific knowledge often has implications of a broader strategic and security-related nature. Reconciling the legitimate concerns which follow these implications with the preservation of an open scientific order involves issues which go far beyond this report; but it is clearly of great and growing importance to the efficiency of the research system as a whole.

In a report which laid the stage for postwar science policy, Vannevar Bush referred to science as "the endless frontier". Even in the subsequent periods of more limited means, policy makers clearly recognised this same potential and developed the scientific infrastructure to a degree that has exceeded even the most optimistic projections of earlier years. Today, the scientific community faces new and complex pressures, and its best hope lies in ensuring that the science infrastructure itself is responsive to outside stimulus and is flexible in adjusting to changing circumstances. Inevitably, this is not always easy to reconcile with the scientific community's emphasis on the advancement of knowledge for its own sake, but – given recent and prospective trends – it is a reconciliation well worth making.

NOTES AND REFERENCES

1. The internationally accepted definition of research and experimental development (R&D) has been elaborated by national R&D experts in co-operation with the OECD and is given in OECD, *The Measurement of Scientific and Technical Activities, Proposed Standard Practice for Surveys of Research and Experimental Development*, Paris, 1981, better known as the *Frascati Manual*:

   "Research and experimental development (R&D) comprise creative work undertaken on a systematic basis in order to increase the stock of knowledge, including knowledge of man, culture and society and the use of this stock of knowledge to devise new applications."

   R&D is a term covering three activities: basic research, applied research and experimental development.

   Basic research is experimental or theoretical work undertaken primarily to acquire new knowledge of the underlying foundation of phenomena and observable facts, without any particular application or use in view.

   Applied research is also original investigation undertaken in order to acquire new knowledge. It is, however, directed primarily towards a specific practical aim or objective.

   Experimental development is systematic work, drawing on existing knowledge gained from research and/or practical experience that is directed to producing new materials, products or devices, to installing new processes, systems and services, or to improving substantially those already produced or installed.

2. A wealth of literature exists on the "market failure" argument for supporting basic research. In particular, see Nelson, R.R., *Government and Technical Progress*, Pergamon Press, 1982; Freeman, C., *The Economics of Industrial Innovation*, Second Edition, Frances Pinter, London, 1982; Nelson, R.R., "The Simple Economics of Basic Scientific Research" in Rosenberg, Nathan (ed.), *The Economics of Technical Change*, Penguin Modern Economics Readings, 1971; Arrow, K., "Economic Welfare and Allocation of Resources to Inventions" in *Rate and Direction of Economic Activity*, National Bureau of Economic Research, Princeton University Press, 1982; Clark, N., *The Political Economy of Science and Technology*, Longman, 1985; Nelson, R.R., "Government Support of Technical Progress: Lessons from History", *Journal of Policy Analysis and Management*, Summer 1983, Vol. 2, No. 4. A particularly useful summary of rationales for government support for basic research can also be found in *Public Investment in Research and Development in Australia*, a report to the Prime Minister by the Australian Science and Technology Council (ASTEC), Australian Government Publishing Service, Canberra, November 1985. See also Submission to ASTEC Review of Public Investment in Research and Development in Australia, Part 2, *Higher Education Research Funding*, Department of Science, July 1986.

3. This new dimension of research is mirrored by the emergence of a variety of denominations, such as "enabling research", "long-term research" or "strategic research". It is interesting to note that the UK Cabinet Office distinguishes in its 1985 Annual Review of Government Funded R&D strategic and specific aims of applied research, where the "strategic" part is defined as "applied research which is in a subject area which has not yet advanced to the stage where eventual applications can be clearly specified".

   On the blurring of the frontiers between basic and applied research, see Committee on Science, Technology and Public Policy of the National Academy of Sciences, National Academy of Engineering Institute of Medicine, *Frontiers in Science and Technology: A Selected Outlook*, W.H. Freeman and Co., New York, 1983; on its implications for Japan, and concern about the future, see Science and Technology Agency, *White Paper on Science and Technology 1985 – New Development of R&D and the Era of Co-operation*, Foreign Press Centre, Tokyo, December 1985.

4. Ben-David, J., *Training for the Professions*, Yale University Press, 1975.

5. Polsby, N.W., *Political Innovation in America*, Yale University Press, 1984, Part II.

6. In 1985, almost three-quarters of the United States R&D outlays were for defence and space programmes, the highest proportion for almost fifteen years. Other countries giving high priority to defence and space R&D are the United Kingdom, where this objective absorbed over half of total government R&D funds in 1985, and France, where it absorbed a quarter.

7. See the country reports on scientific instruments submitted to the OECD Directorate for Science, Technology and Industry (DSTI) Ad Hoc Group on University Research at a meeting held on 15th February 1985. See also *Academic Research Equipment in the Physical and Computer Sciences and Engineering*, An Analysis of Findings from Phase I of the National Science Foundation's National Survey of Academic Research Instruments and Instrumentation Needs by Westat Inc., Rockville, Maryland, December 1984. See also National Research Council, "Keeping Research Strong While Reducing the Deficit", *News Report*, April 1986, Vol. XXXVI, No. 4; de Solla Price, Derek, "The Science/Technology Relationship, the Craft of Experimental Science, and Policy for the Improvement of High Technology Innovation", *Research Policy*, 1984, No. 13.

8. It is worth noting that trends in information processing, notably the declining cost of computers and telecommunications, may have gone in the other direction.

9. "Keeping Research Strong While Reducing the Deficit", *art. cit.* in Note 7; OECD, *Industry and University. New Forms of Co-operation and Communication*, Paris, 1984; Hoslock, J.H., "Technological Education for the 21st Century" in *Proceedings of the International Conference on Future Development in Technology, the Year 2000*, London, 4th-6th April 1984, Induscience Enter-

114

prises Ltd., 1985; OECD, *Science and Technology Policy Outlook 1985*, Paris, 1985; "The Role and Functions of the Universities – General Report", prepared for OECD, May 1986.

10. Financial resources consist of current and capital expenditure for R & D. Capital expenditure for R & D consists of gross expenditures on fixed assets for R & D use, i.e. for expenses for land and buildings, instruments and equipment.

11. European Science Foundation, *Employment Prospects and Mobility of Scientists in Europe*, ECE, Strasbourg, 1980. See also Herman, R., *The European Scientific Community*, Longman, 1986; Avveduto, S. and Brandi, C., *Training and Mobility of Researchers: A Study on the European Situation*, National Research Council, Institute for Studies on Research and Scientific Documentation, Rome, September 1984; National Research Council, *Outlook for Science and Technology. The Next Five Years*, National Academy of Science, San Francisco, 1982; Dyring, A., *Swedish Research: Policy, Issues, Organisation*, Swedish Institute, Malmö, 1985; Ministry of Cultural and Scientific Affairs, *White Paper No. 60 (1984-85) on Scientific Research in Norway*, Oslo, January 1986.

12. The growing importance of primarily application- (rather than science-) oriented tertiary institutions, such as Fachhochschulen and technical colleges, has been an additional factor in this respect.

13. An excellent summary of evaluation techniques of research and the difficulties inherent in the peer review procedures to cope with the emergence of new scientific specialities as well as with ranking existing disciplines according to their importance can be found in Gibbons, M. and Georghiou, L., "Evaluation of Research – Synthesis Report", prepared for OECD/DSTI, September 1986. For more details on evaluation procedures, see *Colloque international CPE méthodologies évaluatives de la recherche II - Les programmes de recherche*, Paris, 3rd-4th May 1984, Centre de prospective et d'évaluation, Etude No. 51, January 1985; Mitroff, I. and Chubin, D., "Peer Review at the NSF – A Dialectical Policy Analysis", *Social Studies of Science*, 1979, No. 9.
For a thorough discussion of problems and prospects of research evaluation, see the papers presented at the 17th Special Topic Workshop on Evaluation of Research and Resource Allocation, organised by OECD/Centre for Educational Research and Innovation (CERI) in December 1984 within the framework of their Institutional Management in the Higher Education Programmes – in particular, see Gibbons, M., "Methods for the Evaluation of Research". See also Goldenberg, E.N., "Evaluation as a Management Goal - The Three Faces of Evaluation", *Journal of Policy Analysis and Management*, Summer 1983, Vol. 2; Taylor, M.G., "Evaluation of Research and Resource Allocation", summary of papers and discussions of the 17th Special Topic Workshop organised by OECD/CERI, paper presented at the OECD Workshop on Science and Technology Indicators in the Higher Education Sector, Paris, 10th-13th June 1985; Hill, Chr.T., "Rethinking Our Approach to Science and Technology Policy", *Technology Review*, April 1985; Advisory Council for Applied Research and Development (ACARD), *Exploitable Areas of Science*, HMSO, London, May 1986; *Raising the National Skill Base*, Press Notice 4/86, 8th May 1986; and *The Development of Higher Education into the 1990s*, response by the ACARD to the Green Paper (Cmnd 9524); *Outlook for Science and Technology. The Next Five Years*, op. cit. in Note 11.
For a more specific critique of peer review mechanisms, see Irvine, J. and Martin, B., "What Direction for Basic Scientific Research?" in Gibbons, M. *et al.*, *Science and Technology in the 1980s and Beyond*, Longman, London, 1984.

14. To give one example, in 1981-82 the Science and Engineering Research Council in the United Kingdom allocated, besides fellowship programmes and subscriptions to international research, almost twice as much funds to large research facilities as to universities in the form of peer reviewed research grants. See also Farina, C. and Gibbons, M., "The Impact of the Science Research Council's Policy of Selectivity and Concentration on Average Levels of Research Support, 1965-1984", *Research Policy*, July 1981, No. 10.

15. OECD, *The Research System, Vol. 1, France, Germany, United Kingdom*, Paris, 1972.

16. According to national sources, federal support for basic scientific research is estimated to have increased by 76 per cent between 1982 and 1988 and is expected to realise strong growth in the coming years. In the federal budget proposal for fiscal year 1988, basic research represented $9.7 billion or almost half of the federal budget for *civil* R & D. The increased emphasis in 1988 on basic research is reflected by some 18 per cent more funding for basic research for the NSF, an increase of some 22 per cent in basic research of the NASA, and about 15 per cent for general science programmes of the DOE. These measures are accompanied by programmes aiming at the development of human capital, interdisciplinary research and knowledge transfer to industry.

17. *Outlook for Science and Technology. The Next Five Years*, op. cit. in Note 11.

18. The description of institutional features and their assessment for the United States and the following four countries is largely based, besides national sources, upon: Strategic Studies Center, *Performer Organisations and Support Strategies for Fundamental Research: United States, France, West Germany, United Kingdom, Japan, Soviet Union, Vol. I: Comparative Overview; Vol. II: Country Studies*, Washington D.C., 1985; Tisdell, C.A., *Science and Technology Policy, Priorities of Governments*, Chapman and Hall Ltd., London, 1981.
On the importance of adequate management structures for scientific research, see Keyworth II, G.A., "Priority for Science and Technology", *Technology in Society*, Pergamon Journals Ltd., 1986, Vol. 8.

19. Another significant share of basic and applied research is carried out by the "blue list" research institutes which are jointly financed by the federal and state governments.

20. BMFT, *Faktenbericht 1986 zum Bundesbericht Forschung*.

21. See Strategic Studies Center, *op. cit.* in Note 18.

22. OECD, *Reviews of Innovation Policies: France*, Paris, January 1986.

23. As announced by the government in 1982, recurrent block grants to universities administered by the University Grants Committee (UGC) declined from 1983 in cost terms and are due to fall by 2 per cent a year until 1990.

24. *White Paper on Science and Technology 1985 – New Development of R&D and the Era of Co-operation, op. cit.* in Note 3.

25. For example, in the *United Kingdom* an attempt was made to strengthen the efficiency of resource allocation in applied research. Since 1972, the so-called customer/contractor principle, as recommended by the Rothschild Report, has been adopted. Applied research is now regulated by this principle where government departments act as customers and research councils most often as contractors. This "market-facsimile" approach seems to have worked reasonably well, although it is said to have increased the administrative work-load too much and made it more difficult to pursue some research areas of a longer-term nature.

   In the *Netherlands*, where the share of project funds has traditionally been very low, the approach adopted in the early 1980s to improve allocation procedures for universities consisted in dividing the recurrent block grant into two components, one remaining basically linked to student numbers, the other being conditional, i.e. assessed by external peer review. A similar approach is planned by the British University Grants Committee (UGC), which intends to split university block grant allocations into two elements consisting of a student numbers-oriented floor finance, supplemented by research-oriented additional finance. See also De Clerg, M., "Output Financing Wherever Possible – The Wolfson Committee on the Efficiency and Effectiveness of the Research Factory", *Science Policy in the Netherlands*, December 1985, Vol. 7, No. 5; OECD, *Reviews of National Science and Technology Policies - The Netherlands*, Paris, 1986.

26. The search for more objective methods of performance evaluation than the ones provided by peer review has led to a trail-blazing large-scale experiment in a Dutch university using bibliometric data (publication and citation counts) as an additional means of rationalising evaluation of scientific performance. First results of this experiment have demonstrated the utility of this complementary approach. For a description of this approach, see Moed, H.F. *et al.*, "The Use of Bibliometric Data as Tools for University Research Policy", paper presented at the OECD Workshop on Science and Technology Indicators in the Higher Education Sector, Paris, 14th May 1985. See also Irvine, J. *et al.*, "Charting the Decline in British Science", *Nature*, 15th August 1985, Vol. 316.

27. See *White Paper No. 60 (1984-85) on Scientific Research: Norway, op. cit.* in Note 11; *Science and Technology Policy Outlook, 1985, op. cit.* in Note 9; OECD, *Reviews of National Science Policy: Norway*, Paris, 1985.

28. *Industry and University. New Forms of Co-operation and Communication, op.cit.* in Note 9. See also *Outlook for Science and Technology. The Next Five Years, op. cit.* in Note 11; Stankiewicz, R., "Industry-University Relations" in *Six Countries' Workshop on Industry-University Relations*, Stockholm, 1982.

OECD/CERI and Bundesminister für Bildung und Wissenschaft, *Higher Education and the Community – Relations and Exchange between University and Industry*, proceedings of the Fourth Innovation Exchange Seminar on Higher Education, University of Karlsruhe, 1983. See also Wissenschaftsrat, *Stellungnahme zur Zusammenarbeit zwischen Hochschule und Wirtschaft*, Cologne, 1986; *The Federal Role in Fostering University-Industry Co-operation*, a report by the United States General Accounting Office, 25th May 1983; Kennedy, D., "Basic Research in the Universities: How Much Utility?" in Landau, R. and Rosenberg, N. (eds.), *The Positive Sum Strategy, Harnessing Technology for Economic Growth*, National Academy Press, Washington D.C., 1986.

A good example of growing interest in industry-university links is the emergence or rapid growth of science parks as illustrated by the table below for five European countries.

GROWTH OF SCIENCE PARKS IN EUROPE

	1980		1985	
	Parks	Establishments in parks[1]	Parks	Establishments in parks
United Kingdom	3	76	13	180
Germany	–	–	18	269
France	3	275	8	320
Belgium	4	38	5	76
Netherlands	–	–	3	42
Total	10	389	47	887

1. Establishments include companies and research institutes.
Source: Currie Sunman Partnership.

29. *INFOBRIEF Research and Technology*, 5th January 1987, No. 319, Luxembourg.

30. Martin, B. and Irvine, I., "Output Indicators for Science Policy: An Evaluation of CERN's Past Performance and Future Prospects", paper for OECD, Paris, May 1985. An excellent general discussion of prospects and problems of international collaboration in research can be found in Papon, P., *Pour une prospective de la science : recherche et technologie : les enjeux de l'avenir*, Seghers, Paris, 1985.

31. Thus, the percentage of internationally co-authored articles of all institutionally co-authored articles has risen from 12.7 per cent in 1973 to 17.2 per cent in 1982 for all fields of science for the United States. It is noteworthy that 43.9 per cent of articles in the field of mathematics were co-authored in 1982. Source: *Science Indicators, the 1985 Report*, National Science Board, Washington D.C., 1985.

32. Table 2.1 summarises the research inputs for twenty-one countries in terms of funding and researchers, standardised to population and labour force. Indicators on the international dissemination of technology are given in the last three columns. These dissemination indicators in the form of ratios visualise a country's position vis-à-vis other countries. They furthermore represent different stages in the process of international dissemination of technology and begin with the ratio of numbers of

patents applied abroad divided by the number of foreign patent applications for each country. The second indicator relates to the coverage of payments for technology transfer by corresponding receipts, indicating the dependence on foreign technology and know-how, e.g. a ratio of 0.2 means that this country imports five times more technology than it can sell abroad. The third ratio gives a very approximate idea of a country's export performance in highly R&D-intensive industries, standardized to the overall share of all OECD countries. Although partial in character and incomplete in their explanatory value due to non-technological parameters in play, they may be helpful in drawing a rough picture of the different degrees of national commitment to R&D and at the same time present a general picture of what is commonly called "technological performance".

Chapter 3

THE LABOUR MARKET AND INDUSTRIAL RELATIONS

"The pursuit of full employment is not like the directed flight of an aircraft on a beam; it is a difficult navigation, in which a course must be steered among shifting, unpredictable, and to a large extent, uncontrollable currents and forces."

Beveridge, W.H., *Full Employment in a Free Society*, London, 1944, p. 38.

INTRODUCTION

The rise in unemployment and the prospect that high unemployment may persist is the major economic challenge confronting policy makers in the OECD area. In much of Europe, in North America and in Australia and New Zealand, unemployment reached higher levels during the 1980s than at any time since the mid-1930s[1]. Only Japan and some of the smaller European countries have been able to keep unemployment rates below 5 per cent, and even in most of these countries there are more unemployed than formerly. In Europe, steadily rising joblessness has been paralleled by a stagnation or near-stagnation of total employment. In North America, Australia and New Zealand, the number out of work has increased in each business cycle, despite continued growth in employment overall (Graph S.1).

Unemployment at its present levels inevitably entails widespread individual hardship and economic waste. The OECD countries have, for much of the postwar period, provided generous unemployment insurance; these schemes, however, can hardly counter the human and social consequences of the lengthening of the average time spent unemployed and the erosion of the skills and resources of those out of work. The economic waste that has accompanied this hardship is enormous – in the order of several years of growth, at the growth rates that have characterised the last decade.

On top of the sheer waste of unemployed resources, the inefficient use of labour has held back the growth of real incomes. Thus a second challenge facing policy makers is to ensure that jobs adapt to changing markets and technology and that new jobs are created in areas that make the greatest contribution to the social product.

These concerns – minimising joblessness and improving the efficiency with which human resources are allocated – make labour markets a central focus of efforts to improve the overall functioning of economies. In assessing how labour markets might be made to function better, two perspectives are important. First, outcomes in labour markets must be seen against the background of the broad pressures operating on and within economies. To a considerable extent, these pressures have been similar across OECD economies over the last two decades, but responses have differed across countries. Second, labour markets have several unique features, having to do partly with their nature, which is inherently different from other markets, and partly with their pivotal social, political and economic roles. These perspectives provide a starting point for an examination of systems of industrial relations in Member countries and their effects.

A.   Pressures and responses in labour markets

Over the last two decades, the labour markets of Member countries have had to deal with an accumulation of pressures coming from a prolonged period of high growth and exceptionally low joblessness, followed by a sequence of external shocks and emerging internal constraints that created a growing gap between aspirations and outcomes with respect to real wage levels, with respect to the stability of the workplace in the face of changing market demands and areas of production, and with respect to the security of employment and the availability of jobs.

Differences in the ways in which the labour markets of Member countries could cope with pressures became apparent by the end of the 1950s. Levels of industrial conflict began to diverge significantly within the OECD area: in Japan and in northern European countries, high employment coincided with a stabilization of strike rates at extremely low levels; in the United States and Canada, indicators of the frequency, duration and size of strikes generally reverted to their relatively high prewar levels though important variations occurred over the decade; while in some other countries, strike rates rose rapidly as high employment was achieved[2]. In Italy and

119

France, the strike rate rose owing mainly (at least until 1968-69) to an increase in the frequency of political strikes. Though these involved large numbers of workers, they had extremely short durations, and it is questionable whether they severely disrupted production. But in the United Kingdom, the rise in the number of days lost reflected a steady growth in the incidence of "unofficial" strikes, highly localised to a particular line, plant or firm, and whose frequency and unpredictability seem to have weighed heavily both on the capacity of United Kingdom firms to exploit scale economies and on their reputation as reliable sources of supply[3] – a problem only significantly eased in the mid-1980s, when the number of industrial disputes dropped to its lowest level for almost fifty years.

Continued tight labour markets in the 1960s increased these divergences further. Except in North America, where unemployment did not reach such low levels, wage growth accelerated in the first half of the decade, partly as a result of negotiated settlements, but owing mainly to wage drift as employers bid up wages to retain or attract workers. Direct and indirect pressure from governments slowed this rate of growth in 1964-67 as labour markets eased slightly and a number of countries implemented nominal incomes policies[4]; however, moderation proved unsustainable in the face of continuing high levels of wage aspirations, worker perceptions in some countries of "speed-ups" in production, and the (albeit incomplete) recovery from the "growth recession"[5]. Beginning in 1968, a wave of industrial disputes spread through Europe, Australia and (to a much lesser extent) Japan, with drastic impacts in France and Italy, a somewhat later peak in the United Kingdom, and noticeable effects in Germany and Scandinavia[6].

Thus, labour market institutions in Europe – and notably in the United Kingdom, France and Italy – were already showing clear signs of disfunctioning during the tail years of the period of rapid growth; the major changes which were to come in the economic environment merely compounded the difficulties and generalised them to a broader grouping.

The macroeconomic changes involved are highlighted in Chapter 1: a substantial slowing in the rate of growth of total factor (labour and capital) productivity; sudden increases in prices of raw materials in 1973-74 and again in 1979-80, each of which reduced real income in the OECD area by somewhat over 1 per cent; accelerating inflation as the price and productivity shocks worked their way through the economy; and rising unemployment.

Each of these changes reduced economies' "capacity to pay" – measured in terms of rising living standards – below earlier trends. The costs of adjusting to these developments would have been minimised to the extent that nominal wage growth remained stable, so as to accommodate the reduced capacity to pay without an upward spiral of prices and wages. While the wage responses to these pressures differed greatly across countries and sometimes between episodes, nowhere did adjustment occur without some increase in wage and price inflation and the emergence of a gap between wages and the value of what labour produced. Both these results contributed to the rise in unemployment – the first as demand was constrained to counter inflation, and the second as incentives were inadequate to sustain the creation of new jobs and, in some cases, even to maintain old ones.

The wage responses to these developments in collective bargaining and other wage setting processes must at least partly have been due to the effects of the changes in economic circumstances themselves on the quality of the information flowing to the labour market. Throughout the OECD area, the rise of inflation in the 1970s made it increasingly difficult to define what a "reasonable" inflation outcome might be. Uncertainty as to the trend of real GNP and industrial production probably increased too, particularly in Europe, further complicating the wage bargainers' task. At least until 1979, the signals coming from government policy were also unclear as policy alternated between a primary concern with inflation and fears about unemployment. Finally, within the labour market itself, rising tax wedges between what firms paid for labour and what workers received tended to distort the perceptions of unions and employers alike[7].

Significant as these factors doubtless were, they merely aggravated the central problem wage bargainers had to face – how wage setting systems, accustomed to distributing the fruits of growth, could be brought to bear on the task of smoothly absorbing shortfalls in real income. The problems of union leaderships were made more acute in the early 1970s by the recent wave of worker militancy and industrial unrest at the shop-floor level[8]. But individual employers also faced costs if they appeared to disregard the "implicit contracts" linking them to employees, whether union members or not, because this could lead to a rise in the quit rate, reductions in work effort and increased conflict[9].

The general failure to achieve nominal wage moderation during this period involved both a "prisoner's dilemma" situation and a "public good" problem. A "prisoner's dilemma" arose because, though all wage setters might have been better off if wage moderation had prevailed, any individual group of employees could be significantly worse off if it were to accept wage moderation while other groups continued to demand and obtain large wage increases. Equally, the "public good" problem arose because the benefits of nominal wage moderation would flow not only to the wage setters who bore its proximate costs but also to others – notably in the form of a general reduction in inflation and a general rise in output and employment levels. The public good aspect of wage setting became especially marked as macroeconomic policy was increasingly focused on reducing inflation, since wage claims by powerful unions affected both the credibility of the inflation target and the room for real output growth within any tolerated expansion of nominal demand. As wage behaviour was a significant determinant of the effectiveness with which they could achieve their policy goals, the governments of the day became prime beneficiaries of wage restraint. Depending on relationships between governments and labour movements and the degree of co-ordination within the labour movement, these political stakes on occasion complicated or eased the problem of achieving nominal wage restraint.

B. The labour market as a system of industrial relations

In short, workers and employers had to respond to rapidly changing circumstances, but the functioning of labour markets cannot be assessed as a simple matter of price adjustment to balance supply and demand. In order to understand the difficulties which arose in adapting to external and internal constraints, three distinguishing features of labour markets must be kept at the centre of the analysis.

The first is the inherent imperfection of the labour market as compared with theoretically ideal markets for commodities, given the extreme heterogeneity of jobs and the uniqueness of the individuals who seek and fill them. This feature greatly compounds the information requirements for good labour market functioning; it makes for high transaction costs in matching workers to jobs; and it renders meaningless the concept of a "market wage". The outcome of the labour market is not, then, the outcome of a "market" in the conventional sense but rather the result of agreements between workers, individually or collectively, and their employers, individually or collectively. These agreements are complex and often implicit, given the difficulties of defining the rights and responsibilities of both sides.

The second feature is the direct effect labour markets have on living standards and social relationships. The vast majority of people in advanced industrial societies derive most of their income from dependent employment, and labour is the primary resource they command. Moreover, the institutions and procedures involved in setting labour incomes have a bearing on the social and political environment that goes well beyond the labour market itself. The functioning of labour markets is therefore inevitably embedded in the social and political context – especially in prevailing views about the fairness of access to jobs, about the allocation of risks and rewards arising from economic activity, and about the prerogatives of management and the rights of workers in the workplace.

The third is their macroeconomic impact: labour is an input into production of virtually all goods and services, and its price tends to be roughly co-ordinated across uses. As a result, money wages set a short-term peg for determination of the general price level and, indirectly, for the level of activity. At the same time, the efficiency with which human resources are allocated and utilised over the longer term, and the incentives labour markets provide to acquire and effectively deploy skills, shape the growth of productivity and the scope for rising living standards.

The special features of labour markets are reflected in the development of complex social arrangements – a "web of rules"[10] – relating partners who, in the nature of things, have to continue co-operating yet whose interests generally remain distinct. These arrangements define more or less formal procedures by which participants can resolve disputes of interest – i.e. disputes as to what understandings or contractual commitments should govern employment – and disputes of right, i.e. disputes about how existing understandings and contracts should be interpreted and their provisions applied.

These procedures can be regarded as a type of investment by society. When operating efficiently they yield four major benefits[11]: by standardizing employment relations, they reduce the costs of search and negotiations; by periodically formalizing agreements over the conditions of work, they limit the range of items subject to ongoing disputes; by precluding employees and employers from opportunistically exploiting positions of temporary power, they favour investment in types of skills and capital assets which would otherwise be too risky; and they provide alternatives to conflict and division as a way of resolving differences. In short, these procedures make the large-scale organisation of work more or less manageable and congruent with social values in the areas of fairness, equity and social relationships.

Social arrangements in labour markets, though their operations are in some areas primarily determined by government regulation and in others by the direct action of market forces, hinge on organised negotiation between employers and employees or their representatives. The capacity of employers and employees together to define a framework that allows for the smooth handling of conflict and change at the workplace, and that encourages adaptation rather than resistance to evolving economic realities, has an obvious bearing on the capacity of economies to minimise joblessness and to allocate human resources efficiently.

These outcomes in labour markets – and their relation to institutional structures – are the principal concerns of this chapter. But in examining how well or badly they have been achieved and in exploring the scope for adapting systems to improve performance in these respects, it is necessary to keep in mind the social considerations that are also of concern – concerns, such as equal access to employment, which have not always been well served by existing systems.

C. The approach of the chapter

Given these perspectives, this chapter is focused on the differences across Member countries in systems of industrial relations, their influence on the response of labour markets to the pressures of the last two decades, and the scope for improvement.

Arrangements under which collective bargaining takes place between labour unions and employers are a key feature of industrial relations systems in all Member countries. A framework of custom and law supports and complements these arrangements. This framework defines the rights of employees to associate in trade unions, and of employers to associate for the purpose of negotiating over the conditions of employment, as well as the rights of each to seek the most advantageous outcome through industrial action. In doing so, it not only determines the context in which collective bargaining takes place, but also influences the extent of collective bargaining and employment arrangements where collective bargaining does not take place. In addition, in virtually all countries there are some legislative constraints on the freedom of contract: for example, restrictions on the employment of minors; standards for safety in the workplace; prohibitions on discrimination on the basis of race, religion or sex; and regulation of working hours and minimum wages. The terms on which governments provide unemployment compensation also condition the environment in which collective bargaining agreements and individual employment contracts are concluded.

In Part I the focus is on how these strands are put together and have functioned in different national systems of industrial relations. The focus is on their interaction rather than on the effects of the presence or absence of specific institutional features. There are several reasons for having adopted this approach. First, what bearing a particular legal provision or customary practice has on outcomes is crucially dependent on the context in which it operates. Second, as is made clear in the discussion, whether or not countries have adopted particular practices has been influenced to a considerable extent by the broader institutional context and the way that various pressures have manifested themselves within it. Hence, there are causal relationships running in both directions between outcomes and institutional arrangements. For both of these reasons, it is difficult to clearly isolate, in the data on labour market outcomes in different countries, the effects on economic performance of particular features of systems of industrial relations, such as policies with respect to minimum wages, the extent of unionisation, or the extent of indexation of wages to inflation. And comparing performance across countries on the basis of isolated institutional features is further complicated both by their sheer variety and by the fact that insufficient time has passed for the effects of many recent policy actions directed at freeing labour markets to be identified. Thus, such comparisons are likely to be inconclusive. Indeed, this is the general finding of recent Secretariat work and other work along these lines[12].

The examination of the functioning of systems of industrial relations in Part I is complemented in Part II by a closer examination of labour market performance – in terms of both macroeconomic responsiveness and microeconomic efficiency – and of the constraints that the functioning of labour markets has imposed on overall economic performance. A discussion of ways in which the functioning of labour markets might be improved and adapted to new pressures appears in Part III.

I. INDUSTRIAL RELATIONS IN OECD COUNTRIES

National systems of industrial relations reflect not only a wide range of factors internal to labour markets but also the broader features of each country's social and political institutions, including the prevailing attitudes towards work, conflict and co-operation that have shaped them and are shaped by them. These systems are therefore inevitably a collection of special cases whose functioning can only be characterised in terms of complex variables. Four such variables appear to be of special importance; they are[13]:

- The *breadth* of collective bargaining, in terms of the coverage of major agreements and the level at which they are negotiated;
- The *depth* of these agreements, in terms of the range of detail they specify about the management of the work relation;
- The nature of the *constraints* bearing on collective bargainers, in particular the degree of monopoly representation enjoyed by unions and employers' associations, the legal status of collective agreements, and the procedures used to resolve disputes of interest and of right; and
- The broader *societal role* of the organisations involved in collective bargaining, including their role in shaping government policies with respect to minimum wages, unemployment compensation, working conditions and job security.

Seen in terms of these variables, postwar systems of industrial relations in the OECD area can be classed into five groups; the specific features of each group have had an important effect on the performance of labour markets in recent years. It must, however, be noted at the outset that any typology can only imperfectly capture the variety which characterises groups of countries. Thus, there are numerous borderline cases and some countries' positions in the typology have shifted even over as short a period as two decades. Those considerations have not been fully reflected in the congress as set out; but this does not undermine the usefulness of seeking a broad pattern.

A. Encompassing bargaining

A first group includes Austria, Sweden, Norway, Germany and, more arguably, Switzerland (which shares many features of the "enterprise bargaining" model discussed below)[14] and the Netherlands (where, however, there are multiple union confederations). It comprises countries where, since the early 1950s, industrial relations have been based on bargaining structures with great breadth but little depth. Four features characterise this grouping.

First, bargaining has been encompassing as well as highly centralised, with most employment contracts being determined through collective negotiations, which in turn have hinged on a relatively small number of agreements between national unions and employers' associations. Though certain aspects of employment relations have typically been set locally – through firm or plant level wage drift, enterprise bargaining and contract implementation – there has been a fairly high degree of vertical control in the formal system, thereby circumscribing the extent of local initiative[15].

Second, the lack of depth of collective bargaining in these countries has been in marked contrast to its breadth: negotiated agreements have rarely reduced management prerogatives, which have been protected by tradition (as with the "Article 32" clauses in Swedish collective contracts, which for many years safeguarded the role of management in operational decisions) and by law (as in Germany). The day-to-day running of work relations has been constrained mainly by national legislation and by employers' obligations to consult employees through mechanisms organisationally distinct from collective bargaining. As a result, the restrictive work practices frequently associated with trade unionism in other countries have been rare.

Third, the unions themselves have enjoyed a significant degree of monopoly representation. Levels of unionisation have been high, though Germany is an exception in this respect (see Table 3.1). Most major work sites have been covered by collective agreements, and until recently there has been little or no competition between unions, whether nationally or locally. At the same time, employers' associations have been centralised and well organised; and the common (though not universal) practice of extending collectively bargained contracts to all the firms and workers in an industry has tended to strengthen employer solidarity and employers' organisations more generally, providing an effective check on bargaining outcomes. Monopoly representation has both reflected and permitted a broader governance role for trade unions and employers' organisations: governments, at least until recent years, have not intervened in collective bargaining nor have they set minimum wages; in exchange, unions and employers have been expected to contribute to creating and implementing a consensus on economic and social policies – and most notably to the maintenance of full employment (which has been a far more significant goal for the union movement in these countries than elsewhere)[16].

Table 3.1. **Trade union membership as a percentage of total labour force**

Country	1970	1971	1972	1973	1974	1975	1976	1977	1978	1979	1980	1981	1982	1983	1984
Sweden	—	—	—	—	—	—	—	—	—	75	76	77	77	78	79
Denmark	—	—	51	51	51	55	58	61	63	66	68	69	—	72	73
Finland	—	—	—	—	—	—	—	—	—	—	—	—	—	—	68
Belgium	—	—	—	—	—	—	—	—	—	—	—	63	—	—	—
Luxembourg	—	—	—	—	—	—	—	—	—	—	—	62	—	—	—
Norway	—	—	—	—	—	—	—	—	—	—	—	—	—	56	—
Australia	—	—	43	45	46	46	45	43	43	—	—	—	—	—	43
United Kingdom	—	44	45	45	46	47	47	49	50	50	48	45	43	42	—
Italy	—	—	—	—	—	—	—	39	39	40	39	—	—	—	—
New Zealand	35	—	—	—	36	37	37	37	38	39	40	39	40	39	—
Ireland	—	—	—	—	—	—	40	—	—	40	—	37	—	—	—
Germany	31	—	—	—	—	33	33	34	35	35	35	35	—	—	—
Netherlands	—	—	34	34	35	35	35	35	35	35	34	32	—	—	—
Japan	23	—	—	—	—	24	—	—	22	22	22	22	22	—	—
France	—	—	—	—	—	—	—	—	—	—	—	—	19	—	—
United States	23	22	22	22	22	21	20	20	20	—	—	—	—	16	15

Source: EEC, National Statistical Yearbooks.

Finally, it is this consensus-building role, and the nation-wide structure of bargaining which accompanies it, which has created the major constraints on the behaviour of unions and employers: the systemic consequences of breakdowns of co-operation in highly export-dependent economies where powerful, highly centralised unions face equally powerful and unified employers have engendered strong pressure for agreement to be found, with the result that both sides have usually refrained from testing the limits of their power.

Formal, legal controls bearing on collective bargaining have been significant in some countries (notably Germany), and all the countries in this group have a well developed body of labour law. Nonetheless, legal constraints have had far less impact on collective bargaining than those arising from economic openness and from the broader societal responsibilities of management and labour leaders.

Taken as a group, the countries with encompassing bargaining structures have enjoyed better-than-average records of unemployment over the 1970s and first half of the 1980s, although unemployment in Germany has compared less favourably in the past half-decade. There can be no doubt that external competitive factors – notably the high dependence of these economies on foreign trade – have provided an important source of pressure for internal adjustment in these countries. Particularly in Austria and Norway, these pressures were at times accentuated by the setting of an exchange rate target at a level inconsistent with rapid domestic inflation. Nonetheless, as is clear from the relatively poor performance of Belgium and the Netherlands, the relation between openness *per se* and performance has been a weak one; and the distinguishing feature of the countries in their group lies less in the constraints of openness than in the degree to which they were accommodated by their bargaining institutions.

This is largely because encompassing bargaining structures provided a framework in which the public good and "prisoner's dilemma" problems arising in the negotiated adjustment to real income shortfalls could be resolved. Given the relatively small number of actors and the breadth of the contracts they negotiate, most of the direct benefits arising from nominal wage moderation could be "internalised" in the bargaining unit. At the same time, the risks to each actor that others would obtain higher settlements could be minimised through vertical and horizontal controls on the bargaining process. These factors made it easier for wage moderation to be achieved in the face of reduced capacity to pay.

However, the adjustment process was not entirely smooth or costless. Difficulties arose, in part from prior changes in the structure of industrial relations, which tended to reduce the "governability" of encompassing bargaining systems. The steady growth of white-collar employment and trade unionism, in both the private and public sectors, fragmented the unions' bargaining front[17]. At the same time, the lesser exposure to international competition of the growing share of the labour force in the public and non-traded services sector weakened the external constraints on the bargaining process. But even within the industrial unions, the degree of control had tended to diminish in the years prior to the external shocks of the early 1970s: wage drift in the late 1960s left a legacy of decentralised wage bargaining in systems accustomed to operating with a sole bargaining level (Austria being somewhat of an exception in this respect); and recent memories of "unofficial" industrial action – notably the 1969-70 wave of grass-roots strikes in Germany and Sweden – almost certainly increased union officials' concerns about the practicability of wage moderation[18].

Against this background, the union response, particularly in Scandinavia[19], appears to have been twofold. To begin with, the central union organisations seem to have sought to reinforce the "collective ethos" underpinning centralised bargaining structures. In particular, renewed emphasis was placed on "solidaristic" (i.e. internally redistributive) goals, notably that of reducing disparities in the wage structure; and most obviously in Sweden, successive rounds of wage negotiations were associated with a significant compression of the structure of earnings, both between occupations and industries. This compression has been only partially reversed in the 1980s.

At the same time, unions sought compensation from governments for nominal wage moderation, thereby exploiting the interest of governments in wage moderation that would reinforce their anti-inflationary macroeconomic strategies. And, as noted, the carrots which governments provided through compensatory agreements were sometimes accompanied by the stick of a strong-currency monetary policy. The precise form and content of these agreements differed greatly from country to country; moreover, they were rarely set down in the form of explicit bilateral agreements, so that an overview is difficult to compile. Nonetheless, four instruments appear to have been involved[20]: a general government commitment to maintain a high level of domestic demand; tax cuts or expanded social spending or both; subsidies to firms, regions or industries in difficulty; and direct job creation through government programmes.

Norway provides a particularly striking illustration of this process – and of its limits: from the early 1970s, the government found itself increasingly drawn into the bargaining process, offering a broad range of spending and tax benefits in exchange for moderation in the successive contract rounds of 1975, 1976 and 1977. The capacity of the Norwegian Government to pursue this course was enlarged by government revenues from North Sea oilfields. But despite these benefits, agreement proved impossible to obtain in 1978, forcing the government to change its approach to incomes policy radically and to institute a general wage freeze in September of that year. The wage freeze ended in late 1979, but the following years saw repeated government intervention in the wage setting process[21]. By and large, these interventions proved reasonably successful in countering nominal wage pressures; but they could not be repeated indefinitely, notably as budgetary constraints ultimately came into play and diminished the scope for further tax/wage trade-offs.

Both solidaristic wage setting and union-government bargaining had significant longer-term consequences for the efficiency of industrial relations, notably in the Scandinavian countries. To begin with, the narrowing of wage differentials undermined relations between white-collar and blue-collar unions and encountered growing resistance from the better paid occupations and industries, even within the manual labour force. Already by the early 1970s, collectively bargained reductions in differentials were being at least partly offset by intensified informal negotiations at plant level, which contributed to wage drift[22]. Particularly during cyclical recoveries, "solidaristic" national contracts tended to be followed by wildcat strikes aimed at restoring relativities[23]. Employers too – and notably those in the export industries – were concerned that wage compression would undermine work effort and slow the development of skills; hence they sought greater autonomy from national bargaining structures[24]. The growing diversity of situations among firms as a result of structural change accelerated the tendency.

Overall, the highly centralised structure of negotiations in countries with encompassing industrial relations systems almost certainly facilitated collective bargaining's initial adjustment to slower growth; and it is equally clear that this contributed to considerable nominal wage moderation. However, in Scandinavia particularly, where the levels of centralisation were highest, the internal dynamics of these structures pushed them in two directions which were ultimately destabilizing: that of seeking to strengthen the legitimacy of central bargaining through the pursuit of solidaristic goals; and that of demanding government compensation for wage moderation, thereby steadily expanding the role of government in the bargaining process. In Germany too, the capacity to achieve wage settlements consistent with maintenance of low unemployment seems to have eroded over time – though the system of collective bargaining has proved more stable and resilient than elsewhere.

B. "Job control" bargaining

This picture of "encompassing" interest organisations involved in bargaining that is broad but not deep provides a sharp contrast with a second group consisting of the United States and Canada. Postwar industrial relations in these two countries have been marked by "job control unionism" within a labour market with relatively low rates of unionisation. Four features distinguish these systems.

First, most collective agreements have been negotiated and established at the level of the plant or firm, with intra- and inter-industry co-ordination occurring through informal and somewhat stable "pattern bargaining". This has been reflected in organisational structures; unions have had a national structure, but with a high level of internal decentralisation; employers (with the exception of a few industries) have not sought to co-ordinate their bargaining positions.

Second, collective agreements, in addition to stipulating wage levels and structures, have usually covered a wide range of personnel practices setting "the rules of occupancy and tenure of the employment opportunities"[25]. Conditions laid down in collective agreements have generally ensured both greater opportunities and greater protection for workers with higher seniority; and they have at least partly compensated for lower levels of social insurance by mandating company schemes for medical care, compensation in case of lay-offs, and old-age pensions[26]. But collective bargaining has not generally constrained the right of management to reduce its labour force in the face of weak demand for output.

Third, these countries' industrial relations systems have been characterised by a high degree of legalism. Federal and State (in Canada, Provincial) laws establish procedures by which unions can obtain rights of representation, set down the enforceability of collective agreements as legally binding contracts, and hence limit recourse to industrial action during the term of an agreement. The relatively long and rising duration of contracts, which currently are most often for three years[27], and their binding status have led negotiators to seek provision against unforeseen internal and external contingencies: within the firm, the agreements have typically mandated elaborate procedures for the settlement of grievances and disputes; similarly, the risks arising from external shocks have been met by seniority-based lay-off rules and widespread reliance on automatic cost-of-living adjustments to wage rates during periods of inflation.

Finally, though job control has been far-reaching in unionised plants and enterprises, trade unions themselves and indeed the broader system of collective bargaining have had a low level of institutional protection. While the legal framework has been permissive, it has not uniformly encouraged or facilitated unionism. Indeed, union behaviour is constrained in a number of important respects, notably as regards disputes[28]. Collective bargaining in the United States has never had the ideological legitimacy which it has enjoyed elsewhere[29], and the unionised parts of the economy, where the collective bargaining model prevails, have faced constant competition. As a result of a host of economic, regulatory and social developments, there has been a substantial erosion of unionisation in the United States (but not in Canada) in recent years. This has led central labour movement organisations to seek broader coverage and higher levels of minimum wages through the political process, at least partly so as to contain this competition. As in the unionised sector, non-union firms typically manage employee relations through highly standardized and generally quite rigid procedures, but these are unilaterally set by the employer and implemented through the internal hierarchical structure of the firm[30].

In many respects, the adjustment problem was less severe in the United States and Canada than elsewhere because the post-1968 fall in factor productivity growth rates – though starting from a lower trend – was smaller, the increases in energy prices had a less marked effect on the terms of trade, and wage pressure had not built up to the same extent as in Europe – partly because unemployment had been relatively high earlier. Nonetheless, these countries experienced periods of wage pressure and high unemployment following the shocks of the 1970s. But real wage trends moderated significantly (and fairly rapidly) as unemployment rose and the subsequent declines in unemployment were substantial.

At least until recently, wage flexibility was considerably greater in the non-union sector than in the collectively bargained parts of the economy[31]. This was partly because wages in unionised firms often involved automatic cost-of-living adjustments to inflation[32] as well as considerable inertia in responding to labour market circumstances. More generally, however, the extensive decentralisation of bargaining, the low degree of horizontal and vertical co-ordination in the bargaining structure, and union officials' concern about contract rejections (situations in which members vote against proposed agreements)[33] presumably made a union-led strategy of concerted wage moderation virtually unfeasible, whatever the views of national union leaderships. At the same time, the costs to employers of seeking a reassessment of wage levels – in terms of apparent violations of "implicit contracts" with employees leading to declines in work effort and increases in industrial conflict – were probably greater in unionised than in non-unionised firms[34]. However, the pattern of three-year contracts in North America helped to stabilize wages in the face of rising prices as indexation generally provided for less than full adjustment of wages to price changes and was not universally included in collective bargaining arrangements.

One outcome of the decentralised and heterogeneous wage setting pressures in North America was a rising spread in wage rates within the labour market. Thus, the union/non-union wage differential for manufacturing production workers, adjusted for differences in employee characteristics, increased in the United States from around 13 per cent in 1973 to 20 per cent in 1978[35]. The inter-industry spread in wages also tended to rise slightly, partly reflecting differences between industries in the degree of unionisation[36]. And there was a significant decline in the relative earnings position of younger male workers[37] as demographic trends interacted with differences in degree of protection under collective bargaining.

These tendencies were partially reversed in the early 1980s as "concession bargaining" spread subsequent to the Chrysler contract. The extent of the change in wage behaviour should not be exaggerated, however; for though the union/non-union wage differential did decline in 1979 and 1980, it rose from 1981 to 1983, only to decline again subsequently. In parallel to these changing and rather unstable patterns of wage setting, there was some movement away from the traditional rigid emphasis on highly formalized job control at plant

level, typical of American unionism; and though it would be premature to assess the changes as long-lasting, they do appear to have persisted longer than similar cyclical swings in bargaining patterns in the past[38]. Overall, the evidence suggests that adjustment in the United States occurred largely through the direct and indirect effects of competition between a unionised and non-unionised sector, the unionised sector adjusting to changed circumstances with a considerable lag.

C. "Enterprise" bargaining

The system of collective negotiations in Japan, as in the United States and Canada, has been highly decentralised; however, it has not had the depth of bargaining typical of the North American model and has been subject to even tighter internal and external controls. Four features stand out[39].

First, as in North America, collective agreements in Japan have been negotiated at the enterprise level, though the guidelines set and arrangements made by industrial federations and national centres affect enterprise level outcomes. Indeed, enterprise unions have accounted, on average, for 80 per cent of collective agreements and 90 per cent of union members. In the 1950s, there was relatively little co-ordination between enterprise level negotiations on the union side. (Employers, on the other hand, have tended to co-ordinate their position fairly effectively and have generally displayed a high level of employer solidarity.) The absence of co-ordination between union negotiations was altered somewhat by the development of the *Shunto* or "Spring Offensive" (which involves concerted targets for wage increases in annual renewals of over two-thirds of collective agreements) and of *de facto* industry-wide bargaining in some key export-oriented industries; but the pattern of settlements has not proved stable.

Second, in contrast with the North American practice, the range of items subject to collective bargaining has been limited: wage structures within unionised firms have broadly reflected supply and demand trends rather than "solidaristic" goals of unions; and issues relating to work practices and to personnel policies have generally been dealt with by consultation rather than through formalized bargaining or adjudication[40].

Third, union bargaining power has frequently been constrained by competitive pressures and management initiative. The capacity to pay of the enterprise seems to have served as a check on wage demands, especially in small and medium-size firms employing four-fifths of the labour force or more. Even in large firms there have been competitive restraints on wage demands – in particular, their extensive networks of smaller subcontractors and their use of "casual" and "temporary regular" workers may have provided ways to reduce dependence on "regular" employees covered by collective bargaining agreements[41], though these have at times of strong labour demand been partly offset by a tendency for other wages to increase in line with those paid to "regular" employees. In addition, management has intervened in union affairs by sometimes, but less often in recent years, encouraging changes in representation[42] and through the not uncommon practice of providing retired union leaders with senior management positions[43], though the latter practices may be viewed as simply meaning that union leaders are not excluded from enterprises' promotion systems.

Finally, the social context of employment relations in Japan has moderated the incentives for employees in larger enterprises to exploit whatever market power they may have: despite its limited coverage[44], the "life-time" employment system has fostered an association between the interests of individual workers and those of their firm – an effect accentuated by the role of bonus payments, seniority increments in the wage structure, and company pensions. Company bankruptcy would have severe consequences for lifetime employees, and these must have made union members wary of pursuing unreasonable strategies. In addition, the low degree of occupational differentiation in job definitions and pay structures (and especially the lack of a clear split between white- and blue-collar workers) seems to have engendered a greater sense of community within the company[45].

Overall, the Japanese model has displayed a finer balance between the carrot and the stick than either its advocates or its critics would contend; but in general, Japanese collective bargaining (at least in its traditional quasi-adverserial sense) has been both relatively limited in scope and restrained in intensity.

After the 1974 *Shunto* (which, in the midst of the first oil shock, increased nominal wages by 33 per cent), the collective bargaining system of Japan adjusted fairly quickly to a path of persistent nominal wage moderation. In part, this moderation presumably reflected the close identification between employees and their firms, which made wage moderation more of a "local public good" than it would otherwise have been, and the significance of bonus payments dependent on each company's profitability and economic circumstances[46], which ensured that employees would be compensated if their moderation led to significant increases in profit levels – thereby easing the "prisoner's dilemma". At the same time, union negotiating strategies took account of the dangers which accelerating inflation could create for overall employment and income levels, as well as for the lifetime employment system – a perception highlighted in tripartite consultative procedures at industry and national level. These procedures were strengthened in the early 1970s and provided a forum in which unions could be brought to see the advantage of moderation as a bargaining strategy[47].

Nonetheless, despite these factors which promoted moderation in collective bargaining, the greatest adjustments occurred outside the unionised sector[48]. Thus, over the period 1980-85, the average annual rate of increase in wages was around 5 per cent in establish-ments with more than 100 employees, 4.5 per cent in establishments with 30 to 99 employees and 4 per cent in those with less than 30; it is questionable whether the different trends in skill levels and productivity were sufficient to account for these disparities. Moreover, within the labour force the relative wage position of the workers least represented in collective bargaining tended to deteriorate: the earnings gap between men and women (many of whom work part-time) widened; the structure of male earnings became more unfavourable to younger recruits and to older workers; and the inter-industry wage spread increased.

In short, collective bargaining responded to changed circumstances more readily in Japan than in the United States – but in both countries the broadly decentralised nature of the wage adjustment process played an important part, though acting in rather different ways.

D. "Fragmented" bargaining

In the systems discussed above – be they of encompassing, job control or enterprise unionism – a single level of bargaining dominates; but industrial relations in a fourth group of countries has been distinguished by widespread competition between unions, the existence of multiple and largely unco-ordinated levels of bargaining, and a lack of strong formal or informal controls on the collective bargaining process. Most markedly, but in quite different ways in the United Kingdom, Italy and France, these features have tended to interact, generating unstable and (at least in the past) highly conflicting systems.

For different reasons, the union structures of these countries did not undergo the rationalisation in the immediate postwar period that occurred elsewhere in Europe. In the United Kingdom, the continuity of union organisation over an extended period of time has left craft, industrial, and general (or "open") unions surviving side by side[49], although the number of unions has declined considerably over the longer term. In France and Italy, the primary factor has been political, as competing union confederations have distinguished themselves largely by ideological affiliation; religion has been an additional distinguishing element in Belgium and the Netherlands.

The most obvious result of fragmentation is that employers have had to deal with several unions. Although there are now growing numbers of single union deals, the United Kingdom case has historically been extreme: in the early 1970s, labour-management negotiations in nearly 60 per cent of large establishments involved at least three unions, and 20 per cent involved five unions or more[50]. Placed in this situation, unions have tended to compete with one another and press narrow sectional interests within the labour force, making labour contracts difficult to reach and enforce.

The consequences of fragmentation in union organisation have been exacerbated by a proliferation of bargaining levels. A trend in this direction occurred during the 1960s, when centralised bargaining was eroded by wage drift not only in those countries but virtually everywhere in the OECD area. The distinguishing feature of the United Kingdom, Italy and France was that the upper levels of the bargaining structure proved unwilling or incapable of defining a stable division of responsibility as between plant, enterprise and industry negotiations. The lack of vertical control tended to reflect the weakness rather than the strength of union organisation: the small size and limited means of union staff relative to the number of shop stewards and unpaid officials[51], and the lack of either rewards or sanctions available to central organisations with which to command their member unions or branches.

The absence of a common front has also been evident in employers' organisations, which have rarely been capable of implementing common negotiating positions across the full range of their members. Employer solidarity has been weak or even poorly defined – in Italy, for example, as between public and private firms. This has itself accentuated the trend to multi-level bargaining, as unions seek to "generalise" the results of the best settlements obtained at one level of bargaining through negotiation at others.

The centrifugal tendencies inherent in vertical and horizontal fragmentation have been strengthened by a lack of internal and external constraints on unions and collective bargaining. In this respect, the absence of an adequate legal framework for regulating collective bargaining has been a striking feature of industrial relations in the United Kingdom, Italy and France. In the United Kingdom, collective agreements have not normally had the status of legally binding contracts since the Trade Disputes Act of 1906. In practice, the negotiation of agreements has never been more than a phase in a continual conflict over wages and conditions and procedures for settlement of disputes of right, i.e. differences over the interpretation of contract terms, without ensuing industrial action[52]. In Italy, it has not proved possible to define and give effect to coherent legislation regulating industrial disputes, despite constitutional provisions to this effect. As a result, the system has relied on interpretation by the courts of a highly uneven and significantly incomplete complex of labour laws which have largely served to strengthen the power of the stronger side in each episode[53]. In France, the relative weakness of union organisation and the lack of stable differentiation between the industrial relations system on the one hand, and political decision-making on the other, has been reflected in a legal framework that until recently relied primarily on nation-wide regulatory instruments (covering issues as diverse as occupational gradings and minimum wages): at least until the early 1980s, the legal status of collective bargaining itself was poorly defined, with the obligation to reach and abide by collective agreements being recognised neither by employers nor by unions[54].

Finally, the social and economic constraints bearing on collective bargaining have been exceptionally weak. By and large, employers and especially unions have not perceived their role as being one of contributing to overall economic performance; this has most obviously been the case not only in France and Italy where major sections of the union movement have been ideologically hostile to the market economy, but even in the United Kingdom where distinctions of status between union members and managers have clouded perceptions of common interest. At the same time, the market environment has not been such as to impose effective restraint: in the United Kingdom, an early industrial lead, the persistence for many years of colonial outlets, and pervasive price-fixing and collusion has had the effect of blunting employers' incentives to resist union pressure[55]; in France and Italy, far-reaching government regulation of competition in the domestic market has had similar repercussions; and in all three countries, union bargaining with state enterprises has been relatively uninhibited by concerns about corporate profitability or indeed viability. In short, the fragmented nature of bargaining has provided few means to resolve ongoing tensions; and the external and internal constraints which might have steered the process towards better outcomes have been largely lacking.

The vulnerability of fragmented systems of industrial relations was evident in the responses to slowing growth and rapidly rising prices of oil and other commodities in the 1970s. The response, as it occurred, was partly conditioned by the legacy of 1968-1971. By and large, labour had emerged strengthened from the worker unrest of that period, but – especially in Italy and the United Kingdom – the increased strength largely escaped the control of central trade union structures. At the same time, the widespread perception of the events of that period as a grass-roots rebuff to the central structures made union officials wary of exposing themselves to further incidents by adopting policies of wage moderation – whatever they thought of such a course otherwise. Governments too were sensitive to the risk of triggering a repetition of the 1968-1971 wave of strikes, and adopted macroeconomic policies that were basically accommodating, thereby creating room for an acceleration of cost-push inflation in the wake of the first oil shock[56].

But by the time of the first oil shock, the cost-push process was already well under way. In Italy, the 1969 contracts – which came into effect in early 1970 – stipulated a 19 per cent average increase in manufacturing earnings; this was some five percentage points more than could have been expected on the basis of historical relations between wage increases, inflation and unemployment[57]. Wage increases in the 1973 collective agreement raised the trend rate of inflation by even more, exceeding their anticipated level by six to seven percentage points[58]. In the United Kingdom, the rapid growth of nominal and real wages in the period 1970-1972 was followed by a two-year period of mandatory wage restraint; though initially successful, restraint gave way to a wage explosion in early 1974, when the newly elected Labour government granted the mineworkers a 29 per cent wage increase, more than three times the previous year's inflation rate. In France, though wage growth slowed after the 1968 Grenelle agreements, wages rose more rapidly than nominal GDP in every year from 1968 to 1973[59].

The inflationary consequences of the first oil shock obviously accelerated this process; but perhaps more significantly, they made it more difficult to reverse. Thus, in 1974-1975, nominal wages increased more than econometric wage determination models would have led one to expect in the United Kingdom and France[60]; but by then, real wages were in any case well out of line with productivity adjusted for the terms of trade, thereby creating the so-called "real wage gaps". These gaps, measured relative to 1973, were to persist to the early 1980s; and, taking account of large wage increases in the late 1960s and early 1970s, the relationship between wages and productivity has still not returned to where it was in the mid-1960s.

The widespread recourse to wage indexation was a significant factor in this respect. Of the countries in this group, only the United Kingdom did not have comprehensive wage indexing in place during the second half of the 1970s[61]; and of the countries outside this group, only Australia and Denmark, and to a very much lesser extent Norway and Finland, had wage indexation provisions covering most of the labour force. Moreover, even among that part of the labour force covered by wage indexation, the degree of indexing (the proportion of registered price increases transmitted into wages) was very much higher in the countries in this group than elsewhere[62]. In this sense, comprehensive wage indexation was a distinctive feature of countries with fragmented bargaining structures.

Indexation might have facilitated wage moderation in fragmented systems of industrial relations if dealing with the inflation of the 1970s had been a simple matter of reversing excessively expansionary macroeconomic policies. The "prisoner's dilemma" obstacle to wage moderation – and hence to the then gradual abatement of inflation – would have been solved. But reducing inflation was also a matter of bringing wage settlements into line with the reduced capacity to pay. The indexation mechanisms that were put in place made this more difficult to accomplish because they made inflation largely ineffectual as a mechanism for correcting initial disequilibria between wage and productivity levels. At the same time, they reduced the incentives which powerful groups in the labour force had for pursuing wage moderation, since full indexation guaranteed that real gains would not be eroded by subsequent inflation. The evolution of the Italian economy in the period between the oil shocks clearly illustrates the problem: a national policy of nominal wage moderation was at least

implicitly in effect from 1976 to 1978, but the wage indexation system which was set up in 1975 maintained the wage/price spiral. And the decline in the trend of real labour costs was consequently minimal – certainly insufficient to correct the discrepancy between wages and productivity which had opened up in the previous period[63].

Even aside from indexation, wage setting institutions in these countries demonstrated an inherent tendency to push the growth of nominal earnings beyond the levels supportable by prevailing macroeconomic conditions. This was clearest in the United Kingdom, where periods of "free" collective bargaining (in the sense of collective bargaining unconstrained by incomes policies) in 1974-1975 and from 1978 onward were associated with increases in nominal wages, notably in highly unionised activities[64], far above those which could be absorbed at current inflation and rates of increase in overall productivity. In France, where government setting of the minimum wage (the SMIC) had a significant flow-through into the overall level of nominal earnings, the desire to avoid industrial conflict led to inordinately large wage increases in 1974-1975 and again in 1981 and 1982.

Characteristically, the inflationary pressures coming from excessive rates of growth of nominal wages led governments to "freeze" prices and wages in attempts to break inflationary wage/price spirals. Thus, in the United Kingdom, incomes policies were implemented in 1972-1974 and – as a result of government negotiation of a "Social Contract" with the Trades Union Congress (TUC) – from 1976 to 1978. In France, the Barre government sought to influence wages indirectly from September 1976 until the election of a Socialist government in 1981[65]; this government, having substantially raised minimum wages in its first two years, announced a wage-price freeze in June 1982 and, as from 1983, enforced *ex ante* limits on inflation adjustments of wages. In the Netherlands, wages were controlled in 1976 and then from 1980 to 1982. In Belgium, government wage guidance in national collective bargaining has been strong since 1980, extending to direct control of wages and the suppression of indexation of wages above the minimum wage in 1982-83; direct controls on wages were imposed in 1983. Finally, in Italy, an incomes policy of sorts was implemented in late 1981 when the employers' association – with at least tacit government approval – refused to re-negotiate more than a hundred national collective agreements which were about to expire.

These attempts to solve the "prisoner's dilemma" through government intervention in wage setting did not bring about lasting reductions of inflation. One problem during the 1970s was the inadequacy of complementary macroeconomic policy restraint. More recently, wage policies aimed at securing moderation have been accompanied by restrictive monetary policies: in Belgium from 1983; in the Netherlands from 1985; in France from late 1982; and in Italy from 1980 (though fiscal policy continued to be expansionary). These have been more successful, but more favourable terms-of-trade developments have also eased the capacity-to-pay problem and thereby facilitated disinflation. In the United Kingdom, after 1978 the government did not seek to impose direct controls on private sector pay; rather, primary reliance was placed on reducing inflation through monetary instruments. Though at a rate which differed greatly from country to country, the shift to less accommodating macroeconomic policies and a movement away from wage indexation led to some narrowing of real wage gaps, but by then the disequilibria between increases in nominal wages and productivity growth had lasted more than a decade in the United Kingdom and Italy and only slightly less in the other countries.

The very high unemployment rates of these countries are attributable not only to wide wage gaps, but to the failure of labour market mechanisms to respond to the initial rise in unemployment caused by the recession; in particular, the fragmented but nonetheless broad union coverage has hampered wage responses to this unemployment though in France the primary factor for reducing wage flexibility was until recently the statutory minimum wage). Unions representing relatively small groups of workers, often enjoying regulatory job protection, have pressed wage claims with little regard for the cost in terms of employment opportunities for others. Without the internalisation of these costs, as in the encompassing bargaining countries, or without the safety valve of a large non-union sector, as in the United States, the unemployed have grown in number and they have become increasingly cut off from economic opportunity. Indeed, the concentration of unemployment among the young and older long-term unemployed is especially marked in these countries.

This concentration of unemployment also reflects major changes which have occurred in the microeconomic functioning of the labour market in these countries. Two such changes in which government policies have played a role have been of particular significance.

First, the interaction of wage indexation and incomes policy led to a substantial compression of *wage differentials* in virtually all the countries in this group. In Italy, the narrowing of differentials began in 1969; but it was greatly accelerated by the 1975 official indexation agreement, whereby cost-of-living adjustments were to take the form of lump sum increases set equally for all wage-earners. In the United Kingdom, a significant reduction in occupational pay differentials began in 1968[66] and further compression occurred under the "Social Contract" of 1976-78[67], although a very large part of the original comparison was subsequently upward. In France, differentials narrowed steadily over the period from 1968 to 1983, as increases in the minimum wage outpaced increases in overall earnings[68].

Second, tighter regulatory and contractual restrictions were imposed on *labour utilisation*. These were partly a response by governments to the rise in unemployment following the first oil shock: legal restrictions on redundancy were significantly strengthened in Italy in 1970, 1973 and 1975; in France in 1973 and 1975; and in the United Kingdom in 1975[69]. At the same time, notably in Italy and France, collective agreements increasingly contained provisions limiting overtime, shift working and internal mobility[70]. Many of these legislative and contractual constraints were eased in the early 1980s[71], but by then the economies concerned were well into recession.

In short, fragmented systems of collective bargaining had great difficulty in adjusting to changing economic circumstances. By and large, they entered the period with a wage-gap problem and serious wage/price spirals. These problems were exacerbated by the oil shocks; and it has taken more than a decade of rising unemployment, reinforced by a sharp shift in the stance of macroeconomic policy, for the wage policy disequilibria to recede, and even then not fully – but unemployment still remains unacceptably high.

E. "Fragmented" bargaining with compulsory arbitration

Many of the features of multi-level unionism can also be found in the apparently more centralised structures of compulsory arbitration characteristic of Australia and (until the early 1970s) New Zealand. In particular, union organisation and bargaining patterns in these countries have resembled the United Kingdom model in some respects, though differing from the model in others: the coexistence of a large number of unions organised on craft, industrial and general (multi-industry) principles has given rise to frequent demarcation disputes; central union hierarchies and employers' organisations have been fairly weak relative to their constituent parts (though less so than in the United Kingdom); bargaining levels have coexisted, though during the periods where collective bargaining has dominated (as 1973-74 and 1981-82), settlements have generally been at industry level; and there has at times been a tendency for each level to seek to improve on the terms negotiated at the level immediately above, with comparability claims spreading the results of generous settlements throughout the economy[72]. The system of compulsory arbitration and conciliation evolved in parallel to this structure; and one of the system's effects may have been to perpetuate fragmentation, both by granting legal recognition to the existing structure and by shielding it from pressures for change[73]. Moreover, the intimate historical links between a regulated labour market and a highly protected product market may well have blunted manufacturing unions' and employers' perceptions of the need to adjust to changing external circumstances[74].

Nonetheless, compared with unregulated multi-level systems, arbitration and conciliation has had three major advantages. First, it has laid down procedures for the orderly settlement of disputes of interest and of right, limiting (though by no means eliminating) recourse to industrial action[75]. Second, since the arbitration courts have sought to ensure consistency in the treatment of claims across sectors and levels of the structure, they have frequently set out the principles of wage fixation that would govern their decisions; these principles have defined a yardstick against which unions and employers could themselves assess the reasonableness of their demands. Third, arbitration has been a mechanism by which broader economic concerns could be brought to bear on industrial relations outcomes, notably through the determination of national wage cases.

The weakness of the compulsory arbitration system in practice has been the tendency for it to be circumvented or abandoned in periods of relatively strong labour demand. In the late 1960s and early 1970s, wage increases in Australia surged ahead of the awards of the Arbitration Commission as unemployment fell to 1.4 per cent. In 1973-74, only 20 per cent of the rise in the minimum weekly wage rate for males arose from increases in the National Wage Case – down from over 50 per cent in 1969-1970[76]. Wage determination was recentralised in the second half of the 1970s as a result of wage indexation. But once again, as labour markets tightened in the late 1970s, fragmented bargaining and wage increases to attract workers returned to the fore.

A breakdown of wages policy and an overall deterioration in economic conditions led the Liberal-National Party government to introduce a federal public sector wage freeze in December 1982, which was subsequently extended to the private sector. A new Labour government then re-introduced wage indexation in early 1983, having reached a broad-ranging agreement (the "Accord") on economic and social policy with the central trade union organisation, the ACTU, prior to the election. As in the 1975-1981 period, implementation of the Accord entailed a significant recentralisation of wage policy in the hands of the Arbitration Commission, which again proved effective in engineering a substantial moderation of unit labour costs[77]. Nonetheless, the period since 1983 has been primarily distinguished by the willingness of the ACTU to negotiate reductions in the degree of indexation with a Labour government on the basis of changing economic circumstances, introducing an element of flexibility in what could have been a system based on excessively rigid rules. As a result, containment of most labour costs has been achieved *despite* a significant tightening in the labour market.

Overall, compulsory arbitration has replaced certain of the internal and external controls characteristic of industrial relations in less fragmented systems. Taking the system's history as a whole, this has allowed it to smooth the consequences of the violent swings in the bargaining power of unions and employers to which primary exporting countries seem prone[78]; but despite its legal status, the system's effectiveness as a mechanism of control has been highly vulnerable at any point in time both to the state of the labour market and to the degree of consensus between unions and the government.

II. THE LINK TO ECONOMIC PERFORMANCE

The extent to which a system of industrial relations contributes to or impedes economic performance is largely a matter of the effectiveness of adjustment mechanisms operating within it. The foregoing description of types of industrial relations systems and their functioning in the past is indicative of important differences in these respects. In this part of the chapter, the adjustment mechanisms in national labour markets are compared from three additional perspectives: the macroeconomic aspects of wage adjustment; the efficiency of the allocation of labour resources; and third, when put in the context of other medium-term macroeconomic relationships, what both of these imply for sustainable rates of economic growth and employment. The results broadly confirm the observations made earlier about the strengths and weaknesses of different national systems. They also serve to identify the ways in which adjustment mechanisms need to be improved if economic performance in the future is to be better than in the past. Nonetheless, collective bargaining is by no means the sole factor affecting wage setting; indeed, in several countries, e.g. the Netherlands, lack of responsiveness in wage setting behaviour appears to have been mainly due to regulatory interventions in labour markets, notably through minimum wages and unemployment compensation schemes. As a result, the relation between collective bargaining structures on the one hand, and aggregate outcomes on the other, is neither simple nor direct but must be viewed in the light of changing regulatory contexts.

A. Macroeconomic responsiveness

Seen from a macroeconomic perspective, how labour markets adjust to disturbances and to indications of emerging disequilibrium is an important determinant of whether wages are maintained on a path that is in line with an economy's capacity to pay, without persistent high unemployment or accelerating inflation. Three adjustment mechanisms may play a role:

- The response of nominal wages to prices, i.e. the extent of indexation, whether formal or implicit, in the wage bargaining process and the lags involved;
- Adjustment of wages to changes in economic conditions that affect an economy's capacity to pay – in particular, changes in productivity trends from new technology or the efficiency with which

labour and capital are used in production, and changes in international terms of trade;

- The response of nominal wages to labour market conditions, in particular to the level of unemployment.

Macroeconomic wage adjustment equations seek to measure these relationships to the extent possible, given the limitations of aggregate time series analysis of individual structural relationships within macroeconomic systems. These have evolved through the introduction of additional variables into the Phillip's curve relationship between nominal wage growth and unemployment. Extensive effort has been devoted to the estimation of such relationships for Member countries. While this body of work has produced a considerable range of estimates for individual measures of responsiveness[79], there has been considerable convergence over time on key points. Secretariat work in this area[80] has produced results that are broadly representative; exploration of the relative importance of various adjustment mechanisms that follows is based on this work. It can only be illustrative because there is a considerable margin of error around the empirical estimates.

Before examining the adjustment processes from this macroeconomic perspective, it is important to note that they do not tell the full story about the capacity of economies to maintain high levels of employment and price stability. For one thing, the frequency, intensity and nature of the disturbances that push an economy away from a high-employment, stable-price path are as important as the strength and nature of the restoring forces that bring it back. Some enduring changes in the economic environment, such as a deteriorating trend of overall productivity growth which reduces an economy's capacity to pay, may pose especially difficult adjustment problems. For another thing, the extent to which labour market adjustment processes are effective depends in part on how other adjustment mechanisms in the economy are functioning – in product markets (price adjustment mechanisms), in financial markets (interest rate and exchange rate responses) and in the response of macroeconomic policy itself. It is also worth noting at this point that the measures of responsiveness do not by themselves provide an answer to the question: how high is the feasible employment and output path of an economy in the absence of disturbances? This too depends both on the long-run properties of the wage adjustment equation and on other long-run macroeconomic relationships. Some evidence bearing on this question will be reviewed under the heading "sustainable employment performance".

In the long run, the rate of growth of nominal wages seems to adjust more or less fully to sustained changes in price inflation, holding constant other macroeconomic variables that may affect wages; the empirical work of recent years leaves little room for doubt on this point. But there are significant differences in the speed of this adjustment as between countries, as indicated by the average adjustment of nominal wage growth to inflation

in the first year following a change in the rate of price inflation. Secretariat estimates of these wage growth reponses are shown in Table 3.2. The differences do not appear to be systematically related to differences in forms of industrial relations set forth in Part I. But they do reflect differences in institutional arrangements. In Italy and in several smaller European countries, for example, the high degree of formal indexing of wages has led to very rapid wage adjustment to inflation. Nevertheless, the response of wages to inflation appears rapid in Germany as well, where wages are not formally indexed. In Japan too, the response is very rapid owing to annual bonus payments which tend to rise when higher prices improve profitability, and to an apparent tendency for annual wage settlements to incorporate and even anticipate inflation. At the other end of the spectrum, the speed of wage adjustment to inflation in North America is relatively slow because collective bargaining agreements normally have a life of three years and indexation is neither universal nor complete.

Table 3.2. **Percentage of total adjustment of nominal wage growth to changes in inflation**

	In the first half-year	In the first year
United States	14	28
Japan	67	100
Germany	75	100
France	50	100
United Kingdom	34	67
Italy	60	100
Canada	20	40
Australia	50	100
Austria	34	67
Finland	34	67
Netherlands	50	100
Spain	25	50
Switzerland	50	100

Source: Secretariat estimates.

A slow adjustment of wages to inflation may contribute to labour market adjustment even if wage growth eventually fully reflects any change in the rate of inflation. This is because an acceleration of inflation will reduce the level of real wages during the period that nominal wages are adjusting to the increase in inflation and conversely to a decline in inflation. The evidence suggests that catch-up following such an adjustment is incomplete. Moreover, the stickiness of nominal wages tends to provide some inertia that inhibits a pick-up of a wage/price spiral in the face of a transitory inflationary impulse. These considerations have led governments to discourage or even prohibit formal indexation of wages, or at least to reduce the size or frequency of adjustments. To the extent that the pass-through of price increases into wages were reduced, real wages could be brought more readily into line with a reduced capacity to pay, but at some cost in terms of sustained higher inflation. On the other hand, this same inertia may make it more painful to reduce inflation once it has acquired momentum – slowing inflation would not translate so immediately into a slowing of wage increases.

Table 3.3. **Adjustment of wages to productivity and terms of trade developments**
Percentages

Countries for which the wage response to productivity is statistically significant:	
United States	0.27
Japan	0.65
Germany	0.65
Finland	0.91
Spain	0.82
Switzerland	0.26
Countries for which the wage response to the terms of trade is statistically significant:	
Japan	0.82
Austria	0.79
Switzerland	0.41

Note: Terms of trade are measured by the difference between the growth of the private consumption deflator and the GNP deflator.
Source: Secretariat estimates.

A lowering of wage settlements (relative to price inflation) in response to changes in economies' capacity to pay provides the most painless labour market adjustment to many of the disturbances that seem to have contributed to persistently higher rates of unemployment over the past fifteen years – declines in rates of overall productivity growth, and adverse terms-of-trade developments, notably the two oil shocks. Indeed, in the economies for which wage adjustment equations have been estimated, productivity developments appear to influence wage-bargaining outcomes in a number of countries that have had relatively good employment performance, namely the United States, Japan, Germany, Finland and Switzerland. Similarly, in Japan, Austria and Switzerland, changes in the terms of trade, as measured by the growth of consumer prices relative to output prices, seem to have some influence on wages (see Table 3.3). Nonetheless, the estimated responses are incomplete, and to the extent that labour productivity has been maintained in some countries by increasing the ratio of capital to labour, the capacity to pay has not kept pace with productivity as a larger share of output has been required to meet capital servicing costs. Thus, much of the pressure for adjustment has remained on other mechanisms, and mainly on increases in unemployment.

It is interesting that these responses – to changes in productivity performance and shifts in the terms of trade – are evident in several countries that more or less fit the encompassing bargaining model of industrial relations, and in those with decentralised bargaining systems. One would expect that in encompassing systems, the capacity to internalise the benefits from adjusting wages to favourable and unfavourable developments in the economy's capacity to pay would strengthen such mechanisms as compared with fragmented bargaining. In decentralised systems, aggregate wage outcomes appear to reflect to some extent the aggregation of responses to changes in the capacity to pay of individual enterprises. By contrast, these adjustment mechanisms seem particularly ineffectual in countries with fragmented bargaining systems. But the evidence on this issue is incomplete, and these observations cannot be taken as more than indicative of the relative strength of direct wage responses to changes in the capacity to pay under alternative bargaining models.

Given the fairly strong tendency for wage growth to adjust to price inflation and incomplete direct feedback from changes in economies' capacities to pay to wages, pressure has built up on the third macroeconomic wage adjustment mechanism – the response to unemployment. Table 3.4 gives estimated responses of nominal wage growth to the level of unemployment for twelve Member countries.

The estimates reported in Table 3.4 show an especially high response of wages to unemployment for

Table 3.4. **Decrease in nominal wage growth resulting from a one-percentage-point increase in the unemployment rate**
Percentages

United States	0.60
Japan	0.88
Germany[1]	0.05
	0.14
France	0.33
United Kingdom[2]	0.15
	0.44
Italy	0.60
Canada	0.51
Australia	0.39
Austria	0.42
Finland	0.49
Netherlands[1]	0.12
	0.32
Spain[1]	0.08
	0.23

1. For these countries the responsiveness of wages decreases as the level of unemployment rises. The first figures given are based on 1986 levels of the unemployment rate; the second on average unemployment rates for the sample period.
2. The second figure for the United Kingdom is from an estimated equation where only changes in the unemployment rate affect wage growth and hence the impact is only transitory.
Source: Secretariat estimates.

133

Japan – a one percentage point increase in unemployment reduces nominal wage growth in that country by 0.9 to 1.9 percentage points. This finding, together with the consistently good unemployment performance of Japan, lends support to the view that this adjustment can play an important role in correcting the path of wages and reducing unemployment following a range of disturbances that initially tend to raise it – a fall in aggregate demand, a slowing of productivity growth or adverse terms-of-trade developments. Other countries that show a relatively high sensitivity of wages to unemployment are the United States and Italy. The United States has succeeded also in reducing inflation and unemployment relatively rapidly following shocks by virtue of the moderating influence of wages on unemployment and the fact that labour shedding takes place there rather rapidly in response to demand weakness. For Italy, the finding suggests that one must look to the intensity of adjustment pressures and to other structural factors for an exploration of the tendency for inflation and unemployment to remain relatively high.

In a number of countries, notably Germany, the Netherlands and Spain, the data seem to indicate that the response of wages to unemployment is non-linear, i.e. as the level of the unemployment rate rises, the moderating influence on wages of further increases in unemployment diminishes. This means that disinflation can be achieved at less cost in cumulative unemployment over time, albeit more slowly, with moderate levels of labour market slack than by permitting unemployment to rise to high levels. It should be noted that for Germany, Spain, and Finland, the sensitivity of wages to productivity serves substantially to strengthen wage adjustment in periods of demand weakness, since productivity growth tends to slow then. As a result, these countries have overall cyclical wage responses comparable to those of Japan and the United States.

The United Kingdom and the Netherlands stand out as having both a low sensitivity of wages to unemployment and no discernible influence of productivity or the terms of trade on wage growth. In the case of the United Kingdom, this may reflect a fragmented system of industrial relations in which groups which are relatively well protected from job loss press their wage demands without much regard for general labour market conditions. Indeed, the data for France, also a country with a fragmented system, indicate only moderately greater sensitivity of wages to unemployment, partly as a result of minimum wage regulation which has increased downward wage rigidity. It should also be noted that tests of an alternative form of the wage-adjustment equation reveal a tendency for wage behaviour in the United Kingdom to respond substantially to changes in unemployment, but to be relatively insensitive to persistent high rates of unemployment. A sort of equilibrium seems to be established at the prevailing rate of unemployment – a phenomenon that has come to be labelled "hysteresis" in current academic literature[81].

As a consequence, any fall in unemployment from high levels would seem to entail greater risks of renewed wage pressures in the United Kingdom than in countries where an elevated rate of unemployment would continue to exert downward pressure on wages.

Although the precise magnitudes of the adjustment responses for a given country are subject to considerable uncertainty, with the results somewhat sensitive to the form of the equation fit to the data and to the time period selected, the results are indicative of various adjustments that occur in labour markets in response to pressures. From an overall view, the labour markets examined, with the possible exception of the United Kingdom, show evidence of adjustment mechanisms that tend to bring wages into line with the capacity to pay of an economy over time, and that allow unemployment to be restored to sustainable levels without a re-acceleration of inflation. But accelerating the pace with which this could occur would require changes in industrial relations systems – including government policies more favourable to adjustment – in order to strengthen these adjustment mechanisms and lower the unemployment cost of adjusting to pressures on labour market. The question of what is a sustainable level of unemployment in the absence of shocks depends not only on the macro wage adjustments but also on productivity and terms-of-trade trends and hence on the micro functioning of the labour market, which will be examined before returning to this question.

B. Labour market efficiency

In addition to the processes summarised by the macroeconomic responsiveness of wages, employment outcomes have been significantly affected by changes in the microeconomic efficiency of labour markets. These changes may have distorted the price signals facing employers and employees, altered the extent to which labour markets can effectively allocate workers to jobs, and reduced the incentives employers have to recruit workers with few skills – thus impairing both the ability of the unemployed to find jobs and the productivity of economies.

The trends involved are numerous. Some of them – notably the growth of non-wage labour costs – arise largely from government revenue policy rather than from labour market institutions. Others – such as increased regulatory controls on redundancy or the tightening of occupational health and safety regulations – are partly the outcome of collective bargaining but are mainly due to legislative action. Yet others, in particular the compression of occupational and industrial pay differentials, occurred largely through collective bargaining, but minimum wage legislation has played a role in some countries.

These trends have been particularly marked in Europe, and extensive empirical work has been done on what effects each of these, taken individually, may have

134

had on the rise in unemployment. The results have not been conclusive. This is partly because these trends developed in a period when the labour market was in any case heading towards major supply-demand imbalances, but it is also because the impact of any one trend is difficult to assess independently of the others. Moreover, although these trends have been reversed in recent years, insufficient time has passed to discern the extent to which the capacity of economies to sustain better employment performance has been enhanced as a result.

In essence, the efficiency of labour markets relates to the functioning of incentives, the flow of information in the labour market, and the presence or absence of constraints on workers and employers to act on them. Relative wage rates are important in these respects but they are not the whole story. Even in periods of high unemployment, the natural turnover of personnel, the fact that some firms are expanding while others are contracting, and the broader differences in growth rates between occupations or regions mean that the number of vacancies (though declining absolutely) generally remains high. Both the level and the persistence of unemployment are significantly affected by the extent to which these vacancies and the characteristics of those looking for work correspond, i.e. the extent to which wages for different types of labour encourage employers to create vacancies for the skills or groups in excess supply, and the ease with which workers move to occupations, regions or firms seeking to recruit.

It is important to note in this respect that the growth of European unemployment has been associated with a significant compression of pay differentials and a decline in labour mobility, as measured by turnover rates, by the geographical movement of workers and by the degree of mobility between occupations. Moreover, it is clear that wage differentials are now narrower in many European countries than in the United States (Table 3.5), labour turnover is lower (Table 3.6) and the labour force less geographically mobile (Table 3.7).

Table 3.5. **Industry wage differentials;**
coefficients of variation in average wages and salaries for 3- to 4-digit manufacturing industries

Country	1958	1961	1964	1970	1973	1979	1980	1982	1983
Japan	—	—	—	35.5	34.0	34.0	—	—	—
United States	21.4	24.2	22.3	21.6	23.7	26.8	27.1	—	—
Canada (prod. workers)	—	24.5	23.8	23.3	23.4	23.2	23.1	—	—
France	—	—	—	16.7	24.0	23.9	21.6	22.7	—
United Kingdom	—	—	—	20.1	20.2	20.4	—	—	—
Sweden	—	—	15.4	14.1	13.6	12.8	13.0	13.8	14.3

Source: OECD Employment Outlook, 1985, op. cit. in Note 37, pp. 84-91.

Table 3.6. **Labour turnover and job tenure**

Country	Annual new hires per 100 employed					Per cent share of workers with current job tenures[1] of:			
	1971	1973	1978	1981	1983	Less than 1 year	Less than 2 years	More than 10 years	More than 20 years
United States*	47	58	49	39	—	27	39	27	10
Australia	—	—	—	—	—	25	39	19	7
Canada	—	—	—	—	—	23	33	27	9
Japan	29	28	20	21	20	10	21	48	22
Japan*	25	24	16	18	18	—	—	—	—
Finland	—	44	28	36	36	16	—	32	9
France	21	—	19	16	—	—	18	35	13
France*	22	—	15	13	—	—	—	—	—
Germany	29	34	28	28	—	—	19	38	15
Italy*	28	33	11	9	—	—	13	37	9
Sweden*	—	28	15	13	15	—	—	—	—
United Kingdom*	28	32	23	12	16	14	24	31	12

1. Australia 1981; United States, Canada, Finland 1983; Japan 1982; the United Kingdom 1979; France, Germany, Italy 1978.
   An *asterisk* (*) indicates that the turnover data refer to *manufacturing* industries only. Otherwise, the turnover data refer to the whole private sector, with various minor exceptions, or (for France) to the whole labour market.
   The *tenure* data for EEC countries except the United Kingdom come from surveys of certain establishments in manufacturing, mining, building, trade and finance. For all non-EEC countries and for the United Kingdom, the tenure data refer to all employees.
Sources: OECD, *Labour Market Flexibility*, Paris, 1986; OECD, *Flexibility in the Labour Market. The Current Debate*, Paris, 1986.

Table 3.7. **Geographic mobility: persons who changed country or region of residence in certain years in per cent of total population**

Country	Regional unit	Average population of regions	Regional movers (%)		Immigrants from abroad per year (%)		Total rate of migration (%)	
			1970	1980	1970-1975	1976-1983	c. 1970	c. 1980
United States	State	4 mn	3.4	3.3	0.2	0.2	3.6	3.5
Japan	Prefecture	2 mn	3.6	2.6	0	0	3.6	2.6
Canada	Province	2 mn	1.9	1.8	0.7	0.5	2.6	2.3
Australia	State	1.5 mn	1.7	1.8	0.8	0.6	2.5	2.4
Germany	Land	6 mn	1.8	1.3	1.2	0.7	3.0	2.0
France[1]	Region ZEAT	7 mn	—	1.3	0.5	0.2	—	1.5
England and Wales	Standard Region	7 mn	1.5	1.1	—	—	—	—
Sweden[2]	County Block	1 mn	1.5	1.3	0.5	0.4	1.9	1.7

1. Regional mobility rates refer to labour force only; ZEAT regions have been defined specifically for the purpose of labour market analyses.
2. Administrative data, which include multiple and return moves made within a year.
Sources: OECD, *Labour Market Flexibility; Flexibility in the Labour Market. The Current Debate, op. cit.* in Table 3.6.

In analysing these data, it must be recognised at the outset that there is no single pattern of differentials or mobility that can be considered "optimal". Thus, the adequacy of labour mobility needs to be assessed with reference not only to the willingness of workers to change employers but also to the frequency with which movement occurs in the internal labour market of the firm. And, given the importance of "learning by doing", high levels of labour mobility should not be viewed as desirable for their own sake. Moreover, assessing the role of wage differentials in promoting efficiency is as much a matter of their direction (notably whether they accurately reflect the existence of demand-supply imbalances and not the exercise of market power by workers in some sectors) and their predictability as of their size. Finally, it is clear that earnings differentials will tend to be greatest in economies where differences in educational attainment within the labour force are large, where private costs in shifting from one job to another are high, and where employers have little way of assessing the capabilities of employees before hiring them. Thus, the persistence of large wage differentials may be a reflection of micro labour market imbalances, poor information about the availability of jobs and the suitability of individuals for them, and constraints on mobility as well as a mechanism for directing labour to most productive use. Indeed, in the absence of such "imperfections" in labour markets and differences in the opportunities or capacities of individuals to acquire skills, one would expect wage differentials to be small and transitory.

In the light of some of these considerations, a reduction in wage differentials was a natural outcome of underlying trends in Europe up to the end of the 1960s. Historically, the evolution of pay differentials over time has followed a pattern commonly referred to as the "Kuznet's curve", in which skills are in short supply and wage premiums for skills rise during phases of rapid industrialisation and fall subsequently[82]. Germany,

where occupational differentials have been exceptionally stable and relatively small, has to some extent been an exception to this pattern; but elsewhere in Europe, differentials were substantially compressed during the war and immediate postwar years[83] and increased in virtually all countries in the period 1955-1969[84], until by the mid-1960s they were significantly greater than differentials in the United States (Table 3.8). Several developments would have been expected to induce a subsequent fall in occupational differentials: the rise in the average levels of skill attainment of the European labour force (at a rate admittedly about half that in the United States)[85]; the diminishing outflow of unskilled labour from agriculture; the decline in the participation rates of the infirm, the very young and the very old (who have generally been at the bottom of the earnings distribution); and the shifting pattern of labour demand both within manufacturing and between manufacturing and services[86].

Table 3.8. **Occupational pay differentials: years around 1963**

Country	Earnings differential[1]	GDP per manhour ($)[2]
Italy	6.0	2.1
France	4.0	2.87
Denmark	3.5	2.45
United Kingdom	2.8	2.99
Norway	2.1	3.04
Germany	1.6	2.72
United States	1.5	5.41

1. Average earnings of male higher administrative staff and professional staff as a ratio to those of male skilled and semi-skilled manual workers; calculated from Economic Commission for Europe, *Incomes in Postwar Europe*, Geneva, 1967, Table 5.16.
2. GDP per manhour in 1960, calculated using 1970 United States relative prices; derived from Maddison, A., *Phases of Capitalist Development, op. cit.* in Note 1, Table 6.10, p. 212.

Some decline could equally have been expected in regional and industrial pay differentials. Thus, regional pay differentials have tended to decline on a secular basis as communications and information have improved[87]. Inter-industry pay differentials – though their pattern has been surprisingly stable over long periods of time – have also tended to decline as labour markets have become more unified, the occupational differences between industries have narrowed (notably in terms of the ratio of manual to non-manual employees), sex discrimination in employment has become less acute, and collective bargaining (especially where it has been encompassing) has imposed a more uniform wage structure. The United States has been an exception in this respect, with the inter-industry wage spread changing little over the course of this century[88].

Finally, secular forces have also been at work in the observed fall in the industrial and geographical mobility of the labour force. Seen over the longer term, the development of labour markets internal to firms has at least partially replaced the external flow of workers between firms. Thus, on most estimates, labour turnover in the United States declined by as much as two-thirds over the fifty years to 1970; this was closely related to the rise of rules and procedures governing mobility within firms[89]. In continental Europe, labour mobility appears to have been exceptionally high in the late 1950s, largely because casual labour remained a significant source of employment[90] while internal and external migration swelled the pool of highly mobile individuals[91]. The growth of internal labour markets, together with broader trends (such as rising home ownership, the diversification of employment opportunities in larger metropolitan areas, and the re-emergence of two-income families), contributed to bringing mobility rates down. Moreover, in a more short-term perspective, there is considerable evidence that mobility levels decline in periods of high unemployment, as employees become reluctant to leave their present job until they have an assured offer of employment elsewhere; but since they continue to search for a better job while employed[92], the observed decline in mobility considerably overstates the actual fall in the number of workers who would be willing to move to more promising opportunities if they were available.

Nonetheless, the observed changes in differentials and mobility cannot be fully accounted for by equilibrating responses to secular and cyclical shifts in supply and demand. In particular, though little solid empirical analysis is available, the extent of the decline in wage differentials in Europe seems greater than that which could have been expected on the basis of supply and demand trends alone. Thus, it would be consistent with prior experience for skill differentials to have widened somewhat as unemployment rose, even though their secular trend might be to decline[93]; this point is underscored by the fact that while the relative supply of better educated employees has increased, unemploy-ment rates for these employees have remained below average[94]. In this sense, the narrowing of earnings differentials must at least partly have been due to trade union wage strategies[95], the results of which were certainly accentuated by higher rates of inflation[96] and, in a number of countries, by the operation of minimum wages. Equally, it is likely that the observed decline in labour mobility has resulted not only from the longer-term growth of internal labour markets and the cyclical pattern of quit rates, but also – given that migrants tend to be more highly mobile than the native-born – from the effects of regulatory restrictions on immigration (the sharp fall in immigration levels in Europe being in marked contrast to the continued importance of migrant inflows to the United States)[97] and from the rising importance of non-transferable, seniority-dependent fringe benefits in the total labour compensation[98].

In summary, it can indeed be argued that regulatory policies and collective bargaining outcomes have contributed to altering the signals bearing on the microeconomic functioning of European labour markets – especially in Europe. It is a narrowing of wage differentials or slowing of mobility as a result of constraints imposed by regulation and collective bargaining that would seem to pose a problem for the efficiency of labour markets, rather than a narrowing that could also arise from improved mobility between regions or industries or a more flexible response to changing skill requirements.

One area in which increasing constraints on wage differentials seems to have impaired the functioning of labour markets is in the longer time taken by new entrants to the labour force and displaced workers in finding jobs. The growth in unemployment in the major European countries has been less a reflection of larger numbers becoming unemployed than of the increasing time it has taken the unemployed to find jobs. In the United Kingdom, France and Italy, this decline in "employability" has been especially marked for workers with few skills, the young and those close to retirement.

Constraints on differentials may have played an important role in this outcome by reducing opportunities for the unemployed to offer their labour for low wages as a path to higher-wage jobs. Employment at relatively low wages partly serves to "screen" or "filter" the quality of employees[99]. This role is especially marked in labour markets where pay rises with seniority or where previous work experience has a significant effect on future employment prospects. In these situations, lower wages are to some extent a "bond" (or deposit) employees pay to show what they can do in order to compete for higher earnings in years to come; and the existence of jobs at low pay will be of particular importance to workers with few certified skills, since employers bear an obvious risk in recruiting them – a risk which the payments of a lower wage may offset. From the employer's point of view, therefore, wage differentials act to share the risk involved in the initial recruitment decision, and (when earnings rise with tenure) to encourage workers to act in such a way as to retain their job; while as far as the employee is concerned, they are an investment in work experience and seniority.

This function of earnings differentials is clearly borne out by analysis of international and inter-industry patterns of pay. Thus, in Europe, wage differentials – both within and between occupations – have generally been greater in countries lacking nation-wide, certified vocational training than in those with comprehensive training structures (see Table 3.9); moreover, earnings have tended to rise more sharply with age and seniority in the former rather than in the latter group of countries[100]. Equally, in the United States, large pay disparities at least partly reflect the lack of certified, transferable skills in the labour force. This fragments the market for labour and makes it virtually impossible for a uniform rate to emerge for a given set of skills, even within industries; but wide pay differentials have also traditionally provided young employees with a set of low-paid "stepping stones" into secure employment[101]. Finally, in Japan, the seniority wage system is consistent with low levels of formal vocational training and certification in the labour force and the corresponding need for large firms to gradually develop employees' skills through costly internal training programmes over long periods of time. Correspondingly, seniority differentials are wide.

Seen in this perspective, constraints on pay differentials will have two effects: first, notably in countries where large parts of the labour force have few certified skills, it will increase the burden of unemployment on workers with few qualifications; and second, it will make the rise in unemployment cumulative, since those who have been jobless for some time will appear to present greater risks to a potential employer, risks which only progressively growing wage differentials could offset.

It is extremely difficult to test empirically these effects of constraints on wage differentials on overall unemployment since one cannot measure directly the extent to which constraints have distorted differentials. Nevertheless, it is indicative that the overall increase in joblessness and the incidence of unemployment among the young and the less skilled has been especially marked in countries characterised both by pay compression and by a general lack of vocationally certified skills in the labour force – in particular the United Kingdom, France and Italy[102]. Moreover, there is evidence, at least for the United Kingdom, that the probability of re-employment has tended to decline with the length of unemployment, so that a rising share of those out of work can no longer effectively compete for mainstream jobs[103]. This may be related to the tendency, noted earlier, for higher unemployment to have a relatively short-lived effect in moderating wage trends in the United Kingdom. The tightening of redundancy laws and (more recently) of contractual provisions on individual and collective dismissals has almost certainly increased the importance of these imperfect information effects in labour markets, notably by making hiring decisions less reversible[104].

In France and Italy, the declining effectiveness of screening and incentive mechanisms in labour markets has provoked an offsetting reaction in the growth of semi- or unofficial employment. Thus, the evidence suggests that in France, employers have made growing use of part-time or temporary jobs as a means of screening potential recruits (as well as a way of obtaining greater flexibility in employment levels), while for employees they are an important way of obtaining work experience[105]. Equally, in Italy, though the factors making for the growth of the "underground" economy are complex[106], there is little doubt that it has provided pay structures considerably more varied and performance-related than those prevailing in the larger, more highly regulated firms. Similarly, in both France and Italy, there has been a significant shift in employment towards smaller firms. This trend must at least be partly due to the greater flexibility these firms have in setting pay structures and conditions of employment, in recruiting and dismissing employees, and in monitoring individual performance on the job[107]. Nonetheless, these unconventional forms of employment can hardly compensate for deficiencies of mainstream labour markets operating under constraints; and to their efficiency costs must be added the inequities which come from the deepening segmentation of the labour force into "insiders" and "outsiders".

Table 3.9. **Wage dispersion and training programmes**

	United Kingdom	France	Italy	Netherlands	Germany
a) Hourly pay dispersion (coefficient of variation) in industry (1972)[1]	32	31	27	24	22
b) Percentage of 17-year-olds enrolled in schools or apprenticeships[2]	65	75	70	86	97
c) Percentage of 17-year-olds in apprenticeships (years around 1984)[2]	35	10	23	10	46

1. Coefficient of variation in the hourly earnings of individual manual workers in industry; from Saunders, C. and Marsden, D., *Pay Inequalities in the European Community*, Butterworths, London, 1981, Table 2.1.
2. See Chapter 1 on human capital.

C. Sustainable rates of unemployment

What rates of unemployment can be sustained in an economy in the absence of large disturbances is partly a matter of the functioning of labour markets as summarised by the wage adjustment equations discussed earlier. These equations can be used to calculate what rate of unemployment would be sustainable for any growth rate of real wages. This is a macroeconomic reflection of the microeconomic efficiency of labour markets. In order to assess what unemployment rate can be sustained, this information must be put together with trends in economies' capacities to pay. These are the outcome of capital formation, terms of trade, price behaviour given competitive conditions in product markets, technological advance, and the efficiency with which labour is allocated and used in production. Thus, the sustainable unemployment rate in the absence of macroeconomic disturbances is a property of the economic system and not of the labour market alone.

One indicator of this sustainable rate is the non-accelerating inflation rate of unemployment (NAIRU) derivable from wage adjustment equations, taking account of factors affecting the evolution of prices in the economy. Two sets of such estimates for several recent sub-periods are given in Table 3.10. Both are based on the wage-adjustment equations similar to those discussed earlier and thus assume no structural change in labour market functioning over the period. The first column of estimates shows NAIRUs calculated by taking actual import price developments during that sub-period. The second column of NAIRU estimates is based on the average trend of import prices over the entire period. Both sets of estimates incorporate actual productivity performance. Unfortunately, estimates are available only for the largest member countries. No estimate is given for the United Kingdom since, as noted earlier, the relationship between the rate of wage increase and the *level* of unemployment for that country seems unstable.

Three observations about these estimates are especially important from the standpoint of assessing labour markets. First, as seen by the differences between the two columns of figures, import price behaviour has had an important effect on which unemployment rates could have been sustained without accelerating inflation. Second, removing the effects of import prices, NAIRUs have generally risen from the early 1970s to the mid-1980s, owing mainly to falling productivity growth. Third, average levels of NAIRU estimates for the

Table 3.10. **NAIRU estimates**

| | Time period[1] | Actual rates | NAIRU estimates based on: | |
			Actual import prices in each sub-period	Average import price change in whole period
United States	1971-1976	6.3	6.6	5.4
	1977-1982	7.2	8.3	5.7
	1983-1987	7.5	2.7	6.0
	1986 I	7.0		
Japan	1971-1976	1.5	0	1.3
	1977-1982	2.2	3.6	2.5
	1983-1987	2.8	0.5	2.5
	1986 I	2.8		
Germany	1971-1976	2.1	1.5	1.1
	1977-1982	4.2	5.0	3.1
	1983-1987	8.0	3.7	6.0
	1986 I	8.0		
France	1971-1976	2.5	3.8	0
	1977-1982	6.3	5.3	4.3
	1983-1987	10.1	0.4	6.0
	1986 I	10.3		
Italy	1971-1976	5.9	8.7	7.6
	1977-1982	7.8	8.7	7.0
	1983-1987	10.7	4.1	7.3
	1986 I	11.0		
Canada	1971-1976	6.2	7.3	6.5
	1977-1982	8.3	11.0	8.3
	1983-1987	10.4	8.3	8.9
	1986 I	9.8		

1. 1986-1987 are Secretariat projections.
Source: OECD (1986).

mid-1980s are below current unemployment rates in all of these countries.

The third observation suggests that there is scope in all of these countries for some durable reduction of unemployment, given the micro functioning of these economies and the low rates of inflation that have been achieved, but this scope is limited. Reducing the NAIRUs themselves, and hence the sustainable unemployment rates, would require better functioning of labour markets, or better productivity performance, or both. Improvement in industrial relations structures that resulted in capacity to pay or unemployment or both receiving greater weight in wage bargaining would help. But without parallel improvements of the processes of matching skills and job requirements and enhanced access of the unemployed to jobs, market pressures on wages would emerge as unemployment was reduced, limiting the gains. As noted earlier in the discussion of Australian experience with national arbitration of wage settlements, such pressures can rapidly erode wage moderation as labour markets tighten. Better microeconomic functioning of labour markets could be expected to contribute to productivity performance, thereby reducing sustainable unemployment rates through a second channel.

III. IMPROVING LABOUR MARKET STRUCTURE

If sustained employment growth is to be achieved in the OECD area, labour market institutions will have to contribute to better macroeconomic wage adjustment to changes in economies' capacity to pay, facilitate the efficient allocation to jobs of those seeking work, and encourage the development and fullest use of skills. How can labour markets be improved in these respects?

It should be noted at the outset that in no OECD country have labour markets functioned outside the framework of a socially structured system of industrial relations. Even in Japan, where adversarial negotiations have been in some respects more limited than elsewhere, a structure of collective bargaining has functioned alongside far-ranging consultation between employers and employees. And in the United States, where unionisation is less pervasive than in most other countries, collective bargaining nevertheless plays an important role, both in governing key sectors and in influencing labour relations beyond the unionised sectors. Indeed, above and beyond their broader social role, the institutions of collective bargaining have performed and continue to perform important economic functions – notably in reducing the transaction costs involved in the employment relationship. It may therefore be taken as a premise that collective bargaining will remain at the centre of labour markets in OECD countries.

Second, it is clear that some systems of industrial relations have dealt with changing conditions better than others. These differences are apparent in aggregate wage adjustments to changes in countries' capacity to pay, both directly and through their response to unemployment, as well as in the efficiency with which labour has been redeployed in the face of structural change in patterns of demand and production techniques. In both respects, the Japanese system of enterprise bargaining has proved relatively flexible. At the same time, it must be noted that the large adjustments from an export-led economy to an economy directed more towards satisfying domestic demands may pose greater challenges to this structure than those it has faced in the past. The countries with encompassing and "job control" bargaining structures have exhibited moderate flexibility, but they have also shown signs of strain – the former in a tendency for solidarity to weaken and for bargaining to become more decentralised, and the latter in the stronger growth of non-union jobs. It is unclear at the present time whether these trends will prove durable or whether they will be arrested or reversed if the present adjustment pressures on labour markets ease. Finally, on both the micro- and macroeconomic indicators, the economies with fragmented bargaining structures have exhibited the least flexible labour markets, while the Australian experience highlights both the possibilities and the limitations of improving the functioning of an essentially fragmented union structure through national arbitration of wage claims.

Third, it is in the nature of collective bargaining that each party has an element of power which it may use to the detriment of the broader interest – the prisoner's dilemma and public good aspects of labour market outcomes; and the observed differences in performance can largely be traced to the effectiveness of the constraints which different national systems impose on these power relations. Thus, by and large, systems of industrial relations have relied on three factors to limit abuses of power: internal constraints coming from organisational structure and ideology; the regulating framework of the law, including the delineation of the rights of workers to organise as a counterweight to the power of employers; and the pressures of competition. All of these shape the incentives and opportunities of participants on both sides of the labour market; but the balance between these factors has differed greatly from case to case.

Thus, in countries with encompassing bargaining structures, the constraints have been largely internal, arising from the ideology of social partnership, the broader societal role of unions and employers' associations, and the fear of the high costs of a breakdown for both parties in such a system; but exposure to international competition has also been a major factor. In North America, the legal framework has partly played this constraining role (as it has in Australia and New Zealand), but the dominant element has been competition from a large, non-unionised sector. The system of industrial relations in Japan has combined features of the North American model and of encompassing bargaining. The market-place constraints have been particularly significant; but in the larger firms at least, they have been buttressed by the internal pressures for restraint arising from the perceived commonality of interests between employers and their firms – similar to the internal controls typical of encompassing bargaining. Lastly, the distinctive feature of the United Kingdom, France and Italy has been the weakness of each of the three elements of control: the structure of unions and employers' organisations has not been such as to permit internal controls to operate; it is only recently that an explicit legal framework for collective bargaining has evolved; and a tradition of protected and (publicly or privately) regulated markets has reduced the pressures of competition. The absence of controls does not in itself ensure poor performance; but it has made poor performance difficult to contain and correct.

Finally, patterns of production are changing in ways that place a higher premium on flexibility of the deployment of labour within the firm. Production technology, both in manufacturing and in services, is shifting away from reliance on narrowly defined job tasks geared to the production of standardized products, towards an increasingly broad definition of individual skills and functions more appropriate to producing diversified and rapidly changing outputs[108]. The effective implementation of new production technologies depends on the internal mobility and flexibility of the labour force, and especially on the willingness of employees to alter their skill base and work practices several times in the course of working life.

These conclusions, taken together, point to the contribution that reforms in a number of areas could make to better functioning of labour markets in the private sector. At the same time, governments are increasingly drawn into industrial relations through their role as very large employers and by a fairly widespread rise in public sector unionisation[109]. The policy issues posed in this area require separate attention. Finally, whether institutions that function better can command broad support and are able to evolve will depend crucially on community understanding of what labour market institutions can and cannot do. The remainder of this chapter addresses these aspects of improving labour market performance in turn.

A. Improving industrial relations in the private sector

The degree of *coherence of bargaining structures* has a major influence on how well labour markets adjust. This is clearest in the relatively poor performance of countries with fragmented bargaining structures. But the evident pressures toward decentralisation in at least some of the countries with encompassing bargaining systems, and the differential performance of union and non-union

sectors in the United States, highlight tensions in these systems as well.

There are some signs, although by no means unmistakable, that bargaining structures in a number of countries are changing in the direction of decentralised, enterprise-level bargaining – a system to which the Japanese bargaining structure corresponds in some respects, though the role played in Japan by national co-ordination and consultation mechanisms should not be underestimated. The Japanese system has served that country's workers well in providing long-term growth of incomes and employment opportunities. But could such a system work as well in other economies or cultural settings? And if it is a promising approach, what role should governments play in fostering evolution in this direction?

There are several reasons, aside from Japanese success, for believing that decentralisation of collective bargaining to the enterprise level (together with consolidation of representation within each enterprise in countries with fragmented union structures) would improve labour market performance in many countries. Decentralised bargaining provides a setting in which the conditions and prospects of individual enterprises bear on wage outcomes. Although the considerations bearing on the wage strategies of both firms and workers under such a system are complex and consequently the pattern of resulting wage differentials might not have a simple explanation, decentralisation would contribute to smoother adjustment to changing patterns of labour demand: wage differentials would induce labour to move from enterprises in declining sectors with poor wage prospects to those with better ones. Those workers who were most mobile would seize those opportunities, thus reducing the likelihood that those who are less mobile, either geographically or with respect to skills, would be displaced. At the same time, it would provide a setting in which workers could choose to extend the duration of threatened jobs by accepting lower wages or instead opt to extract a higher wage, recognising that by doing so they would accelerate the adjustment process[110]. Finally, to the extent that collective bargaining agreements concluded in individual enterprises reflected the prospects of each enterprise, aggregate wage trends would better reflect the capacity to pay of the economy as a whole.

However, the benefits of decentralised bargaining will not flow automatically, nor is decentralisation sufficient to ensure the better performance of collective bargaining. Although strains have appeared, encompassing bargaining structures have allowed unions and employers to develop and act on a broader view of their responsibilities and to come to agreement on aggregate wage levels, and have taken into account countries' capacity to pay; both theoretical analysis[111] and the postwar history of industrial relations does not support the inference that more decentralised systems always function better. Thus, the experience of the United Kingdom until recent years, and of Italy in the late

1960s and 1970s, highlights the damage which can be wreaked by narrow and self-serving pockets of power in fragmented systems of bargaining.

Strengthened employer solidarity could contribute to more balanced outcomes from decentralised collective bargaining. Thus, in economies where unionisation levels are high – exceeding 40 per cent or more of the labour force – the attainment of reasonable economic outcomes over long periods of time depends not only on the ability of unions to take a broad view of their responsibilities but also on the degree of employer solidarity, i.e. on employers' capacity to establish a reputation as united and tough bargainers, willing to bear the costs of resisting unreasonable demands[112]. Nonetheless, it must be recognised that employer solidarity is most likely to operate when bargaining is highly centralised; and that decentralised bargainers, if they are not subject to the restraining influence of competition from a non-union sector or from imports, can find themselves drawn into a spiral of unsustainable and inflationary outcomes.

Equally, decentralised bargaining in the United States, by imposing a broad range of constraints on employers, has narrowed the scope for reorganising production processes. Thus, flexible enterprise-level bargaining would need to embody more developed procedures for joint consultation, so that management and employee representatives can adapt work practices and recruitment procedures to implement technical advances and raise productivity growth on a mutually acceptable basis. Such procedures should permit both the "numerical" flexibility of a firm's work-force, i.e. the ease with which labour can be recruited and discharged, and its "functional" flexibility – the degree to which human resources can be redeployed within the firm – to be brought more closely into line with the realities of changing technologies and globally competitive markets.

A number of other institutional developments are therefore needed to underpin better labour market functioning against a background of evolution towards decentralised enterprise bargaining – but they are also of relevance to improving industrial relations more generally.

The first, and one in which governments play a central role, is to ensure that collective bargaining occurs in the context of a *legal framework* – a "constitution" – which sets down implementable rules of the game and reduces the uncertainties and risks bearing on each of the parties. The importance of the legal framework becomes all the greater as bargaining is decentralised, for two reasons: the internal controls which limit disputes in encompassing systems – most notably the fear of the high costs of a breakdown that are perceived by both highly centralised unions and employers' associations – will operate less effectively as these systems shift to decentralisation; and the large number of bargaining situations inherent in decentralised bargaining makes the gains in transaction costs achievable by standard-izing the procedures to be followed even greater than they would otherwise be.

It is striking in this respect that collective bargaining has proved least effective as a means of avoiding industrial conflict in the countries where relatively decentralised bargaining coexists with a largely informal, or poorly elaborated, system of labour law – most notably the United Kingdom, France and Italy. In each of these countries, considerable progress has been made in recent years; but the changes are still short of comprehensive reform[113]. In particular, it can be argued that the continued exemption in each of these countries of a broad range of industrial disputes from liability for civil damages not only increases strike frequency but also reduces the value of collective agreements to both workers and employers. Notably but not solely in the United Kingdom, the legal protection granted for strike action taken during "disputes of right", i.e. differences over the interpretation of existing collective agreements, has encouraged attempts to alter the terms of agreements during their lifetime, often at a level of bargaining different from that where agreement was originally reached; and this – together with the lack of effective vertical control within unions and employers' associations – has severely limited the effectiveness of collective agreements in providing a stable context for corporate planning.

The establishment of more suitable legal frameworks is not simply a matter of a government's prescribing laws. The framework must have broad support within society if it is to remain in place and function effectively. This may require moving by stages. Thus, efforts in the United Kingdom to progress in this direction suffered a major setback when comprehensive legislation under the Industrial Relations Act of 1971 met widespread resistance in implementation and was ultimately repealed – though more recent efforts have been considerably more effective. The need for labour legislation to have broad support could be further illustrated by examples from almost every country.

Second, the effectiveness of the legal framework in promoting harmonious industrial relations also depends on the *incentives* facing workers and managers. Economically and socially desirable outcomes can hardly be expected if unions and employers – be it on the shop-floor or in the negotiating process – perceive their relations as a basically "zero-sum" game, in which the one's gain is merely the other's loss. Realisation of the interdependences of their interests and a recognition of the interests of the unemployed are clearly factors in the performance of labour market institutions; but this perception is most easily lost when bargaining is fragmented or decentralised, introducing a "prisoner's dilemma" into wage negotiations. In practice it may be extremely difficult to alter the incentives bearing on the system of collective bargaining so as to correct this inherent flaw of decentralised structures. Hence in small, relatively heterogeneous labour markets where the importance of external competitiveness effectively constrains wage bargaining, it may prove possible and desirable to resolve the tensions within encompassing bargaining structures and retain their advantages within coherent systems of collective bargaining. Elsewhere, several approaches could be considered to enhance the functioning of more decentralised bargaining structures.

Profit-sharing is one approach to making more tangible the interdependences of interest between employees and their firms and between individual employment units and the macroeconomy. It has recently been argued[114] that profit-sharing could eliminate unemployment by enhancing the incentives of firms to take on additional workers, because part of the cost of hiring would be absorbed by the pool of profits shared among workers. Even setting aside such strong claims, profit-sharing could provide an element of wage flexibility in response to external shocks, thus reducing labour shedding. In addition, it has long been thought that if employees shared in their firm's profits they would be less resistant to productivity-enhancing innovations and would welcome (possibly even initiate) corporate decisions aimed at increasing competitiveness[115].

Though appealing in the abstract, practical experience with profit-sharing plans is mixed[116]. This is partly because relative interest in profit-sharing is too often looked at narrowly: in particular, employers tend to favour it only when profits are low, while union leaderships often view it as a threat to collective bargaining. However, two more fundamental problems are also involved. First, for the individual employee, the relation between his or her individual decisions and corporate profitability is extremely weak, particularly in a large firm, so that the incentive effects of profit-sharing on work effort are frequently minor. Second, profit-sharing may significantly complicate rather than simplify collective bargaining: the profit-sharing formulas which emerge from collective bargaining are typically highly complex and inflexible. Profit-sharing arrangements can, of course, be introduced outside the framework of collective bargaining and thus, its effectiveness in such a context raises questions which presently available data are insufficient to answer.

These arguments suggest that profit-sharing is likely to prove most successful when several highly specific conditions are met: workers have other strong motivational reasons for maximising work effort; and collective bargaining is either insignificant, largely non-adversarial and/or employer dominated. These conditions are clearly more generally met in Japan than elsewhere in the OECD area; but even in the case of Japan it is questionable whether, taken on its own, profit-sharing has been as distinctive a feature of industrial relations as some of its advocates claim[117].

"*Productivity bargaining*" is another approach to improving the incentive structure of collective bargaining. In productivity bargaining, improvements in pay and conditions are traded off against changes in work practices which will increase productivity; the link between earnings and performance is typically made at the level of the individual plant or even smaller work unit, rather than at that of the company as a whole (as occurs in profit-sharing).

Productivity bargaining first became widespread in the mid- to late 1960s, originally in the United Kingdom, partly as a reaction to the pervasiveness of restrictive work practices, but also because it was one of the few avenues for raising wages at a rate exceeding the targets set down by the incomes policies then in effect. It is not clear that productivity bargaining has, in and of itself, brought about significant improvements in the functioning of industrial relations[118]. Some of the most obvious drawbacks in this respect are macroeconomic: the widespread acceptance of productivity bargaining makes it difficult to alter obsolete work practices without increasing compensation, even when such increases are not justified by labour market conditions; more generally, it discourages the passing on to consumers of productivity gains and may – through "comparability" claims – impart an inflationary dynamic to wage negotiations. But even from the point of view of the individual firm its results are not entirely satisfactory: it reinforces the narrowly economic and largely adversarial perceptions of employment relations; and it limits the scope for improving work practices in periods of financial restraint when it would be difficult to pay higher wages. Nonetheless, recent experience with "concession bargaining" suggests that needed changes in work practices may be secured through collective bargaining when the viability of entire plants or companies is at stake.

In short, there are no simple formulas which can reconcile the social and microeconomic functions of collective bargaining with its macroeconomic responsibilities. This makes it all the more essential that collective bargainers be exposed to signals that can guide them towards economically desirable outcomes and help correct departures from efficient and sustainable behaviour. It is, in other words, desirable that the system of industrial relations be subject to *constraints* that enhance its self-correcting capabilities.

Competition in product markets has an essential role to play in this respect. Experience and analysis confirm that distortions in labour markets become most pervasive and resistant to correction when employers are sheltered from the discipline of competitive markets: thus, employment practices in regulated industries have frequently served to transfer to employees the monopoly rents arising from restraints on competition[119]; and trade restrictions have allowed protected industries to maintain wage levels and work practices inconsistent with an efficient allocation of resources, most visibly in steel and automobiles[120].

More generally, competition in product markets is partly an indirect form of competition between labour markets; and when for a particular country, wages in an industry have been "taken out of competition" (in

Webbs' celebrated description of the function of collective bargaining in an earlier era), the consequences of labour market behaviour will in the first instance be felt through changes in international market share. How effective these can be in disciplining collective bargaining depends *inter alia* on the size of an economy and the extent of its reliance on international trade; but the impacts can be presumed to be weak in the largest economies as well as on the non-traded goods sectors more generally. It is in these cases that *competition in factor markets* becomes of greatest significance; and it is difficult in this respect to deny that the existence of a sizeable non-union sector in an environment of relatively competitive markets contributed to the adjustment process in the United States and, to a lesser extent, in Japan. The reform of regulations which limit flexibility in labour markets, notably in the face of external shocks, can make an important contribution in this regard.

B. Bargaining in the public sector

Special problems arise with respect to collective bargaining in the public sector. But the priorities are similar to those in the private sector: clarifying the legal framework, improving incentives and enhancing external constraints.

The pressures coming from the growing numbers in public employment have been accentuated by a fairly widespread rise in public sector unionisation[121]. Governments, regardless of their relation to the broader issues of industrial relations, are increasingly drawn into collective bargaining through their role as very major employers; at the same time, governments have found this role increasingly uncomfortable, as they have sought to reconcile the search for equitable and broadly acceptable public employment practices with their broader responsibilities for fiscal restraint and for promoting wage moderation.

The problems of public sector bargaining are partly structural. On the one hand, public employees have a considerable degree of monopoly power: they enjoy uniquely high levels of employment protection; their products are not generally exposed to competition, whether sold in markets or provided as public goods; their employer is not subject to a traditional budget constraint, or at least is faced with one much looser than that bearing on the private sector; and there is great scope for altering the results of bargaining through political intervention. But at the same time, the public sector as an employer is also relatively powerful: the legal constraints on public sector bargaining are generally much tighter than those applicable in the private sector; the government is the sole or principal employer of significant occupational groups, e.g. teachers and, in most countries, nurses; and traditionally there have been strong cultural and ideological pressures against industrial militancy among public employees. These factors have tended to roughly offset each other; but this balance has become increasingly difficult to maintain, partly because the size of the public sector itself has grown and partly because economic circumstances have become less favourable. The result has been rising industrial conflict in the public sector, most markedly in Scandinavia but also elsewhere.

Efficient dispute settlement procedures are one key to stable public sector labour relations. The practice of compulsory arbitration and conciliation is already well established in the public sector. In recent years there have been significant innovations in this respect, of which the most interesting is "final offer arbitration" (in which the arbitrator is required to choose between the final offers made by the parties to a dispute with no modification of those offers being allowed); and the evidence, though limited, suggests that these innovative procedures operate reasonably well[122]. Nonetheless, faced with budgetary constraints, governments have in some cases sought to modify the outcomes of arbitration and conciliation; and this may adversely affect the longer-term credibility of the arbitration process as a whole. It would be preferable for governments to accept arbitration-determined wage scales – but to vary public sector employment levels (rather than compensation) in line with pre-announced cash limits, thus altering the incentives their employees have to press excessive wage demands.

Ultimately, this approach implies that the level of provision of public services is made dependent on costs. Of fundamental importance in this regard is budgetary discipline. The credibility of government as a disciplined employer will also be strengthened to the extent that it is able and willing to draw on outside sources to supply services, should labour costs in the public sector rise relative to productivity. In this sense, greater competition in, or recourse to, the "contracting out" of public services may provide an essential check on public sector pay demands. This clearly implies an increase in the uncertainties and constraints bearing on public employees; but it also entails an obligation on governments to adjust more readily the overall remuneration to providers of services (taking into account broader differences in the conditions of service) to the levels prevailing in the next most efficient source of supply.

C. Attitudes and responsibilities

Labour market institutions are shaped not only by national history and aspirations but by the economic circumstances of their time. The changes now under way in collective bargaining reflect a response, however partial, to the pressures from exposure to external shocks, the realities of global competition and the evolving role of the public sector. Whether institutions emerge that function better will depend on community understanding of the scope and limits of collective bargaining.

The critical factor in this respect is a realistic perception of what labour market institutions can and cannot do.

To begin with, income which does not exist cannot be redistributed; so that when external shocks reduce the community's real income, the only alternatives to reducing the average real compensation of employers are to curtail investment (hence eroding competitiveness and long-term growth) or to allow unemployment to rise (thus reducing the wage bill in total) or both.

Second, labour market institutions cannot costlessly correct the differences in income which arise from disparities in education, skill and motivation. There is no reason to believe that relative earnings solely reflect accurate economic valuations of the opportunity cost of labour – and it would be difficult to deny that vast distortions in the structure of pay arise from the persistence of restrictions on entry into many occupations, notably the professions. But the broad pattern of earnings, notably in industry, does appear consistent with the allocative and "screening" functions of relative pay[123]. It follows that the burden of achieving a narrower spread in earnings must primarily rest with the system of education, training and retraining; and the evidence surveyed above suggests that attempts to narrow disparities through government regulation or collective bargaining (rather than through more equal opportunity) may actually increase inequality by forcing those with few skills into long-term unemployment.

Finally, it is clear that no firm can compete or public sector institution survive if it cannot respond to rapidly shifting conditions of demand and supply. The growing intensity of competition for world markets makes this need all the more pressing; and the changes now under way in production technology create the potential for greater flexibility in products and processes than could be achieved in the past. These imperatives may conflict with unions' traditional emphasis in some countries on "job control"; but the industrial relations system hardly has the option of preventing them from occurring.

In a market economy, open to international competition, these trends can impose themselves even against the will of individual unions or employers. But it is obvious that the costs of change are minimised and the opportunities can be seized only if a measure of understanding and consensus can be obtained. This is largely in the self-interest of unions and employers, and the primary responsibility for developing such an under-standing must rest with them. Consultative procedures at firm and industry level have a clear role to play in ensuring that employees are aware of changing constraints and opportunities and that the legitimate concerns they may express are taken into account; and the empirical evidence suggests that such procedures contribute both to greater productivity on the shop floor and to better collective bargaining outcomes[124].

Governments too have a responsibility for improving community understanding of economic circumstances and their consequences. The primary role of macroeconomic policy in this respect is to set a clear and predictable medium-term framework for the growth of nominal incomes – and it has been emphasized above that the failure of many governments to do so contributed to the deterioration in economic performance in the period immediately following the first oil shock. However, as the Japanese experience strikingly demonstrates[125], government involvement in ongoing consultation at a national level with unions and employers' associations can complement a medium-term orientation of economic policy, even in collective bargaining structures which are decentralised and where co-ordination among unions is relatively loose. Yet the history of consultative mechanisms shows that improved understanding can do little if the incentives and constraints bearing on the system of industrial relations are not such as to promote adjustment[126].

Diverse as it doubtless is, the experience of the last decade demonstrates that good labour market performance has been most easily achieved and sustained when the institutions of collective bargaining are subject to internal and external controls which limit the scope for error and correct it rapidly when it occurs. In present economic circumstances, enhancing these self-correcting capabilities must primarily entail a greater degree of competitive control in product and labour markets, but in the context of a legal framework which sets down clear and enforceable "rules of the game". The persistence of high unemployment makes reform in this direction all the more important, notably in the countries where the industrial relations system has clearly found it most difficult to respond to change. But the need for greater responsiveness in labour market institutions is not solely theirs – it is general to a world which is inherently complex and uncertain, and which must therefore rely on more decentralised and hence more pluralistic decision-making to steer it to better outcomes.

NOTES AND REFERENCES

1. In mid-1936, the unemployment rate for an aggregate of fifteen OECD countries – excluding (because of unavailability of data) Japan, Spain, Portugal, Greece, Turkey, Ireland and New Zealand – was 7.8 per cent (calculated from Maddison, A., *Phases of Capitalist Development*, Oxford University Press, 1982, Tables C.5 and C.70); in mid-1986, it was 8.8 per cent.

2. The change in strike incidence was particularly marked in Sweden which, in the inter-war period, had been the most strike-prone country in Europe. As regards countries with multi-level bargaining systems, a major difference should be noted between France and Italy on the one hand and the United Kingdom on the other. In France and Italy (at least until 1968-69), strikes have largely been political demonstrations aimed at putting pressure on the government; the postwar increase in strike incidence was mainly due to a growing frequency of very short stoppages involving large numbers of people. By contrast, in the United Kingdom, the size of stoppages (in terms of the number of strikers participating in the average stoppage) has declined, as has their duration; the increase in strike incidence has been largely due to a rise in the number of "unofficial" stoppages, involving short, sharp action at individual plants. Finally, strike patterns in North America have been remarkably stable (correcting for cyclical fluctuations in the economy) and have had a distinctive shape: average duration – about fifteen days – has been very high (compared to other OECD countries); the average stoppage has involved some 500 workers; but at five to six strikes per annum for each 100 000 in the non-agricultural labour force, the strike frequency has been moderate to low. See especially Shorter, E. and Tilly, C., *Strikes in France, 1830-1968*, Cambridge University Press, 1974, Chapter 12, "French Strikes in International Perspective"; Walsh, T., *Strikes in Europe and the United States*, Frances Pinter, London, 1983.

3. Regression estimates by the Secretariat find (for a sample of the OECD countries over the period 1969-1974) a negative but not statistically significant relation between strike incidence (measured in terms of annual days lost per 100 000 in the labour force) and productivity growth in manufacturing, correcting for other major factors affecting productivity trends. The disproportionate strike proneness of larger establishments in the United Kingdom may have accentuated the relation in that country. See Prais, S.J., "The Strike-Proneness of Large Plants in Britain", *Journal of the Royal Statistical Society*, 1978, Vol. 141, Part 3, pp. 368-84. See also Caves, R.E., "Productivity Differences Among Industries" in Caves, R.E. and Kranz, L.B. (eds.), *Britain's Economic Performance*, The Brookings Institution, Washington D.C., 1980, pp. 160-174.

4. Incomes policies can be described as "nominal" if their primary goal is to act on nominal wages rather than to seek shifts in the distribution of income. European experience with incomes policies in this period is surveyed in Braun, A.R., *IMF Staff Paper*, March 1975, Vol. 23, No. 1; Ulman, L. and Flanagan, R.J., *Wage Restraint*, University of California Press, Berkeley, 1971.

5. See especially Soskice, D., "Strike Waves and Wage Explosions, 1968-1970: An Economic Interpretation" in Crouch, C. and Pizzorno, A. (eds.), *The Resurgence of Class Conflict in Western Europe Since 1968*, Vol. 2, Holmes and Meier, New York, 1978.

6. It is worth noting that the sharply higher levels of industrial conflict attained in 1968-1971 persisted in most European countries until the late 1970s. It was only after the second oil shock that strike levels reverted roughly to their pre-1969 levels.

7. McKee, M. *et al.*, "Marginal Tax Rates on the Use of Labour and Capital in OECD Countries", *OECD Economic Studies*, Autumn 1986, No. 7, Paris.

8. This was also true for governments, as the McCracken Report noted: "Perhaps, in retrospect, policy making in the period from 1969 to 1971 was too much affected in some countries by the sense of unease to which the discord in labour markets – and in the streets – had given rise. But it is important not to underestimate the influences that this sense of unease may have had on those who held the responsibility for economic policy as unemployment began to rise." (McCracken, P. *et al.*, *Towards Full Employment and Price Stability*, OECD, Paris, 1977, p. 52).

9. The role of "customer" pricing, implicit contracts and their macroeconomic consequences are explored in Okun, A., *Prices and Quantities: A Macroeconomic Analysis*, The Brookings Institution, Washington D.C., 1981 (see especially pp. 104-5 on union wage setting).

10. This term, though it had been used in earlier research reports by the same project, is generally associated with Kerr, C. *et al.*, *Industrialism and Industrial Man*, Harvard University Press, 1960, especially pp. 41-42. Surveying the effects of rapid growth on the pattern of industrial relations, Clark Kerr and his associates concluded (p. 41) that "A network of relationships between managers and the managed and a complex of substantive rules is required to make the industrial system operative at the work place, quite apart from the issues concerned with who formulates or promulgates these rules. At any one time, the rights and duties of workers and of managers, indeed of all those in the hierarchy, must be established and understood by all those involved in the hierarchy...The industrial system (therefore) creates an elaborate 'government' at the work place and work community."

11. See especially Freeman and Medoff in *The Public Interest*, Autumn 1979; for the formulation in terms of idiosyncratic investment and the structure of property rights, Salais, R., Baverez, N. and Reynaud, B., *L'invention du chômage*, PUF, Paris, 1986.

12. See the work on micro labour market policies done by the OECD Department of Economics and Statistics.

13. See especially Clegg, H., *Trade Unionism Under Collective Bargaining. A Theory Based on Comparison of Six Countries*, Basil Blackwell, Oxford, 1976; and the important study by Tarantelli, E., *Economia politica del lavoro*, UTET, Turin, 1986.

14. Germany has a somewhat more decentralised and less encompassing system of industrial relations than Austria, Sweden or Norway, but it shares the other features of these countries. See for example, Streeck, W., "Neo-Corporatist Industrial Relations and the Economic Crisis in West Germany" in Goldthorpe, J. (ed.), *Order and Conflict in Contemporary Capitalism*, Clarendon Press, Oxford, 1985, pp. 291-314. Switzerland is a considerably more complicated case, given the weakness of trade union organisations; a strong and largely convincing argument for including it in this group (as a one-sided variant of neo-corporatism) is made in Katzenstein, P.J., *Corporatism and Change*, Cornell University Press, Ithaca, 1985. Though this argument may be valid as a description of the functioning of Swiss society, the Swiss system of industrial relations also has many of the features of Japanese "enterprise unionism".

15. Thus, Flanagan, R.J. *et al.* note that while the structure of wage negotiations in Austria is "...by European standards decentralised", trade unions have placed great emphasis on integrating shop stewards into formal organisational structures (Flanagan, R.J. *et al.*, *Unionism, Economic Stabilisation and Incomes Policies: European Experience*, The Brookings Institution, Washington D.C., 1983, p. 80). On vertical or horizontal integration in systems of collective bargaining, see more generally, Lehmbruch, G., "Concertation and the Structure of Corporatist Networks" in Goldthorpe, J. (ed.), *Order and Conflict in Contemporary Capitalism*, *op. cit.* in Note 14.

16. The analysis of Switzerland and Austria in Katzenstein, P.J., *Small States in World Markets*, Cornell University Press, Ithaca, 1985, is illuminating in this respect: "An analysis of the policy networks linking interest groups with state bureaucracies...suggests that the boundary demarcating state and society is virtually impossible to identify. Producer groups and state bureaucracies are inextricably linked through institutions...In both countries the state is relatively passive and lacks autonomy from the major producer groups. (But) the political limitations under which both state bureaucracies operate are compensated for by the elaborate search for consensus both within and between peak associations." (p. 126)

17. Thus, in Sweden, public employment as a share of the work-force increased from 15 per cent in 1951 to 38 per cent in 1981; in the United States, it remained virtually constant. In 1980, nearly 90 per cent of public sector employees in Sweden were unionised, compared to 82 per cent of private sector employees (Rose, R. *et al.*, *Public Employment in Western Nations*, Cambridge University Press, 1985, p. 40, Table 1.16).

18. Flanagan, R.J. *et al.*, *op. cit.* in Note 15, p. 329.

19. "Solidaristic" wage policies played little role in Austria (of which it has been said that "...the durability of the Austrian 'social partnership' may rest in part on its lack of emphasis on redistributional objectives..." – Flanagan, R.J. *et al.*, *op. cit.* in Note 15, p. 81) and in Germany. Equally, at least since the breakdown of "concerted action" government has not been involved in directly influencing collective bargaining outcomes in Germany.

20. *Ibid.*, pp. 660-664.

21. *OECD Economic Surveys – Norway*, Paris, 1975, 1976, 1977 and 1979.

22. *Ibid.*, 1975, p. 18.

23. Flanagan, R.J. *et al.*, *op. cit.* in Note 15, p. 329.

24. *Ibid.*, p. 357.

25. Perlman, S., *A Theory of the Labor Movement*, Macmillan, New York, 1928, p. 278. Perlman provides probably the clearest and most influential statement of the philosophy of American unionism, which he expressed as follows: "...the ideology of the AFL...was based on a consciousness of limited job opportunities – a situation which required that the individual...should not be permitted to occupy any job opportunity except on the condition of observing the 'common rule' laid down by his union. The safest way to ensure this group control over opportunity...was for the union, without displacing the employer as the owner of his business and risk taker, to become the virtual owner and administrator of the jobs. Where such an outright 'ownership' of the jobs was impossible, the union would seek, by collective bargaining with the employers, to establish 'rights' in the jobs, both for the individual and for the whole group, by incorporating in the trade agreement, regulations applying to overtime, to the 'equal turn', to priority and seniority in employment..." (pp. 198-199).

26. See Garbarino, J. in *Industrial Relations*, Fall 1985, p. 280.

27. Notably in the United States, the average duration of collective agreements increased markedly up to the 1980s and then declined slightly. Thus in 1956, only 22 per cent of major contracts lasted three years or more; by 1973, this had risen to 73 per cent, remaining at that level to 1980; it then declined to 50 per cent in 1984. The length of United States contracts contrasts with the situation elsewhere: except in Austria and Scandinavia, where many contracts last two years, collective agreements in most other countries last one year. See Cullen in *International Labor Review*, May-June 1985, Vol. 124, No. 3; and, for an attempted explanation, Gray in *Journal of Political Economics*, February 1978.

28. United States law is probably unique in setting down a duty of "fair representation" whereby unions which have secured exclusive representation in a bargaining unit may be sued by individual workers who believe that their interests have not been fairly represented. The effects of United States labour laws on union organisation are examined in Freeman, R.B., "Why are Unions Faring Poorly in NLRB Representation Elections?" in Kochan, T. (ed.), *Challenge and Choices Facing American Labor*, MIT Press, Cambridge, Mass., 1985, pp. 45-65; Cooke, W.N., *Union Organizing and Public Policy*, Upjohn Institute for Employment Research, Kalamazoo, Michigan.

29. See for example, Phelps Brown, H., *The Origins of Trade Union Power*, Oxford University Press, pp. 207-211.

30. See especially Garbarino, J. in *Industrial Relations*, Winter 1984, Vol. 23, No. 1, who highlights the extent to which non-unionised firms in the United States do in fact operate employee relations through complex and highly organised "webs of rules"; these in many respects emulate the elaborate grievance procedures found in the unionised sector. See also Faulkes, F.K., "Large Non-Unionised Employers" in Stieber, J. *et al.*, *US Industrial Relations, 1950-1980: A Critical Assessment*, Industrial Relations Research Association, Madison, Wisconsin, 1981, pp. 128-157.

31. *OECD Economic Surveys – United States*, Paris, 1985.

32. The proportion of United States workers under major union contracts covered by COLA clauses increased from 26 per cent in 1970 to 49 per cent in 1976 and has remained at that level until now. Of the total wage increases taking place each year under all major union contracts, both newly and previously negotiated, the proportion resulting from COLA clauses averaged 32 per cent in the high inflation years 1979-81 and then declined to 18 per cent in 1982-83. See Cullen, *art. cit.* in Note 27, p. 304.

33. On average, some 10 per cent of tentative bargaining agreements have been rejected in recent years – a slight decline relative to earlier periods.

34. Quit rates are typically lower in union than in non-union plants, presumably at least partly because workers in the former plants consider themselves as having a more long-term "commitment" type relation to their employer. See Freeman in *Quarterly Journal of Economics*, June 1980, pp. 643-673.

35. Kosters, M.H. and Ross, M.N., *Union/Non-Union Wage Differentials: Their Magnitude and Trends*, American Enterprise Institute, Washington D.C., 1985.

36. Krueger, A.B. and Summers, C.H., *Reflections on the Inter-Industry Wage Structure*, NBER Working Paper No. 1968, 1986.

37. *OECD Employment Outlook*, Paris, 1985, p. 77.

38. Cullen, *art. cit.* in Note 27; Jacoby in *Industrial Labor Relations Review*, October 1983; Derber, M., "Are We in a New Stage?", *Proceedings, 35th Annual Meeting of Industrial Relations Research Association*, Madison, Wisconsin, 1983; Reuben, G., "The Labor Management Scene in 1986", *Monthly Labor Review*, January 1987, pp. 37-48.

39. See Dore, R., *British Factory-Japanese Factory: Origins of National Diversity in Industrial Relations*, University of California Press, Berkeley, 1973; Levine, S.B., "Labor Markets and Collective Bargaining in Japan" in Lockwood, W. (ed.), *The State and Economic Development in Japan*, Princeton University Press, 1965; OECD, *The Development of Industrial Relations Systems – Some Implications of Japanese Experience*, Paris, 1977; Koshiro, K., "Development of Collective Bargaining in Postwar Japan" in Shirai, T. (ed.), *Contemporary Industrial Relations in Japan*, University of Wisconsin Press, Madison, 1983.

40. In 1977, 71 per cent of establishments, covering 82 per cent of all employees, had standing committees for labour-management consultation: 51 per cent of enterprise unions participated in such consultation bodies. Though "...the boundary between joint consultation and collective bargaining is generally indistinct" (Shirai, T., "Recent Trends in Collective Bargaining in Japan", *International Labor Review*, May-June 1984, Vol. 123, No. 3, p. 313), the latter gives rise to enforceable and reasonably specific agreements, while the former does not.

41. As late as 1959, short-term employees accounted for a fifth of the labour force in larger establishments: see Taira, K., *Economic Development and the Labour Market in Japan*, Columbia University Press, New York, 1970, pp. 180-181.

42. See Cook, A.H., *Japanese Trade Unionism*, Cornell University Press, Ithaca, 1968, pp. 97-98.

43. Postwar Japanese unions have not made a rigid distinction between representation of different levels of a company's labour force: in larger companies, most recruits into managerial positions have tended to join the enterprise union; and in the formative years of enterprise unionism, management staff have often played an initiating role. It is now not uncommon for the most senior union officials in larger enterprises to obtain high-level management positions when they retire.

44. See Tachibanki, T., "Labor Mobility and Job Tenure" in Aoki, M. (ed.), *The Economic Analysis of the Japanese Firm*, North Holland, Amsterdam, 1984, who estimates that lifetime employment applies to no more than 10 per cent of the non-public sector labour force, mostly at higher levels of educational attainment.

45. It is worth noting that the sociological literature has tended to criticise the paternalism-lifetime commitment model classically used to characterise the Japanese firm; thus, a number of studies suggest that the hypothesised relationship between the different features of the model, e.g. "familistic management" and seniority pay structures, cannot be found in the data. See especially Marsh, R.M. and Mannar, H., *Modernization and the Japanese Factory*, Princeton University Press, 1976.

46. Wages as set through employment contracts account for only two-thirds of total cash earnings for the average employee, with overtime and bonuses making up the rest. In theory, bonuses depend on profitability, but in practice they are downwardly rigid (in nominal terms); nonetheless, *increases* in profitability do lead to increases in bonus payments.

47. Thus, in 1975, the Ministry of Labour forecast that an increase in nominal wages would inevitably lead to a large rise in unemployment; the *Nikkeiren* emphasized that this would entail a fall in the number of "permanent" jobs. In fact, trade union wage requests in the year were less than half the previous year's level.

48. *OECD Economic Studies*, Spring 1986, No. 6, Paris.

49. "...the shape of British trade unionism in general might be described as one in which open, expansionist unions have spread around islands of stable closed unionism." (Turner, H.A., *Trade Union Growth Structure and Policy*, Allen & Unwin, London, 1962, p. 244.)

50. Thompson, A.W., "Industrial Relations in Britain During the Period of the Recession, 1974-1978" in Tarantelli, E. and Wilke, G. (eds.), *The Management of Industrial Conflict in the Recession of the 1970s*, Alphen Van Der Rijn, Sijthoff, 1981. The incidence of fragmented unionism in the United Kingdom also reflects the lack of provision for sole representation at the workplace (as mandated by law, for example, in the United States).

51. Thus, in the United Kingdom in the early 1980s there was one full-time union official per 4 000 members; the ratio was even lower in France and Italy (Tarantelli, E., *op. cit.* in Note 13, p. 360). Again in the United Kingdom, full-time shop stewards outnumber union officials in the private sector by two to one (Roberts in *International Labor Review*, May-June 1984, Vol. 123, No. 3, p. 296). Comparable figures for Italy are not available but would certainly be even higher.

52. See especially Phelps Brown, H., *op. cit.* in Note 29.

53. See Giugni, G. in *International Labor Review*, April 1965, pp. 273-291; October 1971, pp. 307-328; October 1984, pp. 599-614. The law has also generally served to legitimate *ex post* the outcome of collective bargaining; the *Statuto dei Lavoratori* is a case in point.

54. As Delorme, R. and André, C. (*L'état et l'économie*, Editions du Seuil, Paris, 1983, p. 479) put it, both employees and employers have preferred to see these problems as primarily political rather than tractable at the level of the firm or industry. This has been consistent with the mainly political strategy pursued by the CGT and has allowed employers to circumscribe the degree of union involvement in the day-to-day running of labour relations at plant and firm level. However, it has entailed three major problems (see Reynaud, J.D., *Les syndicats, les patrons et l'état*, les Editions Ouvrières, Paris, 1978): first, a significant grey area has existed between what is negotiable and what is subject to management prerogative; second, the distinction between "negotiating" and "informing" has been vague; third, the French collective agreement bears little relation to a contract. For more recent trends, see Caire, G., "Recent Trends in Collective Bargaining in France", *International Labor Review*, November-December 1984, Vol. 123, No. 6, pp. 723-741.

55. Phelps Brown, H., *op. cit.* in Note 29, p. 209.

56. Belgium and the Netherlands were partial exceptions in this regard, with broadly restrictive policies being in effect in 1974-75.

57. Modigliani, F. and Tarantelli, E., "Market Forces, Trade Union Action and the Phillips Curve in Italy", *BNL Quarterly Review*, March 1977, pp. 3-37.

58. Tarantelli, E., *op. cit.* in Note 13, p. 369.

59. Flanagan, R.J. *et al.*, *op. cit.* in Note 15, p. 264.

60. Malinvaud, E., "Les causes de la montée du chômage en France", *Revue Française d'Economie*, 1986, No. 1; Flanagan, R.J. *et al.*, *op. cit.* in Note 15, p. 370.

61. In France, indexing basically operated through revision of the statutory minimum wage, the SMIC, rather than through comprehensive indexing in collective agreements.

62. Tarantelli, E., *op. cit.* in Note 13, p. 359.

63. *Ibid.*, pp. 370-374.

64. Layard, R.G. in *Economica – Supplement*, 1986, p. 5123, Figure 3(b).

65. Flanagan, R.J. *et al.*, *op. cit.* in Note 15, pp. 636-645.

66. Elliot and Fallick in *Economic Journal*, June 1979, pp. 377-84.

67. Flanagan, R.J. *et al.*, *op. cit.* in Note 15, p. 428, Table 7.7.

68. Oliba, M. in *Problèmes Economiques*, July 1986, pp. 3-10.

69. Gennard, J., "Job Security: Redundancy Arrangements and Practices in Selected OECD Countries", report to the OECD, September 1985.

70. On Italy, see Giugni, G. in *International Labor Review*, September-October 1984, Vol. 123, No. 5, pp. 599-614; on France, Caire, G., *art. cit.* in Note 54.

71. Gennard, J., *op. cit.* in Note 69, Appendix.

72. Walker, K.F., *Australian Industrial Relations Systems*, Harvard University Press, 1970.

73. This should not be taken to imply that significant change has not occurred. Thus, in Australia, the growth of the Building Workers Industrial Union (BWIU) and the Amalgamated Metalworkers (AMWSU) has involved considerable union amalgamation, largely (but not solely) on industrial grounds. But, as noted in the 1985 report of the Commission of Inquiry into Industrial Relations in Australia, chaired by Professor Keith Hancock, the structure of unionism remains highly fragmented. Employers' organisations have also been highly fragmented, no stable or dominant pattern of representation evolving over time. See Tsokhas, K., *A Class Apart? Businessmen and Australian Politics, 1960-1980*, Oxford University Press, Melbourne, 1984.

74. In his classic study, *Australia*, Sir Keith Hancock referred to restrictive immigration, compulsory arbitration and trade protection as the three "ring fences" cementing the Australian polity. An account of the relation between the rise of compulsory arbitration and the "new protection" can be found in Barnard, G., Butlin, N. and Pincus, J., *Government and Capitalism: Public and Private Choice in Australia, 1901-75*, Allen & Unwin, Sydney, 1982.

75. Until the mid-1960s, arbitration awards in Australia typically contained specific provisions prohibiting strike action during the lifetime of an agreement. These so-called "penal clauses" (whereby arbitration courts fined unions striking in breach of an agreement) were of at best mixed effectiveness, a large backlog of unpaid fines accumulating by the early 1960s. The system of "penal clauses" came to an end subsequent to a systematic campaign against it by the Victorian Tramways Union and the Amalgamated Metalworkers; action by these unions led to the jailing of a prominent union official, creating a situation which (coming in a particularly tight labour market) could have jeopardised the arbitration structure as a whole. The official was freed and the clauses subsequently disregarded. More generally, compulsory conciliation may itself have encouraged some strike action by unions as a means of ensuring that issues are brought into the

system; of course, it has also been common for strikes to occur when the courts have difficulty in defining a mutually acceptable agreement.

76. Hancock in Alexander (ed.), *State and Economy in Australia*, Oxford University Press, 1985, p. 248.

77. Gregory, R. in *Economica – Supplement, op. cit.* in Note 64.

78. See especially Howard, W.A., "Trade Unions and the Arbitration System" in Head, B.W. (ed.), *State and Economy in Australia*, Oxford University Press, 1983, pp. 238-251; Phelps Brown, H., *op. cit.* in Note 29, pp. 279-281.

79. Examples of work in this area include Artus, P., "Formation conjointe des prix et des salaires dans cinq grands pays industriels : peut-on comprendre les écarts entre les taux d'inflation ?", *Annales de l'INSEE*, January-March 1983, pp. 267-311; Englander, A.S. and Los, C.A., "Recovery Without Accelerating Inflation", *Quarterly Review*, Federal Reserve Bank of New York, Summer 1983, pp. 19-28; Grubb, D., Jackman, R. and Layard, R., "Wage Rigidity and Unemployment in OECD Countries", *European Economic Review*, March-April 1983, pp. 11-39; Modigliani, F. and Tarantelli, E., "Forze di mercato azione sindacale, e la Curve di Phillips in Italia", *Moneta e Credito*, June 1976; Santomero, A.M. and Seater, J.J., "The Inflation-Unemployment Trade-Off: A Critique of the Literature", *Journal of Economic Literature*, June 1978, pp. 499-544.

80. The results presented are based on an as yet unpublished update of earlier work presented in Coe, David T., "Nominal Wages, the NAIRU and Wage Flexibility", *OECD Economic Studies*, Autumn 1985, No. 5, Paris, pp. 87-126.

81. See for example, Blanchard, D.J. and Summers, L.H., *Hysteresis in Unemployment*, NBER Working Paper No. 2035, October 1986.

82. Kuznets, S., "Economic Growth and Income Inequality", *An Economic Review*, 1955, Vol. 45, No. 1, pp. 1-28; Williamson, J.G., *Did British Capitalism Breed Inequality?*, Allen & Unwin, Boston, 1985.

83. See especially Roberts, B.C., *National Wages Policy in War and Peace*, George Allen & Unwin, London, 1958; Lanzardo, L., [FIAT book, 1969].

84. Paci, M., *Mercato del lavoro e classi sociale in Italia*, il Mulino, 1973, Chapter 6; Okbaz, M., *Problèmes Economiques*, June 1986, No. 1977, p. 6, Graph 3.

85. Williamson, J.G., *op. cit.* in Note 82, p. 101.

86. See especially Williamson, J.G., "The Sources of American Inequality", *Review of Economic Studies*, 1976, Vol. 58, No. 4, pp. 387-397.

87. Phelps Brown, H., *The Inequality of Pay*, University of California Press, Berkeley, 1977, p. 280.

88. Krueger, A.B. and Summers, C.H., *art. cit.* in Note 36.

89. Jacobs, S.M., "Industrial Labor Mobility in Historical Perspective", *Industrial Relations*, 1983, Vol. 22, No. 2, pp. 261-282.

90. See for example, Chambart de Lauwe, P., *La vie quotidienne des familles ouvrières*, CNRS, Paris, 1956, especially Chapter 1.

91. Paci, M., *op. cit.* in Note 84: Chapters 2 and 5 provide data on comparative mobility of migrants and non-migrants.

92. See Cézard, M. and Rault, D., "La crise a freiné la mobilité sectorielle", *Economie et Statistique*, January 1986, pp. 41-62.

93. Keat, P.G., "Long-Run Change in Occupational Wage Structure, 1900-1956", *Journal of Political Economy*, 1960, Vol. 68, No. 6, pp. 584-600; OECD, *Wages and Labour Mobility*, Paris, 1965.

94. See for example, Meraud, J., *Productivité, croissance, emploi*, Rapport au Conseil Economique et Social, Paris, 1984.

95. This strategy is consistent with the view that unions seek to maintain the support of their median member which, under normal income distribution, makes wage compression strategies attractive.

96. Thus, studies for France find that blue-collar earnings adjust more rapidly to inflation than white-collar earnings, so that income gaps tend to narrow in periods of high inflation. Malinvaud, E., *op. cit.* in Note 60.

97. See OECD, *Flexibility in the Labour Market, op. cit.* in Table 3.6, pp. 67-68.

98. *OECD Employment Outlook*, Paris, 1986, study on non-wage labour costs.

99. Flanagan, R.J., "Labour Market Behaviour and European Economic Growth", paper prepared for the *Conference on Impediments to European Economic Growth*, 9th-10th October 1986, The Brookings Institution, Washington, D.C.

100. Saunders, C. and Marsden, D., *op. cit.* in Table 3.9, Chapter 7.

101. Buchelo, P., "Jobs and Workers", unpublished Ph.D. thesis, Harvard University, 1975; Wilkinson, F. (ed.), *The Dynamics of Labour Market Segmentation*, Academic Press, New York, 1981.

102. See the youth unemployment rates reported in *OECD Employment Outlook, op. cit.* in Note 98.

103. Blanchard, O.J. and Summers, L.H., *Hysteresis and the European Unemployment Problem*, NBER Working Paper No. 1950, June 1986.

104. Though see the paper by Burgess to the Brookings *Conference on Impediments to European Growth* (*cf.* Note 99).

105. Heller, J.L., "Emploi et chômage en mars 1985", *Economie et Statistique*, December 1985, No. 183, pp. 21-37.

106. CENSIS, *Dal sommerso al post-industriale*, Franco Angeli Editore, Milan, 1984.

107. The impact of labour market regulatory policies on the structure of employment by firm size is analysed in Lang, G. and Thélot, C., "Taille des établissements et effets de seuil", *Economie et Statistique*, 1985, pp. 3-16.

108. See Garbarino, J., "Symposium Introduction and Overview", *Industrial Relations*, 1985, Vol. 24, No. 3, pp. 289-294.

109. Rose, R. *et al.*, *op. cit.* in Note 17; Freeman, R.B., "Unionism Comes to the Public Sector", *Journal of Economic Literature*, March 1986, Vol. 34, pp. 41-86.

110. Lawrence, C. and Lawrence, R.L. called attention to the strategic option for unions of pushing up wages in declining industries in "Manufacturing Wage Dispersion: An End Game Interpretation", *Brookings Papers on Economic Activity*, 1985, No. 1, pp. 47-106.

111. See especially Johansen, L., "The Core as a Solution in Cooperative Game Theory", *Journal of Economic Behaviour and Organisation*, 1982, Vol. 3, pp. 1-37; and "The Bargaining Society and the Inefficiency of Bargaining", *Kyklos*, 1979, Vol. 32, No. 3, pp. 497-522.

112. Flanagan, R.J. *et al.*, *op. cit.* in Note 15, pp. 237-250.

113. Caire, G., *op. cit.* in Note 54, pp. 723-741; Treu, T., "Evolution récente du droit du travail en Italie", *Travail et Société*, January 1985, Vol. 10, No. 1, pp. 29-47; Lord Wedderburn, "Les nouvelles lois sur les relations professionnelles en Grande-Bretagne", *ibid.*, pp. 49-68.

114. Weitzman, M.C., *The Share Economy*, Harvard University Press, 1984.

115. This conception was popularised in the 1950s under the name of the "Scanlon Plan".

116. Lupton, T., *Payment Systems*, Penguin, 1974.

117. Though see Freeman, R. and Weitzman, M., *Bonuses and Employment in Japan*, NBER Working Paper No. 1878.

118. Brown, W. (ed.), *The Changing Contours of British Industrial Relations*, Oxford University Press, 1981.

119. Ehrenberg, R.G., *The Regulatory Process and Labor Earnings*, Academic Press, New York, 1979.

120. OECD, *Costs and Benefits of Protection*, Paris, 1985, Chapters 3, 5 and 7.

121. Rose, R. *et al.*, *op. cit.* in Note 17; Freeman, R.B., *art. cit.* in Note 109.

122. Freeman, *ibid.*, pp. 70-74; Sahenfelter, O. and Bloom, D., "Models of Arbitrator Behaviour: Theory and Evidence", *American Economic Review*, 1984, Vol. 74, No. 1, Chapter 10.

123. Phelps Brown, H., *The Inequality of Pay*, Oxford University Press, 1977, Chapter 10.

124. See for example, Faxén, K.O., "Disembodied Technical Progress: Does Employee Participation in Decision-Making Contribute to Change and Growth?", *American Economic Review*, 1978, Vol. 68, No. 2, pp. 131-148.

125. Shirai, T., *art. cit.* in Note 40, pp. 307-318, especially pp. 315-316.

126. A survey of experience in this respect can be found in OECD, *The Search for Consensus*, Paris, 1982.

Chapter 4

THE FINANCIAL SYSTEM AND THE FINANCING OF INDUSTRY

INTRODUCTION

Government policies in most OECD countries during the last decade have been aimed at modernising financial systems and markets. In part, this has meant adapting traditional policy approaches and regulations in financial markets to new technologies and changed competitive environments. These policies have also attempted to ensure that markets operate more efficiently and better meet the changed financial needs of each country's economy.

This chapter examines these two developments in OECD Member countries' financial policies. It assesses the effects these policies have already had, looks at options still confronting governments and discusses possible new areas for international and OECD co-operation.

The analysis is in four parts: Part I examines the major functions of financial markets, particularly their role in economic growth and industrial adjustment. Part II summarises the way new government policies have changed the development of financial markets over the past decade and details the new competitive conditions that have frequently emerged. Part III looks at the impact of these developments on structural adjustment initiatives and industrial strategies, while Part IV outlines the policy options still confronting governments, especially in the field of international co-operation.

I. THE ROLE OF FINANCIAL MARKETS IN ADVANCED ECONOMIES

In any market economy the financial sector plays a triple role:

i) It provides a *payments system* for commercial transactions;

ii) It provides a structure for *safeguarding savings*; and

iii) It operates as a vehicle for the *allocation of the economy's financial resources*, at a national and international level. Modern economies have made considerable progress in each of these areas. The financial sector has also acquired an increasingly sophisticated role in *monetary policy* implementation.

As the payments system has evolved, it has become increasingly intangible, shifting from cash to bank notes and then to cheques. More recently, the credit card and electronic fund transfer systems have further facilitated, speeded up and reduced the cost of payments operations[1]. Debit and credit transfers, and Eurocheques in Europe, have also facilitated international payments.

For the safeguarding of savings, deposit services available have expanded with the development of retail banking networks. These services have been diversified and adapted to suit the needs and requirements of different categories of savers. The proportion of the population with bank accounts has accordingly reached a very high level in most OECD countries[2].

However, the greatest progress from the point of view of macroeconomic growth and development has occurred in the allocation of the economy's financial resources. A number of poor financial decisions are unavoidably made in all advanced economies and these seemed to increase in the 1970s in certain areas (less developed country loans, farm loans, real-estate loans, etc.). Nevertheless, overall development in OECD capital markets increased the capabilities of the financial sector as regards financing structural change in industry.

The channelling of savings into the most profitable investment opportunities is, in general, a prerequisite of macroeconomic efficiency. In under developed financial markets, resources tend to be reinvested in activities from which they originated[3]. In an efficient financial system, funds are accumulated, investment risks diversified and investment opportunities compared and selected. Internationally integrated-capital markets promote such optimisation at the international level. Fulfilling this role, the financial system has played a central role in the successive waves of industrialisation and economic growth in OECD countries[4].

There are two components to the financial market's function in resource allocation, both important in the context of structural change. The first is the role of financial markets in determining the structure of production and economic activity – that is, their role in *allocative efficiency*. The second role of financial markets is to determine the efficiency of each line of production – their role in *technical efficiency*[5].

A. Financial markets and allocative efficiency

Financial markets collect household and company financial surpluses and reallocate them to households, firms and public institutions in need of funds. This financial flow has steadily been increasing in OECD countries, which reflects a remarkable degree of flexibility in the recycling of savings. Table 4.1 shows the total quantity of funds passing through the financial markets in relation to the total national wealth in seven OECD countries.

Table 4.1. **Funds redistributed by financial markets as a percentage of GNP by category of borrower (1985)**

Percentages

Country	Category of final borrower			
	Business sector	Household sector	Public sector	Total
United States	3.8	7.5	8.8	20.1
Japan	9.9	2.1	6.3	18.3
Germany	4.7	2.6	2.4	9.7
France	6.8	4.0	4.5	15.3
United Kingdom	3.0	7.1	2.9	13.0
Italy	9.1	0.9	16.6	26.6
Canada	4.9	4.8	9.3	19.0

Source: National accounting data, Bank for International Settlements.

Table 4.2. **Development of financial intermediation in 22 countries, 1977-1983**

Percentages

Country	Ratio financial assets held by residents[1] to Gross National Product		
	1977	1980	1983
OECD countries			
United States	227	222	213
Japan	205	256	304
Canada	188	253	232
Sweden	144	168	222
United Kingdom	155	163	209
Netherlands	150	166	205
Germany	143	153	186
France	115	139	136[2]
Spain	131	129	134
Portugal	84	129	162
Greece	71	72	79
Turkey	45	..	..
Newly industrialising countries			
Hong Kong	188	470	443
Singapore	210	305	336
Israel	222	342	329
Korea	71	108	110
Brazil	61	50	72
Argentina	34	56	..
Developing countries			
Bolivia	16	15	13
Indonesia	19	22	27
Kenya	53	64	63
Morocco	36	43	..

1. Bank deposits + financial securities.
2. 1982 data for bank deposits.
Source: International Finance Corporation, World Bank.

As this table indicates, a substantial share of business and household savings is reallocated to new uses via capital markets. The financial intermediaries – banks, insurance companies, pension funds, investment trusts – play a central role in the collection of these funds from depositors and their selective reallocation to investors.

The importance of financial intermediation is shown in Table 4.2 by comparing the financial assets and liabilities accumulated in several national economies. The table shows how the development of financial activity sets the OECD area apart from the less developed regions of the world. The Newly Industrialising Countries are a notable exception, since some of them are now as financially sophisticated as the most advanced OECD countries.

Ensuring that available funds are channelled into the most profitable branches of industry, businesses and investment projects is the central function of financial markets. By virtue of their capacity to *identify*, *assess* and *choose* from among the competing demands for funding, financial intermediaries are assumed to ensure that the economy's resources are recycled into the most

productive areas. Through their performance in intermediation, they play a central role in macroeconomic *allocative efficiency*[6].

B. Financial markets and technical efficiency

As well as allocating funds to new uses, efficient financial markets protect their investments by ensuring the effective implementation of these new projects.

This occurs most clearly in the financing of industrial enterprises. Table 4.3 shows various forms of company financing in six OECD countries, in terms of equity participation (shares) and credits (loans and bonds). Each of these financing methods involves specific monitoring mechanisms to check enterprises' efficiency.

Company directors and managers represent shareholders' interests and have a duty to look after these interests by maximising the value (discounted total profitability) of the firm. In dealing with creditors, they

Table 4.3. **Financing sources of non-financial enterprises in six countries (percentage of total liabilities, 1983-1984)**

Country	Capital base (equities, reserves and provisions)	Short-term debt	Long-term debt	Total
United States	60	19	21	100
Japan	17	60	23	100
Germany[1]	36	41	17	100
France	27	56	17	100
United Kingdom	45	45	10	100
Italy	32	45	23	100

1. The total for Germany adds up to 94, owing to a residual category of unclassified liabilities.
Source: OECD.

must maintain the firm's credibility and solvency, which are dependent on the profitability of the enterprise. Although professional managers are responsible for most of the economic activities in OECD countries, they frequently do not behave in line with the above-mentioned pattern, as regards both shareholder control[7] and creditors[8]. Control is nonetheless exercised[9]. It is exercised most effectively when financial markets operate openly and competitively, information circulates freely and financial investors behave rationally.

In a properly functioning financial market, *shareholders* react to the competitive performances of firms. They intervene either "actively", by participating in the appointment, renewal or replacement of management, or "passively", by reselling their securities on second markets when company performance fails to attain the expected rate of return. If a large number of shareholders react passively and sell their shares at the same time, a firm's market value will fall to a level at which other shareholders interveneactively by means of takeovers, reorganisation of the firm and design of a new competitive strategy. Numerous empirical studies have shown that firms with active shareholders have better profit performances[10]; the evidence is less clear on the impact of takeovers, but most studies suggest that such action is largely positive[11].

A firm's *creditors* also exercise control over company efficiency and performance. In the case of bank lending to enterprises, this control takes the form of direct assessment by the bank of the firm's solvency and subsequently of returns on investments. This control is intensified when deterioration of the firm's performance increases the credit risks for the lenders[12]. Efficient lenders then intervene to encourage reorganisation, in order to put the business back on a viable financial footing.

Control by creditors may be exercised by their participation on the board of directors, in countries where this is legally permitted. A recent study carried out in Germany – where this relationship between banks and industrial firms is the most highly developed – demonstrated how closely the relationship is linked to good company performance[13]. Case studies in Japan, the United States and the United Kingdom have also shown the positive impact of this type of creditor control and negative consequences when it is lacking[14].

In the case of more anonymous credit relationships between a company and the holders of its securities (bonds, commercial paper, etc.), financial market control is less direct. The financial soundness and competitiveness of a company are monitored by the financial community, either by major investors or by specialist assessment companies, e.g. credit rating agencies. The risk premium (bonus) and market price of each firm's securities are fixed on the basis of this assessment. Accordingly, competitive companies find their capital costs reduced and their investment stimulated, while less profitable ones are encouraged to reorganise and introduce new competitive tactics.

By exercising such control over company behaviour, properly functioning financial markets help maximise the technical efficiency of each firm and, consequently, of the entire economy.

II. THE DEVELOPMENT OF FINANCIAL MARKETS, 1975-1985

Over the past decade, financial markets in OECD countries have undergone major changes. These have affected the structure and operation of the markets, the instruments used in financial transactions, methods of fixing the prices and yields of financial assets, and correspondingly, the price and cost of balance sheet liabilities of fund users. These changes have altered the interaction between the financial and industrial sectors and have made the role of financial markets more important to the overall economy.

These changes originated because of three factors:

i) *Government policies* strengthening competition in financial markets;

ii) Introduction of *new financial instruments* allowing bigger and more risky financial investments; and

iii) A substantial buildup of resources, skills and competitive strategies in *financial enterprises*.

A. Government deregulation and competition policies

Financial markets and industries are among the most regulated of all economic activities in OECD countries. Problems of interdependence and mutual vulnerability among financial institutions (the so-called "systemic risk" in financial systems) and problems of information faced by depositors, creditors and shareholders of financial institutions (the so-called "asymmetry of information" factor) led all governments to set up highly developed regulatory frameworks. These regulations, mainly devised in the wake of the 1929 crisis, were broadened and refined during the 1940s and 1950s. Changed financial requirements arising from postwar economic and social reconstruction, and subsequent political pressures in the 1960s for better information and protection for savers also strengthened the regulations controlling the financial industry.

Early in the 1970s, many OECD countries still had highly fragmented financial systems, with a limited degree of competition. In a number of countries, universal banks collecting funds on different market segments and investing simultaneously in industrial debt and equity, household loans and government debts, created a more integrated capital market. However, most financial institutions had tight constraints on the structure of their liabilities (sources of finance) and assets (investment areas). The rates applied by these institutions – including deposit and borrowing interest rates and their service commissions – were also highly regulated. Consequently, the majority of financial enterprises were specialised in administratively protected market segments, where a type of oligopolistic competition based on fixed rates and service differentiation used to operate[15].

In many countries, governments also made available subsidies, tax deductions, public guarantees and refinancing to selected industries and sectors, e.g. agricultural credits, housing credits, sectoral interest rate subsidies, etc.[16, 17] Taken as a whole, the capital market was no longer functioning as a comparative selection system for the optimal investment projects (in line with the principles outlined in Part I), but instead as a number of more or less watertight fund collecting and allocation circuits under regulatory control[18]. This compartmentalisation has been less far-reaching in countries with relatively unified and homogeneous universal banking systems.

During the last ten years, there has been a growing political reaction to this state of affairs in countries suffering such rigidities. Most governments have consequently reappraised their financial policies. This change was also encouraged by the development of new borrowing requirements in the economy (particularly in the public sector itself), the emergence of an unregulated financial sector (especially internationally) and the growth in financial institutions under concurrent regulatory frameworks, e.g. savings and loan associations, pension funds, building societies, etc., which competed effectively with the traditionally regulated institutions. In most countries this has resulted in substantial and fairly prompt changes in financial regulations.

These changes have taken four main directions:

i) The deregulation of interest rates;
ii) The deregulation of financial service prices;
iii) The decompartmentalisation of markets; and
iv) The opening up of markets to foreign competition.

1. Deregulation of bank interest rates

The liberalisation of short- and long-term bank interest rates has now begun to be based more closely on the conditions of supply and demand for funds, on domestic and international markets. In countries where interest rate regulation existed, the liberalisation was first introduced for large deposits, but the tendency has been to lower the deregulation thresholds and increase the number of depositors with access to non-regulated rates[19]. At the same time, the introduction of new securities and services at non-regulated rates, such as certificates of deposit, money-market funds, cash-management accounts and sweep accounts have also contributed to a *de facto* liberalisation of interest rates.

2. Deregulation of financial service prices

The deregulation of financial service prices affects underwriting spreads in primary issues, and brokerage

Table 4.4. **Cost differentials of bond issues in domestic markets, 1982-1983**

Country[1]	Maturity of bonds referred to (years)	Size of issues (in millions $)			Total issue cost (as a percentage of the total issue)		
		Small	Medium	Large	Small	Medium	Large
United States	20	15	60	200	1.45	1.08	0.98
Japan	10	10	45	160	3.5	3.5	3.5
United Kingdom	20	15	60	175	1.83	1.15	1.08
Canada	10	20	65	105	2.5	2.1	1.75
Germany	10	25	50	80	3.6	3.6	3.6
Australia	5	10	30	70	1.57	1.61	1.60
France	10	15	75	150	3.3	3.2	3.2
Switzerland	10	10	35	75	2.85	3.0	3.0
Netherlands	10	20	30	55	2.7	2.5	2.4
Belgium	8	20	45	110	4.2	4.15	4.10

1. Classed in order of size of financial market.
Source: International Finance Corporation, World Bank, 1985.

commissions in secondary dealings. Underwriting spreads, traditionally settled by implicit consensus among security houses, came under pressure with increased competition among these enterprises, as well as with the use of auction-type fee fixing by big public sector borrowers. Brokerage commissions in secondary dealings were liberalised by joint action by government regulators and stock exchange authorities, as in the United States in 1975 (May Day), Canada in 1983, the United Kingdom in 1986 (the Big Bang) and in the Netherlands in 1986 (for block transactions).

Table 4.4 shows the impact of regulations on bond emission costs in a number of countries in 1982. Issuing costs were noticeably lower in the United States, which was the only country at the time of the survey with deregulated underwriting commissions. The United States is also the country where economies of scale – which are considerable in this field – are clearly reflected in lower costs[20].

3. Decompartmentalisation of financial markets

Financial institutions are encouraged to diversify their areas of investment (assets) and their financing sources (liabilities) and compete against each other in a more integrated financial market. This policy of market decompartmentalisation has been particularly innovative in countries where commercial banks, investment banks, insurance companies, pension funds and sectoral banks used to collect and allocate their funds in rigidly confined markets. Those countries with federal structures which used to limit the geographic area of activity of financial institutions have also begun to reduce these limitations.

4. Opening up to foreign competition

In order to speed up the modernisation of the financial system by increasing competition and larger transfers of financial technology, a number of OECD countries, whose frontiers were initially closed, have opened up

their markets to international financial institutions[21]. This has mainly concerned commercial and investment banks, whose operation at local level also promotes capital inflows[22]. Several countries have now admitted international institutions into the local financial markets[23]. The OECD Codes (of Liberalisation of Current Invisible Operations and Liberalisation of Capital Movements) have played a notable role in fostering consensus and international co-operation in this area.

B. New instruments and new financial markets

The second major change in OECD financial markets has been the emergence and spread of many new financial instruments[24]. The use of these instruments and services is creating new market segments where suppliers and borrowers of funds are, in part, new players in financial markets.

Table 4.5 lists and classifies the most significant of these innovations, according to the new functions they introduce into markets. Some of these instruments have existed previously but are listed here as innovations since they have only recently come into widespread use, especially at the international level.

Virtually all these new instruments are used for *hedging against and spreading risks* in the financial system, which explains their spectacular upsurge in the past few years. They also created opportunities for taking on more and wider risks by particularly risk-prone investors and speculators. This is due on the one hand to the increase in risk exposure on credit and foreign exchange markets, because of volatility in interest and currency rates, and on the other hand to the increase in credit risks involved in lending to industry, which has become distinctly less stable with higher profit performance variability and higher bankruptcy rates. Innovations have therefore improved the pricing and distribution of this increased amount of total risk borne by the financial sector.

Table 4.5. **Financial innovations since 1970**

New fund collecting techniques (for borrowers)			New risk management techniques (for investors)	New financial advice and support techniques	Automatisation of traditional services
Direct debt	Bonds	Equities			
— Floating rate loans	— Floating rate bonds — Zero-coupon bonds — Eurobonds — Junk bonds — Convertible bonds — Commercial paper — Interest rate swaps	— Venture capital finance — Secondary and tertiary market listings — Convertibles and other equity-linked bonds — Non-voting shares	— Securitised assets — Mutual funds (securities and money market instruments) — Options (securities and currency) — Futures (securities and currency)	— Note issuance facilities — Credit enhancing guarantees — Leverages for buy-outs	— Electronic fund transfer — Electronic security markets — Computerised cash management — Programme trading — Global trading

Source: OECD.

157

Graph 4.1. Increasing volatility of long-term interest rates in OECD countries, 1970-1986

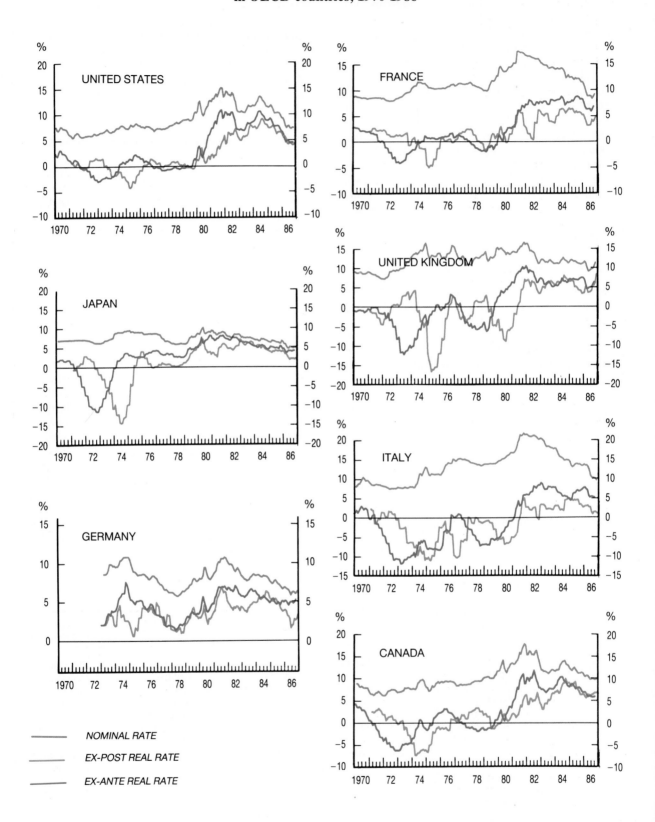

NOMINAL RATE

EX-POST REAL RATE

EX-ANTE REAL RATE

Source: OECD.

Table 4.6. **External financing structure of the domestic non-financial sectors in seven countries (1969, 1976, 1984)**

Percentages

Net borrowing per type of instrument	United States			Japan			Germany			United Kingdom			France			Italy			Canada		
	1969	1976	1984	1969	1976	1984	1969	1976	1984	1969	1976	1984	1969	1976	1984	1969	1976	1984	1969	1976	1984
Short-term securities	9.1	5.4	8.2	2.7	0.2	0.2	-8.1	-3.3	-4.4	-10.6	-7.0	4.1	-2.1	2.1	10.2	1.3	17.7	5.4	8.0	4.5	16.6
Short-term loans	39.3	18.5	32.1	-	-	-	35.4	11.2	14.3	-9.5	23.1	28.5	45.0	25.7	12.3	35.5	42.6	29.4	-	-	-
Bonds	14.0	38.5	40.3	11.5	29.5	31.6	-0.3	12.9	35.9	25.6	30.1	19.8	1.9	6.9	19.4	23.9	9.2	40.8	48.1	33.2	39.0
Equities	3.8	4.1	-11.7	5.3	2.2	3.3	3.4	3.6	2.9	8.3	4.6	1.1	8.9	6.9	12.4	9.7	6.7	10.3	8.9	2.5	12.9
Long-term loans	33.7	33.4	31.1	80.4	68.1	64.8	69.6	75.5	64.3	86.2	49.2	46.6	46.2	58.5	45.7	29.6	23.9	14.2	2.4	20.1	10.5
Total securities[2]	27.0	48.1	48.5[3]	19.5	31.9	35.1	3.4[3]	16.6[3]	25.8[3]	33.9[3]	34.7[3]	25	10.9	15.9	42.0	34.9	33.5	56.4	65.0	40.2	68.5
Total	100	100	100	100	100	100	100	100	100	100	100	100	100	100	100	100	100	100	100	100	100

1. Added to long-term loans.
2. Short-term securities + bonds + equities.
3. Without deducting redemptions of shares and other equity and debt certificates.

159

1. Management of interest rate risks

The volatility of interest rates on capital markets (see Graph 4.1) has made it particularly risky to enter into long-term contracts to lend or borrow at fixed nominal rates. Yet such contracts have always accounted for a large proportion of financial transactions in most OECD countries. A whole series of new instruments, such as floating rate loans, floating rate bonds, interest rate options and interest rate futures now provide borrowers and lenders – who are prepared to pay the price – with the possibility of hedging against such risks. These innovations have played a major role in the further pursuit and development of long-term financial transactions in OECD countries.

2. Management of credit risks

Another distinctive feature of the past decade has been the large amount of risks associated with extending credit to industry. Technological progress, stiffer international competition, structural changes in companies, the creation of many new market entrants, large-scale redeployment operations, etc. have all considerably broadened the credit risks involved with industrial investment. Yet, here too, the available financial instruments have helped greatly to spread and transfer these risks. Options and futures contracts relating to industrial securities (shares and bonds), along with hybrid financial instruments such as convertible bonds, non-voting shares and subordinated loans, offer industrial investors, at a price, a variety of risk-hedging and transferring facilities.

3. The increase in marketable securities

The underlying trend in the use of these new financial instruments has been the gradual replacement of traditional bank loans by marketable security issues (equities and bonds) on which virtually all the new instruments are based. This "securitisation of credit", as this move towards greater liquidity of financial assets is known[25], is clearly measured in Table 4.6. It first developed in the 1970s (in connection with public sector borrowing in most countries), where the scale of loan issues and the practically risk-free nature of the investments made bank intermediation between fund suppliers and users superfluous in many cases. The practice then spread to include borrowing by large, highly reputable and reliable businesses, and subsequently to companies where the risks were greater. Gradually, and unexpectedly, marketable securities have turned out to be an effective funding instrument for industrial risk-spreading and management. Unlike direct bank loans, these securities allow risks to be split among a large number of investors, who can moreover manage them in a more dynamic and flexible manner, because of their more liquid character.

C. Growth and competitiveness of financial enterprises

In the wake of these financial developments, new opportunities have arisen for financial enterprises as new market segments have opened up for the collection and placement of funds. Also the number of investors and borrowers using the new financial instruments has increased rapidly[26]. High inflation rates, the erosion of returns from traditional fixed-income assets, and householders' desires to optimise their financial portfolios[27] have created new business opportunities for financial enterprises – as well as challenged their traditional lines of activity. The need of fund users to minimise costs and to manage their liabilities in a more sensitive way has added further incentives, while lastly, the arrival of new big-size borrowers (particularly international and public sector borrowers) has increased opportunities for sophisticated and larger-scale financial intermediation[28].

1. The development of new financial institutions

Table 4.7 shows changes that have occurred in the composition of household and non-financial enterprise financial portfolios in five countries between 1976 and 1985. It reflects the increased competition between various deposit-collecting institutions and highlights the competitiveness of non-bank financial enterprises. These have fewer restrictive regulations than banks and have direct access to the most advantageous investment areas (especially money markets) as well as to the most attractive sources of finance (in particular private fortunes and large firms' cash resources). As a result, their growth rate has been exceptional. With their economies of scale and specialist skills, these organisations represent the new, sophisticated and aggressive face of financial intermediation[29]. The most rapidly growing, and possible most innovative, category of all non-banking financial institutions in the United States has been mutual funds (see Graph 4.2).

The role of non-bank institutions in financial markets has recently been the cause of two areas of political and economic concern in the OECD:

i) The impact of these institutions' specific portfolio strategies on the stability of capital markets; and

ii) The impact of these strategies on the behaviour of industrial companies controlled by institutional shareholders and creditors.

The first concern stems from the fact that these institutions have portfolios made up almost exclusively of marketable assets (equities, bonds and similar instruments). They can introduce large quantities of these securities onto the market at any given moment, since they continually maximise the market value of their portfolios. It is believed this can bring about greater fluctuations in prices of these assets than are justified by

Table 4.7. **Portfolio composition of the private non-financial sector**[1]

Percentages

Country and items	1976	1977	1978	1979	1980	1981	1982	1983	1984	1985
	As a percentage of gross financial assets									
United States										
Deposits	33	34	35	33	32	33	33	32	34	32
Bonds[2]	10	10	10	10	9	9	9	9	10	11
Shares	20	18	17	18	20	18	18	18	16	17
Institutional investment[3]	20	20	20	20	21	21	22	23	24	25
Japan										
Deposits	51	53	53	52	51	51	52	51	49	49[4]
Bonds[2]	4	5	5	5	5	6	6	6	7	6[4]
Shares	9	8	9	8	8	8	8	9	10	12[4]
Institutional investment[3]	7	7	8	8	8	8	9	10	11	11[4]
Germany										
Deposits	57	57	58	57	55	55	54	53	51	48
Bonds[2]	9	9	9	10	10	11	11	11	13	13
Shares	12	12	12	10	10	10	10	11	11	15
Institutional investment[3]	9	9	9	10	11	12	12	12	12	12
United Kingdom										
Deposits	33	32	32	32	32	33	31	30	29	29[5]
Bonds[2]	6	6	5	5	5	4	5	4	4	4[5]
Shares	12	14	13	12	12	11	11	12	13	12[5]
Institutional investment[3]	19	21	23	23	25	25	28	29	30	30[5]
Canada										
Deposits	31	32	32	32	32	31	31	29	29	29[4]
Bonds[2]	8	8	8	7	6	6	7	8	8	9[4]
Shares	17	17	18	17	18	17	17	17	16	16[4]
Institutional investment[3]	15	16	15	15	15	16	16	17	18	18[4]

1. On the basis of non-consolidated balance sheets for the household and business sectors: in the case of the United States, except for sole proprietors and agriculture. The sum of the sub-totals does not add up to 100 because some items, such as commercial credit and direct investment abroad, are not included.
2. Except for directly held mortgage debentures.
3. Mutual funds, pension funds, assets management funds and insurance company funds not classed as deposits.
4. Estimates.
5. Third quarter.
Source: National balance sheets data, Bank for International Settlements.

the basic economic factors underpinning their value. The use of big-size (block) trading techniques, like arbitrage and programme trading, could also increase such volatility of stock prices. Fluctuations of this kind could distort information and cause unwarranted risks for other investors and borrowers. However, recent empirical studies have shown that excessive price volatility is an age-old characteristic of capital markets[30], and that this volatility has not increased in recent times[31]. Moreover, major financial institutions' decisions on investment and disinvestment are likely to differ from each other, as well as from the generally imitative behaviour of small investors[32]. This could also contribute to greater capital market stability in the future.

The second concern involves constraints that these non-bank institutions impose on companies of which they are shareholders or creditors. Since the main aim of these institutions is to maximise the immediate market value of their portfolios, they may be reluctant to finance firms' risky, longer-term or infrastructural investment projects[33]. It is certainly true that during the early stages of their development, most institutions have had speculative-type investment policies aimed at exploiting the price differentials of their assets on the short term, without paying much attention to the basic value and long-term returns of their investments. Speculative profits of this kind are typical of a period of financial market reorganisation, and should diminish as these markets become more competitive, information more open, and the behaviour of transactors more rational. Many financial institutions are indeed starting to undertake long-term investment in industry by making increased use of their assessment, follow-up and supervisory skills. These are considerable, particularly when compared to those of individual investors[34, 35, 36].

Graph 4.2. The growth of mutual investment funds in the United States

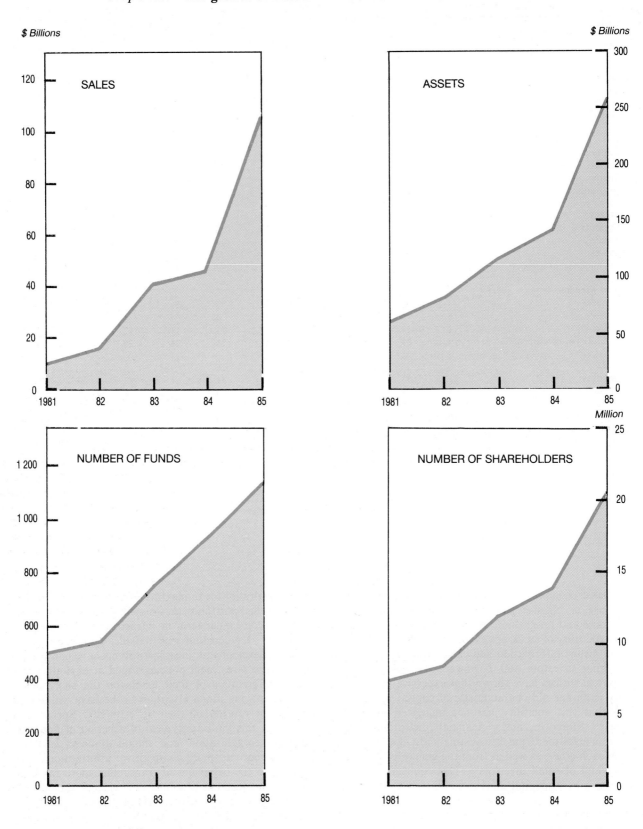

Source: Company Investment Institute, United States.

2. The overall growth of the financial industry

With this increased competition and new opportunities, the entire financial industry has grown remarkably in all OECD countries. Cross-country calculations single out this particular branch from among 18 other manufacturing and service sectors as the one which has experienced the most rapid growth from 1975 to 1983. This is well-illustrated by both the growth of value added and total employment in the sector. This trend is

Table 4.8. **Value added volume: actual growth rates (1973-1983)**

Percentages

Sectors	Countries													
	NLD	NOR	BEL	DNK	FIN	SWE	FRA	GER	ITA	UK	CAN	US	JPN	Total
BMI	-10.50	0.52	-0.09	1.06	5.90	0.47	-0.21	-0.81	0.89	-3.87	—	-4.82	0.08	-2.14
CST	-2.98	2.96	-1.36	-4.37	0.98	0.61	-1.01	-0.96	-0.21	-2.13	0.31	-1.75	-0.63	-1.14
MNM	—	-1.58	-1.39	-4.17	3.26	-2.25	0.41	-0.60	1.41	-3.06	—	-1.13	-1.74	-1.06
TEX	-4.86	-4.62	-0.81	0.21	1.32	-5.55	-1.53	-1.69	1.13	-3.53	—	0.96	2.88	0.14
WOD	—	-0.90	0.17	-0.09	0.34	-1.50	—	-2.18	1.89	—	—	0.56	—	0.24
AGR	4.52	2.31	0.67	3.14	1.25	0.48	0.49	0.97	1.95	1.92	1.51	0.31	-1.25	0.55
FOD	1.87	-1.12	1.51	3.01	2.33	0.47	2.62	1.41	2.64	0.43	—	0.43	1.59	1.25
PAP	1.57	0.38	-0.41	-0.16	2.40	0.74	1.87	0.31	1.57	-1.78	—	1.40	3.41	1.25
PGS	-0.16	5.30	2.36	4.11	4.49	3.07	—	2.21	1.63	1.11	1.64	1.07	3.68	1.69
MOT	—	-11.79	0.02	-0.57	2.48	-4.36	0.75	-1.51	1.62	-3.70	—	0.50	3.30	1.84
MIN	-0.58	24.07	-3.64	19.73	4.44	-5.92	—	-2.85	—	12.58	-2.26	1.08	1.58	1.93
CHE	—	1.58	6.44	4.38	2.63	1.37	2.76	1.15	2.84	0.09	—	1.42	5.13	2.02
EGW	-0.16	4.29	2.65	5.26	3.87	3.42	2.77	2.92	0	1.52	4.48	1.80	4.72	2.29
TRS	—	2.97	0.54	0.22	2.87	2.78	2.59	3.32	3.11	0.91	3.27	2.65	2.38	2.31
RET	-0.01	2.33	1.24	1.35	1.69	1.81	2.14	1.33	2.28	-0.32	2.50	2.31	5.91	2.52
MEQ	-1.64	0.01	2.10	1.95	5.04	1.46	3.26	1.48	1.75	-1.32	—	1.60	8.79	2.80
SOC	—	2.98	3.15	1.49	1.70	2.08	4.26	3.80	—	2.65	4.39	2.80	3.59	3.01
FNS[1]	3.73	0.92	5.96	-3.01	5.11	1.91	2.92	3.73	2.78	3.88	4.68	2.29	4.43	3.41
Total	-3.37	4.15	1.70	1.57	2.74	1.56	2.22	1.56	1.86	0.95	1.98	1.40	3.72	—

1. Financial services (includes real estate).
Source: OECD.

Table 4.9. **Employment: actual growth rates (1973-1983)**

Percentages

Sectors	Countries													
	NLD	NOR	BEL	DNK	FIN	SWE	FRA	GER	ITA	UK	CAN	US	JPN	Total
TEX	-9.62	-6.87	-6.85	-4.55	-2.51	-6.67	-3.97	-5.41	-0.68	-5.78	0.27	-2.53	-3.55	-3.24
BMI	-3.11	-1.92	-3.36	-4.65	1.01	-2.49	-2.11	-2.43	0.45	-4.98	-0.17	-4.19	-1.89	-2.91
MNM	-3.68	-2.08	-5.06	-5.30	-0.35	-3.57	-2.25	-3.05	-0.50	-3.96	0	-1.81	-2.01	-2.20
AGR	-1.24	-2.36	-3.19	-2.49	-2.87	-2.49	-3.04	-3.24	-2.58	-1.41	0.24	-0.63	-2.42	-2.12
WOD	-4.52	-1.94	-4.44	-2.93	-1.32	-2.75	-0.84	-2.38	0	-2.93	2.44	-1.26	—	-1.28
MEQ	-2.12	-0.68	-2.34	-1.03	1.15	-0.82	-0.83	-1.28	-0.34	-2.93	0.52	-0.39	0.10	-0.70
CHE	-1.51	-1.00	-0.95	-0.31	0.07	-0.30	-1.15	-0.75	-1.03	-2.68	2.73	0.27	-1.94	-0.69
FOD	-2.27	-0.82	-1.88	-1.47	-0.61	-0.91	-0.37	-1.23	0.04	-2.05	1.92	-0.71	0.07	-0.66
MOT	-3.72	-4.61	-3.36	-1.44	-1.62	2.38	-1.49	-1.42	0.25	-3.16	6.79	-1.15	0.21	-0.35
CST	-3.46	0.79	-2.86	-3.73	-1.77	-1.97	-1.76	-2.12	-0.35	-2.32	0.49	0.42	1.14	-0.33
PAP	-1.20	-0.77	-3.03	-1.79	-0.10	-0.20	-1.19	-2.99	-0.31	-1.57	3.37	1.15	-1.45	-0.12
TRS	1.01	0.54	0.15	0.68	0.58	0.98	1.10	-0.57	1.36	-0.91	1.04	0.80	0.33	0.46
MIN	-2.01	5.11	-4.29	-2.20	2.29	-2.22	-3.76	-1.19	—	-1.29	3.48	4.08	-2.74	0.96
EGW	0.83	1.66	-2.18	1.06	2.53	1.65	0.43	0.61	1.21	-0.39	1.84	1.73	1.27	0.97
PGS	1.75	3.26	2.32	4.11	4.18	3.72	—	1.79	2.10	0.74	—	1.03	1.47	1.43
RET	-0.49	1.27	-0.01	-1.49	0.04	0.20	0.80	-0.21	2.03	—	2.83	2.20	1.48	1.61
SOC	2.41	1.76	3.30	0.18	0.77	0.69	3.25	2.09	—	1.19	3.15	2.64	3.35	2.53
FNS[1]	1.44	2.36	1.90	3.20	2.60	1.27	2.19	1.18	3.79	2.60	4.38	3.43	3.22	3.14
Total	-0.42	0.74	-0.41	0.24	0.25	0.64	-0.26	-0.69	0.60	-0.42	2.39	1.20	0.67	—

1. Financial services (includes real estate).
Source: OECD.

continuing despite the reduction in profit margins (and, consequently, value added) owing to increased competition, and considerable productivity growth (labour saving) due to the extensive use of information technology[37] (Tables 4.8 and 4.9).

3. Increased stock-market activity

The growth of the financial industry, combined with the increasing share of marketable securities used in financial transactions (securitisation) and the lowering of transaction costs, has brought about an exceptional surge in recent stock-market activity. Table 4.10 shows the extent of this phenomenon in the eleven largest stock markets in the world, ten of which are in OECD countries. Table 4.11 supplements this information by showing the size of the secondary (resale) markets for securities in relation to their primary markets (original issues). The big size of secondary markets is due to the intense level of activity among financial institutions, who have become more active and expert in optimising their portfolios and grasping fleeting investment opportunities.

Table 4.10. **Turnover on major stock exchanges**

Billion $

		Total value of turnover					
		1985	1984	1983	1982	1981	1975
United States	New York SE	970.5	755.9	751.3	459.4	395.0	133.7
Japan	Tokyo First Section	321.2	267.1	213.8	141.2	217.8	51.2
Germany	All exchanges	75.5	29.7	32.9	14.0	13.5	11.1
United Kingdom	London	70.2	48.4	42.5	32.3	32.7	19.6
Canada	All exchanges	39.3	25.3	28.7	16.5	23.6	5.4
France	Paris	17.8	10.2	12.4	8.9	12.1	7.3
Netherlands	Amsterdam	17.1	11.9	10.0	4.8	3.9	2.5
Australia	All exchanges	15.6	10.8	9.3	5.1	8.2	0.7
Italy	Milan	14.3	3.8	3.8	2.8	9.7	2.1
Hong Kong	All exchanges	10.0	6.2	5.2	7.6	18.9	2.1
Sweden	Stockholm	9.9	8.5	9.9	4.3	3.6	0.5

Source: Euromoney.

Table 4.11. **Domestic corporate securities markets[1]**
Largest share of secondary transactions

$ millions

	1982 primary markets				Secondary markets		Secondary transactions/ Primary issues	
	Gross new issues of shares		Gross new issues of corporate bonds		Domestic[2] share trades	Domestic[2] corporate bond trades	Percentages values	
	Number of issues	Amounts	Number of issues	Amounts	Value	Value	Shares	Bonds
Australia	260	2 601	25	1 658	(8 179)	(38)	314	2.3
Belgium	12	492	0	0	1 034	..	210	..
Canada	70	846	110	5 442	17 988	..	2 126	..
France	66	533	..	1 309	(8 403)	..	1 576	..
Germany	35	535	2	49	(13 470)	360	2 517	735
Japan	192	3 288	149	6 361	(266 426)	(5 710)	6 852	90
Netherlands	2	15	17	667	4 826[3]	8 946	32 173	1 341
Switzerland	109	276	103	3 372	(15 537)	..	5 629	..
United Kingdom	80	3 108	39	1 687	32 737[3]	2 131	1 053	126
United States	1 320	23 399	552	42 296	603 861	7 073	2 580	17

1. All amounts have been converted to $ at the respective average annual exchange rates.
2. Traded on the stock exchange(s); figures in ( ) represent 1981 results, at 1981 end of year exchange rates.
3. Netherlands and United Kingdom trade values represent one-half of reported figures, to make them conform to other country reporting practices, and also include foreign shares in the case of the United Kingdom.
Source: International Finance Corporation, World Bank, 1985.

4. Internationalisation of financial enterprises

The growth of the financial industry and its increased sensitivity to investment opportunities has encouraged many financial enterprises to become international. Commercial and investment banks have extended their networks internationally where the relaxing of host countries' regulations has permitted. Investment funds have also broadened their international activities so as to spread their risks, as well as to take on new risks by taking advantage of international investment opportunities. Advances in modern information and communications technologies have also enabled many financial institutions to operate world-wide on an integrated basis. International centralisation of fund-raising and investment decisions (global trading) and non-stop, 24-hour trading have now become a standard for most competitive financial enterprises.

Structural change in the finance industry has turned it into a high technology service sector. Since its resources (in particular its professional skills) are now very sophisticated and costly, new competition is being waged on an international scale. Financial markets of OECD countries are now both the principal home and host markets for international financial enterprises[38]. Subsequent international capital movements are also developing primarily between OECD countries, mainly in the form of intricate networks of cross flows[39].

Tables 4.12 and 4.13 describe this process, showing the considerable growth in the share of international investment and borrowing by banks (Table 4.12). They also show the exponential growth and geographical cover of the activities of SWIFT (the Society for Worldwide Interbank Financial Telecommunications) – the organisation controlling international interbank communications (Table 4.13).

Table 4.12. **Relative importance of foreign business of deposit money banks**

Percentages

Country	Assets		Liabilities	
	1970	1981	1970	1981
Australia[1]	..	0.6	..	1.1
Austria[1]	10.7	24.5	9.8	27.8
Belgium[2]	33.4	57.8	39.0	68.7
Canada[3]	19.8	17.3	14.3	27.1
Denmark[2]	6.7	29.1	7.0	28.1
Finland[1]	4.4	11.5	5.6	17.5
France[1]	15.9	33.7	17.0	32.3
Germany[1]	8.8	10.2	5.6	8.1
Greece[2]	3.5	7.8	4.7	22.0
Iceland[1]	1.0	2.9	2.7	17.2
Ireland[2]	36.0	47.1	29.8	49.2
Italy[1]	12.6	12.6	12.6	15.9
Japan[1]	3.7	6.6	3.1	7.9
Luxembourg[1]	84.2	97.5	57.5	90.4
Netherlands[1]	27.0	39.8	25.9	39.2
New Zealand[3]	7.1	7.0	1.1	2.3
Norway[1]	7.4	6.0	5.5	10.9
Portugal[1]	5.6	7.7	0.8	27.7
Spain[1]	3.5	8.5	4.2	14.9
Sweden[2]	7.0	9.7	5.4	18.2
Switzerland[4]	33.7	50.1	28.9	42.8
Turkey	..	4.7	..	0.3
United Kingdom[1]	46.1	67.9	50.2	69.9
United States[2]	2.6	15.1	6.2	11.3
Total OECD	12.1	23.7	11.3	23.4

1. All deposit money banks.
2. Commercial banks.
3. Chartered or trading banks.
4. All banks, including trust accounts. Balance-sheet data include domestic interbank deposits.
Note: Data are not fully comparable across countries.
Source: OECD, *The Internationalisation of Banking,* Paris, 1983, *op. cit.* in Note 22.

Table 4.13. **Growth of SWIFT's activities**[1]

	Message traffic volumes		Geographic structure of message flows (figures to mid-year, 1985)		
	Average daily traffic volumes	Cumulative traffic volumes (millions)	Area	Outgoing (× 1 000)	Ingoing (× 1 000)
1978	121 000	24.7	Europe	92 266	87 204
1979	164 000	59.3	North America	24 426	25 505
1980	218 000	106.5	South America	1 418	1 487
1981	285 000	169.1	Asia/Pacific	9 201	8 877
1982	346 000	248.6			
1983	480 000	400.1			
1984	566 000	529.9			
1985[2]	650 000	680.0			

1. Society for Worldwide Interbank Financial Telecommunications.
2. Estimate.
Source: Financial Times, 21 October 1985.

Table 4.14. **Geographic and market segment penetration**

Countries with financial futures markets:
United States, Canada, United Kingdom, Netherlands, Japan, France, Australia, New Zealand, Sweden, Singapore

Selected instruments with financial futures traded:	
Currencies:	£, SF, DM, Yen, C$, FFr, Guilder, ECU
Equity indices:	US Equity Market Indices, FTSE 100 (UK)
Bonds:	US T-Bond, Japanese T-Bond, US T-Note, US Municipals, UK Gilts, Dutch Government Bonds, Swedish Government Bonds
Interest rates:	T-bills, Eurodollar, Certificates of Deposit
Other:	US Consumer Price Index

Source: Cooper, I., "Innovations: New Market Instruments", *Oxford Review of Economic Policy,* 1986, No. 4.

Nevertheless, this rapid internationalisation of financial markets and enterprises has not yet led to either a complete integration of markets or to a full diffusion of financial innovations. Unequal international spread of new instruments (see Table 4.14) has meant that no more than ten OECD countries yet have financial future markets, where a mixture of eight international currencies, five types of government bonds and two national stock indexes are traded.

III. FINANCING STRUCTURAL ADJUSTMENT IN INDUSTRY

In view of the role played by financial markets in advanced economies (Part I) and the important changes that have taken place during the last ten years (Part II), it is important for governments to monitor and understand the impact of these developments on industrial investment and adjustment. Investment in both the manufacturing and service sectors is considerably affected by these developments.

In order to make an assessment of these impacts, three types of investment could be looked at:

i) Investment for the redeployment and growth of expanding firms;
ii) Investment for restructuring and reorganising declining firms; and
iii) Investment for creating new businesses in new manufacturing and service sectors.

A. Investment for the redeployment and growth of expanding firms

As discussed in the industrial adjustment chapter, a large number of expanding businesses in all OECD countries are carrying out major investment programmes, stimulating overall structural change in the economy. These are generally large and highly competitive international manufacturing and service companies, with considerable technological, organisational and financial strength. Their strategic scope and financial resources enabled these companies to go ahead with massive redeployment investment during the 1975 to 1985 period[40].

1. Intangible investment

The distinction between redeployment investment and traditional capacity-widening investment is that the former renews the basic human, technological and organisational assets of the enterprises. It is structural in character and paves the way for future growth[41].

This special trait of investment during the last decade can be seen in its distribution by operational areas. The share of investment in machinery and equipment is shrinking while investment in research and development, training, organisation, software and marketing is increasing steadily and becoming dominant in many industries. Table 4.16 illustrates this trend over the last decade in five OECD countries[42]. Yet since most of this investment is intangible and is usually entered in company accounts as current expenditure rather than capital assets[43], much of this trend has been virtually imperceptible in capital formation statistics.

Table 4.15. **Development of large businesses' financing structure**
Increasing role of security issues

As a percentage of borrowing requirements

	United States		Japan		France		Italy		Canada	
	Security issues	Borrowing	Security issues	Borrowing	Security issues	Borrowing	Security issues	Borrowing	Security issues	Borrowing
1975-1976	35.3	64.7	7.7	92.3	8.5	91.5	8.8	91.2	32.2	67.8
1983-1984	54.7	45.3	18.2	81.8	23.9	76.1	40.1	59.9	52.1	47.9

Method of calculation: Security issues include equity, bond and commercial paper issues. Borrowing covers all other forms of financing, including commercial credits. The ratios have been calculated solely on the basis of net positive issues.

Table 4.16. **Development of investment structure in five countries**
(Investment in intangibles/Gross fixed investment, 1974-1984)
Percentages

	France			United Kingdom			Germany			United States			Japan		
	1974	1980	1984	1974	1980	1984	1974	1980	1984	1974	1980	1984	1974	1980	1984
Intangible investment/ Gross fixed investment *of which:*	19.3	21.4	30.9	25.4	28.9	38.4	11.9	14.2	17.8	40.7	47.1	66.8	11.6	16.3	20.9
Research/GFI	10.1	10.9	14.8	13.3	14.7	17.1	7.5	8.8	10.5	17.2	18.6	24.1	6.4	8.4	11.4
Publicity/GFI	7.2	7.2	9.4	10.4	11.7	15.4	4.1	4.4	5.0	20.1	22.3	30.0	4.4	6.1	6.5
Software/GFI	2.0	3.4	6.7	1.7	2.5	5.9	0.4	1.0	2.3	3.3	6.2	12.8	0.8	1.8	3.0

Source: Crédit National estimates.

Large companies in both the manufacturing and service sectors are undertaking this type of infrastructural investment. In France, for example, the 50 largest industrial groups account for 60 per cent of the overall research effort and, in 1983, expenditure on training represented 3.20 per cent of the total wage bill in the case of firms with more than 2 000 employees – yet which pay higher salaries – and only 1.20 per cent in the case of firms with fewer than fifty employees[44].

Since investment of this kind is strategic and has a long amortization period, any decision to go ahead with it does not have to be linked to either recent company profits or expected income in the near future[45]. Managements should therefore be able to plan such investment – assuming properly functioning capital markets – without linking it directly to their current performance and cash flow. When companies do not have sufficient cash resources or when assets are tied up in more immediate investment projects, this strategic investment must be undertaken by borrowing on external capital markets[46].

Recent capital market developments – in particular, securitisation and internationalisation – facilitate external financing of this type of investment[47].

2. *Financing by securities issues*

Financing by securities issues (shares, bonds and hybrid instruments) plays a key role in this connection:

i) It enables the high risks associated with this type of investment to be spread among a large number of investors[48]; and

ii) Investors in securities may be at greater liberty to decide on the basis of companies' long-term profit prospects[49]. Traditional banking finance is not systematically disadvantaged compared to security finance in these respects – especially that due to loan syndication and securitisation facilities and the sometimes better information of lenders – but risks remain more concentrated overall in bank loan arrangements and the role of recoverable tangible assets as collateral in loan decisions remains higher[50, 51].

Loan seeking companies – especially major enterprises in both the manufacturing and service sectors – considerably increased their securities issues during the 1975 to 1985 period. This helped them finance investment projects with correspondingly lower capital costs[52].

3. *International financing*

Large companies have also benefitted from the internationalisation of financial markets. In particular, they have made use of the Euromarkets, where the intense level of competition and favourable tax conditions have reduced borrowing costs even lower than on domestic markets. New floating-rate instruments, options, swaps, etc. are also widely available on these markets, and have been particularly important for companies whose local capital markets do not yet have such a wealth of instruments. Graphs 4.3 and 4.4 show the appreciable growth of bond issues and more recently equity issues on Euromarkets.

However, these developments still concern only the very large, competitive and expanding enterprises. Size, reputation and credentials are essential conditions for raising funds on international markets, and recent estimates suggest that about one hundred European firms and several hundred American and Japanese companies meet all the requirements[53, 54].

Graph 4.3. The growth of Eurobond emissions

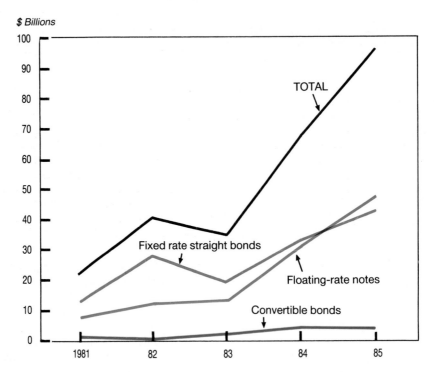

Source: OECD/Bank for International Settlements.

Graph 4.4. The growth of Euroequity emissions

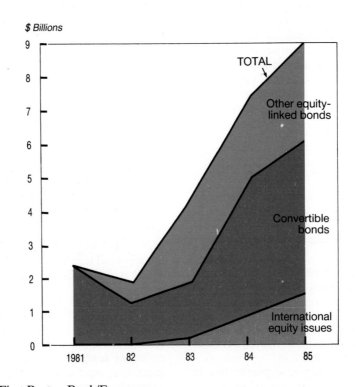

Source: Crédit Suisse First Boston Bank/Euromoney.

B. Investment for restructuring and reorganising declining companies

Companies in difficulties, especially in declining sectors, are faced with different kinds of investment and financing problems. Yet financial market developments concern them just as directly.

The problem for such firms is generally the combined result of difficulties with the company's *technical efficiency* (notably inefficient management) and its *composition of assets* (poor structural adjustment). Recent capital market developments affect both problems and go some way towards solving them by:

i) Improving control of companies' efficiency;

ii) Facilitating industrial restructuring operations; and

iii) Enabling company ownership structures to adapt to the new characteristics of their activities.

1. Monitoring company efficiency

When capital markets function correctly, they are a major instrument for detecting inefficiency in company operations. Often management teams are the first to be informed of, and to foresee, the firm's structural difficulties, but constraints and vested interests often may prevent them from carrying out all the necessary changes, and with the required speed, because the social or organisational costs are too high. In contrast, the principal objective of these companies' shareholders and creditors is to maximise the value and solvency of the enterprise. Consequently, they are usually the first to sound the alarm when difficulties arise.

Company problems are detected at an early stage by well-informed and rational shareholders and by financial institution creditors pursuing commercial objectives. When shareholders are ill-informed, passive or governed by basically non-economic motives (such as many government shareholders)[55], and when creditors are guided by political instructions or guarantees, capital market control is weakened. Recent analyses of structural adjustment delays in many industries show the weaknesses of this type of capital market control[56].

The major development in this field has been the impact of "securitisation" on efficiency control mechanisms.

Traditionally, companies' creditors include principal banks who monitor the performance and financial soundness of the business and whose credit and investment decisions are used as a yardstick by other financial institutions. However, in the past decade, this efficiency control by banks has flagged in several countries, with social and political factors playing a more important part in decisions to grant loans. A similar weakening of control also occurs when the number of a firm's creditor banks increases, or become more international, with the result that there are no main creditors left who have a substantial and direct interest in the soundness of the business[57].

Recent growth of security financing has accentuated this new and dispersed creditor pattern. The reaction of a company's securities holders when performance deteriorates is usually not to assume the costs involved in analysis and corrective measures (since these efforts would mainly benefit other holders of these securities), but quite simply to resell them on the capital market. However, the increased part played in these markets by big financial institutions, that accumulate huge quantities of a given company's securities (in particular, those of large companies) and who have developed the necessary skills and resources to monitor them, should be expected to strengthen control mechanisms rather than encourage silent decisions to resell[58]. The first signs of this kind of strategic development are apparent in a number of financial institutions[59]. The development of takeover attempts through security financing and junk bonds could also be seen as an increase in control mechanisms.

2. Reorganisation of assets

Another problem faced by most enterprises in difficulties is the composition of their activity portfolios. These generally include a number of activities that are not sufficiently productive or are not properly integrated into overall operations, and whose contribution to the performance of the firm is negative. At the same time, many companies lack certain critical activities and resources, technological and commercial in particular, which would be a useful addition to their existing assets and would better enable them to exploit economies of scale and scope. Therefore, the main problem is the unsatisfactory structure of overall assets, which can only be improved by shedding some and developing or acquiring others.

Capital markets play an important role in restructuring programmes, once these changes have been decided and designed by shareholders and management. The possibility of living off certain assets (lines of activity, production units, etc.) without this necessarily meaning liquidations and write-offs depends on the capacity of capital markets to assess, value and finance the transfer of these assets. These transfers have to be made towards organisations that are able to make more efficient use of them, whether they be industrial enterprises or financial groups. Similarly, the enterprise must be able to transfer from outside or develop inside the activities that are critical to its future competitiveness and growth, even if this involves heavy financial costs[60].

Financial institutions skilled in the recognition and organisation of such operations play a major role in these initiatives. The flexibility and efficiency of capital markets *vis-à-vis* industrial restructuring largely depends on their professional capabilities and skills[61].

Such operations developed remarkably in OECD

169

countries during the 1975 to 1985 period, despite considerable variation in number and organisational diversity between countries. In some countries, particularly in Europe, many mergers consisted of the takeover of small firms by larger ones, and the absorption of firms in difficulties by successful companies – in the latter case frequently on government guidance and with government funding. This type of public intervention in the industrial asset redistribution process may be a political response to the insufficient development of such operations in capital markets.

Table 4.17 compares the number of mergers and takeovers in seven OECD countries in 1982 and 1985, and highlights differences between countries. Differences might appear even greater if it were possible to single out the larger operations involving real industrial reorganisation.

Table 4.17. **Industrial mergers and acquisitions in seven OECD countries**

1982 and 1985 (numbers of)

	1982	1985
United States	2 346	3 001
Japan	1 044	..
Canada	491[1]	712
Germany	603	709
United Kingdom	463	..
Netherlands	328	318
Spain	80[2]	..

1. 1981.
2. 1980.
Source: OECD.

Recent increases in mergers, acquisitions and takeovers have caused political concern in several countries, in particular when financed by borrowing (leveraged buy-outs). The impact of this trend on firms' debt ratios increases their financial risks while also producing systemic risks affecting the financial system[62]. This fear is justified when loans are granted without appropriate evaluation and diversification of the risks assumed. But, provided the loan is used to finance an economically justified merger or takeover, even a resulting high debt ratio after a successful asset reorganisation can be positive from the structural adjustment standpoint.

3. *Adjustment of ownership structures*

The third area where capital markets are involved in restructuring operations concerns company buy-outs by their managers and employees. For some firms recovery often means sacrifices on the wage front, adjustments in productive structures, and increased flexibility of work organisation, all of which require consensus and active involvement on the part of managers and employees. In such cases, a buy-out of the firm by its employees may be an efficient way of adjusting the company's ownership structure, since it provides the parties concerned with a stake in the company and a direct interest in putting it back on a sound footing[63].

A similar situation exists in all firms – not just those in difficulties – whose most important assets are human resources and whose competitiveness depends principally on its employees' motivation and active involvement[64]. In such cases it may be useful to provide key professionals with a direct stake in company profitability – an incentive similar to the traditional bonus and stock options available to senior managers – by encouraging insider stock-ownership[65]. This approach has been used in many OECD countries in the last decade, and has frequently resulted in improved company performances. It is however difficult to draw a distinction between "wage" and "incentive" effects of employee ownership in these experiences[66].

Capital markets play a major role in this type of ownership adjustment when employees buying stakes in their companies do not have adequate personal capital. This means they have to borrow on capital markets with the only collateral usually offered being the company's assets. These assets are intangible when they consist mainly of the "good will" of workers.

A special type of external credit arrangement is therefore necessary. The lenders either provide long-term credit directly or, when the amounts and the risks involved are very high, issue securities in order to spread the risks. Techniques for assessing buy-out proposals and arranging appropriate financial packages have become a complicated task with high risk – all operations being financed by credit with practically no collateral. The design and organisation of such schemes has thus become a sophisticated financial skill area.

This sector of the finance industry is unevenly developed at international level. Two OECD countries, the United States and the United Kingdom, account for the majority of the financial companies specialising in this field.

C. **Investment for creating new businesses**

The third major category of structural adjustment-related investment is the setting up of new businesses. New enterprises greatly increased their output and employment in the whole OECD area throughout the last decade. They play a particularly important role in high technology industries and also in services[67].

1. *Particular combinations of risk/liquidity/profitability*

Investment for the setting up of new enterprises is notable for being particularly risky and having a long amortization period. But it can also, in the long run, be exceptionally profitable. Recent studies in the United States show that bankruptcy rates can be twice as high amongst small firms as amongst large firms[68], but that small firms were much quicker to increase their output, employment and profitability over the 1972 to 1982 period[69].

Investment risks in these firms are particularly high because they usually do not have any former organisational, technical and commercial experience. Their managers may be experienced, but the firms as such do not benefit from any learning economy. Also, they often produce entirely new products and services that have not been market tested. In the case of high technology firms, these high risks are reflected in bankruptcy rates of between 30 to 40 per cent of the total number of firms established, even in countries with the greatest experience in these fields.

The amortization period for investment in new enterprises is also, on average, particularly long. Creation of the company's basic resources, such as its product and service technology, its brand image, production units and sales networks involves infrastructural investments that are spread over several generations of products and services. In addition, these enterprises may need investment for several consecutive years without making any profit. Recent estimates show that high technology start-ups – if they survive – reach financial equilibrium only after five to six years. In the 1970s this period was shorter, usually three to four years.

New enterprises can also show exceptional profitability once past the initial growth risks and the setting-up phase. But it is difficult to distinguish between temporary difficulties (in particular, in the acceptance of new products and services by the market, which calls for financial reserves) and difficulties of a more structural nature that require changes in strategy. If the firm can manage this extended phase of risks and uncertainties efficiently, it will acquire the know-how and a niche in the market where it may exploit innovation-related rents for several years. This scenario will produce very high profit ratios and, in the event of the business going public or being bought by a large company, a considerable increase in the market value of the enterprise in relation to the initial investment. In the high technology sectors, this capital gain ratio has in many cases easily reached 30 to 40 times the initial investment in the enterprise.

2. Specific techniques and services relating to venture capital

Financing such new businesses is a high-risk investment, with capital almost completely tied up for several years. This situation necessitates financing by investors with relatively uncommon preferences as regards to risks, maturities and earnings, and/or portfolios sufficiently extensive and diversified to leave room for this type of longer-term investment.

It is essential for the investor to monitor and assess these new operations continually, as there is a considerable likelihood of bankruptcy and the residual (recoverable) value of assets is very low. Because of this specific risk structure, investment in new enterprises often has to take the form of financing through insider participation – by those who set up and participate in the management of the firms. Long-term credit and capital inputs by distant shareholders and creditors are not efficient forms of financing for start-ups.

This type of insider-financing has become a specific and separate financial service, known as venture capitalism. It is made up of small investment units managed by investors partially managing their own funds and, more generally, funds invested by large financial institutions. They are small because their business is monitoring and providing *ad hoc* management guidance to a limited number of start-ups – each by definition small in size.

The specific skill and technology of venture capitalism lies in this ability to evaluate, monitor and participate in the management of fledgling enterprises. The venture capitalist takes an active part in the organisation of the new enterprise, and in the design of its production, marketing and financial strategies.

Obviously this is as much a management as a financial technique, which is why venture capitalism has developed unevenly in OECD countries (Table 4.18). The United States leads with total venture capital investment in the range of $20 billion in 1984. It is followed in Europe by the United Kingdom, with more than $3 billion of investment in 1984. In other European countries, as in Japan, a large number of venture capital investment funds were set up in the 1980s, but very few have managed to develop the resources and specific services that are characteristic of venture capitalism[70]. The main problem has been not so much to raise funds in a high risk/high potential profit context, but to develop the know-how necessary for this type of investment[71].

Table 4.18. **Unequal development of venture capital industry in different countries**

December 1986

	Number of venture capital enterprises	Total capital of venture capital enterprises (million $)
United States	550	20 000
United Kingdom	110	4 500
Canada	44	1 000
Japan	70	850
France	45	750
Netherlands	40	650
Germany	25	500
Sweden	31	325
Norway	35	185
Denmark	14	120
Ireland	10	100
Australia	11	50

Source: Estimates by Venture Economics.

Capital markets also play a part in the later growth phases of new enterprises, when larger sums involving less risk have to be raised. These second- and third-round financings imply less participation and lower management costs on the part of investors. Investment funds partly akin to venture capital funds are used in these financings.

At the last stage when new enterprises go public, the services of financial intermediaries are again useful. They organise the first securities issues at an optimum price for both owners and new investors. They also help private companies going public to comply with the necessary accounting and financial regulations[72].

The roles played by the capital market in the growth of new enterprises call for specific skills and techniques. These are becoming more sophisticated with the increased variety of financing instruments available, the internationalisation of fund sources and investment areas, and the difficulty of assessing the technical value and potential competitiveness of new projects in international markets.

It is unavoidable that these sophisticated skills and knowledge should have developed unevenly in different national financial environments. The existence of dynamic second- and third-tier equity markets is notably an important factor, which facilitates going-public operations for start-up companies and makes venture capital investments more liquid. Further internationalisation of financial markets and venture capital firms, and the subsequent transfers of financial technology, should help gradually bridge these gaps. Although the amount of capital committed to the venture capital industry remains marginal in quantitative terms, this is an area where the interaction between financial market innovation and industrial development proves most significant.

IV. FINANCIAL POLICY OPTIONS AND INTERNATIONAL CO-OPERATION

A. Financial policies as structural adjustment policies

The industrial structures of OECD countries are going through a period of far-reaching and multiform adjustment resulting in:

i) Inevitable obsolescence and scrapping of capital assets under the impact of technical progress and the stepping up of competition – in particular at the international level;

ii) A series of entirely new investment opportunities in the traditional sectors (linked in particular to the use of new technologies) and in the new manufacturing and service activities;

iii) Very tight competitive constraints that imply strict control of firms' management efficiency and the optimisation of their range of activities and diversification of projects.

The first three parts of this chapter showed the role of capital markets in these structural adjustment processes. Firstly, they serve as a connecting link in channelling the economy's savings resources into the best investment projects. Secondly, they contribute to the transfers and redeployment of assets leading to more efficient organisational structures. Finally, capital markets exercise continuous control over the efficient management of companies.

The role of capital markets in industrial adjustment and efficiency has been somewhat overshadowed in OECD countries during the last decades. As a result of relatively regular growth and investment in various sectors, large companies' own cash resources and internal management control tended to predominate. But capital markets are now, once again, playing an active role in structural change, in the development of new sectors and technologies and in the international reallocation of saving resources.

Capital markets do not simply act as a neutral and anonymous arena for matching large numbers of initial investors with final borrowers. Financial enterprises acting as intermediaries play an important co-ordination role, since they can more efficiently identify opportunities for collecting and investing funds and assume rising investment management costs in a complex and changing industrial environment. They also derive considerable benefits from aggregating and spreading risks[73]. The resources of these institutions and their activities are now steadily growing; their information, know-how, financial techniques and assessment capabilities are becoming more advanced; and a large number of specialist areas are developing within the financial sector, the whole process being very akin to a typical industrial (re)organisation process.

Financial industry is the most rapidly expanding industry of the 1980s, both in the OECD area and internationally. The inevitable – although in part temporary – consequences of this growth and buoyancy are commercial fluctuations, concerns associated with the increasing number of risks, a plethora of duplicated, non-standardized innovations, and uncertainties as to the impact of these developments on macroeconomic policies.

Under these circumstances, it is the critical role of financial policies to encourage the growth, innovative capacity and competitiveness of financial industries, while maintaining the soundness of the global financial system. It is only by this stimulation that capital markets will fulfil their allocative role as well as their role in monitoring technical efficiency – both of which are essential to the structural adjustment of our entire economies. The promotion of an integrated and competitive capital market at the domestic level, open to foreign competition and technology transfers at the international level, should therefore continue to be a major policy objective.

B. Reconciling efficiency and stability objectives

This policy orientation must comply with a basic principle – the preservation of the credibility and soundness of the financial system at macroeconomic level[74].

Despite being technically diversified, most financial regulations in force in OECD countries aim to meet this objective. They are aimed at protecting the overall soundness of the financial system against the risk of bankruptcy amongst the constituent firms (minimisation of systemic risks) and protecting savers and users of financial services against any possible lack of information, lack of liquidity and conflicting interests among the suppliers of these services (compensation for the asymmetry of information). Financial policies also have more general objectives, such as the efficient transmission of macroeconomic policies (in particular monetary policies) and the limiting of excessive concentration of financial power.

These fundamental public policy objectives remain valid in all industrial and financial contexts and for all OECD Member countries. They can also be considered more important since the emergence of new risks in the financial system. These are linked to interest and exchange rate volatility, sectoral and geographic concentration of credit risks, and increased macroeconomic fragility[75].

The major challenge facing governments is to pursue policies that will stimulate and modernise capital markets and open them to foreign competition, without sacrificing these prudential concerns. Reconciling the two objectives of efficiency and stability means modernising the instruments of prudential policies and gradually eliminating their protectionist and anti-competitive elements.

C. Modernising prudential instruments and techniques

The decisive stage in this modernisation process is that of dissociating the fundamental objectives of financial policies from the traditional instruments and techniques developed to implement them in particular historical and market situations.

Until recently, financial policies gave priority to maintaining the market structure in domestic financial services as a means of ensuring the stability of the system. Limiting competition via regulated prices (fixed interest rates and commissions), administrative compartmentalisation of markets, restrictions on new entries and the limitation of international competition – notably by limitations to the right of establishment – preserved the sector's market structure and stability. But this was largely at the expense of competition, competitiveness,

technology transfer and overall efficiency in the financial system. In several countries the system's organisational rigidity has also reduced its capacity to absorb shocks (because of the concentration of risks in certain sectors in regional, farm and international credits for example) and the high level of implicit government guarantees.

Many governments are now searching for more flexible techniques to assess the health and soundness of financial enterprises, without jeopardising responsibility, competition and innovation in the financial sector. The use of market monitoring techniques (of the financial audit type) in place of more administrative methods (such as checking compliance with rigid assets/liabilities structures) is in particular prompting these changes in supervisory techniques. International prudential co-operation on a wider scale is also furthering modernisation and is facilitating the opening up of markets to international competition without the hampering of national prudential concerns.

The most important step forward in this direction has been the recent development in many Member countries, of techniques for assessing the financial health of banks. The new approach assesses more precisely the particular risks associated with different types of investment and bank credit (their geographic distribution, their sectoral structure, the particular characteristics of the borrowers, etc.). An additional component of improved risk appraisal is that off-balance sheet activities which are an increasing proportion of bank activities (swap agreements, options and futures contracts, commitments to subscribe to securities issues, etc.) are taken into account.

The new regulatory system in the United Kingdom, as is already the case in the United States, uses a series of self-regulating organisations operating within a statutory framework, to enhance the role which the professional communities themselves can play in ensuring the soundness of the financial sector. This approach may facilitate the adaptation of prudential supervision to the changing conditions, instruments and activities of the different segments of the financial system. Industry-wide co-operation is also, in certain cases, a prerequisite to the implementation of systemic technological changes – as in the case of standardizing interbank computerised networks, automated teller machines, point-of-sale terminals, etc. Self-regulation should not however become an instrument to limit market entry and to promote collusive behaviour in industry.

D. The need for international co-operation

Co-ordination of prudential regulations is essential for the continued internationalisation of financial markets and the development of equal and fair international competition between financial enterprises[76]. Liberalisation of trade and investment in financial services is a major complement to, yet a distinct element from, liberalisation of international capital movements. This liberalisation will fully achieve its purpose only if the underlying transactions and operations which give rise to capital flows are not impeded more than is consonant with appropriate supervision and national treatment. Significant obstacles related to prudential supervision still limit the financial services trade, even in countries having liberalised capital movements fully. This calls for better international co-operation and harmonization in prudential regulations.

International regulatory co-ordination is also necessary to avoid imprudent over-deregulation in the present context, with governments encouraging more of these very mobile international service industries to be located in their own countries. Too rapid a deregulation might also cast doubts on the stability and effectiveness of the system, which might in turn slow down or halt liberalisation policies at the international level.

Although fundamental objectives of most countries' financial regulations are similar, both the techniques employed and their structural consequences are at present very different. Nevertheless, over the past decade, there has been appreciable progress made in co-ordinating these regulations, particularly in the field of banking[77,78]. Member countries should make it a priority to pursue these efforts, which ought to be extended to the whole financial sector. Much still remains to be done in the rapidly expanding area of marketable securities.

1. Supervision of the banking sector

Prudential Supervision in Banking has been a major field of multilateral information and consultation in the OECD area since the early 1980s. A report on the Financial Markets Committee's assessment of recent trends in banking was published in 1985[79], followed by a monograph on Prudential Supervision in Banking in 1987[80]. These activities facilitated continuous consultation among OECD governments on developments in this area.

Two important co-operative initiatives at an operational level concerning banking regulations have been those taken by the European Economic Community and the Bank for International Settlements.

European co-operation developed in the context of the EEC Programme of Convergence of Banking Legislation. The co-operation resulted in several Community directives and recommendations. The first banking co-ordination directive, dating from 1977, lays down common principles for the authorisation of credit institutions, and stipulated in particular that the supervisory authorities of the country where a credit institution's head office is located should exercise overall supervision of the institution's operations throughout the Community. Another directive, dated 1983, on the supervision of credit institutions on a consolidated basis provides for the supervision of financial institutions on the basis of the consolidation of all their activities, and requests the removal of all legal impediments to the cross-border flow of information necessary for the consolidation. Recently, in December 1986, a directive concerning the annual accounts of banks and other financial institutions was adopted, which imposes a uniform structure on the balance sheets of credit institutions. At present a proposal for a second banking co-ordination directive is being discussed. This directive should deal with the following issues: the scope of banking activities to be supervised; the further harmonization of licensing conditions; phasing out of the endowment capital requirement for branches; and the implementation of the freedom to provide services. Initiatives of this kind are contributing to the establishment of a common legal base and shared procedures for prudential banking policies in Europe. They rest in particular on the binding nature of the directives adopted by the Community for its Member States. Besides these legal instruments, the co-operation on EEC level is realised by institutionalised consultations. The Banking Advisory Committee, a Contact Committee and *ad hoc* working groups are responsible for the monitoring of directives, advising on proposals and co-drafting proposals.

The work of the Bank for International Settlements (BIS) in improving co-operation is based more on the principles of goodwill and informal consensus. This originally involved only the Central Banks of BIS Member countries, but has gradually expanded worldwide to include the supervisory institutions of other countries and regions. It is a forum for the exchange of information, ideas and experiences between different countries' supervisory institutions and aims at developing common principles which may become the basis for future national policies within the framework of local laws. The furthest initiative in this direction was the drawing up of the document entitled "Principles for the Supervision of Banks' Foreign Establishments", better known as the "Basel Concordat".

This report was first adopted in 1975 and then extensively revised before finally being distributed to supervisory authorities world-wide in June 1983. Its preparation reflects the complexity but also the flexibility and effectiveness of informal and voluntary international co-operation. First endorsed by the Group of Ten Governors, it later was approved by the BIS's Offshore Group of Banking Supervisors and met with general consensus at a bigger international conference in September 1984.

The Basel Concordat develops and puts forward technical supervision procedures based on two principles: *i)* no foreign banking institution should be permitted to be in a legal vacuum and escape prudential regulations; and *ii)* the supervision implemented should be effective and adequate. An international study currently in progress is intended to determine the extent to which the different countries' supervisory legislation and procedures enable these guidelines to be put into practice.

The Bank for International Settlements has also

carried out studies from a prudential perspective on country risk, foreign exchange risk, liquidity and capital adequacy, etc. At the request of central bank Governors of the Group of Ten Countries, a study group recently produced a major assessment on the impact of Financial Innovations on Banks' Off Balance Sheet Risks[81].

2. Supervision of the securities markets

So far as the monitoring and supervision of dealings in negotiable securities are concerned, the international situation is quite different. Although there is already considerable co-operation between stock markets in certain technical areas, international supervision of the securities markets and the institutions operating therein remains underdeveloped. Yet institutions of this type are growing very rapidly at international level and accumulating investments and financial liabilities; the soundness and risk level of the latter are still not fully appreciated. Although "conflict of interests" and "insider trading" problems within this type of institution are controlled domestically in many OECD countries, they are still inadequately monitored at international level.

The EEC has made some significant steps towards a closer alignment of Member State rules concerning securities markets[82]. In 1979, a directive was adopted co-ordinating the conditions for the admission of securities to official stock exchange listing. This directive was supplemented in 1980 with another directive co-ordinating the requirements for the drawing up, scrutiny and distribution of listing particulars to be published for the admission of securities to official stock exchange listing. Another directive, aiming also at improving the transparency of the securities markets, dating from 1982, contains provisions with regard to information to be published on a regular basis by companies whose shares have been admitted to official stock exchange listing. At present, discussions are taking place on a proposed directive providing prospectus requirements for the public offering of securities. This directive tries to achieve at the same time the mutual recognition of both the offering prospectus and the listing prospectus throughout the EEC. As in the banking sector, also in the securities sector there exists a high-level co-ordinating committee, which discussed international co-operation between supervisory authorities as well as new proposals of the EEC Commission on harmonization.

On the basis of a conference held in 1986, the International Organisation of Securities Commissions has also reactivated international co-operation on these questions. There is a programme designed to overcome the preliminary problems of defining the sectors and financial activities to be supervised, notably in relation to the sectors monitored by the banking authorities – a difficult task in view of the gradual integration of all these activities. Co-operation between regulatory bodies of different countries also necessitates a consensus on risk levels and the information that financial businesses are required to publish – a question that is viewed differently from one country to another. Lastly, the legal status of the supervisory bodies differs considerably from country to country, with government bodies, central banks and trade associations not carrying the same weight. Accordingly, international co-operation in this field cannot be envisaged and organised either as an exclusively intergovernmental co-operation scheme, or as co-operation solely between central banks or, obviously, as a mere matter for co-ordination and liaison between stock-market institutions and professional associations. One can note recent progress in international co-operation on a bilateral basis in order to counter fraudulent practices and insider trading (Agreements between the US and UK, US and Canada, for example). It is desirable that these initiatives be extended at the multilateral level.

Consequently, there is difficult yet urgent work to be undertaken in this area. Because of its flexible and open structures, the OECD could continue to act as a catalyst. The Organisation's Committee on Financial Markets is in the process of initiating related consultations.

3. Impact on the continuation of liberalisation policies

Progress in discussions and in the national and international consensus on prudential questions is very important, not only for ensuring that the financial system remains effectively stable, but also for the continued liberalisation of financial markets at national and international levels.

At national level, the security offered by a modern and effective supervision system will enable governments to move ahead with the liberalisation of markets.

At the international level, the harmonization of policies will help to make financial industries more open to foreign competition by enabling host countries to authorise a greater number of international financial institutions to trade on their territory. They will also encourage countries of origin to adopt a more liberal stance towards the intensified international activities of their financial enterprises, as they will be assured of the quality of control abroad. The OECD Codes on the Liberalisation of Capital Movements and of Current Invisible Operations will be important elements of this new international policy approach.

Thus, modernised regulations should not be seen as a natural limit to, but rather as a new basis for, further liberalisation of financial markets.

NOTES AND REFERENCES

1. Revell, J.R.S., *Banking and Electronic Fund Transfers*, OECD, Paris, 1983; Centre de Recherches en Economie Industrielle, *L'électronisation des flux monétaires*, ministère de l'Industrie/ministère des Postes et Télécommunications, Paris, 1983.

2. Bröker, G., "Competition in Banking" (mimeo), OECD, Paris, 1986.

3. According to M. Allais, the excessive retention of income by firms and a high self-financing ratio are not a sign of economic health and efficiency, but more an indication of poor allocation of the economy's savings resources. See Allais, M., *L'impôt sur le capital et la réforme monétaire*, Hermann, Paris, 1973 (preface by R. Aron). M. Jensen has recently developed a similar analysis in the framework of agency theory, interpreting retained income as resources that are poorly monitored by their owners: Jensen, M., "Agency Costs of Free Cash-Flow, Corporate Finance, and Take-overs", *American Economic Review*, May 1986.

4. See Schumpeter, J., *Business Cycles*, McGraw Hill, New York, 1939, especially Chapter XIII – Central Market and Stock Exchange; Goldsmith, R., *Financial Structure and Development*, Yale University Press, New Haven, 1968; Gille, B., "Banking and Industrialisation in Europe, 1730-1914" in Cipolla C. (ed.), *The Industrial Revolution*, William Collins, Glasgow, 1973; Townsend, R., "Financial Structure and Economic Activity", *American Economic Review*, December 1983; Rosenberg, N. and Birdzell, L., *How the West Grew Rich?*, Basic Books, 1985, Chapter VII – Technology, Trusts and Marketable Stock.

5. The relevant economic literature has in the past not accounted for these efficiency problems by assuming perfect information and functioning of the financial markets. The classical theory from this viewpoint is: Modigliani, F. and Miller, M., "The Cost of Capital, Corporation Finance and the Theory of Investment", *American Economic Review*, June 1958. See also Stiglitz, J.E., "On the Irrelevance of Corporate Financial Policy", *American Economic Review*, December 1979. However, the model is of theoretical rather than explanatory interest for the purposes of analysing the links between the capital markets and industrial investment (as is recognised by Marsh, T.A. and Merton, R.C., "Dividend Variability and Variance Bound Tests for the Rationality of Stock Market Prices", *American Economic Review*, June 1986). More empirical models have begun to be developed on the basis of more realistic assumptions, in particular using the research effort conducted for ten years by the National Bureau of Economic Research in the United States. For an excellent overview and discussion of the results of this research, see Friedman, B., "An Overview of the NBER's Research Project on the Changing Roles of Debt and Equity in Financing U.S. Capital Formation" in Friedman, B. (ed.), *The Changing Roles of Debt and Equity in Financing US Capital Formation*, University of Chicago Press, 1982. See also Myers, S.C., "The Capital Structure Puzzle", *Journal of Finance*, July 1984.

6. See Arrow, K., "The Role of Securities in the Optimal Allocation of Risk-bearing", *Review of Economic Studies*, April 1964; Fama, E., "Efficient Capital Markets: A Review of Theory and Empirical Work", *Journal of Finance*, May 1970; Tobin, J., "Capital Market Efficiency", *Lloyds Bank Review*, July 1984; Revell, J., "Efficiency in the Financial Sector" in Shepherd, D., Turk, J. and Silberston, A. (eds.), *Microeconomic Efficiency and Macroeconomic Performance*, Ph. Allan, United Kingdom, 1985.

7. Berle, A.A. and Means, G.C., *The Modern Corporation and Private Property*, Macmillan, New York, 1932.

8. Kornaï, J., "The Soft Budget Constraint", *Kyklos*, 1986, No. 1. For the weakening of bank constraints under the impact of political factors, see Pastré, O., "La modernisation des relations entre les banques et les entreprises", *Revue d'Economie Industrielle*, 1986, 1st quarter.

9. The maintenance of control of financial markets despite these inevitable phenomena of efficiency loss is the subject of the modern theory of agency costs. See Fama, E. and Jensen, M., "Separation of Ownership and Control", *Journal of Law and Economics*, June 1983; Williamson, O., "Organisation Form, Residual Claimants, and Corporate Control", *Journal of Law and Economics*, June 1983; Jensen, M., "Agency Costs of Free Cash Flow, Corporate Finance, and Take-overs", *American Economic Review*, May 1986. There is also a theoretical synthesis in Pratt, J. and Zeckhauser, J., *Principals and Agents: The Structure of Business*, Harvard Business School Press, Cambridge, Mass., 1986.

10. Demsetz, H. and Lehn, K., "The Structure of Corporate Ownership: Causes and Consequences", *Journal of Political Economy*, 1985, No. 6; Shleifer, A. and Vishny, R.W., "Large Shareholders and Corporate Control", *Journal of Political Economy*, 1986, No. 3.

11. There is disagreement in economic and financial literature concerning the impact that takeover threats and actual takeovers have on firms' competitiveness. On the basis of statistical analyses of comparable quality, all carried out in the United States, J.M. Scherer argues that these threats weaken companies' competitiveness by reducing their (long-term) strategic investments, whereas D.H. Ginsburg and J.F. Robinson find that the capital markets value this type of investment perfectly and so do not in any way penalise firms that make them (by turning them into buy-up targets). Ginsburg and Robinson find, on the other hand, that takeover bids target on under-performing companies, and that takeovers, once completed, have a positive impact on company performance. See Scherer, J.M., "Takeovers: Present and Future Dangers", *The Brookings Review*, Winter-Spring 1986; Ginsburg, D.H. and Robinson, J.F., "The Case Against Federal Intervention in the Market for Corporate Control", *ibid.* A Canadian statistical study

also supports this second "optimistic" interpretation of takeovers: Eckbo, B.E., "Mergers and the Market for Corporate Control: the Canadian Evidence", *Canadian Journal of Economics*, May 1986. The two points of view are also defended, on a more qualitative but instructive basis, by Drucker, P., "Corporate Take-overs – What is to be done?", *Public Interest*, Winter 1986; and Boone Pickens, T., "Professions of a Short-termer", *Harvard Business Review*, May-June 1986.

12. See Arnold, J.H., "Assessing Capital Risk: You Can't be Too Conservative", *Harvard Business Review*, September-October 1986.

13. On the impact of control by the main banks over companies' management efficiency, see Cable, J., "Capital Market Information and Industrial Performance: The Role of West German Banks", *The Economic Journal*, March 1985. For an instructive professional viewpoint, see Galzy, G., "Le profil du banquier d'entreprise dans les années 1980", *Banque*, September 1983.

14. Reich, R.B., "Bailout: A Comparative Study in Law and Industrial Structure", *Yale Journal of Regulation*, 1985, Vol. 2.

15. The impact of price regulations on the financial businesses' competitive strategies has been analysed in Silber, W.L., "Towards a Theory of Financial Innovation" in Silber, W.L. (ed.), *Financial Innovation*, Lexington Books, Lexington, Mass., 1975.

16. In the United States, funds allocated by "loan agencies under government control" amounted to $72.1 billion in 1984, i.e. 8.7 per cent of all funds going through the credit market (OECD Financial Statistics, III.4.c, 1985). In Japan, 13.9 per cent of new credits for investment in machinery and equipment were granted by government financial institutions in 1983, as against 18.6 per cent in 1978 (figures supplied by the Bank of Tokyo). In France, government-subsidised loans accounted for 60 per cent of long-term credit to enterprises in 1983; this proportion has been noticeably reduced since the reform of the financial system. See Ministère de l'Economie et des Finances, *Livre blanc sur la réforme du système financier*, Paris, 1985.

17. On the more general influence of technological and industrial policies on fund allocation by the capital markets, see Joint Economic Committee, Congress of the United States, *Monetary Policy, Selective Credit Policy and Industrial Policy in France, Britain, West Germany and Sweden (A Staff Study)*, June 1981; Cox, A. (ed.), *State, Finance and Industry – A Comparative Analysis of Post-War Trends in Six Advanced Industrial Economies*, Harvest, Sussex, 1986; Rybczynski, T.M., "Industrial Finance System in Europe, U.S. and Japan", *Journal of Economic Behavior and Organization*, September 1984.

18. For case studies of the distortions introduced in capital markets by various regulations, see Council of Economic Advisers, *Economic Report of the President of the United States*, 1986, Chapter VI – The Role of the Federal Government in Credit Markets; *Livre blanc sur la réforme du système financier, op.cit.* in Note 16; Ministry of Finance, *The Regulation of Canadian Financial Institutions: Proposals for Discussion*", Ottawa, 1985.

19. See OECD, *Trends in Banking in OECD Countries. Committee on Financial Markets – Expert Group on Banking*, Paris, October 1985.

20. See Gill, D., *Financial Intermediation Costs*, International Finance Corporation, Washington D.C., 1983.

21. For cases illustrating the technology transfer contribution of international financial institutions – a subject neglected in the theoretical literature – it is necessary to refer to press reports: "Stockmarket Funds – Trust in Foreigners for Tokyo", *The Economist*, 9th August 1986; "Grüezl Frankfurt" (entry of Swiss Banks into German capital markets), *Euromoney*, July 1986; "U.S. Venture Funds are Moving Overseas at Ever-Growing Rate", *Wall Street Journal*, 21st February 1986.

22. Pecchioli, R.M., *The Internationalisation of Banking. The Policy Issues*, OECD, Paris, November 1983, II.2.2a; "International Trade in Services: Securities", report to the OECD Committee on Financial Markets, 1986.

23. See OECD, *International Trade in Services: Banking. Identification and Analysis of Obstacles*, Paris, August 1984; "International Trade in Services: Securities", *op. cit.* in Note 22.

24. For an in-depth description and analysis of the financial innovations in the 1980s, see Study Group by the Central Banks of the Group of Ten Countries, *Recent Innovations in International Banking* (Cross Report), Bank for International Settlements, Basel, 1986.

25. This phenomenon is also known as "disintermediation". However, this term is inappropriate, since the financial intermediaries still play an important (or even increasing) role, both as organisers and as subscribers, in funding through securities issues. It is the role of traditional bank credits that is diminishing, in the form of the constitution of bilateral, non-tradable assets and liabilities.

26. For the influence of a competitive and diversified financial system on the development of household savings, see *Le développement et la protection de l'épargne – Rapport au Ministre de l'Economie et des Finances* (Rapport Dautresme), Documentation Française, Paris, 1982.

27. For reports of the growing sophistication (optimisation) of the behaviour of households and industrial enterprises in savings allocation, see Davis, E.P., *Portfolio Behaviour of the Non-Financial Private Sectors in the Major Economies*, Bank for International Settlements, Basel, 1986; Gönenç, Rauf, "Retirement Savings and Capital Markets" in Gabrielli, G. and Fano, D. (eds.), *The Challenge of Private Pension Funds*, The Economist Publications, London, 1986; for examples on the active role of the new financial services and technologies in the development of this behaviour, see "Personal Financial Advice Spreads as Corporate Benefit", *Wall Street Journal*, 2nd July 1986; "Artificial Intelligence-Based Financial System Allocates Assets Based on Goals", *Computerworld*, 17th March 1986.

28. The impact of public borrowing on the rise in interest rates, and on the various segments and instruments of the financial market, is analysed in: Friedman, B., "Postwar Changes in the American Financial Markets" in Feldstein, M. (ed.), *The American Economy in Transition*, University of Chicago Press, 1980. See also Friedman, B., *Crowding-out or Crowding-in? – Evidence on*

Debt-Equity Substitutability, NBER Working Paper No. 1565, February 1985.

29. Original types of financial institutions are also developing according to local company organisation traditions. See for example, Hashi, I. and Hussain, A., "The Employee Investment Funds in Sweden", *National Westminster Bank Quarterly Review*, May 1986.

30. The excessive volatility of the prices of securities in relation to their natural value (companies' net discounted profits) has been demonstrated in a study covering a long period (1870 to 1970) of the American stock-markets: Shiller, R., "Do Stock Prices Change Too Much to be Justified by Subsequent Changes in Dividends", *American Economic Review*, June 1981. See also West, K., *Dividend Innovations and Stock Market Volatility*, NBER Working Paper No. 1833, 1986.

31. An analysis of price cycles on the New York Stock Exchange over the period 1970 to 1986, carried out by Salomon Brothers, shows that volatility rates have not increased in recent years (report in *The Economist*, 20th September 1986).

32. Nevertheless, a large number of institutional investors continue to follow and imitate others, although more subtly than individual investors. See Shiller, R. and Pound, J., *Survey Evidence on Diffusion of Interest among Institutional Investors*, NBER Working Paper No. 1851, 1985.

33. See Hayes, R.H. and Abernathy, W.J., "Managing our Way to Economic Decline", *Harvard Business Review*, July-August 1980; J. Tobin also took this question into account in: Tobin, J., "Capital Market Efficiency", *Lloyds Bank Review*, July 1984. See also the concern expressed in the financial press: "Playing with Fire – As Speculation Replaces Investment, Our Economic Future is at Stake", *Special Report, Business Week*, September 1985; Greenhouse, S., "U.S. Firms Obsessed with Earnings – Long Term is Forgotten in Quarterly 'Scramble'", *New York Times*, 5th March 1986.

34. For the sophistication of the financial institutions' investment strategies, see Munnell, A., *The Economics of Private Pensions*, The Brookings Institution, Washington D.C., 1982, especially Chapter V – Pension Plans as Financial Intermediaries; Litvak, L., *Pension Funds and Economic Renewal*, Studies in Development Policies, Washington D.C., 1982; "Global Strategy: U.S. Institutions Profit by Investing in World Markets", *Wall Street Journal*, 5th June 1986; "U.S. Mutual Funds to Increase Use of Stock-Index Futures, Options", *Wall Street Journal*, 20th May 1986; "Why Fidelity is the Master of Mutual Funds", *Fortune*, 1st September 1986; Coudert, V., *Les mutations du système financier japonais*, Centre d'Etudes Prospectives et d'Information Internationales, Paris, 1986; "Japanese Pension Funds to Seek Improved Investment Returns", *Financial Times*, 11th April 1986.

35. The ability of competitive financial institutions to identify investment and growth opportunities even in declining industries, and the unavailability of information concerning these opportunities, is a subject that is not discussed in theoretical writings. See press reports: "The New Aces of Low Tech", *Dossier Business Week*, 15th September 1986; "Portfolio Talk – No Blue Chips in this Picks", *Fortune*, 1st September 1986; "An ITT Refugee Builds an Empire" (by leveraging companies that need management skill, not financial magic), *Fortune*, 18th August 1986.

36. The possibility of this sort of development of financial markets had been perceived – and hoped for – by J.M. Keynes following the 1929 crisis. In *The General Theory of Employment, Interest and Money* (1935) he wrote: "If I may be allowed to appropriate the term *speculation* for the activity of forecasting the psychology of the market, and the term *enterprise* for the activity of forecasting the prospective yield of assets over their whole life, it is by no means always the case that speculation predominates over enterprise!" In a market where most of the actors are well-informed and rational, the opportunities for profits from speculation on the price of financial assets diminish, while profits from accurate forecasting of the actual performance of real assets in industry grow. See, for an assessment of recent trends along these lines, Marver, J.D., "Trends in Financing Innovation" in Landau, R. and Rosenberg, N. (eds.), *The Positive Sum Strategy*, National Academy Press, Washington D.C., 1986.

37. For the impact of information technology on employment in the banking system, see Petit, P., "Automatisation of Services: The Case of the Banking Sector", report to the OECD Committee on Information, Computer and Communications Policy in 1984.

38. For the internationalisation of banks in OECD countries and, in particular, the speed of the internationalisation of their asset and liability structures, see Pecchioli, R.M., *The Internationalisation of Banking*, *op. cit.* in Note 22.

39. For the structural impact of the recent growth of capital imports on the American markets, which are particularly developing the short end of the market, see Friedman, B.E., *Implications of the US Net Capital Inflow*, NBER Working Paper No. 1804, 1986.

40. For the risk and maturity characteristics of strategic basic investment and its growth as a proportion of the total investment of 84 large American companies, see O'Connor, R., *Facing Strategic Issues*, Conference Board Research Report, 1986. The development of the phenomenon at macroeconomic level has been identified in Einstein, M.E. and Franklin, J.C., "Computer Manufacturing Enters a New Area of Growth", *Monthly Labor Review*, US Department of Labor, Washington D.C., September 1986. For an analysis of the growth of this type of investment in Japan: Japan Development Bank, "Private Fixed Investment in Japan in 1984-1985 – Fixed Investment Continues to Run Strong Centering in High Technology" (mimeo), Tokyo, 1985; Gönenç, R. and Lecler, Y., "L'électronisation industrielle au Japon", *Sciences sociales du Japon contemporain*, 1982, No. 1.

41. Bitards, D. and Fishman, A., "Linking Technological and Business Planning", *Research Management*, November 1981; Ellis, L.W., "Viewing R&D Projects Financially", *Research Management*, March 1984; Hayes, R.W. and Abernathy, W.J., "Managing our Way to Economic Decline", *Harvard Business Review*, July-August 1980.

42. These tables have been drawn up on the basis of non-official figures taken from the most systematic study of this question today by the French Crédit National.

43. Recent changes in accounting conventions in a large number of OECD countries are starting to remedy this distortion of information. However, they are not yet reflected in macroeconomic statistics.

44. Kaplan, M.-Ch., "La montée de l'investissement intellectuel", *Colloque ECODIX sur l'investissement des entreprises en France*, Université de Paris X, 1st-2nd October 1986.

45. This aspect of strategic investment is discussed in Donaldson, G., "Financial Goals and Strategic Consequences", *Harvard Business Review*, May-June 1985.

46. The role of financial intermediaries in launching very large-scale, high-risk techno-industrial projects was particularly important in financing the aircraft industry. For a report of these experiences in the 1960s and 1970s, see Reed, J. and Moreno, G., "The Role of Large Banks in Financing Innovation" in Landau, R. and Rosenberg, N. (eds.), *The Positive Sum Strategy*, op. cit. in Note 36. Similar financing arrangements will be necessary for the development of a private space industry in the 1980s and 1990s. See Marsh, P., "The U.S. Space Business", *Financial Times*, 26th August 1986; Gump, D., "U.S. Space Shuttle Subsidies Ground Firms", *Wall Street Journal*, 7th August 1986. The fear that the European financial system might not have the capacity to evaluate and finance this type of project – which might in part explain the need for public patronage of the aircraft industry in Europe – is expressed by Pierson, J. (Chairman and General Manager of Airbus Industries), "Airline Finance Systems Unlikely to Cope with Forecast Demand", *Financial Times Conference on World Aerospace*, 27th August 1986.

47. The "basic investment" nature of technology modernisation investment not linked to specific product lines creates a problem of *economic evaluation and appraisal*, even within the companies carrying out the investment. This indicates how critical the efficient working of *external financial markets* is in this field for financing such investment and valuing the enterprises concerned. See for example, National Academy of Engineering, "Corporate Attitudes Toward Introducing the New Manufacturing Technology" in *Education for the Manufacturing World of the Future*, National Academy Press, Washington D.C., 1985. See also Kaplan, R.S., "Must Computer-Integrated-Manufacturing be Justified by Faith Alone?", *Harvard Business Review*, March-April 1986; Canada, J.R., "Non-Traditional Method for Evaluating CIM Opportunities Assigns Weights to Intangibles", *Industrial Engineering*, March 1986. A similar question is raised with respect to the economic justification and capital market financing of energy savings investments. See Association for the Conservation of Energy, Commission of European Communities, *Market for Energy Services Stifled by Lack of Finance*, Brussels, 1986 (report cited in *Financial Times*, 19th March 1986).

48. The difficulties of forecasting the investment costs of innovative projects considerably increase their financial risks. These costs can easily be double or even triple the forecast estimates, thus significantly reducing the actual profitability of the projects compared to their expected profitability. See Merrow, E., Phillips, K. and Myers, Ch., *Understanding Cost Growth and Performance Shortfalls in Pioneer Process Plants*, The Rand Corporation, Santa Barbara, 1981 (cited in Davis, D., "New Projects: Beware of False Economies", *Harvard Business Review*, March-April 1985).

49. For the gradual improvement of financial institutions' ability to analyse and "value" industrial firms' intangible assets, see "Leveraged Buy-Outs aren't just Daredevils Anymore – Staid Wall Street Firms are Jumping in Too", *Business Week*, 11th August 1986.

50. For a series of cases illustrating the differing viewpoints of investors in securities and bank creditors, see Arnold, J., "Assessing Capital Risk: You Can't be Too Conservative", *Harvard Business Review*, September-October 1986.

51. The link between the proportion of intangible investments in companies' total assets, the relative difficulty of financing them through external loans, and their consequent recourse to equity financing, is discussed in Long, M. and Malitz, I., *Investment Patterns and Financial Leverage*, NBER Working Paper No. 1145, June 1983. On the specific aspects of financing intangible investment, see also de Mautort, L., *Investissements dans le domaine des technologies avancées : premières réflexions à partir de l'expérience de la B.E.I. en Italie*, Cahiers de la Banque Européenne d'Investissement, October 1986.

52. In many OECD countries in 1986, large enterprises were able to raise funds on the securities market at rates close to or even lower than the bank base rates in force. See "A Borrower's Paradise", *The Banker*, October 1986.

53. For the traditional differentiation between large and small firms in admission to the capital markets and the most advanced funding instruments, see Jaffe, D.M., *Credit Rationing and the Commercial Loan Market – An Econometric Study of the Structure of the Commercial Loan Market*, Wiley and Sons, New York, 1971; Gramigna, J.E., "Financial Innovation, Financial Deregulation, and Their Effect on Small Firm Financing" (mimeo), New York University, 1986; Afriat, Ch. and Lecler, Y., *L'automatisation des petites et moyennes entreprises japonaises et son financement*, Centre de Prospective et d'Evaluation, Ministère de l'Industrie et de la Recherche, Paris, 1986; Berger, M., "Segmentation et flexibilité du marché des capitaux externes pour les entreprises industrielles", *Revue d'Economie Industrielle*, 1986, 1st quarter.

54. For the gradual spread of the beneficial effects of buoyancy of the capital markets towards small and medium-sized enterprises, see Curran, J., "Big Hopes for Little Stocks – Analysts say the Shares of Emerging Growth Companies, Laggards till Now, are Poised for a Big Leap", *Fortune*, 19th September 1986; "Small Companies Using Impact Loans to Decrease Fund Raising Costs", *Japan Economic Journal*, 14th June 1986.

55. For the generally unsatisfactory performance of government investment companies and the industrial enterprises in which they take holdings, see Hindley, B. (ed.), *State Investment Companies in Europe – Picking Winners or Backing Losers*, Trade Policy Research Centre/MacMillan Press, London, 1983.

56. For case studies from the automobile industry, see Anderson, M., "Financial Restructuring of the World Auto Industry", *Future of the Automobile Program*, MIT, Cambridge, Mass., 1982; Womack, J.P., "The Competitive Significance of National Financial Systems in the Auto Sector", *ibid*. The impact of the financial environment on competitiveness in the semiconductor industries is discussed in: Chase Financial Policy, *US and Japanese Semiconductor Industries: A Financial Comparison*, Semiconductor Industry Association, 1980; Flaherty, T. and Itami, H., *Financial Institutions and Financing for Growth*, project on US-Japanese Semiconductor Industry Competition, Stanford University, 1983; Office of Technology Assessment, *Financing: Its Role in Competitiveness in Electronics*, Washington D.C., 1983.

57. According to a 1985 survey of 400 large and medium-sized enterprises in the United Kingdom, the latter work with an increasing number of banks (17 per enterprise on average), seven of which can be considered as "main banks". See *United Kingdom Corporate Banking 1985*, Greenwich Associates, 1985 (cited in *Financial Times*, 12th August 1985).

58. For the benefit of active involvement on the part of major shareholders and the positive impact this has on company performance, see the statistical analysis in Demsetz, H., "Corporate Control, Insider Trading and Rates of Return", *American Economic Review*, May 1986.

59. Case studies show that a pertinent analysis of the value of industrial enterprises, in particular when they are in difficulty, demands very sophisticated resources and skills on the part of financial investors. These resources and skills are rare, even in the most advanced financial systems, and constitute the comparative advantage of competitive financial enterprises. See for example, Casey, C.J. and Bartczak, N.J., "Cash Flow – It is not the Bottom Line – Operating Cash Flow Information fails as a Thermometer in Gauging Corporate Health", *Harvard Business Review*, July-August 1984; Walsh, F.J., "Measuring Business Performance", *Conference Board Research Bulletin*, 1984, No.153.

60. A large proportion of transfer operations stem from decisions to sell off lines of activity judged to be "non-central" by firms rationalising their asset structure. In 1985, about 1 000 of the 3 000 sales and mergers carried out in the United States were the result of such restructuring initiatives. See Ginsburg, D.H. and Robinson, J.F., "The Case Against Federal Intervention in the Market for Corporate Control", *The Brookings Review*, Winter-Spring 1986.

61. Major asset reorganisation is also taking place within the financial system, with financial institutions adding to their resource and skills by purchasing assets from complementary financial institutions. This movement, that developed rapidly in the United States in the 1970s, is now growing in Europe and Japan. See Andersen & Co., Arthur, *The Decade of Change: Banking in Europe – The Next 10 Years*, Lafferty Publications, 1986 (cited in *Financial Times*, 7th February 1986); Coudert, V., *Les mutations du système financier japonais, op. cit.* in Note 34.

62. See Aglietta, M., *Structures économiques et innovations financières*, Centre d'Etudes Prospectives et d'Informations Internationales, Paris, 1986.

63. Questions are now being raised about the "fairness" of certain leveraged buy-outs (LBOs), in light of the spectacular recoveries in profitability and asset values that have occurred in extremely short time spans. Critical observers are questioning whether previous shareholders were not abused by managers and others involved in the deals. Yet, in this case, the capital structure change can be seen as a rational reaction of capital markets to inefficient shareholder control.

64. For the importance of human resources as the main assets in high technology enterprises and their valuation by the financial markets, see Collins, G., "The Art of Software Takeovers", *Datamation*, 1st July 1986. For a more general theoretical discussion of the problem, see Easterbrook, F.H., "Insider Trading as an Agency Problem" in Pratt, J.W. and Zeckhauser, R.J., *Principals and Agents : The Structure of Business*, Harvard Business School Press, Cambridge, Mass., 1985.

65. According to an original analysis, the development of this kind of internal buy-out, in particular in the American economy, is making companies move towards competitive strategies based on long-term investment and substantial employee involvement – factors which are responsible for the specificity and competitiveness of Japanese firms. See Roberts, D.N. and Ames, W.L., "U.S. Leveraged Buy-Outs Spawn Japan-Style Strategy", *Japan Economic Journal*, 18th October 1986.

66. For a discussion of the prospects of this practice, see Oakeshott, R., "The Beginnings of an Employee Owned Sector", *Lloyds Bank Review*, January 1985; "Employee Ownership", *Dossier Financial Times*, 8th April 1986.

67. See OECD, *Venture Capital in Information Technology*, Paris, 1985, Section X.5.b.

68. Birch, B.L. and MacCracken, S., "The Small Business Share of Job Creation: Lessons Learned from the Use of a Longitudinal File" (mimeo), MIT, Cambridge, Mass., 1982 (cited in OECD, *Employment Outlook*, September 1985).

69. Centre de Prospective et d'Evaluation, *Capital-risque et développement technologique aux Etats-Unis*, ministère de l'Industrie et de la Recherche, Paris, May 1984.

70. See "Special Survey on Japan's High-Tech Start-ups and Venture Capital Firms", *Japan Economic Journal*, 27th September 1986.

71. OECD, *Venture Capital in Information Technology, op. cit.* in Note 67.

72. For an instructive monograph on the key role of merchant banks in the quotation and first issues of securities of new high technology enterprises, see Uttal, B., "Inside the Deal that made Bill Gates $350 000 000" (the going-public of Microsoft), *Fortune*, 21st July 1986. For a general discussion, see S.H. Lewis, "Should a High-Tech Company Go Public – A Comparison of Public Offerings and Venture Capital Offerings", *The Scott Report*, March 1985.

73. The relative advantages of the various types of co-ordination by competitive markets and by administrative organisations have been analysed by Williamson, O., *Market and Hierarchies – Theory and Anti-Trust Implications*, University of Pennsylvania Press, 1978. The application of this model to the capital markets has not yet been made, however.

74. See Lamfalussy, A., *Reflexions sur les relations entre les innovations financières, la politique monétaire et la stabilité des marchés*, Bank for International Settlements, Basel, 26th November 1985; Lamfalussy, A., "Is Change Our Ally?", *The Banker*, September 1986.

75. For two different viewpoints on the growth or lack of growth of the risks currently affecting the capital markets in the OECD, see Rybczynski, T.M., "Financial Systems, Risk and Public Policy", *The Royal Bank of Scotland Review*, December 1985; Aglietta, M., *Structures économiques et innovations financières, op. cit.* in Note 62.

76. OECD, *Trends in Banking in OECD Countries, op. cit.* in Note 19.

77. Pecchioli, R.M., *Prudential Supervision in Banking*, OECD, Paris, 1987.

78. See also Crossick, S. and Lindsay, M., "European Banking Law: An Analysis of Community and Member State Legislation", *Financial Times Business Information*, 1983.

79. Pecchioli, R.M., *op. cit.* in Note 77.

80. *Ibid.*

81. *Recent Innovations in International Banking* (Cross Report), *op. cit.* in Note 24.

82. A recent NBER study of relations between ownership structures and the performances of the 500 largest American companies in 1980 shows that the most profitable amongst them are those whose managers hold between 5 and 20 per cent of the capital value. See Morck, R., Schleifer, A. and Vishny, R., *Management Ownership and Corporate Performance*, NBER Working Paper No. 2055, 1986.

II.   THE OPERATION OF PRODUCT MARKETS

Chapter 5

AGRICULTURE

INTRODUCTION

Thirty years ago, one person in four in the more industrialised OECD economies* worked in agriculture; today, the figure is below one in seventeen. Yet, over the same period, agricultural production in the OECD area increased by more than 60 per cent – nearly three times faster than the growth of population. Pessimism about the overall adequacy of world food supplies – so forcefully expressed by the Club of Rome's 1972 report on *The Limits to Growth*[1] – now appears to be decisively discredited. However, despite this achievement, the difficulties and pressures bearing on the agricultural sector of the advanced economies have, if anything, increased; and concerns about mounting agricultural surpluses have joined the more long-standing issues of low agricultural incomes and unstable agricultural markets.

Why have agriculture's problems proved so intractable? This chapter argues that government policies have a major responsibility in this respect. Policies which shelter farmers from market signals have singularly failed to meet their objectives, while creating large-scale imbalances in agricultural markets, distorting world trade, imposing rising costs on consumers and taxpayers, and reducing economic growth overall. Attempts to contain the adverse effects of these policies without fundamentally revising their basic principles have also failed. The chapter concludes that the only durable solution to the sector's problems is to return farming to a freer market.

The structure of the chapter is as follows. Part I examines the origins, aims and instruments of agricultural policy, highlighting the growing importance of price and income supports. Part II analyses the impacts of these policies, and shows how they have failed to meet their income maintenance objectives, while at the same time creating massive over-production. Part III surveys recent attempts to cope with over-production through output quotas and similar schemes, and finds that they have often been ineffectual and always economically costly. Finally, Part IV argues that agricultural policies

need to be adapted to the realities of modern farming which, as in other sectors, requires a greater role for market forces.

I. THE ORIGINS, AIMS AND INSTRUMENTS OF POLICY

Widespread intervention in agricultural markets predates this century. After a brief period of virtually free trade in agricultural products – from around 1850 to 1870 – the arrival onto European markets of low-cost grains from the Americas and Australia and the associated sharp reduction in wheat prices led to intense rural agitation and to the imposition of tariff duties on farm products, notably in Belgium, Germany, France and Italy. Agricultural protection persisted into the 1920s, with average tariff rates in continental Europe of between 20 and 30 per cent[2]. The concerns underlying protection were familiar: the political power of the farmers (at that time especially of the larger landowners) and the fear of acute social conflict involving the peasantry.

However, agricultural policy as it now operates was primarily shaped in the world depression of the 1930s. Coming on top of the specifically agricultural depression of the 1920s, the sharp falls in world income of the early 1930s had a dramatic impact on agriculture: from 1929 to 1932, the net income of United States agriculture fell by 70 per cent, largely because of a 56 per cent fall in the index of the prices received by farmers[3]; similar declines were recorded elsewhere[4]. These compounded more long-standing problems of rural poverty and unrest.

Already in the years immediately preceding the crisis of the 1930s, politicians and economists associated with the agricultural community had developed a range of policy proposals aimed at stabilizing farm incomes and alleviating rural poverty. Originally rejected as excessively interventionist both by the agricultural interests themselves and by broader political forces, many of these proposals came to be implemented during the Depression and war years as part of a broader reassessment of the role of government in the economy. Some of the other policies entailed by this reassessment have receded – for example, detailed attempts at industrial

* Excluding Turkey, Greece, Yugoslavia, Spain, Portugal and Ireland.

planning – but the agricultural policies proved outstandingly resilient[5].

These policies were partly aimed at addressing the perceived structural bases of rural hardship: the excessive agricultural specialisation of rural areas and their lack of appropriate infrastructure; presumed inequities in land tenure; inefficiencies in the development of agricultural technologies and in their application. Particularly during and immediately after the war, concerns about food security also had a major impact on farm policy. But in addition to altering the framework within which the rural sector operates, the policies also sought to correct apparent deficiencies of agricultural product markets: namely, excessive price instability combined with a long-term adverse trend in the agricultural terms of trade[6].

These deficiencies were taken as fundamental because it was argued that they arise from demand and supply elasticities which are inherently low – on the demand side because of food products' status as "necessities", on the supply side because of the importance of largely fixed land and labour factor inputs[7]. Given these low elasticities, it was thought that major swings in prices would be needed to equilibrate even fairly small

Table 5.1 **An overview of agricultural policy instruments**

Policy	Major rationale	Example
I. Framework measures		
A. Rural development	Externalities involved in reducing regional disparities; congestion costs	Regional subsidies
B. Provision of agricultural infrastructure	Indivisibilities in provision and large capital requirements	Irrigation, electrification of rural regions
C. Tenure and land ownership arrangements	Asymmetries in bargaining power between landlords and tenants; social desirability of dispersed land ownership	Restrictions on land acquisitions above a certain scale
D. Central provision of agricultural services	Market failures compounded by fragmented industry structure	
i) Research, development and extension	Limited appropriability of the gains from innovation	Publicly funded agricultural R&D
ii) Quality control and product promotion	Low product differentiation leading to limited appropriability of gains from advertising and product quality	Levy-funded advertising campaigns
iii) Setting and enforcement of health standards	Negative externalities arising from the spread of disease and infections	Mandatory product inspection
II. Price stabilisation		
A. Stockpiling and similar buffer schemes	Extreme price variations arising from low supply and demand elasticities	Commodity stabilisation arrangements
B. Market flow controls	As above, but applied to perishables which cannot be stocked	Fresh-fruit regimes for certain products in the United States
III. Agricultural income support		
A. Measures which alter price signals	Belief that agricultural terms of trade should be improved	
i) Reductions in input prices		Fertilizer subsidies; mortgage and interest rate subsidies; tax relief
ii) Increases in output prices		Price supports; deficiency payments; border measures
B. Measures which alter demand and supply elasticities		
i) Reductions in the elasticity of domestic supply		Output and acreage controls
ii) Increases in the elasticity of domestic demand		Consumption subsidies; VAT exemption
C. Direct income maintenance		
i) Related to scale of operation		Direct payments
ii) Aimed at increasing income security		Supplementary of subsidised social security

186

Table 5.2. **Public expenditure related to the implementation of agricultural policy**[1]

	1979	1981	1983	1984	1985
United States					
Expenditure ($ million)[2]	22 000.0	27 300.0	47 600.0	39 100.0	57 000.0
Expenditure per capita	97.8	118.6	202.7	165.0	238.2
Share of government spending[3]	2.9	2.7	4.0	3.1	4.1
Share of value added in agriculture[4]	28.5	32.6	71.7	45.4	67.3
Index in constant prices[5]	96.2	99.9	157.5	124.6	175.8
Japan					
Expenditure ($ million)[2]	11 126.0	13 279.7	14 010.2	13 753.4	12 971.2
Expenditure per capita	96.0	112.9	117.5	114.6	107.4
Share of government spending[3]	5.3	4.5	3.8	3.5	3.1
Share of value added in agriculture[4]	29.3	33.7	31.6	29.0	26.6
Index in constant prices[5]	100.0	100.0	94.4	89.0	83.1
Canada					
Expenditure ($ million)[2]	1 505.4	1 914.4	2 458.6	2 561.8	2 624.0
Expenditure per capita	63.3	78.6	98.7	101.9	103.4
Share of government spending[3]	1.6	1.5	1.6	1.5	1.5
Share of value added in agriculture[4]	14.8	15.7	21.6	20.7	20.5
Index in constant prices[5]	14.8	15.7	21.6	20.7	20.5
Australia					
Expenditure ($ million)[2]	179.0	231.8	295.8	291.1	372.0
Expenditure per capita	12.3	15.5	19.2	18.7	23.6
Share of government spending[3]	0.5	0.5	0.5	0.5	0.5
Share of value added in agriculture[4]	2.1	2.8	3.2	3.3	3.8
Index in constant prices[5]	95.6	103.7	120.4	115.3	140.5
Austria					
Expenditure ($ million)[2]	268.5	332.3	392.7	394.7	..
Expenditure per capita	35.6	43.9	52.0	52.3	..
Share of government spending[3]	1.1	1.1	1.1	1.0	..
Share of value added in agriculture[4]	10.7	11.5	13.2	12.2	..
Index in constant prices[5]	98.2	101.8	108.0	104.7	..
Germany[6]					
Expenditure ($ million)[2]	5 208.9	5 045.0	6 091.2	6 400.1	6 819.8
Expenditure per capita	84.9	81.8	99.2	104.6	111.8
Share of government spending[3]	2.2	1.7	1.8	1.8	1.8
Share of value added in agriculture[4]	41.7	36.1	41.3	39.6	47.5
Index in constant prices[5]	107.3	87.0	93.9	95.4	100.1
France[6]					
Expenditure ($ million)[2]	5 677.8	7 273.4	7 747.6	7 847.5	8 099.0
Expenditure per capita	105.9	134.2	141.6	142.8	146.8
Share of government spending[3]	2.8	2.7	2.4	2.3	2.2
Share of value added in agriculture[4]	25.6	32.3	29.5	28.9	29.9
Index in constant prices[5]	96.8	104.0	99.0	96.9	96.1
United Kingdom[6]					
Expenditure ($ million)[2]	2 482.5	2 685.6	3 383.8	3 797.8	..
Expenditure per capita	44.2	47.6	60.0	67.2	..
Share of government spending[3]	1.5	1.3	1.3	1.4	..
Share of value added in agriculture[4]	28.9	28.6	31.8	32.4	..
Index in constant prices[5]	105.1	95.6	107.7	116.9	..
EEC - Total[7]					
Expenditure ($ million)[2]	24 606.3	27 587.2	32 127.7	34 736.5	36 786.5
Expenditure per capita	94.6	105.4	122.4	132.1	139.7
Share of government spending[3]	2.7	2.3	2.3	2.3	2.3
Share of value added in agriculture[4]	30.3	31.2	32.2	33.6	36.6
Index in constant prices[5]					
of which: EEC-FEOGA[8]					
Expenditure ($ million)[2]	12 059.1	12 539.8	17 459.9	19 812.1	21 024.4
Expenditure per capita	46.3	47.9	66.5	75.4	79.8
Share of government spending[3]	75.5	65.0	66.7	69.9	72.8
Share of value added in agriculture[4]	14.9	14.2	17.5	19.2	20.9
Index in constant prices[5]	105.0	91.5	114.0	125.0	128.0

1. The purpose of this table is to indicate the broad trends in central government budget expenditure related to the implementation of the agricultural policies in the countries for which detailed data were available to the OECD Directorate for Food, Agriculture and Fisheries in the context of the Ministerial trade mandate (MTM) exercise. As coverage is not the same between countries, the data represent very approximative orders of magnitude. Besides price and income support for farmers, the following expenditures are often incorporated: research, training and advisory services, inspection and disease control, rationalisation of production and rural infrastructure, processing and marketing aid, and consumer food subsidisation. The last item is particularly important in the United States (Food Stamp Programme). Budget spending at the regional, state or provincial level is excluded. In Japan, this omission may be particularly important as around 60 per cent of total agricultural support is at the prefectoral level - *Source:* Japanese Ministry of Finance, "Fiscal Statistics" (unpublished internal document). Also, import duty revenue amounting to about 2 per cent of budget spending passes directly to agricultural support spending and is therefore excluded from the Japanese figures. Finally, some administration costs are included in some countries, whereas other countries exclude expenditure on salaries of Ministry of Agriculture (or EEC) officials.
2. National expenditure in local currency was converted using purchasing power parities (PPPs) for GDP. PPPs rather than exchange rates were used in order to obtain an approximate indicator of the volume of agricultural support spending in a common currency.
3. Agricultural support expenditure in local currency as a percentage of general government current outlays.
4. First line (in local currency) as a percentage of nominal value added in agriculture.
5. Agricultural support expenditures deflated by the GDP deflator, average for 1979-1980-1981 = 100.
6. National expenditure on agricultural support augmented by the country's share in EEC-FEOGA expenditure.
7. The total of spending on agriculture at the level of the Community as a whole (FEOGA), and national outlays on agricultural support in each of the nine (i.e., excluding Greece, Spain and Portugal) EEC countries. National expenditures on a consistent basis across countries are unavailable after 1980. The estimates for 1981-1984 are based on the assumption that the 1980 share of Germany, France and the United Kingdom (which account for nearly 60 per cent of EEC-9 national expenditure) remains constant.
8. FEOGA: Fonds Européen d'Orientation et de Garantie Agricole, the EEC fund for agricultural support. Expenditure is gross: levies on agricultural imports and on sugar have not been subtracted.
9. EEC spending on agriculture as a percentage of total expenditure by the Community.
Sources: OECD Directorate for Food, Agriculture and Fisheries (Table 5 of the MTM Synthesis Paper), December 1986; OECD Economics and Statistics Department (for PPPs, population, and government current outlays); Eurostat (for ECU/$ PPP).

shifts in supply and demand – hence instability – and that over the longer term, farmers would be forced to pass on to consumers a large share of any gains in agricultural products so that the farm sector's terms of trade would deteriorate[8].

Fifty years later, these concerns about the structural bases of low rural incomes and the presumed inefficiency of agricultural markets continue to dominate the agricultural policy agenda. In meeting these concerns, a progressively broader range of instruments has been brought to bear on the farm sector, to the point where policies now impinge on virtually every aspect of agricultural life, reaching from the development of new seed varieties to the terms on which farmers may sell or rent land. Table 5.1 sets these instruments out in terms of three broad categories:

- Those which are aimed at altering the general framework of agricultural activity and notably at increasing agricultural productivity;
- Those which primarily seek to stabilize agricultural markets; and
- Those which – at a given level of agricultural productivity and a given degree of market stability – are intended to increase farm incomes.

But though the objectives of agricultural policies have remained unchanged, the volume of resources devoted to meeting them has increased enormously. The most visible signs have been in growing public expenditures on agricultural policies: in the United States, for example, average annual net public outlays for price support and related agricultural programmes were 70 per cent greater (at constant prices) in the 1981-85 quinquennium than in 1965-69; equally, in France the aggregate national budgetary costs (in constant prices) of agricultural policy rose from a base of 100 in 1962 to 250 in 1980 – going from 30 per cent of agricultural value added in the base year to 75 per cent at the period's end[9]. More recent estimates – summarised in Table 5.2 – suggest further increases in budget expenditure since 1979, notably in the United States, Canada and the EEC[10].

As overall budgetary expenditures have risen, the pattern of expenditure has changed. The objective of increasing agricultural incomes has become progressively more important, to a considerable extent absorbing the other objectives of policy. Price stabilization schemes in particular have sought to maintain farm prices at levels inconsistent with market balance, so that rather than being self-funding – as they would be were they purely engaged in buffer operations – they have accumulated large and growing losses[11]. Overall, policies for the agricultural sector have increasingly emphasised on short-term income maintenance.

This emphasis is apparent in data on the functional distribution of the resources devoted to agricultural policy. Table 5.3 presents estimates of public expenditure for agriculture by broad category of objective for the reference period 1979-1981; except for Australia and New Zealand, where framework policies dominate in budgetary outlays, and Japan, which devotes a large share of recorded budgetary outlays to rural development, the objective of price and income support absorbs fully two-thirds of total expenditures. This objective's actual share of the total economic cost of agricultural policy is even higher than these estimates suggest, for two reasons.

To begin with, the budgetary data used tend to understate the cost of the transfers to primary produc-

Table 5.3. **Financing agricultural policy**
Public expenditure related to the implementation of agricultural policy (1979-1980-1981)

Million ECU and percentages

	Category I		Category II		Category III		Category IV		Category V		Category VI		Total	
	Mill. ECU	%	Mill. ECU	%	Mill. ECU	%	Mill. ECU	%	Mill. ECU	%	Mill. ECU	%	Mill. ECU	%
United States	814.0	4.2	542.2	2.8	1 607.8	8.3	10 581.1	54.6	3 548.7	18.3	2 292.7	11.8	19 386.5	100
Canada	173.5	10.6	66.6	4.1	151.4	9.3	243.6	14.9	847.1	51.8	151.9	9.3	1 634.8	100
Australia	217.0	46.4	84.5	18.1	28.0	6.0	32.8	7.0	101.4	21.7	3.5	0.7	467.3	100
New Zealand	49.7	19.9	44.7	18.0	71.5	28.7	0.2	0.1	83.1	33.3	—	—	249.2	100
Japan	340.3	3.3	36.3	0.4	3 861.3	37.9	163.2	1.6	4 465.8	43.8	1 320.0	13.0	10 186.8	100
EEC - National total	1 263.8	13.0	454.8	4.7	4 733.6	48.7	1 506.4	15.5	1 630.7	16.8	126.2	1.3	9 715.4	100
EEC - FEOGA	4.7	0.0	—	—	391.6	3.4	657.5	5.8	10 378.2	90.8	—	—	11 432.0	100
EEC - General total	1 168.5	6.0	454.8	2.2	5 125.2	24.2	2 163.9	10.2	12 008.9	56.8	162.2	0.6	21 147.4	10

Definitions: Cat. I - Research, training and advisory services.
Cat. II - Inspection services and disease control.
Cat. III - Rationalisation of production, improvement of structures and rural development.
Cat. IV - Processing, marketing and consumer aid.
Cat. V - Price and income support.
Cat. VI - Other, including, in the case of the United States, the total budget expenditure of the separate States, whose breakdown by category of expenditure is not available.

Notes: — In view of the differences existing between the national accounts systems and the types of measures applied in Member countries, any attempt to classify public expenditure is bound to be approximative.
— Budget expenditures incumbent upon the States, Provinces and Länder in the cases of Australia, Canada, Austria and Germany are included in each of the categories indicated. For Australia, State expenditure refers to the year 1981.
— The figures concerning the various categories of national expenditure for the EEC countries concern the year 1980, except for Luxembourg, where the year is 1979.

Source: OECD, Ministerial Mandate on Agricultural Trade - Country reports.

ers. Two such expenditures are of special importance. The first is preferential tax treatment of agricultural incomes: estimates for 1980 suggest that the tax loss

arising from this treatment was equivalent to 70 per cent of national budget expenditures[12] on agriculture in Belgium, 42 per cent in Germany, 21 per cent in Italy and 16 per cent in France[13]. The second regards public subsidies to agricultural social security systems: (again in 1980) these substantially exceeded other public outlays on agricultural policy in Belgium, France and Italy.

Secondly, budgetary data understate the cost of agricultural income support policies because they do not include that part of costs which is borne by consumers, notably through higher prices for food products. Estimates of these costs, drawn from the Secretariat analysis, are presented in Table 5.4. The figures are calculated from a limited number of products and may not represent precisely the actual value. When the costs are added to the expenditures reported in Table 5.3, the share of income and price support in the total of resources used by these countries for agricultural policies exceeds 90 per cent[14].

The transfers to agriculture that these magnitudes involve are very large when set against the size of the agricultural sector. The estimates presented in Table 5.5 imply that, on average, in the period 1979-81, consumers and taxpayers together spent on agricultural policies an amount equivalent to 68 per cent of the sector's value added, with support levels being particularly high in Japan and the EEC. Time series estimates on this basis, however, are unavailable; what data there are suggest that these ratios were considerably higher in 1979-81 than they had been a decade earlier and that they have since increased further, notably (but not solely) in the EEC.

Table 5.4. **Financing of agricultural policy**
Relative magnitude of financial contributions
made by taxpayers and consumers
Average 1979-1980-1981
Billion ECU and percentages

	Taxpayers (1)	Consumers (2)	(2) / (1) %
United States	19.4	7.0	36.1
Canada	1.6	0.9	56.3
Australia	0.5	0.2	40.0
New Zealand	0.2	0.0	0.0
Japan	10.2	16.7	163.7
Austria	0.5	0.9	180.0
EEC	21.1	35.8	169.7

Note: The final contribution of consumers was estimated as the impact of border measures (customs duties or the equivalent) on domestic prices; this impact was calculated by commodity by applying the corresponding tariffs or domestic external price differentials to the respective consumption level and subtracting the consumer subsidies paid by taxpayers. This is a static estimate and does not take into account the dynamic or secondary effects which a change in policy, notably a reduction of border protection, would have on domestic and international prices. The calculation was carried out for the principal agricultural commodities and extrapolated to final agricultural production. The commodities covered in the calculation represented 71.6 per cent of the total value of final production in the United States, 83.3 per cent in Canada, 74.7 per cent in Australia, 79.6 per cent in New Zealand, 58.8 per cent in Japan, 74.3 per cent in Austria and 68.1 per cent in the EEC. The consumer contribution in respect of that part of production not covered in the calculation has been assumed to be equal to the average contribution estimated for the commodities for which the calculation was made. The financial contribution of taxpayers corresponds to the total budget costs shown in Table 5.3.
Source: Secretariat estimates.

Table 5.5. **Cost of agricultural policy**
Some indicators of the level of cost related to the implementation of agricultural policy
Average 1979-1980-1981

	Cost (billion ECU)	ECU/ha	ECU/per holding	ECU/per agric. worker	Compared with			ECU/total population
					GDP %	GVA %	FVAP %	
United States	26.2	61.3	10 810	7 453	1.3	42.1	22.1	115
Canada	2.5	35.9	10 248	4 203	1.2	42.6	23.7	103
Australia	0.6	1.3	3 708	1 558	0.5	9.2	6.1	43
New Zealand	0.2	17.0	3 458	1 778	1.4	13.7	8.5	79
Japan	23.8	4 361.5	5 110	4 090	2.9	104.3	57.6	204
Austria	1.4	384.2	4 584	4 786	2.6	60.4	39.9	188
EEC	56.5	613.4	11 437	7 465	2.8	93.2	49.9	208

GDP = Gross domestic product at market prices.
GVA = Gross value added by agriculture at market prices.
FVAP = Final value of agricultural production.
Note: The cost of agricultural policies is defined as the *sum* of public budgetary expenditures on agriculture (the "taxpayer costs") and of the subsidies to production financed by consumers (generally referred to as the "consumer costs"). This subsidy has been calculated using the method presented in Table 5.4, but in the case of commodities for which a country is less than self-sufficient the tariff or external/internal price differential has been applied to production rather than consumption because in such cases the burden imposed on consumers (Table 5.4) is greater than the corresponding subsidy given to production.
Sources: Secretariat estimates.
Basis statistics: OECD, *National Accounts; Labour Force Statistics;* unpublished data on agricultural accounts.
FAO, *Production Yearbook,* 1983.
EEC, *The Agricultural Situation in the Community,* 1984.

II. THE EFFECTS OF AGRICULTURAL POLICIES

Given the scale of these transfers, it seems plausible to suppose that they would make the agricultural sector better off: that they would bring closer to realisation the long-standing objectives of a modern and prosperous farming community, operating in a reasonably stable environment and providing an appropriate supply of food. Actually, the results have been quite different.

This is largely because price and income supports have created persistent incentives to expand output in a sector facing extremely slow growth rates of effective demand. The mechanisms at work are straightforward:

- Under the various schemes in operation, the average return to a unit of output has been set on the basis of the costs incurred by the average farm in producing that output;
- At that level of return, the more efficient "commercial" farmers have an incentive to increase production, while the less efficient farmers do not face sufficiently strong incentives to withdraw from the sector altogether;
- The resulting increase in output cannot be absorbed by the natural growth of demand, and therefore gives rise to accumulated stocks, to price cutting on the markets open to international competition, and to downward pressures on pre-subsidy incomes;
- Combined, the imbalances thus produced in input and output markets have aggravated the distribution of income both within the sector and more generally, and have made the broad goals of agricultural policy more elusive.

Relatively few studies examining the process of setting support prices are available[15]. It is, nonetheless, apparent that although economic variables intervene – and have become of greater significance in recent years[16] – the process is an eminently political one, centred on bargaining between farmers' organisations and governments. This has two consequences: first, the extent of the support provided differs significantly from farm product to farm product, depending on the political strength of the various producer groups involved[17]; second, and perhaps most importantly, the bargaining process inherently tends towards support prices which appear acceptable to the average farmer, rather than towards those which reflect the economic costs of the average unit of farm output[18].

In this sector as in any other, prices based on costs of the median firm will create strong incentives for the more efficient producers to expand output. The peculiarity of modern agriculture, in this respect, is the persistence of a very wide range of differentials in productivity levels and growth rates between producers.

These differentials arise from the sector's response to the major supply side changes which have affected it in the postwar period[19]. Two such changes are of particular relevance. The first is rapid technical progress which, in addition to substantially raising total factor productivity – according to some estimates by 1.6 to 2.0 per cent a year[20] – has had a distinct labour-saving and input- and machinery-using bias[21]. The second is a substantial increase in the opportunity cost of farm labour, notably in the period 1950-1974, whose effects on relative factor prices have been accentuated by direct and indirect investment incentives[22]. The combined result of these changes has been extensive capital-labour substitution (Table 5.6) which, with a relatively lesser rise in the ratio of capital equipment to land, has entailed a significant increase in the minimum efficient scale of farms[23].

In addition to raising the average size of farms and reducing their aggregate number, these trends have

Table 5.6. **Growth of capital/labour ratio in agriculture[1]**

Average annual percentage change

	1960-1970	1970-1975	1975-1980	1981	1982	1983	1984	1985
United States	7.1	4.4	3.7	1.5	−1.9	−0.1	0.6	2.2
Japan	17.0	17.4	10.8	10.1	7.3	8.6	8.7	5.4
Germany	8.3	6.1	5.3	2.1	0.9	0.6	0	0
France	8.4	9.2	5.5	5.0	5.0	4.6	3.8	3.1
United Kingdom	6.9	6.5	2.6	−0.1	0.8	2.1	1.6	−0.1
Italy	11.3	7.3	6.1	9.5	11.2	2.2	6.5	—
Canada	4.7	5.0	4.2	1.2	9.6	−3.7	1.1	0.1
Finland	7.6	10.3	3.2	4.9	−0.1	5.3	4.2	6.4
Norway	4.9	6.9	1.9	0.3	6.6	7.6	5.6	−2.4
Sweden	8.0	6.4	4.2	1.3	1.7	4.0	—	—

1. The agricultural sector's gross capital stock (except Norway, where net capital stock is used) at constant price divided by agricultural employment. Capital stock generally excludes land and includes breeding stocks.
Sources: OECD, *Labour Force Statistics.*
OECD/ESD Statistics Division file of national estimates, except for Italy where data are from Eurostat, Luxembourg.

induced a growing differentiation within the farm sector itself, basically between two groups of holdings.

A first group comprises the large number of farms which derive much, if not most, of their earnings from non-farm sources, while generating a relatively small volume of agricultural output and income. These are holdings which, faced with the increasingly high capital requirements of efficient farming, have transferred the bulk of their endeavours to other areas or – if they remain in agriculture – receive relatively low incomes.

In principle, low or negative farm incomes should eventually induce these farms to abandon their agricultural operations altogether. Sectoral employment has in fact declined considerably, with the number of farms diminishing at a somewhat slower rate. Nonetheless, marginal producers in agriculture have proved remarkably resilient, probably for two major reasons. First, the agricultural income of these farms may be higher than it appears to be, largely because survey data understate their earnings (particularly from consumption in kind – for example, of farm residences) while overstating the opportunity cost of the resources they use (especially self-employed and family labour). Secondly, in certain countries, tax advantages and especially social security subsidies directed to farmers may create "poverty trap" situations, where farmers leaving the sector face a sharp increase in marginal tax rates – an example being the particularly favourable inheritance tax treatment of agricultural land holdings in Japan.

A second group consists of the large, commercially oriented farms. These have sought to gain an enduring cost advantage by augmenting their acreage, increasing their use of more sophisticated seeds, pesticides and other purchased inputs, and expanding their stock of machinery. Though these farms have generally moved from the polyculturalism typical of the smaller agricultural producer to specialised cropping and livestock practices, the rapidity with which they respond to revenue incentives has probably increased. This is largely for three reasons[24]: operating with a larger equity base, these farms may be less risk-averse than their smaller counterparts; greater reliance on purchased inputs increases the weight of variable costs in their overall cost structure, and hence makes output variation more profitable; and greater access to technical and marketing services from suppliers and distributors, combined with superior technological and management skills[25], increases their degree of flexibility.

This pattern of differentiation is apparent in data on the structure of agriculture. Thus, both in the United States and the EEC, the dispersion of farm incomes remains very large – both absolutely and relative to other sectors of the economy – and appears to have increased[26]. Though they retain a sizeable equity stake in agriculture[27], farmers at the lower tail of the farm income distribution receive a rising share of their income from non-farm sources – in the United States virtually all the income of farms in the three lower classes of the sales distribution comes from non-farm sources[28]; in the

EEC farm incomes are of greater significance for small and medium farmers, but the share of non-farm income has risen significantly[29]. Conversely, farmers at the top end of the distribution account for a disproportionate share of agricultural activity: thus, in the EEC (where the farm size effect accounts for an income disparity of approximately one to eight) the third of firms with the highest farming incomes in 1981-82 accounted for 63 per cent of the industry's inputs and generated 71 per cent of its value added[30]; during the same period in the United States, the top 28 per cent of farms (broadly defined, and hence including a large number of marginal producers) accounted for 86 per cent of cash receipts and 99 per cent of net farm income[31].

Japan differs in some respects from this pattern, notably because of the prevalence of very small farms – 70 per cent of farm households operating less than one hectare of land. More than two-thirds of the farmers are part-time; but even full-time farmers earn close to half their income from off-farm sources. Part-time farmers' total income (from all sources) is, on average, well above that of urban workers, while that of even full-time farmers is only slightly below this level.

Given a high degree of concentration, support prices or deficiency payments geared to the median producer have entailed a broad spread of margins between farmers, *but the bulk of output has been produced at an economic profit.*

Data for the United States clearly illustrate this process: by 1980-82, 60 per cent of farms operated at a loss, implying that prices were below costs of production for the average farmer; however, since 94 per cent of total farm products were produced by the 40 per cent of farms that had positive net farm incomes, farm prices were in fact below costs of production for only 6 per cent of output. Though output concentration levels in EEC agriculture are somewhat lower, rough estimates suggest that the disparities in profitability may be only slightly less than in the United States[32].

In other words, at prices which result in a loss for most farmers (hence creating political pressures for price rises), farmers in the larger size classes face significant incentives to expand output. The reluctance of governments to reduce support prices in line with the growth of total factor productivity on the most efficient farms accentuates this tendency, with three consequences.

To begin with, it leads to intensified intra-sectoral *competition for scarce resources*, notably land. At its simplest, this is because a significant increase in output without an increase in acreage is likely to result in rapidly rising marginal costs. But this is magnified by the fact that support prices not only raise the average expected price of output, but also reduce the uncertainty associated with that price – since whatever happens, farmers' gross revenue per unit of output will not fall below the support value[33]. This "price insurance" will encourage farmers to expand their portfolios of assets involving fixed commitments – of which land is a prime example. The higher support prices are relative to those yielding only normal profit on the bulk of output, the greater these effects will be.

Prices of agricultural land are affected not only by the marginal revenue which can be obtained from an expansion of agricultural acreage, but also by broader economic circumstances – and in particular by the interaction of inflation, exchange rates, real interest rates and tax regimes[34]. Nonetheless, the observed trends are consistent with detailed studies which show that a substantial part of the benefits of support policies are capitalised into land prices. By and large, United States studies suggest that approximately half the sums transferred to the agricultural sector through price supports have been absorbed through increases in land values; the ratios in Europe may be even higher[35]. To the (admittedly limited) extent to which these increases in land values lead to increases in rents on agricultural land[36], the farm sector's costs rise – presumably to the point where further expansion in output and acreage is unprofitable.

Rising land prices, however, will not deter increases in output, when these largely occur through increases in yields – and this *expansion of output* is the second effect

of setting the unit return to efficient farmers high relative to their unit costs. Thus, in the United States, guaranteed milk prices started to rise in real terms in 1974 after eight years of relative stability; by 1977, they were 27 per cent higher than their 1974 level, peaking at 42 per cent above their initial level in 1980. Despite subsequent reductions, the effects of nearly ten years of high guaranteed prices has been to increase investment in raising milk yields, while also encouraging the expansion of herds and of processing capacity. Milk supply, which had remained stable in the early 1970s, increased from 55.8 million tons of milk equivalent in 1978 to 71.8 million tons in 1983.

Given a sufficiently rapid growth rate of productivity, small declines in support prices may be insufficient to counter the incentives for output to expand, since real returns to efficient farmers will still be rising. Thus, over the period 1975-81, dairy prices in the EEC declined in real terms by about 1.5 per cent annually. But with total factor productivity in dairy production increasing in the period at an annual rate of about 2.0 per cent, the real returns to dairy producers were in fact rising, with the greatest increase going to best practice producers.

Table 5.7. **Food consumption per capita: annual averages for selected OECD countries**

Kg per head per year

	Total cereals[1]	Total fish	Total meat	Beef	Poultry	Total milk[2]	Butter[3]	Marga-rine[3]	Cheese	Total fruit	Total veg-etables	Sugar[4]	Total calories
1964													
Australia	84.1	6.0[5]	112.3	44.1	5.2	152.0	7.7	4.2[5]	3.4	73.4	67.2[5]	45.9	3 096[5]
France	89.4	17.3	82.3	20.8	10.5	107.9	7.1	3.3	11.2	69.2	133.3	33.2	3 139
Spain	93.4	29.4	32.0	5.1	6.8	73.2	0.2	0.8[6]	1.6	94.7	138.4	21.0	2 629
Finland	87.1	9.9	42.3	16.5	0.4	304.0	18.0	4.2	3.1	41.7	14.7	39.0	2 977
Japan	32.6	24.7	12.0	2.4	1.9	20.5	0.2	..	0.2	28.5	104.6	17.2	2 421
United States	62.4	6.1	104.7	46.5	17.7	179.3	2.5	9.8	6.3	66.8	89.6	41.0	3 216
1974													
Australia	76.7	6.1	117.4	57.5	13.6	129.8	5.8	5.3	5.1	81.3	54.9	57.0	3 232
France	72.7	18.3	97.7	23.0	14.3	115.1	7.8	3.5	15.0	71.3	113.3	38.3	3 248
Spain	78.5	33.2	58.9	9.5	17.1	109.8	0.5	1.2	2.8	130.6	131.9	29.7	2 995
Finland	74.0	14.7	58.4	22.0	1.9	365.6	13.0	8.1	5.5	66.7	24.5	41.8	3 113
Japan	33.8	37.6	26.3	3.6	6.8	29.9	0.5	..	0.5	57.7	130.4	26.7	2 597
United States	61.1	6.9	113.7	52.9	22.6	150.8	1.6	11.7	8.7	68.8	94.4	40.3	3 268
1984													
Australia[7]	53.2	7.1	102.8	39.6	19.1	162.0	3.3	8.4	7.7	101.7	44.5	47.7	3 093
France[8]	80.7	17.8	110.3	25.2	17.3	148.3	6.6	3.5	21.3	81.9	112.9	34.4	3 526
Spain[9]	80.5	31.5	74.6	8.3	21.7	109.0	0.5	1.3	3.8	143.0	132.8	27.1	3 172
Finland	86.0	13.6	67.0	21.5	4.1	350.5	12.1	6.8	8.2	74.1	41.2	32.4	3 090
Japan	33.4	37.2	37.0	6.2	11.8	39.8	0.5	..	0.8	47.4	128.3	21.0	2 676
United States	48.1	7.5	115.9	48.5	30.6	151.2	2.2	13.5	11.7	66.7	95.0	30.9	3 317

Notes: 1. Direct human consumption, excluding rice.
2. Total milk and milk products, excluding butter, product weight.
3. Fat content, except in Spain and Finland. Product weight, margarine includes processed fats in Australia, France and United States.
4. Refined sugar.
5. 1965.
6. 1967.
7. 1983 data, except for meats and cheese: 1984.
8. 1983 data, except for meats, dairy products, fish: 1984.
9. 1982, except for meats and cheese: 1983.

Sources: OECD, Food consumption statistics, 1964-1978 (1981).
Food consumption statistics, 1973-1982 (1985).
Supply utilisation account data bases, 1975-1984 (1986).

Decreases in input prices (for example, concentrate feeds) also increased profitability at the margin. Total production therefore continued to grow at over 1 per cent a year.

These increases in production elicited by support prices have run into a wall of slowly growing and inelastic demand. Roughly speaking, the trend annual growth in demand for agricultural output[37] in the OECD area is certainly below 1 per cent and may well be of no more than 0.5 per cent. Though growth is somewhat higher in certain commodities, notably cereals, it is even lower in others, including dairy, sugar and beef. Underlying this slow growth are the relatively low growth rates of OECD population and a low income elasticity of demand for food, the combined effect being aggravated by renewed concerns about diet and the development of substitutes for certain important agricultural products (notably sugar and cereals). Food consumption per capita in 1964, 1974 and 1984 for selected OECD countries is shown in Table 5.7; by and large the share of consumers' expenditure spent on food in the OECD area has decreased by about five percentage points since 1970. Demand for food has of course

been rising more rapidly outside the OECD area but the significance of this trend for OECD producers is limited by growing competition from non-OECD sources of supply (notably Argentina, Mexico, Brazil and the USSR), increases in agricultural output in some important markets (especially India, South Korea and China) and by foreign currency constraints on agricultural imports by the African countries.

In principle, reductions in agricultural prices paid by consumers could boost the slow trend growth of demand. In practice, however, the overall price elasticity of demand for food products in the OECD area is now extremely low, probably in the order of 0.25[38], so that very substantial price declines would be needed to have any significant effect on total volumes.

The implications of these demand constraints can be straightforwardly illustrated. Over the last decade, gross agricultural productivity in the OECD area has risen on average by around 6 per cent a year, while agricultural employment has declined by slightly less than 2 per cent a year, yielding a trend annual growth rate of output of over 4 per cent. Absorbing this output at current income levels, and assuming relatively inelastic supply and a

Table 5.8. **The frequency of application of various non-tariff barriers in 1983[1]**

Total agriculture, 16 OECD countries[2]

	Quantitative restrictions	Decreed prices	(of which: variable levies)	Tariff-type measures[3]	Total[4]
Countries					
Switzerland	28.1	13.3	(12.5)	1.3	41.9
Austria	17.7	15.8	(15.6)	15.0	35.0
Finland	28.0	3.1	(3.1)	12.6	33.2
EEC	15.2	16.6	(11.2)	11.1	33.0
Norway	31.5	5.2	(0.0)	2.6	32.5
Japan	25.6	0.6	(0.0)	1.8	27.5
Australia	17.8	0.2	(0.0)	0.0	18.1
United States	4.3	0.6	(0.6)	2.6	6.6
Products					
Sugar and confectionery	21.7	58.0	(58.0)	0.0	70.0
Dairy products	29.6	28.6	(25.6)	6.9	54.6
Meat and live animals	41.0	26.0	(23.8)	12.3	52.2
Other beverages	22.9	18.4	(0.6)	18.5	42.3
Fruit and vegetables	18.7	4.9	(0.8)	15.6	32.8
Cereals	10.9	21.7	(21.7)	1.7	29.0
Other food	16.6	13.5	(13.2)	0.8	27.4
Raw materials	7.5	0.3	(0.3)	0.0	7.8
Tea, coffee and cocoa	4.0	2.5	(2.5)	0.4	6.6
All agriculture	17.2	11.5	(8.2)	8.1	29.7
Manufactures	6.9	0.5	(0.0)	2.0	9.3

1. This table does not show the restrictiveness of non-tariff barriers but merely the proportion of individual import flow subject to the chosen non-tariff barriers. Excluded are monitoring measures which covered more than 20 per cent of agricultural imports into France and Switzerland in 1983, but are inconsequential in the other 14 countries. Trade flows are distinguished both by commodity (at the level at which non-tariff legislation is defined) and country of origin. The measure—i.e. the "frequency ratio"—is defined and discussed in Nogues, Olechowski and Winters, "The Extent of Non-Tariff Barriers to Imports of Industrial Countries", World Bank Staff Working Paper No. 789, Washington, D.C., 1985.
2. "Total agriculture" is composed of all items in Chapters 01 to 24 of the CCC Nomenclature system for classifying traded goods. Prepared foodstuffs such as flour and confectionery are included.
3. Two types of non-customary tariff measures are distinguished. First, "tariff quotas" apply to goods where two tariff rates operate: the higher rate being applicable once the quantity of imported goods exceeds a certain limit. Second, different seasonal tariffs are applied to the same agricultural good according to the time of year.
4. The total will be less than the sum of the three components if some flows are subject to more than one barrier.
Source: Table 1 of Winters, A.L., "Industrial Countries' Agricultural Policy: How, What and Why", Discussion Paper No. 118, Centre for Economic Policy Research, London, 1986.

stable net contribution by OECD producers in world food demands, would require a real reduction in OECD agricultural prices of at least 6 per cent a year (given a trend growth rate of OECD demand of 0.5 per cent). In actual fact, the average prices paid to producers in the main OECD countries, though fluctuating cyclically, declined over the period 1970-1984 at less than a third of this rate. *On these admittedly very rough calculations, support prices have created a gap of around 2.5 per cent a year between the decline in the returns actually obtained by producers and the rate of decline warranted by market developments.*

Combined, these trends have resulted in an enormous shift in market balances, notably in the EEC. Thus, a comparison of actual 1985 outcomes with OECD projections made in 1968[39] shows that for each of the main commodity groups examined, a net EEC[40] import requirement has been transformed into significant net export availability.

As domestic self-sufficiency has increased, individual countries have sought to absorb the growth of domestic production by reducing imports, generally at the expense of lower-cost producers elsewhere. The extent of agricultural protection is highlighted in Table 5.8 which shows that in 1987 non-tariff barriers affected nearly 30 per cent of agricultural imports to sixteen OECD countries – a share three times higher than that applying to manufacturing. As a result of agricultural protection, the ratio of agricultural imports to GDP for the OECD area actually declined over the two decades to 1985, while that of non-agricultural imports nearly doubled (Table 5.9). Nevertheless, as national self-sufficiency levels have steadily risen, the scope for absorbing domestic output through further import substitution has declined.

This has, in the first instance, led governments to accumulate stocks of domestic produce so as to maintain prices above market clearing levels. Four commodity areas have been particularly affected – dairy, cereals, beef and sugar; even excluding sugar, these account for over 50 per cent of agricultural output in the United States and the EEC. Table 5.10 provides estimates of stock levels over the period 1972-86; it is clear that much of the increase has occurred in the more recent years, and that current stocks far exceed those needed for the ordinary functioning of markets. Thus, in mid-1986, world stocks of cereals were nearly one-third above the FAO's yardstick of "safe" stock levels to maintain food security, while stocks of dairy products, which were relatively low a decade ago, amounted in the EEC alone to over 1.5 million tonnes of butter and nearly one million tonnes of skimmed milk.

Stock accumulation of this magnitude entails obvious costs in terms of public expenditure, both for acquiring and storing the relevant commodities. So as to reduce these costs, a number of countries have sought to dispose of surpluses on world markets by heavily subsidising export sales. However, rising self-sufficiency and restrictions on imports have tended to shrink those

Table 5.9. **Share of agricultural and non-agricultural trade in GDP**[1]

Percentages of nominal GDP

		1964-70	1971-75	1976-80	1981-85
A.	Agricultural imports				
	United States	0.6	0.6	0.7	0.6
	Japan	1.4	1.5	1.4	1.3
	EEC-10[2]	3.1	3.0	3.1	3.0
	OECD[2]	1.6	1.7	1.8	1.5
B.	Non-agricultural imports				
	United States	2.8	4.7	7.4	8.0
	Japan	7.7	8.6	9.4	9.7
	EEC-10[2]	13.8	17.5	21.2	23.3
	OECD[2]	8.1	11.1	14.1	14.4
C.	Agricultural exports				
	United States	0.6	0.8	1.0	0.8
	Japan	0.3	0.2	0.1	0.1
	EEC-10[2]	1.7	2.2	2.4	2.7
	OECD[2]	1.1	1.4	1.5	1.5
D.	Non-agricultural exports				
	United States	3.4	4.5	5.8	5.3
	Japan	8.6	10.2	11.1	12.9
	EEC-10[2]	14.0	17.7	20.7	22.8
	OECD[2]	8.1	10.9	13.2	13.3

1. Agricultural trade corresponds to section 0+1 of the SITC classification. It covers food, tobacco and beverages, but excludes agricultural raw materials.
2. The aggregates were calculated using current-year exchange rates.
Sources: OECD, *Annual Foreign Trade Statistics By Commodities,* Paris, 1987; *National Accounts.*

markets open to international competition. Large price reductions have therefore been required on the markets remaining open so as to absorb the exported surpluses as well as the produce diverted onto them by growing barriers to trade.

Graphs 5.1 to 5.6 highlight for selected agricultural commodities the contrast between the sharp instability and recent decline in "world" prices (that is, prices in open markets), and the relative stability and even trend increase in domestic support prices at least in nominal terms. As this wedge grows between domestic and world prices, the costs to domestic consumers of being cut off from cheaper world market sources rise, as does the taxpayer expenditure needed to maintain world market share. The net result of this process has therefore been to yet further increase the total resource cost of agricultural policies and the subsidy component of agricultural incomes[41].

In summary, price support policies, implemented directly or through deficiency payments, have had an inherent tendency to create incentives for output expansion, leading to imbalances both in input markets (where land prices have been bid up) and in output markets (which have not been able to absorb the growth of production). In turn, these imbalances have had drastic

Table 5.10. **Stocks of selected agricultural products**[1]

1 000 tonnes

	1972	1973	1974	1975	1976	1977	1978	1979	1980	1981	1982	1983	1984	1985	1986[2]
Butter															
EEC	303	201	148	164	255	194	418	372	240	147	306	553	949	1 124	1 324
United States	89	68	53	45	37	90	128	114	134	230	246	268	234	130	132
Australia	17	9	12	29	11	18	22	13	6	11	15	24	32	29	19
New Zealand	25	13	28	38	31	24	23	32	29	20	27	21	80	90	112
Skimmed milk powder															
EEC	220	166	365	1 012	1 135	965	674	227	230	279	576	983	617	520	757
United States	20	34	89	200	219	278	318	244	249	333	514	636	645	493	449
Australia	17	9	5	57	38	7	6	10	9	18	10	17	24	12	9
New Zealand	114	92	41	183	214	129	64	90	76	80	114	77	75	60	34
Wheat															
EEC	7 600	6 200	7 600	10 600	8 500	8 700	7 700	10 100	8 800	9 300	7 600	10 800	7 500	16 200	18 200
United States	26 800	16 200	9 300	11 800	18 100	30 300	32 000	25 100	24 500	26 900	31 700	41 200	38 100	38 800	51 900
Australia	1 400	500	1 900	1 700	2 700	2 100	800	4 600	4 300	2 000	2 600	2 300	7 500	8 500	5 700
Canada	15 900	9 900	10 100	8 000	8 000	13 300	12 100	14 900	10 700	8 600	9 800	10 000	9 200	7 600	8 500
Beef and veal															
EEC	0	34	225	221	356	292	191	272	310	180	204	368	606	646	481
Australia	85	103	113	106	107	137	136	82	69	67	49	42	36	45	45

1. Butter

		Closing stocks
EEC	Public intervention stocks plus privately aided stocks	31.12
US	CCC plus private stocks	01.07
Australia	Private stocks in cold stores	01.07
New Zealand	Export stocks	01.07

Skimmed milk powder

EEC	Public intervention stocks	31.12
US	CCC plus private stocks	01.07
Australia	Private stocks in cold stores	01.07
New Zealand	Export stocks	01.07

Beef

EEC	Public intervention stocks (product weight)	31.12
Australia	Stocks of frozen beef (carcass weight)	31.12

Wheat

EEC		August/July
US		June/May
Australia		December/November; from 1983: October/September
Canada		August/July

2. Forecast for 1986.

Sources: Bureau of Agricultural Economics, *Commodity Statistical Bulletin,* various issues, Canberra.
Eurostat.
FAO, *Food Outlook Statistical Supplement,* Rome, March 1983 and February 1987.

implications for the broader goals of agricultural policy, notably those of achieving a more equitable distribution of incomes within the agricultural sector, of strengthening the poorest rural regions and of providing a framework of stability for agricultural development.

To begin with, the net impact of the support policies has almost certainly been to aggravate *income and wealth disparities* within the agricultural sector. Though the extent of this effect has differed somewhat between countries[41], five general factors have been at work. First, in many OECD countries, support policies have concentrated on commodities typically produced on large farms, though dairy products are a partial exception in this respect. Second, given significant economies of scale, support levels based on median costs have provided bigger margins to larger producers[42]. Third, the effective elasticity of supply tends to be higher in the larger, commercial part of the farm sector than among smaller producers; hence, the larger suppliers have been better placed to expand their output in response to revenue incentives. Fourth, the size of a farm is an important determinant of its capacity to secure finance to expand, mainly because the equity base per acre rises with size[43]. Finally, land ownership tends to be concentrated among larger farms, so that these farms obtain a disproportionate share of the benefits arising from the appreciation of land values[44].

Simulation studies of the impacts of support policies

Graph 5.1. Domestic and world price indexes for
Wheat

1980 = 100

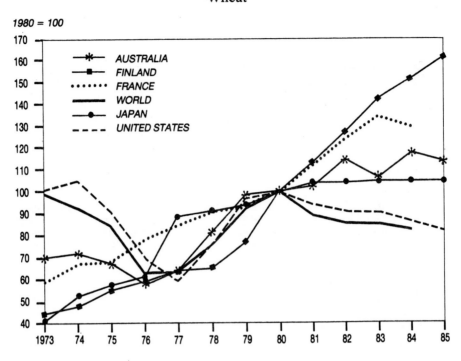

Source: OECD, Directorate for Food, Agriculture and Fisheries. These data are not necessarily the same in all countries and are therefore not comparable between countries.

Graph 5.2. Domestic and world price indexes for
Maize

1980 = 100

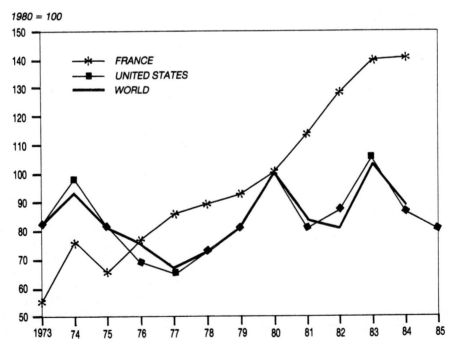

Source: OECD, Directorate for Food, Agriculture and Fisheries. These data are not necessarily the same in all countries and are therefore not comparable between countries.

Graph 5.3. EEC and world price indexes for
Cereals

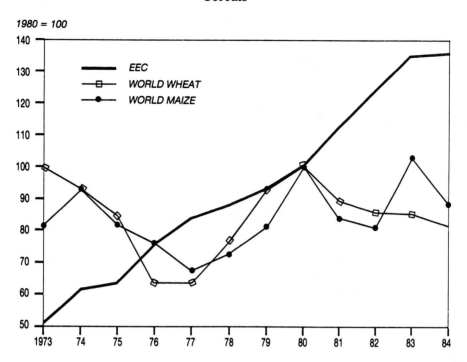

1980 = 100

Legend:
- EEC
- WORLD WHEAT
- WORLD MAIZE

Source: OECD, Directorate for Food, Agriculture and Fisheries. These data are not necessarily the same in all countries and are therefore not comparable between countries.

Graph 5.4. Domestic and world price indexes for
Sugar

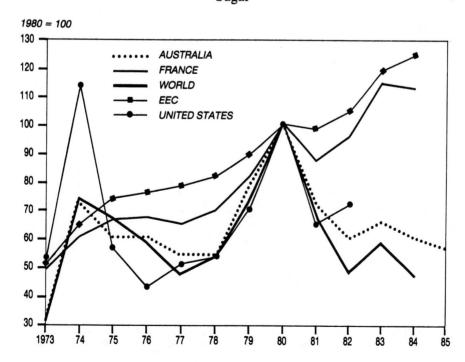

1980 = 100

Legend:
- AUSTRALIA
- FRANCE
- WORLD
- EEC
- UNITED STATES

Source: OECD, Directorate for Food, Agriculture and Fisheries. These data are not necessarily the same in all countries and are therefore not comparable between countries.

Graph 5.5. Domestic and world price indexes for
Beef

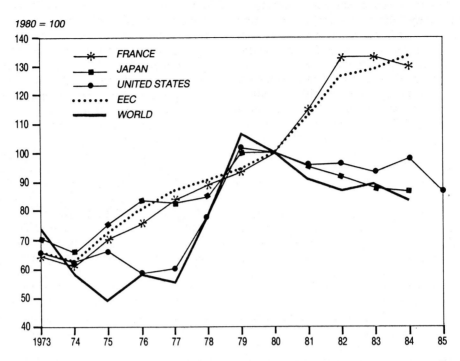

Source: OECD, Directorate for Food, Agriculture and Fisheries. These data are not necessarily the same in all countries and are therefore not comparable between countries.

Graph 5.6. Domestic and world price indexes for
Sheepmeat

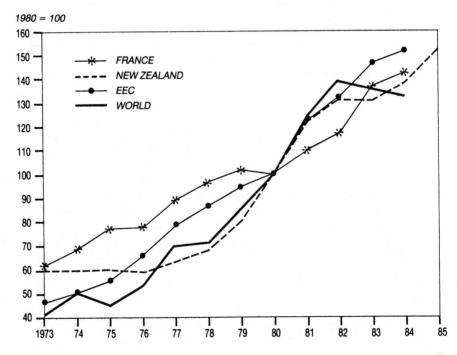

Source: OECD, Directorate for Food, Agriculture and Fisheries. These data are not necessarily the same in all countries and are therefore not comparable between countries.

are particularly useful in illustrating these results. Thus, a study of the distributional impacts over a fifteen-year period of United States corn price support policies found that these allowed large high-equity farms to more than double their acreage, while maintaining annual family consumption high, but that acreage on initially smaller farms remained virtually constant. Over the entire period, the smaller farms' share of after-tax income and family consumption actually tended to fall[45]. Equally, a simulation analysis of the effects of the Common Agricultural Policy (CAP) on the personal distribution of income in German agriculture concludes that the long-run impact of prices maintained 10 per cent above their equilibrium level is to increase the index of intra-sectoral income inequality by nearly 40 per cent[46].

The corollary of a highly skewed allocation of benefits is an increasingly unequal *regional distribution* of farm incomes. This effect has been most marked in the EEC, where very substantial disparities persist both within and between countries in patterns of land use and of agricultural productivity. Given these differentials and a greater capacity to expand output in areas with initially above-average productivity levels, the structure of price supports has entailed large inter-regional income transfers. The regressive impact of these transfers has been aggravated by the fact that (until the early 1980s) support prices tended to be highest for "northern" crops, whose producers had higher incomes to begin with. Overall, the bias in support prices induced Mediterranean producers to shift resources into relatively inefficient (and low-income) production of beef, milk, pigs and poultry (whose combined share in Italian agricultural output, for example, nearly doubled from 1964-65 to 1975-76), while imposing an implicit tax on the commodities where Mediterranean producers have a comparative advantage (notably fruit and vegetables)[47]. Nonetheless, the pattern of transfers under the EEC's Common Agricultural Policy has been changing in recent years, becoming progressively more favourable to Mediterranean producers.

In turn, the worsening inequality of regional income distribution has distorted the process of *rural economic development*. In certain countries – notably Austria, Switzerland and the Nordic countries – agricultural policy has maintained activity levels in rural regions, though at an exceptionally high cost; but this can hardly be claimed for the EEC. Thus, in the EEC's poorest rural areas, the persistence of low agricultural incomes has led to a continued population exodus, biasing the age distribution towards older farmers working marginal plots with no obvious successor[48]. In contrast, in the areas which have largely benefitted from income transfers, and which have received the bulk of agricultural investment allowances[49], intense competition for land has led to sharp increases in land prices, displacing other rural uses of land[50]. Not only is agriculture a more dominant feature of land use in these areas than in the past, but the expansion of highly mechanised agriculture

has occurred at the expense of the amount and variety of cover on land in rural areas, leading to a serious diminution in wildlife[51]. Overall the goal of balanced development of rural areas appears even more compromised now than two decades ago.

Finally, it is questionable whether the policies applied to the sector have in fact led to significantly *greater stability* in its decision-making environment.

In principle, government programmes, given sufficient funding, can stabilize the receipts farmers receive for their crops relative to the variability which these receipts would otherwise have displayed; and some such balancing has in fact occurred[52]. However, this will not entail stability in net farm incomes if the variability of other determinants of costs and revenues rises. This has also occurred, notably in two respects. First, the growing importance of off-farm intermediate inputs has made the sector increasingly vulnerable to external price shocks arising from domestic inflation and exchange rate changes. Second, there appears to have been some increase in output variability, partly because of greater yield variance but also reflecting greater input adjustment to changes in the agricultural terms of trade[53]. As a result, price and income supports have had a limited effect on the stability of agricultural earnings[54]; and, given increasingly high levels of leverage, farm bankruptcy rates have tended to rise, notably in North America[55].

For the agricultural sector as a whole, these trends have been accentuated by the growing importance of export markets. At least in principle, international trade should serve to stabilize the sector's overall revenues, by allowing fluctuations in supply to be spread over a larger consumption base[56]. In practice, however, the use of export markets as an outlet for surplus production, combined with a shrinkage in the market areas effectively open to foreign suppliers, has led to a substantial increase in the instability of world market prices[57]. Notably in the United States (until 1985) and the EEC, farmers have to a considerable extent been protected from this source of instability through price guarantees; but rising budgetary costs are now leading to a reduction in the effectiveness of this insulation[58].

Leaving aside the countries (such as Japan) where the incomes of an agricultural sector largely oriented to the domestic market have been sustained through high domestic prices, there is, therefore, no evidence that the classical goal of stabilizing farm incomes has been achieved. This is partly because the growing integration of agriculture into the international economy has rendered it more liable to external sources of instability; but largely because the policies at work have increased the instabilities in the sector's environment.

Overall, price and income supports have been the central component of agricultural policies over the last two decades; but the very large sums transferred to the sector by consumers and taxpayers have not gone to alleviate the problems of low agricultural income and of the poorer rural regions. Rather, they have provided persistent incentives for the larger and wealthier farmers to expand output, resulting in massive over-production which threatens the prosperity and stability of the sector as a whole.

III. DEALING WITH IMBALANCES

Faced with mounting imbalances, governments have increasingly sought to reduce agricultural output while preserving the broad structure of price supports. The policies applied have taken three basic forms: restrictions on capacity utilisation, for example of land and (in the case of dairy products) of dairy cows; production and marketing quotas; and multiple-part pricing systems, whereby guarantee prices are abated if and when production exceeds a pre-established threshold. In general, these programmes have either proved ineffectual or – where they have attained their objectives – have done so at excessively high economic costs.

The clearest instances of ineffectiveness are provided by programmes aimed at curtailing output through restrictions on inputs. Thus, though *acreage retirement programmes* are among the more widely used instruments of output control in the OECD economies, and have been a feature of United States farm policy for nearly fifty years, the evidence suggests that they have not had a significant effect on the volume of agricultural output. This is partly because their impact in specific years has been offset by unexpectedly good growing conditions; but it is primarily because in a regime of high support prices, they do not eliminate the incentives efficient producers have to expand output. As a result, farmers will generally retire their poorest and least productive land; and, given that they are planting fewer acres, will apply the resources thus freed in more intensive cultivation of the remaining acres[59]. Hence, the general result of these programmes has been to stimulate an increase in yields, so that a considerable part of the rents they create have accrued to suppliers of yield-increasing intermediate inputs.

In contrast, *production quotas*, when rigorously enforced, have usually proved reasonably effective in restraining the growth of output, but have done so at high cost[60]. Consumers, of course, bear these costs most directly through the persistence of price levels above those which would normally clear the market; but the use of quotas also imposes considerable costs on the farm sector. To begin with, reliance on quotas frequently leads to a pattern of output constraint which is regressive in terms of the sector's income distribution. This is because quotas are generally allocated on the basis of prior output levels, so that the reduction in output is distributed roughly proportionately to capacity over the population of firms. In practice, the larger firms will usually have higher supply elasticities at the pre-quota output level and will therefore obtain a greater resource saving from a given reduction in production. The pre-rating of the reduction may consequently impose a greater revenue cost on small producers than would a reduction in output obtained through falling prices.

The rigidities quota systems introduce into the structure of the activity aggravate these biases. When quota rights are not tradable, structural change in the sector is almost inevitably deterred. But even tradable quotas generally have quite perverse effects. In particular, if the system is perceived as durable, the price of quota rights will reflect the capitalised value of the difference between marginal production costs and output prices at the given quota level. The evidence suggests that – in contrast to the imperfect capitalisation which occurs with land prices[61] – the rents arising from excessively high support prices are in fact fully capitalised into the value of traded agricultural quota rights[62]. This has two effects. First, the regressive nature of the schemes in operation is not only accentuated, but also transformed from primarily acting on the distribution of income to acting on the distribution of wealth. Secondly, since (unlike land) quotas have no alternative use, any return to a more liberal arrangement will impose very substantial losses on those who acquired quotas at market prices[63].

The flaws inherent in input controls and output quotas have led to increasing interest in the use of multi-part pricing systems, whereby guarantee prices are abated if and when production surpasses a pre-established threshold. Prominent examples include the EEC's "co-responsibility levies", introduced for dairy products in 1977, and the more recent super-levy scheme, again for dairy products, introduced in 1984. Neither of these systems has had a significant effect on the growth of excess dairy production in the Community mainly because initial quota levels were set too high[64].

The fundamental problem of multi-part pricing schemes is that excess production will persist so long as the weighted average of the prices facing producers is inconsistent with market balance. In practice, with support prices being very high relative to those which would clear the market, the marginal reductions in prices which the schemes have entailed have been insufficient to even prevent stocks from rising. Thus, in 1985-86, the EEC levied a tax on producers whose output exceeded their quota level. In principle, the tax was equal to 100 per cent of the support price but in practice, exemptions reduced it to an average of 30 per cent. In other words, producers could sell an unlimited quantity of milk at 70 per cent of support prices – a net return which still exceeded marginal cost on efficient holdings by some 20 per cent. As a result, over the twelve months to the first quarter of 1986, the Community's production of butter increased by 10 per cent and of milk powder by 20 per cent, while stocks of these commodities rose even more rapidly[65].

Overall, the magnitude of the imbalances confronting the sector is such that these policies – be they acreage controls, output quotas, multi-part prices, or any combination thereof – are likely to be ineffectual. They typically entail high administrative costs and create opportunities for fraud[66], as well as introducing rigidities which slow adjustment in the affected product; and even when they do serve to reduce excess supplies of the commodity, this may simply lead to a transfer of resources – and hence of imbalances – to other agricultural markets[67]. The costs to consumers are high, while the underlying problems remain unsolved.

IV. NEW DIRECTIONS FOR POLICY

Agricultural policies in the OECD economies are locked into a vicious spiral of rising budgetary outlays, mounting supply-demand imbalances, burgeoning stocks of excess products and pervasive subsidisation of agricultural exports. This not only distorts resource allocation on a scale incommensurate with even the agricultural sector's political importance; it also poses a growing threat to the multilateral trading system as a whole. The problems arise first and foremost from domestic policies which provide strong incentives for over-production – and ultimately it is only through the reform of these policies that they can be resolved; but immediate action is also needed, not only domestically but internationally.

Agriculture is now a small sector in the advanced economies. It accounts for some 3 per cent of GDP in the advanced industrial countries and for 7 per cent of employment. But this does not mean that the costs of current agricultural policies are trivial.

These costs are, in the first instance, borne by consumers. Higher consumer prices for food products are clearly in the nature of a tax, the proceeds of which are transferred to agricultural producers. This tax is sharply regressive, first, because in most countries the average food consumer has significantly lower net worth and less net income than the largest farmers (who receive the bulk of the benefits); second, because the share of food in household expenditure (and hence exposure to the tax) is highest in the lowest income groups; and third, because the commodities which have typically been most heavily taxed (cereals and milk) go into products which carry a high weight in the expenditure basket of the poor. Thus, a recent United Kingdom study of the tax rate on each level of income implied by the CAP found that this ranged from only 2.9 per cent on households with an income of over £10 000 a year to 6.0 per cent on households in the £1 000 to £2 000 bracket[68].

To these costs for consumers must of course be added the costs borne by taxpayers. But these are merely the more visible costs. Even more difficult to quantify are the losses which current agricultural policies impose on economies as a whole – by locking resources into inefficient uses, increasing the tax burden (and hence

affecting decisions to work and save) and reducing the disposable income of consumers. Estimates of the magnitude of these effects are inevitably controversial, given the range of assumptions on which they must rest. Nonetheless, losses of up to 1 per cent of GNP appear to be plausible for Europe[69] – a high figure when set against the agricultural sector's size.

Current policies also impose large costs on the countries which depend most heavily on agricultural exports. These countries have had their access to the largest OECD markets – the United States, the EEC and Japan – severely curtailed; and they are penalised by the widespread dumping of surplus agricultural stocks onto those parts of the world market which remain open to international competition. A recent analysis for Australia finds that foreign agricultural policies impose terms-of-trade losses exceeding 1 per cent of GDP[70].

There are costs for developing countries too. In the short run, some developing countries may benefit from access to cheap food imports – but these often dissuade the development of low-cost domestic sources of supply. At the same time, some of the LDCs' most important agricultural exports – including sugar, rice, tobacco, cotton, vegetable oils and beef – are adversely affected by OECD country import restrictions, as well as by the subsidised competition on third markets. Overall, estimates suggest that even a 50 per cent reduction in OECD country tariffs on agricultural products could lead to large increases in the LDCs' export earnings – as high as 75 per cent for beef and nearly 50 per cent for sugar[71].

But ultimately many of the costs are borne by the farm sector itself. Over the years agricultural policies have sought to bring farm incomes closer to those in the rest of the economy – the "parity" goal which plays so fundamental a role in rural politics; yet despite massive subsidies, the relative income position of the farm sector has remained virtually unchanged in most OECD countries (see Table 5.11).

Equally, though many farmers are now extremely wealthy, the gap in living standards persists between agriculture and the areas which depend on it on the one hand, and the rest of society on the other. The data sources available in this regard vary greatly both in coverage and quality; but averaging between countries, and compared to the overall mean for the active population, the average self-employed agricultural worker: receives two years' less schooling; is (except in Japan) about twice as likely to work more than 45 hours a week; has had only marginal reductions in effective working hours in the last decade; is at least twice as likely to have a money income in the lowest quintile of the income distribution; and is still less likely than average to have modern facilities in his or her place of residence[72].

Finally, the growing excess of supply over demand, which agricultural policies have induced and perpetuated, poses a critical threat to the long-term stability

Table 5.11. **Relative income in agriculture[1], 1960-1984, in selected OECD countries**

Agriculture sector income as a percentage of overall per capita income

	1960	1968	1973	1974	1975	1976	1977	1978	1979	1980	1981	1982	1983	1984
Australia	..	103	116	91	80	82	71	103	103	89	80	59	..	..
New Zealand	..	..	110	78	93	104	91	82	103	94	81	72	81	..
United States	47	53	93	83	80	72	76	76	86	75	83	72	57	..
Canada	42	49	71	76	72	66	65	70	70	74	70	71	60	60
Japan	42	40	44	43	43	43	43	39	38	36	35	35	35	36
France	47	46	59	53	49	48	49	50	52	47	46	52	50	49
Finland	47	47	56	57	65	56	58	57	59	64	61	59	60	61
United Kingdom	72	71	93	89	89	89	82	78	77	73	73	74	67	73
EEC[2]	40	42	45	42	42	42	42	42	41	40	40	43	41	42
OECD	30	31	43	40	40	38	38	39	40	37	37	35	32	33

1. Value added in agriculture as a percentage of GDP divided by employment in agriculture as a percentage of civilian employment.
2. Ten countries.
.. = Not available.

Source: OECD, *OECD Economic Outlook - Historical Statistics 1960-1984*, Paris, 1986.

and viability of the sector. As output quotas and similar administrative controls become more important instruments of policy, the policy environment, far from providing a predictable framework for farm planning, has been transformed into a major source of uncertainty.

This gap between the intentions of policies and their outcomes is largely symptomatic of the inherent weaknesses of direct government control of markets. It is only by chance that prices set through the political process could serve to balance supply and demand, while also meeting other objectives of policy; and there is no reason to expect the political process to be more successful in determining agricultural prices than similar processes applied elsewhere in the economy. Nonetheless, the cumulative results of farm policies are also due to the assumptions on which they are based – assumptions which do not reflect the realities of modern agriculture.

In essence, these policies were designed for a pre-modern sector. Resources – in particular, labour inputs – were assumed to be highly rigid in their uses; so that output would respond only slowly to revenue incentives. Given rigidities both on the supply and the demand side, the sector was assumed to be chronically unstable; and it was argued that farms are too small to efficiently spread the risks this entails. The sector was therefore seen as requiring protection from the uncertainties of the market.

The assumptions underlying this case were always questionable[73], but they certainly do not apply to the farm sector in the high-income countries. Studies show that as the number of farms has shrunk, the survivors – and especially the largest amongst them – have been those which use modern management techniques to optimise their response to changing circumstances[74]. Relying on purchased inputs which can be varied in quantity and kind, and on technological assistance from input suppliers and government extension services, these farmers alter cropping patterns, livestock practices and yields in line with market returns, domestically and internationally. As a result, they have steadily raised their share of agricultural output at the expense of smaller producers, who have increasingly turned to non-farm sources of income.

These trends undermine the bases of agricultural policies. In particular, it is by no means clear that modern farmers need to be protected from the operation of market forces – or that exposing them to these forces would result in intolerable levels of instability. Three interrelated factors are involved.

First, though the agricultural sector has become more vulnerable to broad macroeconomic forces, its internal workings have tended to become less inherently unstable. This is largely because the major actors in the sector now respond much more rapidly to changing circumstances than they used to, so that market forces – were they allowed to work – would correct rather than amplify disequilibria. In the United States, for example, changes in supply and demand elasticities over the last two decades have decreased by more than a quarter the ratio of the variance of agricultural receipts to the variance of agricultural quantities[75]. Moreover, greater and more timely information is allowing farmers to base their decisions on data which more accurately reflect overall developments. In particular, studies suggest that access to computer-based information sources and management information systems is already leading to greatly improved decision-making in the agricultural sector[76].

Secondly, the agricultural sector has become more capable of dealing with whatever endogenous instability persists. This is partly because the farms which produce the bulk of agricultural output are now relatively large and – though their leverage has increased – have a sizeable equity base. But it is mainly a result of the increasing integration of primary producers into an agro-food chain, whose other agents also have an interest in greater stability. Processors, like farmers, can be more efficient if they have regular streams of uniform raw materials coming into their plants, at prices which they can reasonably predict. In contrast to earlier projections, this has not led to widespread vertical integration and the end of the family farm; rather, new contractual forms have developed which efficiently spread risk between input suppliers, farmers and industrial purchasers[77].

Finally, farmers can increasingly look to financial markets to help them pool, diversify and spread risk. Options and future markets have of course developed for certain agricultural commodities; but it seems plausible to suppose that they would develop considerably further in a freer agricultural system. Notably in Europe, great scope exists for encouraging or at least permitting the emergence of multi-year futures contracts and of more diversified options on farm products. Compared to publicly operated stabilization schemes, such markets are much less likely to systematically distort the information flowing to the farm sector[78]. Looking to the longer term, a more developed market in farm equity - that is, the "securitisation" of farm assets - could also contribute to spreading the risks farming entails.

Combined, these factors suggest that the agricultural sector could cope with instability; but this does not imply that a move to a freer market in agricultural products would be painless. The evidence suggests that the most heavily indebted farmers are *not* those who receive the greatest transfers from agricultural policies – in fact, in the United States, the opposite is the case[79]. Nonetheless, prices closer to market clearing levels could put some pressure on marginal farmers, as well as eroding the asset base of the larger farmers who have benefitted from price guarantees.

In practice, it is by no means obvious that the reform of agricultural policies would seriously worsen the problems of marginal or low-income farmers. The policies applied to date have done little for producers whose incomes are close to or below the poverty line; in some cases they have aggravated their plight by locking them into the sector. There may be a case for providing these farmers with a direct income guarantee, and – given that they now account for a small share of production – this could be done without aggravating the problems of excess supply. Nonetheless, income guarantees could trap or even attract resources into low productivity uses. An alternative approach – the long-run implications of which might be preferable – would be to re-examine eligibility conditions (such as assets tests) on general income support and social security schemes which may prevent genuinely poor farmers from receiving assistance.

Specific problems arise with the protection of regionally – or environmentally – significant farming activities. By and large, agricultural policies have worsened rather than improved the rural environment, though this is not true in all countries; but there are circumstances in which the survival of small-scale, low-input farming contributes to maintaining the social, regional and ecological balance. The activities involved – for example, farming in mountain areas – generate extremely little output and are hardly a source of excess supplies. It would therefore seem reasonable to provide them with direct subsidies to continue with a cropping and livestock pattern appropriate to their surroundings.

A transition to freer markets could also create considerable difficulties for larger farmers. In particular, these farmers might well face substantial income and capital losses as reductions in support prices cut the value of their output and lead to lower land values. The primary requirements in this respect are policies which facilitate these farmers' adjustment to changing circumstances. During a transition to freer markets this could involve measures such as loans for consolidating land holdings and mobility allowances for those wishing to leave rural areas. Over the longer term, there may be a case for supporting the development and diffusion of agricultural technology, though the mechanisms adopted need to be carefully assessed.

It is less obvious whether farmers should be provided with financial compensation for any income losses arising from liberalisation. Thus it is frequently suggested that the political problems of agricultural policy reform could be dealt with by "buying farmers out" – for example, by providing one-off transfers equal to the capitalised value of the excess profits derived from support prices. However, such schemes would be very difficult to implement fairly – since the future course of market prices (and hence the value of the guarantees) is unknown – and could involve unacceptably high budgetary costs.

A more viable approach would involve a gradual phasing out of all price supports, combined with immediate changes aimed at reducing the distortions they create in production incentives. For example, price guarantees could be replaced by per-acre payments at a level approximately equal to current benefits. These payments would be made to agricultural landowners regardless of the uses to which land was put. Land prices would rise (since they would reflect the capitalised value of the payments) but production decisions would not be biased towards particular crops or output volumes. Even though the payments were being phased out slowly over time, market equilibrium would be restored relatively quickly.

More generally, the income supports provided to farmers – be it as part of a temporary adjustment programme or (in a longer time-frame) as a way of sustaining environmentally or regionally significant farming – should be "decoupled" as far as possible and as rapidly as possible from production incentives. This may increase the budgetary costs of agricultural policies, but there is every reason to expect the gains in improved resource allocation to be even more significant. Nonetheless, over the long term, any policy which provides significant subsidies to persons engaged in an activity is likely to attract resources to that activity and hence add to output. It is consequently essential that any income support provided be subject to careful limits in terms of eligibility and degressivity, and that "decoupling" be accompanied by a transition to realistic and market-based prices.

The process of change in agricultural policies will inevitably be gradual. But if a gradual transition is genuinely to ease adjustment, the timetable it sets out must be credible. Producers will take decisions now so as to adapt to tomorrow's policy environment only if they know that the reforms announced will in fact be implemented.

Multilateral trade agreements have a key role to play in this respect – and the new GATT Round provides an exceptionally important opportunity for progress. The experience of three decades of trade liberalisation confirms that these agreements, once entered into, are generally implemented. By their nature, trade agreements create powerful coalitions between the domestic interests which would suffer were governments to disregard their commitments. The balance of advantages they provide to countries gives them substantial public legitimacy, complicating the task of sectional interest groups. In short, by committing themselves to such agreements, governments can lend credibility to domestic policy changes which will only be phased in over a period of several years.

But a multilateral and multi-commodity approach to the problems of the agricultural sector also has substantial economic advantages. Estimates made for the Secretariat's study of agricultural trade show that compared with unilateral liberalisation, a co-ordinated multilateral approach would lead to a smaller reduction in domestic prices in the more highly protected markets. The expansion of world trade induced by a co-ordinated strategy would minimise the adjustment burden on any single producer; and would maximise the gains to the world economy as a whole.

The multi-commodity nature of the approach is also important. Agricultural product markets are closely interdependent; and liberalisation confined to one market – say dairy produce – could have significant repercussions on others – in this case, beef. In addition to its obvious political advantages, ensuring that markets are liberalised in parallel would limit the adjustment costs on individual sectors and reduce the risk of induced distortions in agricultural trade.

Nonetheless, it is clear that trade liberalisation and the reorientation of domestic agricultural policies towards a greater emphasis on market forces will be gradual processes, spread over a period of years. Yet there are pressing problems which policy makers must address.

It is essential that the immediate measures taken be consistent with the medium-term reorientation of agricultural policies, both domestically and internationally. While correcting the current situation of massive overproduction, they should help redirect world agricultural markets towards a more rational use of resources, based on an increasingly important role for the price mechanism in the sector's decision-making.

A primary requirement is that governments commit themselves to not exceed the levels of trade-distorting support now being given; and to accompany such a commitment with early moves to place agricultural markets on a surer footing. Three criteria are of particular importance in this respect.

First, *excess stocks must be worked down in a gradual and disciplined manner and with a view to avoiding further market disruption.*

Second, if the current problem of excess stocks is not to recur, agricultural output must be reduced. *These reductions should occur first and foremost in the countries where current levels of trade-distorting support are highest.*

Third, *for imbalances to be durably reduced, domestic support prices must be brought progressively into line with world market levels.*

This does not mean that reductions in output levels should be sought solely through price adjustments: given low or even perverse supply elasticities in the very short term, more direct control mechanisms may also be needed. Nonetheless, experience demonstrates that output controls are unlikely to function correctly if prices provide continuing incentives for over-production. Moreover, it is important that the measures adopted should not create new distortions which it will be difficult to remove. Thus, though production quotas may have some role to play, these should not serve to create new vested interests, which could obstruct a shift towards a more competitive environment. This requirement is best met if quotas, if put in place, are short-lived, tradable and accompanied by significant price adjustments.

Combined, these initiatives would create a more favourable context for reforming agricultural policies. These policies must be reformed – not only because of global concerns but because they are basically unsustainable. The high costs they create now visibly exceed their scarce benefits. They are hardly a desirable example to other sectors of the community who must cope with the realities of international competition. And they have fundamentally failed to meet their objectives. More than any textbook, they illustrate the cumulative consequences of policies which distort the functioning of markets.

NOTES AND REFERENCES

1. The Club of Rome, *The Limits to Growth*, Potomac Associates Book, NY Universe Books, 1972.

2. Tracy, Michael, *Agriculture in Western Europe. Challenge and Response, 1880-1980*, Granada, London, 1982, p. 25.

3. Paarlberg, Don, "Effects of New Deal Farm Programs on the Agricultural Agenda a Half Century Later and Prospect for the Future", *American Journal of Agricultural Economics*, 1983, Vol. 65, No. 5, p. 1163.

4. Tracy, *op. cit.* in Note 2, Chapter 6.

5. Rasmussen, Wayne D., "The New Deal Farm Programs: What They Were and Why They Survived", *American Journal of Agricultural Economics*, *op.cit.* in Note 3; Petit, Michel, Determinants of Agricultural Policies in the United States and the European Community, International Food Policy Research Institute, Washington, 1985.

6. Two American studies of the 1920s were particularly important in this respect: Peek, G.N. and Johnson, H.S., *Equality For Agriculture*, Moline, 1922; Black, J.D., *Agricultural Reform in the United States*, New York, 1929.

7. In the traditional theory of "peasant" agriculture, it is argued that labour inputs are quasi-fixed because family labour (the primary source of labour input) has a very low opportunity cost; see for example, Franklin, S.H., *The European Peasantry. The Final Phase*, Methuen and Co. Ltd., London, 1969, pp. 1-20.

8. It is easily shown that the rate of price decline arising from a given rate of cost reduction is (at a given degree of monopoly power) an inverse function of the price elasticity of demand.

9. Alphandery, P., Bitoun, P., DuPont, Y. and Roger, C., *Les concours financiers de l'Etat à l'agriculture de 1945 à 1980*, Institut National de la Recherche Agronomique, Paris, 1982.

10. Estimated from Howarth, Richard W., *Farming for Farmers?*, The Institute of Economic Affairs, London, 1985, p. 73.

11. Sugar price "stabilization" both in the United States and the EEC provides a particularly striking example of the use of buffer stocks for income maintenance purposes: in 1985, United States loan rates for raw cane sugar stood at 18 cents a pound, while world prices ranged from three to six cents per pound; operating with an equally large disparity between internal and world market prices, the EEC's sugar regime rapidly accumulated a loss of over 400 million ECUs.

12. It is important to note that this excludes FEOGA, i.e. EEC, outlays in the countries referred to.

13. EEC, *Public Expenditure on Agriculture*, Brussels, November 1984, p. 229.

14. However, estimates which seek to exclude all double counting from transfers (and hence only comprise *net* transfers to agriculture) yield a figure of around 60 per cent for the share of income and price support in agricultural transfers.

15. On the United States, see Paarlberg, D., *Farm and Food Policy*, University of Nebraska Press, Lincoln, 1980; Gardner, B.L., *The Governing of Agriculture*, Regents Press of Kansas, Laurence, 1981; and on Europe, Coulomb, P., *Recherches sur l'élaboration de la politique agricole*, INRA, Paris, 1977; Petit, *op. cit.* in Note 5; Howarth, *op. cit.* in Note 10; Neville, Rolfe E., *The Politics of Agriculture in the European Community*, Policy Studies Institute, London, 1984.

16. See for example, on the United States, Infanger *et al.*, *American Journal of Agricultural Economics*, February 1983.

17. See for example, Howarth, *op. cit.* in Note 10, pp. 60-61, and Paarlberg, *art. cit.* in Note 3, pp. 1164-5.

18. See especially Bullock, Bruce J., "Future Directions for Agricultural Policy", *American Journal of Agricultural Economics*, 1984, Vol. 66, No. 2, pp. 234-239.

19. See especially Day, Richard H., "The Economics of Technological Change and the Demise of the Sharecropper", *The American Economic Review*, 1967, Vol. 57, No. 3, pp. 427-449; Barkley, Paul W., "A Contemporary Political Economy of Family Farming", *American Journal of Agricultural Economics*, 1976, Vol. 58, No. 5, pp. 812-819; Gardner, B. Delworth and Pope, Rulon D., "How Is Scale and Structure Determined in Agriculture?", *American Journal of Agricultural Economics*, 1978, Vol. 60, No. 3, pp. 295-302; Kislev, Yoav and Peterson, Willis, "Prices, Technology, and Farm Size", *Journal of Political Economy*, 1982, Vol. 90, No. 3, pp. 578-595; Walford, Nigel, "The Future Size of Farms: Modelling the Effect of Change in Labour and Machinery", *American Journal of Agricultural Economics*, 1983, Vol. 34, No. 3, pp. 407-416.

20. Evenson, Waggoner and Ruttan in *Science*, 1979, pp. 1101-1107.

21. See also Thirtle, Colin G., "Induced Innovation in United States Field Crops, 1939-78", *American Journal of Agricultural Economics*, 1985, Vol. 36, No. 1, pp. 1-14.

22. See Traill, Bruce, "Taxes, Investment Incentives and the Cost of Agricultural Inputs", *American Journal of Agricultural Economics*, 1982, Vol. 33, No. 1, pp. 1-12.

23. Kislev and Paterson, *art. cit.* in Note 19, estimate for the United States farm sector that the ratio of power and machinery input to labour increased from a base of 100 in 1950 to 476 in 1976, while that of power and machinery to acreage rose from 100 in 1950 to 243 in 1976.

24. Askari, Hossein and Cummings, John Thomas, *Agricultural Supply Response: A Survey of the Econometric Evidence*, Praeger Publishers, New York, 1976.

25. See especially Schultz, Theodore W., "The Value of the Ability to Deal with Disequilibria", *The Journal of Economic Literature*, 1975, Vol. 13, No. 3, pp. 827-846.

26. On the United States, see Gardner and Pope, *art. cit.* in Note 19; on the EEC, see "Income Disparities in Agriculture in the Community", *EEC Green Europe Newsletter on the Common Agricultural Policy*, 1985, No. 208.

27. Thus, in the United States, farms in the annual sales class of $40 000 to $100 000 earn more than half their total income from off-farm sources – but net equity per farm in this class is approximately $400 000; see Council of Economic Advisers, *Economic Report of the President*, United States Government Printing Office, Washington D.C., 1986, p. 131.

28. That is, farms whose annual sales are below $40 000; see *Economic Report of the President, ibid.*, p. 132.

29. See Hill, B. in *American Journal of Agricultural Economics*, 1982; Commission du Bilan, *La France en Mai 1981, les activités productives*, La Documentation Française, Paris, 1982, p. 110.

30. "Income Disparities in Agriculture in the Community", *art. cit.* in Note 26, p. 11.

31. Bullock, *art. cit.* in Note 18.

32. The United States data are from Bullock, *ibid.*; for the EEC, see also Tillient, M., "Disparité des revenus en agriculture dans la Communauté Européenne", *14e séminaire européen des économistes agricoles*, Rennes, September 1986.

33. In other words, by truncating the lower tail of the price distribution, support prices reduce the variance of the mean expected price of output. It is worth noting that this effect can be significant even when support prices are set *below* the market clearing level. Thus, assume that prior to support, the expected price distribution is normal, with a mean of 2.2 (corresponding to market equilibrium) and a variance of $(.336)^2$. Setting the support level at 2.1 will decrease the variance to $(.1968)^2$ – a reduction of 65 per cent.

34. Castle, Emery N. and Hoch, Irving, "Farm Real Estate Price Components, 1920-78", *American Journal of Agricultural Economics*, 1982, Vol. 64, No. 1, pp. 8-18.

35. On the United States, see Johnson, D.G., *Farm Commodity Programs*, AEI, Washington, 1973; Boehlje, M. and Griffin, S., "Financial Impacts of Government Support Price Programs", *American Journal of Agricultural Economics*, 1979, pp. 285-296; Johnson, James D. and Short, Sara D., "Commodity Programs: Who has Received the Benefits?", *American Journal of Agricultural Economics*, 1983, *op.cit.* in Note 3, pp. 912-921. For the United Kingdom, see Traill, *art. cit.* in Note 22, and Howarth, *op. cit.* in Note 10, pp. 80-89.

36. In practice, rentals are only loosely related to land values. This is mainly because current rentals must reflect the current value of marginal product, while capitalised values can pick up other sources of gain or loss. Regulations on land rentals, notably in Europe, are also a factor in this respect.

37. That is, output at the farm gate, *excluding* processing, distribution and transport.

38. See Howarth, *op. cit.* in Note 10, pp. 42-43; Von Witzke, Harald, "Prices, Common Agricultural Price Policy and Personal Distribution of Income in West German Agriculture", *European Review of Agricultural Economics*, 1979, Vol. 6, No. 1, pp. 61-80; Tweeten, Luther, "Economic Instability in Agriculture: The Contributions of Prices, Government Programs and Exports", *American Journal of Agricultural Economics*, 1983, *op.cit.* in Note 3, pp. 922-931.

39. OECD, *Agricultural Projections for 1975 and 1985*, Paris, 1968.

40. Balassa, C., "Agricultural Protection" (draft), Washington D.C., 1984.

41. This is simply because reductions in world prices will generally reduce the value of domestic output estimated at world prices; so that for domestic agricultural incomes to remain unchanged, the total subsidy element to agriculture must rise.

42. Thus, in the United States, concentration of benefits has been limited by the fact that many large-scale farming operations produce commodities not covered by direct payment programmes, e.g. poultry, and that usually no single producer can receive payments exceeding $50 000. These have not been significant factors in the CAP.

43. See for example, Carles, R. and Chitrit, J.J., "Les revenus dans les entreprises céréalières", *Revenus agricoles. Systèmes céréaliers, Systèmes laitiers*, INSEE, Paris, 1985, pp. 95-166.

44. Boehlje and Griffin, *art. cit.* in Note 35.

45. In the United States, for example, the smallest 29 per cent of farmland owners – those owning less than ten acres – accounted in 1978 for less than 1 per cent of total farmland owned. The largest 4 per cent of farmland owners, those owning at least 500 acres, accounted for over 50 per cent of total farmland owned. In addition, over 70 per cent of all farmland owned was acquired prior to 1976. Thus, any benefits from land appreciation were highly concentrated. See Dougherty, A. and Otta, R.C., *Farmland Ownership in the United States*, USDA ERS Staff Report, AGES 830311, 1983.

46. Boehlje and Griffin, *art. cit.* in Note 35, and Johnson and Short, *art. cit.* in Note 35, provide a useful survey of the empirical work on this subject, as does Shultze, D.L., *The Distribution of Farm Subsidies*, The Brookings Institution, Washington D.C., 1961 for earlier studies.

47. As measured by the Gini coefficient; Von Witzke, H., *art. cit.* in Note 38.

48. The effects of the CAP on inter-regional income distribution in the EEC are discussed by, *inter alia*, De Benedictis, Michele, "Agricultural Development in Italy: National Problems in a Community Framework", *American Journal of Agricultural Economics*, 1981, Vol. 32, No. 3, pp. 275-286; Bonnieux, F. and Rainelli, P., "Regional Disparities in Western European Agriculture", *European Review of Agricultural Economics*, 1983, Vol. 10, No. 3, pp. 295-301; Weinschenck, Günther and Kemper, Jutta, "Agricultural Policies and their Regional Impact in Western Europe", *European Review of Agricultural Economics*, 1981, Vol. 8, No. 2-3, pp. 251-281; Petit, Michel, "Agriculture and Regional Development in Europe - The Role of Agricultural Economists", *European Review of Agricultural Economics*, 1981,

Vol. 8, pp. 137-153; Tarditi, S. and Croce Angelini, E., "Regional Redistributive Effects of Common Price Support Policies", *European Review of Agricultural Economics*, 1982, Vol. 9, No. 3, pp. 255-270.

49. See for example, Putault, J.P. *et al.*, "Intensification et Systèmes de Production du Lait", *Revenus Agricoles...*, INSEE, *op. cit.* in Note 43, p. 181; more generally, Franklin, *op. cit.* in Note 7, pp. 122-124; and Petit, *art. cit.* in Note 48.

50. See for example, Weinschenck, Günther and Kemper, *art. cit.* in Note 48, especially Table 10.

51. Wibberley, Gerald, "Strong Agricultures but Weak Rural Economies - The Undue Emphasis on Agriculture in European Rural Development", *European Review of Agricultural Economics*, 1981, Vol. 8, No. 2-3, *op. cit.* in Note 48, pp. 155-170.

52. See House of Lords, Select Committee on the European Community, *Agriculture and the Environment*, HMSO, London, 1984, especially pp. xii-xx.

53. Tweeten, *art. cit.* in Note 38.

54. Hazell, Peter B.R., *American Journal of Agricultural Economics*, 1984, pp. 302-311.

55. See for example, Bullock, *art. cit.* in Note 18; Howarth, *op. cit.* in Note 10, p. 68. It has been argued that at a given gearing level, farmers seek a particular level of risk. Government programmes which reduce this risk level will simply be offset as farmers adjust their portfolios to augment the other risks they bear. See especially Gabriel, S.C. and Baker, C.B., *American Journal of Agricultural Economics*, 1980, pp. 560-66.

56. Shepard, Lawrence E. and Collins, Robert A., "Why do Farmers Fail? Farm Bankruptcies, 1910-78", *American Journal of Agricultural Economics*, 1982, Vol. 64, No. 4, pp. 609-615.

57. In other words, the price elasticity of export demand is greater than that of domestic demand; so that a rising export share increases the weighted demand elasticity. In the United States, for example, the growth of exports was the primary factor in the 12 per cent increase in the price elasticity of demand in the period 1950-59 to 1976-82; though modest, this increase implies a 26 per cent *decrease* in the ratio of the variance of receipts to the variance in quantity.

58. Blandford, D. and Swartz, N.E., *Food Policy*, 1983, pp. 305-312.

59. Hazell, Peter B.R., "Sources of Increased Variability in World Cereal Production Since the 1960s", *American Journal of Agricultural Economics*, 1985, Vol. 36, No. 2, pp. 145-159.

60. See Council of Economic Advisers, *Economic Report of the President*, United States Government Printing Office, Washington D.C., 1961, p. 142.

61. It should be noted, however, that there are numerous instances in which production controls have *not* been effectual in curtailing output. In some cases, this is because the quotas have not been rigorously enforced, or because the incentives they provide for illegal supply are sufficiently strong to undermine their overall impact. It has also happened that the quota allocation system provided incentives for producers to exceed their set output level. Thus, in Austria, prior to 1984, annual production quotas were realigned each year with the previous year's output for each producer, *regardless of the quota level*; producers therefore systematically exceeded their quota so as to obtain a larger quota next year.

62. Castle and Hoch, *art. cit.* in Note 34.

63. This is shown by the relatively high prices quota rights elicit; see *Economic Report of the President*, 1986, *op. cit.* in Note 27, for example at p. 150. Note that capitalisation will occur even in schemes whereby quotas are repurchased by a central regulatory authority from producers willing to leave the sector; this is because a repurchase price below the capitalised value of the rents will deter exit.

64. It is worth noting that no system of quotas escapes these flaws. Thus, attempts to use revisable quotas (whereby permitted volumes are altered over time) create uncertainties which increase producer costs, dissuade quota trading and hence slow down structural change. Equally, offers to allow some entry into the sector by providing new farmers with free or otherwise subsidised quota rights may simply encourage churning in the farm population, as quotas are held for the minimum period needed before they can be resold.

65. EEC, *The Agricultural Situation in the Community*, Office for Official Publications of the European Communities, Luxembourg, 1985 and 1986.

66. Papitto, Franco, "Il 'grande botto' della Cee Vernici fatte col burro e latte in pasto ai maiali", *la Repubblica*, 24th July 1986, p. 10.

67. Marsh, J.S., "Economics, Politics and Potatoes - The Changing Role of the Potato Marketing Board in Great Britain", *American Journal of Agricultural Economics*, 1984, Vol. 35, pp. 325-343; EEC, "The Prevention of Frauds against the Agricultural Fund", *Green Europe Newsletter on the Common Agricultural Policy*, 1982, No. 193.

68. OECD, *National Policies and Agricultural Trade*, Paris, 1987.

69. Dilnot, A.W. and Morris, C.N., "The Distributional Effects of the CAP", *Fiscal Studies*, 1982.

70. The Economic Planning Advisory Council (EPAC), *The Medium-Term Outlook for the Rural Sector*, Canberra, 1986.

71. Valdes, A. and Zeitz, J., *Agricultural Protection in OECD Countries: Its Cost to Less Developed Countries*, International Food Policy Research Institute, Washington D.C., 1980.

72. Data drawn from OECD: *Living Conditions in OECD Countries. Compendium of Social Indicators*, Paris, 1986 – Tables 5.2 (education), 10.1 and 10.2 (working hours), 14.3 and 20.1 (income) and 24.2 (housing standards). Income distribution is also covered in EEC, "Income Disparities in Agriculture in the Community", *art. cit.* in Note 26. The problems involved in comparing rural money incomes with incomes in other sectors should be borne in mind.

73. See especially Schultz, T.W., *Transforming Traditional Agriculture*, Yale University Press, New Haven, 1964.

74. Tolley, G.S. in *American Journal of Agricultural Economics*, 1970, pp. 485-93.

75. This is because the ratio of the variance of receipts to the variance of quantities is a function of the sum of the absolute values of the supply and demand elasticities. When these elasticities rise, agricultural incomes become more stable. For estimates of changes in these parameters over time, see Tweeten, *art. cit.* in Note 38.

76. Proceedings Symposium, *American Journal of Agricultural Economics*, 1985.

77. Barkley, *art. cit.* in Note 19.

78. Gardner, B.C., *The Governing of Agriculture*, Regents Press of Kansas, Lawrence, 1981.

79. *Economic Report of the President*, 1986, *op. cit.* in Note 27, pp. 155-156.

Additional references consulted:

Avery, Graham, "Guarantee Thresholds and the Common Agricultural Policy", *American Journal of Agricultural Economics*, 1984, pp. 355-364.

Bonnen, James T., "Historical Sources of US Agricultural Productivity: Implications for R&D Policy and Social Science Research", *American Journal of Agricultural Economics*, December 1983, pp. 958-966.

Braden, John B., "Some Emerging Rights in Agricultural Land", *American Journal of Agricultural Economics*, 1982, *op. cit.* in Note 34, pp. 19-27.

Breimyer, Harold F., "Conceptualisation and Climate for New Deal Farm Laws of the 1930s", *American Journal of Agricultural Economics*, 1983, *op. cit.* in Note 3, pp. 1153-1173.

Cordts, W., Deerberg, K.-H. and Hanf, C.-H., "Analysis of the Intrasectoral Income Differences in West German Agriculture", *European Review of Agricultural Economics*, 1984, Vol. 11, No. 3, pp. 323-342.

Delorme, Robert and Andre, Christine, *L'Etat et l'économie*, Editions du Seuil, Paris, 1983.

Dobson, N.D., "Future Directions for Agricultural Policy: Discussion", *American Journal of Agricultural Economics*, 1984, *op. cit.* in Note 18, pp. 240-241.

EEC, *The Agricultural Situation in the Community*, Office for Official Publications of the European Communities, Luxembourg, 1983.

Farrell, Kenneth R. and Runge, Ford C., "Institutional Innovation and Technical Change in American Agriculture: The Role of the New Deal", *American Journal of Agricultural Economics*, 1983, *op. cit.* in Note 3.

Heien, Dale, "Future Directions for United States Food and Agricultural Trade Policy: Discussion", *American Journal of Agricultural Economics*, 1984, *op. cit.* in Note 18, pp. 232-241.

Josling, Timothy E., "Future Directions for United States Food and Agricultural Trade Policy: Discussion", *ibid.*, pp. 248-249.

Krueger, Anne O., "Protectionism, Exchange Rate Distortions, and Agricultural Trade Patterns", *American Journal of Agricultural Economics*, 1983, *op. cit.* in Note 3, pp. 864-871.

L'Hardy, Philippe, "La consommation des ménages, 1960-1990", *Futuribles*, 1984, No. 76, pp. 15-36.

Newby, Howard, "Rural Sociology and its Relevance to the Agricultural Economist: A Review", *American Journal of Agricultural Economics*, 1982, Vol. 33, No. 2, pp. 125-165.

Plaxico, James S. and Kletke, Darrel D., "The Value of Unrealized Farm Land Capital Gains", *American Journal of Agricultural Economics*, May 1979, pp. 327-330.

Raymond, W.F., "Options for Reducing Inputs to Agriculture: A Non-Economist's View", *American Journal of Agricultural Economics*, 1984, pp. 345-354.

Schuh, Edward G., "Future Directions for Food and Agriculture Trade Policy", *American Journal of Agricultural Economics*, 1984, *op. cit.* in Note 18, pp. 242-247.

Chapter 6

STRUCTURAL ADJUSTMENT IN INDUSTRY

INTRODUCTION

All the squalls that have swept the world economy in the past fifteen years have transformed industry, while being themselves largely due to the technological or other changes that have taken place in the manufacturing and service sectors. Against a background of slower world economic growth, increased interdependence and more uncertainty, almost all industries and businesses have been forced to reconsider their product ranges, production technologies, geographical locations and marketing strategies.

As a result, industry's role in the social fabric and economic development of OECD Member countries has been radically changed. The sharp decline in some sectors, the rapid emergence of new industries, intensified competition and the "industrialisation" of many service activities have sent powerful and disruptive shock waves through society. Governments and opinion groups are now taking a fresh look, in direct contrast to the decline of interest in industry during the high-growth period of the 1950s and 60s, when industrial aspects of economic development were sometimes considered to be a "logistic" question of only secondary importance.

The revival of interest in industrial adjustment stems from two major concerns. The first relates to the decline in the contribution of manufacturing industry to job creation, and the second to industry's central role in the generation and exploitation of new technological opportunities. This renewed interest initially tempted governments to introduce an active industrial policy where there had been none before – witness the lively debate on the subject in the United States – or to strengthen existing industrial policy. Governments introduced a host of measures intended to shape this industrial adjustment; the "interventionist" wave peaked in the early 1980s.

In recent years, and particularly due to budget constraints, more and more countries have been questioning the effectiveness of industrial policy measures. Historical and comparative analysis of the scale, direction and causes of changes in industrial structures and the way in which governments have responded to the problems that have ensued should help clarify the underlying reasons for this change in attitude. It should

then be possible to identify some future policies that would be more successful than previous ones have been in achieving and reconciling some essential objectives – holding down the social costs of industrial adjustment and sharing them fairly, but without unduly slowing the adjustment process; arriving at a better balance between policies affecting the environment in which firms operate, and those applying directly to the adjustment process; and minimising the socio-economic pressures that result from industrial change in each country, while avoiding increased international economic tensions.

This chapter comprises three sections and an annex. Part I shows the diversity of national paths of industrial adjustment, analyses the reasons for this diversity and reconnoitres the boundaries that each country's policies are likely to come up against sooner or later. Part II is a critical analysis of government policies in the industrial area, pinpointing the main reasons why they were a failure or a success. Part III, in conclusion, broadly outlines the directions that the desirable reform of those policies might take. The Annex, in two parts, first examines the influence of the monetary and financial environment on structural adjustment, showing that differences in the structure and efficiency of financial systems from one country to another are a significant factor in explaining international disparities in industrial performance, and then goes on to analyse the implications of contemporary technological change for industry, illustrating the adjustments that it forces, the new modes of adjustment that it allows, the impediments to adjustment that it reveals and the new conditions it creates for government action.

I. NATIONAL PATHS
OF INDUSTRIAL ADJUSTMENT

In attempting to grasp *the most fundamental* differences between national paths of industrial adjustment – and thus the main reasons for international disparities in industrial performance – it is important not to conclude, from the extreme diversity of the factors that determine structural change, that the differences are all relative. For example, differences in responses to common pressures, such as those from the newly industrialised nations (NICs) or the energy market, do not seem to be *the prime reason* for the different types of structural adjustment encountered internationally.

They seem to be explained more satisfactorily by comparing the type of technological adjustment in industry, that is, by examining the way in which industry in individual countries gradually manages to master technical and organisational innovations and uses these to defend and consolidate its international position in response to changing conditions of competition and altered domestic and world demand.

The features and limitations of the "path of technological adjustment" of the three leading world industrial powers will be examined first, starting with the country that has shown the most vigorous growth, Japan. The medium-sized countries, such as France and the United Kingdom, and the smaller OECD countries will then be examined.

A.   Japan

Japan today has a comparative industrial advantage which is somewhat similar to that enjoyed by the United States in previous decades in mass production sectors, but which is better adjusted to the technological conditions of the 1970s and 80s. The United States advantage was based on the size of its domestic economy and on its advanced industrial organisation (extreme type of Taylorist production and advanced management techniques which allowed the co-ordination of production in several locations, in diversified firms and in multinational operations). However, as world economic integration has made a large domestic market less of an advantage, and new production methods arising from technical progress and the growing sophistication of demand have made Taylorist-type production systems much less effective, competitiveness in many industries now depends primarily on changed factors. The first is the capacity to implement new forms of production organisation that allow technological opportunities to be rapidly and commercially exploited, while the second factor relies on the existence of conditions that promote fruitful interaction between the national and international innovation processes, and the diffusion of technology at national level.

Japan has been more successful than any other country in achieving the right mix of technological and organisational innovation. It has been helped by some features of its economy which cannot easily be transferred elsewhere. For example, the traditional structure of Japan's industry, which strikes a balance between competition and co-operation, has also allowed it to exploit intersectoral synergy to full effect without foregoing the benefits of competition. The system of lifetime employment practised within diversified industrial groups has made possible a job mobility policy that does not deter employers from investing in training. Since 1973, the high dependence on imported energy has

created stronger pressure than in other countries to switch resources to lighter industry. However, other less specific factors have also been at work – for example, its education system is geared to changing economic needs, its general and industrial policies have created a stable environment which encourages rapid structural and behaviour adjustment, and the substantial appreciation of the dollar in the early 1980s also played a part[1].

The remarkable vitality of Japanese industry in the past fifteen years has been based on the exploitation in an exceptionally wide range of industries of a new type of comparative advantage in "manufacturing know-how" -intensive goods. This advantage has several specific characteristics. First, it stems from Japanese firms' readiness to rapidly grasp the new dimensions it offers when traditional factor endowments are similar, i.e. the importance of product differentiation, of scale and learning economies, of R&D and workers' skills (the role of government policies is discussed in the next Part). Second, it cuts across a large group of industries which all utilise complex manufacturing processes, but which differ in the pattern of inputs used and in the degree of R&D intensity. Third, it is a cumulative advantage in that it tends to increase as an industry moves up the learning curve, and investment is more dynamic than in competing countries (record growth of gross fixed capital formation has allowed technical progress to be mastered more rapidly – see Graphs 6.1 and 6.2) and to spread to new industries located increasingly close to the leading edge of technology.

However, Japan is rapidly approaching a new strategic turning-point, just as important as the one that many years ago led to the adjustment process described above. If Japanese industry continues on the same course, its dynamism will inevitably be adversely affected, for three main reasons.

First, there are economic and political limits to the kind of rapid industrial growth that generates big trade surpluses, notably in sectors where world demand is growing at only an average rate; and here account has to be taken of the curb imposed by certain countries' import policies and tightened by experience of the difficulties of penetrating the Japanese market. In 1983, products for which world demand was growing at only an average rate – that is between 2 and 3 per cent over the past ten years – accounted for 43 per cent of total Japanese exports. And between 1972 and 1983, Japan's share of the total OECD market expanded more in this category than in high-growth products – 6.1 per cent compared with 5.6 per cent. Second, competition from the NICs is stepping up in part of this product range with the rising yen adding to the pressure[2]. Third, to offset this loss of growth potential, Japan must reinforce its position in high-growth market segments, which are generally high technology segments and which are not yet dominated by Japanese manufacturers. It will have to move into sectors where the sources of comparative advantage and conditions of market access are quite different from those in other sectors, e.g. the importance

Graph 6.1. **Rate of investment in manufacturing**[1]

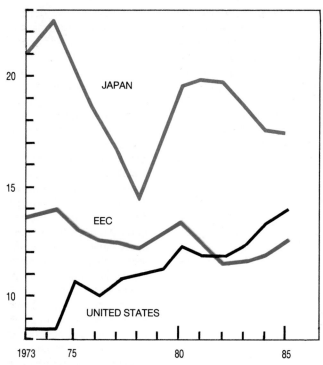

1. Share of gross fixed capital formation in manufacturing value added.
Source: EEC.

Graph 6.2. **Trend of gross fixed capital formation in manufacturing**
(at 1975 prices)

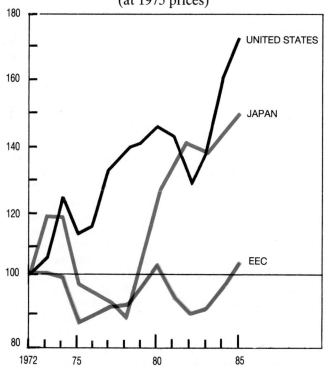

Source: EEC.

211

of domestic basic and pre-competitive research capability and of government procurement, particularly of defence contracts, etc.

In keeping with its forward-looking approach, the Japanese Government became aware of this challenge several years ago, and has already started to adjust the direction of its industrial policy, encouraging a broadening of the range of indigenous technological capacities (note, for example, the position Japan has acquired in new materials) and placing more emphasis on basic research. However, given the breakdown of basic research expenditure in the OECD area shown in Table 6.1, and also the present weakness of university/industry links, the task is likely to be a long one.

Table 6.1. **R&D expenditure by main OECD area (1981)**
Percentages

	Basic research expenditure	Total R&D expenditure
United States	44	46
EEC	36	30
Japan	10	16
Other	10	8
Total	100	100

Source: OECD.

Basic research must be expanded to create both the economic conditions necessary for the change of direction from one adjustment path to another, and the right political environment for that change. Japan could go some way towards maintaining or obtaining an appropriate access to markets by contributing to the production of this international public good on a scale more commensurate with its economic power.

B.   United States

Industry in the United States shows a different pattern of technological adjustment from Japan, closer to the "product cycle" model as applied to international specialisation[3].

With the increasing exposure to foreign competition and the loss of competitiveness of United States industry in several traditional or mass consumption sectors – the effects of which on the trade balance have varied with the fluctuations of the dollar – the trend towards moving resources out of these sectors into those high-growth sectors where the US has a comparative advantage has been accelerated. These comparative advantages exist primarily because of the size and features of the country's scientific and technical capability. This trend – dictated by market forces – has been particularly pronounced in recent years and was accentuated by the steep rise in the dollar's value in the early 1980s. It is reflected in the changes seen in manufacturing trade balance (Graph 6.3) or in total exports.

However, these data give only an approximate and probably underestimated picture of the trend since they group together indiscriminately all products with an above-average R&D intensity, including those in which the United States has become less competitive, such as consumer electronics or some types of semiconductors. The sectors primarily concerned are those in which innovating capability both has the greatest impact on trade performance and depends the most directly on unique features of the US economy. These include its vast reservoir of scientific and technical skills, into which R&D funds (especially government funds for defence research) are continually pumped, a very large supply of skilled personnel[4], unique close links between universities and industry[5], the ease with which R&D personnel move between firms, and the number[6] and variety[7] of firms capable, in a stimulating competitive environment, of participating in the technical design and market testing of new products with high direct and indirect R&D content.

If the direct spin-off to industry as a whole from major national research programmes seems small, it is because the impact is concentrated in "leading edge" sectors (in particular, computers, aerospace, and new generation electronic components). It is precisely in these sectors characterised by a rapid rate of technical advance and by large-scale R&D spending that US firms enjoy a dominant position.

However, it is not certain if this pattern of adjustment will be viable in the medium and long term, for both economic and other reasons.

Recent history has clearly shown that advances in leading-edge industrial sectors are not enough to offset, e.g. in terms of jobs in industry or foreign trade, the effects of a fall in competitiveness in more traditional sectors. In addition, various obstacles are likely to be encountered in the pursuit of such a technological lead.

First, increasing specialisation in high R&D investment activities, where the accelerating pace of obsolescence makes it necessary to recoup costs more and more rapidly, implies a growing dependence on foreign markets which may not be as open and/or dynamic as desired[8]. Yet, in general, high technology sectors are those in which the "dematerialisation" of products has gone the farthest, while the liberalisation of trade in services tends to lag far behind that of trade in goods.

Second, this type of specialisation requires a technological lead which is partly non-economically motivated. This makes it potentially vulnerable to policy changes, particularly shifts in national defence policy[9].

Third, on account of its specialisation and the nature of its comparative advantage, US industry seems more sensitive than its competitors to changes in the appropriability of innovations. This could either be because

Graph 6.3. **Share of high technology trade in the manufacturing trade balance[1]**
(%)

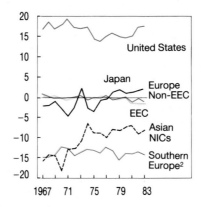

1. For a given area, this indicator is defined as:

$$CONT = 100 \times \frac{(X^{HT} - M^{HT})}{(X + M)/2} - 100 \times \frac{(X - M)}{(X + M)/2} \times \frac{(X^{HT} + M^{HT})}{(X + M)}$$

X^{HT}, M^{HT}: high technology exports and imports for a given area.
X, M : manufacturing exports and imports for a given area.
The indicator allows the trend of the high technology trade balance to be compared with that of the manufacturing trade balance. When the indicator is positive, this means that the balance of high technology trade is more favourable than its share of trade would suggest.
2. Spain, Portugal, Greece, Turkey, Yugoslavia.
Source: CEPII.

Table 6.2. **Share of high technology exports in total exports**
Percentages

	1967	1980	1983	Change 1967-1983
United States	32.3	35.9	42.6	10.3
Japan	21.8	27.4	32.1	10.3
EEC	21.2	22.7	25.0	3.8
Asian NICs	9.4	24.1	24.9	15.5
World	20.4	23.3	26.2	5.8

Source: CEPII.

balance which worries so many United States policy makers is obviously not entirely attributable to the classical and macroeconomic factor of competitiveness (that is, factor cost and productivity, exchange rates, etc.). It also reflects a gradual weakening of the competitive position of many sectors, which has microeconomic structural causes.

It is important to understand why United States firms in these sectors have found it difficult to exploit new technological opportunities as rapidly and on the same scale as their competitors, especially Japanese firms. This has in turn made it hard for the United States to adopt the best production and commercial practices at world level, in the wide range of mass-produced goods

American research advances spread more and more rapidly internationally or simply because the period during which technological superiority ensures a commercial superiority has become shorter (semiconductors are a striking example of this).

Such considerations underlie many of the policies recently adopted by the United States Government on international economic issues (trade in services; transfer of sensitive technology, foreign participation in government-funded R&D programmes, etc.).

However, the domestic dimension should also be borne in mind. The trend of the manufacturing trade

Table 6.3. **Market shares of US, European and Japanese firms in some high technology industries, 1981-1982**
Percentages

	American firms	European firms	Japanese firms	Total
Computers and data processing	82	9	9	100
Software	89	10	1	100
Data transmission services	62	29	9	100
Satellites and launchers	81	13	4	100

Source: Datamation.

which still account for the bulk of trade. Indeed, the weakening of the United States' competitiveness not only adversely affects the trade balance, but also reflects a relative decline in United States manufacturing know-how which fairly rapidly may jeopardise the growth of all sectors, including service and leading-edge sectors. This is particularly true now since there is a rapid increase in functional interdependence, e.g. between design, manufacturing and marketing capability, and in sectoral interdependence, e.g. between services and industry and between innovating sectors and user sectors, such as the obvious link between Japan's domination of the consumer electronics market and its progress in the semiconductor sector.

C. Other Member countries

The changes in industry structure in Europe, Canada and, to a lesser degree, Australia are, even more than in the United States, directly related to changes in international competitiveness. This is due to the very high dependence upon international trade of the manufacturing sector in these countries and areas (see Table 6.4).

Table 6.4.   **Degree of manufacturing industry dependence on international trade[1], 1985**

	High R&D intensity	Medium R&D intensity	Low R&D intensity
United States	31.3	26.7	10.2
Japan	35.1	26.9	12.0
EEC[2]	52.4	38.3	29.9
Sweden[3]	91.1	81.4	53.5
Australia	56.7	43.4	25.1
Canada	83.1	84.9	29.5

1. This indicator is equal to $ER + (1 - ER) MP$ or to $MP + (1 - MP) ER$, where ER = proportion of output exported, and MP = import penetration rate.
2. Excluding intra-EEC trade.
3. 1984.
Source: OECD.

These changes reflect a significant shift in the pattern of international specialisation, as shown by the data in Table 6.5. European countries have increased their competitive advantage in low R&D-intensive sectors during the past fifteen years, but have lost it in medium-intensive sectors, while their international position in high R&D-intensive activities has worsened rapidly this decade, after remaining steady during the 1970s. Slower and less judicious technological adjustment (innovating capability, effectiveness of technological diffusion) than its main competitors would largely appear to explain Europe's difficulties in holding its ground in international markets that are changing rapidly on account of globalised and increased competition. For example, in the ten years between 1973 and 1983, Europe's share of world manufacturing trade fell from 56 per cent to 49 per cent, while that of the United States and Japan remained unchanged, and that of non-Member countries increased substantially from 25 to 32 per cent.

This general diagnosis is amply confirmed by the debate on the causes of this so-called "Eurosclerosis". The most important factors that are considered to impede technological progress in the European economies are the slower growth and fragmentation of demand into small national markets; insufficient competition in many sectors, especially those under direct government control (in public ownership) or indirect control (government procurement); slower regeneration of the industrial fabric (greater impediments to market entry and exit, particularly for small and medium-sized firms); bottlenecks in the education and training system; inadequate capital markets in some countries; price distortions inhibiting the effective allocation of resources and technological diffusion; and that adjustment in mature industries is slower than that of its overseas competitors.

However, this general diagnosis covers a wide range of situations. In particular, national paths of technological adjustment are far from identical in all the countries concerned.

For example, as regards the medium-sized/major economies, the mode of adjustment in German industry

Table 6.5.   **Apparent comparative advantage of manufacturing industry**

OECD average = 100

	High R&D intensity			Medium R&D intensity			Low R&D intensity		
	1970	1980	1985	1970	1980	1985	1970	1980	1985
United States	146	142	149	108	107	96	67	66	67
Japan	114	128	133	77	100	105	120	86	68
EEC[1]	88	85	75	108	103	100	98	104	116
Sweden	68	71	63	83	85	87	135	135	144
Australia	16	24	17	66	54	83	175	198	187
Canada	51	39	40	123	108	126	97	122	108

1. Excluding intra-ECC trade.
Source: OECD.

contrasts sharply with that of its French, British or Italian competitors.

1. Germany

While *Germany* has lost ground in its established world market sectors, especially to Japan and the NICs, and has not been able to gain ground in the leading-edge sectors dominated by the United States, it has markedly increased its lead in intra-European trade. This has led to an exceptionally favourable trend in its trade balance (see Table 6.6)[10].

Table 6.6. **Trend of trade balance**
As percentage of GDP; annual averages

	1971-1973	1974-1979	1980-1983
Germany	1.9	3.9	4.4
France	− 0.7	− 0.1	− 1.8
Italy	− 4.7	− 1.3	− 2.1
United Kingdom	− 3.6	− 1.5	− 0.6
EEC	− 1.6	0.2	0.5

Source: EEC.

Table 6.7. **Specialisation by niche of manufacturing industry**[1]

	High R&D intensity		Medium R&D intensity		Low R&D intensity	
	1970	1983	1970	1983	1970	1983
United States	105	103	101	97	97	95
Japan	109	127	105	118	105	102
Germany	117	113	127	146	98	95
France	99	101	102	105	101	98
Italy	101	100	107	118	102	110
United Kingdom	107	96	113	98	96	93

1. Specialisation by niche measures the degree of self-sufficiency, i.e. the ratio of production to domestic demand.
Source: OECD.

The main explanation is that Germany has managed to successfully defend its position in those industries where historically it has had a comparative advantage[11]. Most of these industries are of medium R&D intensity (motor vehicles, engineering and chemicals), as is clearly shown by the trend of specialisation by niche, i.e. the ratio of production to domestic demand (see Table 6.7).

If Germany has been successful, it is because its positions in these sectors have solid foundations in its socio-economic structure and are the outcome of a learning process and reputation built up over a very long period. For example, Germany's strength in the chemicals sector is outstanding, since it is the only traditional

and complex manufacturing sector in which Japan has not outperformed its rivals in the past ten years. It is also because Germany has managed to offset the relative disadvantage of being specialised in medium-trend growth sectors by moving early into upmarket segments[12].

However, this was only achieved by pursuing a type of technological adjustment that placed the emphasis on dissemination, thereby allowing the technology in pace-setting sectors to be continually updated. As in the case of Japan, Germany's scientific and technical potential for several decades has been oriented primarily to commercial applications, one of the main reasons for this being the relatively small scale of its defence research. However, this is far from the entire explanation. Another important factor is that the infrastructure of technological generation and dissemination (the education and training system, and the system of standards and applied research) was geared primarily to the specific economic requirements of those sectors in which Germany was traditionally strong[13]. It is thus not surprising that it has tended to promote a type of adjustment that has strengthened the traditional specialisation of its industry. However, there are potential drawbacks to this adjustment pattern.

First, Germany's "poles of competitiveness"[14] – however strong they may be – are not invulnerable in the medium and long term. The experience of the difficult period it went through in the early 1980s, even though the situation has improved since then, should be carefully borne in mind. The threat is threefold. In emerging market segments, e.g. biotechnology and new materials[15], German industry does not have as strong a position as in the related traditional sectors that are potentially threatened. Established market segments with a high scientific and technical content and a high innovation rate are under continuous competitive pressure from countries such as Japan; in some sectors, Japanese industry even seems to be eroding, and even usurping, the reputation that for a long time has cushioned German industry fairly well against outside competition. Finally, in the more "mature" market segments, like bulk chemicals and conventional engineering, competition from the less developed countries – the NICs, East European nations and oil-producing countries – poses a real threat to Germany's position.

Second, a technological diffusion strategy and research policy that concentrates too strongly on the requirements of a few major sectors and large firms may, in the long term, handicap other sectors which also need to update their technological capability[16]. This concern was undoubtedly a factor behind the recent change of direction in Germany's research policy. However, other policy areas are also involved, especially education and training, where it is now necessary to reduce the vast range of specialised apprenticeships offered in an attempt to teach more general skills with greater flexibility for final employment opportunities and better geared to changing technology.

2. The other medium-sized countries

Countries such as *France*, the *United Kingdom* and *Italy* are facing a difficult challenge. Their industrial structures will have to change if they are to find an international role compatible with that of the world's three major industrial powers. But this change will have to take place within the constraints of foreign trading and without any slip down the technical-industrial "learning curve", which would mean an erosion of the industrial fabric and a subsequent decline in economic and social prosperity. The oscillation in France's industrial adjustment strategy in the past decade (between *"redéploiement"* or "market niche" policy with the emphasis on deepening international specialisation, and "modernisation" or *"filière"* policy with the emphasis on strengthening national capability in broad groups of interrelated activities) illustrates the nature of the dilemma at least as much as the differences in economic philosophy of successive governments. This (as the United Kingdom's experience shows) does not mean that policy thrust is not important. The check in the slide towards de-industrialisation there at the beginning of the 1980s is probably partly attributable to the change in policy orientation that took place at that time.

It is clear that these countries do not have the structure of specialisation that adjustment on the German pattern requires (see Table 6.8).

Table 6.8. **Number of major branches of industry[1] with very high export/import ratios[2] and their share of exports (1980)**

	Germany	Japan	United Kingdom	Italy	France
Number of major branches (16)	7	6	5	2	2
Exports of major branches as percentage of total exports	61.6	68.2	21.3	20.4	16.7

1. On the basis of a breakdown of industry into 75 branches, each comprising a set of interdependent industries.
2. Export/import ratio over 120 per cent.
Source: INSEE.

As the "strong sectors" in the United Kingdom, France and Italy are scattered through the industrial fabric, the linkage effects between interdependent industries are much weaker than those which operate within the "poles of competitiveness" in Germany. This was not a major impediment to industrial development when world demand was expanding strongly in the 1960s – to the point even where supply sometimes had difficulty keeping pace with it[17]. However, the situation has changed since competition has increased in world markets which are growing more slowly and unevenly[18]. These markets are often characterised by overcapacity, and success depends more than ever on the effective dissemination of innovation and technological know-how via a network of inter-industrial linkages. However, the disappointing results of the policy implemented within "groups of industries" *(politique de "filières")* in France in the early 1980s show that a structural adjustment policy must accept that there is no short-term solution to this source of relative disadvantage.

Besides being scattered, the "strong sectors" in these countries are more fragile than those of the leading industrial powers. This is shown, for example, by the steady weakening of many of such sectors in a country like France[19] and, at a broader level, by the trends in trade balances[20] (see Graph 6.4) or the indicator of adjustment to world demand[21]. When only trade with the most advanced economies is considered, most of these sectors appear less "strong".

Established international trade theory is incapable of explaining the geographical pattern of such international specialisation in industrial activity. Neither its remote origins, which are as much geopolitical as economic, nor its specific dynamics (which are a matter for concern in the present context of rapid technical change) are explained satisfactorily by this theory. The position of the "medium-sized" countries in world trade remains ill-defined, and theories differ on the interpretation of the pattern of their exports[22].

Nonetheless, it is an established fact that, for two reasons, this pattern of exports is a source of vulnerability. First, the export markets of these countries are often less dynamic than, for example, those of German industry, and are at times extremely volatile. Second, as these markets are usually less sophisticated and competitive[23], the technical and commercial learning opportunities for exporting firms are smaller. However, a significant shift in this export pattern can only be achieved in the long term, and it would be pointless to make it a short-term objective of adjustment policy. Goal-oriented policies have shown their limitations in this respect – for example, the policy of government backing for exporters implemented for a time in France clearly did not live up to expectations.

For numerous and still more obvious reasons, Japanese-style adjustment is also not possible in the immediate future for countries like France, the United Kingdom and Italy which, like many others, simply

Table 6.9. **Export/import ratio for capital goods**

	Japan	Germany	United Kingdom	Italy	France
1973	441.4	340.7	154.5	133.2	111.3
1976	669.5	317.9	173.1	168.6	143.0
1980	582.6	237.7	139.2	140.6	128.6
1982	677.3[1]	251.0	121.4	165.6	122.5

1. 1981.
Source: INSEE.

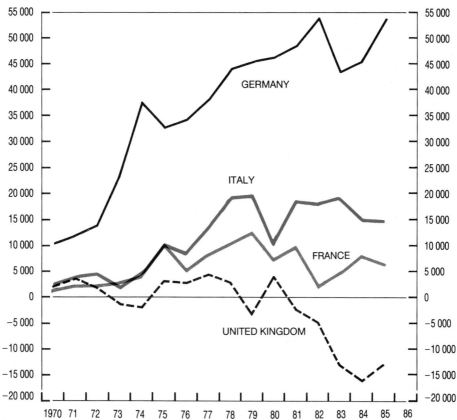

Graph 6.4. **Manufacturing trade balance**
(million dollars)

Source: OECD

do not have the special strengths that have enabled Japan to master advanced manufacturing techniques better than its competitors and to acquire the peculiar type of comparative advantage that it has today. Their relative weakness in the capital goods sectors is indicative in this respect (see Table 6.9), but their delay in adjusting human capital to the changing requirements of technology is probably an even more important factor.

Finally, a go-it-alone United States-style "dash" by these countries into leading-edge technology would probably soon come up against insurmountable barriers, given the importance of R&D economies of scale in the sectors concerned.

For a long time, however, science and technology policies, and to some extent industrial policy in both France and the United Kingdom, tended towards this end, although, in sharp contrast, other policies tended to slow down the process of withdrawal from ailing traditional industries.

In France and the United Kingdom, the pattern of R&D spending has been markedly influenced by mili-

tary requirements. These countries' science and technology mirror, too, their industrial structures and the traditions that shaped their industrial policy. For decades, government measures to promote technology reflected above all a predilection for large-scale programmes, for the concentration of resources needed for design and application (via the "national champions") and for the centralisation of monitoring and assessment procedures. This is still true today, though perhaps to a lesser degree, since a real effort to redress the balance has been made over the past few years (notably in the United Kingdom). The figures in Table 6.10 speak for themselves and show that government funding of R&D is highly concentrated in a few advanced sectors, especially aerospace, nuclear engineering and electronics.

In France, the perception of national independence as extending to economic matters, and the special features of the training system that produces its top-level technocrats, largely explain the French preference for a technological development strategy centred on large-scale programmes conceived, directed and implemented

217

Table 6.10. **Government R&D funding of manufacturing industry**

	United States	United Kingdom	France	Germany	Japan
Government funding as percentage of total R&D expenditure (1983)	31.6	31.8[2]	23.6	13.6	1.5
Government funding as percentage of total R&D expenditure in high R&D-intensive sectors[1] (1983)	42.7	44.0[2]	36.2	19.0[2]	0.9
Share of high R&D-intensive sectors[1] in total government funding (1983)	94.8	96.3[2]	91.3	67.0[2]	25.7
Defence R&D expenditure as percentage of total government funding (1983)	64.3	49.6	32.7	9.6	2.4
Share of government-funded R&D performed in the public sector (1983)	26.0	39.0	47.0	32.0	..

1. Aerospace, computers, electronics (including telecommunications), pharmaceuticals, scientific instruments and electrical engineering.
2. 1981.
Source: OECD.

either by teams of top civil servants appointed specifically for that purpose or by large, often public, enterprises working hand-in-glove with government, partly because they depend on government funds and partly because of the close bonds uniting those who hold the reins of technology and government[24].

The results obtained have sometimes been disappointing. Alongside France's undeniable successes, which include the nuclear and telecommunications industries, there have been major set-backs, especially where government has only limited control over demand (as in the case of computers). Moreover, these strategies have had an adverse impact on technological adjustment in other sectors of industry. Policy makers have given insufficient attention to the diffusion of technology, since the modernisation of industry has tended to be equated with the acquisition of technological independence. The channelling of financial and human resources into very large-scale programmes has, in fact, inhibited the spread of technology.

Given the limitations of the present strategy of technological adjustment in countries such as France or the United Kingdom, it is worth considering the main prerequisites for a gradual transition towards a more promising path of adjustment.

The first shortcoming is that these countries only have a strong foreign trade position in scattered areas, while their productive system is highly concentrated (although production units are often too small or badly located). For various reasons, some of which are considered in Part I of the Annex on the financial environment, their industrial organisation is not optimal in terms of economic efficiency, and especially with regard to the requirements of contemporary technology. The competitive incentive is blunted and many giant firms do not have clearly defined production and technological focus.

This is because they have often been formed by a series of mergers and takeovers, the aims of which are not always to promote efficiency.

In the second place, if policies are to be changed to speed technology diffusion, the first step must be to identify a suitable way of changing policies involving major projects. Closer international and European co-operation seems to be a must in this respect (see Chapter 2). The precedent set by the aerospace industry is encouraging, especially since it shows the necessity and benefits of reconciling the two levels of co-operation. But other requirements must also be met. The most important concern the mobility, flexibility and inter-sectoral allocation of human resources[25]. In particular, the tendency to build up advanced knowledge within agencies responsible for the major technological programmes classified as being in the "national interest" should be reversed. But it is also necessary to adapt the education and training system to the needs arising from technological change[26], in order to catch up in this field with the more advanced countries.

3. The smaller economies

It is pointless to generalise about the smaller economies because of the variety of economic situations and development levels. However, very broadly speaking, the countries can be placed in two categories – developed countries with a sound national technological base, and countries in the process of industrialisation with a limited national technological base.

The problem of structural adaptation may initially seem less complex for countries in the first category than for the "medium-sized" countries, since their limited domestic economies have forced them to learn very early how to adapt to external constraints – particularly those

Graph 6.5. **Total R&D expenditure by manufacturing industry**
1975 dollars (PPP)

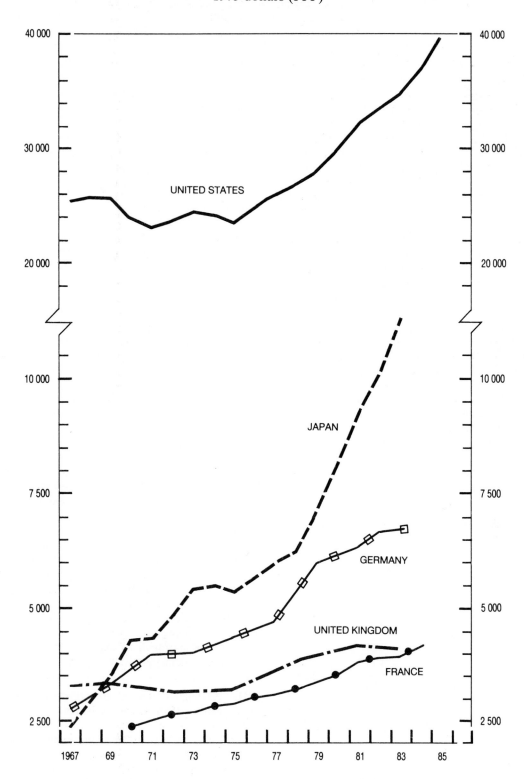

Source: OECD.

constraints arising from the changing specialisation of the major industrialised nations.

In the case of countries like *Sweden* or *Switzerland*, it is possible to speak of a German-style adjustment strategy adapted to the needs of a small economy and mainly implemented by industry itself. The emphasis is thus placed on the dissemination of modern technologies rather than on their development, which tend to permit an ongoing technical modernisation process in the traditionally strong industries geared to the high value-added slots in the world economy[27]. The reasons for the temporary difficulties affecting adaptation in the early 1980s, and the factors that have enabled this strategy to succeed, as well as the limiting factors, are much the same as those for Germany. However, the special significance of Sweden's industrial and macroeconomic policy changes in the late 1970s must be mentioned (see Part II).

But the picture is not so rosy in other countries with the same degree of development, such as the *Benelux countries* (which are more exposed to foreign competition than any others) or *Austria*. They are handicapped by their excessive specialisation in sectors that are not technology-intensive, are quite mature, e.g. metallurgy, basic chemicals, secondary energy sector, or have a growth potential well below average, e.g. food industries. The adjustment of these industries to changes in world demand and new production techniques depends greatly, especially in the Netherlands, on the ability of a few major firms holding the bulk of the nation's industrial, technological and commercial assets to make the necessary strategic responses.

The problem is obviously quite different for *the less developed countries in the OECD area*. The main obstacles holding back their industrialisation during the past fifteen years have been: the slowing of world growth; the emergence of the NICs competing in home and external markets; the tremendous increase in energy costs; and technology advances which have devalued the advantages of a large low-cost unskilled labour force.

Industry in these countries is geared internationally according to the principles of "graded comparative advantages". They tend to predominantly export low or medium skilled labour-intensive products to the most developed regions (especially textiles), and to export capital-intensive and/or skilled labour-intensive products to the markets of the less advanced countries, or to markets of secondary priority or that are less accessible to the exporting firms of the dominant countries. (For example, Spain and Greece are major exporters of cement, particularly to Africa and the Middle East.) In this context, industrialisation consists of gradual cross-substitution in the export structure between this type of market and product. On the import side, in addition to raw materials and energy, the main item is technology. It can be in the form of imported goods embodying technology or by the actual transfer of knowledge and skilled personnel. [For example, in Spain, the technological payments for these transfers are 1.5 times the total national R&D expenditure (see Table 6.11).]

Each stage in industrialisation is marked by both the financial capacity needed to acquire this foreign technology and also by the country's ability to assimilate it, adapt it and utilise it so that comparative advantages may materialise. To advance from one stage to another – or just to prevent a slipback in the world hierarchy of comparative advantages under pressure from both the NICs and the new global marketing strategies by companies of dominant countries[28] – the attempt at "domesticating" foreign know-how must be supplemented by the development of national technical and scientific infrastructure. This should make it feasible to successfully import increasingly sophisticated technologies and achieve maximum benefits from the associated learning effects.

Direct investments have a role to play here, although their importance should not be overestimated as has been done in the past in some countries. Their experiences show that although investments involving the manufacture of high technology products can be attracted, often the corresponding R&D activities are not. This modern direct investment sector has also not stimulated as much as expected the more traditional parts of national industry.

D. National structural adjustment and internationalisation of industrial activities

Most of the paths to national industrial adjustment, the diversity of which has just been described, were opened up many years ago. The present shape of these trajectories is therefore still largely due to structural inertia. But the direction of these trajectories may change if the new forms of internationalisation of industrial activities – particularly the international gen-

Table 6.11. **Technological and development level for smaller countries**

	Per capita GDP in dollars (1985)	Export/import ratio of technological payments (1983)	Technological payments as percentage of business enterprise R&D expenditure (1981)
Switzerland	14 002	..	..
Sweden	11 369	2.19	3.8
Denmark	10 690	1.50	22.8
Finland	10 493	0.64	26.4
Netherlands	8 534	0.60	41.9
Spain	4 192	0.21	158.2
Greece	3 380	..	..
Portugal	1 905	0.10	154.1
Turkey	1 018	..	..
For comparison:			
United States	15 346	32.74	1.3
Japan	10 457	0.86	7.2
Germany	10 025	0.50	10.2

Source: OECD.

eration and dissemination of innovations, the development of world-wide computerised communication networks, and the rapid development of co-operation between firms in the R&D, manufacturing and marketing fields – act to modify the underlying principles of international trade.

The ambivalent theories used in the past to account for international trade, e.g. the mobility of products versus immobility of the factors of production; exports of products versus exports of capital; market transactions versus internal trading within a multinational enterprise, have already been undermined and now have to be replaced by explanations that are more complex and refined.

First, the trend towards the increasing service content of products, the changes in production organisation at a world level and the diversification of market penetration processes mean that the movements of products, capital, services and knowledge are now almost inextricably merged. World trade flows have become increasingly hybrid and increasingly difficult to analyse with the statistical standards in use. For example, is the distinction between balance of trade in services and balance of trade in goods still relevant when the value of the services included in the goods traded or resulting from their use is rising extremely rapidly in some sectors, e.g. in the case of computers?

Second, with the changes in the international mobility of certain factors of production, major determinants of the geographical location of industrial activities are being modified. Some of the current trade flows can now be explained by the contrast between the increasing ease of transfers of technology and knowledge, and the persistent difficulties of transferring a number of factors on which the ability to exploit this technology and knowledge commercially depends. But the degree of this non-transferability is not well known, nor how far it will persist into the future. For this reason, developments like the Japanese/United States joint ventures in the car industry should be very carefully studied to assess more precisely how effective is this international transfer of manufacturing know-how and to see more clearly the type of limits such a transfer is likely to encounter[29].

Third, the changes in competition for access to world factor and product markets is increasingly marked by new objectives set by internationally active firms and corporations. They tend to search for opportunities for complementary functions: the ability to control the pace at which technical advances are introduced so as to avoid over-rapid depreciation of physical and human capital; and the minimisation of commercial and financial risks in terms of the R&D and investment input needed to produce and sell goods rapidly at world level on fast changing markets. This explains the emergence of new, global inter-company networks involving a great many actors and many types of transaction, ranging from the pure market relationship to full internalisation (see Graph 6.6).

Graph 6.6. **Types of foreign participation and relative level of transaction costs and monitoring costs**

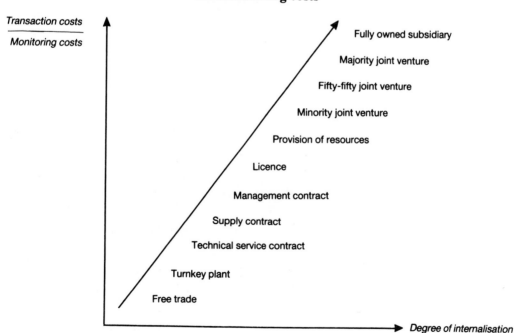

Source: Mason, R. Hal in Mucchielli, J.L., "Les firmes multinationales. Mutations et nouvelles perspectives", *Economica*, 1985.

221

The nature of trade flows is thereby modified, since the search for complementarity through contractual relations in extremely varied sectors – ranging from textiles, e.g. outward processing traffic[30], to electronics, e.g. the scheme for original equipment manufacture[31] – results in an increase in structural interdependence between the various national industries. This imposes a further limit on the capacity of governments to influence trade flows without endangering the strategic interests of firms and without ultimately weakening national industrial drive. For example, it has been estimated that 40 per cent of Japanese exports to the United States already came under long-term agreements between the two countries' firms[32]. It is of great importance to recognise that certain imbalances in international economic transactions and subsequent macroeconomic problems are partly due to the process of international integration at the microeconomic level between firms. Therefore, the elimination of these imbalances ultimately will depend on the direction in which this integration process develops. This, in turn, will depend on how quickly the obstacles preventing international dissemination of the best productive practices are removed.

The relationships between direct investment flows and flows of goods and services are also modified, although this process is not yet clearly understood, despite efforts to fit them into pre-established frameworks. In this respect it is sufficient to notice how far the recent wave of Japanese direct investment, especially in the last few years (see Graph 6.7), differs from earlier waves originating in the United States in the 1960s and more recently in the EEC countries. First, at this relatively early stage in its cycle, and though encouraged recently by the lifting of trade barriers and the appreciation of the yen, Japanese direct investment replaces exports to a lesser degree than has usually happened in the case of the other major economic powers. Second, the kind of contribution it makes to re-establishing the international balance of industrial forces reflects the specificity of the comparative advantage enjoyed by Japanese firms. Whereas United States direct investment in the 1960s considerably helped the international dissemination of a very wide range of technological and organisational know-how, the transfers involved in Japanese investment at the present stage seem to be more limited, since they mainly concern assembly operations[33]. However, the content of these transfers may be expected to become richer as direct investment flows swell, the stock of such investment matures and the recipient countries' ability to assimilate new production techniques improves.

All in all, then, the present phase in the internationalisation of industrial activities has brought a further change in the principles of trade, which now combine complementarity of goods exchanged (as traditionally in international trade) with the intra-product competition typical of more recent times. But this apparent return to

Graph 6.7. **Japan's direct investments**
(billion dollars, as of 31 March)

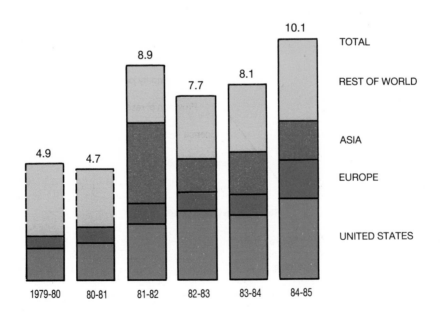

Source: Japanese Ministry of Finance.

222

the past is only an illusion, since complementarity now concerns more companies' skills (in the field of R&D, production, marketing) than products[34].

Are we to suppose that the importance of the national dimension in the industrial adjustment process is thus greatly reduced? In other words, is the question of the paths to national adjustment becoming irrelevant?

The impact of the new competitive contests is still being measured at the national level and assessed on the basis of the requirement for macroeconomic balance. But it is often believed that since firms can now draw on an international pool of know-how in response to their own weaknesses, their success and contribution to national economic progress depends more on their astuteness in positioning themselves in world networks than in their own national environment. For two main reasons, a much more balanced view should be taken.

First, competition precedes co-operation in the growth of world networks. To obtain a good position within these networks, it is necessary to first have certain strategic assets. These are most often established on the firm's own home front, e.g. Japanese manufacturing know-how, or the capacity of the United States for advanced design work.

Second, from the viewpoint of national spin-off, there is a hierarchy in these assets exchanged in between-company agreements. For example, the provision of a marketing network does not lead to the same benefits for the industry's own country as the provision of manufacturing or research capabilities[35]. This hierarchy seems to be closely linked to the hierarchy of national industrial strengths which explains the existence of varied national adjustment paths.

If there is any misunderstanding, it is probably due to the confusion between two distinct aspects of the problem. The question of the changing role of government must not be confused with the more general issue of the influence which specific national factors affecting competitiveness have on the structural adjustment of world industry.

With regard to the first point, it is clear that a move towards international production reduces a government's possibilities for directly influencing the trend in structural adjustment[36].

With regard to the second, it is no less clear that industry's national or regional environments are still responsible for the creation of a firm's main strengths and weaknesses which are then revealed in competition at world level.

But overriding this apparent contradiction is a more basic general policy implication. The decline in the potential effectiveness of direct intervention policies on the adjustment process highlights the vital necessity of looking first to the quality of the competitive environment created for industry – whether deliberately or not – by all the general government policies in other areas.

II. GOVERNMENT POLICIES AND INDUSTRIAL ADJUSTMENT

Monetary, energy and technological upheavals have meant stormy times for all economic players but especially for governments. Pulled in every direction by interest groups, governments have found it difficult to sort out their priorities and evaluate their actions in the industrial field.

The changing role of governments has to be seen in a wider framework: that of the search for a new national and international consistency between modes of production, competition, consumption, distribution and government intervention[37]. The far-reaching economic and social transformations that are required – especially in the industrial sphere – are bound to be relatively slow, because of the inertia of existing structures and the inevitable resistance to change in society. Economies and industries world-wide have entered a period of uncertainty rife with the danger of distortions which, when they occur, tend to linger on. Looking at government intervention in industry (not the least frequent potential source of distortion), it can be seen that the past fifteen years have been a gruelling, and not always conclusive, test of governments' abilities to:

- Tackle a succession of new problems while maintaining and acting within their existing industrial policies and frameworks, using instruments that have proved successful in the past;
- Adapt their industrial strategies, not only to changing socio-economic priorities, but also to meet the changing effectiveness of the various types of intervention needed to accommodate the internationalisation of industrial activities and technological change.

This Part looks first at the main characteristics of OECD Member countries' government intervention systems and at the new industrial problems that have confronted governments over the past fifteen years. After giving an account of the major shifts in government action, this chapter will assess the results of these actions and, in conclusion, identify the broad directions which seem to hold most promise for the future.

A. Industrial policies: different national approaches in tackling common problems

Part I shows quite clearly that the specificity of each country's situation – in terms of its national assets, the size of its domestic economy, its specialised industrial structures and the economic power wielded by governments – makes it impossible to assess governmental roles in the industrial adjustment process in a simplistic manner. It cannot be judged according to supposedly universal standards which are far removed from the socio-economic realities of any country.

1. Defining industrial policies: a difficult and by no means clear-cut task

Such is the variety of measures that can interfere with market forces, so relative (in our mixed economies) the value placed on the market-place, and so varied the extent and visibility of the impact of such measures, that any comparative study of the national and international effects of government policies on the development of the industrial system must sooner or later come up against problems of definition, if not of semantics.

If we take industrial policy in the narrowest sense of the term, the only measures to be considered would be those expressly designed to promote – by reinforcing or countering market forces – an industrial adjustment process held to be desirable by government in the name of political and socio-economic imperatives. This, however, would place too much emphasis on only a few Member countries and disregard all the *ad hoc* measures taken by governments outside the framework of any overall plan, especially in times of radical change. Alternatively, the mode of intervention may be regarded as the most important criteria. For instance, a distinction is frequently made between domestic measures (especially those most easily quantified) and trade measures, since the former are supposedly the only ones relevant to industrial policy. However, given the importance that some governments have recently assigned to trade policy as a means of intervention, shortsightedness and partiality of another kind are inevitable. In other approaches, the principal criterion is the intentional selectivity of the measures taken, but this ignores more general programmes, e.g. tax incentives. Or again, the criterion may be the *de facto* selectivity of action of any kind, although this would mean taking into account an extensive range of measures including some whose purpose is clearly macroeconomic.

When it comes to international comparisons, in practice the choice made usually, and rather unsuccessfully, hides behind arguments of a technical nature either some more equivocal intentions or else snap judgements as to effectiveness at home and the harmlessness abroad of the various types of intervention. This obviously does not make open and fruitful discussion of the real problems caused by government intervention in industry any easier.

In the absence of any universally accepted definition of the term "industrial policy", it is best to take a pragmatic approach, imposing no prior limits to the field of investigation and acknowledging that it is bound to vary according to each country's institutional and policy setting.

2. Government intervention on the domestic front: the diversity of permanent features

Government-industry relations have to be seen in the broader and more permanent context of the political and social system that, in each country, defines national interests and reconciles various individual interests. It is not the aim of this report to examine in detail the origins, characteristics and potential for marginal change in this system. However, a brief reference to political science is necessary in order to define the limits of such an economic analysis of the effects of government policies on industrial development. This avoids the debate becoming bogged down in misleading considerations which confuse the effectiveness of the various modes of intervention with the legitimacy of the political and social values embodied in each government's policy instruments and underlying philosophies.

Despite many common features, the Western democracies do not all agree on the exact role of government[38] as a regulator and arbitrator of economic processes, as a supplier of public goods, as leader or direct participant in economic life and in adjusting the distributional effects – across regions, sectors or occupational groups – of structural change dictated by market forces. Yet each of these functions affects industrial policy. As a result, government intervention varies widely from one country to another as to scale, accumulated expertise, organisation of economic authorities, their permanent terms of reference (explicit or implicit), the extent of their statutory and informal powers that influence the competitive sector, and the nature of their preferred policy instruments. Although these institutional and psycho-sociological structures are gradually changing, notably as a result of economic pressures, they still generally constitute "invariants" which restrict the range of policy options which can be discussed on pure economic criteria alone. They confer "comparative advantages" on government policy, advantages which may be used to enhance or mitigate the effects of more orthodox comparative advantages that exist due to certain economic attributes[39].

There are two extremes in Western society of varying political and institutional intervention. One tends to favour market solutions, while the other extreme favours more mixed solutions involving government intervention and/or the concerted actions of private agents. Most Member countries are in a situation midway between these two extremes, epitomised by the United States in the former case and Japan in the latter.

In the United States, two interdependent factors combine to ensure the predominance of market solutions. First, the size of the domestic market and the exceptional flexibility and dynamism of structures and economic factors (labour mobility, wage flexibility, highly developed capital market, entrepreneurial tradition, etc.) guarantee, more than elsewhere, the effectiveness and foolproofness of market mechanisms. Second, the country's political and administrative system makes it hard to imagine – or at any rate to implement – a policy of direct, selective and co-ordinated government intervention in industry. There are four main reasons for this. First, so far as the economy is concerned, the only obligation devolving upon central government under the "social contract" is to ensure that the macroeconomic climate remains healthy and that the microeconomic "ground rules" are met. Second, because the decision-making process is fragmented, the potential for blocking proposed measures which would severely penalise organised groups is considerable. Hence the preference for horizontal measures affecting a wide cross-section of interests, e.g. tax concessions, or for selective measures concentrating benefits but spreading costs, e.g. trade measures. Third, American history has not allowed the development of a federal bureaucracy with the same independence, expertise and prestige enjoyed by national civil services in countries with a more interventionist tradition. Fourth, the federal government has no instruments of a general nature (like, for example, direct or indirect control over the banking system, as in France or in Japan) which enable it to force the private sector to implement detailed structural adjustment programmes or to follow guidelines laid down by the authorities. For all these reasons, United States government policy on industry has always been indirect, non-targeted or decentralised, e.g. a spin-off from major civil or military R & D programmes, the role of the individual states, with no central co-ordination and no industrial strategy – not even an informal one – and with great importance attached to competition policy. In such a context, trade policy is especially important and in recent years has often been made to encompass assignments which in other countries would have been covered by industrial policy proper.

In Japan, the tradition is diametrically opposed to that of the United States, not so much because of the scale of government intervention (many European countries are just as "interventionist" as Japan) but due to the role of central government in formulating a clearly defined, coherent and forward-looking national industrial strategy. The formulation of such a strategy in co-operation with all the industrial partners is a constant and cornerstone of a Japanese policy originally aimed at catching up economically with other countries[40]. However, it does not imply (as is often believed) a general lack of confidence in the capacity of market forces to promote structural change to the long-term advantage of the nation. While the central government does act as a catalyst in reaching consensus on desirable main lines for development, it has never – or at least not since the end of the reconstruction period – sought to exercise detailed planning powers. Nor has it tried or been obliged to take on the role of entrepreneur. This is borne out by the very small scale of government participation in the competitive sector.

In the general framework set up to facilitate the desired changes – a framework that has proved itself to have remarkable adaptability – the Japanese Government has always ensured that competition is encouraged and that the overall industrial environment (education, macroeconomic climate, etc.) remains of high quality. The success of Japanese policy is largely due to its ability to galvanise and direct, without ever inhibiting, the quite extraordinary capacity of the private sector, both producers and consumers, to respond to opportunities.

However, the nature of the more selective direct incentives used – though by international standards these have never amounted to much[41] – reveals another essential dimension of the philosophy underlying Japanese policy. While lack of competition may make government incentives less effective, too much competition and too shortsighted an approach to the problems involved in adjusting industry to sudden shocks may lead to high social costs in the longer term. This absence of dogmatism and consequent ability to spot at once any market failures is also essential to the Japanese policy of accelerated industrial change, which anticipates and moves with market currents rather than trying to swim against the tide.

The basic factors explaining the distinctive features of Japanese industrial policy seem to be the stability and unity of decision-making, the pyramidal structure on which national economic and industrial consensus is built, and a powerful, expert, well-informed and influential civil service which plays a central role in the birth of this consensus and ensures that it is subsequently translated into practice. The credit of the civil service is high and it is well able to persuade or stimulate. The powers of the economic and industrial authorities, particularly the Ministry of Finance and MITI, have no equal elsewhere in the OECD area, since their legitimacy derives from long historical tradition[42]. This tradition became stronger in the wake of World War II, not only because of the urgent need to rebuild the country but also because the new primarily economic bureaucracy tended to fill the vacuum left by the disappearance of the military and by a number of institutional reforms. It took over, for instance, some of the powers of co-ordination previously held by the "Zaibatsu"[43].

The Japanese Government, playing as it does such a major role in the economy and pursuing a policy whose principles reflect the desire to shake loose from the antagonism between liberalism and *dirigisme*, is the instrument of an enduring effort to reconcile opposites. The interaction of opposites also seems to have been one of the prime factors in promoting industrial development – by playing off competition against co-operation, rigidity and stability of many economic and social practices against exceptional ability to adapt to change, and strong social cohesion and economic unity against the dualistic nature of the productive structures.

No other OECD Member country has economic and political characteristics like those of the United States which restrain its government from intervening through domestic microeconomic measures in influencing structural change in industry. Nor does the government of any other country possess the characteristics that would allow it to play the same unique role as the government of Japan in the collective steering of an industrial growth that is rooted in the exceptional dynamism of the private sector.

In Europe, five main factors seem to be broadly involved in the long term:

- Over the years, and particularly during periods of strong growth, European governments have accumulated commitments to the various actors who have gained or lost through structural change. They have had to face the fact that Europeans are less willing than Americans to take economic risks; and they have tended to assume the role of protector that in Japan largely devolves to employers in the framework of a long-term contractual relationship between private parties, e.g. the lifelong employment system[44];
- Governments have inherited economic and industrial prerogatives from the past, e.g. Colbertism in France – such as those affecting supplies and production because they were considered strategic to national defence and political considerations. These prerogatives have been recast and updated in the postwar reconstruction period, used to catch up with the United States in the rapid growth phase and, more recently, have served in the context of restructuring policies;
- In addition to having these prerogatives and a historical inclination to use them to meet the "extended commitments" provided for under the "social contract", the typical European government (as compared to the United States) is more liable in times of sweeping change to be confronted with an even stronger surge of demands for assistance or protection. This occurs because industrial structures are less flexible and economic agents less adaptable (for example, with regards to labour mobility, the rate at which firms are created or disappear, wage flexibility, etc.). High barriers to entry and exit in many sectors – partly as an unintentional result of earlier policies, such as those encouraging the concentration or the recruitment of foreign labour – hamper spontaneous and rapid adjustment to market changes. Failing a genuine lowering of these barriers, governments are supposed to bear the costs of delayed adjustment;
- In many countries, political instability has given greater autonomy to the civil service, which over time has acquired its own views on industrial development needs and created an "old-boy network" with the most powerful and organised industrial groups;
- In smaller countries governments sought, especially in the 1960s, to promote concentration to achieve economies of scale and to contain the costs of the resulting monopolies through regulation or direct involvement in the management of the companies or industries concerned;
- Lastly, the growth of the EEC has restricted Member countries' discretionary powers over trade policy and thus modified the weight of the different instruments in the range of purely domestic policy measures, even though the EEC, for its part, has sought to keep national industrial policies in line, in particular by trying to ensure that they did not conflict with the objectives of the Community's competition policy, and has had some success in this regard (witness the progress made on several fronts – steel, synthetic fibres and, more recently, shipbuilding).

For all these reasons the industrial policies of most European countries, with the notable exception of Switzerland, have a number of common denominators. These include:

- The substantial weight of the state as entrepreneur or shareholder in the competitive sector;
- The scale of direct financial aid to industry;
- The undeniable and, until very recently, increasing propensity of government to slow the pace of developments liable to add to its already heavy commitments involved in redistributing the costs and benefits of industrial change. Contrarily, most European governments had a predilection for interventionist policies, replacing market mechanisms, so as to force resources to be redeployed to "mission-oriented activities" considered to be either insufficiently exploited or potentially unexploitable by the private sector.

Of course, countries differ greatly. In illustration we may take two examples: France, whose tradition of government intervention is frequently compared to that of Japan; and Germany, whose more liberal economic policy options are sometimes likened to those of the United States.

France may seem to be close to Japan because it has long felt the need to establish a government strategy for industry in the framework of its national Plan. It also has a powerful civil service with a wealth of experience and human capital and a wide range of instruments enabling it to shape industrial development. However, here the analogy must end, because the French public sector plays an industrial role in a different socio-economic context (affected, for example, by the chronic weakness of the French entrepreneurial base), a role that is in many ways totally unlike that of its Japanese counterpart. In particular:

- In France, despite certain recent reforms, policy planning and implementation are still highly centralised, whereas in Japan the process of implementing public decisions is largely decentralised;
- But centralisation does not mean unity of government powers in the industrial field. There is much less unity in France than the existence of such a strategic co-ordinating body might lead one to suppose. In recent times, problems related to the co-ordination and harmonization of the various elements of macroeconomic and industrial policy have been chronic and usually ill-resolved. Policy conception and implementation is divided among

a number of different government-level organisations whose powers partly overlap, whether they be ministries, relatively autonomous administrative units such as the DGT (Direction générale des Télécommunications) or quasi-government bodies (public institutions or enterprises);

— The rivalry between these different organisations, each strong in technical know-how and political influence, plays at least as great a role in determining the lines of industrial policy as do the bodies theoretically responsible for policy making and co-ordination. This stems partly from the competition which exists between the institutional groups which control policies (for example, the "grands Corps d'Etat"), and which, for a wide range of industrial activities under direct government control, act as a sort of poor substitute for the competition between private interests that derives from and is regulated by market forces;

— More generally speaking, the French Government has largely taken over from private initiative, whereas Japan prefers administrative guidance of market forces.

The German tradition of industrial policy cannot be so neatly catalogued. It combines an interventionist bent, that is due to motivations similar to those of most other European countries but which is satisfied in a manner peculiar to Germany, with a liberal slant whose existence and persistence cannot be explained in exactly the same way as the similar slant of United States policy. In fact, Germany's liberalism can be clearly understood only by reference to the country's specific "social economy" ("soziale Marktwirtschaft"), in which the strictness of market mechanisms is tempered less by government than by co-operation between private actors (industry/trade unions/banks):

— Even when most strongly tempted to do so – for example in the late 1960s, when the success of France's industrial policy gave all its partners food for thought – the government of the Federal Republic of Germany, when establishing its microeconomic strategies, never overstepped the bounds of the tripartite co-operation framework set up in 1966. And that co-operation only served to strengthen the social consensus, not to resist the irreversible changes in comparative advantage then occurring, and to step up competition in a country haunted by the spectre of domination by cartels or excessive concentration[45]. It is this policy line that underlies almost all actions by the Ministry for Economic Affairs, despite the rare deviations from it exemplified by coal-mining and shipbuilding subsidies, or the few concessions made, after stubborn resistance, in the context of Community policy [the Multi-Fibre Arrangement (MFA), the steel plan];

— Federal government intervention has been mainly confined to regional policy (tax concessions for Berlin and the frontier zone with the German Democratic Republic); and to R & D, in line with a policy of promoting sunrise industries and aid for SMEs. Until quite recently, the main interventionist arms of the federal government have been the Ministry of Research and Technology (the BMFT) and the other agencies responsible for technology. These agencies have long taken actions not very different from those carried out in the same area by governments in other countries;

— However, the most original feature of the German system of selective government intervention is not so much its discretion as its decentralisation. The States (Länder) and the city councils (communes) are very largely responsible for planning, financing and implementing specific aid schemes. Once this is taken into account, it can be seen that transfers from the public to the private sector in Germany are more substantial than is generally supposed[46].

3. Solving common problems

Since the end of World War II, the economies of almost all OECD Member countries have passed through three distinct stages, during which priorities for government action underwent fundamental changes:

— The reconstruction period, which in Europe and Japan lasted until the end of the 1950s and was remarkable for the tremendous effort – supported by the United States and encouraged or undertaken directly by the different governments concerned – to overcome shortages by restoring the industrial base and developing essential economic and social infrastructures (communications, energy and raw materials production, housing, etc.). During that period, the productivity drive took precedence over any other consideration such as specialisation or international competitiveness;

— During the second period, which came to an end in the early 1970s, this was no longer the case. This phase saw strong growth fostered by the expansion of international trade due principally to the creation of free trade zones (EEC, EFTA) and, more generally, by the liberalisation of world trade[47]. Winning an advantageous position in this emerging international economy became every country's prime concern. In the United States this process took place spontaneously and primarily involved the rapid establishment abroad of industrial concerns making the most of their technological and managerial edge. In Europe, the top priorities were to catch up with United States technology and to develop national production capacity so as to be able to compete, first at home and then internationally, with the American multinationals in fast-growing sectors. To this end, governments almost everywhere encouraged mergers so that businesses could achieve the "critical mass" needed on the international market. They often sought to control foreign investments while supporting the development of their own national champions, and sometimes (as in Ireland) set out deliberately to attract foreign investment. In Japan, the 1960s saw the climax of the policy of promoting growth sectors in the context of an overall industrial restructuring strategy, which has since that time been much attenuated;

- The current structural adjustment phase began many years ago, probably even before the first oil shock, when the first signs emerged of overcapacity in a number of highly capital-intensive sectors[48]. This phase of adjustment of industrial structures to pressures emanating from a number of areas (energy, monetary matters, technology, competition), and in a context of sluggish economic growth, raised problems common to all Member countries and quite different from those dealt with in the past. Thus, government priorities are no longer the same; nor is the relative effectiveness of the various modes of intervention, and hence the pattern of "comparative advantages" in the specific field of government options to which reference was made earlier. The strong pressures for adjustment are testing not only the flexibility of government policies – and even, in some cases, the malleability of the political and institutional frameworks within which they have to be established and applied – but also the flexibility of productive systems' structures themselves.

This present phase of structural change in world industry has brought new problems for governments. Some changes are now a part of industrial history in modern times – for example, there is nothing novel about some industries reaching their full maturity while other new ones emerge. Nor is there anything revolutionary in the fact that it may be necessary to redeploy labour resources that have become less productive as changes in supply and demand occur, directing them towards activities that offer a better return, whether inside or outside the manufacturing sector.

What really is novel is that i) industrial adjustment has to take place in unusual circumstances; and ii) it tends to upset some of the economic and social balances guaranteed by governments in both the short and the long term. This brings unprecedented dilemmas that are difficult to resolve since profound changes in the mechanisms of microeconomic change and in the relationships between micro- and macroeconomic developments occur. This then affects the ability of governments to gain overall mastery of the economic and social adjustment process by using instruments traditionally at their disposal, notably in the industrial policy context.

i) Since 1973, a combination of factors – slower and more hesitant economic growth, a general slowdown in productivity gains, ebbing average returns on industrial capital and increasingly internationalised production and trade – has created a difficult climate for industrial adjustment, while at the same time showing how urgently this adjustment is required. As long as growth was rapid, some of the rigidities prevailing at microeconomic level were no hindrance to the structural adjustment process. For instance, the downward inflexibility of real wages mattered little, as long as productivity gains continued at a brisk pace. Nor did high exit barriers in many industrial sectors really matter, as long as adjustment caused a redistribution of additional resources among the various sectors, rather than an absolute reduction of productive resources in some of them. Or again, inflexibility of producer prices due to overconcentration or to other factors cost little before the arrival on the market of new competitors who did keep their prices flexible – and made the most of that advantage.

ii) The industrial adjustment dictated by world market forces creates and exacerbates certain disequilibria in economic and social structures. This necessitates the adjustment of one structure after another in a chain reaction that no government, whatever its views on intervention may be, can afford to disregard. Because of the scale of the problems involved, all governments have been tempted to tackle them at their roots by intervening in the industrial adjustment process itself and seeking to make the pace of this adjustment compatible with the pace of the changes in the rest of society:

- Quantitative and qualitative labour market disequilibria. In the best situation (Japan), total employment in industry remains more or less stable. However, in most other countries, the number of jobs in industry has for years been steadily declining. Moreover, the structure of labour demands by qualification has radically changed, and this means that frictional unemployment, too, is at a higher rate and tends to last longer – a clear sign that education and training systems are inadequate;
- Regional disequilibria. In all countries, the crisis industries (above all textiles, shipbuilding, metal and heavy chemicals) tend to be highly regionally concentrated;
- Social disequilibria. The costs and benefits of industrial adjustment are usually inequitably shared, since some parties more than others can avoid the costs and reap the benefits. This depends if the parties are in sectors exposed to international competition or in sheltered sectors, are SMEs or large firms, or are in highly unionised or less unionised sectors;
- Disequilibria in foreign trade. It takes a long time to adapt the structures of international specialisation to the new conditions of competition on world markets. In the short-to-medium term, the will to adjust usually has to contend with balance-of-payments constraints, except in countries with

a structural trade surplus for manufactures (Japan, Germany).

B. The policies at work

Over the past fifteen years, there have been two major policy shifts on the part of most OECD Member country governments. Following the first oil shock, there was a spate of direct or indirect government aid to the productive system. Then, in some countries from the early 1980s, in others later, there has been a reversal of this trend as governments began to retreat on a number of fronts.

1. The rise of interventionism

Using available indicators showing the most visible and most easily quantifiable forms of intervention – that is, financial transfers from government to industry and trade barriers – interventionism was rife throughout the 1970s and peaked in the early 1980s, when protectionism and subsidies to industry were simultaneously at their highest.

Table 6.12.   **The rise of subsidies in the OECD area, 1960-1983**

	As percentage of GDP	As percentage of operating surplus
1960	0.72	2.63
1970	1.15	4.71
1975	1.52	7.18
1976	1.52	7.10
1977	1.56	7.27
1978	1.63	7.44
1979	1.63	7.48
1980	1.66	7.89
1981	1.69	8.05
1982	1.77	8.51
1983	1.87	8.67

Source: National accounts of OECD countries.

Table 6.12 shows that *subsidies* to the productive sector as a whole usually followed a rising trend. Data on transfers specifically to industry are harder to find and, above all, raise such difficult problems of international comparability that it has not so far been possible, despite some attempts[49], to produce figures sufficiently comparable to construct consistent aggregate indicators. Nonetheless, the examples below provide a broad illustration of the growth in government assistance:

- In many European countries there has been a marked rise in government aid to industry. For example, aid as a percentage of industrial value added increased from 2 per cent in 1970 to 5.1 per cent in 1983 in France; from 5.7 per cent in 1976/77 to 7 per cent in 1981/82 in the United

Kingdom; from 3.3 per cent in 1977 to 5.9 per cent in 1982 in the Netherlands; and from 1.2 per cent in 1975/76 to 5.0 per cent in 1982 in Denmark. Or, expressed as a percentage of GDP, from 2.1 per cent in 1978 to 3.6 per cent in 1983 in Italy, and from 0.2 per cent in 1975/76 to 2.9 per cent in 1982/83 in Sweden;
- In a more limited number of countries, the rise was more moderate, although still significant, since the initial level was not low. This was the case, for example, in Germany and Canada, where aid as a percentage of industrial value added rose respectively from 1.6 per cent in 1977 to 2.0 per cent in 1981, 1982 and 1983[50] and from 1.1 per cent in 1975/76 to 1.5 per cent in 1982/83;
- Lastly, in the countries where the level of such subsidies had always been low, there was also a substantial rise in support (except in Japan, where levels have remained more or less the same for the past ten years). In the United States, aid doubled during the second half of the 1970s, and in Switzerland, after being hardly worth mentioning for years, more than doubled in the three years to 1983 to 0.5 per cent of industrial value.

As far as *trade* is concerned, the lowering of tariff barriers – which has not perhaps been as effective in reducing protection as might be suggested by the trend in nominal rates alone[51] – has been offset, particularly since the early 1980s, by the proliferation of non-tariff barriers in sectors beset by adjustment difficulties or targeted by sectoral promotion policies. Such non-tariff barriers include quotas, orderly marketing agreements, administrative measures requiring approval of imported products, agreements between private trading partners tacitly endorsed by the public authorities and discriminatory public procurement policies. Looking solely at quantitative controls – and thus confining ourselves to a restrictive definition of non-tariff barriers which underestimates their real impact, particularly in high value-added and technology-intensive industries – it can be seen that non-tariff protection has tended to affect a growing proportion of trade.

- Between 1980 and 1983, restricted imports as a share of total imports of manufactures rose in the United States from 6.2 per cent to 12.7 per cent and in the EEC area from 10.8 per cent to 14.9 per cent. Over the same period, the percentage of restricted exports from Japan and the Asian NICs increased symmetrically, from 15 per cent to 30 per cent;
- Non-tariff protection has affected a growing proportion of total trade and the number of products or countries subject to restriction in each sector has increased. The Multi-Fibre Arrangement is a particularly striking example; for instance, in the case of the EEC area, MFA I included bilateral agreements with 33 countries on 23 specified products, whereas MFA III covers 43 countries and 48 products;

- The range of affected industries has also widened. Quantitative restrictions, initially imposed in certain older industries, e.g. textiles, clothing and steel, have recently been extended to other sectors (cars, machine tools and electronics).

The main reasons for this spate of government intervention seem to have been:

- First, the need to reduce the short-term costs of adjustment, which were considered socially and politically unbearable. Clever attempts were sometimes made to rationalise this concern by analysing the possible divergence between the social and the private costs of adjustment. But it is likely that the social, and hence political, advantages in the short term (rather than the medium- and long-term economic costs) of maintaining certain activities carried more weight with governments often pressed by electoral considerations;
- Broadly speaking, most governments have succumbed to the temptations of "industrial physiocracy". This has led them to reassess the role of industry in the overall economic and social development process and, as a corollary, to reconsider their own industrial policy strategies. This revival of concern for manufacturing industry is partly the result of the shock caused by the numerous crises in sectors which had always been central to national or regional economies in terms of jobs, inter-industry linkages and social relations (the automobile, steel, basic chemical and textile industries). But the renewed concern for industry arises not merely from "nostalgia" but because industry occupies a special place, situated as it is at the interface between national economies and an increasingly integrated and competitive world economy. Industry is also responsible for the production and diffusion of most of the technologies that shape and give impetus to the socio-economic changes now taking place;
- Governments have had to contend with the weakening of some of the mechanisms that regulate industry's macroeconomic environment, e.g. the instability of the international monetary system, and of certain markets, e.g. the destabilization of the oligopolies referred to in Part II of the Annex. Many governments were increasingly convinced that market shortcomings do exist and that preventive or corrective action is therefore warranted;
- As certain industries shrink (steel and shipbuilding in almost all countries, basic petrochemicals and non-ferrous metals in many), strategic considerations have taken on increasing importance. The idea of strategic interest has permeated the maze of inter-industrial relations, with some industrial policy approaches stressing the importance of inter-sectoral linkage effects for national industry as a whole. In France, for example, the idea of grouping interconnected industries was briefly in vogue (cf. "la politique des filières");
- Such ideas have been brought into service in a singular and debatable attempt to deal with a universal problem – the higher macroeconomic costs resulting from the mismatching of industrial structures with demand as international competition changes. In seeking to remove the "external constraint" on macroeconomic policy options, many governments have developed a closer interest in structural change in industry, and have thus been led to intervene energetically at microeconomic level;
- Lastly, the competitive pressures exerted by the newly emerging industrial countries have frequently been seen as evidence of the potential of industrial strategies which combine market forces with powerful incentives and/or protectionism. This consideration has been at the centre of public debate in the United States on whether a more active government industrial policy should be adopted. But it has certainly also been at the back of decision-makers' minds in most other Member countries too.

These inducements to governments to intervene in industrial affairs have carried varying weight in different countries. In a climate where interventionism was generally popular, national intervention policies have been either i) strikingly similar or ii) quite different as regards intensity, preferred methods, procedures and time-span.

i) *The common features*

First, in nearly every country in the 70s and early 80s, there was a surge in all kinds of assistance to help industry adjust to the energy crisis. This was added to by the considerable effect on industry of government energy pricing policies[52] and energy restructuring schemes with a view to developing alternative fuels such as coal and, above all, nuclear energy. In all countries, a policy of real-cost energy pricing was the most powerful and effective incentive to industrial energy saving and fuel switching. But no government was prepared to leave it entirely to private initiative to achieve this end purely by obeying undistorted market signals. All governments played a role in supplying information and in providing incentives[53]. Most of them resorted to the systematic use of financial or tax incentives to encourage investment in energy saving and fuel switching, and to promote energy-related R&D.

Second, there was almost as general a move towards a rapid increase in export assistance, especially export credits. Chapter 7 looks at this in detail; here we shall mention only a few striking examples. In France, from 1970 to 1978, export aids accounted for between 4.5 per cent and 6 per cent of the value of capital goods exports. In 1979-1980 this proportion rose to 8 per cent, and in

1981-1983 to around 10 per cent. In Denmark, export assistance as a proportion of steadily rising total aid to industry increased from 2.3 per cent in 1975 to 20.5 per cent in 1980 and to 28.4 per cent in 1982. In the Netherlands, the corresponding average figure rose from 3 per cent between 1975 and 1978 to 8 per cent between 1980 and 1982, and in Sweden from under 1 per cent in 1976 and 1977 to nearly 10 per cent in 1981.

Third – and perhaps most importantly – intervention became increasingly selective, focusing on a small number of sectors in difficulty and reflecting a shift in government strategies towards defensive positions. This occurred particularly in countries which, in the past, had shown a marked preference for non-discriminatory horizontal measures at sectoral or enterprise level. Sweden is the most striking example. Breaking with the practices of the 1960s, when economic and industrial development was in the main supported solely by means of macroeconomic and tax policy, the Swedish Government began to apply in the 1970s an active industrial policy to which by 1982/1983 it was devoting almost 3 per cent of GDP. This policy was also a highly selective one, since more than half the aid granted went to specific enterprises or industries. Germany's move in the same direction, while less spectacular, was equally significant. Between 1977 and 1983, subsidies as a proportion of total federal aid to industry (which had previously consisted mainly of tax benefits granted in the framework of regional policy) more than doubled, increasing from 6.6 per cent to 16.5 per cent.

For both subsidies and trade protection the tendency was inceasingly to concentrate on a few ailing sectors:

– The available figures on subsidies speak for themselves, although total amounts tend to be underestimated because substantial transfers via regional aid budgets do not appear. In Germany, the proportion of aid to shipbuilding and steel (expressed as a percentage of total federal industrial subsidies) rose from 23 per cent in 1977 to 50 per cent in 1983. In France, the same two industries took one-quarter of government aid between 1973 and 1983. In Denmark, a maximum of 51.2 per cent of government aid to industry in 1976 and a minimum of 36.4 per cent in 1983 went to shipbuilding. In the United Kingdom steel, shipbuilding and mining together received one-quarter of total aid to industry in 1982/1983, against only 7.5 per cent six years earlier. Other examples abound;

– As regards trade protection, the preferred and often the only instrument used in some countries, e.g. the United States, or in some sectors, e.g. textiles, concentration on a few industry sectors is equally apparent. The most blatant non-tariff barriers were introduced in certain traditional sectors such as steel, textiles and clothing, where tariff barriers were already higher than average. It has been estimated that between 1968 and 1983

the proportion of world trade subject to restrictions rose from 31 per cent to 73 per cent in the case of steel and from 53 per cent to 61 per cent in the case of textiles and clothing. Yet there was only a slight rise (from 13 per cent to 15 per cent) in all other industry sectors combined. Moreover, even that slight rise reflected mounting protectionism in a single sector, the automobile industry, where the proportion of trade subject to restriction grew between 1973 and 1983 from less than 1 per cent to almost 50 per cent[54].

ii) *The differences between countries*

Besides many common intervention policies and features, the substantial differences between countries as to the way the content and nature of government intervention have developed also deserve consideration. There are three main reasons for those differences, although it is not easy to assess their relative importance in each case:

– The intensity of the pressures on industrial structures, the scale of the adjustments those pressures made necessary, and the structural inertia were not the same everywhere. In particular, certain industrial structures inherited from the early 1970s had placed too much emphasis on energy-intensive heavy industry and relied too heavily on unskilled labour; they proved to be more vulnerable than others to changes in demand and in the international conditions of supply. Furthermore, the macroeconomic and financial environments of industry were different, and the mechanisms for redeploying productive resources across sectors worked better in some countries than in others;
– Government/industry relations and industrial policy traditions varied widely internationally;
– Even when their interventionist traditions were similar, governments did not always approach similar new problems the same way.

First, even though the growth of interventionism in the vast majority of countries followed much the same pattern – that is, the stepping up and redeployment of existing means of intervention – in a few countries the process led to a complete break with past practices. The case of Sweden has already been mentioned. The United States was tempted to resort to an industrial policy – something it had never before had – although finally the government kept to its traditional policy approach, simply applied more systematically than before. By contrast, industrial policy in Japan appears to have entered a new, less active phase in the 1970s. Significantly, Japan is almost the only country where direct financial aid to industry has not grown over the past ten years, nor trade protection for ailing sectors systematically increased. While this may be due to the success of earlier and particularly strong interventionism, this atypical trend is worth noting, since it disproves certain simplistic, but still far too prevalent, theories put forward to explain Japanese industrial performance over the past fifteen years.

Second, intervention was wider and more intense in some countries than in others[55], although it increased in almost all cases. This surge of interventionism produced no international current impelling all general industrial policy approaches to converge.

Third, the national specificity of government interventions persisted to a striking degree. Assistance to ailing sectors, to exports and to adjustment on the energy front was superimposed rather than substituted for intervention in other areas. Such intervention still differed sharply from one country to another. This was especially true of policies to promote growth industries, which were a main plank of selective action in many European countries, whereas in the United States, government support for them continued to be non-targeted, non-selective and indirect, via civil and military R&D programmes and government procurement.

Fourth, favourite interventionist instruments differed, and so did the way they were used. As far as federal action was concerned, the United States and Germany preferred tax expenditures, while most other countries resorted mainly to granting subsidies or low interest loans. Again, direct implication of government in company management was a notable feature in some countries where the government was a major shareholder, but negligible in others. Intervention also tended to be decentralised in some countries (Germany and Japan are obvious examples) and highly centralised elsewhere.

2. The ebb of government intervention

The interventionist tide in Europe has recently receded, and there are even signs that it has been falling back to its lowest pre-crisis level. This has been accompanied by a questioning of the validity of some of the principles on which government industrial policy has for so long been based.

Almost all OECD Member countries have begun to retreat on a number of intervention fronts, especially on i) subsidies supporting specific industries or enterprises. Furthermore, ii) the institutional and regulatory frameworks ensuring governments' control over industry have been made more flexible and sometimes even abolished ii). It would, however, be premature to conclude that these still embryonic developments herald a new era in government/industry relations in the OECD area as a whole. Recent changes in domestic policies have taken place for reasons not always sufficiently unequivocal to allow unreserved extrapolation and, in any case, iii) these changes have not yet proved sufficient to justify or facilitate a real reversal in trade protectionism.

i) Apart from the few countries where a scaling down of industry assistance occurred much earlier[56], no evidence yet exists to show the extent of government disengagement on the subsidies front (in spite of the trend in Sweden illustrated in Graph 6.8). In a very few cases, for example in France, this disengagement does not yet show up, even in the most recent statistics.

ii) Deregulation and privatisation are the two main and sometimes intersecting roads along which many governments have for some time been tempted to discard, in the name of economic efficiency, some of the prerogatives they have long enjoyed. Chapter 8 looks at this important development in depth, showing how this movement began in the United States and spread fairly rapidly to the rest of the OECD area[57]. It has been principally the service sector so far that is concerned by selective "economic" deregulation – that is, the relaxation of government control over price and supply structures in certain industries. Such moves are motivated either by the decline of certain natural monopolies due, among other things, to technical change, e.g. telecommunications, or to second thoughts about competition being "destructive", e.g. road transport. However, the resulting change has a considerable impact on the industrial sectors that contribute to the activities concerned. Blanket "economic" deregulation reducing government intervention in market operations as a whole, e.g. the repeal of price control legislation in France, undeniably affects all industrial sectors. There is also "social" deregulation, which seeks to relax the frameworks determining the general conditions for all productive activities (protection of dependent workers or of the environment, standard-setting and quality control). This also clearly has an immediate effect on industrial firms' freedom of action.

Privatisation, whether or not related to deregulation, more specifically concerns industry. Most governments are currently seeking to redefine public sector frontiers and, especially, to reassess the costs and benefits of direct government involvement in management of the competitive sector. Many have begun to sell to the private sector their holdings in various manufacturing industries[58]. Paradoxically, recent experience in France shows that while this has become an increasingly imperious necessity, it is less affected than is sometimes claimed by the political and ideological colour of the government in power. After the wave of nationalisations in 1982, it was not long before privatisation crept in by the back door as parts of public enterprises were sold off and share flotations launched. When the government changed, this movement was stepped up, and it was decided to repeal the measures taken in 1982 and to plan for the privatisation of enterprises that had for a long time, if not always, been government controlled.

However, changes in ownership are by no means the only way to improve the efficiency of public enterprises. Indeed, modifications of policies affecting these enterprises may suffice, e.g. scaling down subsidies in exchange of greater freedom and independence for management. This has been considered by several countries, in particular Canada, Australia and New Zealand[59].

Graph 6.8. Trend of government aid to industry in Sweden

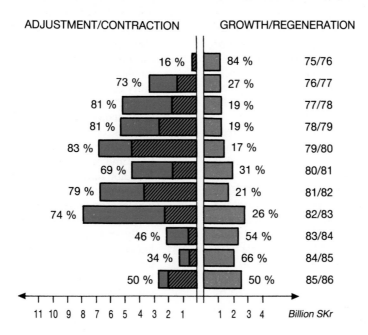

Notes: [hatched] Aid to shipbuilding.

Adjustment/Contraction = temporary measures + sectoral aid.
Growth/Regeneration = aid to R&D, regional development, exports and SMEs.
Source: Swedish Ministry of Industry.

iii) It is tempting to believe that some of these recent changes in government attitudes are the first signs of what may prove to be a genuine move towards an unprecedented international convergence of policy approaches. This, in turn, would help reconcile national industrial interests by creating a favourable climate for the dismantling of trade protection. However, prudence is required, since it is not yet possible to untangle the widely differing causes that have led to this world-wide review of microeconomic policies. Undeniably, this review has come about partly as a by-product of changes in macroeconomic priorities, and has been prompted by the desire to reduce the direct budget costs of assistance to industry. Thus, it may not arise primarily from an in-depth reassessment of the overall social and economic costs and benefits of that aid. Moreover, the scaling down of assistance to industries in crisis (shipbuilding, for example) has sometimes been the logical consequence of a refusal to increase such aid, given the irremediable deterioration of the industry's position, rather than the result of a fundamental policy shift.

There is, therefore, no absolute guarantee that in changed circumstances industrial policies will not fall back again into the same old interventionist rut. It remains to be seen whether there has been any real and lasting change in government thinking and in public opinion as a result of the hard schooling of the past five years. The following section is a brief account of what should be learned from this experience to encourage the present hopes to be fulfilled.

C. The effects of industrial policies

In considering the impact of government policies on industrial adjustment, it is first necessary to seek answers to a number of key questions. To what extent have these policies been able to control the cost and burden of adjustment without unduly slowing down its pace and thereby generating higher long-run economic and social costs than those they were designed to obviate? Have they brought about a sound equilibrium and a modicum of compatibility between policies affecting the business environment and those aimed at directly influencing the adjustment process? Have they succeeded in diminishing the socio-economic pressures generated by changes on the domestic front, without exacerbating tensions internationally?

More broadly, the question of effectiveness of industrial policies may be posed in the following terms. A weak market – due to the existence of a monopoly or externalities, the lack of a solidly based market-place, government intervention on the international market or a supposed dearth of private initiative – does not in itself warrant government action. It is necessary to ascertain beforehand that such action can be more effective than the market solution, however imperfect, and that the appropriate means can indeed be mobilised.

The broader lesson to be drawn from the past fifteen years' experience is that many Member countries have tended to overrate the risks and costs of such market failures and to underestimate those associated with "government failures". These government failures have often resulted from an inclination to underrate the stringent conditions required. These requirements are that the objectives be clear and realistic, that the means match the ends, that the measures be compatible with other policies and that the seed sown by government falls on fertile ground. On this latter fundamental point, government programmes have often been hampered by a lack of receptiveness and/or capacity to respond to incentives – factors which hinge on the quality of the macroeconomic, financial and educational environment of industry. The same basic reasons explain both the weaknesses of the market and the inability of governments to remedy matters through the preferred use of selective measures.

In most countries selective measures – that is, those that provide some form of public subsidy on a selective basis to individual sectors or firms – constitute the hard core and the most specific component of industrial policies. These measures have been greatly expanded over the past fifteen years and have also given rise to serious problems since they often lack transparency and may even be harmful internationally and ineffective at home. These problems exist irrespective of the policy framework, be it emergency assistance to ailing industries or promotion of growth sectors.

1. The limits of industrial policies

At a time when governments felt forced to resort increasingly to such intervention expedients, several developments (especially technological change and the internationalisation of production and trade) were making it increasingly difficult to design and implement effective, carefully targeted industrial policies – hence the need to impart a new thrust to government policy, the extent of which is not always fully appreciated.

i) Policies that are becoming increasingly difficult to design

From the policy planning stage, governments have hit an increasing number of obstacles:

- The growing internationalisation of production and trade is narrowing governments' "discretion-ary" options; this applies to both trade and domestic policies;
- The "decisive impact" of sector-targeted government measures is dispersed because of the rapidly blurring frontiers between sectors. In Europe, for example, plans in the 1970s to support the machine tool industry failed because of an inability to foresee the extent, pace and implications of the "electronic revolution" in this sector. Similarly, today, doubts may be harboured as to the outcome of policies that seek to treat the telecommunications and data processing sectors as distinct and separate industries;
- It is not easy for governments to define sectoral strategies to which the firms concerned can wholeheartedly subscribe, because of their widely varying performance and strategic interests, especially in the declining industries where the gap between the best and the average production practices has tended to widen over the years. This has been particularly problematical in sectors with a low degree of concentration such as textiles and machine tools; but the same also applies in other sectors, particularly when policies must be framed multinationally within the EEC;
- Defining most of the government programmes implies looking ahead, a much more difficult and risky business than in the past. In the 1950s and 1960s, the stability of the business environment and the steady pace of general economic growth made forecasting an easier task. Since then, the chances of bad misjudgements have been much greater and the consequences of these misjudgements all the more serious since government policies are claimed to be more finely tuned.

ii) Policies that are hard to control over time

If governments are able to overcome these obstacles, they may still find it hard to maintain sufficient control over their means of action for any length of time. Written large in all government programmes is the necessity of acting promptly, following up policies and their impact, altering their thrust – even discarding them – in the light of market circumstances or of an ongoing process of evaluation. Experience has shown, however, that intentions are one thing and practice quite another.

By nature cumbersome and slow-moving, government procedures generally act more as a brake and a stabilizer than as an accelerator of change. Lately, with the development of modern communication techniques, the decision-making process has tended to be faster in the private sector than in the public sector. Governments have sometimes reacted by delegating greater powers to civil service task forces vested with some degree of autonomy and greater flexibility than the central administration, but they may have lost in co-ordination what they have gained in efficiency, possibly strengthening the power of certain lobbies to influence government decision-making.

The experience of many European countries and, to some extent, that of the United States, has shown that once they have been introduced, measures to support industry often have an irresistible tendency to be self-perpetuating and to spread outside their initial terrain. When a particular measure fails or has damaging side-effects, most OECD Member governments have frequently been inclined to take further corrective measures rather than back-pedal – something they are reluctant to do, more for political and social reasons than on economic grounds.

First, once they have approved an outlay, governments tend to wish to "protect" their initial "budget investment". Second, every measure rallies its own lobby and generates other organised interest groups seeking to obtain equivalent treatment or redress. The government is therefore all the more unlikely to resist these pressures in that it can spread the costs of its decisions by shifting part of the burden to the least organised members of society, e.g. consumers and taxpayers. The bulk of subsidies thus increasingly goes to the major enterprises – partly because of the latter's influence on government policy making – a trend which is likely to continue and gain ground as measures are renewed and extended.

Third, government and industry do not enjoy the same access to information, nor do they have the same negotiating clout. It is much more difficult for governments to set time-limits on its subsidies or to make these dependent on specific commitments by the recipients than is usually assumed. Industry is often able to enjoy a real advantage as to access to the relevant technical and economic data, and is able to devote greater intelligence resources and other powers of persuasion (including the mobilisation of lobbies such as the unions or banks) to put across its particular view than the authorities, whose responsibilities are far more wide-ranging.

From an industrial policy standpoint, the idea of a government monopoly with a wide range of disparate beneficiaries is purely illusory. The reality is that there are a large number of government agencies, each with limited independent powers of evaluation, dealing with influential lobbies each able to put forward a good case for obtaining the "fix" to which the government has involuntarily accustomed them. The surge in interventionism has in large measure responded to this "sedimentation" of government subsidies, with each stratum originating in government policy, but changing under the effect of social and political forces into an inescapable obligation.

iii) *Policies with limited intrinsic effectiveness*

Even when the dangers of perpetuation and proliferation of measures can be averted, a number of general factors limit on the domestic front the likely effectiveness of industrial policies. Internationally, these policies

often give rise to distortions – and hence to less and less efficient allocation of resources among the world industrial community. Although in some cases (for instance in Japan) institutional patterns and socio-economic traditions offer more scope than elsewhere for efficient and effective government action, experience in most countries shows that such action usually comes up against the following difficulties:

- Government intervention in industry has become so complex and comprises such a wide variety of programmes and measures that the risk of a conflict of goals is considerable. The ability of governments to appraise the measures' direct or indirect effects, other than on the budget, is also more limited;
- The lack of transparency of government policy cannot but arouse international mistrust and increase the government's vulnerability to the most powerful lobbies. Thus, whatever the intentions at the outset, the distribution of public favours will ultimately be influenced as much by economic and social power relationships as by cost/benefit considerations;
- In most countries, industrial policies display a marked bias in favour of the largest enterprises, especially those where the nationalised sector plays an important role[60];
- While detrimental to the other actors, this concentration is not always beneficial to the major enterprises. For example, several governments have been tempted to use public enterprises as a prime policy instrument, often giving them broad and contradictory mandates, e.g. to create jobs and promote more balanced regional development, while at the same time streamlining their activities with a view to spearheading the export drive. Or governments may encourage or constrain firms to depart from their initial industrial objectives in order to take over ailing enterprises or launch into growth areas in which they have had insufficient experience;
- While financial transfers from government to industry tend to be modest from a macroeconomic standpoint (at most around 3 per cent of GDP), they have a particularly distorting effect on the market because of their concentration on certain sectors or firms. For example, in the declining sectors they penalise the most efficient firms nationally and internationally by permitting the survival of production capacity that is no longer competitive; at the same time they divert resources from more profitable uses in other areas of the economy;
- Lastly, one of the worst cumulative effects of many industrial policy measures is that they are internationally contagious. As the disease spreads – as it has many times in the past, shipbuilding probably being the prime example – it distorts the cost/benefit balance of support. At the same time

as increasing the allocation costs for the world economy as a whole, it erodes any benefits to the national economy. This is true both of policies to shelter and assist ailing sectors and of those encouraging too headlong a stampede towards new growth areas.

iv) Co-ordination problems that soon become insurmountable

As industrial policy measures multiply, problems of co-ordinating macro- and microeconomic policies increase exponentially as does the risk of incompatibility between these two types of government action.

Seldom is the link between macroeconomic and industrial policy clearly defined, even though each is recognised to have a decisive influence on the other. In particular, changes in the quality of the international macroeconomic climate largely explain why apparently similar industrial policies may not necessarily have the same success in all countries. Japanese industry, in this respect, enjoys a clear advantage over its competitors since the country's growth has been faster, steadier and less inflationary than elsewhere as a result of a remarkable continuity and consistency of policy.

Rather than making possible microeconomic consequences one of the criteria in determining macroeconomic policy options, the tendency has been to resort afterwards to microeconomic measures to correct any undesirable effects. But the resources reallocated in an industrial policy framework can provide only scant compensation, especially for the less-favoured enterprises or industries, for the costs that may be imposed by policy options in other areas. For instance in France, when industrial prices moved down by just one point against those of other sectors, this resulted in an estimated transfer of FF 7 to 8 billion to the latter, equivalent to 20 per cent of total aid to industry in 1983 and half the export assistance paid out that year. (Between 1973 and 1980, the price differential averaged −1.2 per cent, against only −0.1 per cent over the same period in Germany, primarily because higher inflation in France benefitted protected industries to the detriment of the competitive sectors, and probably also because of price controls.) Another example, also for France, illustrates the disproportion between the costs and benefits for industry of macroeconomic policies and microeconomic adjustment measures, when the lowering of employers' social security contributions from 57.4 per cent in 1977 to 49.2 per cent in 1983 brought the costs borne by industry down by twice the amount of total aid to industry.

The lack of consistency between industrial and macroeconomic policy is one of the main and chronic causes of the ineffectiveness of many efforts to intervene directly in the industrial adjustment process. Examples of contradictions or lack of consistency between the aims pursued and the means employed by these policies over the past fifteen years abound. Some of the most striking are monetary depreciation versus the drive to promote high technology sectors; macroeconomic policy to cool off the economy versus the promotion of industries producing certain capital goods; price controls to reduce corporate profit margins versus the industrial investment drive; macroeconomic policies with the overall effect of subsidising capital and taxing employment or tax policies favouring investment in plant and machinery over structural investment or investment in human resources versus sector plans aimed at maintaining industrial employment.

2. Strategies to support ailing sectors

Support to ailing sectors has taken up a substantial and, until recently, growing share of microeconomic resources. Valuable lessons can be drawn from the past record in this respect for, as well as confirming the limits of selective measures, it provides a closer insight into the possible causes of failure and the required conditions for the success of government intervention in industry.

First, it is clear that purely defensive policies aimed at eluding the consequences of the underlying market trends or even changing them have failed, irrespective of whether the instruments used were subsidies or trade barriers. No country has been able to avoid a slump in employment in such sectors as iron and steel, textiles or shipbuilding (see Table 6.13). It is telling that, in the textile industry, Germany – whose policies have been among the least interventionist – has not suffered any more job losses than its European partners, notably France and the United Kingdom.

Table 6.13. **Employment trends in three ailing sectors**

	Iron and steel 1985 (1974 = 100)	Textiles 1984 (1974 = 100)	Shipbuilding 1985 (1975 = 100)
United States	45.5	64	..
Japan	80	63	52
Germany	66	60	45
Benelux	59.5	49	56[3]
France	52	64[1]	57
Italy	76	81	35
United Kingdom	31	42	25[3]
Austria	71	62	..
Norway	53	65[1]	29
Sweden	62	62[2]	11
Switzerland	50	..	..

1. 1983.
2. 1982.
3. 1984.
Sources: OECD, COMITEXTIL, ILO, GATT, MITI.

A key policy objective in this area has been to limit the risk of dislocating regional economies as a result of the decline of geographically concentrated industries. It must also be admitted that many countries have been unsuccessful in achieving this objective. The industrial

236

Table 6.14. **Share of the textiles industry
in total industrial employment in selected regions, 1978-1982**

		1978	1982
France	Nord/Pas-de-Calais	17.5	17.1
	Rhônes-Alpes	8.4	9.4
Italy	Lombardia	14.4	17.6
	Piemonte	13.6	12.0
	Toscana	21.7	24.3
	Veneto	16.3	17.3
United Kingdom	North-West	12.0	10.6
	East Midlands	17.7	18.2
	Yorkshire/Humberside	12.8	10.7

Source: COMITEXTIL.

and social policies they have pursued have not been able to save the jobs under threat or to achieve the desired diversification of job opportunities, as may be seen from the figures in Table 6.14.

i) *Why policies have failed*

With hindsight the disappointing results of many policies to support ailing sectors or enterprises may be put down to two main causes.

First, the marriage, rather than the simple co-ordination of social and industrial policies, has proved to be something of an unholy union generating a vicious circle of mutual problems condemning both to costly impotence.

The majority of Member countries have yielded to the temptation of using industrial policy for social policy gains. Subsidies dependent upon the maintenance of employment have been by far the most pernicious form of confusion of these objectives.

Second, the chances of the "marriage" working were particularly slim since the support measures generated unwanted and unforeseen effects, compounding both industrial and social problems.

In the case of trade measures, this question was well documented in the recent OECD report on *Costs and Benefits of Protection.* It is noteworthy that in the textile industry the benefits of protectionism have tended either to go partly to the distribution side (as in France) or to be used to increase capital intensity. This in turn speeded up labour-shedding in the most highly protected segments of the industry, which, paradoxically from a positive industrial adjustment standpoint, have been those producing downmarket goods (a trend particularly noticeable in countries such as France and the United Kingdom where the textile industry was concentrated).

Direct subsidies or exemptions from social overheads have had a similar if not greater effect on capital intensity. Furthermore, sectors where the work-force is highly organised, e.g. the steel and motor vehicle industries, have often succeeded in capturing a substantial share of government hand-outs, as can be seen from the trend in inter-sectoral wage differentials. This has done nothing to improve the international competitiveness of the enterprises concerned in the short term, and in the longer run exaggeratedly boosts the substitution of capital for labour, destroying job opportunities and adversely affecting resource allocation.

It has been noted, as in the case of the German shipbuilding industry, that wage increases due to government subsidies sometimes tend to spread to the region where the subsidised enterprise or industry is located, exacerbating the problem of creating alternative jobs which would have made the withdrawal of subsidies easier.

Government support for employment reasons generally has worsened overcapacity problems in many industries, both in those where entry barriers are the weakest, e.g. textiles, and in those where exit barriers are blocking adjustment, e.g. steel, aluminium and petrochemicals. In the capital-intensive sectors, the unit cost of job-saving can prove astronomical both for taxpayers and for participants in the world market for the goods in question that have suffered a ruinous slump in prices. The response of the world market to demand and supply-side disequilibria has often been on such a scale that the oxygen pumped in by the authorities has rapidly been burnt up.

ii) *Conditions for success*

However, it would be wrong to conclude that there should be no kind of government involvement in the adjustment of ailing sectors and to have a blind confidence in the absolute effectiveness of market forces. Experience has shown the usefulness of a few isolated measures, and even some broader strategies have proved to be of genuine value.

In bailing out individual enterprises or sectors, the golden rule is that assistance should be given for a strictly limited period and, if possible, with strings attached[61]. In certain institutional and socio-political settings there is a higher probability that this rule will not be applied – paradoxically they are often those where strong ties exist between central government and industry. Others, by contrast, lend themselves to *ad hoc* and more short-term co-operation between the authorities and specific private interests.

The rescue of Chrysler in the United States is a good example. However, it is a case often cited to show that, in the matter of government intervention, the United States is not as far removed from Europe as commonly supposed. This is to disregard a distinctive and crucial feature of this rescue operation. The company and those having a claim on it (creditors and the work-force) had no precedent in law or practice to claim any assistance from the government and so had to convince the government by making concessions which are estimated to represent in discounted terms double the loan guaranteed by the government. This is a far cry from the aid on tap given to certain European motor vehicle manufacturers.

The same lesson may be drawn from United States trade protection experience. When the government showed itself receptive to lobbying by strongly organised industries, it decided – sometimes against the opinion of the International Trade Commission – to take protectionist measures whose effects on the adjustment process were debatable. These measures subsequently took on a permanent character (as in the case of textiles), had a more distortionary impact than expected (voluntary restraints in the automobile industry) or were accompanied by sometimes clumsy government interference in the sector's economic decision-making (as in the steel industry where the government made assistance contingent upon modernisation and investment programmes which, given the industry's overcapacity, were highly risky). On the other hand, the trade measures taken via the quasi-statutory channel of the International Trade Commission – which were directed at sectors that were not necessarily any less hard hit by foreign competition but certainly had less political clout – appeared to have better cushioned the shocks, and so creating a propitious climate for inevitable, if difficult, adjustment[62]. Not only has the ITC displayed real independence of judgement in firmly refusing the majority of representations made to it[63]; it has also usually managed to avoid the perpetuation of protectionist measures[64].

The American example shows that the weakness of the traditional links between government and industry may provide an effective "natural" antidote to "government failings" in the framework of an *ad hoc* intervention policy. But the Japanese example makes it easier to understand the precise conditions where the existence of such links may help to solve the problems posed by the decline of certain sectors, in the framework of a comprehensive strategy for accelerating adjustment.

Without going into the detail of the means employed in Japan (as specified in the 1978 Act on the stabilization of ailing sectors and the 1983 Act on the improvement of the sectoral structures)[65], it may be useful to summarise briefly the type of approach taken, the type of instruments used and the results obtained. We shall then seek to identify what general lessons may be drawn from the Japanese experience.

The Japanese approach was based on the profound conviction that when sudden and unpredictable changes, such as the oil shocks, hit sectors with a poor capacity to respond in the short term (for instance, because of insufficiently mobile factors of production), adjustment by way of market forces alone would lead to destructive competition, affecting the sound long-term allocation of productive resources. It was therefore necessary for the authorities to bring about an "orderly" adjustment, in close co-operation with the enterprises concerned. This began with a phased reduction in capacity with due regard to considerations of technical efficiency and with the burden equitably distributed between the actors, so as to avoid being trapped in the "prisoner's dilemma" that can block the adjustment of demand and supply in capital-intensive sectors[66].

Apart from the consensual determination of the scope[67], aims and timetable of action, the main feature of the Japanese measures was the concerted action by the parties concerned – public and private – to reduce capacity and even remodel the supply structure of the sectors concerned. Neither financial assistance nor trade protection played such a key role as they did in similar programmes in most other countries, although it is admittedly true that loan guarantees have generally been forthcoming, as well as limited subsidies in a few cases, e.g. in the shipbuilding plan.

The results have been undeniably positive, given the initial difficulties. The extent of the phasing down of excess capacity relative to needs, as well as the speed at which it all took place, was without precedent in the OECD area. The nature of the instruments used also served to minimise any unwanted effects on other economic sectors. To cite only the most striking examples: in just the three years between 1978 and 1982, primary processing capacity of aluminium was reduced by almost 55 per cent and by almost 50 per cent for urea processing capacity; the later 1983 Act reduced ethylene capacity by over a third in only two years.

A number of features specific to Japan help explain the form of assistance chosen and its effectiveness. These include the particularly severe adjustment problems faced by the energy-intensive sectors; the exceptional dynamism of sectors offering alternative employment; the ease of redeployment of manpower which reduced resistance to change thanks to the presence in the ailing industries of major groups with highly diversified interests; and the high quality and versatility of the trained workers to be redeployed. Nonetheless, a number of general lessons can be drawn.

First, the notion of "market failure" was defined in a narrow sense, and specific eligibility criteria for all sectors were laid down. Second, industrial and social aspects were clearly delineated to the extent that they come under two different sets of laws. Third, unlike last-ditch *ad hoc* measures, the policy has been one of coherent and flexible adjustment, with rules and well established procedures applying to all the sectors, although with some differentiation between them. This reduced the scope for unco-ordinated lobbying with a view to obtaining maximum concessions from the authorities. Fourthly, all the parties concerned, including the unions, were from the outset involved in the consensual decision-making process; employment and redeployment problems could thus be taken into account well before capacity was actually reduced. This was made possible, in particular, by the reasonable acceptance of the sectoral forecasts drawn up jointly by government, industry and independent experts. Finally, the Act, particularly as amended in 1983, was not confined to phasing down production in the industries in question but also concerned the revitalisation of these industries, notably by way of technological adjustment.

3. Promoting promising sectors and technological adjustment

A criticism frequently levelled at support policies for ailing sectors is not so much that their effectiveness is often dubious, but rather that they distract government attention and scarce budget resources from the higher priority of promoting activities with real growth potential, particularly the high technology industries. According to this thesis, a desirable industrial policy reform would be to redeploy available means to provide more assistance to sectors making the biggest contribution to the nation's wealth and employment.

This approach is off the mark, for it underestimates the ability of individual governments, in the prevailing technological and market conditions, to promote the growth of these spearhead sectors. What is required in a number of countries is a more fundamental break with tradition and a thorough review of industrial policy practices and instruments, and of the relationship between industrial policy on the one hand and financial, competition and education policies on the other. This would make it easier to derive the best advantages, both nationally and internationally, from the new opportunities afforded by technological progress and the changing pattern of demand.

Without wishing to dwell on what has been said earlier on the general limits of selective policies, it must be restated that many of these limits are particularly constraining in the case of growth sectors. This is particularly true in industries where demarcations are blurred by technological progress and which are more affected than others by the internationalisation of business activity and the globalisation of corporate strategies (see Part II of the Annex).

The main conclusions for government action can be drawn from the reasons outlined in Part I for the different approaches countries have taken to technological adjustment. Three countries would seem so far to have been the most successful in their course of action: the United States, Japan and Germany (whose approach may be likened to that of smaller countries such as Switzerland or Sweden). By contrast, countries like France and the United Kingdom have been less able than the United States or Japan to harness technological progress to develop their industrial structures in line with changes in world demand or to consolidate their traditional strong points on the international market in the same way as Germany.

i) The golden rules for success

The American and Japanese approaches, however different they may be, show that certain fundamental and universal conditions are necessary for a successful public policy to support growth sectors, be it direct or indirect, targeted or not.

Government intervention must not inhibit the forces of competition that now more than ever play an irreplaceable role, particularly in sectors in the throes of rapid technological change, in selecting innovations with the greatest market potential and in allocating productive resources to those areas where they will be used to best effect. Early internationalisation of activities and maximum exposure of the domestic market to outside competition is imperative, particularly for those countries that are too small to avoid the creation of national monopolies in sectors characterised by economies of scale and scope.

In this competitive setting, the enterprises concerned must have access to the appropriate technological, financial and human resources. The channels for technological dissemination must be efficient, the market must allow for sufficient labour mobility, and the education and training system must be able to help workers adapt speedily to new needs. Additionally, the financial market must be sufficiently flexible and innovative to cater for high risk ventures with unconventional investment requirements involving substantial intangible investment (see Part II of the Annex).

ii) The American example

In the United States, government R&D support programmes and contracts, particularly in the defence industry, have played and continue to play a major role in boosting the development of many high technology industries. They are probably the main arm of the country's implicit industrial policy. Despite their intrinsic failings (notably their cumbersome nature), they have imparted new life to the competitive sector, for three main reasons[68]. First, these programmes were designed and undertaken in a way that ensured very broad participation by a wide range of private actors in their implementation. Thus, only a small portion of government-funded research is undertaken by the public sector, unlike the situation in other countries where defence spending is on an equally large scale[69]; government contracts go to a large number and a great variety of enterprises, and the results of research commissioned by the government are widely and rapidly disseminated[70]. Second, even if unsuccessful, government programmes seem to have only a limited "crowding out" effect on other R&D efforts, because of the gigantic scale of the American scientific and technical system. Third, the general industrial environment is highly favourable to the rapid exploitation of new opportunities, including those to some extent deliberately created by federal programmes (a mobile and plentiful scientific work-force; a receptive capital market; competitive pressure strongly encouraging innovation, etc.).

iii) *The Japanese example*

The Japanese example shows that there is more than one road to success and that a policy quite different from that of the United States can produce excellent results in a whole host of areas. But on closer scrutiny, the marked dissimilarities of Japanese and United States policies and their field of application mask a number of significant resemblances. In particular, neither the Japanese Government nor the United States Government has ever sought to play an entrepreneurial role, and firms and private ventures have taken on the task, in a highly competitive environment and with or without government assistance, of developing the growth sectors. In both countries, the dissemination of scientific and technical knowledge across enterprises and sectors is extremely effective as is the capital market, even though the reasons for this efficiency are not identical.

In reality, the role played by the Japanese Government, and in particular MITI, has often been inflated particularly by sections of opinion seeking to justify interventionist policies in other countries. It is nonetheless far from negligible, despite the contention of other groups whose ultra-liberalism has difficulties in countenancing such a blatant exception to the rule that economic performance is strictly inversely proportional to government involvement in industry. Not only have the Japanese authorities largely followed the golden rules referred to above, e.g. by looking after the educational and macroeconomic environment surrounding industry and encouraging competition at home, they have also created other conditions making for much faster technological adjustment by national industry than would have been possible under the impetus of market forces alone. But they have also gradually eased and are even slowly dismantling the support and protectionist measures instituted to promote the target sectors, once these have become sufficiently mature to compete internationally.

The Japanese policy of promoting growth sectors is now a standard feature of the industrial economy, but the caricatures it engenders can inspire the wrong kind of ventures in countries tempted to follow a recipe they only half understand and without having all the ingredients to hand. Much emphasis tends to be placed on its protectionist aspects, as regards both imports and direct investment, as well as on the filtering and monopsonistic impact of the government on imports and foreign technologies, or on the major borrowing leverage enjoyed by the growth industries. Far more disregarded are other equally important aspects: the fact that MITI can also make mistakes, but that the consequences of any errors of judgement are attenuated by the consensual nature of decision-making (the most typical example being the motor industry's past resistance to government concentration schemes); the fact that it has always sought in its policy of controlling the import of technologies to avoid creating an anti-competitive situation; that government procurement, because of the low level of defence spending, is not such a major policy instrument as in most other countries; that the "target" sectors have been fairly loosely defined at government level, and that central government is hence not tempted to involve itself in private decisions in regard to specific goods or groups of goods.

Lastly, before considering how the Japanese example may be transposed to other national settings, it is necessary to weigh up the four other features of the private Japanese economy which have vitally contributed to its success in building up and conquering international markets in a large number of sectors. These features are the extraordinarily dynamic and prompt response of private domestic demand (the pace of penetration of new consumer goods in Japan has outstripped that in any other country); the extreme flexibility of industrial prices which has greatly facilitated foreign market penetration[71]; the remarkable capacity for organisational innovation displayed by the business sector; and the special links between the manufacturing and distributive sectors which limit conflicts of interest and power imbalances between the two.

iv) *The German variant*

Germany's experience, and that of other countries which have pursued a strategy of consolidating strong international market positions, suggests that the way out does not lie solely in participating in the greatest number of high-growth market areas. It more shows that a strategy for technological adjustment must reflect the nature of the country's comparative advantages. Using foreign trade performance as a judging tool, it can sometimes pay off to give priority to technological dissemination and to updating technologies in the more traditional sectors, leaving it to the market-place and private initiative to identify which high technology areas can be exploited most successfully.

Significantly – after having sought in the 1970s to promote such specific sectors as electronics – the German government has lately backtracked in the face of mixed results[72]. Thus, German technological adjustment policy once again comprises the following broad thrusts: a bias in favour of general incentives such as tax relief; decentralisation of the process of defining specific technological objectives and of distributing government financial assistance[73]; provision of the back-up necessary for innovation and technological dissemination (education; standardization; co-operative research infrastructures); and assistance to the SMEs to help them use this back-up to best advantage, e.g. the demonstrably successful scheme to assist SMEs in recruiting scientific and technical personnel.

v) *Counter-examples*

Looked at over the long term, the French and British examples, for their part, show all too clearly the limits of the policies applied, especially those intended to "create" competitive advantages in sectors designated as strategic. Those policies prove successful only in sectors where central government firmly controls demand by way of government contracts[74], and have generally shown themselves to be ineffective elsewhere[75] and even to be detrimental to sectors and industries other than those targeted.

The dominant traits of these policies have been centralised identification of objectives, direct government involvement in the management of the enterprises designated to achieve them, the red tape attendant on the allocation of resources – particularly managerial and financial resources – and their concentration on a limited number of national front runners exposed to a minimum of domestic competition. Each constitutes a breach of the golden rules referred to earlier, and their relative lack of success is further evidence of the stringency of these conditions.

Moreover, the marked bias of technological policies in favour of the generic technology sectors has indirectly weakened and distorted the process of technological dissemination and modernisation in the rest of industry. This has been to the detriment of a wide range of activities and, involuntarily, has enfeebled their international competitiveness. In particular, the crowding out effect of the "major" technological programmes would seem to have been much greater in these medium-size countries than in the United States, particularly from a human resources standpoint. It would seem to have amply outstripped the "spin-off" effects, which were far weaker than expected and sometimes even negative[76]. Finally, the energy, resources and hopes invested by the authorities in these major programmes could not go to other equally crucial areas, and notably to providing the necessary back-up for innovation throughout industry, e.g. education and training, and to creating the right sort of climate for such innovation.

The governments concerned are now patently aware of these undesirable effects, and have for some years been trying to overhaul their policies accordingly. In the United Kingdom, the change of direction in 1979 was particularly perceptible. It began with a gradual increase in the share of support devoted by the Trade and Industry Department to industrial R&D in the civilian sector under the Support for Innovation Programme and a change in that programme's priorities. Greater emphasis was placed on the promotion of co-operative projects and the dissemination of leading-edge technologies in user sectors, and less importance was attached to support for projects undertaken by individual firms. Nonetheless, in the United Kingdom as in France, time and perseverance will be needed before there can be any complete turn-round in the time-hallowed administrative and entrepreneurial practices that have shaped institutional and industrial structures for centuries.

III. CONCLUSIONS

Over and above individual national situations, a number of broad lessons may be drawn from the review of the nature, development and impact of OECD Member countries' industrial policies over the past fifteen years.

The changes that have taken place inside and outside industry – slower growth, increased uncertainty on the monetary and energy fronts, an international *rapprochement* of patterns of consumption, the internationalisation of production and trade, technological development – have created conditions for government action that are radically different from those in which industrial policy instruments and options were framed in the 1950s and 1960s.

In most countries selective approaches, sector by sector and even product by product, have lost much of their effectiveness in solving problems that are increasingly assuming a trans-sectoral and transnational dimension. On the other hand, the importance of the general determinants of industrial performance and adaptability is growing, both as regards the flexibility and efficiency of the factor and goods markets, or the other parameters favouring industrial innovation generally, and the inter-sectoral and international spread of technological progress.

In other words, the chances of success for industrial policies, however legitimate their goals, are likely to become increasingly remote unless certain basic conditions, ensuring a swift and adequate response from private agents both to government incentives and market pressure, are met. Among these conditions which it would seem increasingly utopian to expect selective policies to replace, the most fundamental are the following:

- The quality of the environment created by macroeconomic policies must minimise the uncertainties surrounding the choices of industrial agents and be sufficiently neutral in its microeconomic effects as not to distort these choices. This is particularly important for the choices concerning production technologies and hence the industrial mix and the make-up of investment (see in particular the tax policy recommendations in Chapter 10);
- A financial system capable of responding flexibly and inventively to the changing needs of industry and of assuming fully its role in allocating resources to the most productive uses (see recommendations in Chapter 4);
- An education and training system able to supply – and retrain whenever necessary – the manpower to meet the technological demands of present-day production and innovation (see recommendations in Chapter 1);

- A labour market giving all enterprises proper access to such manpower (see recommendations in Chapter 3);
- The existence in each industrial sector of a market providing for a minimum degree of competition, without which there is no spur to excel and without which built-in advantages would have free rein, distorting the allocation of both financial and human resources.

Any improvement in these key areas would diminish the perceived need for corrective measures either by sectors or enterprises, and hence the risk inherent in any microeconomic measures. Experience has shown the difficulty of correcting distortions at this level without unwittingly creating others and thus being obliged to pile on measures to increasingly uncertain effect.

Promoting the quality of the overall environment and the competitive setting of industry hence amounts to relieving industrial policy of one of its most debatable and daunting tasks, namely that of compensating for the shortcomings of the financial market. But it is precisely because it is a prerequisite for success on other fronts that governments continue to deem it necessary.

The country-by-country analysis in the previous pages shows that the specific nature of national settings calls for some international differentiation in industrial policy objectives, in the policy instruments used and in how they are applied. What does clearly emerge, however, is that certain features are common to all policies that have proved effective and that, equally, a number of others would invariably seem to be a sure source of failure.

First, *industrial policy objectives must be realistic.* The prime imperative here is that they do not flout the rationale of comparative advantage. While admittedly the mix of such advantages may vary over time, notably under the impact of technical progress, this is no reason to give way to the lure of substantially overestimating governments' capacity to "create" such advantages wherever and whenever they so choose and to maintain costly protectionist measures in certain sectors, pending a hypothetical reversal of competitive positions.

Second, it is necessary to *avoid a proliferation of industrial policy objectives and hence a dilution of priorities.* This is vital to any policy evaluation and to ensure that the industrial policy measures are compatible in themselves as well as with measures on the economic and social front.

Third, the *combination of industrial and other policies must form a coherent whole.* It is important to clarify industrial as distinct from other policy objectives. Confusion of industrial and social policy objectives would seem to be undesirable.

Fourth, this does not imply that industrial policy should be defined without reference to its social implications. In framing industrial policy options, *there should be due consultation between all the parties concerned,* including the social partners, so that any accommodating social measures that may be needed can be put in hand as early as possible. If a sufficient social consensus can be constructed at the policy planning stage, the chances of success will be considerably enhanced.

Fifth, the more industrial policy decision-making and implementation is decentralised, the greater the effectiveness of this consultation. *Some degree of decentralisation, however small,* makes for easier policy appraisal, finer tuning and a fairer distribution of government aid.

Sixth, industrial policy often errs in its over-generosity towards the major enterprises, often to the advantage of the best-organised corporations, and not necessarily those that most need help. In many countries it is important that *government assistance be made more transparent, more accessible to small and medium-sized enterprises* and less subject to pressure by lobbies.

Seventh and finally, *policy evaluation procedures must be strengthened,* through recourse, wherever possible, to impartial arbitrators, especially when central government is itself a participant in the industrial competitive sector.

NOTES AND REFERENCES

1. See in particular, the study by Dore, R.P., *Structural Adjustment in Japan, 1970-1982*, International Labour Office, Geneva, 1986.

2. The recent trend in Japanese exports confirms that the effect of the rise in the yen on the competitiveness of Japanese products is inversely proportional to their degree of technological sophistication (see "High Technology Beats Yen; Other Industries Suffer", *The Japan Economic Journal*, 16th August 1986).

3. See the work by R. Vernon.

4. Proportion of personnel employed in R&D in 1981 (per thousand employees):

United States	6.2	United Kingdom	3.9
Japan	5.4	Norway	3.8
Germany	4.7	France	3.6

Source: OECD.

5. Between 2 and 3 per cent of the United States engineers and scientists move every year from universities to industry, or vice versa (as compared with only about 0.5 in France). In addition, industry makes a substantial contribution to the funding of university research, as well as awarding more research contracts and consultancy work than in other countries.

6. In the United States, over 15 000 firms have R&D laboratories, compared to only 1 500 in France and 800 in the United Kingdom.

7. Since the "birth rate" of firms is very high, the ideas neglected by major firms are more likely than in most other countries to be rapidly exploited by new companies.

8. Some of these markets are still not soundly established like, for example, the launch vehicle market (see OECD, *The Space Industry*, Paris, 1986). Several others depend greatly on national policies concerning deregulation/privatisation for survival, like the telecommunications market. See for example, the study on structural adjustment in telecommunications done in 1987 by the OECD Directorate for Science, Technology and Industry (DSTI).

9. The past and present importance of military research programmes in the development of sectors such as computers or semiconductors is well illustrated, e.g. by the work of Professor John Zysman, University of California, Berkeley. See also the recent study by Flamm, K., *Targeting Technology, National Policy and International Competition in Computers*, The Brookings Institution, Washington D.C., December 1985, and the work by F.R. Lichtenberg who recently estimated that 30 per cent of private R&D expenditure in the United States industrial sector in 1984 was linked to government, especially military orders (*cf.* NBER Working Paper No. 1974, July 1986).

10. See for example, Orléan, André, "L'insertion dans les échanges internationaux : Comparaison de cinq grands pays développés", *Economie et Statistique*, January 1986.

11. After a period of uncertainty in the early 1980s – when the temporary difficulties of adjustment in sectors such as mechanical engineering (especially the machine tool sector) were compounded by the effects of the world crisis in chemicals – German industry has improved its position by catching up on the technological progress of its mechanical and electrical engineering sectors.

12. The example of the car industry is obvious. More generally, as early as 1970 the unit value of 75 per cent of exports in the German mechanical engineering sector already exceeded the average, as compared with only about 35 per cent in France or the United Kingdom.

13. One such example is the apprenticeship and co-operative research system in the fragmented sector of mechanical engineering (see the analysis by Ergas, H. in *Does Technology Policy Matter?*, CEPS Paper No. 29, Centre for European Policy Studies, Brussels, 1986).

14. On the concept of the "poles of competitiveness", see in particular the analyses by Aglietta, M. and Boyer, R., "Pôles de compétitivité, stratégie industrielle et politique macro-économique", *CEPREMAP*, 1983, No. 8223.

15. The case of fine ceramics is typical, particularly because of the importance of its potential use in the car industry. Although efforts have recently been stepped up, German firms are still far behind their Japanese competitors, who hold a well-established position on the world market. They have a market share of about 50 per cent and have powerful research facilities to maintain this lead in the future.

Number of research personnel working in the fine ceramics industry (1983):

	Engineers	Technicians
Japan	2 000	2 000
United States	1 000	1 000-2 000
Europe	500	..
Canada	50-100	..

Source: M.K. Murthy Consultants International.

16. The major branches concerned are:
   - in Germany: metallurgy, mechanical engineering, land transport equipment, computers and office and precision equipment, electrical and electronics engineering, plastics and chemicals;
   - in Japan: the same, except for chemicals;
   - in the United Kingdom: non-metallic mineral products, metallurgy, mechanical engineering, rubber, plastics and chemicals;
   - in Italy: metallurgy and mechanical engineering;
   - in France: metallurgy and transport equipment.

17. When studying the inflation problem in the early 1970s, the OECD turned its attention to the increase in the number of bottlenecks in the productive system.

18. For example, growth is particularly sluggish in the area of capital equipment contracts for underdeveloped countries – an industry in which France holds a strong position.

19. See for example, Delattre, M., "Points forts et points faibles du commerce extérieur industriel", *Economie et Statistique*, July-August 1983.

20. The favourable trend in the Italian trade balance is drawing attention to the particularities of this country's specialisation structure. First, it is a hybrid one in that its trade pattern combines that of semi-industrialised countries (as shown by the importance of textiles to its trade balance) and that of the most developed countries. Second, more than all its European partners, Italy's imports are concentrated in its weak areas and its exports in its strong areas, which are more numerous than in all other European countries except Germany. Furthermore, for the purposes of international comparisons, it must be remembered that the United Kingdom's trade balance, which has been strongly affected by non-industrial factors such as North Sea oil, high oil prices and volatile exchange rates, is an unreliable indicator of industrial performance.

21. See on this subject the work by the Centre d'Etudes Prospectives et d'Informations Internationales (CE-PII).

22. See for example, the explanation in terms of "graded comparative advantages" proposed by B. Lassadrie-Duchêne and J.L. Mucchielli and contested by C. Clair, O. Gaussens and D.L. Phan (*cf. Revue Economique*, May 1979 and March 1984).

23. In addition to other factors (such as changes in exchange rates, or the tendency of forms to maximise their unit profits rather than increase their market shares, and particularly specialisation in lower-productivity sectors where prices tend to rise more quickly than in innovating sectors), the fact that France's export markets are less competitive probably partly explains why the deterioration in its terms of trade has been less marked than for other countries:

Trends in terms of trade (indexed, 1970 = 100)

	France	Germany	Italy	United Kingdom	EEC
1971-73	102.6	102.2	95.5	99.2	99.9
1974-79	94.5	94.7	80.8	87.8	89.6
1980-83	94.9	87.4	78.1	97.0	88.2

Source: EEC.

24. See the recent report by the OECD Committee for Scientific and Technological Policy on *Innovation Policy, France*, Paris, 1986.

25. The requirement for greater mobility between industrial sectors, between universities and industry, and between the public service and industry is essential, but also particularly difficult to achieve. It is necessary to reverse a trend, as is well illustrated in the case of France in a recent study by Cézard, M. and Rault, D., "La crise a

freiné la mobilité sectorielle", *Economie et Statistique*, January 1986.

26. For instance, in France and the United Kingdom, about 40 per cent of children leave the education system without any kind of certificate or qualification, against only 10 to 15 per cent in Germany and 20 per cent in the United States.

27. See Ergas, H., *op. cit.* in Note 13.

28. Firms in the most advanced countries tend to exploit their competitive advantage simultaneously at world level, and not sequentially on the basis of an implicit market hierarchy.

29. See Fuss, M. and Waverman, L., *The Japanese Productivity Advantage in Automobile Production – Can it be Transferred to North America?*, University of Toronto, September 1985.

30. Outward Processing Traffic is an extensive practice in Germany (particularly for trade with the GDR) and in the United States (for trade with Costa Rica, Honduras and Mexico).

31. According to the OEM scheme, an importer markets foreign products under his own trade mark on the basis of a long-term supply contract.

32. See Yoshimura, K., "The Friction of Convergence", *Journal of Japanese Trade and Industry*, 1986, No. 2.

33. For an interesting, although provocative, paper on this subject, see Reich, R. and Mankin, E., "Joint Ventures with Japan Give Away our Future", *Harvard Business Review*, March-April 1986.

34. See Joffre, P., "De la vente internationale au partenariat mondial", *Chroniques d'actualité de la SEDEIS*, 15th March 1986.

35. See Doz, Y., Hamel, G. and Prahalad, C.K., *Strategic Partnership: Success or Surrender; The Challenge of Competitive Collaboration*, INSEAD, London Business School, University of Michigan, 1986.

36. See Doz, Y., "Government Policies and Global Industries", in Porter, M.E., *Competition in Global Industries*, Harvard Business School Press, 1986.

37. Rather like the blend of Taylorism, Fordism and Keynesianism in the 1930s.

38. In some countries, for lack of private initiative, central governments have taken over certain economic or industrial functions (France, for example, does not have a particularly strong entrepreneurial tradition). Moreover, government implication in economic and industrial fields has sometimes simply been an extension of certain of its sovereign powers (for example, in the case of armaments and allied industries). Paradoxically, government involvement has also sometimes been due to the historic decline of some of those powers, rather as a firm with "a surfeit of managerial capacity" (to use C. Penrose's phrase) may find itself forced to diversify. This has occurred, especially, in the ex-colonialist countries (France, the United Kingdom), and in Japan, where the economic and industrial bureaucracy has in a way replaced the former military power structure.

39. See Weaver, R.K., *The Politics of Industrial Change*, The Brookings Institution, Washington D.C., 1985.

40. In 1965, Japan's GDP still amounted to no more than half the average for the OECD area as a whole, and only one-third that of the United States.

41. Contrary to general belief, direct financial assistance has never amounted to more than a very modest fraction of government aid. For example, subsidised loans by the Japan Development Bank accounted for only 1.4 per cent of total bank loans to the steel sector between 1961 and 1970 (3.8 per cent between 1971 and 1980), while in the electrical engineering industry (including computers and semiconductors) the corresponding figure was 0.7 per cent. In the late 1970s, when the latter industry made such a spectacular entry on the international scene, the Japanese Government was financing only about 7 per cent of total R&D expenditure in that sector. Another example is the automobile industry, which over the past 20 years has received neither tax concessions nor loans on special terms. See Tresize, P.H., "Industrial Policy is not the Major Reason for Japan's Success", *The Brookings Review*, Spring 1983.

42. See Crawvour, E.S., "The Tokugawa heritage" in Lockwood (ed.), *The State and Economic Enterprise in Japan*, Princeton University Press, 1965.

43. See Boltho, A., "Was Japan's Industrial Policy Successful?", *Cambridge Journal of Economics*, 1985, Vol. 9.

44. This explains certain general measures (comprehensive regulations on dismissal rights) and others more specific (industrial policies intended to slow job losses in certain sectors or enterprises).

45. As early as 1957, Germany passed legislation prohibiting cartels. This law was supplemented in 1973 by provisions controlling mergers and acquisitions. Germany was one of the first countries in Europe to adopt such legislation.

46. For example, in the textile industry, investment subsidies and low-interest loans by regional government agencies in 1980, 1982 and 1984 accounted respectively for 7.5 per cent, 8.8 per cent and 9.5 per cent of total investment costs. (See the recent DSTI study on textiles.)

47. Between 1965 and 1975, customs duties in the OECD area were, on average, halved (customs revenue as a percentage of import values fell from 6.8 per cent to 3.3 per cent).

48. For instance, in petrochemicals, production capacity had begun to far outpace demand by the end of the 1960s, although this was not generally realised at the time since general economic activity was so buoyant (see OECD, *Petrochemical Industry. Energy Aspects of Structural Change*, Paris, 1985).

49. See recent work on this subject by the OECD Industry Committee.

50. Federal subsidies, i.e. excluding transfers financed and executed by the territorial authorities.

51. See OECD, *Costs and Benefits of Protection*, Paris, 1985.

52. The wide international differences in electricity pricing policies for major industrial users also substantially affected competitiveness in various sectors, particularly non-ferrous metals (see for example, OECD, *Aluminium Industry. Energy Aspects of Structural Change*, Paris, 1983) and inorganic chemicals, e.g. chlorine.

53. See the many IEA studies on industrial energy saving.

54. See OECD, *Costs and Benefits of Protection, op. cit.* in Note 51.

55. For instance, financial transfers to industry in 1983, when government interventionism was at its height, were ten times larger in France (5.1 per cent of industrial value added) than in Switzerland (0.5 per cent). Moreover, transfers in Switzerland related almost entirely to export promotion costs.

56. For example, in Denmark, government aid as a proportion of industrial value added, after peaking at 5 per cent in 1982, was down to 2.6 per cent in 1983 and 2.9 per cent in 1984. In the United Kingdom, aid to shipbuilding and steel fell from £971 million in 1981/82 to £223 million in 1985/86; subsidies to the nationalised industries were also substantially reduced over the same period (for instance, aid to public sector enterprises under the authority of the Department of Trade and Industry was cut from £404 million to £115 million).

57. See also the report by the OECD Committee on Restrictive Business Practices, *Competition Policy and Deregulation*, June 1986.

58. Examples abound. Most European countries are taking the same road as the United Kingdom and proceeding to denationalise industrial assets in one way or another. In *France*, the new government plans to denationalise the five industrial concerns that were nationalised in 1982 and also to privatise in the longer run other enterprises that have long been in the public sector. In *Germany*, the government sold in 1984 its holdings in VEBA, the country's biggest industrial group. It also plans to privatise VIAG, which produces aluminium, chemicals and energy, and IVG, a firm whose many activities include an industrial engineering consultancy division. In *Italy*, a number of nationalised groups such as IRI and ENI have sold off a number of their interests since 1982. In the *Netherlands*, the government reviewed its holdings in 1985 and is expected to reduce some of them; it has already sold its shares in the steel firm Hoogovens. In *Austria*, the public corporation OIAG is being reorganised, and some of the companies it controls are to be sold to the private sector. In *Finland*, the government has sold part of Valmet, an engineering consultancy firm. In *Sweden*, the public corporation Procordia has sold off several companies to private buyers. In *Spain*, reorganisation of the INI portfolio has already resulted in the privatisation of certain firms, and the government has sold its majority shareholding in SEAT to Volkswagen. In *Turkey*, a major privatisation programme is also under way. (This short account is drawn from a United Kingdom Treasury study, *Privatisation Overseas*, Economic Programme Report, March-April 1986.)

59. See *OECD Economic Outlook*, December 1986, No. 40.

60. For example, in France some 80 per cent of financial aid in recent years has gone to the nine nationalised industrial groups. Moreover, the share of these nine groups in government procurement rose from 18.4 per cent in 1975 to 28.5 per cent in 1980.

61. See OECD, *Positive Adjustment Policies: Managing Structural Change*, Paris, 1983.

62. See Lawrence, R.Z., *Industrial Policy in the United States and Europe: Economic Principles and Political Practices*, Brookings Discussion Papers, November 1985, No. 41.

63. Out of 53 applications received since 1975, there have only been 13 requests for protectionist measures and six requests to help workers affected by a deterioration in trade.

64. Out of 30 sectors that have benefitted since 1954 from protection by the ITC, only two are still enjoying such protection today.

65. For a concise and impartial description, see Laumer, H. and Ochel, W., "Industrielle Strukturanpassung: das Japanische Modell", *IFO - Schnelldienst*, 26th October 1985.

66. In many capital-intensive countries and sectors, it has frequently been noted that the least profitable enterprises are unwilling to bear the brunt of a reduction in capacity from which others derive the benefit.

67. Twenty-two sectors or sub-sectors were pronounced eligible, among which the biggest employers were electrical steel mills, shipbuilding, cotton mills, synthetic fibres and basic petrochemicals.

68. See analysis of the issue in Ergas, H., *Does Technology Policy Matter?*, op. cit. in Note 13.

69. In 1983, government-funded research equalled 48.8 per cent of all research expenditure in France and almost 40 per cent in the United Kingdom, against 25.7 per cent in the United States.

70. Quite apart from the fact that the large number of participants in government programmes is itself an assurance of this dissemination, it is also fostered by certain statutory provisions or government practices (most of the major government agencies, such as NASA, have set up units to promote technological transfer; the *Patent Law Amendments Act* of 1980, allowing recipients of government contracts to take out patents, is helping to disseminate technologies by way of licensing).

71. It is striking that over ten years and in sectors as different as iron and steel and semiconductors, Japanese enterprises have managed to break into the world market during a cyclical trough, with their price flexibility standing them in good stead. The greater overall flexibility of Japanese industrial prices is brought out in D. Encaoua's study, "Price Dynamics and Industrial Structure: A Theoretical and Econometric Analysis", Working Paper No. 10, OECD, Paris, July 1983.

72. In computer science, for instance, the most spectacular German successes were not achieved by the "national front runner" (*cf*. Nixdorf).

73. The central government agencies delegate the detailed allocation of resources and the framing of specific programmes to industrial associations or co-operative research organisations. Hence the funds go to a wide range of firms and industries.

74. The few attempts by government to steer private demand so as to make it more responsive to supply-side policies have foundered, e.g. the French MECA plan in 1972 for numerically controlled machine tools.

75. See the study by Nelson, R.R., *High Technology Policies: A Five Nation Comparison*, American Enterprise Institute for Public Policy Research, Washington D.C., 1984.

76. Negative spin-off effects often result when government procurement policies giving preference to national suppliers are applied in government-controlled enterprises operating in a competitive sector.

I. MONETARY AND FINANCIAL ENVIRONMENT AND INDUSTRIAL ADJUSTMENT

Two monetary upheavals in the past fifteen years have had an impact on the course of industrial development in Member countries which, though major, is difficult to gauge exactly, so inextricably linked are the effects of specifically monetary factors and those of other determinants of the structural development of industry.

- With discontinuance of dollar/gold convertibility, the effects of which were magnified by the financial imbalances resulting from the first oil shock, there began a period marked by excess liquidity throughout the world, low real interest rates, big exchange rate savings, a rise in the overdraft economy and the acceleration of the inflationary process set in motion in the mid-1960s.
- This trend was reversed in 1979 with the move into an era of disinflation, marked in particular by the surge in real interest rates.

A. Inflation, overdraft economy and industrial adjustment

While the excess liquidity and inflation of the mid-1970s did on the whole offset the recessionary effects of the oil shock and the underlying decline in the economic profitability of industrial investment, the effect on the industrial adjustment process was adverse. This varied in degree, however, from one country to another, depending on the pace of inflation, exchange rate fluctuations and the particular characteristics of each national financial system.

1. Distortions

High inflationary expectations and strong incentives to finance investment through borrowing combined to distort the mechanisms of price formation and resource allocation.

- Inflation encouraged relative price changes which prompted a transfer of productivity surpluses from sectors exposed to international competition (mainly manufacturing) to sheltered sectors (mainly non-manufacturing) or oligopolistic sectors better able to raise their prices in response to increased costs, especially financial.
- The low level of real interest rates meant that they lost most of their effectiveness as a selection mechanism for financial resource allocation. With the break-even point for achieving positive leverage very low, the incentive to borrow was very strong. Accordingly, a growing proportion of investment resources were distributed on the basis of bank loan supply criteria. However, applying such criteria did not always facilitate rapid adjustment of industrial structures to the new conditions of supply and demand, banks often tending to favour the capital assets aspect to the detriment of entrepreneurial options, large firms rather than small- and medium-sized ones, etc. This, for example, is how the overdraft economy of the 1970s contributed to overinvestment in a number of heavy industry sectors which, some years later, found themselves weighed down by excess capacity.

- On the demand side, an important consequence of the development of the overdraft economy was that it was accompanied, in non-Member debtor countries, by a spectacular take-off in demand for imports of manufactures, especially civilian and defence capital goods. This acceleration in demand was sufficiently long-lived for there to have been a significant increase in the supply of these products in many Member countries, but sufficiently precarious in the long term for the industrial structures of those Member countries that had banked too heavily on these new outlets to be made more fragile as a result.

2. Differential effects between countries

The harmful effects just referred to were not felt everywhere to the same degree, the cost to industry in the countries where they were most severe having been heightened by the slippage in competitive positions that they helped to cause or accentuate. In this connection, the main distinguishing factors to be taken into account are the following: inflation differentials, productivity and wage trends, and the individual structural aspects of industrial financing channels.

- The adverse effect on industrial profitability of the unfavourable trend in relative prices was offset by favourable developments in productivity and wages, and also the strengthening of international price competitiveness resulting from the cumulative effect of the relative easing of industrial prices and the general rate of inflation – the case of the export sectors in Japan as of 1976.
- In countries such as Japan and Germany with the lowest inflation, real interest rates were considerably higher than elsewhere, with the result that the least economically profitable sectors/firms had little incentive to borrow.
- Broadly speaking, there was less borrowing in countries where, structurally, there is a marked propensity for self-financing, e.g. the United States, and/or the financial market is a prime source of external funding for industry, e.g. the United States or United Kingdom.
- Lastly, in the countries which traditionally have substantial recourse to bank borrowing, e.g. France, Italy and Japan, there are appreciable differences as to the nature and flexibility of bank/industry/government relations and also as to the degree of openness of the domestic capital markets to the influences of the international monetary environment. From this point of view, Japan is in a unique position and has been more successful than any other country in using debt as an instrument with which to underpin its medium- and long-term industrial strategy.

All in all, the monetary environment in the wake of the first oil shock, i.e. at a turning point in the contemporary history of industrial adjustment, tended in some countries to increase the stability of industrial structures, thereby contributing significantly to the initial build-up of an adjustment backlog which was to weigh heavily later on. In these countries, of which France and Italy are perhaps the most representative examples, a vicious circle formed between a variety of factors (high inflation/debt/bank conservatism/monetary depreciation) and this helped to perpetuate the pre-crisis resource allocation system[1]. Some years later, the lower contradiction between this homothetic growth in resources and non-homothetic demand growth was to become blatant.

In other countries, this vicious circle had one or more weak points which correspondingly lessened its adverse influence on the industrial adjustment process. For example, because it is not so open to the rest of the world, American industry has been less sensitive to exchange rate fluctuations than have its European counterparts. Moreover, its financing structures have remained notable for the relative importance of self-financing and, more generally, equity capital, with the result that it is less vulnerable to the short- and long-term implications of indebtedness.

A third group of countries – Germany, Japan, and Switzerland – have in common the appreciation of their currencies in the mid-1970s. All other things being equal, this appreciation has generated pressure for increased specialisation in sectors with comparative advantages[2] and, generally, has acted as an incentive to use part of the terms of trade gains to increase productivity in activities facing international competition, the slower pace of inflation having at the same time limited the extent to which these gains were appropriated by the sheltered sectors[3]. In the second half of the 1970s, industrial developments in Japan were particularly unusual. Contrary to what happened in most other countries, where the 1976 recovery resulted in an almost universal upturn in investment, in Japan it marked time until 1978, although the pattern across sectors did vary considerably. This is evidence of the fact that Japanese industry used this period to implement a far-reaching reorganisation of its structures which enabled it to move from one development path to another. Particular features of the latter were the slower growth rate which was more economical on capital and thus required a lower investment and profit rate. It is important to stress that industry's monetary and financial environment made a positive and significant contribution to this transition.

B. Disinflation and industrial adjustment

As of end-1979, the essential turning point in American monetary policy, a radical change took place in the monetary environment for industry in Member countries. After a final inflationary surge in 1980, prompted by the second oil shock, a new era began which, in contrast with the previous period, was marked by disinflation, high interest rates and the end of dollar undervaluation. This turnabout in trend directly affected the international conditions governing industrial adjustment, and this on three counts. In the first place, the rise in financial costs, coinciding with a cyclical fall in the profit ratio during the 1980-82 recession, made financial restructuring an absolute priority for many enterprises. Secondly, the scissors movement of rising interest rates and falling profitability of fixed capital appreciably reduced the incentive to invest in many Member countries. Thirdly, changes in exchange rates substantially altered the relative competitive positions of the main areas of industrial production.

1. The imperative of financial restructuring

With the rise of interest rates, the debt service burden weighed more heavily on operating results while at the same time – short-term in particular – was in some countries reaching levels such as to squeeze liquidity and limit the possibilities of external financing. Threatened with the simultaneous erosion of both their self-financing capacity and their ability to obtain external financing, the most heavily indebted firms had to strive to restore their financial situation by reducing their overall debt ratio (debt/equity) and improving their liquidity ratio (long-term capital/total liabilities), even at the risk of cutting into their investment potential in the short and medium term.

The manœuvre was less vital and/or easier in countries where industry had less debt, e.g. in the United States, where profit margin trends were more favourable because of the behaviour of unit labour costs[4] or because firms had proved more adept at gaining favourable market positions[5], and where the tax-take on industrial earnings was low, as in the United States[6]. Moreover, the deregulation, modernisation, and internationalisation of the capital markets in that country, which happened earlier and was more extensive than in the rest of the OECD area, broadened the range of financial options available to firms and at the same time reduced their cost in most cases.

In other countries, such as France for example, despite a number of government schemes aimed at putting firms' financial situations back on a sound footing[7], these have on the whole remained fragile and this vulnerability has without any doubt been an obstacle to adjustment thus far (see Graph 6A.1 showing the trend of the debt service burden and structure in a number of countries).

2. The effects on investment incentives

Apart from the impact on the availability and cost of industrial firms' financial resources, the steep rise in real interest rates has affected the trade-off between the various possible uses of these resources.

In one group of countries, foremost among which are the United Kingdom and Italy, for the first time in modern industrial history the rate of return on fixed capital has dropped on average to below the expected real interest rate (see Graph 6A.1)[8]. As a result, the preference for investment in financial rather than physical assets has increased (see Graph 6A.3) and greater priority is being given to rationalisation investment.

In countries such as Japan and the United States, asset yield differentials have on the whole not encouraged financial investments so much and, judging from the development and pattern of gross fixed capital formation in industry, seem not to have had such a significant impact on the composition of investment.

These general trends have varied at the sectoral level, in particular according to the relative level of the return on investment. Here again, the European countries clearly compare unfavourably with Japan and the United States, since the return on capital has in general been relatively lower in those sectors achieving strong growth at world level than in the average of the others.

All in all, as is evidenced by the buoyancy of investment in the United States and Japan, and as a number of recent studies have shown[9], it is not so much the rise in interest rates as the

Graph 6A.1. Change in the financial situation of enterprises[1]

FINANCING STRUCTURES OF ENTERPRISES DURING THE PERIOD 1971-1984[2]

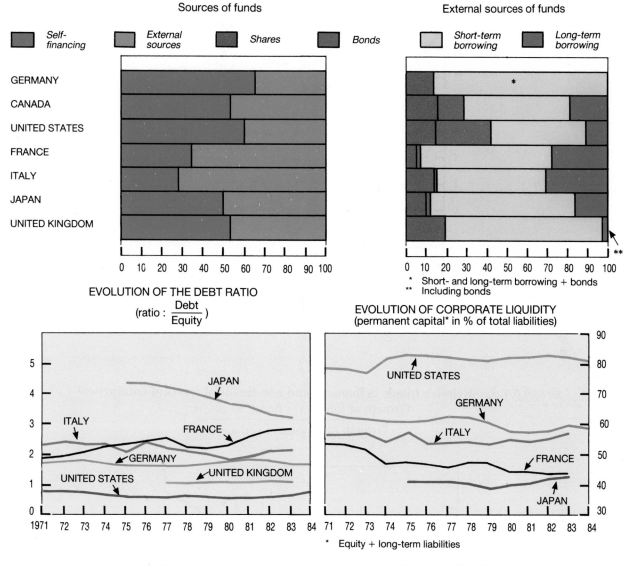

Sources of funds — External sources of funds

Self-financing | External sources | Shares | Bonds | Short-term borrowing | Long-term borrowing

GERMANY, CANADA, UNITED STATES, FRANCE, ITALY, JAPAN, UNITED KINGDOM

0 10 20 30 40 50 60 70 80 90 100

* Short- and long-term borrowing + bonds
** Including bonds

EVOLUTION OF THE DEBT RATIO

$$\text{(ratio : } \frac{\text{Debt}}{\text{Equity}}\text{)}$$

EVOLUTION OF CORPORATE LIQUIDITY
(permanent capital* in % of total liabilities)

* Equity + long-term liabilities

COST OF DEBT IN MANUFACTURING INDUSTRY IN JAPAN AND FRANCE
(financial costs in % of wages)

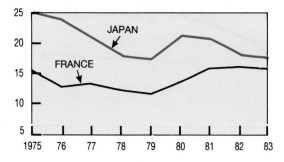

Notes: 1. Germany, Canada, United States, Italy: non-financial enterprises;
France, Japan: manufacturing enterprises;
United Kingdom: large manufacturing enterprises.
2. 1979-1982 for France and Italy; 1975-1983 for Japan; 1977-1983 for the United Kingdom.
Source: OECD financial statistics.

Graph 6A.2. **EEC: net rate of return on capital invested and real long-term interest rate**
(%)

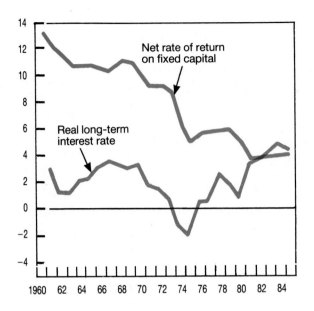

Sources: Bundesministerium für Wirtschaft (Bonn), EEC.

Graph 6A.3. **Relative trends in financial and non-financial assets of enterprises[1]**

$$\left(\text{ratio: } \frac{\text{Growth of long-term financial assets}}{\text{Growth of physical fixed assets}}\right)$$

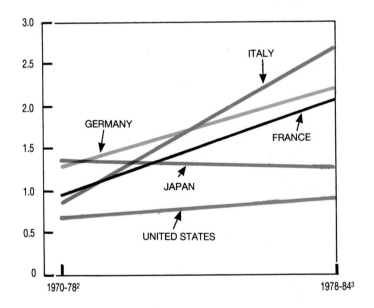

1. See Note (1) of Graph 6A.1.
2. 1975-1978 for Japan.
3. 1978-1983 for France, Italy and Japan.
Source: OECD financial statistics.

Table 6A.1. Gross return on capital stock, 1980-1981

Index 100 for industry as a whole

	High-growth sectors	Total
EEC	71	100
United States	104	100
Japan	108	100

Source: EEC.

erosion of investment yields that has curbed industrial momentum in some Member countries. The main consequence of the rise in interest rates has been to magnify the intersectoral and international effects of yield differentials.

3. Changes in competitive positions

With the spectacular recovery of the dollar in 1981, the process of adjustment to the second oil shock differed from that which followed the first in one important respect. The international competitiveness of American industry was hit, as was reflected in the deterioration in the trade balance, but it did also encourage more active redeployment of resources to activities less sensitive to price competition, especially those with a large innovation content. Thanks to the undervaluation of its currency, Japan was able to reap the benefits of its early adjustment which had been facilitated during the 1970s by the appreciation of the yen. In other countries the effects were more mixed, the recessionary consequences of the higher oil bill resulting from the dollar appreciation tending to outweigh other factors. It is true for example that, except in certain specific sectors such as chemicals, the effect of the improvement in many Member countries' industrial competitiveness vis-à-vis the United States turned out to be slight because of the relatively limited amount of trade with that country and its content (large proportion of high technology products whose competitiveness is not so much determined by prices), and also because Japan's advance often more than wiped out the gains made in the framework of trade with the United States.

To sum up, two main lessons can be drawn from the above.

First, even if latterly industry's monetary and financial environment has tended to become more uniform throughout the OECD area – in particular because of widespread disinflation and the fact that the terms on which funds can be obtained have become more similar as a result of the internationalisation and deregulation of capital markets – over the past 15 years it has generally been sufficiently dissimilar across countries to be one, by no means negligible, explanation for the differences in the pace and course of industrial adjustment at international level.

Secondly, among the many factors that have made industry better able to take advantage of the monetary environment, or mitigate its adverse effects, the structure and working of its financing system would appear to be of special importance. This leads on to a more general comment to the effect that the increased pressure for adjustment has served to reveal the varying structural propensities of domestic financing systems to accelerate back-up or inhibit industrial change. Some have proved able to create both the incentive for such changes and

also the necessary financial resources. Others have however tended rather to act as a force of inertia, encouraging the preservation of existing structures, and the defects of these systems have undoubtedly been one of the objective reasons for the increase in government intervention.

C. The efficiency of industrial financing systems: an international comparison

The network and nature of the channels through which a proportion of saving is allocated to industrial development have always differed substantially across countries. Although the details of and reasons for these differences do not fall within the compass of the present chapter, it is nonetheless essential to consider whether these various financing methods are still as efficient, in the new context of industrial adjustment, as they were in the 1950s and 60s. There are many reasons for thinking that this has not been the case in a number of countries where, consequently, financial reform needs to be one of the first priorities of policies designed to promote industrial adjustment.

International differences in industrial financing methods relate to the propensity for self-financing, the range of the financial markets (equities, bonds, venture capital), the extent of recourse to bank lending, the strength and nature of the links between industry and banks, and the degree of government influence on the financial system. Countries may be divided into three broad categories.

The first includes those countries, such as the United States or the United Kingdom, where the self-financing rate is relatively high, the financial markets are very developed and are a prime source of firms' external funding[10], banks have a comparatively limited role in the framework of unstructured relations with industry[11], and the government has very little direct influence on how financial intermediaries decide to allocate funds. The second group comprises countries such as Japan, Germany, and Sweden, where self-financing is considerable, the financial markets are smaller[12], banks traditionally play a vital role in the framework of close relations with fund users[13] and where also, in the case of Japan, the government has a marked influence on the way the financial system allocates funds to industry[14]. Lastly, in a third group comprising France and Italy in particular, a chronic lack of equity capital (explained by the low rate of self-financing and the narrowness of the financial markets) is offset by substantial borrowing from financial intermediaries that are closely constrained by government directives but do not have close structural relations with industry.

Closer examination reveals a number of other individual features which allows still finer distinctions to be drawn. By comparison for example with their British counterparts, American financial intermediaries are more numerous and more decentralised, less attracted towards the international financial market and more inclined to enter into long-term commitments with industry. A distinction also needs to be made between Japan and Germany. Bank/industry relations in Japan are part of a unique system of contractual relations which largely take the place of the transactions between independent entities that are typical of the market economy, and which bind together manufacturers, suppliers, customers and financiers; these relations are at their closest and most solid within the "keiretsu"[15]. In contrast with the situation in Germany, moreover[16], bank loans to industry are mainly short-term but are almost systematically refinanced. From the firms' point of view, this reduces financial uncertainty while at the same time maintaining interest rate flexibility and so avoiding the collection of financial rents from industry during periods of disinflation.

The relative merits of the various financing systems can be gauged by first of all examining the general influence they have exercised on industrial structures; and then by assessing their capacity to contribute positively to the two types of structural adjustment that have been commonest in recent years: the restructuring of firms in difficulty on the one hand; and the development of activities with high growth potential on the other.

1. The effects on industrial structures

In some countries the financial environment has been one of the factors encouraging the abnormal development of industrial structures, typified by excessive concentration in a number of sectors, corresponding to forms of integration/diversification – notably of the conglomerate variety – that are not as advantageous as schemes dictated purely by considerations of economic efficiency. This phenomenon has been particularly prominent in a number of European countries, particularly France and the United Kingdom. It may be interpreted in some degree as a response on the part of industrial structures to the shortcomings of certain markets, in particular capital markets[17].

2. The rescue of firms in difficulty

In all countries in recent years the acceleration of industrial change has caused acute adjustment problems in certain firms which it would have been socially unacceptable to allow to close down, so serious would the external effects have been. Hence the need for emergency aid, including some in the form of government intervention. Some of the most significant examples in this respect are to be found in the automobile industry, and analysis[18] shows that the types of solution arrived at, their cost and the way this is split between the various parties concerned (shareholders, employees, banks, and taxpayers), have largely depended, inter alia[19], on the particular features of the financial environment of the firms in question[20].

Over and above the specific features of each concrete example, financing the restructuring of firms in difficulty poses a major general problem - the possibility of imperfections in the capital market. When for various reasons bankruptcy is not considered an acceptable solution, part of the benefits of renewal investment, in particular the increase in the firm's market value, will go not to the party that financed it but to earlier investors, including those whose bad decisions are the cause of the difficulties[21]. As a result, the flow of capital for the revitalisation of firms in difficulty will tend to be less than optimal and government intervention may seem inevitable. However, the Japanese example shows that certain types of co-operation between private parties, and especially between banks and industry, may spare the need for this kind of intervention and thus avoid the concomitant risks, e.g. distortion of the mechanisms of competition in the sector concerned, lack of efficiency owing to the difficulty of maintaining the right balance between the need to supervise the use of public funds and the need to avoid excessive administrative interference in private management decisions, etc.

3. Financing new activities

With regard to the capacity of financial systems to contribute effectively to the development of new activities with a high technology content, here too it would seem that there are major differences across countries which partly explain the differences in industrial performance. The systems – the American and the Japanese – which represent two virtually opposite philosophies regarding relations between productive and financial activities, seem for different reasons to be the systems that offer industry the greatest advantages.

In the United States, the large and buoyant stock market and abundant supply of venture capital encourage the setting up of new firms. By making the threat of new market entrants credible, the system forces existing firms to be more competitive. Moreover, by offering a wide range of opportunities for the sale or purchase of firms, it limits the dangers inherent in diversification by reducing the exit barriers[22].

In Japan, where the market for the sale and purchase of firms is by contrast very limited and where there is less venture capital available, the financial infrastructures have other characteristics which compensate for this relative deficiency. The development of new activities, mainly through the diversification of existing firms and the creation of new ones within the general framework of subcontracting or contractual relations between suppliers/producers/customers, has the benefit of dependable financial support organised by banks linked structurally to the groups concerned and backed by the Japanese Government using its influence selectively with respect to bank loan allocations. Inter-bank links and links between banks and government institutions spread the risks incurred by lenders ("multi-umbrella system"), and so reduce their inhibitions as regards high risk projects, particularly the most innovative ones[23]. Lastly, it should be noted that not only does their financial environment encourage Japanese firms to engage in profitable activities, it also favours an entry strategy which attaches priority to winning long-term market shares.

In most other OECD countries, the picture is more mixed. Of those where the financing system is akin to the American model, not one has a financial market with the drive and staying power of the American market. In particular, the effect of changes in the supply of funds, with the constant increase in the number of financial institutions having a marked preference for safe investments as a source of steady income, is felt all the more in that the latter are not counterbalanced by the same vigorous growth in new instruments for financing innovation – particularly venture capital – that the United States has witnessed. In countries where there are close links between banks and industry, these links do not guarantee adequate funding for innovative projects to the same extent as in Japan, inasmuch as they only concern firms of a certain size, and are not therefore part of the close-knit network of inter-firm relations that exists within the pyramid shaped structure peculiar to Japanese groups. Lastly, some countries combine the drawbacks of an inadequate financial market and of banking channels that have failed to adjust.

4. Conclusion

In terms of both structures and the way it operates, the capacity of the financing system to underpin effectively the industrial adjustment process has varied considerably across countries, and the efforts many countries have made to overhaul the system have not so far succeeded in stopping this possible source of comparative disadvantage. Being unable really to eliminate the deficiencies of the capital market, governments have generally tended over the past fifteen years to tolerate and try to counteract them by means of direct financial intervention – with arguable results. It is worth noting in this connection that countries cannot be singled out by virtue of having an interventionist tradition or otherwise: Japan, together with the United States, is the country where government/industry financial transfers have been least substantial. Without underestimating the role played by the Japanese Government in allocating funds to industry, it has to be stressed that it has basically been indirect and non-discretionary, taking place in the framework of close triangular co-operation between government and private banking and industrial entities. In contrast, the weaknesses of financial infrastructures are measured in many countries by reference to the substantial financial assistance granted to industry over many years. However, government assistance does not seem to have been as effective as the most efficient financial systems operating in certain rival countries. It follows that, if the structural adjustment process is to be given a free reign, many Member countries – particularly in Europe – will have to step up their efforts to modernize and adjust their financial channels (see Chapter 4). Amongst the considerations attaching to financial reform, however, it is also important that due priority be given, alongside macroeconomic constraints (such as balance of payments equilibrium, public deficit, financing, etc.), to the need for efficiency in financing the productive sectors, especially industry.

II. TECHNOLOGICAL DEVELOPMENT AND INDUSTRIAL ADJUSTMENT

Industry is both the main source and the first point of impact of the wave of innovation in recent years[24]. The force of the latter has been such as to undermine several of the pillars which supported the dynamic equilibrium of industry in previous decades.

Whether the scale or "revolutionary potential" of this wave of innovation has been greater than in earlier periods of modern economic history is a question that will probably remain a matter of debate for a long time, if it ever receives a definitive answer. Therefore, in the present context it is of greater import to ask a question of more limited scope: how and why does technical change, in its current phase, interact in new ways, on the national and international plane, with the other forces of change at work in industry?

As in the past, during the recent decade technological innovation has been one of the main driving forces of economic change, and particularly of industrial change; however, on account of the modifications that have taken place in its content and in the manner of its generation and application, it has tended to play a qualitatively different, and in many respects completely new, role compared with that in earlier periods of economic development. This has obviously altered the conditions in which consistency between policies, industrial structures and corporate strategies are sought.

The links between growth and innovation can be perceived more clearly at the microeconomic level of the firm, or of the industry, than at a more aggregated level. This is due primarily to the difficulty involved in defining conceptually and/or measuring statistically the innovation effort and its results[25]. It also stems from the fact that innovation takes various forms (product/process, major/minor innovation), is disseminated via various channels and sometimes has conflicting effects on several mechanisms of growth (demand, productivity, international and intersectoral competitiveness). In addition, it is somewhat arbitrary to seek to establish an order of one-to-one casual relationships between phenomena that are closely interrelated; the explanatory factors of innovation are for a large part the very factors, the changes in which are supposed to show the impact of innovation.

It is thus not surprising to find that the numerous attempts made to isolate and quantify the role of innovation in the overall process of industrial growth have, by and large, been disappointing inasmuch as they have been unable to provide clear-cut empirical data that would make it possible, once and for all, to get beyond theoretical postulates or personal convictions[26]. More than ten years after, it is still possible to subscribe to the opinion of R. Gilpin: "Unfortunately, although economists have come to recognise the importance of innovation for economic growth, the economic theory of innovation is still in its infancy"[27], insofar as the sometimes substantial progress that has been made at the microeconomic level[28] has still not been incorporated successfully into macro- or mesoeconomic analysis of structural change and growth. At best, the ability of this analysis to throw light on policy choices, particularly in respect of support for R&D, thus remains limited; at worst, it is highly questionable, when it creates a dangerous confusion between highly imperfect tools of analysis of economic interrelationships, and concepts for policy formulation.

A. Innovation and industrial adjustment: new conditions of interaction

Given the shortcomings of the analytical framework and the empirical data, it is difficult to give due weight to the technological dimension of industrial change, in the formulation of policy. A prerequisite for this is a correct qualitative assessment of the reasons for innovation being a catalyst of development which, although it is not perhaps intrinsically more active than in the past, now operates and is produced in new ways.

This stems mainly from the fact that some contemporary flows of innovation feed through to the entire production system, often radically reshaping methods of production and the terms of competition. The past 15 years have seen the rapid development, and an increase in the number of applications, of information and communications technology. This has led to the emergence of new industrial sectors, whose extremely fast growth has partly offset the decline of some traditional industries. Also, and perhaps most significantly, the way in which most manufacturing industry operates has been affected, and in some cases it has been radically transformed.

1. The emergence of new sectors

The *direct* impact of the development of the new information and communications technology sectors on the overall level of industrial activity, and thus on the supply of industrial jobs, should not be overestimated. True, they have grown very rapidly, but the scale of their operations remains fairly small, even in those countries that have been at the forefront of their development.

Table 6A.2. **Output of information technology industries, 1984**
In billion 1983 dollars

	Value of output	As percentage of GNP
United States	164	1.4
Japan	86	2.3
Germany	21	1.3
United Kingdom	15	0.9
France	14	1.1
Italy	8	0.9
Canada	5	0.3
Switzerland	3.6	0.6
Sweden	3.3	1.1
Australia	1	0.5

Sources: McKintosh Yearbook; OECD.

The same remark is also valid for other new sectors, such as new materials, as shown by the following data for the country that is probably the most advanced in this field – Japan.

Table 6A.3. **Output of new and conventional materials**
Billion yen

	1983	Projection for 1990	Annual growth 1983-1990
1. New materials[1]	1 021	3 200	18.0
2. Conventional materials[2]	65 985	79 700	3.0
1/2 (%)	1.5	4.0	

1. Fine ceramics, engineering plastics, new metals, composite materials.
2. Steel, non-ferrous metals, ceramics, chemicals, textiles, pulp and paper products.
Source: IBI; MITI.

At a more general level, analysis of the trend of sectoral shares, ranked by R&D intensity, in the value of industrial output, confirms that technological advances do not *directly* produce a major change in the structure of industry.

2. The impact on existing sectors

Although the face of industry has not been as radically changed by the growth of new technology sectors as is

Table 6A.4. **Composition of manufacturing output**
In percentages

	High R&D intensity		Medium R&D intensity		Low R&D intensity	
	1970	1983	1970	1983	1970	1983
United States	14.9	16.6	31.7	30.8	53.2	52.5
Japan	14.4	16.2	32.2	34.1	53.2	49.6
Germany	12.3	12.8	32.2	40.7	51.9	46.4
France	10.6	12.7	28.5	33.8	60.8	53.5
United Kingdom	12.5	11.4	29.7	28.1	57.6	60.4
Italy	11.7	10.9	28.6	32.2	59.4	56.8
Belgium	6.8	7.0	30.3	37.1	62.8	55.7
Netherlands	13.2	12.5	19.6	25.4	67.1	62.0
Australia	7.3	7.2	29.2	35.4	63.3	57.2
Canada	8.6	7.1	28.3	32.1	62.9	60.6
Finland	3.6	4.9	18.7	18.8	77.6	76.1
Norway	5.9	5.9	21.3	25.5	72.7	68.5
Sweden	9.8	9.8	27.0	29.1	63.1	61.0

Source: OECD.

sometimes imagined, the way industry functions has been changed far more than is usually realised by the application of new technology across virtually the whole spectrum of existing industries[29]. The new flows of generic innovation, particularly in information and communications technology, coupled with the technical progress in each sector, allow industry to broaden the technological base of process and product design. Via the creation of new "vectors" that apply and disseminate the new technology, e.g. CAD/CAM, robotics, the new base can be exploited rapidly on a wide scale. This often results in a complete remodelling of methods of production, and in corresponding changes in the industrial structure and in the terms of competition at national and international level. The most significant features of the current phase of technological change that should be taken into account in policy formulation appear to be the following.

3. A new pattern of generation and diffusion of innovation

The sectoral pattern of sources of "primary" innovation, and the intersectoral dynamics of the generation and dissemination of innovation, have changed. Electronics and closely related sectors, such as that of scientific instruments, account for an increasing share of industrial innovation, taking over from sectors such as the chemicals and engineering industries in which the major technological breakthroughs took place in the 1950s and 60s. New intersectoral technological links have also been established in a context of growing technological interdependence between industrial activities[30]. The birth of "mechatronics" in the mid-1970s out of the merging of innovation from four separate sectors (mechanical engineering, precision engineering, electrical engineering, and electronics and communications), is no doubt the most striking example of the new multisectoral poles of "secondary" innovation which play an increasing role in the process of development/dissemination/adaptation and application of "primary" innovation[31].

A vital prerequisite for the technological progress of industry is thus the growth of innovation "clusters"[32], such as those now being formed around information, communications and automation technologies; not only do they give an impetus to the development of the most innovative sectors, but they also, when the intersectoral transmission mechanisms are functioning properly, catalyse technological adjustment throughout the economy by stimulating innovation in supplier sectors and over an increasingly wide spectrum of user sectors[33].

However, this should not be taken to mean that it is possible to single out "leading-edge" sectors, and that by promoting them individually the overall level of technology will be ratchetted up more or less automatically and the range of industrial activities will be widened. The dynamism of the innovation process hinges increasingly on the intensity and the quality of the interaction between productive sectors and user sectors[34]. Furthermore, while it is true that the intersectoral network of generation and dissemination of innovation comprises some strategic nodes, they are not always upstream from the dissemination process[35]; and also their importance changes over time for reasons that it is difficult for governments to take account of in forward planning, since it depends on the way a large number of actors in a large number of sectors perceive constantly changing technological opportunities.

4. The rapidity of technical progress

With the increase in the number of sources of innovation, the technology front is moving forward more and more rapidly in a growing number of sectors, as a result of which the costs and risks involved in R&D investment[36], together with the uncertainty for potential users, are increasing. The trend to shorter technological life cycles has, in particular, speeded up the rate of obsolescence in the existing stock of physical and human capital, especially in highly specialised manufacturing equipment; as a result, it has become more worthwhile economically to introduce modular and flexible plant in many sectors. In addition, on account of the uncertainty that it creates amongst users, in a given geographical area the propensity to innovate may not be matched by a similar propensity to adopt the innovation rapidly. In other words, uncertainties about the trend of technology may sometimes inhibit the decisions of users the more closely located they are to the innovator. It has been proved empirically that this happens in some sectors[37]. Although one should not generalise, this does at least show that the control of innovation does not always constitute an advantage for disseminating technology at national level.

5. The internationalisation of technological development

Technological factors both operate in a context of the internationalisation of production and help to create it. In addition to the intersectoral dimension of technological interdependence, there is thus an international and transnational dimension that is becoming increasingly important. This is shown indirectly by the increasing number of international patent applications since the late 1970s[38], and directly by the multinational origin of the components of most high technology products[39]. There are several reasons for this trend.

The first is that the multidisciplinary and multisectoral nature of innovation, the increasing costs and risks involved in R&D, and the global scale of its commercial application make transborder co-operation agreements between firms indispensable[40] (see Table 6A.5); moreover, such agreements are encouraged by intergovernmental initiatives, e.g. EUREKA, ESPRIT, etc. The second reason, which is related to the first, is

Table 6A.5. **Inter-firm co-operation agreements[1], 1982-1985**

	Number	Percentage	
	A. INTRA- AND INTER-AREA PRODUCTION AGREEMENTS		
Intra-area			
EEC	134	14	38
United States	236	24	
Inter-area			
EEC - United States	253	26	
EEC - Japan	81	8	62
United States - Japan	128	13	
With other areas	142	15	
Total	974	100	
	B. PURPOSE OF AGREEMENTS		
Technology transfer	165	16.9	43.1
Integration of R&D activities	254	26.2	
Integration of production	156	16.0	
Supply agreements	55	5.6	
Distribution and marketing agreements	272	27.9	56.9
Other	72	7.4	
Total	974	100	

1. Agreements concluded between firms in the most advanced industrialised countries (excluding East European countries, but including the NICs of South-East Asia and China) in the electronics, computer, telecommunications, aerospace, scientific instruments and pharmaceuticals sectors.
Source: FOR/Montedison.

that to remain technologically competitive, many firms are obliged to strengthen their multinational operations in order to keep close track of, and exploit rapidly, the technological opportunities that arise.

Other reasons relate to the international conditions of, not production, but the dissemination of innovation. In this respect, it should be noted that the growing dependence of firms on external technology sources does not show up clearly in the overall trend of the standard indicators of the intensity of international trade in technology[41], since it is accompanied by a shift in the relative importance of the various channels of international diffusion of technological know-how. In particular, transactions outside, or on the fringe of, the market proper are increasing, especially those involving direct investment and inter-firm co-operation agreements, because corporate strategies for technological development and for reaping the economic benefits of innovation have evolved.

Also, a growing share of technology transfer implicitly comes under international trade in manufactured products. High technology trade is expanding much more rapidly than

Table 6A.6. **Growth of international high technology trade in the OECD area[1]**

1970-1983: Annual growth rate in value

Exports of high technology products	15.1
Total manufacturing exports	13.1
Demand of high technology products	10.8

1. Canada, United States, Japan, Australia, Germany, Belgium, France, Italy, Netherlands, United Kingdom, Finland, Norway, Sweden.
Source: OECD.

average manufacturing trade, and especially much more rapidly than world demand for high technology products (see Table 6A.6). As a result, competition has stepped up in the high technology sectors, to the benefit of user industries. Provided that the latter have the financial, technical and managerial ability to apply the new technologies wisely, they can hope to strengthen their competitive position, and in consequence their earnings may quite possibly exceed those that the sectors with higher R&D intensity earn from their technology rents in domestic and foreign markets[42].

6. New conditions of appropriability of innovation

The conditions under which R&D funded and performed by industrial firms, universities and/or government agencies is exploited commercially, have changed. The inter-firm, inter-sectoral and international pattern of the economic gains made possible by technical progress – which should continue to provide an incentive to innovate while encouraging the dissemination of innovation – has shifted in the past ten years, as a result of two main factors.

First, the rapidity of technical change, the increase in the number of actors with a level of know-how close to that of innovators, and the accelerating pace of dissemination of scientific and technological information, have considerably shortened the period during which a firm can hope to exploit a purely technological superiority commercially without at least having to share the technology rent with some competitors. Note that except in a few sectors, such as chemicals and pharmaceuticals, firms can do little about this trend, since patents and other forms of protection of technological property, e.g. trade secrets, are highly ineffective[43].

Second, on account of the shorter technological life cycle of products, rising R&D costs have to be recouped more rapidly. Command of the most advanced mass production techniques and the ability to market output rapidly in large markets, often on a world scale, are more and more a prerequisite for reaping the benefits of innovation, in a continually expanding range of activities and at an increasingly earlier point of the product life cycle[44]. Innovative firms that do not have this capability to the same degree as their competitors or trading partners are inevitably forced to forfeit all or part of the technological rent[45].

It does seem that in recent years the ability of firms to manufacture advanced products has been one of the most important factors that have reshaped international competition in the industrial field, because it has determined their capacity to transform a potential advantage in new product design into a position of lasting market strength.

This trend obviously creates problems when, contrary to the assumptions of the orthodox theory of comparative advantage, manufacturing expertise tends to be geographically concentrated. The resulting channeling of technological rents to specific areas accentuates trade imbalances and may eventually weaken and distort the innovation process at international level[46]. The firms/countries that have a "sovereign" manufacturing know-how – which grows by the cumulative effects of learning, scale and sectoral cross-fertilization – seem well placed to continue to "internalise externalities" at an increasingly rapid rate and at decreasing cost, and thereby to take an even larger share of the value added made possible by technical progress in an ever-growing number of activities; in contrast, competitors tend to be relegated to design, assembly and marketing functions[47].

Such a widening of the differentials in performance would inevitably increase the strains on the multilateral framework of trade; however, it can be avoided. The prerequisite for achieving a new international equilibrium is further modernisation of production in most OECD countries; this can be facilitated by stepping up international transfers of manufacturing know-how by means of direct investment or co-operation agreements between firms.

B. Impact on the structure and functioning of the industrial system

For the broad reasons set out above, technological change is modifying – sometimes in spectacular fashion, at other times more subtly – the functioning of many of the mechanisms that govern structural change in industry. A thorough rethinking of industrial analysis, and thus of the industrial policy it is supposed to inform, is therefore required.

1. The new pattern of industry

Technical progress shifts, blurs or makes more porous a number of the conventional boundaries between industries. As a result, selective policies directed at specific sectors may prove difficult to frame, since it is not easy to focus measures on an area whose boundaries are becoming less clear-cut and liable to shift a great deal as time goes on.

i) New links between industry and services

Technical progress is transforming the nature of the relationship between manufacturing industry and the service sector, as a result of which they are becoming increasingly complementary. Indeed, it is one of the major causes of the growing service content of manufactured goods[48], sometimes referred to as the "dematerialisation of products"; at the same time it promotes the "industrialisation" of services. For manufacturing industry, this "industrialisation" has numerous positive aspects since it improves quality and the variety of specialised services offered, creates external economies at a broader level, and widens the market for many products, especially those with a high innovation content[49].

ii) A more relative concept of maturity

Within the manufacturing sector, the boundary line between mature sectors and growth sectors has become increasingly difficult to draw. When framing policy, the very concept of maturity should be treated with extreme caution, since technological change is weakening considerably this bipolar structure of industry. First, the extremely rapid pace of technical progress gives rise to hybridisation in some sectors; the same family of products may thus exhibit simultaneously the features of both mature and growth industries. The semiconductor industry is probably the most obvious example of this[50]. Second, the application of new technologies coupled with other forms of innovation, allows some long-established sectors to be revitalised.

It is important, however, to be clear about what this means. It is very seldom that an injection of new technology suffices to remove the ageing symptoms of the oldest industries. As a rule, it is powerless by itself to reverse the underlying trends of demand when they reflect a growing saturation of markets. On the other hand, it can have a major impact on the conditions of supply, by enabling the competitiveness of traditional industrial areas to be restored, or by stopping it from declining further[51]. It would however be hazardous to conclude that adjustment is always facilitated by speeding up modernization, and particularly by the provision of government incentives. In those sectors in which excess capacity is the major adjustment problem, excessive incentives to carry out modernization may increase the mismatch between supply and demand still further[52].

iii) New boundaries within industry

In addition, technical progress exerts both a centripetal and centrifugal effect on a sector's structure. Technological change sometimes increases interaction between sectors to such a degree that it results in the virtual merger of activities that were formerly separate. It is for this reason that it has become difficult to draw a clear-cut line between telecommunications and computers, and that it is increasingly questionable whether it is possible to adopt a separate policy approach for each of them. Conversely, technical progress can initiate a process of specialisation that accentuates the differentiation of industrial structures. Thus, the software industry has emerged partly as a result of the progressive withdrawal of users and hardware manufacturers from software design[53].

2. Changes in modes of production

In most industrial sectors, technological advances have led to changes in methods of production that reflect a radical remodelling of organisational and economic principles. In particular, it has changed the quantity and quality of factors of production required for industrial development, and the way in which industrial structures respond to the pressures of their environment, including those from government.

i) New modes of production

Indeed, the emergence of new technologies did not initiate, but rather removed the impediments to, speeded up and disseminated the process of change in methods of production that had started in the 1960s, but which had come up against several obstacles, not the least of which were the limits of the technology of the time. The production system came under increasing strain as a result of the contradiction that had arisen between, on the one hand, the new pattern of demand calling for product diversification and shorter product lifespans[54] and, on the other, the prevailing type of production organisation resulting from the extension and internationalisation of assembly line and taylorist scientific management methods, geared to the mass production of undifferentiated products which were marketed for local, homogeneous and supply-dominated markets. The existing methods of production found it difficult to respond to the change in general economic conditions after the first oil shock, especially to the new pattern of slower and less stable demand; they thus received their death blow at the very moment when technological breakthroughs were making it possible to renew them. Since then, new methods of production based on a new generation of technology (see Table 6A.7), and more closely integrated with the other economic functions of the firm than before, have been introduced in most sectors, especially in the processing and assembly industries[55].

In consequence, some of the "iron laws" underpinning

Table 6A.7. **Industrial electronics sales in the United States, 1981-1986**

In million dollars

	1981	1982	1983	1986[1]
Numerical control systems	198.5	265.0	371.7	998
Automated test equipment	969.3	1 108.6	1 421.1	2 676
Measurement systems	197.7	239.6	269.1	394
Process control equipment	1 288.6	1 481.0	1 604.1	2 529
Computerised energy management equipment	440.5	571.2	721.3	1 550
Industrial robots	191.2	217.1	290.2	537
CAD systems	312.4	450.9	744.6	1 801

1. Estimates.
Source: Electronics.

industrial adjustment strategies in the 1950s and 60s ceased to be relevant, or at least they now operate less inflexibly. In particular, in many sectors the trend over past decades to a larger and larger minimum economic size of production unit was halted, and in some cases even reversed[56]; the use of flexible, multi-purpose plant coupled with modular product design, on the principle of postponed differentiation, allowed strategic objectives that before were often incompatible to be reconciled. It has become possible to seek simultaneously economies of scale and product differentiation, as well as quality and low costs. In addition, the adoption of modern forms of production organisation, and of computerised management of flows and stocks of raw materials, semi-finished and finished products, making possible lower production and marketing costs, influences the way industry responds to changes in final demand, and thus the impact of macroeconomic policies of demand management.

ii) The impact on industrial organisation

The impact on the organisation of industry has been considerable. Firms have implemented new technology and production policies which have reshaped many sectors[57]. By concentrating exclusively on a few high technology industries, e.g. aerospace or pharmaceuticals, there is a tendency to over-emphasize the fact that technological change, by raising steeply the cost and/or risk of innovation, is conducive to industrial concentration, since large firms need the monopoly rents it creates to have the resources and financial incentives to carry out R&D. In doing so, two other important aspects of the effects of technical progress on the structure of industry today are underestimated.

First, as the technology front widens rapidly, large firms are increasingly incapable of exploiting all the opportunities for innovation that exist in their particular field. In focusing on specific areas, they have to make a trade-off that obliges them to neglect some growth opportunities. There are thus an increasing number of "technology slots" that can be filled by small and medium-sized firms[58]. Furthermore, it is not always in the interest of large firms to seize every opportunity for innovation open to them, either because they prefer to leave the risks of the technical and commercial teething troubles to smaller firms[59], or because they have too large a stake in the manufacture of products that may be threatened by the innovation.

Second, in quite a few sectors, technological change results directly in the vertical disintegration and decentralisation of production, allowing small firms to recover a comparative advantage in certain market segments[60].

The ability of each country to exploit technological opportunities to the full thus depends to a large degree on the absence of rigid organisational structures in its industry, and particularly on the vitality of its small and medium-sized firms. This vitality however varies greatly from one country to the next; by and large, it is greater in Japan and the United States than in the other Member countries:

Table 6A.8. **Business start-ups and closures in 1984**
As percentage of total number of firms

	Births	Deaths
Japan	4	3.6
United States	3.6	3.6
Germany	3.4	1.2
France	1.9	1.2

Source: OECD.

iii) *Impact on the demand for, and utilisation of, factors of production*

Technological change has a no less greater impact on the demand for, and management of, factors of production. Attention focuses naturally on the effects on employment, but other related aspects also merit consideration, such as the way capital requirements are changed. In order not to get bogged down in detailed analysis of the complex relationship between technology, employment and investment, we shall only summarise the main, converging findings of the large number of studies on the subject.

First, a reductionist conception of technical progress and its effects seems to underlie the "technological pessimism" about employment. However, it is incorrect to equate, as is often done more or less implicitly, technical progress with higher productivity, and higher productivity with increased competitiveness[61]. In fact, by shifting the boundaries of production and demand, major technological change creates entirely new job and investment opportunities as well as allowing existing demand to be met more efficiently, leading to an increased need for replacement investment and less, but not always, demand for labour. The rapid growth of manufacturing investment observed in recent years in Japan and the United States was probably due in part to the speed of the technological change in their industry, while the slower technological adjustment in Europe, which nonetheless resulted in large productivity gains, no doubt accounts partly for the persistent sluggishness of investment.

Thus, the fear that technological change *by itself* wipes out jobs at an overall level seems unfounded[62,63]. First and foremost, it produces a shift in the sectoral pattern of, and a qualitative change in, job opportunities[64] in the entire productive system, including service industries. At national level, it is rather the failure to bring technology up to date at the requisite pace, and to make the job cuts involved in certain sectors, which worsens the employment situation in the medium term. This inability stems largely from the inadequacies of the

education system, and the shortcomings of the retraining system for employees whose skills have been made redundant by technical progress[65].

Second, with the increasing role of human capital and the growing technological interdependence between sectors, job mobility, particularly of skilled personnel, has become an even more important means of disseminating technical know-how between firms and between industries[66]. When wage differentials are too far out of line with changes in productivity and in labour supply and demand in the various sectors and skills[67], they are likely to impede job mobility or to distort its sectoral pattern.

Third, new areas of complementarity are growing up between investment and employment. Non-physical investment, the share of which in total investment is increasing (cf. Graph 6A.4), is directed to skilled labour-intensive activities, e.g. R&D, or even to upgrading human capital, training); also, it is increasingly performed outside the firm, as technological change strengthens intersectoral links, e.g. innovating firms devote an increasing amount of resources to customer training[68].

However, this change in the content of investment – as a result of which the conventional analysis of the effect of technical progress on the complementarity/substitutability of capital and labour becomes less relevant[69] – may be inhibited by factors whose effect is to increase unduly the relative preference for physical investment, and especially for investment in rationalisation measures. The excessively rapid rise in real wage costs in relation to capital costs is a case in point[70]. All the fiscal, industrial and other policies whose effect is to subsidise capital excessively and/or tax employment are, from this point of view, liable to stand in the way of balanced technological adjustment in industry.

In this respect, it should be noted that when the external prerequisites for the effective dissemination and application of new technologies do not exist (flexible labour and capital markets, appropriate education and training systems, etc.), the main effect of too forceful policies of modernisation, e.g. increasing financial incentives for adopting new plant, is very probably to give a further boost to the general process of the substitution of capital for labour resulting from relative factor price movements at national level, rather than to encourage firms to exploit fully the possibilities that technical progress offers to respond more effectively to changes in demand and supply at international level[71].

Fourth, and lastly, the new nature of technological change amplifies the potentially negative effects of many of the imperfections of factor markets, and thus makes it even more urgent to eliminate them. This is true of the capital market, and perhaps especially of the labour market, whose continuing rigidity is a major impediment. By reducing job mobility, labour market rigidities inhibit technological development and dissemination. By retarding organisational innovation, they slow down the process of application of new technologies, and by distorting relative factor price movements, they set the process in the wrong direction by placing excessive emphasis on the defensive strategies for controlling costs through capital/labour substitution[72]. In doing so, they are likely to prevent a virtuous circle of technical progress, qualitatively balanced growth of investment, enhancing of the stock of human capital and net creation of jobs, from forming or operating fully. They may even help to create a vicious circle in which technological backwardness, investment centred on rationalisation, depreciation of the stock of human capital, and a net decrease in job opportunities, reinforce one another.

Graph 6A.4.   Trend of investment in France

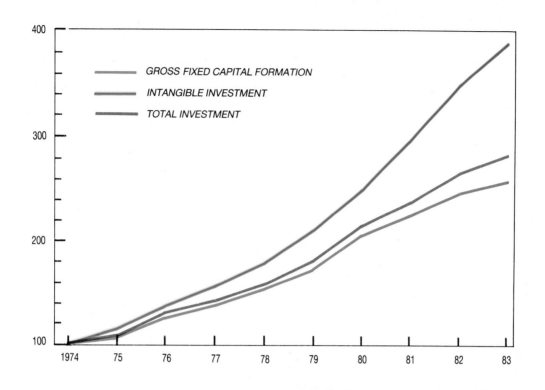

Legend:
- GROSS FIXED CAPITAL FORMATION
- INTANGIBLE INVESTMENT
- TOTAL INVESTMENT

Structure of intangible investment (1974-1983)
(%)

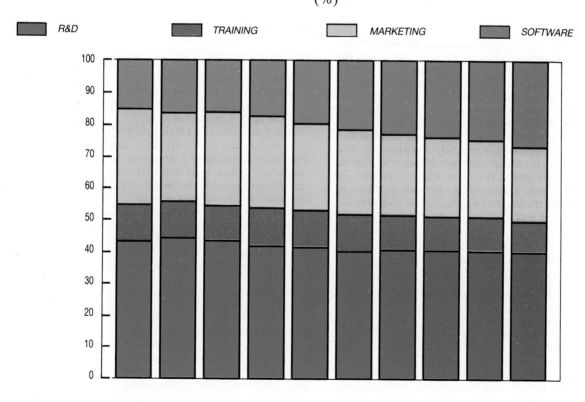

Legend: R&D — TRAINING — MARKETING — SOFTWARE

Source: Crédit National.

259

3. The emergence of new competitive strategies

Firms in most sectors are confronted with more and more numerous and rapid technological changes that alter the boundaries between activities, the conditions of competitiveness and barriers to market entry; in consequence, they must adjust their strategies. In many markets this gives rise to the emergence of new competitive strategies; any firm that does not follow this movement, either because of its intrinsic market weaknesses, or because its environment limits its scope for strategic manœuvre (thereby posing a problem for governments), finds itself placed at a disadvantage.

i) In traditional sectors

In some traditional sectors, such as the textile or chemicals industries, technological change is a factor, and not one of the least important ones, that contribute to the increasingly marked duality of markets. In the section of the market that is increasingly dominated by non-Member countries – mass-produced standardized products manufactured with well-established technology – the most competitive firms are those that have a competitive advantage in production costs. In the other section of the market, the pace is set by the firms that gear their technical and commercial capabilities to a policy of product differentiation[73] and specialisation in high value added market segments, which are less saturated and in which there is less competition; at the same time, they ensure a sufficient volume of business for reaping economies of scale by globalising their marketing and/or production strategy. Firms that are incapable of finding or creating their "market niche" in this new context find it very difficult to keep afloat.

In addition, the wave of technological and organisational innovation may be strong enough to dislodge long-established oligopolies in some sectors. The most striking example of this is probably the electrical engineering oligopoly that existed for over 50 years before being broken by the emergence of the electronics industry. There are other examples, especially that of the motor vehicle industry; in the past ten years, the dynamics of international competition have been radically transformed, largely on account of technological change. By exploiting the new technology rapidly and effectively, Japanese manufacturers have made a major breakthrough into world markets, thereby putting an end to the long-standing regulation of the world market by means of national and regional oligopolies operating in relatively closed markets. At a more general level, the accelerating pace of technical progress in medium- or slow-growth sectors, in which there are high barriers to merit exit, widens the gap between the best and average practices, thereby making oligopolistic co-ordination of the market, and especially cartel agreements, more difficult[74].

ii) In the high technology sectors

But it is in the cluster of activities on or near the leading edge of technology that competitive strategies are changing the most rapidly and radically. First, technological change, particularly in the telecommunications industry, is expanding the potential market, while contracting that of regulated natural monopolies[75]. Second, the internationalisation of markets and sources of innovation, and the increasing complexity and broadening of the scientific and technical base of manufacturing, require firms to adopt new technological, production and commercial strategies.

The resulting changes in the conditions of competition obviously vary from one sector to the next, but two broad trends may be observed in all sectors: corporate strategies are increasingly framed in global terms, and inter-firm co-operation agreements are on the increase and becoming more diversified. As a result, the way in which firms, and thus national industries, operate within the international economy is changing; it is quite different from the way they mostly operated until the mid-1970s[76], and to which most government measures were geared. However, two broad types of activities should be clearly distinguished.

In the most R&D-intensive industries located at the interface of science and industry, such as certain segments of the computer, semiconductor, telecommunications and bio-technology industries, firms are increasingly unable to develop on their own the entire scientific and technical base they need in order to grow, while the conditions in which the results of R&D are exploited commercially are changing; they must therefore adopt strategies that allow them to acquire sources of innovation outside their own laboratories, while retaining a minimum amount of control over the innovation process. Co-operation with universities or private or public laboratories is particularly important in this context.

In industries that are oriented primarily towards the application, and not the development, of generic technologies, such as the consumer electronics industry, the movement towards global and co-operative strategies is dictated more by the needs of production and marketing. What counts is to know how to produce and sell products, which are fast becoming obsolescent, more and more rapidly and on a world scale[77].

C. Implications for international manufacturing trade

The validity of many of the explanatory theories of the functioning of the economy on which private and public policy making has been based for a long time has been called into question by contemporary advances in technology that have produced, or speeded up, changes in industrial structures, methods of production and conditions of competition. It seems especially difficult to interpret developments in international manufacturing trade in terms of established economic theory, or in the light of experience alone.

Theory has difficulty keeping pace with the changes that have taken place in the last decade in the geographical pattern, content and dynamics of international trade (see Chapter 7), particularly as regards the implications for policy making. For example, no sooner had the "new theory of trade" been devised to account for increasingly marked features of the development of trade which classical and neo-classical models were incapable of explaining[78], than it was undermined, or at least its scope and predictive power were considerably diminished, by the emergence of new forms of internationalisation of production, such as the growth and diversification of inter-firm agreements.

This theoretical disarray, although not surprising in a period of rapid and sweeping economic change, is disquieting insofar as it erodes the conceptual foundations on which to build a basic international consensus on how to achieve effective, coherent and compatible industrial, technological and trade policies at national and international level.

The blurring of a common frame of reference gives rise to large grey areas in which clashes of interest are likely to occur both within and outside national boundaries. It is to be feared that the worsening of the trade climate in recent years is not

Graph 6A.5. **R&D expenditure by business enterprises**
(Share of the major geographical areas)
1969-1983

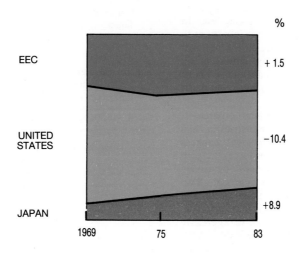

Trend of manufacturing industries market shares
1970-1984

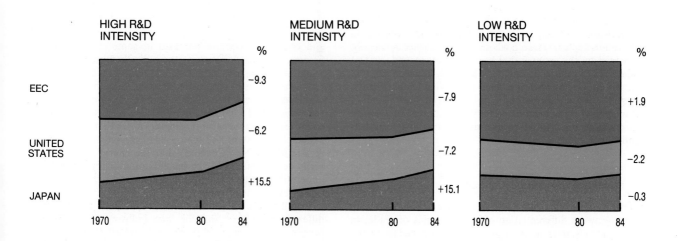

Source: OECD.

only of a "frictional" nature, the kind of temporary disturbance that is inevitable during a period of structural transition. It also probably reflects the existence of growing differences about the basic interpretation of the current phase of internationalisation of production and trade, about how the cost/benefits of it should be assessed from the national standpoint, and about the ways in which national interest and corporate strategic interests can be reconciled at policy-making level. In order to achieve more harmony in this area, it is important to pursue further joint discussions on the future of international manufacturing trade, and to begin with, by making a full assessment of the impact that technological change will have on such trade. The following remarks point to areas that merit closer consideration.

To understand the way in which technical progress is influencing the competitive position of the industries in each country, a paradox has to be explained: technological change is one of the major forces, if not the major force, shaping structural change in the industries of the most developed countries, but at the same time, the link at aggregate level between *intra muros* R&D effort and national industrial performance seems to be becoming less weak than before.

This development, which is confirmed both at aggregate level (see Graph 6A.5) and at sectoral level (see Table 6A.9), is a major source of concern to the countries that raise the largest quantitative contribution to the growth of world science; it cannot be explained solely by non-economic, e.g. factors, the scale of military research, or by international differences in the sectoral pattern of research (see Table 6A.10). It also stems from the fact that the findings of basic and pre-competitive research are increasingly becoming a *de facto* international public good and that the ability of the industries in each country to exploit new technological opportunities to strengthen their existing comparative advantages or to create new ones varies greatly.

This gives rise to two major problems: first, that of preserving in many OECD countries, in a context of budget restraint and mounting unemployment, sufficient incentives to pursue non-applied research whose economic benefits may not be reaped by the country that carries it out; second, that of maintaining a minimum amount of harmony between national industrial interests at a time when a growing share of trade seems to depend increasingly on the speed and mode of technological adjustment in industry, and thus less and less on the classical mechanisms operating automatically towards equilibrium.

1. Plurality of the principles of trade

Technological change is one of the main factors contributing to the growing differentiation of the principles of trade; in particular, this means that the mechanisms provided for by the monistic theories of international trade that have underpinned multilateral agreements until now (factor prices, exchange parities, etc.) are less and less capable of ensuring balanced international industrial growth founded on an expansion of trade which brings benefits for all partners that outweigh the costs of adjusting their industries.

In some industries, in which the overall competitive position of Member countries has been eroded by non-Member countries, relative factor endowments and prices (capital, labour, energy and raw materials) still explain the trend to international specialisation on the basis of intersectoral complementarity[79] – for example, not only in the primary energy

Table 6A.9. **Research expenditure and market shares in computer and instrument industries in the United States and Japan**

	Computers		Instruments	
	1970	1983	1970	1983
Market share (% of world exports)				
United States	31.4	31.0	21.6	23.5
Japan	11.1	20.2	14.2	25.5
	1975	1981	1975	1981
Share of R&D expenditure (%)				
United States	83.6	54.3	75.3	83.7
Japan	9.2	7.2	6.5	10.2

Source: OECD; National Science Foundation.

Table 6A.10. **Sectoral breakdown of industrial R&D, 1981**

	United States	Europe	Japan	Other OECD countries	Total
Total BERD[1]	50.2	32.6	15.0	2.2	100
Electrical/electronic	46.1	35.0	16.9	2.0	100
Chemical	40.9	41.0	16.0	2.1	100
Aerospace	75.3	23.1	—	1.6	100
Transport	47.2	29.4	22.7	0.7	100
Metals	35.7	30.6	30.3	3.4	100
Machinery	62.0	24.8	12.3	0.9	100
Services	38.8	36.4	18.5	6.3	100

1. R&D expenditure of business enterprises.
Source: OECD.

and commodity sectors but also in some energy-intensive processing industries such as the bulk chemicals or primary aluminium industries, or in labour-intensive industries such as certain segments of the textile industry. Only the trade of less developed and less diversified economies is primarily based on the principle of complementarity. However, some Member countries with large natural resources also exhibit, although to a much lesser extent, the same kind of specialisation (Canada, Australia and New Zealand) that the energy crises temporarily accentuated, but the benefits of which are now being undermined by technological developments and by the evolution of the terms of trade.

In other sectors, international trade operates on a quite different principle – that of intra-industry competition in products that cannot be readily substituted for one another (either because of their innovation content or for other reasons), and which are traded between countries at a comparable level of development and similarly endowed with productive resources. There is nothing new about this since it has probably been the most marked feature of the trend of international manufacturing trade for the past 30 years. What has changed in the recent period is that the relative importance of the factors underlying this development, i.e. which determine the way in which it is reflected in the international specialisation of each country's industry, has changed. The factors are more numerous and complex than those that shape trade on the basis of intersectoral complementarity. Being of a purely microeconomic nature, many of them cannot be reduced to the more macroeconomic concepts which are used, for example, in theories of general equilibrium to identify those conditions in which the dynamics of comparative advantage are the most likely to contribute to the harmonious economic and industrial development of the countries engaged in world trade.

2. Equilibrium of intra-industry trade and technological change

The main explanation for the growth and geographical and sectoral pattern of intra-industry trade lies not in international disparities in the availability of "classical" factors of production, but in factors of a technological order (capacity for innovation, conditions of international and intersectoral dissemination of technical progress), and in the characteristics of methods of production (such as economies of scale) and of markets (imperfect competition, degree of product differentiation demanded by consumers). It is both the effect and cause of a process of specialisation that might have been expected to have produced a convergence in the pattern of international trade of the industries of the most developed Member countries as trade was liberalised, economic regions were integrated, levels of income, patterns of consumption and scientific and technical skills drew closer together, technical progress increased the possibilities of product differentiation in a wider range of sectors, and the very expansion of trade helped to reduce the imperfections in factor and product markets.

If this had been the case, there would have been no more reason than in the case of trade conducted on "classical" principles to have posed the question of whether structural factors can cause international incompatibility of national paths of industrial adjustment; although not often formulated explicitly, this question nonetheless underlies much of the concern caused by persisting and worsening trade imbalances. Trade would then have developed along the lines of trade theory according to which, even when economies of scale, imperfect competition and product differentiation exist, there is an optimal national and international path for industrial adjustment, along which expansion of intra-industry trade, economic growth and increasing specialisation of national economies mutually reinforce one another[80].

A key element in these theories is that competitive equilibrium is continuously ensured along this growth path by the fact that the demand expressed by consumers for differentiated products limits the extent to which producers can exploit economies of scale. However, it may be asked whether it is not precisely technological change that makes this balancing mechanism much less effective since, as was pointed out above, economies of scale and product differentiation are no longer incompatible in many sectors. Moreover, given that technological progress depends increasingly on the quality and intensity of interaction between sectors, particularly between innovative and user sectors, and that long-term learning effects and/or national external economies (university/industry links; vitality of small and medium-sized innovative enterprises, etc.) still determine in some industries (either traditional, such as the chemical industry, or new leading-edge industries) the capacity to generate and/or assimilate technical progress, the link between changes in international trade and changes in industry at national level, needs to be completely reconsidered. Intra-industry trade in a large number of industrial products would seem to exhibit features that are similar to the effects of scale and of scope that create competitive advantages at the microeconomic level and that may be cumulative for the firms that have the resources and the capability to exploit them by a better strategy of specialisation, diversification and integration than that of their competitors.

Thus, while the similar factor endowment of the most developed Member countries contributes to the development of intra-industry trade at an increasingly specialised level, major disparities between individual countries in respect of the structural factors that determine how effectively their factor endowment is used, inhibits a similar trend in international specialisation, even perhaps to a point where international industrial growth is becoming imbalanced. The new conditions of technological development amplify considerably the importance of these "structural" factors of competitiveness, which include not only the characteristics of the industry but also

Table 6A.11. **Breakdown of exports and imports by product category in 1980**

In percentages

	% of total exports/imports[1] with trade ratios that are				
	Insignificant	Low	Balanced	High	Total
Exports					
France	2.5	25.2	20.0	52.3	100.0
Germany	3.2	14.6	9.3	72.9	100.0
Italy	1.9	30.6	7.4	60.1	100.0
United Kingdom	3.9	18.0	42.8	35.3	100.0
Japan	16.2	3.0	1.8	79.0	100.0
Imports					
France	1.8	58.7	15.8	23.7	100.0
Germany	2.4	55.4	10.0	32.2	100.0
Italy	1.7	77.9	5.9	14.5	100.0
United Kingdom	2.9	39.8	41.0	16.3	100.0
Japan	7.1	82.4	1.7	8.8	100.0

1. On the basis of 121 products classified by trade ratios as follows: insignificant (export/import ratio below 20 per cent); low (export/import ratio below 80 per cent); balanced (export/import ratio between 80 and 120 per cent); high (export/import ratio over 120 per cent).
Source: INSEE.

those of its environment (labour and capital markets, education system, etc.), i.e. a number of parameters that do not adjust automatically in response to market forces alone[81].

Actually, the trend of trade has proved quite different from that predicted by theory. In particular, the pattern of the international trade of the most advanced industrialised countries has not become more uniform, quite the contrary. Japan's foreign trade has remained strongly polarised in certain sectors. The United States shows a surplus in the group of high technology industries, but a deficit in other sectors. The foreign trade of European countries is more marked by intra-industry specialisation, but Germany has a pattern of exports that is much more polarised than that of its partners (see Table 6A.11).

Differences in national paths of technological adjustment, which are described in Part I of this chapter, explain to a large degree the trend of comparative advantage that underlines developments in the pattern of international trade.

NOTES AND REFERENCES

1. Allowing for the increase in energy saving or fuel substitution investment.

2. In particular, the increase in relative wage costs resulting from currency revaluations prompted an early withdrawal from some of the most labour-intensive industries.

3. Germany is the only country where the rate of inflation between the two oil shocks was lower than before the first shock.

4. Reflecting the improvement in productivity (United States, Japan and the United Kingdom) or the slower pace of real wages (Germany).

5. Thanks in particular to product differentiation, the development of customer services, increased market shares, etc. which allow price trends to be more closely tailored to costs, or owing to reappraisal of the product range resulting in consolidation of profit margins.

6. In the United States, the weight of direct taxation in relation to the gross operating surplus fell from 23 per cent in 1980 to 14 per cent in 1984.

7. In the form of government financial assistance or by a series of measures intended to broaden the base of the financial market and encourage consolidation of bank lending to firms.

8. See for example, "Profitability, Relative Factor Prices and Capital/Labour Substitution in the Community, the United States and Japan, 1960-1983", *Economie Européenne*, July 1984.

9. As for example, in the case of Germany, the study of Dicke, Hugo and Trapp, Peter, *Investment Behaviour and Yields in Some West German Industries*, Working Paper No. 205, Institut für Weltwirtschaft an der Universität Kiel, October 1984.

10. In the United States for example, the financial markets not only attract a substantial proportion of savings but they also serve a wide range of firms, the ten leading companies accounting for only about 16 per cent of total capitalisation on these markets.

11. In the United States, as in the United Kingdom and Canada, there is legislation restricting the extent to which banks can acquire shareholdings in corporate capital.

12. For example, total capitalisation on the financial market is three times lower in Germany than in the United Kingdom.

13. In Germany in 1980, banks held 63 per cent of the equity in the seventy four largest companies, the three main banks alone holding 35 per cent of these equities. In Japan in 1984, insurance companies, banks and other financial institutions held a total of 38 per cent of stock market listed shares; some ten per cent of banks' assets were made up of equities and bonds.

14. The Ministry of Finance, the Central Bank and the Ministry of International Trade and Industry (MITI) have traditionally used their considerable influence to channel the substantial savings of Japanese households towards selected uses, including industry where some firms have been able as a result to incur exceptionally high levels of debt and/or benefit from exceptionally low interest rates. In 1980, for example, the main Japanese manufacturers of semiconductors had a debt/equity ratio of 1.5 to 2.3, compared with an average of 0.2 in rival American companies. It should however be noted that government influence over the industrial development process, exercised through financial control, has diminished during the past 15 years as a result of the relative decline in firms' financial requirements following the slowdown in investment, the rise in the self-financing ratio and increased recourse to international financing facilitated by gradual capital market deregulation.

15. For example, the Mitsui Bank holds between six and ten per cent of the capital of the various firms comprising the Mitsui Group.

16. Between 1970 and 1979, 80 per cent of German firms' external funding was in the form of fixed interest loans with terms of ten years or more.

17. It should for example be noted that the British financial market, the main source of long-term corporate capital, is less broad-based than its American counterpart, with the result that conditions of access represent an objective, incentive to concentrate industrial activities following a line of reasoning that is more financial than industrial. France's heavily concentrated banking system, with its highly centralised allocative procedures, has always tended to favour large firms to the detriment of smaller ones.

18. See for example, Reich, Robert B., "Bailout: A Comparative Study in Law and Industrial Structure", *Yale Journal on Regulation*, 1985, Vol. 2.

19. Other decisive factors included managerial skills and industrial relations.

20. Two examples at either end of the scale can be given: British Leyland and Toyo Kogyo. In the case of British Leyland, the lack of effective co-operation between management labour organisations and creditors meant that the restructuring which started in 1974 basically took the form of massive labour cutbacks, with relatively little redeployment of activities. The cost of operation was borne mainly by the government, essentially because the unions and creditor banks were unwilling to agree to some of the sacrifices that were necessary. The case of Toyo Kogyo, on the other hand, illustrates how effectively active co-operation between the parties involved (as part of organised and stable relations between the parties, particularly banks and firms, such

that reciprocal concessions can be made without delay) can help to put the firm back on an even keel at a social cost which is lower in that it consists more of redeploying assets than reducing them and does not involve massive government intervention.

21. In the case of bankruptcy, the shortcomings of the capital market are not relevant since the new investor can acquire the company's capital at a reduced price. On the other hand, the shortcomings of the labour market may be an obstacle to reconstituting the company if legislation on collective agreements imposes too many restrictions on the buyer's freedom to fix re-employment terms on the basis of the necessities of competitiveness.

22. See Ergas, H., *Why do Some Countries Innovate More than Others?*, CEPS Paper No. 5, Centre for European Policy Studies, Brussels, 1984.

23. See Nagawa and Ohta, *The Japanese Economic System: A New Balance between Intervention and Freedom*, Foreign Press Center, Tokyo, 1980.

24. See for example, Robson, M., Townsend, J. and Pavitt, K., *Sectoral Patterns of Production and Use of Innovations in the UK: 1945-1983*, Science Policy Research Unit, Sussex, May 1985.

25. In particular, some aspects of the innovation process are considerably underestimated because of the tendency to equate, for statistical convenience, technological intensity with R&D intensity.

26. Although work such as that of P. Patel, L. Soete, Z. Güliches or J. Mainesse represents a significant progress in a good direction.

27. Gilpin, R., *Technology, Economic Growth and International Competitiveness*, 1975.

28. See for example, the work of P. David, C. Freeman, E. Mansfield, R. Nelson, N. Rosenberg, D. Teece.

29. For example, recent OECD studies show that between 60 and 65 per cent of manufacturing firms in the United Kingdom, France, Germany and Japan adopted some form of microelectronic technology in 1984.

30. See *Sectoral Patterns of Production and Use of Innovations in the UK: 1945-1983*, op. cit. in Note 24.

31. Other examples may be cited, e.g. biotechnology cuts across the chemical, pharmaceutical and food industries; new ceramics have been developed as a result of the collaboration between the traditional ceramics industry, and the mechanical, electrical and chemical industries (*cf.* Kodama, F., "Japanese Innovation in Mechatronics Technology", *Science and Public Policy*, February 1986).

32. See in particular, the analysis of Freeman, C. in *Unemployment and Technical Innovation: A Study of Long Waves and Economic Development*, Frances Pinter, London, 1982.

33. At an empirical level, the importance of the intersectoral dimension in the innovation process is shown by the fact that a positive correlation may be observed between the propensity of each sector to innovate and its propensity to use the innovations made by other sectors (see *Sectoral Patterns of Production and Use of Innovations in the UK: 1945-1983*, op. cit. in Note 24).

34. The development of the semiconductor industry shows how effective the virtuous circle created by improvements in a new product (and the lowering of its cost) and by an increase in the number of its applications can be. Also, the systematic character of contemporary technology draws manufacturers and users more and more closely together. This is true of semiconductors (see OECD, *The Semiconductor Industry*, Paris, 1985) and of new materials; the latter's structures are often designed specifically for the shape of the parts in which they are to be used.

35. For example, the application of electronics in the motor vehicle industry has given birth to a new integrated system of design and manufacturing processes, the main features of which can be transposed to almost all assembly industries. Likewise, computer-aided design grew out of the computerisation of the aircraft industry.

36. See for example, the study on structural adjustment in telecommunications done in 1987 by the OECD Directorate for Science, Technology and Industry (DSTI).

37. See Antonelli, C., *Technological Expectations and the International Diffusion of Process Innovations. The Case of Open and Spinning Rotors*, Polytecnico di Milano, 1986.

38. See OECD, *Science and Technology Indicators*, No. 2, Paris, 1986.

39. For example, the total cost of an IBM PC breaks down as follows: 44 per cent of Japanese components, 27 per cent of American components, 19 per cent of components manufactured in Singapore and ten per cent of Korean components.

40. For a recent analysis of these co-operation agreements, see the recent work by the OECD Committee for Scientific and Technological Policy, (CSTP).

41. In particular, the technological balance of payments (see *Science and Technology Indicators*, op. cit. in Note 38).

42. Several studies show that in the United States there is no correlation between the profitability of firms and their R&D intensity. At international level, it is clear that it is in medium R&D-intensive sectors (motor vehicles, consumer electronics, etc.) that a country like Japan has reaped most of the benefits from rapid technological adjustment.

43. The cases where the specific features of a technology allow firms to keep their know-how confidential for a long time are the exception rather than the rule. For example, a recent study of a sample of 100 US manufacturing firms shows that, on average, it does not take more than a year for competitors to obtain detailed information about a new product, and not more than six months for a third of the firms surveyed; with the exception of the chemical industry, competitors generally get hold of the details of process innovations less than 15 months after they have been introduced (see Mansfield, E., "How Rapidly Does New Industrial Technology Leak Out?", *Journal of Industrial Economics*, December 1985). A survey carried out in the United States on 650 research directors in 130 industries confirms that in most sectors, including the most R&D-intensive sectors, patents are considered one of the least effective ways of appropriating the benefits of innovation (see Levin, R. *et al.*, *Survey of Research on R and D Appropriability and Technological Opportunities*, Working Paper, Yale University, July 1984).

44. See in particular, Teece, D.J., *Capturing Value from Technological Innovation*, University of California, Berkeley, March 1986.

45. The commercial development of the CAT scanner is a good example of this.

46. Weaken it by making it less worthwhile economically to invest in R&D, and distort it by encouraging firms to direct their innovation more and more exclusively to improving productivity, and governments to focus their R&D expenditure on activities in which they control the market.

47. See in particular, Reich, R.B., *The Next American Frontier*, Penguin Books, New York, 1983; Zysman, J. and Tyson, L. (eds.), *American Industry in International Competition: Government Policies and Corporate Strategies*, Cornell University Press, Ithaca, 1983.

48. Manufactured goods now have a considerable service-content, e.g. it has been estimated that three-quarters of the value added of the manufactured goods sector is created by service activities in the sector (US National Study of Trade in Services). The application of new technology tends to increase this service content; thus, software accounts for a growing share of the purchase price and installation cost of a lot of equipment incorporating new technology. It has been estimated that the relative shares of software and hardware research in the average R&D budget of seven representative US computer manufacturers changed from 35 to 65 per cent in 1981 to 55 to 45 per cent in 1985 (OECD, *Software: An Emerging Industry*, Paris, 1985).

265

49. For example, in 1982 80 per cent of information technology (including computers) and communications equipment sales in the United States were to the service sector. In the United Kingdom, 70 per cent of computer sales in 1984 were to the same sector.

50. Several generations of products coexist in the integrated circuit market. The conditions of competition are different for each generation; some (as in the case of 64k memories) are similar to those found in many so-called mature industries (price competition, emphasis on process rationalisation, etc.). See *The Semiconductor Industry, op. cit.* in Note 34.

51. For example, in several segments of the textile industry and in the motor vehicle industry (see the recent DSTI studies on these two sectors).

52. See the recent DSTI study on steel.

53. See *Software: An Emerging Industry, op. cit.* in Note 48.

54. For example, in the European car industry, the average lifespan of models fell from 15 years for vehicles brought out in 1960 to seven years for those brought out in 1975. In France, the number of inventory items held by department stores increased by 10 000 per year in the 1960s (see Plaud, P. and Tarondeau, J.C., "Technologies flexibles et rentabilité", *l'Expansion*, Summer 1984).

55. There seems to be a renewed emphasis on the production function: it is ceasing to be the logistic appendage of other functions, such as marketing, which were the cornerstone of industrial strategy in the previous period. Today, the production function is recovering its strategic importance with the development of new approaches that integrate the various aspects of a firm's activity, and analysis in terms of the "market-product-process triangle" (see Tarondeau, J.C., "Le 'come back' des producteurs", *Revue française de gestion*, September-December, 1984).

56. For example, the use of robots in the motor vehicle industry reduces the minimum economic size of production units and makes possible more flexible production (see OECD, *Industrial Robots – Their Role in Manufacturing Industry*, Paris, 1983).

57. See in particular, Ergas, H., "Corporate Strategies in Transition" in *European Industry: Public Policy and Corporate Strategy*, Clarendon Press, 1984.

58. See the analysis of Momigliano, F., in *Economia industriale e teoria dell'impresa*, Bologna, 1975, which follows on from that of Penrose in *The Theory of the Growth of the Firm*, Oxford, 1963.

59. IBM's strategy in the microcomputer market is a good example of this.

60. See the DSTI study on textiles (*cf.* Note 51).

61. Today, the competitive advantage in many sectors depends less on the ability to cut costs than on the ability to improve the quality and the range of products and services offered to customers, to deliver on time, the speed with which investment, production and marketing decisions are taken, the flexibility of production capacity, etc. Furthermore, excessive concern with maximising productivity in the narrow sense of the term (output per employee) deflects minds and resources from the main means of raising competitiveness (see in particular, Skinner, W., "The Productivity Paradox", *Harvard Business Review*, July-August 1986).

62. The trend of employment in Japan and the United States is significant in this respect. For example, between 1970 and 1980, in Japan and the United States nine new jobs were created for every ten new job applications, compared with only four in Europe.

63. This is confirmed by macroeconomic studies such as that by P. Dungan and A. Younger, "New Technology and Unemployment: A Simulation of Macroeconomic Impacts and Responses in Canada", *Journal of Policy Modeling*, 1985.

64. Not only a change in the relative demand for different levels of skills, but also a change in the nature of the tasks at each level; in particular, there is an increasing emphasis on multi-skilling, as the following table shows:

Number of tasks carried out by operators of numerically controlled machine tools in 970 Japanese industrial firms

	Total (%)	*Of which* large firms
Large number of skills I	26.5	43.9
Several skills II	40.1	39.8
Single skill III	22.5	13.0
Did not reply	11.0	3.2
Total	100.0	100.0

Large number of skills I:	Operator performs five to seven tasks
Several skills II:	Operator performs three to four tasks
Single skill III:	Operator only tends machine

Source: Survey of in-firm training, Ministry of Labour, Tokyo, 1983.

65. Includes private and public in-firm or outside training and retraining, as well as the structural determinants of job mobility within or between established or new firms.

66. Inter-firm or geographical job mobility, which have tended to decline markedly in all countries over the past 15 years, are much lower in Europe that in the United States. Also, in contrast with the United States, in Europe it is generally lower among scientific workers and engineers than among other categories of workers (see the study on labour market flexibility done in 1985 by the OECD Directorate for Social Affairs, Manpower and Education).

67. There has been little long-term change in the distribution of hourly wage costs between industrial sectors in most European countries, indicating that there are rigidities which prevent wages from responding to the trend of productivity differentials and of the labour market situation in each sector. Across-the-board wage indexation agreements and the existence of a minimum legal wage in all industrial sectors have thus had a strong levelling effect in Europe that is not found in the United States and Japan (for further details see a study by the Commission of the European Communities, "The Determinants of Supply in Industry in the Community", *Economie Européenne*, September 1985).

68. The following table shows the amount of training provided by manufacturers when they supply numerically controlled machines to the engineering industry in Japan (findings of a survey conducted by the Ministry of Labour in 1980).

Number and percentage of firms[1]

	Number	%
Total number of firms	1 503	100.0
In-firm training by the firm itself	757	50.4
Outside training by government training centre	40	2.7
Training provided by microelectronic machine manufacturers	1 003	66.7
Other	98	6.5

1. As the questionnaire was based on several replies, the separate data do not add up to the total on the first line.

69. This analysis is based on investment statistics which, in line with the practice of the tax authorities, do not take account of

non-physical investment, which is treated implicitly as current expenditure.

70. The contrast is striking between the trend of the content of investment in Japan and the United States and of that in Europe. It is significant that it reflects fairly closely the trend of unit labour costs.

71. That the risk is a real one is clearly demonstrated in the case of Italy by Antonelli, C. in "Le politiche della diffusione" in Momigliano, F., *La politica industriale*, Bologna, 1986.

72. See Skinner, W., *art. cit.* in Note 61.

73. This differentiation takes several forms. However, note in particular a trend to add an increasing amount and quality of service to the product; the trend is particularly evident in the chemical industry, especially in fertilizers.

74. See for example the recent DSTI study on steel (*cf.* Note 52).

75. See Chapter 8.

76. International integration as a result of direct investment by multinational firms and technology transfers under licence agreements.

77. Changes in conditions of competition in the video recorder or RAM industries are illustrative of this.

78. See in particular, Dixit, A. and Norman, V., *Theory of International Trade*, Cambridge, 1980; Krugman, P.R., "Increasing Returns, Monopolistic Competition and International Trade", *Journal of International Economics*, 1979; Helpman, E., "Increasing Returns, Imperfect Markets, and Trade Theory", *Handbook of International Economics*, 1984, Vol. 1, Amsterdam, North Holland.

79. International trade reflects the natural resource endowment (Ricardian goods) or the relative "classical" factor endowment (Heckscher-Ohlin goods) of exporting countries.

80. See in particular, the work of Dixit and Stiglitz and the work of Krugman following on from it.

81. See for example, the work done by the OECD CSTP on *technology and competitiveness* which clearly shows how technological change increases the importance of the "structural factors" in competitiveness (size of national economy, organisation of production, etc.) while diminishing the importance of "classical factors" of competitiveness.

Chapter 7

WORLD TRADE

INTRODUCTION

The liberalisation of world trade on a multilateral basis was one of the outstanding successes of international economic co-operation in the first twenty years of the postwar period. The process of liberalisation has still a long way to go, indeed it has in some significant respects been reversed in more recent years; but the experience of the past few decades makes it clear that greatly widened opportunities for trade, once durably established, have substantial positive effects on economic performance.

At its simplest, this is because international trade provides a uniquely powerful source of pressures for structural change. The *constraints* trade imposes are obvious: in an integrated world economy, the option of not adjusting no longer exists. But the *incentives* that access to global markets creates to develop new and more efficient products and processes are no less important.

Like other forms of structural change, the growth of international trade brings significant material gains to the societies involved in it. At the same time, specific changes arising from it are often harmful to particular interests and groups. Here as elsewhere, competition creates problems, as well as incentives, opportunities and rewards.

This chapter – which focuses largely on manufacturing – analyses the processes and mechanisms by which the growth of trade has encouraged structural change and bettered living standards. By casting familiar data into a new form, it argues that greater interdependence has allowed the fuller exploitation of the economies of large-scale production while steadily increasing the variety of products available to consumers (Part I). These gains have hinged on firms' willingness to make large and irreversible investments for world markets; and this in turn has depended on confidence in the continued openness of the international economy. Up to the mid-1970s, the process of multilateral liberalisation itself encouraged this confidence; but the process of liberalisation has been largely reversed in recent years, growing recourse being made to forms of protection falling largely outside the effective discipline of the GATT (Part II). This has increased the risks investors face – and hence the costs consumers must bear

(Part III). Reversing these trends requires strengthening existing instruments and extending them to meet new challenges (Part IV).

I. THE CHANGING FUNCTION AND STRUCTURE OF TRADE

In 1950, imports accounted for a twentieth of supplies of finished manufactures in the OECD countries; by 1984, they accounted for a quarter (Table 7.1 and Graph 7.1). Yet, contrary to what might have been expected, the spectacular growth of interdependence over this period did not primarily lead to far-reaching inter-industry specialisation – that is, to each country coming to depend largely on imports for the products of certain industries while concentrating its output and exports on others. Rather, the industrial countries' patterns of trade and output tended to converge, with most countries increasingly producing and exchanging similar commodities[1]. But the growth of trade did fundamentally reshape industrial structures in four inter-related respects.

To begin with, increasing trade flows made it possible to implement production technologies where competitiveness depends on *large scale*, either because large plants are needed and/or because unit costs fall as cumulated production rises. In the mid-1950s, production runs in Europe were frequently less than a quarter of the United States average, even for relatively standardized products[2]; yet, notably in the process industries, technology was in the throes of changes that in many cases more than doubled the efficient scale of plants[3]. Even in a context of rapid growth, most countries – and especially the smaller ones – could not have reaped these economies of scale without access to world markets. At the same time, markets permitted efficiency gains through a finer division of labour – that is, by allowing individual firms and establishments to specialise in particular components and processes. These sources of improvement in efficiency tended to interact as greater specialisation increased the length of production runs, so that scale economies could be more fully exploited even in small plants and firms.

Second, rising incomes entailed growing demand for *product variety*: that is, for an increasing range of goods

Graph 7.1. **Volume indexes for exports and production**
(1950 = 100)

Semi-log. scale

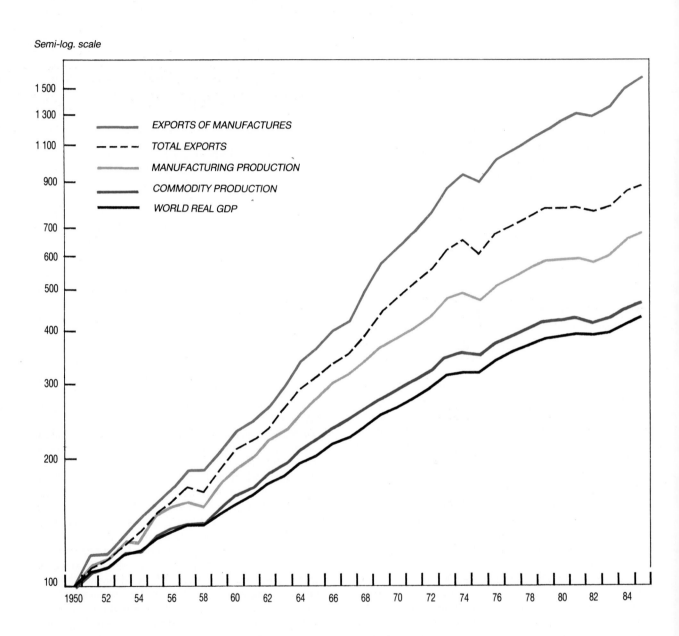

Source: GATT, *International Trade 1986,* Geneva, 1987.

Table 7.1. **Import content of "supplies" of finished manufactures[1], 1899-1985**

Percentages

	Maizels[2]					Batchelor[2]		OECD estimates[3]			
								1971		1985	
	1899	1913	1950	1959	1963	1963	1971	A	B	A	B
United Kingdom[4]	16	17	4	6	7	9	16	12	16	29	36
France	12	13	7	6	12	12	19	17	19	27	34
Germany[5]	16	10	4	7	10	9	17	16	16	26	29[6]
Italy	11	14	8	8	13	13	15	12	16	20	27
United States	3	3	2	3	3	3	8	9	9	24	24
Japan	30	34	3	4	6	4	5	4	5	6	7
Total	9	8	3	4	6	6	11	10	11	21	23
Belgium/Luxembourg	26	24	14	15	24	25	34	43	46	55	62
Netherlands	..	..	33	33	39	35	44	40	46	55	62[6]
Norway	..	35	33	34	34	35	44	50	52	61	61
Sweden	8	14	12	17	17	18	22	37	35	46	47[6]
Canada[4]	20	23	16	20	18	22	32	37	36	45	45
Australia[4]	..	39	25	15	16	20	26	19	22	33	32
Total[7]	..	..	18	21	24	25	33	36	38	47	49
Total industrial[7]	..	10-11	5	6	8	8	14	14	15	25	27

1. "Supplies" are defined as gross value of production of non-food manufactures free of duplication, plus cif value of imports of finished manufactures (goods not normally subject to further processing). The figures of Maizels and Batchelor *et al.* were based on production data (value added) which were inflated by the ratio of net output to gross output (excluding taxation and items sold by one part of the manufacturing sector as inputs to another part), both valued at factor costs. The data on intra-manufacturing purchases and sales which are needed for computing this ratio were available only for a limited number of countries in individual years. Maizels based his calculations partly on the ratios which he had been able to compute for individual countries (mainly relating to the early 1950s) and partly on a "rule of thumb". Batchelor *et al.* used a regression based on the investment/output ratio to calculate gross output. (For a further exposition of the methodologies used, see Batchelor.) The OECD data for production are based on gross domestic product at market prices for total manufacturing, excluding food, beverages and tobacco (for the United Kingdom and Canada, gross domestic product for total manufacturing at factor costs) and are converted into dollars, using purchasing power parities and dollar exchange rates respectively. Import data are based on cif value of imports of "finished manufactures" which is a separate category in the Brussels Nomenclature and were converted to and calculated on the SITC (Rev. 1) basis. The import content ratio is based on current prices because volume data for production and imports of non-food finished manufactures, free of duplication, are not available.
2. 1955 prices.
3. Current prices; first column (A) conversion with purchasing power parities for GDP, and second column (B) conversion with dollar exchange rates.
4. For United Kingdom, Australia and Canada, gross domestic production of total manufactures for OECD estimates.
5. Federal Republic of Germany from 1950 on.
6. For Netherlands, Sweden and Germany, GDP for 1985 is calculated by the ratio non-food manufacturing/total manufacturing of the latest available year, since for 1985 no breakdown was available.
7. Australia is not included in totals for small and industrial in the figures from Maizels and Batchelor.
Source: Maizels, A., *Industrial Growth and World Trade*, Cambridge, Mass., 1963; Batchelor, R.A. *et al.*, *Industrialisation and the Basis for Trade*, Cambridge, Mass., 1980; OECD, *National Accounts;* compatible trade and production data base.

and for more variants of each type of good. Greater trade made it possible to meet this demand without sacrificing scale economies; so that reductions in the number of domestic suppliers did not lead to a decline in the range of models on offer[4].

Third, global sales were an increasingly important means of recouping high and rising investments in *research and development*. These were of greatest significance in the industries most directly based on the application of science to product and process design – in chemicals, aerospace and electronics. Already by the early 1960s, the fixed R&D outlays required to be competitive in these industries were too great to be recouped in even the largest country[5] and since that time, industrial R&D expenditures have risen consistently more rapidly than value added. The openness of world markets not only made these outlays economically feasible but encouraged specialisation and hence efficiency in R&D efforts (since no firm or country had to

"cover the waterfront", though some did seek to for other reasons) as well as facilitating the rapid diffusion of technology.

Last, but not least, exposure to foreign rivals increased the *competitive discipline* bearing on large and small firms alike. The decline in world trade and foreign investment in the inter-war years had been associated with the pervasive cartelisation of domestic and international markets[6]. Postwar governments attached much greater weight to the maintenance of competition and legislated accordingly; but there can be little doubt that the growing importance of static and dynamic scale economies and of product differentiation tended to raise the entry barriers facing new competitors – creating scope for the abuse of dominant positions. However, these barriers were a far weaker deterrent to entry by importers – who could penetrate or withdraw from a foreign market by gradually modifying output levels at their home plant, rather than incurring the great risks involved in setting up an entirely new, large-scale operation. Equally, entry barriers proved a far less significant obstacle to new competition from foreign direct investment, since foreign firms could draw on the know-how they had accumulated elsewhere to rapidly acquire a presence in a new market. The growth of foreign trade and international investment therefore made domestic markets increasingly *contestable* – that is, vulnerable to entry even in the presence of transient profit opportunities[7]. The results were felt not only through constraints on profit margins but through constant pressures to innovate.

In short, trade has acquired new functions intimately linked to the dynamic processes which raise the efficiency of resource use; and it is these functions which have primarily shaped the composition and direction of economic integration. Thus, new sources of gains from trade have been added to the long-recognised benefits of exploiting the comparative advantages stemming from differing national endowments of natural resources, capital and labour. Three trends emerge from the trade data in this respect.

First, the OECD countries' trade has increasingly involved products characterised by significant economies of scale in production, extensive product differentiation or close links to the science base – rather than those where trade primarily reflects factor endowment (see Box 7.1 for an important discussion of terms and methodology). Thus, from 1962 to 1985, the share of production-intensive and science-based goods in total OECD manufacturing trade (exports plus imports) increased from 53 to 65 per cent, with growth rates of the latter category being particularly high in the most recent period (Table 7.2).

Second, the growth of trade has mainly (though by no means exclusively) entailed specialisation within industries, rather than between them – most obviously because a global market, in which products can be differentiated without sacrificing scale economies, is capable of sustaining a large number of competing suppliers. Table 7.3 sets out an index of intra-industry trade, based on the ratio of gross trade to net trade (see Annex 7.B for a fuller definition); this index can be viewed as representing the share of intra-industry trade

Table 7.2. **Average shares of six categories[1] of manufactures in total value of exports[2], imports[2] and production of manufacturing for 14 OECD countries[3]**

Percentages

	Imports[4]			Exports[4]			Production[4]		
	1970-1971	1977-1978	1984-1985	1970-1971	1977-1978	1984-1985	1970-1971	1977-1978	1984-1985
Resource-intensive industries	30.6	28.2	22.5	15.3	14.4	13.5	27.5	28.0	27.5
Labour-intensive industries	15.3	16.4	15.1	12.8	12.3	9.8	15.6	13.6	12.4
Production-intensive industries	46.9	48.2	51.7	58.7	62.4	61.1	46.8	49.7	49.2
of which:									
Scale-intensive industries	30.2	30.4	30.9	33.3	35.3	33.8	29.6	31.9	30.2
Differentiated goods industries	16.7	17.8	20.8	25.4	27.1	27.3	17.2	17.7	19.0
Science-based industries	7.1	7.2	10.6	13.1	11.0	15.5	10.1	8.8	10.9

1. The industries making up these categories are described in Annex A.
2. Imports/exports consist of trade with the whole world thus including trade between these 14 OECD countries.
3. Australia, Belgium/Luxembourg, Canada, Finland, France, Germany, Italy, Japan, the Netherlands, Norway, Sweden, United Kingdom, United States. These countries accounted for 77 per cent of world exports of manufactures in 1985. The respective shares are a weighted average of each country on the basis of their respective shares in total trade of all 14 countries.
4. The calculations are based on the International Standard Industrial Classification (ISIC).
Source: Secretariat estimates.

Table 7.3. **Adjusted intra-industry trade, all commodities (averages)**

Percentages

	Grubel and Lloyd			Secretariat estimates				
	1959	1964	1967	1964	1967	1973	1979	1985
Canada	29	37	49	37	49	57	56	68
United States	43	48	52	48	52	48	52	72
Japan	17	23	22	23	22	24	21	24
Belgium/Luxembourg	54	62	63	62	66	69	73	74
Netherlands	58	64	61	65	66	63	65	67
Germany	42	44	52	44	51	60	60	65
France	47	63	67	64	67	70	70	72
Italy	38	49	45	49	45	54	48	55
United Kingdom	35	46	71	46	55	71	80	76
Australia	15	17	17	18	17	29	22	25
Mean of above countries	38	45	50	46	49	55	55	60

Note: The table shows the percentage of intra-industry trade in total trade with the rest of the world. Calculated on SITC (Rev. 1) 3-digit level; adjustment is made for aggregate trade imbalances of the respective countries. See Annex 7.B for methodology.
Source: H.G. Grubel and P.J. Lloyd, *Intra-industry Trade*, London, 1975; Secretariat estimates.

in total trade. With the important exception of Japan, this index increased significantly for all the countries listed, the average for the group as a whole rising by more than two-thirds over the period 1959-1985. This has partly reflected more rapid growth in the trade categories with relatively high ratios of intra-industry trade; but there have also been significant increases in the extent of intra-industry trade within major categories, especially in the production-intensive and science-based groupings.

It does not need to be emphasized that the distinctions between groups are not hard and fast. Moreover, competitiveness usually depends on a mix of characteristics – e.g. applying scientific advance is also important in activities which are resource-based.

Equally, in practice the skills involved in "scale-intensive" and "differentiated goods" industries increasingly overlap, so that the aggregate of these two groups is included in the tables presented in this chapter under the heading of "production-intensive" (Annex 7.A provides a detailed concordance between this classification and the SITC).

Bearing these caveats in mind, the main advantage of the approach adopted here is that it provides a natural link between the way product groups are defined and the main types of economic benefits which flow from trade:

– Trade in resource- and labour-intensive products brings the allocation of resources within countries more closely into line with the international pattern of factor endowments (for example, by freeing countries with high energy costs from having to smelt bauxite);

- In scale-intensive products, trade allows firms to increase plant size and lengthen production runs, thus reducing costs;
- Through trade in differentiated goods, consumers can benefit from great product variety without sacrificing the advantages of large-scale production;
- Finally, trade in science-based products makes it possible to spread the high fixed costs and risks of R&D over a larger market, while also ensuring that the benefit of new products and processes are rapidly diffused.

In this respect, the classification is entirely consistent with the modern theory of international trade[8] and of foreign investment[9], as well as with recent work on the dynamics of technological change and industrial competition[10].

Third, this emerging pattern of specialisation has been accompanied by major shifts in the geographical structure of trade. Thus, throughout the 1950s and 1960s, trade occurred primarily between industrialised countries, which share broadly similar factor endowments and patterns of demand (Annex Table 7A.4). Moreover, trade grew particularly rapidly between closely located countries, mainly the United States and Canada on the one hand and the European OECD countries on the other.

These trends were partially reversed in the 1970s and early 1980s. Within the OECD area, trade between closely located countries declined in significance; as the process of trade creation within Europe slowed[11], Japan dramatically increased its share of world exports and the United States became a very major market for imported manufactures. At the same time, the role of the OECD countries as a centre of gravity in world trade was eroded, to some extent by the rapid growth and later decline of the OPEC market for manufactured goods but mainly by the emergence of the Newly Industrialising Countries (NICs) who, by 1985, accounted for fully 8 per cent of OECD manufactured imports.

But the extension of interdependence to new trading partners did not weaken the major tendencies affecting the structure of manufactured trade. Thus, by the end of the period, nearly 40 per cent of OECD imports from the NICs were not in labour- or resource-intensive products, but in products characterised by significant scale economies or extensive product differentiation (see Annex Graphs 7A.1 to 7A.3, and Annex Tables 7A.1 and 7A.2). And intra-industry trade – which had been a marginal factor in OECD trade with developing countries in the late 1960s – accounted for fully 31 per cent of the NICs' manufacturing trade with the OECD area in 1985, confirming that they too were increasingly drawn into the dynamic functions of trade.

Underlying those broader developments were significant changes in competitiveness. These changes can be analysed using a "constant market share" decomposition of exports; such a decomposition seeks to identify the extent to which shifts in an individual country's share of world export markets results from the initial pattern of its trade or from its capacity to adapt this pattern to changing demand conditions in world markets (see Box 7.2).

The aggregate outcome of this analysis, carried out for the period 1964-1985, is summarised in Table 7.4. There are some largely predictable differences between countries – Japanese industry's success in adapting the commodity composition and geographical distribution of its exports to changing patterns of demand is particularly striking. But perhaps the more significant result of the analysis is that for all countries (though less so for Japan than for the others) the dominant factor affecting export performance overall is change in the "market share effect" – that is, changes in competitiveness across the board, holding constant the commodity composition and geographical distribution of exports. This suggests that export performance mainly reflects more general determinants of efficiency rather than a specialisation in one set of product lines against another, for example "high" versus "low" technology.

II. THE EVOLUTION OF OECD TRADE POLICIES

The growing significance of scale economies, product differentiation and R&D in shaping world trade and output has partly been the natural consequence of rising incomes and the emergence of new technologies; but it has also been significantly affected by the scope and pattern of trade liberalisation.

At its simplest, this is because world trade could never have reached its present levels had far-reaching liberalisation not taken place. At the end of World War II, dutiable manufactured imports to the industrial economies faced an average legal tariff of around 30 per cent; but even these very high levels were largely irrelevant as bilateral agreements, preferential systems and quantitative restrictions, together with other non-tariff barriers, had a pervasive effect on trade flows. By the early 1960s, most of the non-tariff border barriers had been eased or even removed; and tariffs on dutiable manufactures had on average been cut to around 13-18 per cent. The Kennedy Round reduced this average to 8-11 per cent; and a further fall, to 6 per cent or less, was secured in the Tokyo Round. At the same time, the binding[12] of multilateral tariff reductions – perhaps the most significant innovation of postwar trade liberalisation – meant that exporters could view the decline in tariffs as a permanent feature of the

Box 7.2

ANALYSING CHANGING MARKET SHARES

The change in an exporting country's share in world imports can be split into several underlying effects. A Constant Market Share Analysis (CMSA) analyses those effects individually for each country or group of countries. The analysis which is limited to trade in manufactures is based on initial year weights with all data in current prices. The following five sources of change in market share are distinguished:

a)   *Market share effect*

Total change in the *exporting* country's share in the imports of each partner country, weighted by the initial commodity composition of each partner country's imports and by each partner country's share in total world imports. This is the change in share due which would have occurred *in the absence* of any change by the exporting country of the commodity composition or geographical distribution of its exports.

b)   *Market distribution effect*

Total change in the shares of *partner* countries in total world imports, i.e. the market distribution of exports. This is the effect on the exporting country's share of world imports of the growth rates of its original export markets as compared to the growth rates of all exports markets.

c)   *Commodity composition effect*

Change in *commodity* shares in total world imports, i.e. the commodity composition of exports. This is the effect on the country's export performance of the relatively slower or faster growth of world trade in the commodities in which it specialises relative to growth rates for all commodities.

The first three terms represent the change in export shares which would have resulted had the country maintained constant market shares in each market. They are generally identified with *demand* factors.

d)   *Relative market distribution effect*

Degree of success of the *exporting* country in adapting the market composition of its exports to the total change in the market composition of world imports – that is, to the geographical distribution of world imports.

e)   *Relative commodity adaptation effect*

Degree of success of the *exporting* country in adapting the commodity composition of its exports to the overall change in the commodity composition of world imports.

The two last effects could be considered as a measure of the adaptiveness of the exporting country with regards to the geographical distribution of export markets and the commodity structure of its exports; they may broadly be identified with *supply* effects. If a zero effect is recorded under each of the share headings, the exporting country is changing its export structure at exactly the same rate as the average of all countries exporting to the markets in question, or at the average of the change in the commodity structure of world imports.

Table 7.4.   **Changes in the share in world imports of manufactures, 1964-1985**

Percentage points

	United States	Japan	France	Germany	Italy	United Kingdom
Commodity composition effect	1.57	0.29	− 0.05	2.38	0.45	0.88
Market distribution effect	− 0.07	1.39	− 0.09	− 2.08	− 1.60	− 0.56
Relative commodity adaptation effect	− 0.37	1.11	0.06	− 0.91	− 0.16	− 0.04
Relative market adaptation effect	− 0.33	1.01	0.06	− 0.45	− 0.19	− 0.29
Market share effect	− 5.71	3.64	− 0.48	0.84	3.40	− 3.81
Total change	− 4.91	7.44	− 0.51	− 0.22	1.90	− 3.83

Source: Secretariat estimates; Calculations based on Fagerberg, J. and Sollie, G., *The Method of Constant Market Shares Analysis Revisited,* Discussion Paper No. 9, 23 May 1985, Central Bureau of Statistics, Oslo.

landscape, and plan and invest accordingly – a fact of obvious importance in the context of rising plant size.

Nonetheless, the opening of markets has been far from uniform. To begin with, certain sectors were largely excluded from the postwar process of trade liberalisation. The most notable exception to liberal trade has of course been agriculture; but services too have not been significantly affected by the multilateral opening of markets within the framework of the GATT (though certain other multilateral instruments, notably those elaborated in an OECD context, have had a significant impact on trade in services).

Moreover, even within manufacturing, the average reductions in protection concealed significant sectoral disparities. These were, of course, of least significance within the regional trading areas and common markets; and it is no coincidence that the greatest increases in intra-industry trade occurred within Europe. But as far as inter-regional trade was concerned, tariff and non-tariff barriers declined most and most durably for products characterised by extensive product differentiation and close links to the science base, and declined least and least durably for products with relatively high labour intensity, with scale-intensive products falling between these extremes (Annex Table 7A.5 illustrates these sectoral trends with reference to the long-term evolution of Most Favoured Nation (MFN) tariffs on a range of products).

By and large, tariffs on *highly differentiated* products had been relatively low at the outset and were steadily reduced both in the process of regional integration (notably in the setting of the EEC's Common External Tariff) and in the multilateral rounds. Moreover, the decision taken early on that the binding of a low tariff would be considered equivalent, for negotiation purposes, to a tariff concession encouraged countries to commit themselves to a liberal regime for these products.

The *science-based* products also benefitted greatly from the liberalisation process. By the late 1950s, these products generally entered under tariff lines which had been bound at relatively low levels, partly because they initially accounted for a small volume of trade. Moreover, the procedures by which binding was implemented made it particularly difficult for countries to introduce higher duties through tariff reclassification as markets grew – a tactic frequently applied to new products in the inter-war years.

The picture with respect to *scale-intensive* products was more mixed. In some areas – for example, passenger motor vehicles and steel – significant reductions in protection on an MFN basis were secured in the early trade rounds, largely under United States pressure (the United States being a major exporter of these products in those years). But in other scale-intensive products – notably petrochemicals – tariffs remained high virtually throughout the period. A similar pattern emerges with respect to *resource-intensive* products; effective rates of protection were reduced by an initial compres-sion of tariff escalation[13]; but the degree of escalation stabilized somewhat in later years and effective protection tended to fall by less than the declines in nominal rates (see Annex Tables 7A.6 and 7A.7)[14].

However, the greatest divergence from the overall trend towards durable liberalisation occurred in *labour-intensive* products. MFN tariffs on these products – notably on clothing, as well as on textiles (which are less labour-intensive) – remained relatively high; and the significance of even these tariffs was progressively overshadowed by the spread of quantitative restrictions to trade, as a "special regime" regulating trade first in textiles and then in clothing was put in place[15]. Moreover, while trade liberalisation had provided other producers not only with access to an integrated world market but (and perhaps most significantly) with good grounds for assuming that openness would last, the trade regime facing exports of labour-intensive products continued to be characterised by pervasive uncertainty. Frequent changes in regulations governing market access; more or less unilateral extensions of the range of goods subject to control; and growing recourse to mechanisms aimed at preventing sharp increases in importers' market share: all undermined exporters' capacity to plan[16].

In short, the process of market opening was a highly uneven one – and there were areas where little progress was made, or where steps forward were soon reversed. Yet, to the end of the 1960s, the underlying trend was to liberalisation – and the sectors excluded from this trend could be considered exceptions. Events subsequent to the first oil shock have broadly reversed this picture: progress in trade liberalisation has become increasingly difficult to achieve while the range of exceptions has grown ever wider.

This is not to deny that in some areas significant results have been achieved. The Tokyo Round of Multilateral Trade Negotiations led to a further reduction in overall tariffs and to agreements on subjects which previously had either not been covered by the GATT or covered inadequately – including public procurement, technical barriers to trade, customs valuation and anti-dumping and countervailing duties. But these results were obtained against a backdrop of overall deterioration in the trading system, in terms of the range of goods affected by trade distortions and of the general willingness to abide by the basic principles of the GATT.

The problems have been most acute in agriculture, where the mounting over-production engendered by domestic support policies has led to widespread dumping on the narrow markets open to international trade and accentuated protectionist pressures on home markets. However, even within manufacturing, trade barriers have become increasingly pervasive. Thus, the net of regulations limiting trade in labour-intensive products has become ever tighter, while little progress has been made in reducing the relatively high tariffs which still bear on these products. At the same time, quantitative restrictions (almost always applied on a discriminatory basis) have come to affect a growing range of scale-intensive, differentiated and even science-based goods. Indeed, estimates suggest that non-tariff barriers now cover at least 27 per cent of the imports of the sixteen major industrial countries[17].

The spread of these restrictions has been intimately associated with growing recourse to forms of protection which can be imposed and altered outside the effective discipline of the multilateral trade system. The pace-setters in this respect have been the successive Multi-Fibre Arrangements (MFA), within the terms of which importing countries have imposed import restrictions unilaterally, arbitrarily revised product classifications so as to obtain a greater restrictive effect, and (even within the lifetime of bilateral agreements) implemented provisions reducing previously set import quotas[18]. Though they cannot be considered as a breach of multilateral discipline (since the possibility of a review of terms was included in the decisions taken at the outset), similar practices have eroded the effectiveness of the Generalised System of Preferences (GSP), with a tendency for the preferential tariffs initially granted to be withdrawn without compensation when trade volumes in a particular product (and notably labour-intensive products) become quantitatively signifi-cant[19].

Both the MFA and the GSP apply to developing countries; however, the greater use of non-conventional forms of protection has also introduced a considerable degree of uncertainty to trade relations within the OECD region. The spread of discriminatory quantitative restrictions to previously less or unaffected products (such as automobiles, electronics or steel) is of course familiar; but the growing recourse to "contingent" protection and to anti-dumping and countervailing duty action is of no less significance. Even within the internal market of the EEC, the evidence suggests that Member States are making more frequent use of administrative measures which distort trade; and a recent study finds that it is the uncertainty associated with these measures, rather than their restrictiveness, which primarily concerns exporters[20].

Finally, notably in the late 1970s, the predictability of trading relations was eroded by the effects of subsidies on international trade. The most direct impacts arose from the competitive subsidisation of exports, especially of capital goods; and though substantial progress has been made over the years in reducing the subsidisation of officially supported export credits (Annex Table 7A.8), subsidisation through the mixing of aid with export credits has become increasingly widespread. However, an important influence was also exerted by subsidies to domestic output. These went partly to the industries experiencing acute adjustment difficulties – especially textiles, automobiles, steel and shipbuilding. But though subsidies to these industries were somewhat reduced in the early 1980s, those provided to so-called "high technology" industries have remained in place or even risen.

The postwar trade regime was distinctive not only because of its largely liberal thrust but because the procedures for liberalisation, the initial adherence to the "tariffs only" principle of the GATT and indeed the spirit in which market opening was obtained were such as to sustain confidence in the irreversibility of the liberalising trend. In this area, as in others, golden ages do not exist; but the evidence clearly suggests that in the last ten years, the protectionist tendencies prevailed, eliminating part of the benefits of the earlier shift to liberal trade. Overall, the principle of the Most Favoured Nation, which was both central to earlier liberalisation efforts and vital to the stability of trade relations, has been very significantly eroded.

III. THE EFFECTS OF TRADE POLICIES ON ECONOMIC PERFORMANCE

Seen with hindsight, there can be little doubt that the growth of world trade contributed greatly to raising the efficiency of resource use in the OECD area. Yet this proposition has proved exceedingly difficult to quantify or rigorously model. This is partly because it hinges on data which are rarely available – such as the extent of cost savings consequent on greater production volumes – or even poorly defined – such as the effect of increased product variety on consumer welfare. But it is also because so much of the benefits of open trade have come from greater confidence – and notably from producers' confidence that reduced cost or improved quality would lead to greater world market share, while failure to innovate would rapidly be sanctioned by market forces.

Nonetheless, the evidence supporting the general proposition is strong. It is first and foremost microeconomic – in the sense of coming from detailed studies of individual products, firms and industries. Thus, recent estimates[21] suggest that the cost savings permitted by scale economies in the integrated European market increased productivity in the major EEC countries by nearly 12 per cent – five to ten times more than the studies carried out around the time of the Rome Treaty thought possible[22]. Clearly, exploiting these scale economies required a willingness to invest for foreign markets; and detailed studies of individual firms suggest that this was closely linked to the perception that the opening of markets was a largely irreversible process – a perception which reshaped corporate strategies[23].

But there is also strong macroeconomic evidence – that is, bearing on entire national economies and industrial structures. Thus, it is a striking feature of postwar growth (and one which sets it apart from the inter-war years) that small countries – which rely most heavily on international trade – generally grew more rapidly than their larger counterparts. Moreover, their growth depended heavily on products characterised by economies of scale in production (Annex Table 7A.9) – products in which they could hardly have been efficient without access to foreign markets; while a large share of their imports consisted of goods characterised by great product variety – so that consumers in smaller economies benefitted from the same range of choice as in the largest national markets[24]. It is not surprising, therefore, that recent estimates using computable general equilibrium models suggest that the impact of trade liberalisation on domestic efficiency in small economies may be much greater than had earlier been thought[25]. And it is illuminating, in this respect, to compare the experience of the small countries which opened their markets to international trade (such as the Scandinavian countries) substantially more than others (such as Australia and New Zealand)[26]: the former had significantly higher rates of growth of manufacturing productivity than the latter; and this was closely linked to the fact that they became increasingly specialised both within industries and between them, concentrating resources onto a narrower range of traded items. Moreover, interdependence made the small open economies not more vulnerable to shocks (as is often claimed) but less, for it allowed them to spread risks over a larger and more diverse set of markets.

These gains provide a bench-mark against which the costs of the recent trend away from liberal trade can be assessed. (A detailed review can be found in the study on the *Costs and Benefits of Protection* published by the OECD in 1985.) At a microeconomic level, the costs are most probably those of foregone specialisation – that is, of the benefits lost by not adapting the international structure of production to that of factor endowments. The poorer countries clearly do account for a rising share of OECD imports of labour-intensive manufactures; but growth rates of these imports declined by far more than those of other categories of imports after 1973, excepting the resource-intensive industries (whose growth rates in world trade were adversely affected by

price and demand trends) (Table 7.5). Yet the gap in production costs – and presumably even more so in comparative costs – between developing and OECD countries remains enormous (for some clothing products being in the order of one to two)[27] and the scope for increased trade is highlighted by the large rents which protectionist measures create.

But protection also entails significant, though still less easily quantified, losses in terms of scale economies, product differentiation and R&D efficiency. These are most readily assessed when markets are durably fragmented, forcing manufacturers to adapt their product lines to diverse national requirements – a recent study, for example, finding that the fragmentation of the European telecommunications equipment market by conflicting technical and regulatory norms increases R&D costs in certain products by as much as 40 per cent[28]. The uncertainties created by administrative or contingent protection also impose efficiency losses, as firms opt for more flexible but less cost-effective production and marketing strategies. There is little quantitative evidence in this respect; but case studies of particular industries – notably textiles, steel and consumer electronics – discern a growing risk-averseness in export-oriented firms[29].

Ultimately, however, the greatest costs may come from the erosion of competition. Over the last twenty years, underlying trends in technology have tended to raise the size of plants and firms, reinforcing the oligopolistic character of a broad range of product markets[30]. In this environment, the pressures to increase productivity, upgrade products and processes, and reduce prices have increasingly come from international competition – from the ease with which an established foreign firm could enter a market through lower prices or more innovative products[31]. The spread of controls over imports has a drastic impact in this respect: for it has become increasingly common for discriminatory measures to be applied against foreign firms whose competitive behaviour is considered too aggressive, for anti-dumping and countervailing actions to be employed

Table 7.5. **Growth rates of trade and output at current prices in six categories of manufactures for 14 OECD countries**[1]

Percentages

	Imports		Exports		Production	
	1970/1971-1977/1978	1977/1978-1984/1985	1970/1971-1977/1978	1977/1978-1984/1985	1970/1971-1977/1978	1977/1978-1984/1985
Resource-intensive industries	17.1	7.3	17.8	6.1	13.2	8.1
Labour-intensive industries	19.6	9.5	18.3	3.6	10.8	7.0
Production-intensive industries	18.9	11.9	20.0	6.7	13.9	8.2
of which:						
Scale-intensive industries	18.6	11.0	20.0	6.4	14.2	7.5
Differentiated goods industries	19.5	13.3	20.0	7.2	13.4	9.4
Science-based industries	18.7	17.0	15.9	12.5	10.7	11.8
Total manufacturing	18.5	10.8	18.9	7.0	12.9	8.4

1. See notes to Table 7.2.
Source: Secretariat estimates.

to harass importers who cut prices, and for officially negotiated "price undertakings" to be used to control the competitive process.

The costs this entails are also macroeconomic. The large macroeconomic distortions and disequilibria of the last ten years – high unemployment, large external imbalances and unprecedented swings in real currency values – have, of course, accentuated protectionist tendencies. But policies directed at alleviating particularly acute pressure points have not and could not be expected to correct problems that are at root a reflection of major savings investment imbalances, heightened uncertainty about inflation and financial prices, and the broader deterioration of macroeconomic performance. At best, trade interventions have redistributed the burdens of these macroeconomic problems, and they have even exacerbated them by further weakening adjustment processes.

Thus, there is considerable econometric evidence that exposure to international competition increases the responsiveness of factor and product prices to changing market circumstances[32]. This shifts the burden of adjustment from quantities (and notably output and employment fluctuations) to prices, facilitating the task of macroeconomic policy in achieving sustainable, non-inflationary growth. Especially in the sectors of the economy which set the pace for nominal wage increases, shielding firms from price competition can only lead to higher inflation and decreased competitiveness, and thus make higher levels of employment more difficult to attain – as well as compromising the growth of living standards.

IV. STRENGTHENING THE TRADING SYSTEM

Looking to the future, the scope for gains from trade will, if anything, increase. The experience of the last three decades confirms that as countries' factor endowments become more similar, they benefit from interdependence by better exploiting economies of scale and product differentiation, which cumulate with the long-recognised advantages from specialisation in line with differing patterns of resource availability. Trends in technology are likely to raise these potential benefits further.

This is basically because the process of technological change now under way (and surveyed in more detail in the chapter on industrial structures of this report) opens a myriad of new product opportunities across a wide range of sectors. These will increasingly involve differentiating goods and services to better meet the needs of narrowly defined customer groups; and new design and production technologies are making smaller production runs more cost-competitive[33]. Yet far from leading to a disappearance of the advantages of size, the (albeit

limited) evidence suggests that fully exploiting these opportunities requires large markets: partly because new design and production equipment, though flexible among models, entails high and indivisible initial outlays; but especially because the effective use of this equipment, and the marketing of its products, involves considerable "economies of scope"[34]. As these new technologies come on stream, the nature of the efficiency gains from access to larger markets may change; but the extent of these gains is hardly likely to diminish.

Securing these gains requires a strengthening and extension of the open, multilateral trading systems. Three priorities stand out in this respect:

The first is to dismantle the protectionist measures which – having been put in place to ease immediate sectoral problems – have become an enduring feature of the landscape. The regulation of agricultural trade – dealt with in Chapter 5 – is of special importance in this respect; but the Multi-Fibre Agreement and the differing trade restrictions with which it is associated stand out in the industrial context. When the current Agreement expires, fully thirty years will have passed since the first derogations of textiles trade from the ordering discipline of the GATT – derogations which were intended to be stricly temporary. While there has indeed been considerable structural change in the OECD clothing and textiles industries, there is little evidence that the MFA has contributed to the efficiency of this process or of its outcomes, while the costs the MFA engenders – not only for consumers but for the economy as a whole – are increasingly widely recognised[35].

A second priority is to restore the confidence of traders and investors that reductions in cost and improvements in quality will be rewarded through increases in world market share. Even removing the major protectionist measures now in place will not suffice in this respect. Rather, this will require an assurance of greater discipline by all trading partners in their future behaviour, including progress as regards forms of protection which at present escape international obligations. The objective of granting foreign competitors a treatment no less favourable than that accorded domestic producers remains paramount; the manner in which safeguard options in world trade are implemented is of utmost importance in this respect, as is the use more generally made of administrative protection and of anti-dumping action.

Finally, the full benefits of interdependence will not be secured if the world trade regime is not brought into line with the changing character of trade flows. The albeit slow increase in the share of science-based products in world trade creates new challenges to trade policy – challenges associated with the importance which technical norms and standards and the protection of intellectual property have in encouraging the rapid diffusion of goods based on new technologies. Equally, the scope for specialisation in services is becoming increasingly apparent – but securing the benefits of specialisation in this area will require an important extension of multilateral trade liberalisation, as well as a review of the countries' domestic policies (such as restrictions on entry and pricing) which effectively limit foreign competition.

Combined, these measures would contribute to preserving and strengthening the role of trade as a powerful agent for structural change. But the desirability of these measures hardly implies that trade – or indeed structural change – is or ever will be entirely painless. Recognition of the difficulties change can create for individuals or groups in the community does not, however, provide an argument for protection. Thus, the empirical evidence suggests that protectionist policies have not only generally hindered the adjustment process, but have done little to alleviate the difficulties of the individual workers and communities adversely affected by foreign competition[36]. There is every reason to believe that the difficulties associated with structural change are most efficiently addressed through the more general instruments of labour market and social policy.

Although there is widespread agreement at a general level on the harmfulness of most if not all restrictive trade measures, trade policy formation has become increasingly vulnerable to the pressure of sectoral interest groups. Options need to be identified and analysed for better management of this process, widening its base and increasing its transparency. To begin with, trade policy authorities should be encouraged to adopt more open decision-making procedures or processes so as to allow those affected to express their views. At the same time, efforts should be made to systematically promote economic evaluations – on a public and independent basis – of specific trade policy measures[37]. The scope for improvement in these respects remains particularly large in Europe, where there is a need for more frequent systematic evaluation of the external trade policies of individual countries and of the common policies implemented in the framework of the European Community.

* * *

Thirty years ago, international trade was of primary significance to the smaller economies, and the economic performance of the larger countries was mainly shaped by domestic policies and circumstances. But as is abundantly clear from the data presented here, the growth of trade has dramatically altered this picture; and in today's highly integrated world, the outlook for small and large economies alike depends on access to global markets – access which enhances both microeconomic efficiency and macroeconomic responsiveness. The changing composition of trade indicates many of these gains are associated with investment: in larger plants, more specialised processes, more differentiated products, and in research and development. These investments are necessarily of a long-term nature; so that it is not only the degree of openness which is at issue but also the confidence with which firms can plan on open access persisting. The trend of recent years cannot but undermine this confidence; restoring it is surely a major challenge facing the new GATT round.

NOTES AND REFERENCES

1. See for example, ECE, *Structure and Change in European Industry*, New York, 1977.

2. Scherer, F.M. *et al.*, *The Economies of Multi-Plant Operation*, Harvard University Press, Cambridge, Mass., 1975; Owen, N., *Economies of Scale, Competitiveness and Trade Patterns within the European Community*, Clarendon Press, Oxford, 1983.

3. Carlsson, B., "The Content of Productivity Growth in Swedish Manufacturing", *Research Policy*, 1981, Vol. 10, pp. 336-354, especially p. 350.

4. The European automobile industry strikingly illustrates this process: the number of suppliers declined by nearly half in the postwar period, as the search for economies of scale led to higher levels of concentration; but the range of models available in individual countries continued to rise, largely because national suppliers expanded into each other's markets. Mosconi, A. and Velo, D., *Crisi e Restrutturazione del Settore Automobilistico*, il Mulino, Bologna, 1982.

5. Freeman, C., *The Economics of Industrial Innovation* (2nd ed.), Frances Pinter, London, 1982.

6. Edwards, C.D., *Cartelization in Western Europe*, GPO, Washington D.C., 1964; Stocking, G.W. and Watkins, M.W., *Cartels in Action: Case Studies in International Business Diplomacy*, Twentieth Century Fund, New York, 1946.

7. Bailey, E.E. and Friedlaender, A.F., "Market Structure and Multiproduct Industries", *Journal of Economic Literature*, September 1982, Vol. XX, pp. 1024-1048.

8. Ethier, W.J., "National and International Returns to Scale", *American Economic Review*, June 1982, pp. 389-405; Krugman, P., "Increasing Returns, Monopolistic Competition, and International Trade", *Journal of International Economics*, November 1979, pp. 469-80; Krugman, P., "Intra-industry Specialization and the Gains from Trade", *Journal of Political Economy*, October 1981, pp. 959-73; Lancaster, K., "Intra-industry Trade under Perfect Monopolistic Competition", *Journal of International Economics*, May 1980, pp. 151-76.

9. Caves, R.E., Porter, M.E. and Spence, A.M., *Competition in the Open Economy: A Model Applied to Canada*, Harvard University Press, Cambridge, Mass., 1980; Caves, R.E., *Multinational Enterprise and Economic Analysis*, Cambridge University Press, 1982.

10. Pavitt, K., *Some Characteristics of Innovative Activities in British Industry*, Science Policy Research Unit, University of Sussex, 1982; and Pavitt, K., "International Patterns of Technological Accumulation" (draft), Science Policy Research Unit, University of Sussex, 24th July 1984.

11. Jacquemin, A. and Sapir, A., "La part des échanges intra-CEE", *CEPS Working Document*, Centre for European Policy Studies, Brussels, 1986.

12. Binding refers to the process whereby countries commit themselves to not altering a tariff level set in the context of multilateral trade negotiations without providing compensation to their trading partners.

13. Tariff escalation refers to the effective protection generated by the structure of tariffs bearing on products of successive stages of processing.

14. Deardorf, A.V. and Stern, R.M., "The Effects of the Tokyo Round on the Structure of Protection", *National Bureau of Economic Research, Conference on the Structure and Evolution of Recent US Trade Policy*, Cambridge, Mass., December 1982; Deardorf, A.V. and Stern, R.M., *Input-Output Technologies and the Effects of Tariffs and Exchange Rates*, Bureau of International Labor Affairs, US Department of Labor, April 1984.

15. *Textiles and Clothing in the World Economy*, GATT document Spec(84)24, May 1984; OECD, *Textile and Clothing Industry. Structural Problems and Policies in OECD Countries*, Paris, 1983.

16. Choi, Y.P., Chung, H.S. and Marian, N., *The Multi-Fibre Agreement in Theory and Practice*, Frances Pinter, London, 1986.

17. Nogués, J.J., Olechowski, A. and Winters, L.A., *The Extent of Non-tariff Barriers to Imports of Industrial Countries*, World Bank Staff Working Papers, No. 789, Washington D.C., 1986.

18. Choi *et al.*, *op. cit.* in Note 16; Aggarwal, Y.K., *Liberal Protectionism*, University of California Press, 1985.

19. OECD, *The Generalised System of Preferences. Review of the First Decade*, Paris, 1983; Pelzman, J., *The US Generalized System of Preferences: An Evaluation and an Examination of Alternative Graduation Programs*, report prepared for the Office of International Economic Affairs, Division of Foreign Economic Research, Bureau of International Labor Affairs, US Department of Labor, September 1983.

20. Berr, Holmes, Reboud, Shepherd, *Comparative Research on Non-Tariff Barriers in Britain and France*, 1986.

21. Owen, N., *Economies of Scale, Competitiveness and Trade Patterns within the European Community, op. cit.* in Note 2, p. 156.

22. Most of these studies – which took little account of scale economies or product variety – concluded that the gains from free trade in Europe would not exceed 0.5 to 1 per cent of European GNP. See Lundgrau, N., "Customs Unions of Industrialised West European Countries" in Denton, G.R. (ed.), *Economic Integration in Europe*, Weidenfeld and Nicolson, London, 1969.

23. Müller, J., "Competitive Performance and Trade with the EEC: Generalizations from Several Case Studies with Specific Reference to the West Germany Economy" (mimeo), 1983; Hood, N. and Young, S., *Multinationals in Retreat*, Edinburgh University Press, 1982.

24. In this respect trade patterns confirmed the projections of Dreze, J., *Quelques réflexions sereines sur l'adaptation de l'industrie belge au Marché Commun*, No. 275, Comptes rendus des travaux de la Société Royale d'économie politique de Belgique, 20th December 1960.

25. Harris, R.G., *Applied General Equilibrium Analysis of Small Open Economies with Scale Economies and Imperfect Competition*, Queens University Kingston, Canada, Discussion Paper, No. 524, 1983; Harris, R.G. (with the assistance of David Cox), *Trade, Industrial Policy, and Canadian Manufacturing*, Toronto Economic Council, Ontario, 1984.

26. See Ergas, H., "Industrial Competitiveness and Restructuration", paper to the *Australian Studies Centre Conference*, London, 1986; Caves, R.E., "International Trade and Industrial Organisation: Problems, Solved and Unsolved" (mimeo), Harvard University, presented to the European Association for Research on Industrial Economics, Bergen, August 1983; Caves, R.E., "Scale, Openness, and Productivity in Australian Industries", *The Brookings Survey of the Australian Economy Conference*, Canberra, 9th-11th January 1984; Pratten, C.F., *A Comparison of the Performance of Swedish and UK Companies*, Cambridge University Press, 1976.

27. OECD, *Costs and Benefits of Protection*, Paris, 1985, p. 119.

28. Müller, J. *et al.*, *Economic Evaluation of Telecommunications Investment*, DIW, Berlin, 1985.

29. Thus, this is viewed as a significant factor underpinning increasing reliance by OECD firms on contractual arrangements – such as international subcontracting – relative to more conventional forms of foreign investment in developing countries. See especially Oman, C., *New Forms of International Investment in Developing Countries*, OECD Development Centre, Paris, 1984; Grunwald, J. and Flamm, M., *The Global Factory*, The Brookings Institution, Washington D.C., 1985.

30. A review can be found in Scherer, F.M., *Industrial Market Structure and Economic Performance*, Rand McNally, 1980, pp. 81-150.

31. Geroski, P.A. and Jacquemin, A., "Imports as a Competitive Discipline", *Recherches économiques de Louvain*, No. 47, September 1981, pp. 197-208; Jacquemin, A., "Imperfect Market Structures and International Trade", *Kyklos*, 1982, Vol. 35, No. 1; Lyons, B., *International Trade, Industrial Pricing and Profitability: A Survey*, University of Sheffield, September 1979; Pugel, T.A., "Foreign Trade and US Market Performance", *Journal of Industrial Economics*, December 1980, Vol. 29, No. 2, pp. 119-30.

32. Encaoua, D., "Price Dynamics and Industrial Structure: A Theoretical and Econometric Analysis", *Working Paper No. 10*, OECD, Paris, July 1983.

33. Ergas, H., "Corporate Strategies in Transition" in Jacquemin, A. (ed.), *European Industry: Public Policy and Corporate Strategy*, Oxford University Press, 1984.

34. See especially Hicks, D.A., *Automation Technology and Industrial Renewal*, American Enterprise Institute, 1986; Flamm, K., "International Differences in Industrial Robot Use" (mimeo), The Brookings Institution, 1986; Skinner, W., "The Focused Factory", *Harvard Business Review*, May-June 1974, and *Manufacturing in the Corporate Strategy*, Wiley, 1978; Haskett, J.L., "Sweeping Changes in Distribution", *Harvard Business Review*, March-April 1983; Tarondeau, J.C., *Produits et technologies*, Dalloz, Paris, 1982; Gerwin, D., "Do's and Don'ts of Computerised Manufacturing", *Harvard Business Review*, March-April 1982, p. 113.

35. OECD, *Costs and Benefits of Protection*, *op. cit.* in Note 27, Chapter 6.

36. *Ibid.*, Chapter 3.

37. OECD, *Competition Policy and International Trade, OECD Instruments of Co-operation*, Paris, 1987, pp. 28-29.

Annex A

CLASSIFICATION OF MANUFACTURING INDUSTRIES

The five categories of manufacturing industries with their respective ISIC classifications consist of the following sectors:

1. Resource-Intensive Industries

31	Manufacturing of food, beverages and tobacco
323	Manufacturing of leather, except footwear and wearing apparel
331	Manufacturing of wood, wood and cork products, except furniture
3411	Manufacturing of pulp, paper and paperboard
353	Petroleum refineries
354	Miscellaneous products of petroleum and coal
369	Other non-metallic mineral products
372	Non-ferrous metal basic industries

2. Labour-Intensive Industries

321/322/ 324	Textile, wearing apparel and footwear industries
332	Manufacture of furniture and fixtures, except primarily metal
380/381	Metal scrap from manufactures of fabricated metal products and fabricated metal products, excluding machinery and equipment
39	Other manufacturing industries

3. Scale-Intensive Industries

34	Manufacture of paper, paper products, printing, publishing, except 3411

351	Manufacture of industrial chemicals
355	Rubber products
356	Plastic products not elsewhere classified
361/362	Manufacture of pottery, china, earthenware, glass and glass products
371	Iron and steel basic industries
384	Transport equipment excluding 3845

4. Differentiated Goods

3821	Engines and turbines
3822	Agricultural machinery and equipment
3823	Metal and woodworking machinery
3824	Special industrial machinery and equipment excluding 3823
3829	Machinery and equipment except electric not elsewhere classified
383	Electrical machinery, apparatus, appliances and supplies
3852/3	Photographic and optical goods, watches and clocks

5. Science-Based Industries

352	Manufacture of other chemical products
3825	Office, computing and accounting machinery
3851	Professional, scientific, measuring and controlling equipment
3845	Aircraft

INTRA-INDUSTRY TRADE

1. Intra-industry trade is the value of total trade $(X_i + M_i)$ remaining after subtraction of the absolute value of net exports or imports, $|X_i - M_i|$, of the industry i. For comparison between countries and industries, the measures are expressed as a percentage of each industry's combined exports and imports:

$$\text{Measure of inter-industry trade} = \frac{|X_i - M_i|}{(X_i + M_i)} \cdot 100$$

$$\text{Measure of intra-industry trade} = \frac{(X_i + M_i) - |X_i - M_i|}{(X_i + M_i)} \cdot 100$$

$$\text{Aggregated measure of intra-industry trade} = \frac{\Sigma\,(X_i + M_i) - \Sigma\,|X_i - M_i|}{\Sigma\,(X_i + M_i)} \cdot 100$$

See: Grubel and Lloyd (1975), *op. cit.* (Table 7.3).

2. In Table 7.3 the adjusted average (AA) is calculated as:

$$AA = UA \quad \frac{\Sigma\,(X_i + M_i)}{\Sigma\,(X_i + M_i) - |\Sigma\,X_i - \Sigma\,M_i|}$$

$$\text{Where:} \quad UA = \frac{\Sigma\,[(X_i + M_i) - |X_i - M_i|]}{\Sigma\,(X_i + M_i)} \cdot 100$$

See: Grubel and Lloyd, *ibid.*

Annex C

GRAPHS AND ADDITIONAL TABLES

Graph 7A.1. Revealed comparative advantage of NICs in imports of OECD

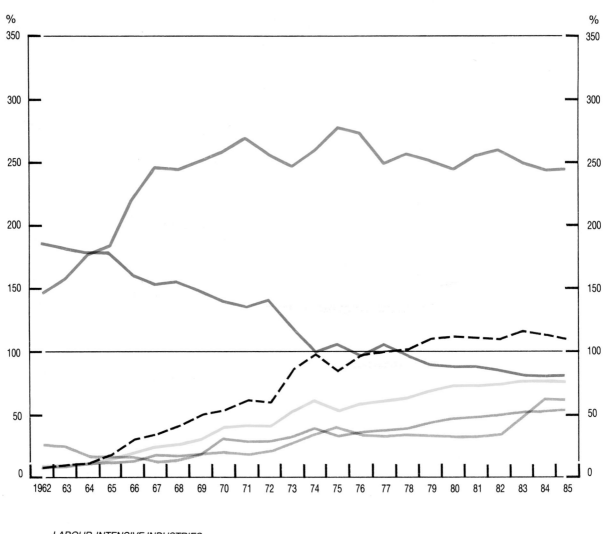

LABOUR-INTENSIVE INDUSTRIES

DIFFERENTIATED INDUSTRIES

RESOURCE-INTENSIVE INDUSTRIES

PRODUCTION-INTENSIVE INDUSTRIES

SCIENCE-BASED INDUSTRIES

SCALE-INTENSIVE INDUSTRIES

Note: The indicator of revealed comparative advantage compares the trend in the structure of exports of an industrial sector in a given country with the structure of exports in the same sector in other countries or in another group of countries. This indicator is equal to the share of an industry's exports in total manufacturing exports in relation to the same share for a group of countries.

Source: OECD.

Graph 7A.2. **Shares in NICs' exports to OECD**

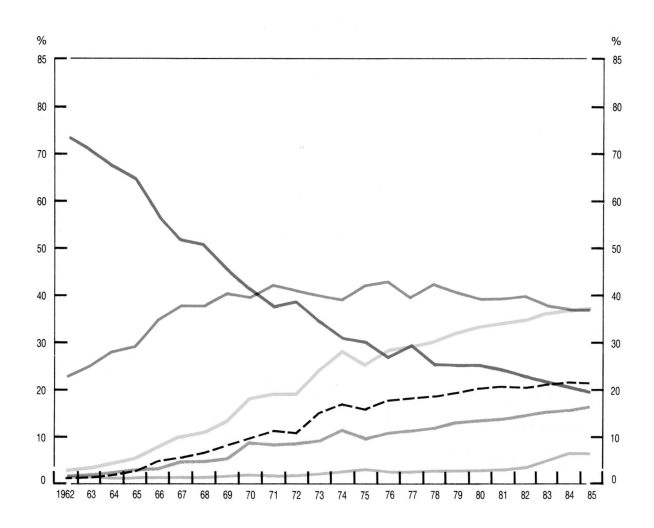

PRODUCTION-INTENSIVE INDUSTRIES
LABOUR-INTENSIVE INDUSTRIES
DIFFERENTIATED INDUSTRIES
RESOURCE-INTENSIVE INDUSTRIES
SCALE-INTENSIVE INDUSTRIES
SCIENCE-BASED INDUSTRIES

Source: OECD.

Graph 7A.3. Share of NICs in imports of OECD (per industry)

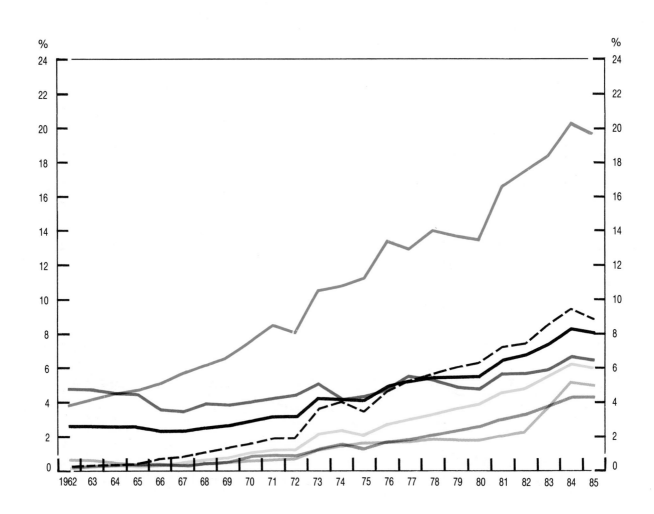

LABOUR-INTENSIVE INDUSTRIES

DIFFERENTIATED INDUSTRIES

TOTAL MANUFACTURING

RESOURCE-INTENSIVE INDUSTRIES

PRODUCTION-INTENSIVE INDUSTRIES

SCIENCE-BASED INDUSTRIES

SCALE-INTENSIVE INDUSTRIES

Source: OECD.

288

Table 7A.1. **Shares of partner countries in total manufacturing exports/imports of declaring countries, 1962-1985**

Percentages

Partner countries[1]

Declaring countries	Exports									Imports								
	1962			1973			1985			1962			1973			1985		
	OECD	NICs	DEVC	OECD	NICs	DEVC	OECD	NICs	DEVC	OECD	NICs	DEVC	OECD	NICs	DEVC	OECD	NICs	DEVC
Resource-intensive industries																		
United States	60.2	3.2	34.5	65.4	6.0	24.3	56.5	9.9	31.5	53.2	9.2	36.6	56.2	6.8	34.6	53.0	10.3	33.7
Japan	67.6	12.4	19.0	49.1	24.7	24.8	36.6	31.4	28.2	52.8	13.3	29.1	47.5	11.6	33.4	44.1	15.9	35.3
EEC (10)	79.2	1.8	15.8	85.4	1.1	10.4	84.0	1.3	12.8	63.6	2.4	27.5	73.2	3.3	17.3	71.8	3.3	17.1
OECD	78.2	2.2	16.9	82.2	2.5	12.0	78.9	3.4	15.2	61.8	4.8	28.5	67.7	5.0	21.6	64.9	6.4	22.0
Labour-intensive industries																		
United States	59.5	2.9	35.1	66.2	9.1	22.8	54.6	9.3	35.3	73.7	7.1	18.0	59.1	24.0	15.0	37.6	41.0	20.2
Japan	50.4	10.7	35.0	46.3	22.9	25.8	46.4	20.8	29.9	83.3	4.2	11.5	45.2	29.2	23.5	38.6	33.5	26.1
EEC (10)	76.4	1.7	18.5	84.1	1.4	10.5	81.7	1.7	14.0	86.7	3.5	7.4	83.2	5.9	6.7	78.2	7.4	10.8
OECD	70.9	3.1	22.7	78.8	4.4	13.0	75.7	4.3	17.3	85.2	3.8	9.0	76.7	10.5	9.5	64.2	19.6	13.7
Production-intensive industries																		
United States	51.3	3.9	37.5	63.5	8.5	23.8	61.9	8.2	8.5	96.9	0.5	1.9	88.3	7.4	3.8	80.4	11.9	7.0
Japan	39.0	15.1	39.5	50.0	14.8	31.4	58.7	11.7	27.2	89.9	0.5	4.2	86.1	7.2	3.5	74.3	16.2	6.8
EEC (10)	69.2	2.4	21.8	76.4	2.3	14.9	75.9	2.3	17.4	94.9	0.1	1.0	94.8	0.8	1.5	93.2	2.3	2.6
OECD	65.5	3.6	25.4	71.3	6.7	18.3	70.5	5.3	20.6	96.5	0.2	1.2	94.2	2.2	1.8	88.6	6.0	4.0
of which:																		
Scale-intensive industries																		
United States	55.9	3.5	38.9	69.7	6.5	22.0	69.6	5.9	22.9	96.0	0.4	2.6	93.1	3.6	2.7	86.4	7.9	4.5
Japan	34.7	15.7	42.8	47.1	12.1	37.4	58.4	8.2	30.7	81.6	0.8	8.2	82.3	6.2	6.3	70.9	15.4	9.6
EEC (10)	70.3	2.2	21.5	79.0	1.7	14.1	79.4	1.8	14.7	94.9	0.1	1.4	95.0	0.6	1.9	93.2	1.5	2.8
OECD	65.9	3.4	25.3	73.2	3.9	18.5	74.3	3.6	18.6	95.2	0.1	1.8	94.5	1.3	2.1	90.3	4.2	3.4
Differentiated goods industries																		
United States	58.1	4.4	36.1	60.1	10.7	25.8	52.8	10.8	5.1	98.6	0.7	0.6	78.5	15.2	6.0	70.9	18.1	10.8
Japan	46.4	13.9	33.6	55.4	19.9	20.1	59.0	15.8	23.1	97.9	0.2	0.3	90.2	8.3	0.5	79.5	17.6	2.6
EEC (10)	67.6	2.7	22.3	72.3	3.3	16.2	70.1	3.1	21.9	98.2	0.2	0.5	96.6	1.2	0.8	93.2	3.5	2.3
OECD	64.9	3.8	25.5	68.4	7.0	18.0	64.9	7.8	23.6	98.5	0.2	0.3	93.6	3.6	1.5	85.7	8.8	4.9
Science-based industries																		
United States	63.7	5.1	29.7	73.1	7.8	17.4	69.7	10.8	18.7	91.8	2.3	5.1	89.2	3.1	7.4	80.3	14.2	5.4
Japan	42.9	23.3	30.7	67.6	15.1	14.1	73.9	12.4	12.4	98.3	0.6	0.7	93.5	4.0	2.1	93.4	4.4	1.9
EEC (10)	69.8	3.0	23.7	76.1	2.6	16.8	79.4	2.6	15.2	95.2	0.6	3.3	96.4	0.7	2.3	94.9	2.4	2.4
OECD	68.2	3.8	24.7	75.2	4.9	16.5	75.9	6.1	15.8	96.0	0.7	2.5	95.9	1.2	2.4	92.1	4.9	2.7
Total manufacturing																		
United States	58.8	3.8	35.7	66.7	8.0	22.7	62.6	9.1	26.9	68.6	6.5	24.0	74.0	9.4	15.3	68.2	16.4	14.2
Japan	46.6	13.4	35.3	50.1	16.4	29.6	58.2	13.0	26.4	77.1	5.6	13.6	61.1	13.6	20.8	59.2	17.2	20.6
EEC (10)	72.5	2.2	19.9	79.4	1.9	13.3	78.8	2.0	15.7	81.0	1.6	13.2	86.6	2.4	7.4	85.1	3.4	7.9
OECD	69.1	3.2	22.8	75.0	4.4	16.1	73.3	4.9	18.7	80.9	2.6	13.4	83.8	4.3	8.8	79.5	8.0	9.7

1. NICs: Brazil, Singapore, South Korea, Taiwan, Hong Kong.
   DEVC: Developing countries.
Source: Secretariat estimates.

289

Table 7A.2. **Shares of industries in manufacturing exports/imports of declaring countries with respect to partner countries**

Percentages

Declaring countries	Partner countries[1]																	
	Exports									Imports								
	1962			1973			1985			1962			1973			1985		
	OECD	NICs	DEVC	OECD	NICs	DEVC	OECD	NICs	DEVC	OECD	NICs	DEVC	OECD	NICs	DEVC	OECD	NICs	DEVC
Resource-intensive industries																		
United States	23.5	19.1	22.2	16.7	12.8	18.2	12.9	15.4	16.7	43.2	78.7	84.8	24.1	23.0	71.6	15.4	12.4	46.9
Japan	17.7	11.3	6.6	4.7	7.2	4.0	2.0	7.6	3.4	23.8	83.2	74.6	33.9	37.1	70.1	30.2	37.7	69.4
EEC (10)	21.7	15.8	15.6	20.7	10.7	15.0	21.0	12.4	16.0	32.9	62.6	87.3	26.5	42.5	73.2	23.9	28.1	61.1
OECD	27.2	16.7	17.9	23.2	11.8	15.8	19.2	12.4	14.6	30.5	73.6	85.1	23.4	34.1	70.8	19.7	19.2	55.0
Labour-intensive industries																		
United States	11.7	8.8	11.4	9.3	10.7	9.4	5.9	6.6	8.6	18.0	18.2	12.5	11.4	36.6	14.0	8.7	39.6	22.4
Japan	38.1	28.3	34.9	12.8	19.3	12.0	5.9	11.7	8.3	17.2	12.0	13.6	16.2	47.0	24.8	9.9	29.6	19.1
EEC (10)	18.5	13.9	16.2	17.9	11.9	13.2	15.7	13.0	13.5	15.9	32.1	8.3	16.0	40.5	15.7	13.8	33.1	20.5
OECD	16.6	15.9	16.2	15.1	14.2	11.6	12.3	10.3	11.0	16.1	22.5	10.5	14.8	39.8	17.3	12.2	37.0	21.5
Production-intensive industries																		
United States	52.9	57.0	57.3	54.7	59.3	58.8	53.8	48.7	57.6	34.1	1.8	1.9	59.2	39.0	12.2	66.7	41.1	27.7
Japan	42.5	57.2	56.9	77.1	69.8	82.1	83.1	73.9	85.0	42.1	3.4	11.1	34.6	13.0	4.1	39.0	29.4	10.2
EEC (10)	53.1	61.0	60.1	54.2	67.3	62.3	51.7	60.1	59.4	43.8	2.9	2.8	49.1	14.9	8.7	49.6	30.8	15.0
OECD	49.2	58.8	58.2	53.5	64.9	64.2	56.2	62.5	64.4	45.9	2.4	3.4	53.5	24.2	9.9	56.1	37.5	20.7
of which:																		
Scale-intensive industries																		
United States	25.5	25.0	29.2	30.8	24.1	28.6	32.7	19.1	25.0	21.8	0.9	1.7	41.9	12.7	5.8	43.7	16.7	10.9
Japan	24.1	38.1	39.3	47.4	37.3	63.8	44.8	28.1	51.9	18.7	2.6	10.7	17.1	5.7	3.8	22.5	16.8	8.7
EEC (10)	33.2	34.5	36.5	34.4	30.0	36.2	33.7	29.2	31.3	26.0	1.4	2.3	29.7	6.1	6.9	31.0	12.9	10.0
OECD	28.7	32.2	33.7	33.5	30.5	39.4	35.6	25.7	34.7	27.0	1.3	3.0	33.2	8.9	6.8	35.3	16.3	10.9
Differentiated goods industries																		
United States	27.4	32.0	28.1	23.9	35.3	30.2	21.1	29.6	32.6	12.3	1.0	0.2	17.2	26.3	6.4	23.0	24.4	16.9
Japan	18.4	19.2	17.6	29.7	32.5	18.3	38.4	45.9	33.1	23.5	0.7	0.4	17.6	7.2	0.3	16.5	12.6	1.6
EEC (10)	19.9	26.5	23.7	19.8	37.4	26.2	18.0	30.9	28.2	17.8	1.6	0.5	19.4	8.7	1.8	18.7	17.9	5.0
OECD	20.4	26.5	24.5	20.1	34.4	24.7	20.6	36.8	29.5	18.9	1.1	0.4	20.2	15.3	3.1	20.7	21.1	9.7
Science-based industries																		
United States	12.0	15.1	9.2	19.3	17.2	13.6	27.6	29.3	17.2	4.8	1.3	0.8	5.4	1.5	2.2	9.3	6.9	3.0
Japan	1.7	3.2	1.6	5.5	3.7	1.9	9.0	6.8	3.4	16.9	1.4	0.7	15.3	2.9	1.0	20.9	3.4	1.2
EEC (10)	6.6	9.3	8.1	7.2	10.1	9.5	11.5	14.6	11.0	7.4	2.4	1.6	8.4	2.2	2.3	12.6	8.1	3.4
OECD	7.1	8.7	7.8	8.2	9.1	8.4	12.3	14.8	10.1	7.5	1.6	1.2	8.4	2.0	2.0	12.1	6.4	2.9
Total manufacturing																		
United States	100	100	100	100	100	100	100	100	100	100	100	100	100	100	100	100	100	100
Japan	100	100	100	100	100	100	100	100	100	100	100	100	100	100	100	100	100	100
EEC (10)	100	100	100	100	100	100	100	100	100	100	100	100	100	100	100	100	100	100
OECD	100	100	100	100	100	100	100	100	100	100	100	100	100	100	100	100	100	100

1. NICs: Brazil, Singapore, South Korea, Taiwan, Hong Kong.
   DEVC: Developing countries.
Source: Secretariat estimates.

Table 7A.3. **Average shares of six categories[1] of manufactures in total value of exports[2], imports[2] and production of manufacturing for 14 OECD countries[3]**

Percentages

Manufactures from	Imports[4]			Exports[4]			Production[4]		
	1970-1971	1977-1978	1984-1985	1970-1971	1977-1978	1984-1985	1970-1971	1977-1978	1984-1985
Resource-intensive industries									
Large countries	32.1	28.6	22.3	12.3	11.5	10.8	26.9	27.2	26.8
Small countries	22.0	25.1	24.7	37.0	37.9	38.3	43.2	46.6	46.6
All countries	30.6	28.2	22.5	15.3	14.4	13.5	27.5	28.0	27.5
Labour-intensive industries									
Large countries	15.2	16.3	15.5	13.0	12.3	10.0	15.7	13.7	12.5
Small countries	15.8	17.3	11.8	11.8	12.2	8.3	12.5	10.7	8.6
All countries	15.3	16.4	15.1	12.8	12.3	9.8	15.6	13.6	12.4
Production-intensive industries									
Large countries	45.5	47.6	51.3	60.4	64.3	62.5	47.1	50.1	49.4
Small countries	55.2	55.4	55.8	46.8	46.3	49.1	40.5	39.2	41.4
All countries	46.9	48.2	51.7	58.7	62.4	61.1	46.8	49.7	49.2
of which:									
Scale-intensive industries									
Large countries	28.9	29.3	29.7	32.9	35.3	33.0	29.5	32.0	30.1
Small countries	37.9	37.6	42.9	36.0	35.9	41.2	30.9	30.4	33.7
All countries	30.2	30.4	30.9	33.3	35.3	33.8	29.6	31.9	30.2
Differentiated goods industries									
Large countries	16.6	18.2	21.6	27.5	29.1	29.4	17.6	18.1	19.3
Small countries	17.3	14.8	12.9	10.8	10.4	7.9	9.6	8.8	7.7
All countries	16.7	17.8	20.8	25.4	27.1	27.3	17.2	17.7	19.0
Science-based industries									
Large countries	7.1	7.5	10.9	14.4	11.8	16.8	10.3	9.0	11.2
Small countries	7.0	5.2	7.7	4.4	3.7	4.4	3.9	3.5	3.4
All countries	7.1	7.2	10.6	13.1	11.0	15.5	10.1	8.8	10.9

1. The industries making up these categories are described in Annex A.
2. Imports/exports consist of trade with the whole world, thus including trade between these 14 OECD countries.
3. Australia, Belgium/Luxembourg, Canada, Finland, France, Germany, Italy, Japan, the Netherlands, Norway, Sweden, United Kingdom, United States. Large countries: Canada, France, Germany, Italy, Japan, United Kingdom, United States; small countries: Australia, Belgium/Luxembourg, Finland, the Netherlands, Norway, Sweden. In 1985 the group of large and small countries accounted for 60 per cent and 17 per cent of world exports of manufactures respectively. The share of "all countries" is a weighted average of large and small countries on the basis of their respective shares in total trade of all 14 countries.
4. The calculations are based on the International Standard Industrial Classification.
Source: Secretariat estimates.

Table 7A.4. **Network of trade[1], all commodities and manufactures, 1963, 1973 and 1985**

Percentage of total world export

Exports from	Exports to					
	Industrial countries		Other[2]		World[3]	
	All commodities	Manufactures	All commodities	Manufactures	All commodities	Manufactures
Industrial countries						
1963	49.7	59.0	17.4	23.3	67.1	82.3
1973	55.1	63.8	15.8	19.3	70.9	83.1
1985	49.8	58.1	16.5	20.7	66.3	78.8
World						
1963	67.1	62.8	32.9	37.2	100.0	100.0
1973	72.2	70.1	27.8	29.8	100.0	100.0
1985	68.2	67.8	31.7	32.2	100.0	100.0

1. Based on export values (fob) in dollars.
2. LDCs and Eastern trading area.
3. Including South Africa, Australia and New Zealand.
Source: GATT, *International Trade 1986,* Geneva, 1987.

Table 7A.5. **Illustrative MFN tariffs on selected products in the mid-1950s, before and after the Tokyo Round**

Percentages

		Denmark	Norway	Sweden	Austria	Switzerland	United Kingdom	Germany	Benelux	France	Italy	EEC	United States	Canada	Japan
60.05	Knitted outer garments	20	17-20	15	28	12	20-33.3	13	24	25	22	21	15-42.5	32.5-35	17.5
			17	15	25	10						18	2	27.5	14
			17	15	25	8						14	2	25	
64.01	Rubber shoes	15-25	10-30	14	28-32	10-13	25	19	24	22	20	21	12.5-20	22.5	10
			6-10	14	28	8.5						20	6[3]	20	10
			3-5	14	28	8.5						20	6[3]	20	
73.13	Sheets and plates of iron and steel simply cold rolled	0	0	6	17	6-8	10	14	3	16-22	23	10	10-13	0-25	7.5
			0	6	15	1.5						7	8-9	10	4.9
			0	5	15	1.5						4.9	5-6.5	6.8	
87.02	Cars assembled	14	30	15	20	14-23	30	17	24	30	40	29	8.5-10.5	15	17.5
			8	10	9.6	9.3						11	3	9.2	18.8
			5.3	6.2	9.6	6.2						10	2.5		3
29.01	Monomeric styrene	0	0	0	0	1-4	33.5	12	12	20	10	13	0-30	0-20	10
			0	11	0	0.1						6.4	13.7	15	8
			0	6.5[1]	0	0.1						6	7.4	7.5	
84.36	Textile machines for spinning and twisting	5	10	10	18	3-5	15	5	6	15	18	11	17-20	5	7.5
			5	5	9	0.6						5	7	0	4.9
			3.8	3.8	6	0.6						3.8	4.7	0	
85.01	Electric motors	7.5	10	10	18-24	2-6	17.5	8	8	20	16.5	12	10.5-15	20	7.5
			5	5	19	1.8						8.5	5-12.5	15	4.9
			3.8	3.8	19	1.5						8.5	0-6.6	9.2	
84.52	Electronic calculating machines	5	10	10	5	4-15	17.5	12	8	20	15	14	13.75	10	15
			5	2.5	2.5	5.2						14	5.5	10	4.9
			3.8	1.8	1.8	3.5						12	3.9	3.9	

1. The MFN duty actually applied is zero.
2. It is not possible to reconstitute comparable figures. However, in this category many very high tariffs (i.e. 42.5 per cent) before the Tokyo Round were reduced to 17 per cent.
3. Other items under the same category have higher rates, also unchanged in the Tokyo Round.

Note: The first row for each country refers to the mid-1950s; the second to immediately before the Tokyo Round (which is equivalent to after-implementation of the Kennedy Round), and the third to after-implementation of the Tokyo Round. Given the diversity of sources and slight changes in national definitions, the figures given are not always strictly comparable from one country to another and over time, but can be taken as illustrative.

Source: GATT.

Table 7A.6. **Weighted average of tariffs by countries and sectors, 1953**

Percentages

	Austria	Benelux	Canada	Denmark	France	Germany	Italy	Norway	Sweden	United States	Average of ten countries
Primary products for food, excluding fish	30	1	4	1	11	11	27	2	5	2	6.9 (12.9)
Manufactured products for food, excluding fish	21	5	7	1	9	21	23	3	3	10	10.7 (18.3)
Fish and fish products	1	14	9	0	9	15	19	1	2	6	8.3 (11.8)
Raw materials, including petroleum products	1	0	2	0	2	2	2	1	0	4	2.1 (3.1)
Products of chemical and allied industries	9	4	7	1	17	15	20	6	3	6	8.4 (12.3)
Leather and products of leather, fur skins, rubber, wood, cork, paper and clothing	10	10	11	4	15	14	21	8	5	2	6.5 (15.1)
Textile products and clothing	21	13	14	4	18	18	22	13	6	18	9.0 (19.0)
Base metals and manufactures thereof	11	4	10	1	6	10	22	3	3	6	6.9 (12.3)
Machinery, electric and transport equipment	23	10	9	4	16	12	23	6	10	6	10.7 (15.9)
Miscellaneous manufactures	11	9	11	5	14	8	20	13	6	16	12.1 (15.3)

Note: The figures are strongly downward biased, as they are weighted by each country's actual imports in 1950 or 1951, including non-dutiable imports, and they use cif valuation. By comparison, the figures in brackets represent unweighted (arithmetic) averages; fiscal duties are excluded throughout.
Source: GATT, *A New Proposal for the Reduction of Customs Tariffs;* Geneva, January 1954; OECD estimates from internal GATT documents.

Table 7A.7. **Tariff averages before (B) and after (A) the Tokyo Round**

Percentages

		Nine tariffs		United States		Canada		Japan		EEC		Australia		Finland		Norway		Sweden		Switzerland	
		B	A	B	A	B	A	B	A	B	A	B	A	B	A	B	A	B	A	B	A
All industrial products	1°	10.3	6.4	11.2	6.3	12.5	7.3	10.1	5.9	9.0	6.4	11.7	8.1	13.2	11.4	8.5	6.6	6.0	4.8	7.7	2.8
(including petroleum)	3°	5.2	3.5	4.4	3.0	11.7	7.3	4.1	2.6	4.0	2.9	7.5	6.3	4.6	3.6	3.1	2.4	3.7	2.6	2.2	1.7
of which:																					
Crude materials	1°	2.9	1.7	3.3	1.8	4.9	2.6	2.5	1.4	1.9	1.6	2.6	1.9	0.8	0.5	1.2	0.9	0.5	0.4	1.8	1.5
	3°	0.7	0.6	0.7	0.6	1.1	0.7	1.9	1.5	0.0	0.0	2.6	1.9	0.1	0.0	0.0	0.0	0.0	0.0	0.1	0.0
Semi-finished manufactures	1°	9.7	6.2	10.1	6.1	11.7	6.6	9.7	6.3	8.9	6.2	10.3	7.3	13.0	11.7	6.7	5.4	6.0	5.1	3.6	2.8
	3°	6.0	4.2	4.4	3.0	11.8	8.3	6.5	4.5	5.5	4.1	5.7	4.7	6.7	5.8	1.7	1.4	5.2	3.2	1.6	1.2
Finished manufactures	1°	11.7	7.0	13.0	6.9	13.6	8.1	11.5	6.4	10.0	7.0	13.4	9.1	14.3	12.0	10.0	7.8	6.6	5.1	4.0	3.0
	3°	9.9	6.4	8.1	5.6	13.6	8.3	12.4	5.9	9.7	6.8	18.3	16.0	7.7	6.0	5.6	4.2	6.5	4.8	3.9	3.0

Note: 1°: unweighted (arithmetical) average, and 3°: weighted average. The tariff averages are the same as in the 1974 Tariff Study, calculated on the basis of 1977 total import data (including non-dutiable imports).
Source: GATT data bank.

Table 7A.8. **Subsidy shares by destination and in total officially supported export credits**

Percentages

	1979	1980	1981	1982	1983	1984	1985
OECD	6.7	13.4	9.9	10.5	4.0	9.5	2.2
NICs	35.4	31.4	26.6	20.8	21.8	28.3	10.3
CPE	26.2	13.2	13.2	11.8	12.8	5.9	1.1
OPEC	11.2	5.0	4.4	4.4	12.1	28.0	22.5
LDCs	20.4	36.9	45.9	52.5	49.3	28.3	63.9
Subsidy shares (all areas)	14.2	19.2	27.5	22.2	15.8	25.4	12.0

Note: Subsidies are calculated as the net present value of credits using actual credit terms and estimated market terms. Data pertain to officially supported credits of over three years' maturity. They do not include the aid component of tied aid credits. Thus, this table gives the subsidy element in officially supported non-aid export credits.
Source: Secretariat estimates.

Table 7A.9. **Index of revealed comparative advantage by product category: small countries versus large**[1]

	1962		1973		1985	
	Large	Small	Large	Small	Large	Small
Resource-intensive industries	86.1	144.8	75.8	169.4	77.2	198.4
Labour-intensive industries	100.0	100.5	96.7	96.8	92.5	102.0
Production-intensive industries	105.2	84.0	107.9	81.1	106.7	77.1
of which:						
Scale-intensive industries	104.2	102.2	106.1	97.1	104.8	91.4
Differentiated goods industries	106.6	58.9	110.9	56.2	109.6	55.5
Science-based industries	108.7	64.5	113.7	55.8	108.7	62.8

1. The index of revealed comparative advantage compares the trend in the structrure of exports of an industrial sector in a given country with the structure of exports in the same sector in other countries or in another group of countries. This indicator is equal to the share of an industry's exports in total manufacturing exports in relation to the share for a group of countries.
  See notes to Table 7A.3.
Source: Secretariat estimates.

Table 7A.10. **Growth rates of trade and output at current prices in six categories of manufactures for 14 OECD countries[1]**

Percentages

Type of industries	Imports		Exports		Production	
	1970/1971-1977/1978	1977/1978-1984/1985	1970/1971-1977/1978	1977/1978-1984/1985	1970/1971-1977/1978	1977/1978-1984/1985
Resource-intensive industries						
Large countries	16.8	7.6	18.1	6.2	3.1	8.3
Small countries	19.2	4.9	17.0	6.0	14.3	5.0
All countries	17.1	7.3	17.8	6.1	13.2	8.1
Labour-intensive industries						
Large countries	19.8	10.7	18.4	3.9	10.8	7.1
Small countries	18.4	−0.3	17.1	0.1	10.6	1.8
All countries	19.6	9.5	18.3	3.6	10.8	7.0
Production-intensive industries						
Large countries	19.5	12.7	20.3	6.7	13.9	8.3
Small countries	16.1	6.1	16.4	6.8	12.5	5.9
All countries	18.9	11.9	20.0	6.7	13.9	8.2
of which:						
Scale-intensive industries						
Large countries	19.0	11.7	20.4	6.2	14.2	7.6
Small countries	16.8	7.2	16.6	7.9	12.8	6.6
All countries	18.6	11.0	20.0	6.4	14.2	7.5
Differentiated goods industries						
Large countries	20.3	14.2	20.2	7.4	13.4	9.5
Small countries	14.4	3.2	15.9	1.9	11.7	3.1
All countries	19.5	13.3	20.0	7.2	13.4	9.4
Science-based industries						
Large countries	19.6	17.6	16.0	12.7	10.7	11.9
Small countries	12.2	11.1	13.7	8.6	11.4	4.4
All countries	18.7	17.0	15.9	12.5	10.7	11.8
Total manufacturing						
Large countries	18.7	11.5	19.2	7.2	12.9	8.5
Small countries	16.9	5.2	16.6	5.8	13.1	5.0
All countries	18.5	10.8	18.9	7.0	12.9	8.4

1. See notes to Table 7A.3.
Source: Secretariat estimates.

III. EFFICIENCY AND EFFECTIVENESS
IN THE PUBLIC SECTOR

Chapter 8

REGULATION AND ITS REFORM

INTRODUCTION

In 1969, an eminent United States specialist concluded a survey of the costs of regulation by noting that though these costs were increasingly recognised, the prospects for reform were slight[1]. Yet, less than two decades later, substantial parts of previously highly regulated industries have been liberalised; and greater use of market forces is widely seen as indispensable if these industries are to have incentives to be efficient and innovative.

Broadly speaking, "regulation" can be defined as the set of processes by which governments issue instructions which directly alter the resource allocation decisions of private agents; the instructions may affect the ownership of productive assets (for example, through nationalisation), the manner in which assets are employed (for example, by the setting of compulsory quality levels), or the terms on which output is sold or otherwise distributed. Within this broad ambit, this chapter focuses on "economic" regulation – i.e. measures aimed at altering outcomes in particular industries – rather than on the "social" regulations (such as environmental controls or occupational health and safety legislation) which set standards applicable across a range of industries. Specifically, the chapter concentrates on the regulatory problems of the public utilities – the industries supplying electricity, gas, water, transport services and communications, and which have generally been seen as "affected with the public interest".

Of course, economic regulation extends far beyond these industries – for example, a recent survey of New Zealand (where the government is engaged in a far-reaching process of regulatory reform) identifies 142 activities into which entry is restricted, excluding cases of occupational licensing and similar professional controls[2]. But a concentration on the public utility industries can be justified on two counts.

The first is their size and economic importance. On average, the public utility industries account for some 10 per cent of value added in the OECD economies and for an only slightly lower share of employment. With only a few exceptions, they are highly capital-intensive, and their assets comprise nearly a fifth of the OECD area's capital stock. They are also growing at above average rates, so that the efficiency and flexibility with which they use resources have increasing bearing on productivity overall.

The second is that it is with respect to the public utility industries that the sharpest changes have occurred in beliefs about and policies for government control of industry. Twenty years ago, it was largely accepted that these industries' economic characteristics justified a high level of government involvement in their operation; a view strengthened, in many countries, by perception of these industries as "strategic" for national economic development. Yet it is now widely thought – and a number of governments have altered policies accordingly – that for certain of these industries, government regulation may be neither inevitable or desirable; while for others, though an element of continuing regulation may be needed, there is a strong case for reforming its scope and content.

In examining this shift in attitudes and policies, it is useful to begin by looking at what sets the public utility industries apart – what it is, in other words, that accounts for these industries being sheltered from the operation of market forces. Traditionally, the economic argument for regulating public utilities rests on the concept of "natural monopoly", i.e. situations where production by one firm is more efficient than production by several. At its simplest, this can arise because the industry's cost function is characterised by significant *economies of scale* at all economically relevant levels of demand; but it may also be due to the efficiency gains obtainable from *economies of scope*, i.e. the cost savings which come from having a single firm produce the full product range of a multi-product industry, rather than relying on more narrowly specialised producers. In either case, costs will be minimised if the industry is operated as a monopoly – but the risks this creates (in particular, that the monopoly will exploit the market power it has over consumers) make some measure of regulation inevitable.

Yet there are many industries which have generally been regulated as public utilities but which are not natural monopolies, e.g. airlines, taxi-cabs or road freight (trucking). The argument generally given for regulating these industries is that competition would be "destructive", in the sense that it would induce recurring bouts of excess capacity, and "unfair", in that it would lead to a pattern of provision inconsistent with broad goals of social equity.

This raises two questions. First, in those regulated industries which are not natural monopolies, is it true that competition is likely to have undesirable economic or social impacts? And second, in the industries which do in fact have natural monopoly characteristics, how can an efficient and flexible use of resources best be secured? This chapter focuses on these questions. Its structure is as follows.

Part I (regulation in structurally competitive industries) looks at the regulated industries – notably in transport – which clearly do not possess natural monopoly characteristics. On the basis of case studies of these industries, it concludes that there is little economic or social justification for their continued regulation – and that the benefits of entirely deregulating them may be considerable.

Part II (the control of natural monopolies: the options) turns to the industries where the conditions of production do provide a *prima facie* case for regulatory intervention. It examines the three major instruments of intervention – public enterprise, franchising and formal regulation (i.e. a formalised process for setting prices and rates of return). It concludes that public enterprise may be afflicted with significant difficulties, largely as a result of the nature of its interaction with government; that franchising, though analytically interesting, is feasible only in fairly narrowly defined circumstances; and that formal regulation – though the most promising of the three approaches – has generally been implemented in a manner which at best blunts, and at worst perverts, the incentives for efficiency and innovativeness.

In short, natural monopoly is a market imperfection; and there is no costless administrative way of correcting it. Yet options do exist for reducing the costs it creates. Drawing largely on the experience of the telecommunications industry, Part III (reforming the regulation of natural monopolies) argues the case for three interrelated changes: placing greater reliance on competition; enhancing the simplicity and transparency of regulation; and accompanying improved product market incentives by reform of the status of public enterprise and increased use of capital market incentives for efficiency.

I. REGULATION IN STRUCTURALLY COMPETITIVE INDUSTRIES: THE TRANSPORT SECTOR

In virtually all OECD countries, most transport modes have been subject to some form of government control over the entry and exit of firms and on market prices and the range and quality of service. Yet the transport industries form a highly heterogeneous grouping; and seen as a whole they certainly do not display natural monopoly characteristics.

Thus, there can be little doubt that railroad transport involves considerable economies of scale and scope and that a local rail network may well be a natural monopoly[3]. However, road freight[4], air transport (for both passengers and freight)[5] and bus services[6] largely display constant returns to scale, and though there are barriers to the entry and exit of firms (especially in air transport), these industries can be considered to be structurally competitive. Moreover, there is significant competition between transport modes – notably but not solely for freight – and cross-price elasticities of demand are high[7]. As a result, in the absence of regulatory intervention, the degree of monopoly power in the transport industries would be limited – not only by the ease of entry and exit of producers into any individual transport mode, but by the pressure which price-setting in the modes which are more competitive, e.g. road freight, imposes on those which are less so, e.g. rail. The attempt to control intermodal competition largely explains the historical tendency for regulatory intervention to spread across the transport industries, new modes being subject to regulation as they challenge the position of established, already regulated, forms of supply. Yet the economic costs of regulation have been high (Section A); and deregulation, where it has occurred, has contributed to efficiency and innovativeness (Sections B and C).

A. The economic effects of transport regulation

Given the heterogeneity of economic characteristics within the transport industries, and the diversity of the constraints imposed on the various modes, it is not surprising that the effects of regulation have varied from mode to mode, as well as varying from country to country. Quantification of these effects is complicated by the interdependence between modes, as the results of any particular distortion, e.g. rail prices not in line with long-run marginal costs, may offset or compound those pertaining to any other form of transport (in this case, collusive fixing of road freight charges). Moreover, relatively few comparative studies are available across transport modes, especially internationally, so that generalisations about the "costs of regulation" are likely to be misleading.

Bearing these caveats in mind, the "established wisdom" about the impacts of regulatory intervention on the transport industries – a "wisdom" largely established during the period when these interventions were in place and heavily reliant on analyses carried out in the United States – can be briefly summarised as follows[8].

1. Price levels

First, prices for regulated transport services (both in individual modes and for transport services as a whole) have been higher than those which would pertain in a competitive market, as well as (on average) exceeding the price levels corresponding to a second-best optimisation, i.e. prices designed to offset distortions arising elsewhere in the economy. This has only partly been due to supra-normal profits – though these have been significant in a few cases[9]. Rather, the additional profits created by regulatory protection have typically been dissipated in excess costs, as producers resort to non-price forms of competition – such as enhanced or more frequent service – to increase their market share, and as some part of the rents from regulation are transferred to suppliers of inputs. Indeed, in the case of rail transport, average prices have frequently been kept *below* average costs by regulatory intervention, direct or indirect subsidies (or debt accumulation) making up the difference; yet average costs – and hence the real resource burden on the economy of obtaining service – have been swollen both by operating inefficiencies and by higher than needed input prices.

2. *Price structures*

As well as affecting the overall *level* of prices, regulation has typically distorted their *structure* relative to that of costs. This in part reflects a tendency of regulatory systems to seek a degree of uniformity in prices on distinct markets – if nothing else so as to minimise the costs of taking regulatory decisions and monitoring their implementation. However, it also arises from the use of price structures as a way of redistributing income, notably from users in low-cost areas to those in areas with higher costs – a phenomenon generally known as "rate averaging". The actual incidence of these attempted redistributions on final incomes is highly uncertain and frequently paradoxical – for example, rail subsidies to areas where service is unprofitable may to some extent be capitalised into the value of land holdings in the locality, and hence actually aggravate the intra- (and possibly the inter-) regional income distribution[10]; and the unpredictable nature of the outcomes is compounded by the fact that the extent and pattern of the cross-subsidies almost always differs across competing transport modes. Nonetheless, it has generally been taken for granted that cross-subsidisation in transport pricing has favoured the poorer, frequently rural, areas, by providing them with service at prices only slightly above or even below long-run marginal cost.

3. *Capacity utilisation*

The distortions this induces in demand patterns have generally been accompanied by distortions in the *structure of supply*. Thus, it has been a widespread practice to oblige certain providers of transport services – and especially railroads – to retain unprofitable capacity in use, notably in lower-income regions and in areas where economic trends have led to declines in demand. This results in persistent excess capacity which – in addition to its financial impact on suppliers – imposes economic

losses measurable by the difference between price and short-run marginal costs. Regional externalities must, of course, be taken into account in assessing whether these losses are matched by gains; but estimates suggest that the welfare costs of excess capacity have been considerable[11].

4. *Technological change*

Finally, there is some, though very mixed, evidence that regulation has been associated with dynamic inefficiencies arising from its effects on technical progress. In some instances, regulatory structures have offered inadequate incentives for the diffusion of innovation and encouraged or permitted the persistence of outdated work practices (the virtually universal overmanning of rail systems being a case in point)[12]. In others, the primary effects have been on the direction rather than on the rate of technical change, with distorted relative prices being the major factor at work: regulated airlines, for example, overlooking the scope for cost reduction on low-density routes largely because returns on these routes have been protected[13] and rail carriers in Europe and Japan concentrating on improving high-speed long-distance passenger trains (where regulated returns are highest) rather than on upgrading local commuter services[14].

B. Deregulation: two case studies

Overall, these findings provide a basis for assessing the likely effects of transport deregulation. More specifically, it can be conjectured that – compared to regulatory outcomes – competitive provision of transport services encourages efficiency gains both through greater capacity utilisation and improved work practices (thus permitting lower prices on average) and by bringing the structure of transport prices more closely into line with the structure of costs; but that the transition to competition may impose incidental losses on the producers and consumers who had benefitted from regulatory protection.

In assessing the extent of these impacts, it is now possible to rely on the experience and evidence of up to a decade of regulatory reform in the transport industries. Two cases are of particular interest, both because they are well documented and because they emphasize similar points but in quite different settings.

1. *Airline deregulation in the United States*

The first is that of *airline deregulation* in the United States, a process initiated by the Airline Deregulation Act of 1978 and culminating in the elimination of all restrictions on entry, exit and pricing as of 1st January 1983.

The consumer gains from deregulation have been considerable: econometric analyses find that on average, competition has reduced the real price of air travel by some 13 per cent; at the same time, the frequency of flights has increased on most routes, so that the overall benefits to air travellers have been greater than the lower fares suggest. On one recent estimate, these gains are equivalent to an annual income increment of $6 billion (in 1977 dollars) – a sum equal to 35 per cent of total airline revenues[15].

These consumer benefits have been obtained not at the producers' expense, but through organisational innovation and consequent increases in efficiency. In essence, United States airlines, faced with competitive pressure, have rationalised their route structure, shifting from a predominance of direct flights to "hub and spoke" networks in which traffic is concentrated at nodes from which passengers take connecting flights to their destinations. This allows airlines to optimise more carefully the aircraft sizes and characteristics used on each route and to more effectively exploit the economies of aircraft size on high-density links[16]. The reduction in the number of direct flights has probably caused some consumer inconvenience, but the development of traffic nodes has ensured that consumers rarely have to change carrier in mid-journey – a time-saving which survey data suggests travellers value highly[17]. The rise in capacity utilisation from improved routing and consequent cost savings has allowed the United States airline industry to – on average – actually *increase* its profitability, a simulation study showing, for example, that had the market been deregulated in 1977, industry profits would have been $2.5 billion dollars higher in that year. The industry did make significant losses in 1983, but these were due to input price increases and the state of the macroeconomy – and they would have been even greater had regulatory restrictions prevented firms from responding to the downturn in demand through route rationalisation and other cost-cutting measures[18].

Nor is there strong evidence that deregulation has had a significant adverse effect on the industry's labour force. Despite large productivity gains, the traffic growth induced by lower fares has raised industry employment levels in virtually all occupational groups. The wages picture is more mixed, partly because the three-year duration of United States collective agreements gives earnings a considerable degree of inertia in responding to changing market circumstances. Nonetheless, it does appear that pilots – who had previously secured exceptionally high pay rates, but have few opportunities for transferring their skills out of the industry – have had to accept significant reductions in real earnings, while mechanics and (at least until 1985) flight attendants have obtained continuing increases[19].

In short, productivity increases and not income redistribution have been the primary source of consumer gains from competition, and the data suggest that these gains have been fairly widely spread.

The evidence suggests that deregulation has led to improved service to many small communities as well and has not led to widespread service cuts. Thus, the shift to hub-and-spoke networking has permitted increases in flight frequency on all route lengths and a rise in the total number of points served. It is true that between 1st June 1978 and 1st June 1983, ninety-five smaller towns lost air service; but the evidence suggests that the major causes were increases in input prices and changes in macroeconomic circumstances, rather than deregulation *per se* – and that the (largely temporary) decline in the number of routes served might have been greater under the prior regulatory regime[20].

At the same time, a side-effect of deregulation has been to significantly reduce the cost of federally subsidised air service[21]. The United States Government has for some time provided subsidies for maintaining air services to small communities; and concern about deregulation led to this programme being substantially extended in 1979. However, increased routing efficiency and the entry of new "commuter" airlines (which specialise in low-density, short-haul links) has brought intensified competition for small communities' traffic, so that the volume of federal subsidies needed to maintain service declined in nominal terms by nearly 50 per cent from 1977 to 1983.

Overall, though deregulation does not seem to have imposed major welfare losses on any significant group of consumers, far-reaching redistribution among producers has occurred, as some carriers have responded better than others to changes in the industry's environment. At least in a first phase, deregulation encouraged entry by a significant number of new producers, eroding the market position and net income of the larger national carriers (the "majors")[22]. However, over the last two years or so, the industry's structure has been in the process of consolidation; and though it would be hazardous to predict this process's final outcome, the number of competing carriers has declined and may continue to do so.

However, the consequences for overall performance of these changes in industry structure should not be exaggerated. The evidence does suggest that there are barriers to entry and exit in the airline industry[23], i.e. the industry will never be perfectly competitive or even fully contestable (in the sense that any supra-normal profits can be bid away by "hit and run" entry). But even under present circumstances, the level of internal and external rivalry is sufficient to keep prices close to their competitive level. Moreover, public policy can further contribute to strengthening effective competition in this industry, notably by ensuring that the limited availability of airport landing slots does not protect encumbent firms (who benefit from "first come, first serve" allocation rules) from the threat of entry. A shift to market allocation of slots – in which carriers would be allowed to buy and sell landing rights – may be desirable in this respect, and has indeed been approved for a number of major airports[24]. A market-oriented approach to the provision of airport services should also encourage the more effective pricing of these services, with peak load

302

pricing of landing slots being used to reduce the present levels of congestion.

2. The deregulation of bus services in the United Kingdom

A similar broad picture emerges from United Kingdom experience with deregulation of *bus services*. The process has occurred in two stages, with liberalisation in 1980 of entry, exit and pricing controls on all long-distance (over thirty miles) coach services and on local bus service in a few "Trial Areas" being followed in 1985 by abolition of all non-safety related controls on bus service outside London. (The 1985 Act also provides for the sale of the state-owned National Bus Company (NBC) to the private sector as a series of sixty separate subsidiaries.)

The effects of these changes must be seen in the context of an industry which had been declining for some time. Thus, the number of long-distance journeys fell by nearly 40 per cent from 1975 to 1980, while local journeys decreased by over 20 per cent. Seen over the longer term, bus fares have risen far more than motor vehicle running costs, and indeed since the early 1970s have outstripped the growth of disposable income per capita. Yet despite rising fares, the net income of bus operators has declined sharply, so that maintaining bus services in operation has required growing public subsidies – the subsidies provided by local authorities increasing thirteenfold in real terms between 1972 and 1982[25]. There is strong evidence that these subsidies were leaking into rising costs (rather than benefitting customers) with the scope for cost reduction estimated as being in the range of 30 per cent[26].

The shift to competition has at least partially reversed these trends. The results are most visible in the long-distance market, which was deregulated earliest. More efficient routing arrangements have been introduced, broadly similar to the hub-and-spoke networking adopted by United States airlines subsequent to deregulation. This appears to have caused passenger inconvenience in some cases, by lengthening point-to-point travel times. However, the resulting efficiency gains have allowed the National Bus Company (the dominant carrier) to increase the number of inter-city services by 17 per cent in the first two years of deregulation, provide numerous frequency increases and reduce fares. At the same time, the quality of services has been upgraded, with new vehicles being introduced and catering and video services becoming standard. The most direct effect of these changes has been to increase the number of passengers on long-distance bus service from nine million in 1980 to fifteen million in 1985. But there has also been a not insignificant impact on British Rail which – faced with an initial marked dip in its traffic – has sought to recoup passengers by developing new fare and service packages.

It is more difficult as of yet to fully evaluate the consequences of deregulation of local bus services, since the provisions of the 1985 Act only came into full operation in October 1986. Nonetheless, early results – including those from the "Trial Areas" deregulated under the 1980 Act – point to an extension in the range and quality of service, notably as smaller operators use minibuses to provide fast point-to-point travel even on low-density routes. The 1985 Act blurs the distinction between taxi and local bus services, and it appears likely that bus operators will increasingly seek to provide service on a more flexible basis[27].

At the same time, there is already significant evidence of gains in the efficiency of local bus service. Under the terms of the 1985 Act, operators must register to provide a particular service on either a commercial (i.e. without requiring subsidy) or non-commercial (will only be operated if a subsidy is available) basis. Local authorities are required to put subsidised routes out to competitive tender, singly or in small groups, and to award the contract to the operator providing the best value for money. Two results have emerged from this system. First, more than 70 per cent of the existing vehicle mileage has been registered as commercial – which suggests that most bus services can indeed be operated profitably[28]. Second, in a parallel to experience in the United States, competitive tendering has allowed local authorities to reduce subsidy costs by as much as 70 per cent while maintaining (at least in principle) the existing level of service[29].

Looking to the longer term, it appears unlikely that the number of operators of bus service will rise significantly. In long-distance service, control of major hubs provides incumbent firms (and notably the National Bus Company) with a clear advantage over potential competitors. Equally, in many local areas, passenger densities may not be sufficient to sustain several local bus operators[30]. Nonetheless, the experience to date highlights the contestability of markets for bus services: the capital costs required to provide busing are low (labour accounts for around 70 per cent of expenses); and virtually all of the requisite investments (especially vehicles) can be readily transferred between markets. As a result, there is little reason to fear that continued concentration will confer undesirable market power on firms in the industry. Moreover, the 1985 Act strengthens consumer protection in this respect by removing the various exemptions which bus operators had previously been granted from United Kingdom competition laws.

C. Conclusions

Overall, the regulation of the transport industries has entailed significant efficiency costs in terms of distorted price levels and structures, reduced cost-effectiveness and innovativeness. Where deregulation has occurred, market forces have induced a move towards a more economically rational pattern of provision, with benefits for consumers and suppliers alike.

Perhaps the most striking overall feature of deregulation is the extent to which it has encouraged organisational innovation – the hub-and-spoke system in the airlines, the growing role of minibuses in urban transit. These innovations were largely unexpected by the economists who examined the transport industries prior to liberalisation; and they have permitted far larger increases in efficiency than originally anticipated, as well as an extension (rather than contraction) in the range of services provided[31]. Fears that liberalisation would lead to the ending of transport services in many smaller communities have, in other words, generally proved unfounded. At the same time, the subsidies needed to maintain service for social reasons on genuinely unprofitable routes have declined, as more suppliers have been able and willing to bid for public service contracts. Nor has any evidence emerged of "destructive competition": the number of suppliers has if anything increased somewhat less than expected, though internal and external rivalry appears sufficient to prevent the emergence of monopoly power. Finally, the deregulation of any one transport mode has probably increased the competitive pressure on others, further extending the efficiency improvements[32].

II. THE CONTROL OF NATURAL MONOPOLY: THE OPTIONS

The regulatory problems of the industries which are wholly or partly natural monopolies are both more complex and more intractable. The arguments for regulatory control of industries which are structurally competitive are questionable; yet few doubt the need for some form of policy intervention in natural monopolies – but the desirable scope and degree of intervention is more difficult to define.

The primary requirement is that the control of natural monopolies provide for the effective representation of the consumer interest in efficient and innovative service – since (virtually by definition) consumers of natural monopoly outputs are unlikely to be able to express their preferences by switching among competing suppliers. There are three policy options in this respect:

– The first is *public ownership and/or operation*. This is intended to protect consumers by eliminating the incentives which profit maximisation creates for their exploitation; it merges the function of representing the public interest with that of providing the industry's capital and monitoring the efficiency of its use;

– The second option is *formal regulation* on a direct or delegated basis, i.e. the grant to a legislative body, a government department or a statutory agency of ongoing powers of review of the prices and quality of service in an industry, so as to ensure that these adequately reflect the public interest;

– Finally, a natural monopoly may be operated as a *franchise*, with the conditions of service being set out in a periodically renegotiated agreement (which is usually legally binding) between the firm providing the service and the state or its representative; the selection of the firm in question may be subject to some form of competitive tendering.

Though not mutually exclusive in theory, there has been a broad tendency for countries to rely on one option or the other.

From an analytical point of view, each of these options can be seen as involving an implicit or explicit contract between the public authority and the entity operating the natural monopoly; and the strengths and weaknesses of each option can be seen as arising from four factors: the extent to which the "terms" of the contract are clear and internally consistent; the scope for adapting these terms to changing circumstances; the degree to which there are built-in incentives for objectives to be achieved; and the ease with which implementation can be monitored and outcomes assessed.

It is by no means easy to set experience with each of the policy options against these criteria. Inevitably, the choice of governing instrument for a particular industry in a particular country will reflect the broader features of that country's institutional framework. Yet there are some similarities in different countries' experiences, and the analysis of these likenesses can provide a useful basis for re-examining policy options.

A. Public enterprise

Public enterprise is intended to provide a framework for reconciling the economically efficient provision of goods and services with broader goals of social responsibility. In the natural monopoly industries – where public ownership has been particularly widespread[33] – this presumably entails cost-effective supply without the abuse of market power. Yet the experience of public enterprise – though varying significantly from country to country – often falls short of this objective[34].

In part, disparities in performance reflect inherent differences between public and private enterprise. In particular, private ownership can provide direct and cost-effective means for defining objectives for an enterprise and monitoring outcomes against those objectives; but this has proved difficult to do in the case of state-owned firms.

Thus, the key feature of private enterprise is the role capital markets play in monitoring the efficiency with which resources are used. This role is clearest when ownership rights in a private firm take the form of tradable equity (an ownership arrangement usually referred to as an "open" corporation) – as is largely the case today and is likely to be more so in the future (see the chapter of this report on financial markets). Investors can then buy or sell ownership rights in a corporation on the basis of their assessment of the firm's current performance and future prospects; and firms which consistently fail to exploit profitable opportunities can expect to find the value of their stock diminishing (so that their cost of capital rises and their scope for growth declines), making them vulnerable to eventual liquidation or takeover[35]. The existence of an active market for ownership rights in private corporations thereby serves three functions:

- It forces managers to concentrate on profitability objectives (since stock-market prices largely reflect expectations of future income streams) though this may at times involve an over-concentration on short-term returns;
- It provides a straightforward means whereby owners can signal their assessment of managerial performance; and
- It ensures that consistently poor performance can be corrected[36].

These control mechanisms, in turn, make owners willing to allow management a high degree of operating autonomy – so that full benefit can be drawn from specialising the functions of risk-bearing relative to those of business decision-making.

Public enterprise differs from this model in important respects. In particular, in the public enterprise context, there are few effective procedures for setting objectives and monitoring performance; and this undermines the scope for specialising the management function.

Thus, there is extensive empirical evidence that the objectives public enterprises are expected to pursue are often poorly set out, and that even when set out, they are extensively altered and reinterpreted through political processes of negotiation; while this may be useful in some circumstances, it frequently gives rise to inconsistent requirements being placed upon the enterprise[37]. At the same time, the lack of a continuing external and public valuation of the firm's assets makes state-owned enterprises highly vulnerable to unreasonable political demands – demands which, were they accepted by a private sector firm, would lead to a sharp fall in its stock-market worth. This vulnerability may create incentives for the government to behave opportunistically relative to its own enterprises, using them as instruments of short-term policy, e.g. for subsidising specific groups, as tools of macroeconomic management and/or as taxing agents[38].

In turn, unclear and conflicting objectives make performance difficult to define and monitor[39] and compound the problems created by the lack of any ongoing external assessment. In some cases, this leads to public enterprises being subject either to little effective control (as has sometimes happened in France)[40] or to detailed administrative requirements aimed at the *ex ante* supervision of procedures and decisions (as has happened at times in Australia)[41].

In short, it has proved exceedi[ng] governments to find a satisfactory bal[ance] need for management autonomy and th[e] rements of accountability.

This has most obviously been the case i[n] where political criteria have dominated ec[onomic] decision-making, e.g. Italy[42], rather than i[n] there is a long tradition of autonomous and transparent management of statutory authorities, e.g. Sweden[43]. However, it can be argued that the economic circumstances of the last ten years have tended to make the difficulties of public enterprise more acute in virtually every country, and that the outlook is for a continuation of this trend.

At its simplest, this is because policy towards public enterprises has so directly reflected dominant macroeconomic concerns. In the mid-1970s, primary emphasis was placed on controlling inflation while protecting employment: and in countries as diverse as the United Kingdom, France, Austria and Italy, public enterprise price rises were constrained while they were at the same time subject to formal or informal instructions to avoid employment adjustments. The result was a significant deterioration in their immediate financial position as well as a loss of longer-term competitiveness[44]. More recently, the focus has shifted to budgetary concerns, with growing emphasis being placed on public enterprise profitability. While this has to some extent contributed to raising the efficiency with which public enterprises use resources, it has had two less desirable impacts: public enterprises have in some cases been used as taxing agencies; and public enterprise investment – which was frequently allowed to rise to unjustifiable levels in earlier periods – has increasingly been subject to fiscal (rather than economic) constraints[45]. Given the medium-term fiscal outlook, it is unrealistic to expect these distortions to be substantially eased.

These distortions presumably affect public enterprises regardless of their sector of activity; yet their consequences are likely to be particularly serious in the industries which are wholly or partly natural monopolies. The long investment lags which characterise these industries make the welfare costs of subjecting them to governments' annual budget cycle high – but this is largely unavoidable (though not obviously economically desirable) in the present context of fiscal restraint. At the same time, the low elasticity of demand for their products and the breadth of their customer base can make them particularly attractive as instruments of indirect taxation – and especially so in periods when "visible" taxation is subject to tight political constraints. But finally, and perhaps most importantly, their monopoly position magnifies the economic costs of these distortions: a public enterprise in a competitive market which did not maintain an adequate level of investment would simply lose market share; in a regulated monopoly the costs of inadequate investment or overpricing are borne by the community as a whole.

all, the problems of public enterprise arise partly [from] the fact that the "regulatory contract" between the state and a publicly owned operator of a public utility is a highly implicit one, where the primary guarantee given consumers is often a purely negative one – monopoly profits will not be maximised; and it is conceivable that these problems could be eased by subjecting public enterprises to some form of explicit, formal regulation. However, public ownership also removes any capital market constraints on inefficiency; and with the objectives to be pursued being frequently unstated or inconsistent, administrative controls over the enterprise's efficiency are not likely to be entirely satisfactory.

B. Franchising

Franchising, in which the right to provide a public utility service on given contractual terms is vested in a single private supplier, is in many respects the polar opposite to public enterprise as an approach to the control of natural monopoly. This is because franchising entails an explicit contract between the state and the service provider; and those who favour this approach generally argue that the franchise should be awarded on the basis of competitive bidding – the franchise going, for example, to the supplier offering to provide a specified level of service at the lowest price. This solution has had considerable support among economists[46], and indeed plays an important role in industries as diverse as water supply[47], television[48] and bus services[49].

The major attractions of franchising, in addition to its presumed simplicity, lie in the fact that through "competition for the field" (in Chadwick's famous phrase) it preserves the incentives for efficiency associated with profit maximisation, while nonetheless subjecting the search for profit to the price and service constraints of the franchise contract. It appears, in this respect, to be a cost-effective approach to the control of natural monopoly – notably in terms of the costs of administration and monitoring.

In practice, however, franchising has rarely proved satisfactory in a natural monopoly context and, in particular, does not eliminate the need for some form of continuing regulatory review[50]. To begin with, it is usually very difficult if not impossible to set out precisely the contractual conditions on which the monopoly is to be operated – and notably the price and grade of service – once and for all or even for an extended period of time, since these will inevitably be affected by changes in input prices, technology and patterns of demand; yet adapting the contractual conditions to shifting circumstances requires a review mechanism which is likely to resemble regulation. Moreover, the conditions of franchise are not self-enforcing – and since individual consumers may be reluctant to incur the costs involved in seeking legal redress, some procedure is needed for monitoring performance against contract terms. Departures from these terms are most common when a franchise is about to expire, since at that time the operator has few incentives to maintain or even more so expand the installations being used, so that the threat that the franchise will be discontinued often aggravates the conflicts between the authorities and the operator. Finally, it cannot be assumed that once the franchise does expire, competition for the new franchise will be perfect: the incumbent firm usually has advantages which derive from having previously operated the service; and there may be collusion among potential operators[51], though this problem could be eased by expanding the field of bidding to new, e.g. foreign, suppliers.

In short, franchising does not generally eliminate the need for a "buyer's agent" with continuing responsibility for oversight; but it can under certain circumstances contribute to more efficient regulation. This is most likely to be the case when:

– The provision of the service can be separated from responsibility for the infrastructure;
– There are significant advantages to local (as against national) provision so that there will be numerous operators at any point in time, facilitating efficiency comparisons and increasing competition for franchises; and
– The service to be provided is sufficiently standardized to be contractually definable.

C. Formal regulation

Formal regulation, at its simplest, involves the continuing supervision of the market by an explicitly constituted "buyer's agent" distinct from the supplier of the service and with powers to alter the terms on which service is provided. In principle, this role can be played directly by a government department or delegated to a regulatory commission; the trend in recent years has been for increasing reliance to be placed on the latter approach, which broadly corresponds to the North American model.

Formal regulation is in many respects intermediate between public enterprise and franchising as a mode of control. The obligations bearing on the service provider are rarely set out in specific terms; rather – as in public enterprise – they emerge from ongoing interaction of the regulatory body and the interested parties. Nonetheless, formal regulation has three broadly positive features relative to public enterprise taken on its own:

– It is consistent with capital market constraints on efficiency (though these are frequently blunted by the form of regulation adopted);
– It is more amenable to transparency and to direct participation by consumer interests; and

- The process of interaction between the regulatory body and the service provider is more explicitly structured – in terms of the frequency of review, the range of variables covered and the scope for redress – than that between a government and its business enterprises.

In theory, therefore, formal regulation allows a clearer and more long-lasting specification of objectives than occurs under public enterprise (at least taken on its own), while permitting a higher degree of flexibility than is feasible in a franchising system.

In practice, however, the formal regulation of natural monopolies has numerous drawbacks, which have been extensively studied in the context of the North American system of control by independent regulatory commissions. This system hinges on rate-of-return (ROR) regulation, i.e. the setting of prices in a regulated industry so as to achieve – and not exceed – a target return on the assets employed[52].

As a practical matter, the procedures required to define and implement a target rate of return are extremely *cumbersome*. Thus, though the desirable rate can in principle be derived from a Capital Asset Pricing Model (i.e. by calibrating the provider's *ex ante* target to the risk involved in the business relative to the pattern of variability of returns on a diversified portfolio), the standard practice is to rely on simpler but necessarily inaccurate comparisons of accounting profitability[53]. But target rates of return are only meaningful relative to a given asset base, and definition and measurement of the allowable "rate base" is by no means unambiguous. As a result, regulatory commissions have frequently found themselves drawn into detailed and lengthy assessments of individual items of capital and current expenditure, which usually require a greater knowledge of the business than is available in the commission's staff.

Moreover, the definition of a target rate of return and an associated set of prices may have undesirable impacts on *efficiency*. Thus, if the target is binding (as it is generally presumed to be) suppliers will have few incentives to increase productivity, since additional profits will have to be entirely passed on to consumers. Even under private ownership, this erodes the effectiveness of capital market constraints on inefficiency, since the potential gains from takeover will be limited. (Moreover, it has been common for United States regulatory commissions to impose restrictions on mergers and acquisitions.)

At the same time, the gap between the rate-of-return target and the provider's cost of capital may create incentives for the regulated firm to select a higher-than-optimal capital intensity so as to expand the total profit earned. The empirical significance of what is generally referred to as the "Averch-Johnson" effect is controversial; but some studies have found evidence of over-capitalisation in the United States electrical utilities[54].

Combined, the administrative complexity of rate-of-return regulation, together with its adverse impact on incentives, make its overall *effectiveness* arguable.

Thus, there is little evidence that it has proved an appropriate mechanism for regulating profitability, thereby protecting consumers and providers of capital from abuse. Comparisons between regulated and unregulated prices and profitability for similar public utility services do not find prices and profits to be lower under regulation – though it is worth noting that these comparisons frequently rely on rather old historical data[55]. Doubts about the effectiveness of regulation also emerge from comparisons between the book value of regulated firms' assets and their stock-market worth: were economic profits zero, these would tend to be roughly equal over time; yet the data show no evidence of this being the case[56] – underscoring the conjecture that even under regulation excess returns may be obtained.

The evidence suggests that under rate-of-return regulation, the profits of regulated firms have depended largely on the overall extent of price inflation. Given inertia in regulatory review, productivity gains achieved during periods of low inflation have been translated into higher profitability; conversely, regulated prices (especially for gas and electricity) have severely lagged behind the GDP deflator in periods of high inflation, leading to significant falls in profitability and investment[57].

The inefficiencies arising from economically undesirable profitability have been compounded by distortions in the structure of public utility prices. The desirable price policy for a utility service provided under conditions of decreasing cost is a matter of much debate; yet it is clear that the price patterns which have emerged from rate-of-return regulation have often been far removed from conventional notions of efficiency. In particular, prices in multi-product industries, notably telecommunications, have entailed far-reaching cross-subsidisation (though this is a virtually universal feature of telecommunications pricing); at the same time, United States public utilities have been considerably slower than their foreign (especially European) counterparts in adopting multi-part and time-of-day prices – thus presumably increasing their capital requirements[58].

In short, formal regulation has certain desirable attributes relative to public enterprise and franchising: while maintaining the functions of "buyer's agent" separate from those of supply, it provides for continuing and open (and hence flexible) review of the adequacy of service provision; and it is consistent with continued capital market control on the effectiveness with which regulated firms use their assets. But, at least when implemented through the regulation of rates of return, many of these advantages are offset by efficiency losses due to the cumbersome nature of the regulatory process and to the weakening of incentives, so that the fundamental question is the extent to which the process of formal regulation can be improved.

III. REFORMING THE REGULATION OF NATURAL MONOPOLIES: EVIDENCE FROM TELECOMMUNICATIONS

Natural monopoly is in essence a market imperfection and there can be no costless way of resolving the difficulties it creates. Each of the administrative mechanisms reviewed above has major drawbacks, but those drawbacks are not entirely unavoidable – and at least some of their adverse consequences can be minimised. The primary requirement in this respect is to find ways of limiting the burden on control mechanisms – to reduce, in other words, the system's vulnerability to the deficiencies of administrative processes. Three interrelated directions for policy appear to meet this goal: *a)* placing greater reliance on competition; *b)* enhancing the simplicity and transparency of regulation; and *c)* accompanying improved product market incentives by increased use of capital market controls over efficiency.

A. Greater reliance on competition

Even in industries which are wholly or partly natural monopolies, there may be considerable scope for competition in product markets. This reduces the burden on regulation: directly, by delegating some part of the responsibility for resource allocation to market forces; but also indirectly, by improving the quality of the information available to regulators and strengthening the incentives for regulated firms to be efficient. In this sense, competition can be an important tool of efficient regulation.

Three broad types of competition are relevant in the context of regulated industries:

- "Internal" competition, which refers to the competitive provision of smaller or greater parts of the industry's range of products;
- "Intermodal" competition, which refers to the provision of similar services using different facilities, e.g. satellite versus cable; and finally
- "Yardstick" competition, which refers to the provision of identical services on a monopoly basis but with each local area being served by a different producer.

The prospects for each of these forms of competition differ significantly from industry to industry. Thus, at one extreme, there can be little economic justification for duplication of costly distribution facilities in the water industry, making the industry virtually a textbook case of natural monopoly. However, there do not appear to be significant economies of scope to providing water on an inter-regional basis, so that few costs are entailed in having a different supplier in each region. This makes it possible to implement yardstick competition, with efficiency comparisons between suppliers being used to set prices and profitability, e.g. by linking the allowed rate of price change to the mean productivity increase (so that suppliers with below-average rates of productivity increase suffer net earnings reductions)[59].

In contrast, in the telecommunications industry, the potential for allowing greater competition at virtually all levels of provision appears to be considerable. Until the 1970s, the natural monopoly features of telecommunications were interpreted broadly, as extending from the supply of equipment (and notably of customer premise or terminal equipment) to the supply of services over the whole network. The picture has changed greatly in recent years.

Thus, by the late 1970s, the supply of *customer premise equipment* (CPE) had been substantially liberalised in a number of countries, notably the United States and France (which had long allowed a relatively high degree of domestic competition in this area); and significant moves to liberalisation have occurred more recently in (among others) the United Kingdom, the Netherlands, Japan and Australia. The experience to date highlights the positive features of competition in promoting supplier cost-effectiveness and encouraging innovation: thus, in the market for Private Automatic Branch Exchanges (PABX – private switchboards located on the customer's premises):

- Fully digital, multi-feature models were introduced onto the United States market some three to five years before they became available in the more regulated European markets;
- Penetration rates for advanced technology PABXs in the United States are consequently more than treble those in Europe; and
- Prices for PABXs (measured in terms of cost per line) are some 20 to 30 per cent lower in liberalised markets (notably the United States, France and Australia) than in the German market – and are declining far more rapidly in the former than in the latter markets[60].

At the same time, detailed assessments do not find evidence that competitive provision of terminal equipment has led to a decline in the quality of service or in any respect harmed the telecommunications network[61]. Nonetheless, tight controls persist on the supply of customer premise equipment in numerous countries, with the average time required to obtain regulatory approval for new models ranging from six weeks in the United States to six to twelve months in Germany; and they are compounded in a European context by major differences between countries in technical standards and regulatory requirements, which fragment European markets[62].

The scope for competitive provision is also considerable in the area of *value added network services* (VANs), i.e. services which use the telecommunications network to enhance or in other ways alter, restructure or resequence the information received relative to that transmitted[63]. These services are typically provided over circuits leased by private companies from the public telecommunications operator (PTO – the common carrier with statutory responsibility for basic service); so that they involve the resale of bulk capacity – an activity which is highly regulated in most countries. The use of leased circuits for VANs has been deregulated in the United States since the early 1970s; and the United Kingdom and more recently Japan have also opened these markets to competition. The primary effect of liberalisation has been to accelerate innovation and the diversification of the range of services available:

- A recent study finds that though there are few obvious differences between the United States and Europe in the extent of potential demand for VANs, sales of VAN services in Europe are approximately a quarter those in the United States; and
- The United Kingdom – which has deregulated the VAN market – is the only European country where the range of services available is comparable to that in North America[64].

It is indeed the case that there are VAN services in which network externalities are significant (in the sense that the value of access to the network to any particular user depends on the number of users already on the network)[65], and which are hence best provided by the dominant common carrier; but recent analyses suggest that involvement by the dominant carrier should be complementary to provision by other firms rather than a substitute for it[66].

In practice, however, the extent and attractiveness of VANs in each country is intimately linked to the regulatory regime bearing on *basic services*, i.e. on the provision of common carrier switching and transmission facilities. At its simplest, this is because VANs are primarily provided over leased circuits – and the degree to which, and the terms on which, these are available at least partly depends on the competitive pressures on the common carrier. Thus, in the United States, where all long-distance traffic is subject to competitive provision, not only is the range of data transmission services greater, but monthly rentals for leased circuits are about 40 per cent below the continental European average (where the average circuit length is much shorter) and 10 per cent lower than those in the United Kingdom; and the price differentials are even greater when the comparisons are made over equivalent distances[67]. However, it is also because the boundary lines between VANs and basic service are increasingly difficult to draw; and technical change is likely to blur them even further in future – as well as blurring the boundary between "network" and "customer premise" facilities[68]. Thus, attempts to allow competition in VANs while preserving a monopoly on basic service – though possibly useful as a transition measure – may not be successful over the medium term.

Yet the constraints on competition in basic services are necessarily tighter than those applying to markets for customer premise equipment and value added services. These constraints arise partly from long-established pricing structures in basic services – notably the cross-subsidisation of residential users (and especially those in rural areas) by business subscribers – discussed in more detail below. However, they also reflect the differing economic characteristics of VANs and CPE on the one hand and basic service on the other.

In particular, there is little evidence that CPE or VANs (at least as conventionally defined) have natural monopoly attributes. But econometric analyses consistently find significant evidence of scale economies in the provision of basic services, with a 1 per cent increase in output typically giving rise to an increase in costs of approximately 0.7 per cent[69]. Moreover, there is only weak evidence that the extent of these natural monopoly attributes is diminishing over time[70]. As a result, it can be argued that allowing competitive provision of switching and transmission facilities may lead to costly and inefficient duplication, as sunk investments are made in excess of those required to serve the market[71].

Nonetheless, this argument needs to be qualified in important respects. To begin with, the fact that econometric cost functions find evidence of natural monopoly hardly implies that an actual monopolist will operate on the production possibility frontier, i.e. will minimise the cost incurred in producing a given volume of output. To the extent that competition strengthens the incentives for technical efficiency, the resulting gains may outweigh the costs of duplicative investment. And, even in a natural monopoly context, competitive supply provides an objective standard for measuring performance, so that allowing a "yardstick competitor" can yield significant improvements in the efficiency of whatever regulatory mechanisms are kept in place[72].

Secondly, the natural monopoly attributes do not apply uniformly throughout the basic telecommunications network. Thus, it has been argued that scale economies are less significant in satellite transmission than in terrestrial transmission media – creating room for intermodal competition[73]. More importantly, the scale economies to common carriage telecommunications arise virtually entirely in transmission; in switching, the gains from scale are exhausted at output levels equal to a small fraction of market size[74]. This has led some analysts to suggest that while retaining a monopoly in transmission, competitive provision could be allowed across the board in switching. The practical feasibility of such a distinction is, however, largely untested.

Finally, there is some evidence that the evolution of telecommunications technology reflects the industry's market structure rather than vice versa – so that the development of technologies most efficiently operated at very large scale is at least partly a result (rather than a cause) of the traditional emphasis on monopoly provision[75]. It follows that a transition to competition might result not only in more rapid innovation but in greater investment in technologies suited to decentralised provision; so that – even abstracting from other factors – the efficiency losses would be below those implied by current production function estimates[76].

Though definitive analyses are not available, recent United States experience with competitive provision of telecommunications services is broadly consistent with these propositions. As far as efficiency gains are concerned, AT&T – which now faces competition throughout the long-distance network – has in recent years sought to significantly increase the productivity of its trunk facilities, not only by eliminating overmanning, but by further extending the digital parts of its network, using the superior signalling[77] capabilities of electronic technology to improve call routing (hence raising capital productivity) while widening the range and reducing the price of digital services. At the same time, by pioneering the development of Virtual Private Networks[78], AT&T has not only secured improved capacity utilisation, but may reverse the trend erosion of the public switched network by private facilities – a trend which (despite regulatory obstruction) is well under way in most countries.

Equally, there is clear evidence that the former Bell Operating Companies (which provide all local and most intra-state service) are shifting to technologies which can be efficiently deployed at smaller scales of output than previously characterised the Bell System. Thus, telecommunications administrations in some European countries are planning the transition to fully digital telecommunications services – the so-called "Integrated Services Digital Network" (ISDN)[79] – in terms of a major effort to replace existing infrastructures (notably for local distribution) by digital facilities – a course of action which entails very high fixed costs[80]; in contrast, local service providers in the United States are developing low cost "add-ons" which allow existing facilities to be used to provide fully digital service[81].

This should not be taken to imply that the manner in which the shift to competition occurred in the United States basic network was optimal. The transition problems have indeed been considerable, notably those arising from the divestiture of the former Bell System into a series of separate companies. (The difficulties arising from changes in pricing structures are discussed below.) Moreover, there are as of yet unresolved issues about the prospects for excess capacity in the United States trunk network, the impact of competition on standardization and inter-operability and the longer-term consequences for national security[82]. The possible extent of these costs has led the authorities in the United Kingdom and Japan – while virtually entirely liberalising entry into markets for value added networks and customer premise equipment – to adopt a cautious attitude to competitive provision of common carrier telecommunications facilities, retaining licensing procedures aimed at regulating the entry of new competitors. Yet some degree of competition has been accepted in this area; and over the longer term, as the boundaries blur between the different types of telecommunications services, and between telecommunications, data processing and media services more generally, the pressures for further liberalisation are only likely to increase.

B. Simpler and more transparent regulation

Overall, in the industries which have traditionally been regarded as natural monopolies, market forces have a greater role to play in promoting efficiency and innovativeness than has generally been believed; but competition in these industries is largely a means of improving the regulatory process, rather than an alternative to it. Regulation will remain important in protecting consumers from the abuse of market power – most visibly in the industries where the scope for competition is very limited (such as the distribution of electricity, gas and water), but also in those where, despite liberalisation, a single provider currently has, and is likely for some time to retain, a dominant position (Sub-section 1). And regulatory mechanisms may also be needed to deal with problems arising in the transition from a purely regulated environment to one providing greater scope for market forces (Sub-section 2).

1. Protecting consumers from the abuse of market power

The problems of designing institutions capable of effectively protecting consumers from the abuse of market power hinge on information and incentives. Experience of rate-of-return regulation confirms that regulatory mechanisms for setting overall price levels and profit rates are not likely to prove adequate in protecting consumers when the information they require for making decisions and monitoring their implementation is complex and not readily available from market outcomes; and when the controls put in place erode the incentives for efficient and innovative provision. The challenge, therefore, is to develop regulatory procedures which require a minimum of information and which preserve rather than dampen market incentives.

The most promising recent development in this respect is the use in the United Kingdom of the "RPI-X" formula as a basis for regulation. This formula determines the allowable rate of price increase for a regulated firm as the retail price index *minus* a fixed amount (the "X" in the formula). It thereby prevents the regulated firm from using its monopoly position to raise the relative price of its outputs relative to its inputs, but preserves the incentives the firm has to increase profitability by reducing costs. This approach is similar in many respects to the proposals made in the context of United States regulatory reform to increase "regulatory lag" (the time between increases in productivity and mandated reductions in prices)[83]; but it is considerably simpler to design and implement. The major complexities lie in the initial choice of "X"; but so long as "X" is chosen such that the firm can obtain sufficient funds on capital markets to operate efficiently, the subsequent enforcement problems are very limited.

Nonetheless, three difficulties arise with "RPI-X" price regulation. To begin with, control of overall price levels is insufficient if the regulated firm can vary the quality it provides. Price constraints must therefore be accompanied by a set of grade of service targets, though these should take into account the fact that a regulated firm may have incentives to provide an excessively high-average quality level[84].

Secondly, it may be difficult to apply an "RPI-X" approach to industries – notably gas and electricity distribution – which are vulnerable to major input price shocks. The desirability of dealing with these shocks through non-discretionary adjustments to the pricing formula is questionable[85]; it appears preferable to re-examine the formula whenever the cumulative change in the price of a key input exceeds a previously determined amount.

Finally, when the formula is to be applied over the longer term, it may be necessary from time to time to review the level of "X"; yet, if the regulated firm knows that above-average profitability will lead to an increase in "X" at its next review (that is, to greater price pressure being placed on the firm), the incentives for efficiency will be blunted – as occurs under standard rate-of-return regulation. There are no easy solutions to this problem; the most promising approach appears to be that of setting the formula for an extended period (say ten years) and at the end of that period carrying out a detailed assessment of the efficiency gains obtained over the preceding decade, on the understanding that the new level of "X" will include a premium (or conversely a penalty) for already realised productivity increases, to the extent to which these exceed (or fall short of) reasonable expectations[86]. The use of yardstick competition is of obvious relevance in this respect, since it provides an objective standard against which the performance of any individual firm can be evaluated.

2. Cross-subsidisation and the transition to a more competitive environment

While the "RPI-X" approach provides a framework for monitoring overall price changes – and hence indirectly regulating rates of return – it does not resolve the specific regulatory problems which arise when competition, on however limited a basis, is introduced into markets which have long been highly regulated. The resulting transition creates concerns for consumers and producers alike.

The issues for consumers centre on *cross-subsidisation*, i.e. the widespread practice in the public utility industries of charging a higher price (relative to cost) to some consumers so as to finance the charging of a lower price to others. This practice would clearly be untenable in a purely competitive environment, since the entry of new producers will force prices down on the more

Table 8.1. **Degree of cost recovery in the provision of telecommunications services to residential and non-residential subscribers**

	Sweden (1986)	Australia (1985-1986)	France (1981)	United Kingdom (1982-1983)
Residential	0.85-0.95	0.61[1]	0.86	0.73[1]
Non-residential	1.05-1.15	0.99[1]	1.40	1.03[1]

1. Access only; in other words, does not include revenues from actual use of the network.

Sources:
  i)   Sweden: Unpublished data from the Swedish Telecommunications Administration;
  ii)   Australia: Unpublished data from Telecom Australia;
  iii)   France: de la Brunetière, J. and Curien, N., "Les transferts de revenus induits par la tarification téléphonique entre catégories d'abonnés et entre types de prestations", *Annales des Télécommunications*, 1984, Vol. 39, pp. 469-486;
  iv)   British Telecom, *Annual Report*, 1982-1983.

profitable routes and rule out a continued cross-subsidy to the higher cost areas.

To illustrate the magnitude of the problem, Table 8.1 reports the ratio of revenues to costs for the provision of telecommunications services to residential and non-residential (mainly business) subscribers in Sweden, Australia, France and the United Kingdom. It is worth emphasizing that the telecommunications network entails pervasive joint costs (typically accounting for as much as 40 per cent of total costs), making it difficult to allocate expenses to particular classes of subscriber. Moreover, the procedures adopted in each country differ, so that comparisons between countries cannot be made. Nonetheless, the data highlight the disparities in average return from household and business customers; and there is evidence that these disparities are even greater between telecommunications users in metropolitan and rural areas[87] and between local and long-distance traffic[88].

Seen over the longer term, there is a strong efficiency case for prices which reflect marginal cost – and significant gains in overall welfare can be achieved by moving from the highly distorted price structures which still largely characterise the public utility industries towards more rational pricing policies[89]. Moreover, it seems reasonable to suppose that common-sense notions of equity – the principle that consumers should be treated equally – and fairness – the principle that an individual consumer should not be charged for resources he or she has not consumed – dictate a preference for cost-based pricing[90].

Yet it is also clear that the inevitability of major price "rebalancing" (the process whereby prices in a liberalised market are realigned with costs) raises significant concerns about the social impact of a shift to competition. Nonetheless, these concerns may be exaggerated in three important respects.

First, in practice, the cross-subsidies provided by no means always best serve broader social goals. Thus, analyses suggest that public utility prices are normally a very blunt instrument of income redistribution, the results of which can be unpredictable[91]. More generally, it has frequently been argued that the goals being pursued would be more efficiently achieved through direct subsidies, which can be more narrowly targeted to particular classes of consumers[92].

Second, even if the cross-subsidy is achieving its proximate goal, the issue is still open of whether service to the favoured group would in fact be curtailed in a more competitive environment. In particular, the experience of transport deregulation reviewed above suggests that organisational and technical innovation in a competitive market can enhance the range of service and minimise the adverse social consequences of cost-based pricing. Thus, early results of competition in telecommunications point to the development of low-cost radio-based technologies for use in rural areas, which could eventually reduce the need for cross-subsidisation as a means of ensuring universal service.

Third, it must nonetheless be recognised that there are circumstances in which cross-subsidisation is indeed a relatively effective means of increasing particular customer groups' access to a service, notably because it entails low administrative costs and induces fewer fiscal distortions than the equivalent income-tax-financed direct subsidy[93]; and in which some degree of continuing cross-subsidy – though perhaps to a more narrowly defined class of users – is necessary to maintain service, at least in the short term. But even in these cases, the desired objective can generally be achieved through a price structure which – while not entirely cost-based – is not incompatible with competitive provision.

Thus, in the telecommunications industry, where the problems of cross-subsidisation have been most acute, there is a strong case for channelling price-induced transfers solely through the fixed charge for connection and continuing access to the network rather than through distortions to usage charges[94]. To the extent to which the access cross-subsidy can be funded by a levy on all suppliers, the entry of new competitors – even if solely on the most profitable routes – should not adversely affect the capacity to finance below-cost service to particular communities.

Ultimately, it is probably the *pace* at which changes in prices occur, rather than the absolute extent of the changes, which may create hardship or disruption. Thus, in the United States, prices for telecommunications services have generally been and indeed remain very low by world standards, both for long-distance and local calls[95]; and the concern about increases in local rates following competition-induced reductions in long-distance charges is largely understandable in terms of the rapidity with which price rebalancing is taking place, rather than of effects on consumer real incomes[96]. In the United Kingdom, where concerns about the pace of rebalancing have also been expressed in the context of telecommunications liberalisation, the regulatory authorities have sought and obtained assurances from British Telecom (the dominant common carrier) limiting increases in residential rentals; these appear to have been effective, allowing the move towards a more rational price structure to occur at a broadly acceptable rate[97].

Issues of the pace of change are also central to the competitive problems of the transition from a highly regulated environment, i.e. to the problems confronting new and established suppliers.

It is a characteristic of the industries which have generally been regarded as natural monopolies that – even once liberalisation occurs – each industry remains dominated by an established supplier, which previously had overall responsibility for the market as a whole. This dominant supplier is typically subject to certain competitive disadvantages – notably the burden of serving areas where provision can only be profitable if subsidised from elsewhere. Yet its sheer size relative to that of actual or potential entrants confers on it an undoubted element of market power. It may use this power to dissuade the development of new suppliers, for example through large and sudden price reductions in the services where entry is easiest, possibly subsidised through price increases in the services where competition remains subject to regulatory restraint.

These issues have arisen with particular force and complexity in telecommunications; and they have been the subject of ongoing review by the Federal Communications Commission and the judiciary in the United States and by the Office of Telecommunications in the United Kingdom, as well as being examined in a recent report by the Fair Trade Commission in Japan[98]. The policy response has to some extent differed. Thus, in the United States, concern about the Bell System's dominant position was a major factor in the decision to divest AT&T of its local operating companies; in the United Kingdom and Japan, the desirability of such fundamental change in industry structure has been questioned, notably given its very large once-off costs and the risks of an enduring loss of economies of scale and scope. Nonetheless, in all three countries there has been a trend towards implementing tighter regulatory control on the dominant carrier than on its newer competitors, notably so as to prevent predatory pricing and discriminatory access to common carriage facilities.

Controls of this type are clearly most easily justified when the dominant supplier retains a monopoly over particular parts of the infrastructure, e.g. over the facilities needed to distribute a service locally; or when the previous regulatory regime induced customers to carry out investments which, in a more competitive environment, render them particularly vulnerable to the dominant carrier's abuse of market power – a problem which has created particular concern in railroad transportation[99]. However, experience highlights the dangers involved in preventing a firm – merely because it dominates a market – from exploiting opportunities to provide a service at lower cost or in an innovative manner; and the recent decision by the Federal Communications Commission easing regulatory controls on AT&T is of significance in this respect. More generally, it can be argued that historical evidence shows dominant positions to be something of a wasting asset, the abuse of which leads to the development of entirely new sources of competition – so that concerns in this respect can be frequently exaggerated[100].

Overall, the regulatory problems of transition to a greater reliance on markets should not entail the creation of a new and cumbersome apparatus of regulation. There may indeed be a case for continuing regulatory review of average price levels and (indirectly) of rates of return – and it has been argued that the "RPI-X" rule is of use in this respect. But the regulatory process is not an efficient mechanism for reviewing individual pricing and output decisions, notably in the complex environment of at least partial competition. This argues for a minimalist and pragmatic approach to regulation – an approach which recognises that its benefits are not always greater than its costs.

C. Privatisation and the role of capital markets

The advantages of the changes recommended above may be increased if they are accompanied by a review of ownership arrangements.

At its simplest, this is because public ownership can entail costs – costs arising largely from the difficulties involved in setting and implementing objectives for state-owned enterprises; and the macroeconomic climate of recent years may have aggravated these costs further. These costs can to some extent be reduced through reform of the public enterprise sector (Sub-section 1); but there may remain positive benefits to be sought from privatisation (Sub-section 2). The specific interest here is in publicly owned utilities; but the arguments are quite general and largely apply to public enterprises more broadly.

1. Reforming public enterprise

The difficulties of public enterprise arise mainly from the peculiar nature of the state-owned firm's relation to its owners: a relation which is both tighter and looser than that typical of a private corporation. Attempts to improve the functioning of public enterprise while retaining state ownership have generally involved modifying this relationship through three key elements.

The first is the provision of greater *management autonomy* to the enterprise by clearly separating its operation from that of government departments. Time series analysis suggests that significant efficiency gains have indeed been obtained by this means[101] and "corporatisation" (the delegation to state-owned enterprises of functions previously exercised by government departments) is for example, an important component of the public sector reform now under way in New Zealand and is part of the proposed reform of telecommunications in France.

A second element is to *clarify t...* *...bilities* of the enterprise in a medi... can take a number of forms includ... broad guidelines applicable across ... – as was most notably the case w... investment rules set out in the 196... White Paper on Nationalised Industi... thrust of recent policy in Finland... formal agreements covering corpora ...gy and objectives between the government as owner and each enterprise's board – as with the system of "planning contracts" in France; or the incorporation of "sunset clauses" into the legislation establishing the enterprise and specifying its responsibilities.

Finally, the clear definition of goals permits a third element, namely the search for increased *accountability* by management for the enterprise's performance. This requires a process whereby performance can be assessed; the periodic efficiency audit, conducted by an independent agency or commission, and rendered public, appears to be the most promising instrument in this respect; but efficiency audits are of greatest use if accompanied by frequent reporting by the enterprise of its performance against a range of targets. Effective accountability also requires that there be sanctions in case of poor performance, e.g. a change in top management[103].

How effective these changes can be in resolving the underlying problems of state enterprise is a matter for debate. There are indeed circumstances in which continued public ownership is a fact of life, e.g. because a transfer to private ownership is economically unlikely (notably in the case of chronically loss-making enterprises) or politically unacceptable. And in these circumstances, it is surely desirable that the framework in which public enterprises operate be rendered as conducive to efficiency and effectiveness as possible. There are obvious national differences in this respect (the conditions and problems of public enterprises in Sweden or Finland, for example, being of a quite different order of magnitude from those needing to be faced in Italy or Austria). But it must also be recognised that the experience with successive efforts at reform has not always been satisfactory, the problems apparently resolved at one level or period frequently reappearing at others[104].

2. The scope for privatisation

Yet the case for reviewing ownership arrangements is not solely negative – it does not rest, in other words, solely on the limited scope for internal reform in the public sector. There may also be positive benefits to be sought from a greater reliance on private ownership. These benefits centre on the gains, discussed above, from more efficient monitoring of the use of resources; and it seems reasonable to suppose that the changes now under way in capital markets make these gains all the greater – notably because even the largest enterprises

...ose which typically operate in the public ...ndustries) are now exposed to the risk of ...ver. Reaping these benefits is of particular impor-...nce in the context of regulatory reform.

This is, to begin with, because reliance on private capital markets as a means of monitoring efficiency can itself improve the regulatory process – both by increasing the flow of information to regulators (who, when a firm's equity is traded, can derive important indications from the market's ongoing valuation of its worth) and by transferring some regulatory responsibilities to the market for corporate control, thus easing the burden on the agency charged with regulation.

At the same time, the room for capital markets to work should itself be increased by regulatory reform. In particular, it is an important feature of "RPI-X" regulation that – in contrast to traditional controls over rates of return – it does not reduce the gains which will accrue to a firm's owners from more efficient operation; so that investors have clear incentives to buy shares in public utilities whose management can secure productivity gains at the rate exceeding the pre-set target (the "X" in "RPI-X") and to sell their shares in others. These incentives are likely to be all the stronger in a more competitive environment, since product market pressures will then act as a further sanction on inefficient suppliers.

But these capital market controls on efficiency will only operate if the firm's equity can be freely traded; and two important policy implications can be drawn in this respect.

The first is that restrictions on the tradability of equity in public utilities not only reduce the value the treasury can obtain from their sale; they also run counter to part of the rationale for transferring assets to private ownership. Restrictions on sales to foreigners are of particular significance in this respect – for public utilities are typically very large firms in a national context, and significant changes in their ownership and management (especially through takeover) may well be impossible without recourse to foreign investors.

Secondly, it may be possible to reap some part of the benefits of capital market competition without transferring the entirety of the assets of a publicly owned firm to the private sector. Thus, even if a relatively small part of a firm's equity is traded, both managers and regulators can obtain valuable information from market valuations of its worth; and if the state, as a residual investor, can credibly commit itself to act as a passive shareholder, changes in management can occur even in companies where only a minority of shares is privately owned.

Moreover, the sale of even a relatively small proportion of a firm's equity to the private sector may substantially modify relations between the firm's managers and central government: attempts by the government to force the firm's managers into economically inefficient courses of action can lead to politically embarrassing and financial costly reductions in share values; at the same time, the firm's managers will be faced with a far more continuous check on their efficiency than can be exercised by government departments, Parliament or voters[105]. There are indeed instances in which these constraints have not prevented governments from effectively destroying the viability of public sector enterprises – the case of IRI in Italy being among the most striking; but the consequence has inevitably been a visible withdrawal by private investors from the enterprise, transferring onto taxpayers as a whole the costs of the government's decisions[106].

If there are constraints on the rate at which share markets can absorb new equity, these considerations suggest that it may be more useful to proceed by transferring to the private sector relatively small shares in a range of state-owned enterprises, than by placing the enterprises in a queue for privatisation as a whole; and it can also be argued that such a step-by-step approach is essential if an appropriate price is to be established for the company's shares[107]. But this should be viewed as a transitional strategy, rather than as a longer-term solution, which needs to be seen in a broader context of overall regulatory reform.

NOTES AND REFERENCES

1. Posner, R.A. in "Natural Monopoly and Its Regulation", *Stanford Law Review*, February 1969, pp. 548-643.

2. Economic Monitoring Group, New Zealand Planning Council, *The Regulated Economy*, Wellington, 1985, p. 21.

3. Cost elasticities for rail transport typically range from .35 to .80; see Keeler, T.E., *Railroads, Freight and Public Policy*, The Brookings Institution, Washington D.C., 1983.

4. Wang, J.W. and Friedlander, A., *Mergers, Competition and Monopoly in the Regulated Trucking Industry*, MIT Working Paper No. 289, 1981.

5. Caves, D., Christensen, L. and Tretheway, M., *The Structure of Airline Costs and Prospects for the U.S. Airline Industry Under Deregulation*, Social Systems Research Institute Report No. 8205, University of Wisconsin, Madison, 1983.

6. Lee, N. and Steedman, J., "Economies of Scale in Bus Transportation", *Journal of Transport Economics and Policy*, January 1970, pp. 15-28.

7. See Winston, C., "Conceptual Developments in the Economics of Transportation: An Interpretive Survey", *Journal of Economic Literature*, March 1985, Vol. 23, pp. 57-94, especially Table 3, p. 74.

8. The best overall surveys are Winston, *ibid.* and Breyer, S., *Regulation and Its Reform*, Harvard University Press, Cambridge, Mass., 1982; but see also Meyer, J.R., Peck, M.J., Stenason, J. and Zwick, C., *The Economics of Competition in the Transportation Industries*, Harvard University Press, Cambridge, Mass., 1959.

9. Rose, N.L., "The Incidence of Regulatory Rents in the Motor Carrier Industry", *The Rand Journal of Economics*, 1985, Vol. 16, No. 3, pp. 299-327; see also Moore, T., "The Beneficiaries of Trucking Regulation", *Journal of Law and Economics*, 1978, Vol. 21.

10. United Kingdom land values study.

11. Friedlander, A. and Spady, R., *Freight Transportation Regulation*, MIT Press, Cambridge, Mass., 1981.

12. Caves, D., Christensen, L. and Swanson, J., "Economic Performance in Regulated and Unregulated Environments", *Quarterly Journal of Economics*, November 1981, Vol. 96, pp. 559-81; Harris, R.G. and Keeler, T., "The Determinants of Railroad Profitability" in Boyer, K. and Shepherd, W. (eds.), *Essays in Honour of J.R. Nelson*, East Lansing Press, Michigan, 1981.

13. Capron, W.M., *Technological Change in Regulated Industries*, The Brookings Institution, Washington D.C., 1981.

14. Mansfield, E., "Innovation and Technical Change in the Railroad Industry" in *Transportation Economics*, National Bureau of Economic Research, New York, 1965, pp. 169-197; railroad innovation study in *Essays in Honour of J.R. Nelson*, *op. cit.* in Note 12.

15. Morrison, S. and Winston, C., *The Economic Effects of Airline Deregulation*, The Brookings Institution, Washington D.C., 1986, pp. 30-31. The economic effects of airline deregulation are also reviewed in OECD, *Economic Surveys: United States*, Paris, 1985.

16. Evidence that previous regulatory restrictions severely hampered route rationalisation is given in Johnson, R., "Networking and Market Entry in the Airline Industry", *Journal of Transport Economics and Policy*, September 1985, pp. 299-304.

17. Carlton, D.W., Landes, W.N. and Posner, R.A., "Benefits and Costs of Airline Mergers: A Case Study", *Bell Journal of Economics*, Spring 1980, pp. 65-83.

18. See Morrison and Winston, *op. cit.* in Note 15, pp. 36-41; similar results are reported by Gomez-Ibanez, J.A. *et al.*, "Airline Deregulation: What's Behind the Recent Losses?", *Journal of Policy Analysis and Management*, Winter 1983, pp. 74-89.

19. See Cappelli, P. and Harris, T.H., "Airline Union Concessions in the Wake of Deregulation", *Monthly Labor Review*, US Department of Labor, Washington D.C., June 1985.

20. Morrison and Winston, *op. cit.* in Note 15, pp. 47-50.

21. See Meyer, J.R. and Oster, C.V. Jr., *Deregulation and the New Airline Entrepreneurs*, MIT Press, Cambridge, Mass., 1985, Chapter 16.

22. See Bailey, E., Graham, D.R. and Kaplan, D.P., *Deregulating the Airlines*, MIT Press, Cambridge, Mass., 1985; Moore, T.G., *United States Airline Deregulation: Its Effects on Passengers, Capital and Labor*, Hoover Institution, Stanford, California, 1985; and *La déréglementation du transport aérien aux Etats-Unis*, ENSAE, Paris, 1985, Chapters 3 and 4.

23. Morrison and Winston, *op. cit.* in Note 15, pp. 59-66.

24. Dorman, G.J., "A Model of Unregulated Airline Markets", *Research in Transportation Economics*, 1983, pp. 131-48.

25. "United Kingdom Experience in the Deregulation of Road Transport" (mimeo), OECD, 1986.

26. *Ibid.*, Annex, para. 12 and references cited on p. 20, Notes 1 and 2.

27. See Fairhead, R. and Balcombe, R., *Deregulation of Bus Services in Trial Areas, 1981-84*, Transport and Road Research Laboratory, Crowthorne, 1984; Walters, A.A., "Externalities in Urban Buses", *Journal of Urban Economics*, 1982, Vol. 11, pp. 60-72; and Mohring, H., "Minibuses in Urban Transportation", *ibid.*, 1983, Vol. 14, pp. 293-317.

28. See Viton, P.A., "The Possibility of Profitable Bus Services", *Journal of Transport Economics and Policy*, September 1980, pp. 295-314.

29. "United Kingdom Experience in the Deregulation of Road Transport", *op. cit.* in Note 25, para. 29.

30. Viton, P.A., "A Translog Cost Function for Urban Bus Transit", *Journal of Industrial Economics*, March 1981, pp. 287-304; and Berechman, J., "Costs, Economies of Scale and Factor Demand in Bus Transport", *Journal of Transport Economics and Policy*, January 1983, pp. 7-24.

31. Douglas, G.W. and Miller, J.C. III, *Economic Regulation of Domestic Air Transport*, The Brookings Institution, Washington D.C., 1974. In a careful early analysis of the United States airline industry, though supportive of liberalisation, the author expected service quality to fall and the consumer benefits to be around $1 billion a year: a considerable underestimate.

32. On other transport modes, see for example, Friedlaender and Spady, *op. cit.* in Note 11; international productivity differentials in the transport industries are examined in Forsyth, P. *et al.*, IFS, 1986; and Dudgson, 1986.

33. Seen internationally, the incidence of public ownership is highest in the natural monopoly industries: Pryor, F.L., "Public Ownership: Some Quantitative Dimensions" in Shepherd, W.G. (ed.), *Public Enterprise*, Lexington Books, Lexington, Mass., 1976, pp. 3-23.

34. See for example, Pryke, R., "The Comparative Performance of Public and Private Enterprise", *Fiscal Studies*, 1982, Vol. 3, pp. 68-81.

35. Jensen, M.C. and Ruback, R.S., "The Market for Corporate Control", *Journal of Financial Economics*, 1983, Vol. 11, pp. 5-50; Ginsburg, D.H. and Robinson, J.F., "The Case Against Federal Intervention in the Market for Corporate Control", *The Brookings Review*, Winter/Spring 1986, pp. 9-14.

36. Williamson, O.E., *Corporate Control and Business Behaviour*, Prentice-Hall, Englewood Cliffs, N.J., 1970, Chapter 6; Jensen, M.C. and Mecklin, W.H., "Theory of the Firm: Managerial Behaviour, Agency Costs, Ownership Structure", *Journal of Financial Economics*, 1976, Vol. 3, pp. 305-60; de Alessi, L., "The Economics of Property Rights: A Review of the Evidence", *Research in Law and Economics*, 1980.

37. Vernon, R., "Linking Managers with Ministers: Dilemmas of the State-Owned Enterprise", *Journal of Policy Analysis and Management*, 1984, Vol. 4, No. 1, pp. 39-55 and references therein.

38. Borcherding, T., "A Positive Theory of Public Enterprise" in Prichard, J.R.S. (ed.), *Crown Corporations: The Calculus of Choice*, Butterworths, Toronto, 1986.

39. Foster, C.D., "Introduction" in *Public Sector Accounting and Research*, Delotte, Haskings and Sells, London, 1984, pp. 1-11.

40. Anastassopoulos, J.-P., *La stratégie des entreprises publiques*, Dalloz, Paris, 1980; Anastassopoulos, J.-P. and Nioche, J.-P., *Entreprises publiques: expériences comparées*, FNEGE, Paris, 1982.

41. Stretton, H., *Directing the Australian Public Sector*, paper tabled in Parliament, 4th October 1984; Department of Finance, *Proposed Policy Guidelines for Statutory Authorities and Government Business Enterprises: Policy Discussion Paper*, Canberra, 1986.

42. For a general discussion of Italian public enterprise performance, see Cottino, G., *Ricerche sulle participazioni statali*, Einaudi, G. (ed.), Turin, 1978; Saraceno, P., "Il sistema delle participazioni statali", *Economia e Politica Industriale*, 1981, Vol. 8, No. 29, pp. 35-72; Ranci, P., "Participazioni statali: due osservazioni in margine al saggio di Saraceno, P.", *ibid.*, No. 30, pp. 9-16; for specific sector on electricity, see Zanetti, G. and Frequelli, G., *Una nazionalizzazione al buio: L'ENEL dal 1963 al 1978*, il Mulino, Bologna, 1979; on telecommunications, Antonelli, C. and Lamborghini, B., *Impresa pubblica e technologia avanzata*, il Mulino, Bologna, 1979.

43. See Stromberg, H., "The Public Corporation in Sweden" in Friedman, W.G. and Garner, J.F. (eds.), *Government Enterprise: A Comparative Study*, Columbia University Press, New York, 1970; Coombes, D., *State Enterprise – Business or Politics?*, George Allen and Unwin, London, 1971.

44. Data on the financial position of public enterprises can be found in International Monetary Fund, *Public Enterprise in Mixed Economies*, Washington D.C., 1984.

45. See for example, Heald, D., "The Economic and Financial Control of the Nationalised Industries", *Economic Journal*, 1980, pp. 243-265; Pryke, R., *The Nationalised Industries Since 1968: Policies and Performance*, Robertson, Martin, Oxford, 1981; and for applications to particular public utilities, Slater, M. and Yarrow, G., "Distortions in Electricity pricing in the United Kingdom", *Oxford Bulletin of Economics and Statistics*, 1983, Vol. 45, pp. 317-338; Ergas, H., *Telecommunications and the Australian Economy*, Australian Government Publishing Service, Canberra, 1986.

46. Demsetz, H., "Why Regulate Utilities?", *Journal of Law and Economics*, 1968, Vol. 11, pp. 55-65; Posner, R.A., "The Appropriate Scope of Regulation in the Cable Television Industry", *Bell Journal of Economics*, 1972, Vol. 3, pp. 98-129.

47. Coquidé, P., "La distribution de l'eau" in Ghédon, M.-J. (ed.), *Sur les services publics*, Economica, Paris, 1982, pp. 67-76.

48. Domberger, S. and Middleton, J., "Franchising in Practice", *Fiscal Studies*, 1985, Vol. 6, pp. 17-32.

49. See the survey in Hibbs, J., *Regulation: An International Study of Bus and Coach Licensing*, Transport Publishing Projects, London, 1985, especially pp. 20-22.

50. Williamson, O., "Franchise Bidding for Natural Monopolies – In General and with Respect to CATV", *Bell Journal of Economics*, 1976, Vol. 7, pp. 73-104; and Schmalensee, R., *The Control of Natural Monopolies*, Lexington Books, Lexington, Mass., 1979, pp. 68-73.

51. As occurred in the French water supply industry in the late 1970s: Coquidé, *art. cit.* in Note 47, p. 72.

52. Particularly valuable surveys in this respect are provided by Schmalensee, *op. cit.* in Note 50; Breyer, *op. cit.* in Note 8, pp. 36-59; Littlechild, S.C., *Regulation of British Telecommunications' Profitability*, Department of Industry, London, 1983.

53. See Kolbe, L.G., *The Cost of Capital: Estimating Rates of Return for Public Utilities*, MIT Press, Cambridge, Mass., 1982 for a survey.

54. Littlechild, *op. cit.* in Note 52, pp. 16-17.

55. Stigler, G.J. and Friedland, C., "What Can Regulators Regulate? The Case of Electricity", *Journal of Law and Economics*, 1962, Vol. 5, pp. 1-16.

56. Baron, D.P. and Taggart, R.A., "A Model of Regulation under Uncertainty and a Test of Regulatory Bias", *Bell Journal of Economics*, 1977, Vol. 8, pp. 151-67.

57. Joskow, P.L. and MacAvoy, P.W., "Regulation and the Financial Condition of the Electric Power Companies in the 1970s", *American Economic Review*, 1975, Vol. 65, pp. 295-301; MacAvoy, P.W., *The Present Condition of the Regulated Industries*, New York, 1979.

58. Bailey, E., "Peak Load Pricing Under Regulatory Constraint", *Journal of Political Economy*, 1972, Vol. 80, pp. 662-79; Joskow, P.L., "Electric Utility Rate Structures in the United States", paper presented at the *7th Michigan Conference on Public Utility Economics*, Detroit, 1977.

59. Schleifer, A., "A Theory of Yardstick Competition", *The Rand Journal of Economics*, 1985, Vol. 16, pp. 319-27; Littlechild, S.C., *Economic Regulation of Privatised Water Authorities: A Report Submitted to the Department of the Environment*, HMSO, London, 1986.

60. See Arthur Little International, *European Telecommunications – Strategic Issues and Opportunities for the Decade Ahead*, Boston, Mass., 1983, Annex B; Ergas, H., *op. cit.* in Note 45.

61. Federal Communications Commission, *Economic Implications and Interrelationships Arising from Policies and Practices Relating to Customer Interconnection, Jurisdictional Separations and Rate Structures: Report on Docket 20003*, Washington D.C., 1986; National Telecommunications and Information Administration, *The Economic Effects of Competition*, Washington D.C., 1986.

62. Müller, J. *et al.*, *Economic Evaluation of Alternative Telecommunications Investment Strategies*, DIW, Berlin, 1985.

63. The precise technical definition of value added services, and their distinction from basic services, is a subject of continuing controversy, surveyed in Bruce, R. *et al.*, *From Telecommunications to Electronic Services*, International Institute of Communications, London, 1986.

64. Commission of the European Communities, Directorate-General, Information Market and Innovation, *Impact of Interconnected National PTT Data Networks on the Users of European Information Services: A Report Prepared by Information Dynamics Limited*, Luxembourg, 1986; similar results emerge from Logica, *European Telecommunications*, London, 1986.

65. See Taylor, L.D., *Telecommunications Demand: A Survey and Critique*, Ballinger, Cambridge, Mass., 1980.

66. See Reid, Ann, "Economic Aspects of the Provision of Value Added Services in the United States, the United Kingdom and Germany" (mimeo), OECD, Paris, 1986.

67. Telesis, *Documentation for the "Business Communications" Working Meeting*, Paris, February 1987.

68. See especially Federal Communications Commission, *In the Matters of Amendment of Sections 64.702 of the Commission's Rules and Regulations (Third Computer Inquiry): Notice of Proposed Rulemaking*, Washington D.C., 16th August 1985, which finds at para. 34, p. 16 that "increasingly it appears that a regulatory policy that turns on service definitions and service attributes – the basic/enhanced and network/CPE dichotomies established in Computer II – is fundamentally flawed".

69. An excellent survey can be found in Curien, N., "Bilan des études économetriques sur les coûts des télécommunications", *Revue Economique* (forthcoming). The only study which conflicts with the result cited in the text is Evans, D.S. and Heckman, J.J., "Test for Sub-additivity of the Cost Function with an Application to the Bell System", *American Economic Review*, 1984, Vol. 74, pp. 615-623. However, the subsequent, but as of yet unpublished, analysis by F. Kiss using the Evans-Heckman data and a Generalised Translog functional form finds that a number of the constraints imposed by Evans-Heckman are rejected by the data; and that all the models accepted by the data yield significant global scale economies and sub-additivity.

70. Charnes, A., Cooper, W.W. and Sueyash, T., *A Goal Programming/ Constrained Regression Analysis of AT&T as a Natural Monopoly*, CCS Working Paper 530, University of Texas, Austin, May 1986.

71. The underlying theory and an application to telecommunications are set out in Sharkey, W., *The Theory of Natural Monopoly*, Cambridge University Press, 1982.

72. Ergas, H., *op. cit.* in Note 45, Chapter 3. The large apparent productivity differentials between telecommunication administrations in different countries underscore this point.

73. In practice, however, the desirability of intermodal competition on this basis is limited by economies of scope between transmission media; moreover, the scale economies in satellite transmission may not be insignificant – for recent econometric estimates, see Quayle, M.J., unpublished D.Phil. thesis, University of Queensland, 1986.

74. Gensollen, M., "Mesure des coûts et déréglementation dans le secteur des télécommunications", paper presented to the *Industrial Organisation and Regulation Seminar at the Direction de la Prévision*, Paris, February 1986.

75. Shepherd, W.G., "The Competitive Margin in Communications" in Capron, W.M. (ed.), *Technological Change in Regulated Industries*, The Brookings Institution, Washington D.C., 1971, pp. 86-122.

76. This is in many respects the dynamic parallel to the distinction made in transport economics between economies of scale and economies of density. See Winston, C., *art. cit.* in Note 7, especially p. 67, Note 1.

77. "Signalling" refers to the internal information flows within the telecommunications network which primarily serve to control the flow of traffic.

78. Virtual Private Networks are private (user-specific) networks based on carrier facilities but which – unlike dedicated circuits – are assigned on demand, so that the circuits can be redeployed to carry other traffic when they are not in use.

79. The Integrated Services Digital Network refers to the integrated provision over fully digital switching and transmission facilities of the full range of telecommunications services. It is, in this sense, an evolution relative to the present situation, where voice, data and other digital services are generally provided over distinct facilities.

80. Müller, J. *et al.*, *op. cit.* in Note 62.

81. See Casse, G.D., *New and Future Technologies in the Local Telephone Network*, CWA Communication Products, Inc., 1986.

82. The transition problems following the dismantlement of AT&T are surveyed in MacAvoy, P.W. and Robinson, K., "Losing by Judicial Policymaking: The First Year of the AT&T Divestiture", *Yale Journal on Regulation*, 1985, Vol. 2, pp. 225-262; concerns about excess capacity are discussed in "The Coming Glut in Phone Lines", *Fortune*, 7th January 1985, pp. 73-78 (though this is by no means solely an American phenomenon); and the perceived adverse implications for network inter-operability and robustness and hence for national security in Bollings, Colonel G., *AT&T: Aftermath of Anti-Trust*, National Defence University Press, Washington D.C., 1985.

83. Baumol, W.J., "Reasonable Values for Rate Regulation: Plausible Policies for an Imperfect World" in Phillips, A. and Williamson, O.E. (eds.), *Prices: Issues in Theory, Practice and Public Policy*, University of Pennsylvania Press, Philadelphia, 1967, pp. 108-23.

84. Crew, M.A. and Kleindorfer, P.R., "Reliability and Public Utility Pricing", *American Economic Review*, 1978, Vol. 68, pp. 31-40; see also Director-General of Telecommunications, *Quality of Telecommunications Services: A Report*, OFTEL, London, December 1986.

85. See Schmalensee, *op. cit.* in Note 50, pp. 121-125.

86. The problems of prolonged "RPI-X" regulation are discussed in Vickers, J. and Yarrow, G., *Privatisation and the Natural Monopolies*, Public Policy Centre, London, 1985, pp. 42-43; Littlechild, S.C., *op. cit.* in Note 52, Chapter 10.

87. Thus, in Sweden it is estimated that the average cost of the 15 per cent of lines classified as rural is double that of the average line. Equally, in Australia the subsidy from metropolitan to non-metropolitan users (for access and local calls only) is equivalent to some 50 per cent of the cost of providing non-metropolitan services.

88. The ratio of interstate to local call charges in the United States in the early 1970s was one to forty; it should have been one to six. Equally, in 1982-83, British Telecom's cost coverage on local calls was 109 per cent; on trunk calls it was 528 per cent. Finally, in 1983, the ratio of local to long-distance call prices in Germany was one to eight; on cost grounds it should have been closer to one to four. See Kay, J., "Telecommunications Tariff Policy" (mimeo), Institute for Fiscal Studies, London, 1985.

89. Examples are given in Brown, S. and Sibley, D., *The Theory of Public Utility Pricing*, Cambridge University Press, 1986, p. 50; Encaoua, D. and Moreaux, M., "L'analyse théorique des problèmes de tarification et l'allocation des coûts dans les télécommunications", *Revue Economique*, Spring 1987.

90. See Baumol, W.J., *Super-Fairness*, MIT Press, Cambridge, Mass., 1986 for a discussion of concepts of equity and fairness.

91. See for example, Arrow, K. and Kalt, K., *Petroleum Price Regulation*, American Enterprise Institute, Washington D.C., 1979; Rolfe, J. *et al.*, *Economic Analysis of Telecommunications Policy Options*, Bell Laboratories, Princeton, N.J., 1979.

92. A review of the literature and a useful critique can be found in Rhoads, S.E., *The Economist's View of the World*, Cambridge University Press, 1985, Chapter 6.

93. See Munk, K.J., "Optimal Public Sector Pricing Taking the Distributional Aspect into Consideration", *Quarterly Journal of Economics*, 1977, Vol. 91, pp. 639-50; Renshaw, E., "On the Distribution of Telephone Communication Subsidies", *Public Utilities Fortnightly*, 21st July 1983, pp. 34-39; Ergas, H., *op. cit.* in Note 45, Annex II.

94. See Curien, N. and Pautrat, C., "Une approche économique de la tarification des télécommunications", *Journal des Télécommunications*, 1983, pp. 187-194; Neuman, K.H., Schweizer, U. and von Weizsächer, C.C., *Welfare Analysis of Telecommunications Tariffs in Germany*, Economic Research Institute of the German Post Office, 1983.

95. See Mitchell, B.M., "The Cost of Telephone Service: An International Comparison of Rates in Major Countries", *Telecommunications Policy*, March 1983, pp. 53-63.

96. National Telecommunications and Information Administration, "Local Service Rates" (draft), Department of Commerce, Washington D.C., 1986, pp. 34-37.

97. Director-General of Telecommunications, *Review of British Telecom's Tariff Changes, November 1986*, OFTEL, London, December 1986.

98. Study Group on Competition Policy in the Information Communications Industry, *Current Policy Issues About Competition Promotion in the Telecommunications Industry*, Fair Trade Commission, Japan, February 1986.

99. See Damus, S., "Ramsey Pricing by United States Railroads: Can it Exist?", *Journal of Transport Economics and Policy*, January 1984, pp. 51-61.

100. See Caves, R.E., Fortunato, M. and Ghemawat, P., "The Decline of Dominant Firms", *Quarterly Journal of Economics*, August 1984; a contrasting point of view is argued in Encaoua, D., Geroski, P. and Jacquemin, A., "Strategic Competition and the Persistence of Dominant Firms: A Survey" in Stiglitz, J.E. and Mathewson, Frank G. (eds.), *New Developments in the Analysis of Market Structure*, MIT Press, Cambridge, Mass., 1986, pp. 55-86.

101. See for example, Ergas, H., *op. cit.* in Note 45.

102. See Ministry of Trade and Industry, *Decision by the Council of State Containing Guidelines for the Administration of State-Owned Companies*, Helsinki, October 1983.

103. Information Canada, *Report*, Royal Commission on Financial Management and Accountability, Ottawa, 1979.

104. See for a survey, Vernon, *art. cit.* in Note 37; see also Rees, R., "Is There an Economic Case for Privatisation?", *Public Money*, March 1986, pp. 19-26.

105. See Garner, M., "Nationalised Industries and Sponsoring Departments", *Public Money*, September 1983, pp. 29-32.

106. See especially the analysis by Prodi, R. (Chairman of IRI), "La crisi delle participazioni statali: conseguenze economiche di faticosi processi di decisione", *L'Industria*, 1981, Vol. 2, pp. 5-20.

107. Kay, J. and Thompson, D.J., *Privatisation: A Policy in Search of a Rationale*, Institute for Fiscal Studies, London, 1985.

Chapter 9

SOCIAL POLICIES

INTRODUCTION

The pursuit of social goals is a fundamental element of the consensus that confers legitimacy on a society. These goals include the protection of citizens against sickness and poverty and the general principles of justice and equity. This chapter is devoted to the three biggest areas of government policy involving major social welfare expenditure: health care, retirement pensions and help for the unemployed. Certain other areas of social policy – such as housing support and policies toward single-parent families, etc. – are not included in the discussion.

In this chapter, we shall consider whether these social programmes are in need of structural reform. The social goals outlined above are not being questioned, rather the effectiveness of the methods that have been applied and the institutions that have been set up to achieve these goals will be examined. Several factors seem to suggest that a review of these policies is necessary and desirable.

Firstly, foreseeable demographic changes are likely to lead to a steep rise in future costs, particularly for pensions and probably also for health care, unless considerable technological progress is made in this last area. It will become increasingly difficult to ignore the pressure for reforms to bring these costs under control.

Secondly, in the next decade the trends in labour markets may be reversed. Demographic developments, combined with an economic recovery, may make it difficult to meet the demand for labour, especially skilled labour, in some occupations. These labour shortages would reveal the inherent disadvantages of social programmes that do not encourage workers to adapt their skills to market requirements, or that encourage them to withdraw from the labour market. It is clearly important to provide incentives and help to those who wish to work or who need to update their skills.

Thirdly, the techniques used to provide the various social services are constantly changing. For example, medical progress has made it much easier to treat many diseases. The costs per day of in-patient treatment are high and, as hospital services have become increasingly sophisticated, have recently risen more rapidly than consumer prices. However, less costly alternatives do sometimes exist: for example, new forms of care for the elderly which may be both cheaper and better suited to their needs. The health status of the elderly also has a bearing on decisions concerning the age of retirement. In addition, major progress in capital markets, notably the development of the financial industry and of competitive and innovative forms of insurance, may well open up new possibilities for the organisation of health and pension schemes (see Chapter 4 on the financial system).

These factors underline the importance of flexibility in the provision of social services. It will be suggested in this chapter that the best way to stimulate flexibility is to strengthen existing social programmes by offering incentives that allow competition and market forces to contribute more to their efficiency. It will be argued that autonomous, medium-sized service organisations geared to economic incentives and control mechanisms could play a greater role and usefully complement the services provided by the public sector. However, the need for greater flexibility and responsiveness to changing needs must be met within the framework of existing systems, most of which are public. A number of proposals in this direction will therefore be examined.

The following three sections deal respectively with the three major welfare fields: health care, retirement pension schemes and income support for the unemployed. The conclusions are presented in the final section.

I. HEALTH POLICIES

A. Development and success of postwar health policies

The expansion of health systems has been a major structural feature of postwar economic growth. The elasticity of the growth of total health expenditure in relation to economic growth has been greater than unity in most OECD countries – on average 1.4 to 1.5 in real terms, depending on the years considered – signifying that health expenditure has grown even more rapidly than GDP over the period. Table 9.1 shows the size of the health sector in OECD economies in 1984, using two indicators: the share of public health expenditure in GDP, and the share of total health expenditure in GDP.

Table 9.1. **Size of health sector, 1984**

In percentages

	Expenditure on public health as percentage of GDP	Total expenditure on health as percentage of GDP
Australia	5.4	7.5
Austria	4.4	7.2
Belgium	5.7	6.2
Canada	6.2	8.4
Denmark	5.3	6.3
Finland	5.4	6.6
France	6.5	9.1
Germany	6.4	8.1
Greece	3.6	4.6
Iceland	6.5	7.9
Ireland	6.9	8.0
Italy	6.1	7.2
Japan	4.8	6.6
Luxembourg	..	6.4 (1982)
Netherlands	6.8	8.6
New Zealand	4.4	5.6
Norway	5.6	6.3
Portugal	3.9	5.5
Spain	4.2	5.8
Sweden	8.6	9.4
Switzerland	..	7.8 (1982)
Turkey	..	..
United Kingdom	5.3	5.9
United States	4.4	10.7
Average	5.6	7.2

Source: OECD, *Financing and Delivering Health Care*, Paris, 1987.

These shares are currently between 5 and 10 per cent in most Member countries; health care has thus become a major industry.

In postwar welfare policies, health services have been regarded as essential "social goods". This has meant that in several countries, especially in Western Europe, a political consensus has grown up around the principle that governments should ensure that health services are accessible to all citizens, irrespective of their financial resources and ability to pay. They have done so by developing three types of health system with different structures and financing arrangements[1]:

- The *National Health Service* system, based on the supply of a comprehensive range of free, or almost free, health services. Central or local governments are responsible for the planning, siting and financing of the infrastructure, while the services are provided by public hospitals and health centres. The system does not prevent private hospitals and private medical practitioners from offering their services to people who are willing or able to pay for them. The United Kingdom and Italy are two countries that have developed this system on a large scale. In theory, the entire population is covered, subject to the actual availability of the services required;

- The *Social Insurance* system is one where governments also finance a large part of health expenditure, but by refunding the cost of care and offering some direct services. In most countries, this system has resulted in the merging of occupational or local health insurance funds. It has been progressively extended to the entire labour force and to dependants (parents, spouses, children, etc.). Health risk cover has also been steadily widened through supplementary insurance schemes, some of which may be quasi-public, e.g. mutual associations. Nevertheless, some sections of the population still have no health cover in a number of countries that have adopted this social insurance system.

Health services are provided by independent medical practitioners and public or private hospitals. Often hospital investment is planned, and the fees of hospitals and medical practitioners set, by negotiation between representatives of professional associations, insurance schemes and government. This means the market does not necessarily function on a competitive basis, since prices and conditions of entry are regulated. Most hospitals remain non-profit-making public bodies, local or attached to universities. This system has been taken furthest in Germany and France, where it currently covers over 90 per cent of the population and refunds about 80 per cent of total expenditure on health;

- The *Private Insurance* system differs from the social insurance system from a financing perspective in that the cover is provided by private insurance firms. Health services remain provided by both public and private organisations. Here again, however, the supply and prices of services, especially hospital, are often regulated and controlled by agreement between government, medical associations and insurers.

Government policy has played an important role in the growth of private insurance schemes. The schemes have been given highly advantageous tax treatment in some countries, which amounts in practice to subsidising private insurance expenditure. Some subsidised public insurance schemes have also been developed for non-active and elderly people and for those not covered by private insurance schemes. The health system in the United States has developed on this basis.

In the first two systems, more than 70 per cent of total expenditure on health is public budget funded. The proportion is the same in the third system when refunds of payments under private insurance schemes are included. Thus social policies result in only a very small proportion of the cost of health services actually being paid for by the users. The share borne by public and private insurance is particularly high in the case of hospital services (the most expensive), smaller in the case of visits to doctors, and smaller still for medicine price refunds. In the United States, for example, the third-party contribution is respectively about 90 per cent, 70 per cent and 45 per cent for these three categories of expenditure, which account roughly for 55 per cent, 30 per cent and 10 per cent of total health expenditure in OECD countries[2].

Mention should also be made of the large manufacturing industries which produce the equipment and medicines required by health services. These industries expanded rapidly during the postwar period due to major advances in health technology and treatment. The value of world production of medicinal products exceeded $100 billion per year in the 1980s. The bulk of these products are made in OECD countries, where the pharmaceutical industry today accounts for between 0.5 and 1.5 per cent of GDP. It is a competitive, unconcentrated, high technology and R&D-intensive industry[3]. Within a regulatory framework that strictly monitors new products – to make sure they have no harmful effects – the industry marketed a big number of new medicines during 1955 to 1985.

Measuring health outcomes is difficult. However, on the basis of readily available indices such as life expectancy, infant mortality, and disease-specific mortality rates, there have been significant improvements over the past 30 years. All OECD countries have registered big progress in the treatment and prevention of infectious diseases (such as tuberculosis, meningitis and poliomyelitis) which caused dramatic health problems only 40 years ago. Progress has also been made in

the treatment of many other diseases (cardiovascular, gastro-intestinal, etc.) and in the treatment of milder disorders. Health prevention and promotion campaigns have also played an important role (such as the compulsory wearing of crash helmets and safety belts reducing road accident casualties, and the addition of fluoride to tap-water improving dental hygiene). In contrast, only limited success has been achieved with chronic and degenerative diseases such as cancer. As an example, Table 9.2 shows a composite indicator of all these improvements: that is, the trend of the perinatal mortality rate, which has been reduced by a factor of three to four in the last 30 years. Unfortunately, one cannot easily attribute those improvements to specific changes in environmental, economic, social, or health system specific characteristics.

B. Structural problems in health policies

Health systems began to encounter certain major difficulties in the 1970s and 1980s. These problems were fairly similar for most OECD countries, despite the different health systems in each. In fact these difficulties were already latent in most of the systems from the time they were designed, but came to the forefront of policy considerations starting in the late 1970s. They may be divided into three categories.

1. Costs

The total cost of health programmes to public budgets consumed an increasing share of national wealth (GDP) in all OECD countries. In those countries that have private insurance schemes, the cost to employers of company insurance schemes has also risen just as steadily. In the United States, for example, total national health expenditure shot up from $215.1 billion in 1979 to $387.4 billion in 1984. The share of GDP devoted to health has increased from an OECD average of 4.2 in 1960 to 7.5 in 1984.

There are four reasons for these soaring costs:

– Advances in health care technology and the mounting costs of equipment and medicine. For example, in the United States, the average daily cost of in-patient treatment in a hospital increased from $217 in 1979 to $411 in 1984;

– The growth in demand for health care as a result of the ageing of the population. Persons aged 65 and older use four times as much health care – by value – as the average population;

– The concentration of health services on problems that require more difficult, protracted and expensive treatment than with diseases of the past which have now been largely eliminated. In France, for example, as much as 65 per cent of total expenditure on health goes to the 10 per cent of the population that suffer from these expensive illnesses or disabilities;

Table 9.2. **Trend of perinatal mortality rate**[1]
Per 1 000 births

Country	1950	1960	1970	1975	1979/1980
Australia	36	29	23	20	15
Austria	47	35	21	21	14
Belgium	..	32	23	20	14
Canada	36	28	20	17	12
Denmark	34	26	18	13	9
Finland	35	28	17	12	8
France	36	31	23	18	14
Germany	50	36	26	19	12
Ireland	..	..	24	22	16[2]
Italy	51	42	31	24	17
Japan	47	41	22	16	12
Luxembourg	..	33	25	16	10
Netherlands	34	27	19	14	11
New Zealand	35	27	20	17	13[2]
Norway	28	24	19	14	11
Portugal	..	41	38	31	..
Spain	..	..	..	21	17[3]
Sweden	34	27	16	11	9
Switzerland	..	..	18	13	10
United Kingdom	39	34	24	20	13
United States	33	29	23	18	13

1. Deaths after 28 weeks pregnancy and under the first seven days of life per 1 000 live births.
2. 1978.
3. 1979.
Source: OECD, *Living Conditions in OECD Countries,* Paris, 1986.

- Pay in the health sector being likely to rise at the same rate as in the rest of the economy in the long run, but that unless offset by improvements in productivity, resulting in higher real costs of health provision. Different remuneration systems, e.g. fee-for-service versus salary, lead to different incentive structures and hence to different effects on efficiency and costs.

2. The suppliers' "dominant influence"

In the three health systems, the planning of capital investment, range of health services, pricing structure and treatment strategy are virtually all determined by the professionals providing the services and by the funding organisations. Those organisations who finance the services – government health departments or public or private insurance systems – do exercise some financial control over the options, but only in a technical and organisational environment where the medical profession has the dominant influence[4]. Users are generally assumed to have neither the information nor the knowledge needed to make rational cost and benefit choices and have to trust to the competence and ethical integrity of the suppliers. Moreover, they have little incentive to be discriminating about costs, since these are borne by third parties.

This relatively asymmetrical relationship between funding agencies and suppliers of health services on the one hand, and between users and the same suppliers on the other, involves a twofold delegation of powers to the medical sector. Users delegate to it their right to choose the health services best suited to their needs. In theory, the funding agencies still have the right to determine their financial commitments, but in practice relinquish that right too, because of the technical complexity of the decisions that have to be taken and because ethically they prefer to set no limit on expenditures when human lives may depend on them. Therefore, the health sector in OECD countries is in the singular position of not merely delivering services, but at the same time acting on behalf of its clients and funding agencies[5].

Governments operating all three types of health system have long recognised and accepted this state of affairs. Only in the 1970s, when costs soared to an extremely high level, was it perceived as a major policy issue. In particular, critics claimed that the medical community does not take sufficient account of the financial implications of its decisions – while acknowledging that doctors have not been trained to cope with this constraint or to regard it as being one of their professional responsibilities. The problem is not a question of competence or professional ethics, but rather one of economic incentives and control.

Another criticism of the suppliers' dominant influence is that current health schemes provide little incentive to develop and apply preventive medicine on a large scale. The medical sector has few financial or professional incentives to invest heavily in prevention, yet this can substantially increase well-being and reduce costs in many health areas.

This does not, of course, detract from the major preventive public health campaigns. These involve legislation, regulations and public information activities rather than individualised medical services. Examples include compulsory vaccinations, anti-drinking and smoking campaigns, prenatal care, regulations ensuring healthy housing conditions, compulsory use of protective equipment in industry and on the road, and so forth[6]. All of these have had a beneficial effect on public health in OECD countries. Nevertheless, such action has not been the result of preventive strategies or services devised by the medical sector in the strict sense of the term[7].

3. Inefficiency in the production and consumption of services

The weakness of economic constraints and incentives in the health sector also seems to have encouraged a degree of economic inefficiency in health delivery. When alternative means of supplying or financing health care were established, it was found that substantial savings could be made by tapping into existing health systems' "productivity reserves". In the United States for example, cost reductions of between 10 per cent and 40 per cent were recorded in many types of care, without any apparent deterioration of quality, after Health Maintenance Organisations (HMOs, see below) were set up[8].

The economic inefficiency of health centres and hospitals has long been recognised. For the wide range of strategies involved in providing a given type and volume of health service – either within a given country or at an international level – it appears that no standards of efficiency have yet been established as they have in competitive industries. Available comparative studies, notwithstanding their methodological shortcomings, indicate that the total annual expenditure per hospital bed in one OECD country may be double that of another and up to six or seven times higher in the most extreme cases. Total daily expenditures on in-patient hospital treatment show roughly the same disparity of costs, which cannot be explained solely by differences in the quality of care. Big international differences in medical practices, e.g. Caesarean as against normal deliveries, total as against partial mastectomies, bypass heart surgery as against treatment by drugs, etc., also seem to indicate that criteria for measuring the effectiveness and cost efficiency of health care are lacking[9].

The basic problem of evaluating differences in expenditure is the lack of measures of health outcomes and the lack of generally agreed upon clinical standards of appropriateness of medical care[10]. Then one cannot readily attribute the large observed differences in medical practice patterns within and between countries to differences in underlying population characteristics, efficiency, quality, or national amenities. In all cases however, professional and economic incentives are important aspects of these differences[19].

C. New approaches in health policy

Confronted with the growing problems of health policies, the strong political incentive to improve their efficiency, and the need to respond to changing demands, most OECD governments are encouraging alternative approaches to health services. Given the highly complex structure of health systems and the knowledge of several decades embodied in their management, these approaches are being taken gradually and often on an experimental basis. If they give good results – and some have already started to do so – it may be expected that they will be adopted on a wider scale in the innovating countries and in others too. Side by side with this approach, traditional cost control techniques like cost/benefit analyses of new health technologies will continue to be used.

The next section will discuss these new experiments which, although still marginal to overall health system management, may be the most interesting and thought-provoking organisational innovations from the structural adjustment standpoint.

New policies have three thrusts that have followed sequentially:

- The containment and rationing of expenditure on health;
- The participation by the consumer in the funding of services;
- More effective interaction between funding agencies and suppliers of services.

1. Containment and rationing of health spending

The first, simplest and most effective short-term way of controlling costs is simply to ration expenditure on health. This results in a slow-down in investment and recruitment in national health systems, in a reduction in authorisations for treatment and in refunds in national insurance systems, and in a reduction in the levels and scope of cover in insurance contracts in private insurance schemes. This policy has contributed to curbing the growth of expenditure fairly rapidly. For example, in 1984 expenditure in the United States grew for the first time by less than 10 per cent, a deceleration largely due to retrenchment but also to a general slow-down in inflation[11].

The problem with this approach is that it may result in an indiscriminate rationing of expenditure, with undesirable individual and social consequences. In times of shortage, it is difficult to allocate available services according to clear-cut priorities, and an across-the-board reduction in expenditure may be a source of social injustice. Although redistributive effects have been more rapid in health services than in any other social service[12], the present distribution is still weighted against the lowest income groups in several countries[13]. Most OECD governments still hope to make further improvements in this distribution pattern[14].

In addition, this policy is not viable in the long term,

since it creates an imbalance between what people justifiably expect and what is actually available from public health services. Queueing (in public health centres) and delayed treatment (pending authorisation by national insurance systems) cannot be a long-term, socially acceptable way of regulating imbalances. There is also evidence that lower income groups may be affected more severely than those able to afford private hospital insurance. A recent study showed that such health service rationing exists to a similar extent in different health systems[15].

Note, however, that rationing may also encourage consumers and suppliers of health care to make some savings. The tighter budget constraints since the mid-1970s probably have not a little to do with the fact that stays in hospitals are now shorter. In spite of the increase in the numbers of long-term elderly in-patients, the average length of stays in hospitals has continued to fall in most OECD countries, from 26 days in the 1960s to about 18 days (international average) in the 1980s[16].

Nonetheless, the pure and simple rationing of expenditure is regarded in most countries as a short-term policy which should be replaced or rapidly supplemented by more structural measures.

2. User participation in health service financing

Most countries are generalising financial participation requirements on a larger scale. Such participation takes different forms, e.g. insurance excess (first instalment of the cost of treatment and medicine is not refunded), "tickets modérateurs" (a fixed proportion of costs is not refunded), or charges for certain services that were refunded or provided free of charge in the past, etc.[17]. But in all countries the share paid by users remains quite small.

Policy aims regarding consumer participation are twofold:

- First, part of the cost of health services can be transferred to the actual users. Although the transfer is small compared to the total costs still defrayed by funding agencies, when multiplied by a large number it makes substantial savings possible. For example, in many company insurance schemes in the United States, employees now pay up to 20 per cent of their routine outlay on health care[17]. In the French social security system the proportion is similar (about 22 per cent), and in Australia around 15 per cent. The user's share of minor expenses, e.g. on medicines, has been increased, but it has been kept down in the case of major expenditures, e.g. hospital treatment as an in-patient. In this connection, it must be remembered that it is not possible to consider imposing payment of any significant share of costs on that 4 per cent of the population whose complex health problems account for 50 per cent of total health spending in the OECD countries;

- Second, these measures aim to change users' attitude to health services. Inasmuch as in all three systems the consumer tends to regard the services as being virtually free (a view that is correct so far as each individual is concerned, but wrong at national level), the new measures should induce users to make savings and rationalise expenditure. The problem is to find the right balance. The share to be paid by each individual must be small enough not to restrict his access to necessary health care, but large enough to make each user understand his own personal interest in cutting costs and in rationalising expenditure.

A related objective concerns not only the volume, but the value, of consumption. Sharing the costs of medical care should, in theory, encourage users to turn to the most efficient suppliers of services, who can offer and charge more competitive prices. Users have always been attentive to the quality of the services they are offered, but the new measures aim also to encourage them to select the most cost-efficient suppliers. Such an inducement works when the user can choose between several suppliers, i.e. insofar as there is no geographical, sectoral or administrative monopoly. It would also be desirable for users to shake off the habit of considering that the most expensive health service is bound to be the best. A certain amount of competition is thus required. Such competition need not be restricted to profit-making organisations. Whatever their status, health organisations should have the margin of manœuvre necessary to adjust their capacity upward when social demand increases and downward when that demand slackens[18].

In economic terms, it may be considered that making consumers bear their share in the financing of services should induce them to act as funding agencies' "agents", optimising the range of services used and holding down costs. However, these mechanisms can work only in fairly routine health care where the consumer can be asked to share the costs (such sharing is both impossible and undesirable where very high expenditures are concerned), and where he can choose between alternative services and suppliers. They work less well in the case of the major, expensive and specialised treatment over a long period that accounts for the biggest proportion of expenditure on health. Subject to these reservations, the most extensive study yet made to assess cost-sharing by users has concluded that cost-sharing reduces expenditures and has only very minimal adverse effects on health outcomes[19].

3. Improving the interaction between funding agencies and suppliers of services

The two policy thrusts described above aim primarily to reduce or to slow down the growth of health spending. The third policy thrust aims to increase the productivity of such spending.

This third group of policies is based on the premise that there is ample scope for productivity gains in all three types of health system – national health service, national insurance system and private insurance schemes. Productivity gains may relate either to finding the best and least expensive treatment in each specific case, i.e. choice of care – surgery, treatment by drugs or in hospital, treatment at home, etc., or to implementing these health strategies, once defined, in the most effective and economical way. Public and private funding agencies, and to a much lesser extent the users themselves, have every reason to optimise and rationalise such expenditure.

Funding agencies are starting to seek productivity gains by means of three different approaches. None of these approaches are really new since all have already been applied to a certain extent in each of the three types of health system. However, as a result of mounting pressures, they are now being reconsidered and adapted in many countries. They include:

- Regulatory measures (price and quantity controls);
- Keener competition between suppliers of services;
- Better interaction between funding agencies and suppliers of services.

a) *Regulatory measures*

This is the most common and widely used approach in OECD countries. The funding agencies – either government departments in national health services, social security bodies in national insurance systems or insurance companies in private insurance schemes – bargain with the suppliers of services to reduce costs and rationalise procedures. Physicians' fees are negotiated with the doctors' professional associations; hospital fees with individual hospitals or their local or national representatives; and drug prices with the pharmaceutical firms. The outcome of these negotiations is generally embodied in price regulations under the national health service and national insurance systems, and in agreements with the insurance companies under private insurance schemes. In certain cases, funders have imposed freezes or ceiling prices unilaterally[20].

Most countries have attempted to control increases in expenditures through regulatory mechanisms. Such mechanisms have included planning laws limiting hospital beds and equipment, tight limits on reimbursement rates and hospital budgets, overall expenditure limits, and reduced coverage of some marginally effective services such as spa treatments and certain pharmaceuticals. The effects of such policies in terms of equity, effectiveness and efficiency have been difficult to ascertain, although strictly from a cost-control perspective some countries appear to have controlled expenditures better than others[21].

What has emerged from the lessons of the past decade is an interest in virtually all countries to use economic

326

incentives to promote efficient production and consumption of health services. While much of the discussion has been blurred by a semantic debate concerning "competition" versus "regulation", the principal point is that most countries are attempting to achieve competitive market type efficiencies, while preserving access. What is clear is that one cannot speak about competitive policies versus regulatory policies in isolation. The real issue is the need for increased competition in an adapted regulatory environment[22].

b) *Keener competition*

Health economists have usually advocated greater competition in the health sector to promote higher productivity and efficiency[23]. But in none of the three systems (private insurance included) has competition ever been very keen[24]. The hospital service sector is largely public or regulated in all countries and is often locally quasi-monopolistic – except in urban areas in some countries, where competition between public and private hospitals does exist. Competition between doctors in the private sector is generally only moderate and is to some extent regulated by their professional bodies, which also exercise ethical and quality control. New entrants in both sectors are usually controlled by means of administrative authorisation and professional certification procedures. New investment by hospitals is also subject to various types of administrative authorisation.

In this environment, the private hospital sector (in the countries where it exists) and the medical profession performed outstandingly well in terms of return on their investment throughout the postwar period. In the case of the medical profession, this good return refers to investment in human capital[25]. Revenues do appear, however, to have fallen in recent years – especially in the United States – as a result of tighter constraints on health expenditures and the surplus of qualified professional personnel in several areas[34].

The idea of stepping up competition to boost efficiency is simple in theory, but difficult to apply in practice. It comes up against unwieldy established economic and administrative structures, and against users' expectations and reactions. In particular, the use of third-party financing, the power of suppliers to create their own demand, the relative ignorance of consumers and the prevalence of local monopolies all make it difficult to promote competition among suppliers or cost-consciousness among customers. It has even been argued, on the basis of economic theory, that users do not desire genuine competition in the supply of health services, because they want to avoid the burdensome technical and moral choices that would be involved[26]. In this context – and although certain health economists may today be warning policy makers and public opinion against "uncontrolled" application of economics to health care[27] – it has to be acknowledged that in most countries too little attention is paid to economic analysis

of the health care sector, especially in terms of industrial organisation and competitive behaviour.

A major reform intended by government to promote competition in the health sector was made in the United States in 1983, when the DRG system (Diagnosis Related Groups) of the Health Care Financing Administration (HCFA) was introduced. Paradoxically, it was not sponsored by the private insurance companies, which in fact had no incentive to achieve higher efficiency in the provision of services, since they could pass costs on to consumers through higher insurance premiums. It stemmed from a new policy of reimbursement for the federal insurance system, Medicare, which was faced with a mounting deficit. Under DRG, fixed, flat rates of hospital reimbursement are set for 467 diagnosis categories. Public, local and private hospitals are allowed to keep any difference between their actual costs and sums reimbursed by Medicare under the DRG system. Quality of care is monitored by a system of Professional Review Organisations (PROs). It is still too early to make a full assessment of this system, but first results do seem promising[28]. However, little is known about the relative efficiency of the DRG system as compared with reimbursement rules in other countries[29].

c) *Better interactions between funding agencies and suppliers of services*

The aim of the policies intended to enhance productivity is to bring about a change in the behaviour of doctors and hospitals (organisation, choice of treatment, treatment techniques, etc.) in line with funding agencies' cost-cutting strategies. Doctors and hospitals, therefore, are to be assigned a more active role in reducing costs, insofar as their functions imply co-operation with the funding agencies in their capacity as the latters' "agents" (see Part II.2). One way of making sure that this role-delegation works effectively may be to group funders and suppliers organisationally, making the latter administratively subordinate to the former. In the health sector, this means grouping the funders and suppliers together in integrated organisations.

National health systems may be considered as a transformation of national insurance systems along these lines. Contributions and public funds are paid to a body which centralises and manages them and also provides the services that they finance. Such a body has complete financial responsibility for the system, funds its expansion out of its own resources, and is supposed to provide health services at the lowest cost. While overall spending is limited, it is not clear that the inherent incentives lead to allocational efficiency at the micro level.

One new development in the United States, the Health Maintenance Organisations (HMOs), applies this vertical integration principle on a microeconomic scale and in a competitive environment. Other similar bodies, the Individual Practice Associations (IPAs) and Primary Care Networks (PCNs), work in the same way[30].

Table 9.3. **A profile of medical-specific inflation rates**

Average annual growth in percentage points

	Institutional care			Ambulatory care			Pharmaceutical sales		
	1960-1970	1970-1980	1980-1985	1960-1970	1970-1980	1980-1985	1960-1970	1970-1980	1980-1985
Australia	1.9	1.3	..	1.7	1.0	..	0.9	0.8	..
Austria	3.1	1.9	1.6	1.9	1.7	0.8	0.3	0.7	0.6
Belgium	2.7	1.2	1.7	..	1.3	0.9	..	0.3	1.0
Canada	2.1	1.2	..	1.4	0.7	1.3	−0.1	0.5	2.1
Denmark	2.3	1.1	1.0	..	0.9	1.0	..	0.7	1.3
Finland	1.2	1.0	0.9	(1.8)	1.1	..	0.4	0.8	..
France	1.4	1.1	0.9	1.2	0.9	0.8	0.3	0.5	0.5
Germany	2.5	1.6	..	2.5	1.5	..	0.9	0.8	2.1
Greece	1.7	1.7	..	0.7	1.5	..	0.9	0.8	0.8
Ireland	2.7	1.0	..	..	1.0	..	..	0.8	..
Italy	2.3	1.1	1.3	2.6	0.8	1.2	0.1	0.3	2.7
Japan	0.7	0.8	1.8	0.7	0.8	1.8	0.2	0.7	2.3
Netherlands	1.3	2.0	1.4	..	1.3	0.3	..	0.5	0.9
New Zealand	1.5	1.2	..	..	..	..	..	..	..
Norway	1.7	1.1	0.9	2.7	1.2	1.0	..	0.9	0.9
Portugal	..	1.1	..	..	1.1	..	..	0.7	..
Spain	..	..	..	..	..	..	..	0.4	..
Sweden	2.0	1.3	..	..	0.5	..	..	0.9	..
Switzerland	..	..	1.9	..	1.2	1.0	0.4	0.4	0.6
United Kingdom	1.3	1.3	..	..	..	..	−0.1	0.9	..
United States	1.6	1.2	1.5	1.5	1.1	1.4	0.0	0.7	1.6

1. Medical specific expresses the rise of medical goods and services' prices above that of national average inflation.
2. The 1980-1985 rates are provisional estimates; 1979-1984 rates have been used when 1985 implicit indices were not available.
Source: Calculated from OECD, *Measuring Health Care - 1960-1983, op. cit.* in Note 2, by J.-P. Poullier, "From Risk Aversion to Risk Rating: Trends in OECD Health Care Systems", *art. cit.* in Note 10.

Graph 9.1. **Growth of HMOs**

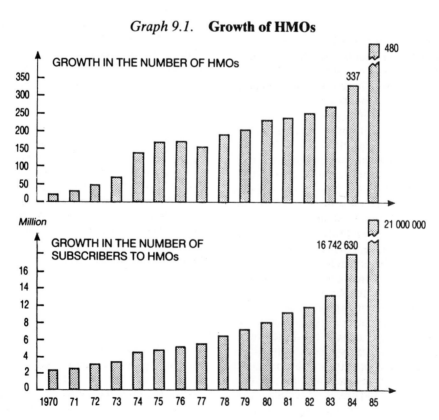

Source: See Note 30.

328

In the HMOs, the insurance/funding function and the care/service function are incorporated in the same, usually profit-making, organisation. Patients enrol either individually or under company programmes and pay an annual fee fixed in advance. In return, the HMO provides all the health care they may need during the period covered. The HMO acts as both insurer and supplier of services[31].

HMOs have taken off in the United States since the mid-1970s. Developed by the private sector, they were given impetus in 1973 by a federal legislative decision (the Health Maintenance Organisation Act), which required employers to include them in their health insurance schemes and granted generous subsidies for that purpose. The subsidies were withdrawn in 1982 when the system had become sufficiently well-known and had acquired enough credibility to continue unaided. Graph 9.1 shows the spectacular growth of HMOs in the United States in the past ten years.

HMOs seek to reduce their costs as insurers and so have a big incentive to provide the most efficient care possible. Since there are a large number of HMOs competing on the market, they all strive to be more efficient in order to lower their premiums, without any drop in the quality of care provided. Because of this specific incentive pattern it is more important for HMOs than for the independent insurance companies and health organisations to maximise their performance in terms of health status/cost ratio. The first studies of the HMOs' actual performances have borne this out. These studies have shown that HMOs have cut treatment costs in many fields by 10 to 40 per cent, while maintaining the quality of service[8]. However, the HMOs cover 9 per cent of the United States population, and there is some concern, on the basis of recent research, about the impact of HMOs on the health status of low income earners at high initial risk of sickness[33]. It is also not clear what the health sector's global supply-side response would be if utilisation rates were lowered on a generalised basis. In contrast, recent research does not confirm the most widely shared reservation in interpreting HMOs' good performance, namely the social and demographic characteristics of the population covered. Population characteristics are to be ruled out in explaining lower hospitalisation rates in HMOs[33].

One potential advantage of the HMOs is their direct incentive to practise preventive medicine. Since they are responsible for all their patients' health care, in theory over a long period, it is in their interests to minimise the total health cost of each individual by using preventive medicine techniques. They are in a good position to do this, since they hold detailed records of the health status of each patient. These data are usually centralised and managed by advanced computer systems, and monitored by traditional family doctor-type general practitioners. For this reason, some members of the US medical community predict that the HMOs will be the driving force behind a new wave of research and development on preventive medicine techniques.

The length of time covered by each subscriber's contract with an HMO is an important issue, as is the financial viability of these organisations. New technologies centred on preventive medicine are typically very costly in the short term, but costs can be written off with remarkable success in the medium and longer term[32]. This means the HMOs will be able to use these new techniques to the best advantage only if their subscribers' contracts cover a long period. For these reasons – and also because of the serious problems that would be raised if an HMO ceased activity without being able to meet its commitments – the regulation governing HMO contracts has become an important policy issue in the United States.

There is also concern that HMOs may provoke a fragmentation of the health system into risk groups and income groups because they may attract and accept low-risk patients with the means to pay, and exclude high-risk and low-income patients with health problems. Thus, while being a remarkably efficient extension of private insurance schemes, they would weaken the welfare and national solidarity component of the health system.

United States law has sought to guard against this "adverse selection" problem by making non-discriminatory pricing of premiums compulsory for the various risk groups, and by making it unlawful to refuse individual enrolments into HMOs. The possibility of discrimination due to inability to pay is diminished somewhat by the fact that most memberships are paid by employers. This does not help the elderly and unemployed, or those in work but whose employer does not run this type of scheme. However, this problem is not specific to the HMOs, but is inherent in any system of private insurance[34]. The growth and sophistication of the private health industry, of which the HMOs are the most economically advanced sector, may in this context accentuate social inequality in health care.

While institutional innovations in the health sector inevitably raise technical, economic and social difficulties, they may also make health systems more efficient. OECD governments – by monitoring current international experiments in health policies, by introducing institutional innovations cautiously but courageously, and by dispassionately assessing their advantages and disadvantages – should be able to make their health systems considerably more effective in the future. This is already becoming a social, political and macroeconomic necessity.

II. RETIREMENT PENSIONS

A. Development of public pension schemes

In many countries, public pension schemes date from the beginning of the century, but their present structures and virtual universality are largely the result of postwar developments[35]. Coverage of the schemes has been extended to all groups in society, retirement benefits have been greatly enhanced and the schemes have grown as the proportion of old people in the population has risen. This development has been accompanied by a marked growth in public outlays on pensions, from about 4.5 per cent of GDP in 1960 to 9 per cent in 1983. Although great disparities in pension levels still exist between OECD countries, the trends have been the same. Except in Australia and New Zealand, state pension schemes operate basically on the insurance principle. Some schemes also guarantee a basic minimum for all.

The contributions paid by employers and employees during their working lives confer an entitlement to retirement pensions. This is comprised of a flat-rate element plus an earnings-related element and is index-linked to the rise in prices or average earnings. However, although the pattern of revenues and entitlements is closely linked to the lifetime earnings and contributions of each individual, most systems currently operate on a pay-as-you-go basis. That is, current revenues cover current outlays irrespective of the future liabilities of the schemes. In three OECD countries (Canada, Japan and Sweden) the funding system continues to play an important – though now diminishing – role. In the United Kingdom funding plays an important and growing role in the state pensions scheme via contracting out.

A number of factors have contributed to the growth of pension schemes:

– The dissolution of traditional family structures and the increasing longevity of retired people, which makes it more difficult for families to provide for their older members;
– The lack of saving and investment opportunities providing a guaranteed real return, the erosion of annuities by inflation and the difficulties due to the varying length of retirement life for all workers;
– The actual or assumed inadequacy of voluntary retirement savings by individuals, due to either improvidence or insufficient resources;
– A determination to provide adequate and equal incomes for all individuals, groups and generations, which has prompted governments to guarantee a minimum income for the old, as well as for the poor in general;
– Political considerations, since pensions commitments are a way of responding to social needs without weighing too heavily on the public purse in the short term.

For all these reasons – as well as because of the long period of economic growth and rising incomes resulting in a more than proportional increase in household assets, much of it in the form of owner-occupied housing – the income levels of older workers and retirees have improved greatly over recent decades, both in absolute terms and in relation to the average earnings of the working population. Until the late 60s, old age often meant poverty. Although a significant minority of the

Graph 9.2. **Pension benefits and labour force participation in five major countries[1]**

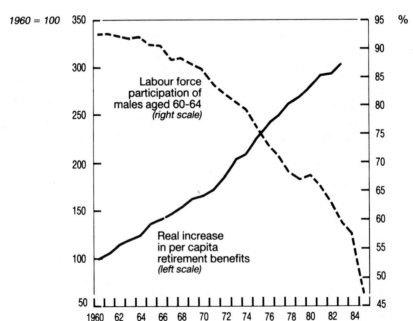

1. Germany, Italy, Japan, United Kingdom, United States.
Source: OECD.

330

elderly still have only a meagre income, people are today much less worried about their financial situation on reaching old age. A large proportion of workers – particularly men – have been able to retire before the normal retirement age under the State pension schemes (usually between 60 and 65) (Graph 9.2). Few retired people are nowadays obliged to live with their children for financial reasons.

B. The problems of public pensions

Following three or four decades of rapid and successful growth, pension schemes are now facing problems. While the general objectives of such schemes continue to enjoy solid social and political support, differences are now emerging about how to achieve these objectives. One of the salient issues under debate is whether the State should provide relatively high pensions for those workers who have enjoyed a substantial income during their working life and who have therefore been in a better position to save and accumulate wealth.

The main concerns underlying the current debate on the reform of public pension schemes are that:

- The growth in outlays on public pension schemes is putting heavy pressure on public finances at a time when governments are making every effort to reduce public deficits and contain the growth of the public sector generally;
- Demographic trends, which must be considered in conjunction with the existing commitments of public pension schemes, suggest that outlays will come under very heavy pressure in most countries, particularly at the forthcoming turn of the century;
- In a number of countries, pension schemes are still some way from maturity. In other words, the improvements and increases in coverage promised to workers still contributing have yet to be fully translated into increased benefits paid to retirees. In some cases, the promised increases in future benefits have not been matched by a proportionate increase in contribution rates. Because of the pay-as-you-go structure of the schemes, contribu-

tion levels will have to be raised, sometimes very sharply, when the time comes to pay these higher benefits.

The future arithmetic is clear when the effects of demographic changes on pension schemes are closely scrutinised. The proportion of people in retirement (expressed as the ratio of those aged over 64 to the working population – usually those aged 15-64) has been steadily growing since 1950 in most OECD countries. This trend is expected to continue, probably up to the middle of the next century, although the load borne by the working population will increase only slightly during the 1980 to 1990 period (see Table 9.4). But the rate of increase will then accelerate, especially during the first 30 years of the next century, being the fastest and most pronounced in Japan among OECD countries.

Demographic trends therefore pose an additional and serious problem for income distribution. Given present productivity rates, retirement entitlements and retirement age, future generations of retirees will absorb an increasingly larger proportion of national income. This depletion can only be at the expense of labour and capital incomes. Just how this additional transfer should be determined, generated and allocated is now the key question for retirement support policies[36].

C. Possible reforms: the potential role of funded schemes

A number of mathematical solutions can be proposed to deal with the problem of the dependency ratios (retiree/worker ratios) shown in Table 9.4:

- A first alternative would be to hold replacement rates at their current level (about 50 per cent in 1980) and to leave the retirement age unchanged[37]. To provide the additional pension resources needed for the growing number of retirees, productivity per worker would then have to increase by an additional quarter per cent per annum between 1980 and the year 2000 and by an additional half per cent per annum between the years 2000 and 2020;

Table 9.4. **Dependency ratios[1] in seven major countries**

	1950	1960	1970	1980	1990	2000	2010	2020
Canada	12.2	12.7	12.7	13.1	15.8	17.3	18.7	25.0
France	17.3	18.8	20.7	21.4	19.6	22.4	22.2	28.3
Germany	13.0	16.0	20.7	22.7	21.1	24.4	31.1	33.4
Italy	12.6	14.2	16.4	20.9	21.4	24.7	26.3	29.2
Japan	8.3	9.0	10.3	13.4	15.9	22.0	28.2	34.0
United Kingdom	16.0	17.9	20.6	23.1	22.9	22.6	23.0	26.8
United States	12.5	15.5	15.8	17.1	17.9	17.6	18.0	23.9
Average for seven major countries	13.3	14.9	16.7	18.8	19.2	21.6	23.9	28.7

1. Ratio of population aged 65 plus to population aged 15-64.
Source: OECD.

- However, these calculations assume increases both in the expenditure ratio (pension outlays as a proportion of GDP) and in contribution levels (employers' and employees' pension contributions as a percentage of wages and salaries). The expenditure ratio would need to rise from about 10 per cent of GDP in 1980 to 12 per cent in 2000 and 16.5 per cent in 2020. Contribution rates would have to rise from about 15 per cent of wages and salaries in 1980 to approximately 25 per cent in 2020;
- A second possible solution would be to hold the expenditure ratio (and hence the contribution rates) constant. Replacement rates would then have to fall to compensate for the demographic shift. In present circumstances, rates would need to fall from, say, 50 per cent in 1980 to 43 per cent by the year 2000 and 33 per cent by 2020;
- A third option would be to raise the retirement age without altering either the replacement or the contribution rates. In that case, and on the same assumptions, the retirement age would have to be raised by three years between 1980 and 2000, and by a further five years between 2000 and 2020;
- Pressures on retirement systems can also be reduced by tipping the balance of social expenditures in favour of the elderly. Such a change of pattern is predicted by current demographic trends. For example, less youth-related investment will soon be required, e.g. for education, and could feasibly be spent on the elderly. Also, to the extent that working-age families have fewer children, their taxable capacity is greater, as is the potential for married women to work. These factors provide additional scope for tipping social expenditure more in favour of the elderly. Another obvious solution would be to make savings elsewhere in the public sector.

Clearly, the above estimates are merely an indication of the magnitude of the problem. The figures vary widely from one country to another and are also affected by the maturation of the various schemes. For example, in France it is thought that the maturation of the system will be the main factor affecting contributions over the next 20 years, but that demographic effects will predominate early in the next century. In Japan, the problems of the maturation of the system and the ageing of the population tend to reinforce each other, with the result that the necessary (and recently initiated) reforms are correspondingly more drastic.

It is clear that unless these trade-offs are clearly explained and accepted by society, inflationary pressures might increase and so upset the balance between the resources available for pensions and legitimate claims. The strain of financing any such deficit out of budget resources, coupled with the upward pressures on employers' and employees' contributions, might bring corresponding pressures on prices and wages.

Apart from these possibilities, considered from a national accountancy standpoint and within the context of existing systems, there is also scope for broadening the institutional basis of pension schemes. Additional retirement income could be secured as capital income on special savings built up during working life. This is the basic principle of the "funded" private supplementary schemes popular in a number of countries, e.g. Australia, Canada, Finland, the United Kingdom and the United States[38].

This practice could be developed further in OECD countries by using a variety of institutional arrangements. Such schemes include company pension funds financed by employers and/or workers, individual working-life savings schemes with banks, insurance companies and other financial institutions, or new pension funds organised on an occupational or geographical basis. These systems could be used to supplement unified public schemes in order to raise future retirement incomes to the level compatible with popular expectations[39]. The actual extent of this additional support will be governed in countries with state insurance-based schemes by the foreseeable deficits in those schemes.

If such supplementary systems became widespread, the issue of pensions would partially become less of an inter-generational income distribution problem and more a question of each generation's working-life savings and long-term returns on capital. The income allocated to pensions would be deducted in both cases from national income, but as a quasi-tax transfer for the pay-as-you-go element, and as capital income for the funded complement[40].

In the long term, many countries are likely to make simultaneous use of various alternatives and may adopt a threefold system combining the flat-rate and proportional benefits of a public scheme with the income produced by a funded system. Notably, the provision of flat-rate universal benefits may become an important component of political consensus and a means of compensating for the inevitably regressive distributive effects of the private schemes. The elements of such a system are already in place in several countries, and others like Switzerland are moving in this direction[41].

Apart from these broad strategic options, the restructuring of national pension schemes is technically complex. It poses two particular problems:

- There is the problem of lead times. Because of the long-term nature of retirement contracts, any attempt to supplement existing pay-as-you-go schemes with funded plans involves very long lead times. If existing obligations and entitlements cannot be tampered with, then the complete restructuring of a system could, in principle, span an entire working life. Those countries whose systems have not yet reached maturity have the advantage that commitments can be frozen at their present level, although this may mean going back on promised improvements;

– There are also the problems of transition. The transitional generation has to bear a double burden on changing from a pay-as-you-go to a funded system since it must not only provide for existing retirees but also build up funds to finance its own pensions. However, the transition does not involve a total transfer but only a partial reallocation of responsibilities between pay-as-you-go and funded schemes. Furthermore, the extra burden to be borne by the transition generation has to be compared with that which would fall on future generations if the system were not changed. In any case, unless the mounting strain on resources is squarely faced and solutions found, inflationary pressures for higher wages and public financing might increase with their associated costs.

Governments would also have to assume a large measure of responsibility for the financial discipline and the tax treatment of pension funds.

Financial discipline is essential to safeguard the savings and assets intended to generate income in old age against the vicissitudes of financial markets and risky investment strategies. It is not easy to promote a competitive environment where pension funds, banks, insurance companies, mutual funds and investment trusts display a dynamic attitude to the collection and management of retirement savings so as to maximise returns while also taking care to minimise the associated investment risks[42]. It will be important to develop prudential supervision and insurance mechanisms adapted to the capital market conditions of each country.

The taxation of retirement savings is an important policy tool since it can provide the necessary stimuli. A tax system which favours contributions to and profits from pension funds may help in promoting these new schemes. At the same time, care must be taken not to create an isolated and excessively privileged sector in capital markets. The collection and management of these large amounts of capital should be conducted in an integrated and competitive financial environment. The ability to transfer pension rights accumulated in occupational pension funds is an important factor here, as are also the indexation of income, tax treatment and socio-political effects[43].

D. Impact on national capital markets

Any large-scale transition to funded pension schemes would have appreciable effects on capital markets, tax policy and savings at the macroeconomic level. Such a move would involve building up financial reserves until the arrival at retirement age of those age groups which started the funded schemes. This would be followed by a period of stabilization (or "maturation") during which the system would operate under conditions of capital flow approximately equal to pay-as-you-go as contribu-

tions (savings) and pension[...] became more evenly matche[...] level. But only in a stable dem[...] nomic environment will it be pos[...] match.

Retirement savings will be in[...] kets. They will be expected to proc[...] at minimum risk and will be su[...] regulations. In the United States[...] private savings stock (total pension[...] rently exceed $1 trillion. This sum [...] nalf the total net equity of all United States corporations and a quarter of its gross national product. In the United Kingdom at the end of 1985, pension fund assets represented over 70 per cent of the equity value of United Kingdom industrial and commercial companies and around 45 per cent of GDP. Consequently, the management of these funds is now central to capital market operation, fund allocation and investment monitoring. The same situation exists, although to a lesser degree, in Japan where private pension funds are major institutional investors. The importance of pension funds as sources of primary finance for industry and government is likely to become a structural feature of capital markets in all countries developing funded pension schemes.

In conclusion, the immediate, short-term prospects for existing pension schemes are favourable. The demographic trends of the present decade are only mildly adverse and, with a recovery in economic growth, most countries should be able to keep the increase in contribution rates within acceptable limits during the next few years. The impending problems do not as yet present a clearly perceived threat for the current generation of workers and contributors. At the same time, the social acceptance of change is an essential prerequisite for the political feasibility of reforms which will inevitably involve a downward revision of retirement expectations. Political conditions for this revision are no simple matter, given the electoral weight of the ever-expanding older age groups and the sensitivity of the issue. Governments might take advantage of the present period of respite to devise, test and progressively promote the new institutional arrangements and the necessary related savings and investment practices by individuals and corporations.

III. HELP FOR THE UNEMPLOYED

The individual's status in society is chiefly determined by his job. Unemployment is not merely a waste of resources but also creates glaring injustices and a feeling of humiliation in individuals who are no longer able to provide for their own needs. The objectives of government policy on unemployment should therefore be the unemployed cope with their loss of ... to facilitate their return to work. The ... problems posed by the employment situation ... have already been discussed in the chapter on ... markets. This section will deal with measures affecting unemployed individuals and will consider both income transfers and the measures aimed at the acquisition of new skills.

A. Income transfers to the unemployed

The economic well-being of most individuals depends on their jobs. It also often takes the earnings of more than one household member to support the family. The social importance of employment is all the greater because of the cumulative character of many of its rewards – the use of one's abilities to the full, promotion opportunities, seniority-based wage systems, insurance and pension entitlement. When an increase in poverty levels is seen in OECD societies, the reasons are usually found in underemployment, primarily affecting those registered as unemployed but also many who have given up looking for a job and quit the labour market, as well as those who unwillingly find themselves in only part-time or casual employment[44].

The deteriorating employment situation over the last 15 years has involved governments in heavy expenditure on income transfers. The cost of unemployment benefits now accounts for more than 1 per cent of GDP in many countries (see Table 9.5), and other expenditure on general welfare, disability pensions and early retirement has also increased substantially as a result of joblessness. In addition, means-tested allowances for housing, education and welfare tend to increase as unemployment figures mount.

Table 9.5. **Expenditure on unemployment compensation**
In percentage of GDP

	1960	1981[1]
Canada	1.5	2.3
France	0.2	1.9
Germany	0.1	1.4
Italy	0.2	0.6
Japan	0.3	0.4
United Kingdom	0.2	1.4
United States	0.6	0.5
Australia	0.1	0.8
New Zealand	0.0	0.5
Austria	0.3	0.5
Belgium	..	2.6
Finland	0.0	0.6
Greece	..	0.3
Ireland	0.6	2.5
Netherlands	0.2	1.0
Norway	0.2	0.3
Sweden	0.2	0.5

1. For Belgium and Greece: 1980.
Source: OECD, Social Expenditure 1960-1990, Paris, 1985.

In almost all OECD countries, standard unemployment compensation takes the form of insurance, which protects persons with a work history against loss of income resulting from involuntary unemployment. Standard benefits are usually boosted by supplementary benefits, although in some countries, e.g. Australia and New Zealand where means-tested income security payments are provided as entitlements, only standard benefits are available. Turkey is the only OECD country which does not provide unemployment compensation benefits[45]. In all other OECD countries, dependent workers are entitled to unemployment compensation. Benefits are typically linked to the wage last received, subject to a certain ceiling: in most countries they replace two-thirds or more of the reference wage in the low and average wage brackets. Benefits are normally of limited duration – in the United States this is six months, in most other countries a year or more. To be entitled to these benefits, the unemployed person must usually be genuinely looking for work.

Both workers and employers usually contribute to the funding of unemployment insurance, although in most countries the system is still heavily subsidised by government. The contributions paid by companies and workers seldom bear any real relationship to the actual risks of unemployment for the various sectors. That is, the funding requirements of most schemes are spread more or less evenly across the whole labour market or, at least, its major areas of activity.

Unemployment insurance schemes have generally proved effective in alleviating the hardship suffered due to temporary spells of unemployment – a fact which has made it easier for governments to exercise fiscal and monetary restraint. However, high levels of longer-term unemployment have recently placed a great strain on these schemes and shown their limitations. As a result, during the seventies it became necessary to make a number of improvements to the cover provided.

In several European countries, the difficulties encountered by the jobless in finding work have increased far more sharply than the risks of unemployment faced by those already in work. As a result, a gulf is widening in some countries between workers in stable employment and outsiders with little prospect of ever meeting the necessary requirements for unemployment insurance benefits.

Those unable to claim insurance benefits include some newcomers to the labour market such as school-leavers and women who have raised their children and now wish to return to outside work. Several governments have introduced special allowances and more generous contribution conditions for these groups, whilst Australia provides standard benefits irrespective of work experience. Furthermore, with the increase in long-term unemployment, many of the jobless covered by unemployment insurance have exhausted their entitlements. However, in France, Germany, the Netherlands and the United Kingdom – where long-term unemployment is particularly widespread – these unemployed who have used up their entitlements may receive allowances paid by schemes other than unemployment insurance, under a means test. In the United Kingdom some unemployed may also receive means-tested benefits in addition to their insurance benefit. In some cases, these benefits are payable indefinitely, such as the allowances paid by the assistance scheme in Australia and by the insurance system in Belgium.

The elderly unemployed are often guaranteed benefits until they reach retirement age, either under the unemployment insurance system or via other schemes. Although most public pension schemes set a fixed retirement age, a degree of flexibility is provided by disability pensions. In Austria, Belgium, the Netherlands and the Nordic countries, medical assessment of "disability" in the case of the elderly always includes an appraisal of their job prospects. In other countries whose legislation makes no explicit provision for this, like the United Kingdom and the United States, disability pensions nonetheless play an important role in guaranteeing the income of the elderly long-term unemployed. In some European countries, the government has also introduced early retirement schemes for elderly workers who release jobs for unemployed youth or for the elderly unemployed[46].

Unemployment compensation places a heavy burden on many countries' budgets and adds considerably to wage costs. A number of governments have recently considered it necessary to institute measures to restrain the growth of this expenditure – particularly as insurance benefits – with substantial cuts in Canada, Denmark, France, Germany and the United Kingdom. Although the main purpose of such measures is to reduce costs, there has also been some concern that high benefits discourage the unemployed from taking jobs.

The debate about the impact of unemployment benefits on the incentive to look for work draws upon a number of studies. However, these are restricted to certain countries and are far from conclusive. The common assumption is that unemployment benefits raise the reservation wage: that is, the lowest wage acceptable to job-seekers. This could exacerbate unemployment in three different ways – by increasing the flow into unemployment through voluntary quitting of jobs and less resistance to lay-offs, by lengthening the time spent looking for work and by pushing up wage levels. But even if all these effects manifested themselves, the impact on unemployment as a whole would not necessarily be great, since the jobs rejected by unemployed persons with good insurance coverage are often accepted by those with little or no coverage, who make up the majority of the unemployed in all countries.

There is little empirical evidence to show that high benefits encourage a flow into unemployment[47]. A possible exception is the United States unemployment insurance system which, in combination with other features of the American labour market, does appear to encourage temporary lay-offs. In most other countries, temporary lay-offs are less common than in the United States in spite of more generous unemployment benefits.

There is strong evidence to support the existence of a link between generous benefits and an increase in the length of unemployment. However, the size of these effects may not be large; the cause and effect mechanism is probably not highly significant and is chiefly limited to workers with good prospects of finding another job. However, for two special groups – workers nearing retirement and members of households where someone else has a higher income – unemployment compensation in conjunction with other factors does appear to have had an appreciable effect. There is also some evidence, notably from the United States, implying that the provision of benefits makes the unemployed reluctant to accept badly paid jobs. This phenomenon has become known as the "poverty trap" – a situation where some workers find short-term unemployment financially preferable to paid work. Unemployment benefits may also act as a "wage floor" by preventing wages from falling.

The benefits paid to the majority of insured workers have not been shown to have any marked adverse effect on the labour supply, although they may occasionally reinforce the reluctance of insured persons to accept jobs which fail to come up to their expectations. The disincentive effect may be greater on those groups of workers getting little satisfaction from their jobs, but within these groups only a small minority are covered by unemployment insurance schemes. The most important exceptions are probably the elderly, many of whom have been induced by the possibility of early retirement to withdraw from the labour market.

Since much of the recent increase in registered unemployment has occurred among uninsured persons, it seems feasible that even lowest benefits available to the unemployed could act as a disincentive to work. The groups in question are extremely heterogeneous. In some cases, the availability of benefits may simply encourage more jobless people to register as such. This would imply that the benefits result in an increased labour supply, at least in statistical terms (if supply is defined as the total number of workers in and out of employment) and also perhaps in reality, since the provision of benefits is conditional on the recipient's search for work. However, for the unemployed with compelling reasons for not working – educational opportunities, children to look after or the poor pay of available jobs – even low benefits may tip the balance in favour of giving up the active search for work with a consequent reduction in the actual labour supply. There is also some cross-country evidence of a positive relationship between the level of long-term benefits and the duration of unemployment.

The broad spectrum of the groups not covered by unemployment insurance also makes it difficult to determine what social assistance they require. The assistance benefits payable to these groups may be inadequate by the yardstick of what is considered normal by society, if the recipient households have no other sources of income. But it is not clear how many people are actually obliged to live on these benefits alone. No country appears to have been successful in defining these target groups or the extent of the assistance they require. From the standpoint of labour market policy, the main purpose of unemployment benefits as compared with general social welfare payments is to stimulate the return to work. Unemployment benefits can be made conditional not only on job search – which may be required even for general welfare – but also on means tests and participation in vocational guidance, aptitude tests, training and other activities provided to help the unemployed return to the labour market. This, however, is not always the case, as certain countries provide universal standard means-tested benefits of rates generally equivalent to other social security pension rates, e.g. Australia.

In general, there does not seem to be much prospect of reducing expenditure on income benefits to the unemployed as long as joblessness remains at its current high levels. The social legitimacy of providing those habitually in work with relatively generous short-term protection against unemployment income loss is firmly established in most countries. Such protection is necessary both on the grounds of equity and in order to maintain a sufficient social consensus about the basic aims of national economic policies. The adverse effect on employment of unemployment insurance benefits does not present a major problem – the benefits, if any, available to unemployed persons not covered by insurance are in any case quite meagre. Nevertheless, in view of the large sums currently spent on unemployment compensation, it is desirable that more help be given to the unemployed to rapidly achieve their main goal of finding a job.

B. Help with finding a job on the labour market

Current unemployment is largely due to the failure of the labour market to adjust to the initial rise in unemployment. One response which would assist adjustment would be an improved matching of the skills of the unemployed to the requirements of the jobs which are vacant.

The ease with which workers are assigned to jobs is essentially determined by structural factors specific to each labour market, such as wages, conditions of employment, training and skill requirements, geographical distances and housing conditions. Each of these factors has attracted selective policy initiatives by governments keen to improve individuals' job prospects. The aim has been to make the unemployed more attractive to employers in terms of skills or wage costs, or, as in the case of relocation grants, to encourage the jobless to accept the jobs on offer. Many schemes have included training programmes, wage subsidies and temporary employment contracts in a variety of combinations designed to suit particular target groups.

The results of such selective labour market intervention have been extremely mixed and difficult to evaluate, with many programmes having been short-lived or subject to frequent alterations. Some schemes have been utilised on a small scale, as has happened with relocation grants[48]. Several programmes involving temporary job contracts, wage subsidies or reduced social security contributions have enjoyed a wide response, but their net impact on employment levels appears to have been modest (as many of the jobs would probably have been created anyway). There is, however, some encouraging evidence (notably from the United Kingdom) which suggests that the effects of well designed schemes could be significant. Such schemes have improved the competitive position of the target groups relative to other job seekers and so have perhaps prevented some jobless from becoming long-term unemployed.

Improving the competitive position of the unemployed relative to others is especially important if many of the jobless lack formal credentials detailing their education and training, or where the credentials they do possess fail to give an adequate picture of their skills. In the absence of documentary evidence attesting to his or her training, a job applicant can only be assessed by a potential employer on the basis of work experience, which tends to put both the young and the long-term unemployed at a disadvantage. Both youth unemployment and long-term joblessness are especially high in Mediterranean countries where many job seekers leave school with few or no qualifications (although this factor is not the only one responsible for long-term unemployment). It would seem that the best way of mitigating the present inequalities in the access to available jobs would be to provide more people with training leading to the qualifications that are demanded and recognised in the labour market.

New forms of training for unemployed young people have already enjoyed considerable success in several countries. In the United Kingdom, for example, the Youth Training Scheme (one of the special employment and training schemes recently introduced in this country) currently offers all 16-year-old school-leavers a two-year vocational training course enabling them simultaneously to acquire practical experience, undergo hands-on training and receive instruction in an educational establishment. This programme is primarily addressed to employers and independent training organisations, who receive subsidies covering part of the costs involved. Australia, too, has recently launched a training programme embodying similar features, although less ambitious in scope than the scheme introduced in the United Kingdom. Elsewhere, as in Canada, Germany and most of Scandinavia, adults who become unemployed have access to a variety of facilities aimed at helping them find other work. The courses provided are usually conducted in special training centres, although frequent efforts are made to enlist the participation of private enterprise[49].

Governments have also initiated a variety of community programmes (many within local councils or departments) to provide temporary jobs for the unemployed. Although, for the workers, it may often be preferable to have a job created by one of these programmes rather than be jobless, these schemes are relatively expensive and fail to resolve the basic problem since the jobs offered are usually only for a limited time.

The involvement of local communities in job creation has spawned experiments promoting the establishment of new businesses offering fresh job opportunities. In some cases, these initiatives have been financed from unemployment insurance funds, while elsewhere special funds have been made available. With few exceptions, these activities are run on far too small a scale to have more than a marginal direct effect on the total unemployment picture, but they can act as a useful pointer for other jobless by encouraging them to look into the feasibility of setting up their own businesses.

All the policy instruments discussed above are habitually administered by labour authorities. The recent extension of labour market policies has put these authorities under considerable strain and has had some adverse effects on their more traditional areas of activity, such as the supply of labour market information, job placement, vocational guidance and adjustment measures to assist the handicapped. However, several countries have already given higher priority to all these services over the last decade, and they have often received additional resources in terms of staff, premises and new equipment such as computer systems.

As the labour market increases in complexity, the need for specialised labour market services will no doubt grow. Several European countries assign all placement services to a single system; this is often seen as necessary to avoid too high a concentration of unemployed persons in the clientele of public job centres. Elsewhere, the authorities rely very largely on private market initiatives to meet the demand for such services[50]. As in other areas – see, for example, the sections on health care and pensions and the chapter on education and human capital – it would be unfortunate if necessary improvements in services of this kind could not be achieved owing to public budgetary constraints or to legislation standing in the way of decentralised and competing initiatives.

As long as unemployment remains high, there will clearly be a need for continuing strenuous efforts to help the jobless find work. Admittedly, such efforts will not resolve the broader problems of the labour market which are largely at the root of present unemployment, but they will help to increase flexibility in matching workers to jobs.

IV. CONCLUSIONS

This survey provides confirmation that two of the three criticisms currently aimed at the social policies of OECD countries are well-founded, firstly, that social policies are putting an increasingly heavy burden on the public budget which cannot continue along the same lines without a parallel increase in tax revenue; secondly, that social policies are beset by important technical shortcomings and that the resources allocated to them are not used in the most efficient way. However, the survey does not lend much substance to the third criticism often made against these policies, since it is only in relatively peripheral areas of labour markets that social welfare benefits appear to act as a disincentive to work, savings and mobility.

The survey emphasizes another point which often fails to attract attention in discussions on the reform of social policies. In spite of the remarkable growth of these policies and their many successes over the postwar period, they are still unable to deal with certain social problems, some of which have been aggravated by macroeconomic trends. In many OECD countries, a section of the population still lives in very poor conditions and has needs in the areas of health care, income supplements and vocational training which are still completely unsatisfied. If nothing is done to assist this social category – which though numerically small and virtually politically powerless, is on the increase in many countries as a result of unemployment – their living conditions and social status will decline even further.

Social policies therefore call for reforms. Such reforms ought not be defined in terms of "more" or "less" of the Welfare State, but in terms of making policies more efficient and relevant. This can be achieved by adapting existing instruments and institutions to solve current economic and social problems, as well as by developing new social policy tools.

The essential requirement for social policies is not, as is sometimes supposed, to find an optimum macroeconomic transfer rate supported by a social consensus. It is to reduce social benefits in those areas where they are no longer required (for example, to subsidise the retirement income of the comfortably off) and to increase them in areas of real need (for example, in helping the long-term unemployed). These readjustments are often made difficult by the disproportionate political weight of those social groups who stand to lose some of their entitlements, as compared with groups with a justified claim to increased social solidarity. Such readjustment is nonetheless necessary if social policies are to keep faith with their underlying philosophy of providing insurance against major risks while ensuring, as far as is practicable, that everyone has similar opportunities and access to resources within a social system that retains its entrepreneurial and competitive character.

The forces of an entrepreneurial and competitive market economy could also be put to more active use in the implementation of many social policies. These policies cover such diverse areas of economic activity as the provision of health care, the financial management of pension funds and the vocational retraining of the unemployed. As these activities need to be conducted with maximum efficiency so as to minimise wastage of highly strained public resources, it is sensible to consider enlisting market forces, competitive stimuli and capital market control in the provision of these services. The potential application of these mechanisms to policies on health, retirement pensions and support for the unemployed has been discussed in the relevant sections of this chapter.

Structural reform of social policies presents many technical, institutional and political problems. As these lie at the heart of the social organisation specific to each country, the reforms must necessarily proceed along different lines. In this delicate area, there can be no magic panacea. However, this fact should not deter policy makers from applying the tool of economic analysis to incentives, management control and technical efficiency in social services. In present circumstances especially, only a rational approach of this kind can enable OECD governments to make vigorous headway truly worthy of the human and economic role of social policies.

Two big political difficulties stand in the way of a critical reassessment and reform of social policies. It should be possible, through clear-sightedness and courage, to overcome them:

– The first difficulty is that of the political price of greater transparency. The social solidarity inherent in cross-subsidies in the different social programmes and the redistributive effects of the so-called "free for everyone" services may be hard to sustain where the services are offered on a market governed by actual costs and prices and are possibly competitive in character. Social solidarity will then have to assume the explicit form of measurable and budgetised subsidies supporting the supply of or the demand for these services,

which may then be politically more difficult to maintain or expand.

Nonetheless, the efficiency gains that can accompany reforms and the intrinsic political and democratic value of transparency may be advantages substantial enough to make it worth meeting the challenge and accepting the political costs. Governments ought not to find it impossible to explain that budgetised subsidies, far from adding to social transfers, would in fact replace previously hidden and unacknowledged transfers. They can point out that most of these had the added disadvantage of reducing the effectiveness of services;

– The second difficulty is to deal with the mistrust and misunderstandings which may result from attempts to reform social policies. Such reactions are unfortunately all too frequent; any questioning of the organisational *status quo* is seen as a retrograde step and an abandonment of the ideals of equity and solidarity that underpin advanced societies. This second difficulty is in a way symmetrical to the first in that proposals for reform are perceived as threatening and reducing social solidarity, rather than as increasing budgetised transfers.

Such reactions may sometimes be fairly strong. But it should be possible to convince electorates, now frequently more intellectually and politically mature than in the past, that reforms can bring greater efficiency and greater equity. It is true on the other hand that the present macroeconomic and social climate, and each individual's own fears and uncertainties about the future, create an environment of tension that makes it difficult to reach social and political consensus in order to reform social policies. Yet reforming governments could justly claim – and show many reasons in support of this claim – that their actions are both positive and progressive. The best way to combat irrational reactions of rejection is to argue forcefully and demonstrate clearly that reform need not mean less social solidarity but can, on the contrary, result in equally generous but more effective and more efficient social action.

338

NOTES AND REFERENCES

1. Certain countries have hybrid health systems which comprise elements from the three pure models, e.g. Australia.

2. The remaining 15 per cent covers purchases of individual medical appliances and peripheral health care. The figures given are strictly indicative as they are greatly affected by problems of measurement technique and by wide international divergences. See OECD, *Measuring Health Care – 1960-1983. Expenditure, Costs and Performance*, Paris, 1985.

3. Globally, concentration in the pharmaceutical industry is low; it is very much higher, however, when each specific market segment where interchangeable medicines compete one with another is considered. The mode of competition in the pharmaceutical industry centres on innovation and the differentiation of products, protected by patent for a 15-20-year period.

4. See for example, Enthoven, A., "How Interested Groups have Responded to a Proposal for Economic Competition in Health Services", *American Economic Review*, May 1980; Sournia, J.Ch., "Quarante ans d'assurance contre la maladie", *Futuribles*, July-September 1985.

5. The freedom of action enjoyed by the suppliers in defining the services and determining their cost is so great that, in strictly economic terms, such delegation is closer to a trustee relationship than to an agency arrangement. For the distinction between the two, see Clark, R.C., "Agency Costs versus Fiduciary Duties" in Pratt, J.W. and Zeckhauser, R.J., *Principals and Agents: The Structure of Business*, Harvard Business School Press, 1985.

6. Recently, AIDS education campaigns became important in several countries.

7. In France, for example, although the Social Security department has been endeavouring for many years to introduce the practice of regular health examinations, and despite the fact that such examinations are available from half the local health insurance institutions, the number of annual examinations actually performed in the mid-80s was no more than 500 000, or less than 1 per cent of the population. See Sournia, J.Ch., "Quarante ans d'assurance contre la maladie", *art. cit.* in Note 4.

8. A study carried out in the US by the Johns Hopkins University on the basis of 80 surveys concludes that HMOs were superior in 53 cases, equal in 19 and inferior in 8, and that they generated expenditure 10 per cent to 40 per cent lower than that of the traditional hospital system.

9. See the work done by the OECD Directorate for Social Affairs, Manpower and Education. The quantitative results are summarised in: Schieber, G.J. and Poullier, J.P., "Comparison of Health Expenditures in OECD Countries" in Vigo, J.M. (ed.), *Restructuring Health Policy: An International Challenge*, International Health Economics and Management Institute, Illinois, 1986; Schieber, G.J. and Poullier, J.P., "International Health Care Spending", *Health Affairs*, Autumn 1986.

10. Poullier, J.P., "From Risk Aversion to Risk Rating – Trends in OECD Health Care Systems", *Health Planning and Management* (forthcoming).

11. See Frumkin, R.N., "Health Insurance Trends in Cost Control and Coverage", *Monthly Labor Review*, US Department of Labor, Washington D.C., September 1986.

12. See "Public Expenditure on Health", OECD, Paris, 1977.

13. See for example, a description of the French situation in Mormiche, P., "Consommation médicale : Les disparités sociales n'ont pas disparu", *Economie et Statistique*, September 1986 and "Pratiques culturelles, profession et consommation médicale", *ibid.*

14. See Reinhardt, U., "Health Insurance and Cost-Containment Policies: The Experience Abroad", *American Economic Review*, op. cit. in Note 4.

15. Aaron, H.J. and Schwartz, W.B., *The Painful Prescription*, The Brookings Institution, Washington D.C., 1984.

16. These average figures conceal wide international disparities in regard to the average length of stay, but the tendency for these to become shorter is universal. See OECD, *Measuring Health Care – 1960-1983*, op. cit. in Note 1.

17. See Frumkin, R.N., "Health Insurance Trends in Cost Control and Coverage", *art. cit.* in Note 11.

18. In the United Kingdom a debate is currently in progress on the possibility of conducting an experiment along these lines within the National Health Service (NHS) by introducing a direct link between the level of public hospital funding and the demand for these hospitals' services by consultants and patients (see also Note 10).

19. Brook, Robert H. *et al.*, "The Effect of Co-insurance on the Health of Adults", *Rand*, Santa Monica, California, December 1984; Keeler, Emmett B. and Rolph, John E., "How Cost Sharing Reduced Medical Spending of Participants in the Health Insurance Experiment", *Journal of the American Medical Association*, 22nd April 1983, Vol. 249, No. 16; O'Grady, Kevin F. *et al.*, "The Impact of Cost Sharing on Emergency Department Use", *Rand*, Santa Monica, California, October, 1985; Keeler, Emmett B. *et al.*, "How Free Care Reduced Hypertension in the Health Insurance Experiment", *Journal of the American Medical Association*, 11th October 1985, Vol. 254, No. 14.

20. Morone, J.A. and Dunham, A.B., "Slouching Towards National Health and Insurance: The New Health Care Politics", *Yale Journal of Regulation*, 1985, Vol. 2.

21. See Schieber, G., *An International Comparison of Health Care Financing and Delivery in OECD Countries*, OECD, Paris (forthcoming).

22. Enthoven, Alain C., "Managed Competition in Health Care and the Unfinished Agenda", *Health Care Financing Review*, Annual Supplement, 1986.

23. See for example, Salterthwaite, M.A., "Competition and Equilibrium as a Driving Force in the Health Services Sector" in Inman, R.P., *Managing the Service Economy – Prospects and Problems*, Cambridge University Press, 1985.

24. Enthoven, A., "How Interested Groups Have Responded...", *art. cit.* in Note 4.

25. See Wilson, Rob, "Changing Pay Relativities for the Highly Qualified", *Review of the Economy and Employment*, Vol. 2, 1985/86, University of Warwick, Institute for Employment Research, Coventry, 1986; Jarousse, J.P., "Une mesure de la rentabilité des diplômes entre 1969 et 1976", *Consommation*, 1985/86, No. 2; Dresch, S.P., "Marginal Wage Rates, Hours of Work and Returns to Physician Specialisation" in Greenspan, N. (ed.), *Issues in Physician Reimbursement*, U.S. Department of Health and Human Services, Health Care Financing Administration, Washington D.C., 1981.

26. Fuchs, V.R., "Economics, Health, and Post-Industrial Society", *Health Soc.*, Spring 1979, quoted by Reinhardt, U., "Health Insurance and Cost-Containment Policies..." *art. cit.* in Note 14.

27. Fuchs, V.R., for instance, writes: "Acceptance of the relevance of economics to health care has grown so rapidly that for some audiences it is necessary to add a few words of warning against uncritical application of general economic principles with insufficient attention to the special characteristics of health and medical care" in *Who Shall Live? Health, Economics and Social Choice*, Basic Books, New York, 1974; quoted by Poullier, J.P. in "From Risk Aversion to Risk Rating...", *art. cit.* in Note 10.

28. Morone, J.A. and Dunham, A.B., "Slouching Towards National Health Insurance...", *art. cit.* in Note 20.

29. Two recent and detailed assessments of the DRG system are: *Medicare and Prospective Payment and the American Health Care System*, Report to the Congress, Prospective Payment Assessment Commission, Washington D.C., February 1986; and *Impact of the Medicare Hospital Prospective Payment System – 1984 Annual Report*, U.S. Department of Health and Human Services, Health Care Financing Administration, Baltimore, Maryland, August 1986.

30. A descriptive summary of these structures will be found in: Enthoven, A., Launois, R., Métais, J. and Viens, G., *Systèmes de santé: Health Maintenance Organisations, Réseaux de soins coordonnés – Comparaisons internationales*, Institut La Boétie, Paris, 1985. An in-depth study of HMOs is included in Luft, H.S., *Health Maintenance Organisations: Dimensions of Performance*, John Wiley and Sons, New York, 1981.

31. Economists – including those in the OECD Secretariat – do not all agree on this economic characterisation of HMOs. It is pointed out, for example, that since HMOs do not commit themselves to providing costly new technology treatments (whose existence could not be foreseen at the time a given contract was signed), the function of the principal insurer still depends on the public sector. Nonetheless, analysis of HMOs as vertically integrated insurance and service organisations has proved methodologically useful.

32. See Russell, L.B., *Is Prevention Better than Cure?*, The Brookings Institution, Washington D.C., 1986.

33. Rand Corporation, "A Controlled Trial of the Effect of a Prepaid Group Practice on Use of Services".

34. It was for this reason that the public insurance systems – Medicare and Medicaid – were set up in the 1960s to help the elderly and disadvantaged. But those two schemes have not solved the problem since in 1986 up to 35 million Americans (15 per cent of the population) were still not covered by any public or private insurance scheme. Some of these people are able to receive treatment free in public hospitals, but many would be in an extremely difficult situation in the event of health problems or hospitalisation. For a report on the most recent work on this subject see Light, D.W., "Corporate Medicine for Profit", *Scientific American*, December 1986.

35. This section is based on a large number of "pension problem" studies carried out by the OECD Directorate for Social Affairs, Manpower and Education. A recent summary of this work will be found in Holzmann, R., "Pensions: More Equity between the Generations", *OECD Observer*, January 1986, No. 138, Paris.

36. The United Kingdom has already made substantial reforms to the State Earnings Related Pension Scheme. The share of national income going to pensioners via state schemes may not rise in the United Kingdom.

37. The ratio of retirement income to real income at end of working life.

38. The United Kingdom, in particular, is currently taking measures to encourage further the private provision of pensions.

39. This is basically a question of managing the cycle of savings and withdrawals during the life of each individual. A private pension fund allows very flexible management, particularly with regard to retirement age and the ratio of the individual's disposable income in work and in retirement.

40. A preliminary survey comparing international retirement funds will be found in Gabrielli, G. and Faro, D. (eds.), *The Challenge of Private Pension Funds – Present Trends and Future Prospects in Industrialised Countries*, The Economist Publications, London, 1986. The OECD also organised an expert meeting on this subject in December 1986 under the title, "The Interaction of Public, Occupational and Private Retirement Provisions". The documents of this meeting will soon be published by the OECD.

41. Japan introduced the flat-rate universal system in 1986.

42. It is important to achieve the highest possible efficiency in the management of private pension schemes. Management costs in these organisations are usually quite high – as much as 6 per cent of total entitlements in pension funds, and 12 per cent of entitlements in insurance companies. The last group of intermediaries usually manages individual schemes.

43. The importance of the competitive character of the markets for optimal allocation of long-term individual savings is discussed in the capital markets chapter in this report.

44. This does not mean that poverty is confined to the unemployed. Even in the richest countries, some workers in full-time employment have incomes which, after tax, are below the generally accepted "poverty threshold" for families or, in the case of unmarried persons, sometimes well below. The families of wage-earners also receive large income supplements by way of such social benefits as family allowances and subsidised housing. It is therefore clear that most of the need for financial benefits to people of working age – which accounted for the major growth in income transfers since the early 70s – is more closely linked to the problem of unemployment than to wage levels and the cost of living.

45. See OECD Secretariat note on "Unemployment Insurance and Other Income Support Schemes for the Unemployed" presented to the OECD Working Party No. 1 on Social Policy in 1986.

46. See OECD Secretariat note on "Early Retirement Policies" (*cf.* Note 45).

47. The studies dealing with the relationship between unemployment compensation and unemployment are examined in "The Role of the Public Sector", *OECD Economic Studies*, Spring 1985, and Blackwell, J., "Social Security Transfers, Labour Supply and Labour Market Flexibility", presented to the OECD Working Party No. 1 on Social Policy in 1985.

48. For aids to re-employment, see OECD, *Flexibility in the Labour Market. The Current Debate*, Paris, 1986, Chapter II.

49. See Chapter 1 on education and human capital.

50. Regardless of the organisation of the employment services, it seems that in every country jobs are mainly sought through the newspapers and by personal contacts.

Chapter 10

FINANCING THE PUBLIC SECTOR

INTRODUCTION

The rapid growth of the public sector in the past twenty years has implied a continuous rise in its financing requirements. This chapter examines the consequences for economic growth of the way in which this financing is accomplished. It focuses mainly on the impacts of the level and structure of taxation for two reasons. First, taxes are, quite simply, the principal way in which public spending is paid for. But, second, financing a sustained level of public expenditure through public borrowing entails future debt servicing costs that also entail higher taxes, taxes whose capital value is roughly equal to the size of public borrowing. Thus, barring a reduction in the size of the public sector, there is ultimately no way to avoid financing through taxes.

The growing public sector imposes costs that must be weighed against the benefits of government action. At its simplest, this is true independently of the financing method – increased government direct spending requires an increased commitment of resources to public use at the expense of the private sector, while transfer spending may be undertaken in ways that tend to inhibit economic growth.

But financing the public sector imposes additional costs. Regardless of whether public sector deficits themselves imply a sacrifice of future growth above and beyond that indicated by the volume of borrowing, servicing the debt of the public sector ultimately requires higher taxes. In this sense, taxes are an unavoidable concomitant of public expenditure, and the most significant costs to economic growth are a product of the level and system of taxation. In effect, high marginal tax rates and patterns of tax rates that discriminate haphazardly between different economic activities lead to an inefficient allocation of resources and inhibit good economic performance.

The scope for reducing the harm imposed by current tax systems can be addressed by answering two questions. First, to what extent can tax systems be reformed in such a way as to maintain current revenue yields while reducing the systems' adverse effects? Second, how great are the remaining, tax-induced inefficiencies, which can be reduced only by cutting the size of the public sector itself? This chapter examines these questions and concludes that, at the margin, tax reform can achieve significant improvements in economic efficiency. However, these gains can be complemented, and may well be overshadowed, by those to be had from a reduction in public sector spending and thus in overall taxation.

These conclusions are derived from a review of country experiences and of recent literature in the economics of public finance. As such, they represent a selective review focusing on long-term growth and do not explicitly address a number of other topics important to the formulation of tax policy. In particular, the chapter does not examine the trade-off between growth and an equitable distribution of the fruits of growth. Tax systems, together with the system of social benefits, are often used in part for redistributional ends, and the evidence from some countries suggests these two systems together sometimes redistribute from the rich to the poor – though the major effects arise from social rather than from tax policies[1]. However, the real questions that need to be answered are, first, whether the tax system is a sharp, or a very dull and costly, tool for achieving redistribution and, second, whether the redistribution achieved, if any, is the one that is really desired. These are questions that would require a separate study.

Complaints about the effects of taxation are as old as taxation itself, and the growth of public expenditure in recent years has exacerbated this resentment. Increasingly frequently, extreme claims are made about the power of taxes to influence human behaviour, claims not generally backed by the mainstream of economic research. In contrast, the discussion and conclusions presented here rest very much in that mainstream. Still, the mainstream itself has moved some distance in recent years, a fact reflected in the notes and references of this chapter, which draw almost exclusively on work done in the 1980s. This movement has come about in large part not only because innovations in computing have allowed a great deal of new flesh to be put on very old and widely accepted theoretical bones, but also because significant improvements have been achieved in the more conceptual aspects of fiscal analysis. The results thus achieved have begun to command increasingly widespread agreement, and it would be a mistake to confuse them with assertions based upon pure abstraction and dogma. Rather, these conclusions are the simple, quantitative reflection of a widely observed fact of life: people try to reduce their taxes, and the higher the tax rates, the more intense their effort to do so.

Part I of this chapter reviews the evolution of public sector finances in Member countries and relates these to developments in tax revenues. It also discusses the consequences of public sector deficits and their relation to taxation. The consequences of taxes for the labour and capital markets are then discussed in Part II. Part III takes an institutional view, reviewing the constraints on tax policy and evaluating the potential for major reforms and the gains to be had from such reforms. Part IV looks more broadly at the potential for linking changes in tax systems to changes in public spending. Finally, Part V sums up the key substantive issues raised in the chapter and reviews the nature and quality of the evidence supporting these conclusions.

I. THE GROWING PUBLIC SECTOR

The last twenty years have witnessed steady growth in the public sector – in the roles it has been called on to perform and the commitments it has been engaged to undertake[2]. This growth is reflected in the ratio of public spending by general government to gross domestic product, a development presented in Table 10.1. The period from 1965 saw the ratio grow in the United States from 27 per cent to 38 per cent, in OECD Europe as a whole from 34 per cent to just over 50 per cent, and in Japan from under 19 per cent to 33 per cent. In addition, the public sector grew in other dimensions not reflected in these statistics: for example, through regulatory activity, the provision of loan guarantees, and the offering of tax incentives.

Table 10.1. **Total outlays of government**
Percentages of GDP

	Annual data						Averages			
	1960	1965	1970	1975	1980	1984	1960-1973	1974-1979	1980-1984	1960-1984
United States	27.5	27.9	32.3	35.6	34.9	38.1[1]	30.0	33.7	36.5[1]	32.0[2]
Japan	..	..	19.4	27.3	32.1	33.1	..	28.5	33.4	28.1
Germany	32.4	36.6	38.6	48.9	48.3	48.2	37.5	47.5	48.7	42.1
France	34.6	38.4	38.9	43.5	46.4	52.6	38.1	43.7	50.2	41.8
United Kingdom	32.4	36.1	39.8	46.4	45.1	48.0	37.0	44.4	47.1	40.8
Italy	30.1	34.3	34.2	43.2	46.1	57.4	33.7	42.9	53.4	39.8
Canada	28.9	29.1	35.7	40.8	40.9	47.5	32.2	39.7	44.6	36.5
Total of above	29.1	30.8	32.8	38.2	39.2	44.2	31.9	37.0	41.2	35.0
Austria	35.7	37.8	39.2	46.1	48.9	50.0	38.7	46.7	50.1	42.9
Belgium	30.3	32.3	36.5	44.5	51.0	55.4	34.1	45.5	54.8	41.0
Denmark	24.8	29.9	40.2	48.2	56.2	60.7	33.8	49.1	59.9	42.7
Finland	26.6	30.8	30.5	36.1	36.5	39.9	30.3	36.3	38.6	33.4
Greece	17.4	20.6	22.4	26.7	30.5	38.9	20.8	28.0	36.0	25.6
Iceland	28.2	28.4	30.7	38.5	31.4	32.5	29.9	34.8	33.4	31.7
Ireland	28.0	33.1	39.6	46.5	50.9	..	34.4	45.1	..	40.3
Luxembourg	30.5	33.3	33.2	48.6	54.8	..	34.1	48.2	..	42.8
Netherlands	33.7	38.7	46.0	56.6	57.4	..	41.6	54.6	..	48.0
Norway	29.9	34.2	41.0	48.4	50.7	49.4	36.7	50.5	50.4	42.7
Portugal	17.0	20.1	21.6	30.3	24.8	..	20.4	33.0	..	25.0
Spain	..	19.6	22.2	24.7	32.4	..	..	26.8	..	25.2
Sweden	31.0	36.1	43.3	48.9	61.6	63.7	38.9	54.4	64.5	47.7
Switzerland	17.2	19.7	21.3	28.7	29.3	31.2	20.3	29.2	30.1	24.4
Turkey	..	20.6	21.9	..	..	..	..	..	..	..
Small European countries	28.1	29.3	33.8	40.7	45.5	49.3	31.5	42.0	48.8	37.5
Australia	22.1	25.6	25.5	32.7	33.2	..	24.9	32.9	..	28.6
New Zealand	..	..	..	..	..	..	..	..	..	..
Total small countries	27.0	28.8	32.6	39.6	44.0	49.3	30.5	40.8	47.1	36.3
EEC	32.0	35.1	37.3	44.6	46.3	51.3	35.9	44.1	49.7	40.6
OECD Europe	31.5	34.5	36.8	44.3	46.3	50.6	35.3	44.1	49.4	40.2
OECD less United States	30.8	33.7	33.2	40.2	42.6	44.9	33.7	40.0	44.5	37.4
OECD	28.9	30.6	32.7	38.4	39.9	..	31.8	37.6	42.0	35.2

1. Data for 1983.
2. Estimated for 1984 by the OECD.
Source: Standard national accounts data from Table 6.5 of OECD, *OECD Economic Outlook - Historical Statistics 1960-1984,* Paris, 1986. Data for 1965 and 1970 are from the same series but not currently published.

Table 10.2. **Net lending of government as a percentage of GDP**

Percentages

	Annual data						Averages			
	1960	1965	1970	1975	1980	1984	1960-1973	1974-1979	1980-1984	1960-1984
United States	0.7	−0.2	−1.3	−4.3	−1.4	−4.9[1]	−0.5	−1.3	−2.9[1]	−1.1[2]
Japan	..	..	1.8	−2.8	−3.9	−2.1	..	−3.4	−3.5	−2.2
Germany	3.0	−0.6	0.2	−5.6	−2.9	−1.9	0.5	−3.0	−2.9	−1.0
France	0.9	0.7	0.9	−2.2	0.2	−2.8	0.5	−0.9	−2.0	−0.3
United Kingdom	−1.0	−1.9	2.5	−4.7	−3.7	−3.9	−0.8	−4.1	−3.6	−2.2
Italy	−0.9	−3.8	−3.5	−11.7	−8.0	−13.0	−3.1	−9.2	−11.4	−6.2
Canada	−1.7	0.4	0.9	−2.4	−2.7	−6.2	0	−1.6	−4.3	−1.2
Total of above	0.6	−0.5	−0.4	−4.4	−2.5	−3.9	−0.4	−2.5	−3.6	−1.5
Austria	−0.5	1.4	1.2	−2.5	−1.7	−2.3	0.7	−2.1	−2.6	−0.6
Belgium	..	..	..	..	..	..	..	..	..	..
Denmark	3.1	1.8	2.1	−1.4	−3.3	−4.3	2.1	−0.2	−6.2	−0.1
Finland	3.9	1.5	4.3	2.7	0.5	0.2	3.0	2.9	0.0	2.4
Greece	..	..	..	..	..	..	..	..	..	..
Iceland	8.2	1.0	1.1	−2.7	1.4	2.9	1.9	−0.5	1.2	1.2
Ireland	−2.4	−4.3	−3.7	−11.1	−11.2	..	−3.5	−8.4	..	−6.1
Luxembourg	3.1	2.9	2.7	0.9	−0.8	..	2.1	2.5	..	1.3
Netherlands	0.8	−0.8	−0.8	−2.7	−3.9	..	−0.5	−2.2	..	−1.8
Norway	3.8	3.2	3.2	2.8	5.1	6.0	4.1	1.6	4.5	3.6
Portugal	0.6	0.3	2.7	−5.5	6.0	..	0.6	−5.3	..	−1.3
Spain	..	0	0.7	0	−2.0	..	..	−0.7	..	−0.6
Sweden	2.0	4.4	4.4	2.8	−3.7	−2.3	3.8	1.3	−4.5	1.5
Switzerland	..	..	..	..	..	..	..	..	..	..
Turkey	..	−0.5	2.1	..	..	..	..	..	..	..
Small European countries	1.7	1.2	1.7	−0.4	−2.0	−0.8	1.5	−0.7	−3.1	0.1
Australia	3.3	1.4	2.2	−2.1	−0.8	..	1.5	−2.0	..	0.1
New Zealand	..	..	..	..	..	..	..	..	..	..
Total small countries	2.1	1.2	1.8	−0.8	−1.8	−0.8	1.5	−0.9	−2.8	0.1
EEC	0.8	−1.0	0.2	−4.8	−3.0	−4.6	−0.3	−3.2	−4.4	−1.8
OECD Europe	0.9	−0.6	0.6	−4.1	−2.8	−4.1	0	−2.8	−4.1	−1.5
OECD less United States	0.7	−0.4	0.9	−3.7	−3.0	−3.6	0.1	−2.9	−3.9	−1.4
OECD	0.7	−0.3	−0.2	−3.9	−2.4	..	−0.2	−2.3	−3.5	−1.4

1. Data for 1983.
2. Estimated for 1984 by the OECD.
Source: Standard national accounts data from Table 6.7 of *OECD Economic Outlook - Historical Statistics 1960-1984, op. cit.* in Table 10.1. Data for 1965 and 1970 are from the same series but not currently published.

The evolution of public sector spending carried with it the need to fund increasing commitments and, with the onset of stagflation in the 1970s, required doing so in economies that were no longer growing as rapidly as before. Governments had, in principle, three tools at their disposal to meet their financing needs: increasing inflation, increasing public sector borrowing, and increasing taxation. The evolution of public concerns to some extent determined the feasibility of using each of these tools. Thus, the fact that inflation was already high and rising in most countries during the 1970s virtually prevented inflation from being used as an intentional tool for funding the public sector. Likewise, although the public in many countries had shown a willingness to accept increasing income tax levels earlier, resistance to increasing such taxes in the later 1970s to some degree left other taxes as well as public sector borrowing as the only politically acceptable ways of funding rapidly increasing commitments. Despite the evident unpopularity of higher taxes, tax revenues funded approximately half the increase in spending.

However, by the turn of the decade, concern over increasing levels of public borrowing had become widespread. Table 10.2 shows the size of general government deficits as a proportion of GDP in recent years, and the trend is quite obvious. But this is only a part of the story, as the outlook for future debt accumulation is equally important in its consequences. A set of projections of public sector debt for the seven largest OECD countries, assuming the continuation of current policies, has recently been prepared[3]. These projections take into account probable increases in public pension payments that stem from the ageing of the population in many countries (and, in Japan and the United Kingdom, from the maturing of pension schemes). They also take into account cyclical changes in budget balances that could be expected from a return to economic growth trends more in accord with historical experience. Beyond these factors, revenues and spending, excluding debt service, are assumed to to a constant proportion of GDP. Two sets of estimates have been presented. In the first, real interest rates are assumed to stay at the late 1986 levels projected by the OECD in early 1986, and in the second they gradually fall until they equal the rate of real economic growth, a level to which they have almost fallen in Japan and Germany already[4].

For all the major countries except France, the estimates imply further sharp increases in the ratio of public debt to output by the end of the century. The problem is acute in Japan and Germany, but it would have been much worse without the consolidation of public budgets undertaken since 1980. For Italy, Canada, and the United Kingdom, the debt problem appears even more acute. However, in Canada and the United Kingdom, stated intentions for policy (a medium-term reduction in the Canadian deficit and a change to the United Kingdom pension scheme) should significantly improve the picture, but the prospect of growing debt remains.

A. The medium-term consequences of deficit financing

These deficits are alarming because there are economic costs associated with financing government spending, costs which exceed the volume of spending. Deficits may themselves entail some of these added costs through what is often called "crowding out" in popular discussion. But, in addition, the deficits entail future tax payments that account for a large portion of the additional economic costs. Yet public borrowing may appear to minimise or eliminate the need for taxes and, in so doing, appear to eliminate the economic costs.

The direct costs of public spending are evident: these arise because increases in public activity require a sacrifice of resources from the private sector. The resources may, nevertheless, be more productive in public use. Thus, like any other activities, government activities are implicitly subject to a cost-benefit calculus, though the practical problems of carrying out such a calculation often prevent its accomplishment.

But the costs of funding government activities do not stop here. Financing through public borrowing, through inflation (which reduces the real cost of public debt), or through taxation all have additional economic costs associated with them. From the point of view of ideal public policy, the choice of financing method would depend upon a balancing of these costs. Focusing only on debt and taxes, for example, it is widely accepted among economists specialising in public finance that temporary

surges in government spending – to pay for wars, for example – are best financed through borrowing. This avoids sharp tax hikes which, for reasons discussed later, bring greater-than-proportional losses in efficiency; taxes are higher over a longer time period, but by a lesser amount. In contrast, permanent increases in spending should be financed through taxes[5].

But, however important, these are theoretical considerations, and actual financing choices are determined in large measure by immediate policy concerns. Three such concerns have been raised by the prospect of mounting public sector deficits, though two of these offer, in fact, little real cause for alarm at this time[6]. One of these latter concerns is that current deficit problems are likely to result in future inflation. In fact, the increase in inflation typically needed to fund a given increase in public debt would be large compared to the needed tax increase, making such a choice unlikely in most countries[7]. As with the risk of inflation, the second of these considerations – the spectre of government insolvency or debt repudiation – does not seem a likely eventuality in the light of realistic calculations of manageable burdens for Member countries[8].

The third consideration, the prospect of "crowding out" of productive investment, is a more justified one, and has been a matter of much recent debate among economists. The question at issue is to what extent deficits, on balance, reduce ("crowd out") total national saving and therefore total national investment. As a matter of simple national accounting, the public sector deficit by itself represents a drain on national saving. However, if the private sector in turn increases its saving to offset this, on balance national saving and investment need not decline, nor will growth.

However, this statement over-simplifies the problem by assuming a direct link between national saving and national investment. In fact, the situation is more complicated – and more difficult to evaluate empirically – because international capital flows have become increasingly important[9]. Thus, a presumption that crowding out occurs would be more nearly correct for the OECD as a whole than for any single Member country insofar as there may be more scope for an inflow of foreign capital to offset a deficiency in the individual country's saving. But this can result in a series of more general macroeconomic imbalances, as recent history has shown[10]. And, although an inflow of capital from abroad may contribute to a country's productive potential, it also means that at least part of the income from production will accrue to foreigners rather than to domestic residents.

In any case, the prospect of crowding out raises the question of the extent to which the private sector as a whole does increase its saving to pay for the future taxes needed to support the servicing costs on a growing public debt, bearing in mind that the accumulation of debt brings with it interest costs whose capital value is roughly equivalent to the debt itself. From a different perspective, this is the same as asking to what extent privately held public debt is seen as a net addition to private sector wealth that can support additional private consumption. If it *is* treated as net wealth, i.e. if the implied future tax liabilities are *not* fully taken into account by individuals, then saving will not be sufficiently increased. If it is *not* treated as net wealth, government borrowing will be matched by increased private saving, and total national saving will not be impaired.

The answer to this seemingly academic question has important consequences for economic activity. In the short run, if public debt is indeed seen as a private asset, government deficits will stimulate economic activity in an underemployed economy by increasing consumption. At the same time, in a longer-run perspective, the fall in national saving will reduce growth by retarding the accumulation of productive assets.

At this point in the debate, two camps can be discerned: those believing that there is no effect whatsoever, and those who believe that there is some effect (with the size of the effect yet to be agreed upon, and perhaps varying according to other aspects of the particular historical situation under study). Both camps have empirical evidence to support their point of view[11]. The development and interpretation of this evidence is made quite difficult by the complexities of measuring changes in the relevant notion of public sector debt and of real interest rates[12]. It is changes in these latter that serve as the proximate evidence for the existence of crowding out.

Ultimately, the two camps may well be reconcilable. Recent evidence seems fairly convincing that prospects for increased deficits do increase long-term real interest rates, at least in the short run, an observation that would accord well with those believing crowding out to be important[13]. However, insofar as these deficits are maintained, they do eventually require increasing tax payments to pay interest. This fact, together with assumptions about the rationality of choice that appear to be plausible, at least in the context of long-term outcomes, makes it likely that saving will eventually rise to pay for the tax payments[14]. This means that, other things being equal, both real interest rates and the stock of capital ultimately will not be changed by public sector deficits.

Such a resolution of this contentious topic, though intellectually satisfying and not without precedent (a similar resolution can be discerned in the long-running debate between "Keynesians" and "monetarists" concerning the impacts of fiscal and monetary policies), nonetheless begs the question for policy makers: for how long and by how much do capital formation and growth suffer before the long run arrives? Unfortunately, this question remains largely open.

In summary, although the issue of crowding out is far from settled, the fact remains that unless public spending is cut, budget deficits must still be financed. That is, taxes must be raised to pay servicing costs, taxes whose capital value is roughly equal to the deficit itself.

Even if private saving were to adjust immediately and completely by the required amount, as a practical matter the actual levying of the taxes brings with it additional inefficiencies that can be quite large. At best, then, deficits only mask for a time this necessary consequence of government activity.

B. The growing burden of taxation

Thus, growth in the public sector unavoidably brings with it tax increases. In recent decades, these tax increases seem generally to have proceeded in two stages[15]. From the onset of rapid growth in the public sector in the early 1960s, and continuing to around 1974 and the first post-oil shock recession, governments and taxpayers seemed generally complacent about growing tax burdens. Perhaps this was a reflection of widespread acceptance of the growing role of government and a belief that government actions in such areas as the relief of poverty or the provision of incentives to investment were effective. It certainly was also supported by the rising after-tax living standards provided by buoyant economic growth. But the period of slowing growth took away the latter support; and taxpayer resistance, particularly to increasing income tax burdens, appears to have grown accordingly.

This pattern can be seen most clearly by focusing first on income tax revenues and, in particular, on income tax increases induced by growth in nominal incomes, which in turn were increasingly driven by inflation as real growth weakened. The existence of progressive income tax schedules in most Member countries meant that individuals whose incomes were rising automatically faced higher marginal income tax rates as they were pushed into higher tax brackets by larger nominal incomes. At the same time, inflation eroded the real value of tax reliefs fixed in nominal terms, and low-income families who had been exempt from tax found their inflated incomes subject to tax. This meant higher real tax burdens, both for individuals and in terms of aggregate tax burdens. The phenomenon was most pronounced in those countries with very progressive rate structures, narrow brackets, tax reliefs fixed in nominal terms, and where inflation was high.

In those countries where this phenomenon, often called "fiscal drag", did occur, it provided an important source of additional tax revenue. Prior to the mid-1970s, when fiscal drag arose as much from economic growth as from inflation, it was welcomed by governments, and taxpayers seem by and large to have been willing to accept the increased payments. Few countries had formal indexing provisions prior to 1974 (the main exceptions being Denmark and the Netherlands), and most other countries did not undertake *ad hoc* measures to offset the fiscal drag. France and Japan are notable exceptions. In contrast, there seems generally to have been less acceptance of these automatic and unlegislated income tax increases after 1974. Between 1974 and 1985 Australia, Canada, Finland, France, Sweden, Switzerland, the United Kingdom and the United States introduced indexing provisions, and many other governments regularly provided adjustments to compensate for fiscal drag[16]. Thus, a recent OECD study shows that over the last ten years most countries have largely offset fiscal drag and this, in part, explains why income tax revenues have generally grown more slowly during this period than prior to 1974[17].

Taxpayer resistance to automatic increases in income taxes posed a dilemma for government financing that generally was resolved by seeking alternative revenue sources, the obvious source being consumption taxes. Thus, the period after 1974 witnessed the introduction of new consumption taxes in a few countries and the broadening of bases and increasing of rates in those countries which had previously adopted value added tax (VAT) systems. In fact, rates in all countries with VAT systems, except for France and Norway, were increased between the year of introduction and 1986. In addition to actions on these broad-based taxes, an increasing number of countries have raised the rates of specific excise taxes such as those on petroleum and petroleum products, as well as those on such items as tobacco and alcoholic beverages. Alternatively, as in Canada, some of these taxes were converted to an *ad valorem* basis. In the absence of these adjustments, the real value of revenues from these taxes declines with inflation, a sort of "negative" fiscal drag. This loss was largely ignored prior to 1974.

At the same time, in many countries there was a growing gap between the projected obligations of social security systems and projected revenues, a phenomenon often linked to the falling real wage and to reductions in employment growth after 1973. In most countries, social security contributions are tied to payroll growth, whereas expenditures are linked more to price increases for consumer goods and services. As prices rose relative to wages (and medical care costs rose relative to other consumer prices) while employment stagnated, shortfalls in social security financing opened up. In addition, benefit increases as well as projections of ageing populations in some countries implied further future deficits. As these systems are typically funded by earmarked payroll contributions, increases in contribution rates and broadening of the contributions base – mainly by removing or increasing ceilings – were frequently required. Italy, France, the Netherlands, the United States, and Japan are examples of such adjustments.

These developments had at least three consequences. First, overall revenues as a share of national product increased, and the composition of tax revenues changed. This can be seen in Table 10.3, which shows the share of tax revenues in GDP, in total and by type, for the years 1965, 1974, and 1984. Thus:

- The growth in overall revenues as a share of national product since 1965 is as much as 15 percentage points in a number of countries. With some exceptions, the big increase occurred in

northern Europe and outside of Europe (except Japan) in the first half of the period, whereas in Japan and southern Europe the increase occurred in the second half;

- Between 1980 and 1984, tax levels reached their highest levels in all countries except Finland, Germany and Turkey. Since then, tax levels have tended to stabilize, though since 1980 only six countries have succeeded in actually decreasing the proportion of GDP accounted for by taxation;

- The share of income and general consumption taxes and of social security levies (particularly on employers) in total tax revenues has increased.

Second, over the period as a whole, average and marginal rates of direct tax, excluding business taxes, tended to increase. The degree to which this occurred differed by country and depended upon the existing structure of taxes in each country, a fact which prevents simple comparisons. Where income tax burdens increased, the process that led to fiscal drag raised marginal and average rates by moving individuals into higher brackets. Rates of social security contributions paid by both the employee and the employer were also raised. At the same time as direct tax rates were boosted, consumption tax rates also increased, thereby reinforcing the effects of increasing marginal and average rates of direct taxes. There is very little data on the evolution of direct tax rates because they require the processing of tax information, a process that only became administratively feasible in recent years. However, Table 10.4 does demonstrate some of this evolution for the United States. It is likely that increases in average and marginal rates of direct tax were much more severe in most if not all European countries than is shown in the table for the United States[18].

Third, both the continued increase in tax levels and continuing pressure from interested groups led to action to relieve certain groups and particular sources and uses of funds from the general level of taxation. This reduced tax bases or lowered the rates for these special groups and created a need for yet higher tax rates on others to maintain revenues. Thus, recent evidence shows that in some countries, non-standard tax reliefs can reduce average personal income tax rates by as much as 30 per cent at the wage level of the average production worker[19]. But special treatment was, and is, not limited to personal income taxes. In particular, growing concern with inflation-induced increases in effective business tax rates and stagnant growth heightened the worry that investment was being needlessly impeded by the tax system[20]. This created pressure in many countries to adopt special tax privileges under corporate income tax to favour capital formation.

The revenue loss from all of these special provisions – "tax expenditures" as they are widely called – led authorities in a number of countries to try to identify and quantify their effects within the budgeting process. Here it is significant that in the mid-1970s, only Germany and

Table 10.3. **Receipts from main taxes as percentage of GDP, 1965, 1974 and 1984**[1]

Percentages

	Total taxes			Personal income taxes			Corporation income tax			Employees' social security			Employers' social security			General consumption			Excises, etc.		
	1965	1974	1984	1965	1974	1984	1965	1974	1984	1965	1974	1984	1965	1974	1984	1965	1974	1984	1965	1974	1984
Sweden[2]	36	43	50	17	19	19	2	1	2	1	1	x	3	7	13	4	6	7	7	5	5
Denmark[2,3]	30	44	48	12	25	24	1	1	3	1	*	1	*	*	1	3	8	10	9	6	6
Belgium[2]	31	38	47	6	11	16	2	3	3	3	3	6	6	8	8	6	7	7	4	3	3
Norway[2,3]	33	45	46	13	14	11	1	1	8	x	2	3	3	8	7	7	9	8	6	7	8
Netherlands[2]	34	42	46	9	12	9	3	3	3	5	7	8	4	8	8	4	6	7	5	3	3
France[2]	35	36	45	4	4	6	2	3	2	2	3	6	9	10	13	8	9	9	5	3	4
Austria[2]	35	38	42	7	9	9	2	2	1	4	4	5	4	5	7	6	7	9	5	6	4
Luxembourg[2]	32	32	41	8	9	11	3	7	6	4	4	4	6	5	6	4	4	5	3	2	5
Italy[2]	27	28	41	3	4	11	2	2	4	..	2	3	..	9	10	4	5	6	7	4	4
Ireland[2]	26	32	39	4	7	12	2	2	1	1	2	2	1	2	4	1	5	8	11	9	9
United Kingdom[2]	31	35	39	9	12	10	2	3	4	2	2	3	2	3	4	2	3	6	8	6	5
Germany[2]	32	36	38	8	12	11	2	2	2	4	5	6	5	6	7	5	5	6	5	4	3
Finland[3]	30	33	36	11	16	16	2	2	2	x	x	x	1	3	3	6	7	8	7	5	6
Greece	31	24	35	1	3	5	*	1	1	..	..	5	..	..	5	2	3	5	7	6	8
Canada	26	34	34	6	11	11	4	4	3	1	1	1	1	2	3	5	5	4	4	5	5
Switzerland	21	27	32	6	9	12	1	2	2	1	3	3	2	3	3	2	2	3	4	3	3
Portugal[4]	18	22	32	..	..	..	..	..	..	2	2	3	2	4	5	1	3	4	8	6	9
Australia	24	29	31	8	12	14	4	3	3	x	x	x	x	x	x	2	2	2	5	5	6
New Zealand	25	30	31	10	17	18	5	4	3	x	x	x	x	x	x	2	2	4	5	4	4
United States	26	30	29	8	10	10	4	3	2	2	3	3	2	4	5	1	2	2	4	3	2
Spain	15	18	28	2	2	6	1	1	1	1	2	2	3	7	9	3	3	4	3	2	3
Japan	18	23	27	4	5	7	4	6	6	1	2	3	2	7	4	x	x	x	5	3	4
Turkey	15	18	14	4	6	6	1	1	2	*	1	*	*	1	1	x	x	x	8	7	5
OECD average unweighted[5]	27	32	37	7	10	12	2	2	3	2	2	3	3	4	5	3	5	5	6	5	5

.. = not available; x = no such tax is levied; * = less than 0.5 per cent.
1. Countries ranking order by 1984 total tax to GDP ratios.
2. Countries with a value-added tax as of January 1984.
3. In these countries, employees' social security contributions are levied on an income tax base and are shown as 1100.
4. Receipts cannot be broken down as between personal and corporation income taxes. For the two combined they are 5, 5, 8 for 1965, 1974, 1984 respectively.
5. Excluding Portugal for 1100 and 1200 and Greece and Italy for 2100 and 2200.
Source: OECD, *Personal Income Tax Systems Under Changing Economic Conditions, op. cit.* in Note 17. 1974 figures taken from OECD, *Revenue Statistics of OECD Member Countries, 1965-1983*, Paris, 1984.

Table 10.4. **Marginal rates of taxation on personal income in the United States**

Percentages

Percentile of returns	Marginal rates[1]				Average marginal tax rates[2]		
	1961	1969[3]	1974	1979	Year	Rate	Including employees' social security contributions
1%	0.00	0.00	0.00	0.00	1950	15.2	..
5%	0.00	0.00	0.00	0.00	1955	16.3	..
10%	0.00	0.00	0.00	0.00	1960	16.4	19.4
25%	0.18	0.15	0.15	0.14	1965	14.0	17.6
50%	0.18	0.23	0.20	0.20	1970	17.2	22.0
75%	0.22	0.25	0.22	0.24	1975	17.4	23.3
90%	0.22	0.28	0.28	0.32			
95%	0.26	0.32	0.32	0.38			
99%	0.38	0.47	0.47	0.50			

1. From Steuerle, E. and Hartzmark, M., "Individual Income Taxation, 1974-1979", *National Tax Journal*, 1981, Vol. 34.
2. From Seater, J., "Marginal Federal Personal and Corporate Income Tax Rates in the United States, 1909-1975", *Journal of Monetary Economics*, 1982, Vol. 10.
3. Includes an approximation for surtax charged in 1969.
Source: Hausman, J., "Taxes and Labor Supply", Chapter 4 in Auerbach, A. and Feldstein, M. (eds.), *Handbook of Public Economics*, Vol. 1, North Holland, Amsterdam, 1985, p. 228.

the United States provided for a systematic accounting of these tax expenditures, whereas by 1985 almost half of the OECD countries had implemented accounts for them[21]. But in practice, even these accounts are typically limited to a review of some aspects of the personal and corporate income tax provisions; they do not customarily include favourable depreciation schedules that are generally available, for example. Furthermore, they do not include discrimination in other taxes that are not properly "tax expenditures", such as the prevalence of multiple rates in value added tax systems, which further aggravate the problem.

Yet even with these qualifications, the budgetary impact of the limited set of identified tax expenditures can be quite large. For the United States, the President's budget proposal for 1987 shows tax expenditures for commerce and housing alone to have been equal in magnitude to a direct outlay of 190 billion dollars in the fiscal year 1985[22]. A simple summing of the revenue losses from these same provisions yields a total of over 120 billion dollars[23]. Neither of these estimates includes the effects of favourable depreciation schedules, which were removed from the list of tax expenditures beginning in 1983. By comparison, actual federal tax receipts were estimated at 734 billion dollars[24].

II. THE CONSEQUENCES OF A GROWING TAX BURDEN FOR ECONOMIC PERFORMANCE

Taxes "distort" economic decisions; that is, they alter the prices faced by individuals and therefore alter their incentives. As a result, demands and supplies are altered and, in particular, the supplies of labour and capital are reduced. In addition, the altered prices tend to cause people to choose tax-favoured activities over those not so favoured. Summed up for society as a whole, this "substitution effect" reduces real incomes by more than the revenue collected from the tax, an excess often called the "deadweight loss" from the tax. Moreover, the deadweight loss increases roughly as the square of the tax rate. Beyond these general observations, the actual magnitude of the impacts depends both on how distorted the signals become and on how sensitive individuals are to the prices they face in any particular decision.

Recent public debate has focused on the effect of taxes on two broad classes of decisions or, more accurately, pairs of decisions, that are fundamental to economic growth: the decisions to supply and demand labour and the decisions to supply and demand capital, i.e. to save and invest. For many years the empirical evidence generally suggested that the aggregate level of employment and capital formation had not been greatly reduced by taxes. However, recent years have seen an accumulation of empirical evidence suggesting the effects to be substantially larger than had been thought[25]. This newer evidence has been based on advances in statistical techniques and on newly available data on the activities of individuals and households over longer time periods. Because of this, it will be some time before the results have been fully examined or confirmed. Nevertheless, one conclusion suggested by both the old and new research is that the adverse impacts of taxation, whether they be relatively large or relatively small, result disproportionately from very high tax rates. Therefore, much of what damage has been done could be undone by reducing the highest rates.

But this is only one aspect of the problem. The composition of employment and capital formation is also important. Tax systems typically do not strike similar individuals and transactions similarly. There is a great deal of discrimination between different kinds of workers and jobs and between different forms of savings and kinds of investment. This discrimination is often intentional, though it is fair to say the effects are often more dramatic and somewhat different than has been intended. At the same time, the discrimination has not infrequently been the result of haphazard decisions, or of decisions taken for reasons which have little to do with economic efficiency and whose economic consequences may be purely unintended but very costly. Discrimination is costly because of the wide variation in sensitivity to price incentives throughout the economy and the attendant fact that, even if the overall magnitudes of employment and capital formation were relatively insensitive to the level of tax rates, the choice between particular workers and jobs, or between particular investments, may be quite sensitive to differences in those rates[26].

A. Taxes and employment

Tax rates alter decisions by introducing a difference at the margin between the price that buyers pay and the price that sellers receive. This difference might be called the "total" marginal tax rate because it is the sum of all the applicable taxes. The net effect of the difference depends on its size and the responsiveness of buyers and sellers to the implied price change, and also to the complex response of all other parts of the economy to these changes. However, to begin to untangle all of these effects it is first necessary to identify the difference itself.

In the labour market the tax-induced difference includes payroll taxes, social security contributions, income taxes, and taxes on consumption, all of which bring about a difference between the gross costs of hiring a worker and the consumption permitted by the employee's wage. Although the way in which tax laws apportion responsibility for paying the tax can affect decisions in the short term, especially when taxes change, the longer-run consequences are most likely to be independent of these institutional arrangements. And it is these longer-run consequences that influence the trend of economic performance.

Table 10.5. **Total marginal and average tax rates on labour use at average production worker level**
Percentage of total compensation including payroll taxes

	Single worker				Single-earner married couple with two children			
	Marginal			Average	Marginal			Average
	1979	1981	1983	1983	1979	1981	1983	1983
Australia	44.37	43.49	42.31	35.85	44.37	43.49	42.31	31.01
Austria	60.63	64.14	63.99	42.44	60.63	64.14	63.99	40.64
Belgium	64.61	65.95	66.86	52.83	62.19	62.05	61.65	48.12
Canada	43.32	45.09	42.72	36.83	41.12	42.96	42.72	29.17
Denmark	68.49	69.04	71.24	57.33	68.49	69.04	71.24	53.41
Finland	63.13	63.08	62.48	48.25	63.13	63.08	62.48	44.03
France	66.92	66.67	68.77	51.74	57.47	57.15	59.70	47.57
Germany	61.13	60.53	60.91	41.31	56.81	56.44	57.02	36.62
Ireland	55.51	57.78	70.21	51.68	55.51	57.78	63.80	44.91
Italy	56.28	59.54	62.66	50.25	56.28	59.54	62.66	48.88
Japan	40.50	43.90	43.68	23.73	35.93	39.41	39.93	19.05
Luxembourg	62.36	63.15	67.21	42.70	47.60	48.68	50.61	32.56
Netherlands	66.75	68.97	73.47	39.16	66.75	68.97	73.47	37.51
New Zealand	43.86	54.32	40.31	36.29	43.86	54.32	55.50	31.98
Norway	72.54	70.52	69.47	54.89	65.91	67.01	63.00	50.36
Portugal	44.03	46.75	46.94	37.77	40.08	43.25	44.29	37.05
Spain	43.94	45.38	46.66	38.64	43.94	45.38	46.66	35.52
Sweden	74.42	73.47	73.02	62.85	74.42	73.47	73.02	61.67
Switzerland	44.42	44.15	42.16	27.00	40.48	42.20	40.21	22.61
United Kingdom	51.33	53.44	54.53	42.17	51.53	53.44	54.53	38.97
United States	47.12	52.87	48.63	34.83	40.19	45.20	42.64	28.21
Average (unweighted)								
OECD Europe	59.79	60.78	62.54	46.31	56.95	58.23	59.27	42.53
OECD Non-Europe	43.84	47.93	43.53	33.50	41.10	45.08	44.62	27.88
Total OECD	55.99	57.72	58.01	43.26	53.18	55.10	55.78	39.04

Note: The rates include payroll taxes, employer and employee contributions for social insurance, personal income taxes, and general consumption taxes and excise taxes.
Source: Secretariat estimates.

Table 10.5 presents some recent sample calculations of the total tax rates affecting the labour market for Member countries. They are calculated for a single employee and for a married worker with a non-working spouse and two dependent children. In each case the worker is assumed to earn the annual average wage of production workers in manufacturing, to enjoy only the standard tax reliefs, those not based on the worker's actual expenditures, to have no non-wage income and, in the case of a married couple, to have a spouse who is not in the labour force. The table shows both the average tax rate – that applying to the whole of the worker's cost of employment – and the marginal rate, that applying to an additional dollar of gross employment cost. Because the tax rates affecting individuals with different incomes and income patterns, consumption patterns and family situations vary quite widely within each Member country, these calculations can only be taken as examples. Still, even as examples, they do indicate the high tax rates impinging on the labour market in most Member countries, especially in Europe[27].

What are the likely effects of such high tax rates? Attention has focused to some extent on the effects on the determinants of overall labour demand, given labour supply, in the belief either that these tax rates tend to discourage labour use in favour of capital use or, to the extent exchange rates do not adjust rapidly, that the taxes damage national competitiveness[28]. There is probably some truth in both of these for Europe in recent years, though no reliable estimates exist to suggest the effect is large. Most likely the effect could have occurred from the tax increases, particularly for social security contributions, discussed above, rather than for maintained high tax rates. Over the longer term, maintained high tax rates, by raising the cost of labour, also raise the cost of capital goods, thereby moderating and ultimately eliminating this adverse effect on labour demand[29]. Likewise, as exchange rates evolve to reflect the added costs, competitiveness should recover.

However, these observations about the lack of permanent consequences need to be evaluated in the light of excessive unemployment in a number of Member countries. In many cases the direct reduction of labour costs that could be achieved through a cut in taxes on the labour market – in particular those taxes paid by the employer – might make a measurable contribution to bringing down unemployment over an extended period. In this case, however, the financing of such a tax cut remains problematical, a matter discussed later in this chapter.

In the context of longer-term economic performance, much more attention has been given to the effects of taxes on overall labour supply. Here there are really several possible dimensions in which supply could be affected: number of hours to work, willingness to take a first or an additional job or to enter the underground economy, choice of occupation and attitudes toward risk-taking, amount of education and training to seek, age of retirement, form of compensation – to name several. Among these, most research has focused on the first because it is the easiest to observe, yet these other dimensions should not be forgotten. Focusing on hours alone, the bulk of the research until the mid-1970s concluded that overall labour supply is relatively unaffected by taxation[30]. This conclusion reflects the balancing of the disincentives provided by the rates themselves with the need to maintain family incomes to pay taxes and maintain consumption levels.

However, research since the mid-1970s has shown notably larger effects. As noted earlier, these studies, primarily American, exploit new data bases and innovations in statistical techniques that incorporate the complexity of the decisions being modelled. The data themselves have often been developed from cross-sectional studies of households, sometimes carried out over a period of several years, as well as from experiments to determine the feasibility of "negative income taxes" as a means of raising the incomes of the poor. This finer attention to microeconomic detail has allowed researchers to divide the potential work-force into more homogeneous groups by sex and income level, so that the differences in responsiveness among different groups is clearer by sex and income level. Although these studies are, relatively speaking, at the frontier of economic research, they are widely recognised among interested professionals as being the best information currently available.

The broad character of such results, at least for the United States, is summarised in a recent paper that is, in itself, quite critical of extreme claims about the effects of taxation on labour supply. The authors, Burtless and Havemann (both active researchers in the field), conclude that[31]:

> "On the basis of the best available evidence...a reduction in labour supply of perhaps 5 per cent and no more than 12 per cent can be attributed to the existing combination of government taxes and transfers."

Though the size of the impact is striking, this summary masks a great deal of variation between husbands and wives and across income groups. Hausman, for example, cites estimates for prime-age men that vary from 4.5 per cent for male workers in the lowest wage quintile to 12.8 per cent for those in the highest quintile[32]. And his estimates for wives range from an increase in labour supply of 30 per cent for those in the lowest quintile to a reduction of 23 per cent for those in the highest quintile.

Of course, these estimates all measure the total impact of the tax system – to eliminate the effects would require eliminating the public sector. Yet other estimates make it clear that much of the adverse impacts could be eliminated simply by a move to proportional taxation. For Hausman, for example, 8.1 per cent out of a total labour supply loss, for prime-age males, of 8.2 per cent could be regained by such a move. Likewise, reducing the level of tax rates would result in more than proportional gains.

Although these results are for the United States, similarly striking results have been obtained for the United Kingdom and for Sweden[33]. For that matter, the results for Sweden may be considered to be even more dramatic. For example, Blomquist has estimated that about half the loss in male labour supply due to the existing tax system could be regained by a move to proportional taxation – even given the much higher level of taxation in Sweden than in the United States.

The estimates of supply responsiveness are one indicator of the possible damage to economic performance from current tax systems – the effect on factor availability. It is also useful to look directly at a measure of the loss stemming from an inefficient allocation of resources: at the deadweight loss in real income, and particularly at this loss as a proportion of the revenue yield. Hausman estimates that, again for prime-age males, the mean ratio of income loss to tax revenue is about 22 per cent, with losses in the lowest decile of about 9 per cent and those in the highest close to 40 per cent – a reflection of the effect of progressivity of the income tax schedule and the "square" rule referred to earlier[34]. With a proportional tax, the overall loss drops to about 7 per cent, a third of its value under the 1983 tax law. For Blomquist's sample the current loss is about 19 per cent, while the proportional tax would lower this ratio to 4 per cent. For wives, Hausman estimates an overall deadweight loss of about 18 per cent from all taxes. This is notably smaller than for men because most of those women not in the labour force (about 50 per cent of all women) would not alter their decision if taxes were changed. They therefore suffer no deadweight loss from taxation.

These studies all focus on the broad middle of the spectrum of workers, though a great deal of public attention has been directed to those at the extreme of the income distribution: the effects of taxes on the very rich and the very poor. For the former, direct surveys of individuals with very high incomes do not seem to show significant reductions of work effort[35]. However, the qualitative nature of these studies makes it difficult to say whether this conclusion is out of line with an extrapolation of the estimates for workers in general. Interestingly, one of the surveys does suggest that high-income individuals spend a significant amount of time seeking ways to avoid tax – a deadweight loss[36].

The response of low-income individuals can also be inferred from the results reported above. But for them, various forms of social welfare payments are often also important. For those facing the loss of benefits when they earn more income, the combination of benefit loss plus taxes can reduce their labour supply as their net incomes may be no higher, and in many cases will be lower, if they work than if they receive benefits. Such estimates have been derived from several studies in the United States, and have reinforced the concerns about "poverty traps" that have been expressed in other countries; for example, France, Denmark, and the United Kingdom, though the number of households involved may be relatively small[37].

To the extent that these results are confirmed by further work, it would seem to have four important implications for policy makers. First, the overall effects of taxation both on labour supply and on efficiency could be large enough to affect economic performance measurably. Second, much, if not most, of the damage that occurs could be alleviated by reducing high marginal tax rates and by altering tax (and benefit) schedules to eliminate discrimination against those most adversely affected. Third, although it may seem that high marginal tax rates affect only individuals with high incomes, in practice wives and second income earners, the unemployed, and recipients of income support payments often face high marginal tax rates as well. Thus, eliminating discrimination is also frequently likely to result in more uniform tax treatment of individuals. Many recent proposals for tax reform move in this

direction. Fourth and finally, notwithstanding the large benefits to be gained from a reduction in high marginal rates, so long as revenue requirements are not changed, there is an irreducible minimum damage that cannot be avoided. This irreducible minimum is simply and directly related to the proportional rate of tax necessary to finance public spending, and therefore to the magnitude of public spending.

B. Taxes and capital formation

Tax rates affecting the supply of saving and the demand for investment goods appear to vary widely, and are often negative on the margin. Although the response to these taxes is simpler in its form than for labour – a straightforward change in the level of saving and the level and composition of investment, rather than a multidimensional adjustment of hours, occupation, retirement, and so on, the response may take a longer time to complete. It is also interwoven with some of these other decisions, risk-taking and retirement, in particular. However, the mobility of saving among alternative uses and, increasingly, across national boundaries means that the wide variation in tax rates on capital formation may have effects at least as critical as those of the level of taxation itself.

Tables 10.6 and 10.7 give some sample calculations of the total marginal tax rates applying to capital formation in Member countries. These tax rates encompass both the tax rates at the business (here, corporate) level and those at the household level. The rates in Table 10.6

Table 10.6. **Total marginal tax rates on capital in 1980**

Percentage of pre-tax return

Inflation rate	Germany		Sweden		United Kingdom		United States	
	0%	10%	0%	10%	0%	10%	0%	10%
Asset								
1. Machinery	38.1	46.6	− 18.1	1.5	− 24.2	− 33.3	3.9	22.8
2. Buildings	42.7	31.2	28.9	37.3	41.5	41.0	35.4	41.8
3. Inventories	57.7	60.8	26.5	71.0	50.5	42.7	50.9	45.5
Industry								
1. Manufacturing	44.7	46.8	8.1	28.3	− 1.7	− 6.9	44.2	55.0
2. Other industry	50.8	57.9	29.6	62.6	4.6	− 2.3	10.0	15.8
3. Commerce	44.6	36.6	12.1	40.7	46.8	39.5	37.9	37.5
Instrument								
1. Debt	12.1	− 33.3	− 12.9	6.4	− 29.6	− 81.7	− 2.0	− 22.2
2. New share issues	56.1	65.7	44.2	93.2	7.6	− 0.9	61.0	104.6
3. Retained earnings	72.0	111.5	40.9	69.5	23.5	29.3	48.4	66.5
Source of finance								
1. Households	59.7	82.0	57.1	108.0	26.6	38.3	44.1	61.9
2. Tax-exempt institutions	17.6	− 17.9	− 39.2	− 52.8	− 5.1	− 33.5	4.0	− 37.2
3. Insurance companies	14.6	− 38.9	− 16.0	22.0	8.7	− 2.1	4.0	44.3
Overall	45.1	46.1	12.9	37.0	12.6	6.6	32.0	38.4

Note: Each entry is a weighted average of rates across other classifications. Thus, for example, the entry for machines is a weighting of the tax rate on investment in machines for all industries, instruments and financing sources.
Source: King and Fullerton *op. cit.* in Note 20, Tables 3.23, 4.20, 5.21 and 6.20.

Table 10.7. Estimate of total marginal tax rates on capital in 1983
Percentage of pre-tax rate of return

	Owner[1]	Zero inflation						10 per cent inflation					
		Equipment			Structures			Equipment			Structures		
		Debt	New share issues	Retained earnings	Debt	New share issues	Retained earnings	Debt	New share issues	Retained earnings	Debt	New share issues	Retained earnings
Australia	HH	−18.1	36.3	4.8	38.2	66.6	50.1	−14.9	83.9	26.6	30.5	108.5	63.2
	TE	−76.4	4.8	−42.3	7.7	50.1	25.5	−121.1	26.6	−59.1	−53.3	63.2	−4.3
Austria	HH	−18.6	23.2	16.9	20.8	49.0	44.8	−10.4	52.5	40.4	15.4	70.8	60.2
	TE	−77.0	−14.7	−24.1	−18.2	23.8	17.5	−114.0	−20.1	−38.3	−75.5	7.1	−8.7
Belgium	HH	−12.2	−13.7	−10.2	20.0	19.0	21.5	−0.5	−3.2	3.1	32.2	29.9	35.3
	TE	−100.3	−42.1	−37.7	−42.7	−1.3	1.9	−158.0	−54.0	−46.1	−99.5	−12.6	−5.9
Canada	HH	6.4	24.5	34.8	21.4	36.7	45.6	3.3	41.4	58.7	5.8	43.5	60.6
	TE	−32.6	−6.9	7.6	−11.3	10.3	23.0	−78.6	−24.6	−0.1	−75.0	−21.7	2.6
Denmark	HH	49.5	59.6	24.9	54.4	63.5	32.0	91.2	111.6	37.8	92.0	112.2	38.9
	TE	−19.6	3.3	−75.4	−8.5	12.2	−59.2	−51.7	−5.5	−172.8	−50.0	−4.1	−170.3
Finland	HH	49.3	25.6	24.5	53.5	30.8	29.5	78.6	40.1	42.7	81.7	45.0	45.9
	TE	−14.9	−61.2	−63.5	−6.7	−51.2	−53.7	−53.4	−128.8	−123.6	−47.3	−119.1	−117.4
France	HH	14.7	38.9	40.9	25.6	47.0	48.8	4.8	56.8	61.3	9.7	60.5	64.9
	TE	−38.1	−3.1	−0.1	−22.3	8.7	11.3	−97.4	−22.0	−15.5	−90.3	−16.7	−10.3
Germany	HH	5.1	18.4	52.8	36.8	45.9	69.5	−31.1	0.1	80.9	−27.3	3.4	82.9
	TE	−39.2	27.5	55.9	4.6	50.3	69.8	−127.0	29.6	96.5	−121.7	32.4	98.2
Ireland	HH	−90.1	−107.8	−178.1	−56.4	−71.8	−124.4	−51.2	−75.8	−176.5	−17.6	−38.9	−122.3
	TE	−245.6	−279.4	−405.6	−184.4	−212.3	−308.1	−256.7	−301.4	−484.5	−195.6	−234.3	−386.0
Italy	HH	−6.8	27.5	34.6	9.9	38.9	44.8	−37.5	38.8	54.5	−32.2	42.4	57.8
	TE	−22.1	−2.1	7.8	−3.0	13.9	22.2	−71.5	−27.0	−4.9	−65.4	−21.9	−0.4
Japan	HH	7.7	52.7	43.5	25.3	61.7	54.2	−11.5	91.5	70.5	−12.7	90.9	69.7
	TE	−23.0	36.9	24.7	0.3	48.9	39.0	−82.0	55.3	27.3	−83.7	54.5	26.3
Netherlands	HH	36.0	65.8	16.3	57.7	77.1	44.0	77.9	135.6	42.4	89.7	141.7	57.4
	TE	−76.4	−3.4	−124.5	−23.1	24.3	−56.7	−118.4	22.7	−205.3	−89.6	37.7	−168.7
New Zealand	HH	24.0	58.2	39.2	35.3	64.4	48.2	28.8	105.9	63.1	22.3	102.2	57.8
	TE	−10.6	39.2	11.5	5.9	48.2	24.7	−49.0	63.1	0.8	−58.5	57.8	−6.8
Norway	HH	29.9	59.9	45.6	41.0	66.6	54.4	30.6	99.8	66.8	34.3	102.1	69.8
	TE	−22.8	25.7	2.5	−4.9	36.5	16.8	−83.0	28.8	−24.6	−76.9	32.4	−19.7
Spain	HH	−42.7	−0.3	−11.1	−14.0	20.0	11.5	−44.5	27.7	8.5	−27.4	39.8	22.0
	TE	−80.6	−27.7	−41.1	−44.8	−2.4	−12.9	−107.6	−17.5	−41.6	−86.3	−2.4	−24.7
Sweden	HH	41.3	24.3	39.0	55.0	39.7	53.7	79.6	48.7	60.5	89.5	63.2	71.7
	TE	−67.9	−42.9	−72.8	−38.8	−20.0	−41.6	−99.7	−55.9	−140.5	−78.6	−34.2	−116.6
Switzerland	HH	21.3	35.2	27.5	24.8	38.1	31.0	32.7	62.1	38.2	34.3	63.4	39.8
	TE	−1.9	15.9	6.0	2.6	19.6	10.5	−15.2	22.4	−8.2	−13.1	24.1	−6.0
United Kingdom	HH	−45.8	−0.0	16.3	−21.1	16.9	31.8	−91.7	−0.1	21.6	−59.9	21.7	42.5
	TE	−108.3	−42.9	−19.5	−73.0	−18.7	2.5	−216.7	−85.8	−54.9	−171.3	−54.7	−25.0
United States	HH	−27.6	35.6	10.1	18.2	58.7	43.3	−32.2	82.7	32.8	10.3	104.2	64.4
	TE	−91.4	3.3	34.9	−22.8	38.0	14.9	−148.4	24.0	−50.8	−84.6	56.3	−3.4

1. Financial asset owned directly by household (HH) or by tax-exempt (TE) institution.
Source: Secretariat estimates.

are limited to four countries and 1980 law, but are available in great detail and rest on a wealth of underlying, comparable data[38]. By comparison, those in Table 10.7 cover most OECD countries under 1983 law but are limited to manufacturing and, given the breadth of country coverage, do not rely on such detailed underlying information[39]. In both cases the tax rates are those applying to an investment of the indicated type yielding a pre-tax real return (net of economic depreciation) of 10 per cent[40]. The tables examine the tax rates applying to the investment in different sectors and using different methods of finance, and financed directly by households or through institutions that are permitted special tax treatment. The results are shown both for the case in which there is no inflation and for that in which inflation is running at 10 per cent.

As with the labour tax rates presented earlier, these estimates are subject to many qualifications, but they do seem "representative" in two important respects. First, the tax rates vary widely within each country according to the type of asset, the method of finance, the institution of ownership and the rate of inflation, and they vary in all of these dimensions from country to country. Second, in many countries the marginal rates are quite low, even negative for some combinations. Interestingly, in many cases these "total" marginal tax rates consist of taxes on the corporation that are low or negative, while taxes on the individual savers are relatively high – though in many countries special forms of saving such as homes, pensions, national savings accounts, life assurance, government bonds, and even equities benefit from favourable treatment that reduces the force of this generalisation. Furthermore, it should be remembered that the tax rates shown in these tables apply only to saving used for corporate investment. In point of fact, in many countries savings channelled into particular non-corporate investments (or into particular industries within the given sectors, or into owner-occupied homes) are also subject to tax treatment intended to give especially favourable incentives that reinforce these two conclusions even as they make the tax systems, and evaluation of them, more complex.

One can identify at least four important possible consequences for capital formation of this pattern of taxation:

- It may reduce overall national saving; given the complex pattern, its consequences for investment in any particular country are ambiguous;
- It will reduce the productivity of investment by channelling it into uses that are tax-favoured rather than those that yield the highest economic returns;
- It will alter the international pattern of investment, and international capital and trade flows will be affected;
- It may support existing rigidities or favour the creation of new rigidities that hinder adjustment.

Just as with the taxation of labour, the consequences of taxing saving will depend both upon tax rates and upon responses to them. But with such a range of marginal tax rates, it is virtually impossible to tell exactly what rate characterises any particular saver or the aggregate of private saving in any country; indeed, any such aggregate may be virtually meaningless. Furthermore, given the increasing openness of financial markets to international capital flows, the world supply of saving and demand for investment may have become more important for most countries than the supply and demand in any single country. This in turn means that it is the configuration of capital tax rates world-wide that are the relevant tax variables. Finally, within this configuration, the degree to which negative tax rates may be exploited is typically limited in each country by regulatory barriers and, in the case of business borrowing, solvency considerations.

Insofar as these rates are positive, they may of course be expected to discourage saving, and the converse for negative rates. Empirical research along this line has focused on private saving, the sum of business and household decisions. In this regard there is reasonably strong evidence that households act as though business

saving were a close substitute for household saving, at least over a medium-term horizon[41]. For household saving, the evidence on the impact of tax rates is far from conclusive. However, as is also the case with research on the responsiveness of labour to taxation, new developments in data and methods seem to be leading to estimates of the impacts of taxation significantly larger than the earlier consensus.

As in the case of labour taxes, simple economic theory suggests that there are two offsetting forces at work. Higher tax rates – and lower returns – serve directly as a disincentive to save, while the need to maintain saving for future consumption and for bequests work to offset the disincentive. There is no a priori reason to suppose that one effect predominates over the other. Until recently, the empirical evidence, invariably based upon aggregate relationships between consumption and income, has generally supported this ambiguity. The "extreme" estimate has been an elasticity of private saving with respect to the real after-tax interest rate of about 0.4 – a 1 per cent reduction in real returns (from a tax increase, for example) would reduce private saving by 0.4 per cent[42]. Thus, for the 10 per cent gross return assumed in Tables 10.6 and 10.7, a tax rate of 20 per cent would reduce private saving by 8 per cent if this tax rate were effective for all households and all investments. But this has been the extreme estimate, and many estimates showed declines in after-tax interest rates leading to increases in saving[43].

In the last five years, however, work on the relationship of saving to taxes has taken a somewhat different turn. Researchers have endeavoured to apply a more sophisticated theory – that of "life-cycle saving" due to Modigliani – in this and other related areas. The theory examines consumers' saving patterns over an entire lifetime. One important implication of this work is that there is a third factor influencing the saving decision, in addition to the two mentioned above: changes in interest rates bring about a revaluation of wealth from future labour income that should also influence saving. In the area of tax policy this could imply elasticities at least two or three times higher than the previous extreme[44]. Another implication is that household responsiveness to interest rates will vary with age, and therefore overall private saving will depend upon the age composition of the population. These considerations are only beginning to be reflected in statistical examinations of individual households that tend to support the larger and varying estimates[45]. Incidental to this work has also been the insight that the "income effect" of taxes – the second and "offsetting" effect mentioned above – would tend to cancel out in tax reforms that do not alter total tax revenues because the incomes of some households would increase while those of others are reduced. This suggests yet greater responsiveness where tax reform is concerned[46]. To the extent that these developments in theory and empirical work are borne out by further research, and to the extent the world-wide configuration of effective marginal tax rates on capital formation is, on balance, positive, the supply of saving has been significantly reduced by taxation.

But whatever may be the overall effect on saving, the way in which governments currently tax capital formation certainly alters investment patterns for the worse. Analysis of this is complicated by the institutional workings of the financial markets and their growing integration. Practically speaking, market interest rates are given (vis-à-vis the tax system), so that savers generally face a positive tax rate on the return from saving by comparison with market interest rates (though saving that finances a home or pension are widespread exceptions). This means that there are only limited opportunities for individuals to take advantage of any total tax rates that may be negative.

On the corporate side, however, the availability of negative tax rates, equivalent to subsidies, for some investment opportunities provides an incentive to undertake projects that pay less than the market rate of interest. Here, there is reasonably strong statistical evidence that private investment is sensitive to after-tax returns[47]. And the marginal social return from these investments – their marginal productivity – will therefore often be less than market rates, reducing overall productivity. Moreover, the effective tax incentives vary widely from project to project and, in virtually every case, there are regulatory or other constraints that limit the degree to which negative tax rates may be exploited. Thus, the pattern of investment is altered in a fairly haphazard way, and many investment projects will no doubt face positive tax rates. There is no reason to believe that the resulting pattern of investment in any way contributes to an efficient allocation of resources.

Available evidence on the magnitude of the efficiency losses arising from this dispersion of tax rates is both limited and subject to wide variation: from as low as 0.1 per cent of GDP to 1 per cent or more[48].

In an international context, the fact that business tax rates on investment vary widely and market real interest rates show a tendency towards convergence across countries (even if personal income taxes on the saver cannot be avoided) creates an incentive for portfolio investment in those countries where tax rates are relatively low, assuming pre-tax returns are not significantly different for similar investment projects[49]. Indeed, it creates an incentive to invest in projects with lower yields – providing the net-of-business tax return is favourable. In an era in which national capital markets are increasingly open to foreign investors, the potential misallocation of resources on an international basis is quite large[50]. Furthermore, the ensuing capital flows can contribute to pressures on the payments and trade accounts. One recent estimate suggests that if the United States were to introduce a tax incentive to investment equivalent to a one percentage point cut in the cost of capital, the world real interest rate could increase by as much as 0.4 per cent, with a cumulative deterioration in the external position of the United

States of $256 billion and corresponding improvement in the rest of the OECD countries[51].

Finally, while the consequences of the heterogeneous taxation of capital formation that have been discussed so far have been long-run consequences, the critical role of capital formation in the adjustment to new economic conditions should not be overlooked. Thus, the incentives created by such taxation can prevent changing market signals from leading to investments in newly profitable industries and sectors and hinder the withdrawal from failing enterprises[52]. But they can also limit international competition, where the potential entry of foreign competitors can serve as a useful check in those industries where domestic competition is lacking[53]. This can occur simply from less favourable treatment in general to investment in the country needing greater competition, or it can come about because existing international tax arrangements may fail to yield identical incentives for domestic and foreign investors.

These dynamic factors have a secondary but very important consequence, a consequence that stems from the fact that changes to marginal tax incentives can bring about a persistent (though not sustainable) revaluation of existing capital: they create capital gains and losses[54]. These gains and losses themselves have no direct consequence for economic growth, but they do encourage interested groups to attempt to manipulate tax policy for their own private benefit. There are two quite obvious indirect consequences for economic growth. First, such manipulation may bring further tax-based discrimination. Second, it may lead to frequent changes in the tax system that raise the level of uncertainty that attends investment. This in turn may also limit the efficacy of tax incentives themselves, since all incentives come to be viewed as temporary[55].

These observations pose at least three challenges for policy makers. The first is the need to reduce or eliminate tax-based discrimination among different investment opportunities so that investments are made in response to their comparative productivity, not their comparative tax treatment. The second is to determine what ought to be the appropriate tax rate to apply to the various investment opportunities, a challenge that must take into account desired saving and capital formation on an area-wide basis, and that requires a multilateral response to avoid beggar-thy-neighbour consequences. The third challenge is to settle on a sustainable system for such taxation that will encourage planning in a longer-term horizon and, then, to maintain that system.

III. ECONOMIC PERFORMANCE, TAX POLICY AND TAX REFORM

In principle, the connection between tax policy and economic performance is straightforward: the level and pattern of total marginal tax rates affecting labour and capital markets reduce the supply of capital and labour and limit the degree to which they can be allocated efficiently. The scope for improving performance is constrained to some degree by government revenue requirements. But, as well, tax policy is formulated within a set of institutions and other constraints that limit the degree to which the connection may be taken into account and thus also, to some extent, determine the agenda for tax reform. There are at least three reasons for this.

First of all, practical discussions of tax policy can rarely address total tax rates directly; rather, such discussions necessarily take place within the framework of a given mix of institutions and existing taxes, and focus on those specific taxes. Thus, the current agenda for tax reform in each country is typically framed in terms of individual institutional problems, whether with personal income taxes, business income taxes, consumption or sales taxes, and so on[56]. This is true even where radical reform is being considered. For example, those countries with income taxes often see a switch toward consumption-based taxation (completely or on a piecemeal basis) as a way of getting around the perceived handicap to saving imparted by the income tax. In Japan, by contrast, with its high saving rate, the current income tax system is seen as exempting too much saving, requiring the elimination of some saving incentives. In other countries, high social security levies are frequently viewed as discouraging employment, leading to a search for an alternative tax base to payrolls. In each of these cases, the resolution must lie in an alternative set of tax structures, from which the "total" tax rate is an outcome.

Furthermore, in evaluating specific reforms the practical problems posed by the transition from one system to another often limit the solutions that can be adopted. These transitional problems are of two kinds. First, governmental institutions and treaty commitments limit the degree to which major changes can be taken at any time. Second, reform can have profound impacts on private institutional and contractual agreements, creating a presumptive need for special treatment. For all of these reasons it is possible that the overall impacts on growth may be lost sight of in practical discussions of tax policies, but it is certain that these impacts are only one factor among many.

Second, beyond the constraints posed by the existing tax system, there are other policy concerns besides efficiency that have to be addressed in formulating tax policy. Primary among these are concerns about equity, both horizontal – that similar taxpayers be treated in similar ways – and vertical, that those with unequal incomes be treated differently. Perceptions of equity differ from country to country and, perhaps, over time as well. It is also more complicated than often recognised: it must take into account equity between those of different ages and, ultimately, different generations.

In many and perhaps most cases, vertical equity has been seen as being achievable only at the cost of efficiency. Thus, progressive income taxation has long been considered a fundamental building block of an equitable tax system in most Member countries. Although the degree of equity such systems have achieved has been increasingly questioned in recent discussions of tax reform (suggesting perhaps that perceptions of equity have changed or pragmatic recognition that the income tax is not the ideal instrument for reducing inequalities), it is clear that these systems necessarily sacrifice efficiency. A similar point can be made about social benefits. Often these benefits are based on an income test, a natural way of enforcing equity, yet it is precisely this sort of test that is one contributor to the high marginal tax rates both on benefits and on additional labour income for recipients.

Unfortunately, in public debate questions of equity often become inappropriately entangled with questions of efficiency. There is clearly a trade-off, but it is often misunderstood or incorrectly brought to bear on particular decisions. Taxes affecting the labour market and those affecting the capital market may frequently be thought of as taxes on the poor and taxes on the rich, though this is not the case. It is quite possible that, to the extent that capital formation is reduced by taxes on the capital market, employment is reduced so that the tax ultimately is borne as a real income loss to workers[57]. And this proposition holds symmetrically for reductions in taxes on capital formation. Likewise, it is fair to say that the existence of a separate corporate income tax, in many countries, is viewed as a necessary component of equity. However, there is no necessary connection between capital income and the usual image of the wealthy; for example, in many countries the retired may be heavily dependent upon capital income derived from lifetime savings. In addition, in those countries such as the United States with a large private pension system, the active working population and retirees hold a significant share of capital through these funds. All in all, these confusions, which too often typify many discussions of a certain tax policy, most frequently arise from believing that the economic consequences of a certain tax can readily be identified by knowing whom the tax law names as the taxpayer[58].

The feasibility of implementation is another consideration in the formulation of tax policy, and one that has many dimensions. The degree to which income can effectively be taxed, for example, differs from country to country according to the availability of appropriate accounting and reporting systems, which depend in part on the sectoral composition of production, and also on social and political traditions. The same considerations enter into the taxing of consumption or of payrolls. In addition, the existing mix of taxes and of supporting institutions and contractual arrangements can limit the degree to which tax systems can be altered, say in going from income-based taxation to consumption-based taxation. Finally, perceptions of fairness enter into calculations of feasibility. These considerations may argue for transparency, but they might also argue occasionally against transparency, as with widespread decisions to augment general consumption taxation more than income taxation over the last decade – perhaps a successful attempt to obscure the increase in the overall tax burden.

Third and finally, governments genuinely have other goals to be achieved, and it is legitimate to consider whether these can better be implemented through the tax system than through other administrative means. Individual tax expenditures or other kinds of tax-based discrimination may often be cost-effective means of carrying out particular policies, even though they can add to the complexity and inequity of the system. Here, political dynamics are very important. Many tax expenditures and other "non-neutralities" may be justifiable on a strict cost-benefit basis, given the goals of public policy. Yet the existence of such justifiable favouritism can in itself serve to legitimise those tax expenditures that are not otherwise justifiable. Negotiations over the recent tax reform in the United States provide a dramatic example of these pressures at work.

Given the wide range of institutions and tax systems, economic situations, and constraints operating in Member countries, it is not surprising that perceptions of problems have varied widely, and proposed reforms have also varied considerably. First of all, there have been proposals based on two broad sets of perceptions: taxes affecting labour/employment are too high, and taxes affecting capital formation are too high.

Unfortunately, so long as one envisages maintaining revenue yields at present levels, there would seem to be a sharp limit on the degree to which either of these concerns can be addressed without heightening the other, a point that takes its force from the construction of the total tax rates calculated earlier and from the composition of national income. For the first perception, barring the removal of tax reliefs and expenditures, there is ultimately no practical way to reduce the overall tax burden on the decisions affecting labour without raising it on those affecting capital (though the burden might be redistributed in a less damaging manner). At the same time, given the relatively small share of capital income in national income and the international mobility of saving, a significant shift of taxation from labour to capital would necessitate such high tax rates on capital formation as to be self-defeating. Nevertheless, the recent tax reform in the United States would seem to imply lower tax rates on the labour market and higher tax rates on the capital market[59]. It remains to be seen to what extent this might result in a shift abroad of capital formation.

In other cases it has occasionally happened that tax reforms have been proposed seemingly with only partial knowledge of the effects of taxes. Thus, suggestions have been made to reduce the tax burden on labour by cutting contributions for social insurance, for example, and gaining the needed revenue through increases in other taxes that ultimately have the same or similar effects. In particular, taxes on income, consumption, and payroll all affect the labour market, so that the total tax rate affecting this market can only be lowered by moving towards taxes on the broadest possible base. This is a different point from that usually discussed as "base-broadening", i.e. the elimination of tax reliefs within any given tax. It is simply that a given revenue can be collected at lower rates from the tax base that is largest, assuming that the same proportion of each base is exempted from the tax. Thus, the average marginal rate can be lower and the effect on labour supplies and demands reduced. Given the usual make-up of national income, the broadest base is likely to be income or payrolls[60].

The second perception – that taxes affecting capital formation are too high – is one more easily dealt with by switching to taxes on labour decisions insofar as the amounts of revenue are typically relatively small (so the implied increase in the total tax rate on the labour market is small). In addition, labour may be less mobile internationally, though concerns about a "brain drain" of highly skilled workers and entrepreneurs from high-tax to low-tax countries have been raised in some Member countries such as Canada, Ireland, the Netherlands and the United Kingdom. Still, such a revenue switch clearly cannot avoid raising taxes affecting the labour market.

A. Moving to consumption-based taxation

The major reform to be proposed as a means of shifting the disincentive effects of taxation from capital markets to labour markets – and, indeed, the reform that is most often viewed as yielding the major alternative to existing systems – has been a switch from income-based to consumption-based taxation. Some analysts have also proposed a "cash flow" tax as a way of retaining business taxes without affecting capital formation[61]. The attractive feature of consumption-based taxation (or at least of a proportional tax on consumption) from the point of view of capital formation is that it has, in principle, no direct effect whatsoever on decisions to save and invest – it is more or less neutral with respect to these. But the fact that a consumption tax is a tax on labour decisions (though this may not be obvious to the casual observer) places the most critical tax conundrum concerning economic performance – whether to reduce the supply of capital or the supply of labour – in high relief.

Although the switch to consumption taxes has often figured in the literature on tax reform as a wholesale reform package, in fact a partial switch has effectively been carried out piecemeal in a number of countries. Thus, the "income tax systems" of many countries are in fact a mix of income and consumption taxation. This has typically been achieved through the device of favouring certain forms of saving, such as for housing or for retirement, in the personal income tax, or limiting or reducing the tax rate on some forms of capital income, usually dividends or capital gains. It is also the import of reductions in the share of business-based taxes, particularly corporate income taxes, in many countries (often carried out by increasing the generosity of depreciation provisions or providing other investment incentives that reduce corporate taxes) coupled with increases in general consumption taxes.

Certainly the single most important consumption tax to have gained attention in Member countries has been the consumption-based VAT. As practised, its economic effects are indistinguishable from a retail sales tax on consumer goods and services, though its capacity as a revenue raiser is greater because it can better cope with evasion and with the taxation of services. The tax was widely adopted early in the development of the European Community as a means of tax harmonization, but one of the arguments in its favour was that it reduced distortions associated with the various cascade, or turnover, taxes in use at that time in some countries.

Because of its early development, few comprehensive analyses of its benefits exist of the type now done using general equilibrium models, though the analysis done by Whalley for the 1973 United Kingdom reforms is an exception[62]. His results do make a very interesting point: although the superiority of VAT to turnover taxes is quite evident, and VAT itself was in principle superior to the taxes it replaced in the United Kingdom – purchase tax and selective employment tax (SET) – the actual replacement of those taxes with VAT damaged economic performance. This occurred primarily because SET entailed distortions in the capital market that tended to offset other distortions from capital income taxation. VAT, because it does not distort saving and investment decisions, eliminated these offsetting distortions, thus worsening the situation. This demonstrates the important qualifications that must attend tax policy, particularly in the context of piecemeal reforms.

More recently, the prospect of new adoptions of VAT with the expansion of the Community, or for other reasons (as in New Zealand, as part of comprehensive tax reform), may well stimulate further analyses. Borges has produced such a study for Portugal, highlighting many of the institutional advantages of VAT for a country with rationed savings, a high current account deficit, and extensive reliance on inflation as a means of financing public expenditures[63].

One widespread feature of existing VAT systems outside Scandinavia and New Zealand, however, is the inequality of rates across various kinds of expenditure. Most countries have two or three rates for different types of goods and services; some items are highly taxed while many are taxed at low rates. In other countries, there are more than three rates, and in still others a large proportion of consumer expenditure is not taxed at all. These rate structures have typically been introduced and defended as a means of achieving progressivity – by exempting food, for example – though the degree to which this goal is achieved is at best limited[64]. The

discrimination among consumption decisions brought about by these rate structures should inhibit economic performance, but estimates of the effect for any existing system appear to be lacking.

One rather indirect piece of evidence on this score, however, is available from a general equilibrium model for the United States. Ballard and Shoven have examined the gains to be achieved from replacing some of the revenue from the (1973 vintage) United States income tax with two alternative, consumption-based VAT taxes. One is a tax with a differentiated rate structure similar to those found in Europe, the other is a flat-rate VAT tax (at roughly 6 per cent) that yields the same revenue as the differentiated tax[65].

The capitalised value of the gain in economic performance from introducing *flat-rate* VAT, measured as consumption plus the value of leisure, varies from more than 0.3 to over 0.6 per cent of performance in the absence of such a change. The exact value depends upon the way in which personal income taxes are reduced. The key point, however, is that when VAT is instead levied according to a more "realistic", European scheme, the change in economic performance is virtually nil: it varies from -0.1 to well under +0.2 per cent.

This last estimate illustrates two points. The first is that tax reforms – and estimates of their consequences – may often be formulated outside the daily pulling and hauling of the political arena. There may be a tendency to compare existing taxes, with all their flaws, to ideal reforms. In practice, the results of a tax reform may in the end lead to consequences just as unpleasant as, though perhaps different from, those that led to the reform itself. The second observation is that tax reliefs and discrimination are themselves the source of many avoidable problems with virtually every major existing tax, not just income taxes.

As a major alternative to income taxes, VAT has met with the primary objection that it is regressive, a point that has often been generalised to all consumption taxes. Tax rate differentiation between different types of goods and services may not significantly improve this. Furthermore, a flat-rate tax is not likely to be progressive in the usual sense, since consumption generally takes a higher proportion of the income of the poor than of the rich. Of course, here one needs to be mindful of the ultimate incidence of the tax, and the dangers of confusing apparent incidence with ultimate incidence, a point raised earlier in the discussion of equity.

Still, consumption taxes could in fact be levied in a way similar to income taxes, and levied progressively, though this approach is not currently favoured in any OECD country. This could be achieved through the creation of "qualified accounts" in which accumulated savings are held, accounts which might themselves cover the broad spectrum of financial and real assets. Net payments into these accounts would be exempted from tax, while net withdrawals would be taxed as consumption. This is in some respects simply an extension of methods used in some countries for exempting retirement saving in specific forms from income taxation. Such a proposal might not be harder to administer than an income tax because it would eliminate certain difficult aspects of income-based taxation, such as the need for depreciation accounting. But it would clearly not have the same administrative simplicity as point-of-sale taxes, and it might be perceived somewhat differently.

Such a tax is not without its own drawbacks. Its progressivity alters the trade-off between present and future consumption in a way that proportional consumption taxes do not[66]. The altering of this trade-off, highlighted earlier in discussions of the taxation of saving, means that it does reduce saving, though perhaps not by as much as does income taxation. It should also be noted that the unilateral introduction of such a tax would pose a number of institutional problems for international tax relations, which typically operate through a complex system of bilateral tax treaties keyed to income taxation. These reflect real economic problems, a point discussed later.

How much might economic performance be improved by switching to progressive consumption-based taxation? One broad set of estimates have been calculated for the United States by Fullerton *et al.* using a general equilibrium model[67]. Some of their results are presented in Table 10.8, which shows the gain in the capital value of consumption (including leisure) as a percentage of its capital value under their base case – the 1973 vintage income tax system. The table, and the study itself, offer a rich set of comparisons among alternative tax systems that treat saving in different ways:

- The base system against which all comparisons are made already excluded roughly 50 per cent of saving, i.e. it was effectively about half-way between a pure income tax and a pure consumption tax. About 30 per cent of saving was directly excluded in the form of pension fund accumula-

tion and additions to life assurance reserves. Another 20 per cent was indirectly excluded in the form of new residential housing, though the treatment did not conform exactly to that under a consumption tax. Finally, the base system had a separate corporate income tax with a number of distortions of the type discussed earlier;
- *Plan 1* excludes all remaining saving: thus, 80 per cent of saving would be directly excluded, and special treatment of housing continued. The separate corporate income tax would also be maintained;
- *Plan 2* takes a very different approach: rather than exempt more saving, it would do away with the separate corporate income tax. It would do so by imputing corporate income to shareholders, who are then taxed at their existing income tax rates. Many other distortions – in depreciation, for example – would presumably be maintained, though within the framework of the personal income tax;
- *Plan 3* combines Plans 1 and 2: 80 per cent of saving would be directly excluded, existing treatment of housing would be maintained, and the corporate tax would be integrated with the new consumption tax so that there is no tax on capital income *per se*;
- *Plan 4* would improve Plan 3 by giving proper consumption tax treatment to housing. It is thus a "pure" consumption tax;
- *Plan 5* is a partial consumption tax, one that would exempt only half of remaining saving directly (for a total of 55 per cent), while retaining special housing treatment and the corporate tax;
- *Plan 6* takes a very different tack: it would "purify" the personal income tax of all saving exemptions and retain the corporate income tax;

Table 10.8. **Estimated long-run gains from moving towards a progressive consumption tax in the United States**

Plan	Percentage of saving directly excluded	Existing housing preference retained	Separate corporate tax retained	Range[1] of long-run gain as percentage of capital value of consumption[2] under 1973 tax law
Base: 1973 income tax	30	Yes	Yes	..
1. Consumption tax	80	Yes	Yes	1.1 to 1.2
2. Income tax *with* corporate integration; capital gains indexed	30	Yes	No	0.6 to 1.4
3. Consumption tax *with* corporate integration	80	Yes	No	1.7 to 2.6
4. Pure consumption tax	100	No	No	2.4 to 2.9
5. Partial consumption tax	55	Yes	Yes	0.5 to 0.6
6. Pure income tax *without* integration	0	No	Yes	−1.1 to −0.5
7. Pure income tax *with* integration	0	No	No	0.3 to 0.5

1. Depends upon method used in model to assure revenue neutrality. Excepting Plan 7, the highest value is for a hypothetical ideal (i.e. lump-sum) tax. In Plan 7, this yields the worst outcome because other methods reduce distortions.
2. Consumption includes an imputed value for leisure.
   Plan 6 in the source document has been omitted from this presentation, and the original Plans 7 and 8 renumbered accordingly.
Source: Ballard, Fullerton, Shoven and Whalley, *op. cit.* in Note 27, Chapter 9, Tables 9.1 and 9.2.

– *Plan 7* improves Plan 6 by integrating corporate taxation into the personal income tax system, as in Plan 2.

The estimates are constructed to hold revenues constant. As consumption is a narrower tax base than income, tax rates must be raised. This can be done in a number of ways, and the range of gains shown in the last column of the table stem from using different rules to adjust the tax rates upward. Thus, some of the improved performance from reducing taxation in the capital market is offset by increases in tax rates on labour decisions. Still, the different consumption tax schemes all lead to net gains in economic performance, gains that are strengthened when taxation of corporate income is done at the personal level. The "pure" Plan 4 shows gains of 2.4 to 3 per cent. Although these gains may be perceived as small compared to the chosen standard (the capital value of all consumption and leisure or, in other words, the total value of all capital, both physical and human), they also represent from 25 per cent to 30 per cent of the capital value of all income tax revenues in the base case[68].

By comparison, purifying the income tax only results in a net gain if the corporate tax is eliminated. This suggests the possibility that savings exemptions, at least, may be one exception to the general presumption against tax discrimination: even exemption of some saving may be economically rewarding. Here, however, it is important to recognise that such exemptions are effective only to the extent they apply at the margin. In contrast, the exemption of flat amounts of saving typically does not have these beneficial effects except insofar as individuals save less than the exempted amount, so that the marginal tax rate on their additional saving is zero.

Some important features of adopting a consumption tax are omitted from these simple model-based estimates. The most important omission here is the redistribution of tax burdens among various age groups that would initially accompany such a reform. In general, saving is carried out by the working-age population, who would find their taxes lowered by such a reform, while the elderly, who tend to consume a greater proportion of their incomes, would find themselves facing higher tax burdens. Indeed, much of the boost to capital formation (by comparison with adoption of a payroll tax, which otherwise has the same effects) comes from this initial redistribution. Although those who start working after the reform is instituted would face the same tax burdens over their lifetimes as in the absence of the reform, the redistribution would affect all those over working age at the time of the reform.

Despite the difficulties raised by transition to the new system, the consumption tax would appear to offer an attractive alternative to income-based taxation. There remains, however, one more significant problem with the tax from the point of view of national governments. The sort of results shown here, though often cited in support of such a tax, do not fully reflect the openness of OECD economies and, in particular, the increasing integration of capital markets. Reflecting this lacuna, the same authors have also estimated the gains when the United States economy is open to capital flows[69]. When it is, the link between domestic saving and domestic capital formation is broken, and the consumption tax itself provides no incentive for domestic capital formation.

Under these circumstances, Plan 1 in the table, the only plan for which estimates are available, often leads to losses in domestic performance rather than to gains. The losses arise because an outflow of domestic saving yields only a return net of foreign business taxes, rather than the gross return available from domestic capital. This evidently presents something of a conundrum for the area as a whole. All OECD Member countries might benefit from the increase in saving that would result from general adoption of consumption-based taxation, but the incentives for any one country to adopt such a tax may be limited, at best, without appropriate reforms in other Member countries.

B.   Reforming income taxes

Although a great deal of academic attention has focused on the possibility of switching from income-based to consumption-based taxation, and some moves have been made in this general direction, it is fair to say that overhaul of existing income taxes remains at the centre of attention, as seen in the recently held OECD symposium on tax reform. This doubtless reflects a general reluctance to abandon a system that has proven its effectiveness in raising revenue, and that generally commands support, in favour of an untested system, however promising. At the same time, it also reflects the importance of income taxes in revenues in most OECD countries and the complexities that accompany the way in which these taxes are currently levied.

In broad outline, proposals for reform of income taxes need to focus both on personal and on business income taxation as well as on their interaction, an interaction that affects returns to saving and investment. For the personal income tax, proposals for reform tend to include three features: a widespread reduction or removal of tax reliefs, particularly those considered to be tax expenditures; a restructuring of the rate schedule that usually involves a sharp reduction in the number of brackets and a lowering of the top scheduled rates; and a more equal treatment of different sources of income, especially between labour and other income and between different sources of income from capital. In general, all of these reforms are viewed together as offering an opportunity to cut the average of marginal tax rates while at the same time reducing discrimination.

A similar thrust is found on the business side, where proposals generally contain four aspects: the widening of the tax base; the removal of tax incentives that bias investment incentives, primary among which are attempts to bring tax depreciation more in line with economic depreciation; the bringing of corporate tax rates closer to personal rates; and the reduction of the discrimination against distributed profits either by charging a reduced rate at the corporate level or by providing credit to the shareholder for a portion of the corporate tax paid.

Several of these aspects of income taxation pose problems for a number of countries: among them, the integration of corporate taxation and the treatment of owner-occupied housing stand out. And, as was seen earlier, these two can pose problems that also demand special attention in the context of a move to a consumption tax. Still, these are only two specific examples of the generic problems: high marginal rates and discrimination. For that matter, the two generic problems are often bound together, as has been discussed: high marginal rates create a demand for exceptions, and the exceptions in turn create a need for yet higher rates. Thus, while it is possible to analyse and, in principle, to correct individual problems, resolving the generic difficulties virtually demands a programme of reform that tackles the two together. Whether such a programme is politically feasible remains an open question, but if the evidence from the recent United States reform offers any general lesson, it is that tackling the two together may be essential to gaining the necessary popular support.

The comprehensive income tax reform in the United States may offer a number of other lessons, though care must clearly be taken in generalising from that one set of institutions, both of taxes and of policy formulation. The key features would appear to be:

- A general lowering of personal income tax rates, especially the highest ones, a task already partly accomplished earlier in the Administration; But many lower-income households were also newly exempted from tax liability;
- A widening of personal tax brackets, thus simplifying the rate structure;
- The reduction or elimination of a number of personal tax reliefs, while those remaining are less valuable due to the lower rates;

- Elimination of favourable treatment of income from capital gains;
- Reduction of the statutory corporate tax rate to accord more closely with personal rates;
- More homogeneous depreciation provisions;
- Elimination of a number of special business tax reliefs, most notably the investment tax credit.

Some of these items are already a part of existing tax laws in other countries; for instance, the United Kingdom has a simplified rate structure with most taxpayers paying at a common rate, and it has already reduced its corporate tax rate substantially. Other items that were among proposed reforms but not part of the final law, such as partial integration of corporate and personal taxes, are also part and parcel of existing laws in some other countries.

Still, the obvious question is whether the gains from this major effort at reform will be significant. It is one matter to speculate on the gains from ideal reform, yet another to see what is possible. And here, the final score will not be known for a long time. Indeed, at this writing there appears to be no comprehensive and systematic estimate of the likely impacts of the final law[70]. However, one careful set of estimates does exist for the forerunner proposals of the final law and, according to one of the authors, the final law is roughly half-way between the two proposals[71]. The estimates, presented in Table 10.9, were prepared using a general equilibrium model, and they focus primarily on the consequences of the business tax changes.

The estimates in the table provide for a range of outcomes based upon plausible alternative values for the responsiveness of different parts of the economy to changes in taxes. One key distinction the authors make is between two views of the impact of taxing dividends. In the "old view", such taxation was believed to be adverse to capital formation; in the "new view" it is not. The different views arise less from any conflict concerning the effects of taxation *per se* than from differences in opinion about the way firms make financing decisions – whether to finance with debt, equity or

Table 10.9. **Welfare gains and capital formation from proposed income tax reform in the United States**

Percentages

		Long-run gain as percentage of capital value of consumption[1] under 1985 law		Long-run change in capital stock[2]	
		Treasury plan	President's plan	Treasury plan	President's plan
I.	New view of dividend taxes				
	A. Standard case	0.1	0.3	−1.9	−0.2
	B. Favourable case	0.6	0.7	−0.5	−0.0
	C. Unfavourable case	−0.1	0.2	−1.9	−0.3
II.	Old view of dividend taxes				
	A. Standard case	0.5	0.6	+1.0	+1.3
	B. Favourable case	1.2	1.2	+1.0	+1.0
	C. Unfavourable case	0.3	0.4	+0.5	+0.7

1. Including the value of leisure.
2. Percentage difference from baseline capital stock after 50 years.
Source: Fullerton and Henderson, *art. cit.* in Note 38.

retained earnings, and under what conditions. The gains from integrating the corporate and personal tax or otherwise reducing the tax penalty on distributing profits clearly depend upon how these decisions are made: it is the difference between an increase in capital formation and a decline.

Yet what is most striking about these results is that, with one exception, economic performance improves even when capital formation is reduced. The reduction in capital formation occurs because the overall impact of these proposals, and of the final bill, is to raise the (average) total marginal tax rate on this activity. Yet performance improves both because there is a larger supply of labour and because the capital stock, while smaller, is used more efficiently. Because many of the important features of the model used for deriving these estimates are essentially identical to that used for the consumption tax estimates shown earlier, it is probably not too misleading to compare them[72]. Thus, they are generally in the range shown in Table 10.8 for improving the income tax, though the actual changes evaluated in Table 10.9 are not examined in the earlier table.

It seems likely that these results understate the eventual gains from the reform. Purely as a technical matter, they do not explicitly model any gains stemming from reform in personal taxes beyond the general lowering of rates made possible by the increase in business taxation. But, more broadly, they do not incorporate a number of other provisions, nor do they attempt to estimate the gains from reduced tax avoidance, or any more speculative benefits from improvements in "fairness" and "simplicity".

IV. REDUCING TAXES AND PUBLIC SPENDING

All of the foregoing discussion focuses on the opportunities for improving economic performance by reforming tax systems while maintaining current revenue yields. One alternative to this approach would be to reduce public spending and cut revenue requirements. Of course, such an approach does not rule out reforming tax systems at the same time. Indeed, it may make it easier since all tax rates can be reduced.

The primary question, though, is to what extent the gains from tax reductions coupled with public spending cuts might exceed the gains from tax reform alone. As was seen in some of the evidence presented earlier, tax reform can substantially improve economic performance, particularly insofar as it reduces high marginal tax rates and discrimination among similar sorts of transactions. But there nevertheless remains substantial scope for tax-induced inefficiency that is linked to the need for revenue, a point clearly made in those estimates of the reduction in deadweight losses attributable to tax cuts that were presented in the section on employment and taxation. And these gains would be reinforced by

any losses to economic growth that may accompany particular public spending programmes.

It is possible to estimate the "excess burden" from taxes or spending, or for both combined, with general equilibrium models. This "excess burden" or, by another name, deadweight loss is the excess of economic cost over the amount of revenue gained. For example, an excess burden of 1 per cent would mean that $1.00 requires the sacrifice of $1.01 in economic efficiency (and similarly for other currency units in other countries). A tax with an average excess burden of 1 per cent would mean that the whole of the tax in question costs, on average, $1.01 per dollar of revenue; and a marginal excess burden of 1 per cent would mean that an incremental dollar raised through a particular tax costs $1.01. Conversely in the last case, a tax cut of $1.00 would improve economic well-being by $1.01.

One can combine taxes and spending to ask how much an average or an incremental dollar of additional revenue costs the economy when the dollar is spent in a particular way. In this way, a marginal excess burden of 1 per cent might be attributed to an extra dollar of tax revenues spent on overall public consumption (according to the existing overall pattern of spending). There are then many possible computations of excess burden linked to various taxes and spending programmes, and the number that can actually be calculated and the accuracy with which they can be calculated depends upon the model used for the calculations.

One final point of interpretation is important. The costs represent the loss of efficiency, typically in terms of total economic output: e.g. as the total loss of economic wealth as shown in Tables 10.8 and 10.9. Such calculations do not tell whether the taxes or spending are worth undertaking. They provide only the cost side of the ledger. The question they pose is whether the benefits to be gained from the taxes and spending – in terms of equity, security or any of a number of other important non economic criteria – merit the sacrifice. Thus, a marginal excess burden of 1 per cent for a given tax and spending item would indicate that the gains from the spending item would need to be $1.01 if the additional dollar of spending were to improve overall well-being.

How does the excess burden from taxes and spending – and therefore the potential gain from reducing spending and taxes together – compare to the gain from tax reform? Several such estimates exist for the United States. First, for example Ballard, et al., using their general equilibrium model, find that the marginal excess burden of existing taxes, when used to purchase goods and services, varies from 17 per cent to 56 per cent of incremental revenue[73]. The exact estimate depends upon the tax as well as the assumed degree of responsiveness. In general, the estimates are highest where tax rates are highest or vary the most widely. And, as may be expected from the discussion in this chapter, the excess burden is higher where activities face high or widely varying tax rates. By way of comparison, they have elsewhere estimated the average deadweight loss for taxes alone at between 13 and 24 per cent[74]. An alternative set of estimates, computed by Stuart using a less elaborate model, generally vary within the range presented by Ballard et al.[75]. Stuart also shows that the costs when linked to income redistribution are higher than when linked to public consumption, primarily because of the adverse effects on labour supply that result from income redistribution.

Estimates computed by Hansson and Stuart and by Hansson for Sweden are still more dramatic, reflecting the much higher tax rates and larger public sector in Sweden[76]. Hannson's calculations show marginal excess burdens varying from 47 per cent to 620 per cent for additional taxes used to increase transfer payments. When cuts in specific expenditures are linked to a change in payroll or value added taxes, the excess burden varied from 0.2 per cent (no cost at all) for expenditures on infrastructure to 127 per cent for transfer payments. The calculations also highlight a significant shrinkage of the tax base in response to tax increases[77].

The estimates of marginal tax burdens for Sweden are of particular interest because they represent some of the very little work done outside the United States on the questions of interest in this chapter. Although the models that are used are simple, they capture certain aspects of conditions that may apply to several other countries in Europe: in particular, the larger public sector, higher tax rates and greater degree of openness to international trade and payments flows.

To the extent that these calculations are robust and supported in further work, they would lead to three conclusions. First, and supporting the conclusions elsewhere in this chapter, tax reform can yield significant gains in efficiency when these reforms are aimed at reducing the highest tax rates and reducing their variation. Thus, uniform taxation can achieve much of the difference between the marginal and average burdens computed by Ballard et al. But, second, greater gains can be achieved by linking tax cuts to spending cuts, as this permits elimination of the most egregious distortions without increasing distortions elsewhere, a problem that attends tax reforms that are revenue-neutral. Third, and finally, those countries with higher tax rates and larger public sectors gain the most from such actions, and the gains are more than proportional. Here the key fact, mentioned much earlier, is of overwhelming importance: the long-run loss of economic well-being is proportional to the square of the tax rate.

V. CONCLUSIONS

The economic costs of funding the public sector are large, larger than is indicated by the volume of public spending itself. It is larger for two reasons. First, the government intervenes in the economy through many channels other than spending, channels whose effects are not examined extensively in this chapter. These channels – loan guarantees and regulations, for example – have consequences for growth and efficiency that are not very different from the consequences of taxation.

The second reason that economic costs are larger is that government spending ultimately requires taxation, and taxation itself impedes economic growth. There are of course other ways to "finance" spending: through inflation or through public borrowing. The former of these, in fact, acts much like an especially capricious tax, but it has not been examined here because practical circumstances today bar extensive use of inflation as a means of public finance. The latter, public borrowing, may reduce growth by crowding out saving, but in any case it is only a temporary financing device that postpones taxes for another day, and perhaps another generation.

Thus, inevitably, sustained public spending must be paid for with taxes. These taxes reduce the supply of capital and of labour and distort incentives, thereby leading to inefficiency. The effect in other ways is to impede economic performance. And in recent years, evidence has begun to accumulate that the economic costs of financing government spending are not as small as was once thought, a finding that is particularly strong at the margin: the costs of increasing the size of the public sector, as well as the gains from reducing it, are significantly larger than the average economic cost of public sector spending.

Although all the costs in question are typically small in comparison with GDP, it would be a mistake to dismiss them on this ground. First of all, although it may be possible to bring about dramatic swings (dramatic in comparison with the effect of tax rates) in national output over a few years by using the tools of traditional macroeconomic policy, these are typically not durable or sustainable gains. By comparison, the gains from improving tax policy, though individually small, are durable and will accumulate over time. Second, GDP is probably not the right standard of comparison in any case. When an extra dollar of government spending costs much more than a dollar, it is well to ask whether the benefits have been appropriately weighed.

The obvious question, then, is what can best be done to ameliorate these problems. But another question must be answered first: is the evidence to be believed? After all, the evidence is relatively recent in origin, rather speculative even by standards of economic evidence, and all too often limited to the United States. Given the immediate personal and political interest of every citizen in the burden of taxation, a policy maker will rightly be cautious about casually entering such dangerous territory. Thus, it is essential to consider the quality of the evidence.

How and why is the evidence changing? Although the study of public finance is one of the oldest fields of economic study, and for obvious reasons, in recent years it has been given a new life by the power of the computer. The study of public finance, like all the areas of microeconomic research, is ultimately based on theories of individual behaviour. These theories have not changed, though they have been augmented and extended, particularly by the life-cycle theory originally proposed by Modigliani to explain macroeconomic behaviour, an area in which it has found widespread acceptance. In this theory, individual decisions are examined in the perspective of a whole, finite and evolving life, rather than instantaneously and timelessly.

The power of economists to analyse actual individual behaviour has changed; indeed, it has been newly born. In earlier times, analysts were required to rely on aggregate data that were the outcome of many events, of which taxes were at any moment a small part, and which data therefore could not reveal the information researchers sought. But the computer has begun to enable researchers to keep track of many families over extended periods of time, and the challenge of analysing these data has served as an impetus to create and refine new statistical methods and to improve economists' theories. The new and higher estimates of the responsiveness of labour and capital supply are the product of these developments.

A second product has been the development and application of models of general equilibrium, models yielding the estimates of "welfare" changes induced by tax policy. Here, economists have long desired to apply the general equilibrium theory – allowing and evaluating long-term adjustment throughout the economy at the microeconomic level – but, once again, computers have only made it possible in the last dozen years. The development and application of such models is still in its infancy. In particular, it is clear that equilibrium is an abstraction, however refined, from real world events, and increasing the realism of such models is very much on the agenda. Moreover, yet a newer class of such models, models with individuals who are born, live and die, have just begun to show their promise. In all these equilibrium models, however, the primary lessons to be learned at this stage are qualitative. Although the text of this chapter has presented numerical estimates from the models, what is of primary interest are the insights to be gained from them, and the occasional order of magnitude or rank ordering of the quantitative results.

Though the newer evidence is still limited, its tendency seems unmistakable: taxes have much more powerful effects than were once thought likely. But much of this evidence is from the United States. Is the United States unique? Perhaps it is, though the more limited evidence from other countries goes very much in the same direction. Surely much more evidence remains to be gathered. But at heart there may be no reason for this evidence to be unconvincing except that it differs from the old evidence. In fact, though the theories and methods from which the evidence derives are sophisti-

cated, their credibility rests on a simple and observable proposition: people do their best to avoid paying taxes, and the higher the tax rates, the greater the effort to avoid paying them. Both the disincentives to supply and the distortions and inefficiencies caused by taxes stem from this fact of human life.

All in all, this proposition seems unarguable, and it also does not seem a phenomenon limited – qualitatively or quantitatively – to the United States. The reason is simple and general: taxes, unlike other private spending, do not directly buy anything. That is, it is the perception of "disconnectedness" between tax payment and benefit received at the margin that is the economic definition of a tax. In contrast, one can think of "taxes" by common definition that they are sometimes seen as buying something and are therefore not, economically speaking, taxes: some social security levies may be this way, as may user fees for particular public services. In the main, though, taxes mean the same to economists as to everyone else: an additional dollar spent on taxes is not seen as buying an additional dollar's worth of commensurate benefit to the individual taxpayer. And this perception is quite accurate, because the benefits of public spending are not apportioned according to who pays. This fundamental observation is the source of tax avoidance, and it applies generally.

If, then, this evidence is quite believable, what can be done? The essential solution is twofold: the first element is to reduce those marginal tax rates that are extremely high because they cause damage far in excess of the revenue they raise. In so doing, all the relevant taxes (and sometimes the schedules of social benefits) need to be taken into account. While concerns about equity are unavoidably bound up in such changes in taxation, it is well to consider whether the pattern of marginal rates actually contributes effectively to the desired redistribution or whether its contribution is primarily symbolic. More generally, it is difficult to believe that the tax system is generally the most suitable tool for achieving income redistribution.

The second element is to eliminate differences in tax rates applying to essentially similar transactions. Such differences ultimately lower revenue, and the occasional benefits they bring are typically overwhelmed by the damage they do to economic growth, to the integrity of the tax system, and ultimately therefore, to the integrity of the political system.

Both of these goals can typically be brought about by reform of existing institutions of taxation, typically by reform of income taxes, with no need to reduce revenues. Indeed, elimination of tax-based discrimination among similar activities may raise revenues, providing room for a general lowering of tax rates.

The evidence for a completely different set of tax institutions – those required by a system based on taxing consumption – is less clear-cut. While theory points to the ultimate and overwhelming superiority of proportional consumption taxes insofar as economic growth is concerned, it is not yet clear that a practical system can be devised and instituted on an international basis, or that such a system would, for several generations to come, yield the rewards that theory predicts for the "pure" tax. At this time, consumption-based income taxes are an idea for the future, but a promising one. And, in any case, they remain an idea towards which many countries have moved incrementally.

Tax policies also need to be seen in their international context. Although taxes, given their tight link with the funding of national governments, may often be seen as purely national matters, it is clear that their economic effects reach well across national boundaries, and even more so as capital markets become integrated around the world. Subsidies to investment, in particular, can lead to large capital inflows, and the encouragement of saving to capital outflows. There may therefore be a temptation to engage in beggar-thy-neighbour tax poli-cies, or to avoid bless-thy-neighbour policies. Both of these could be avoided, and economic performance throughout the OECD area improved, were these matters taken into account on an international basis. There is therefore greater scope for international tax arrangements than merely to eliminate double taxation and limit tax avoidance.

Still, although the reform of tax systems can eliminate a great deal of the economic damage they presently do, the evidence reviewed in this chapter suggests that much more can be achieved by a reduction in public spending and the associated reduction in tax levels. Such an approach can easily provide for a selective lowering of extreme rates, and a general lowering as well. It can therefore make tax reform a much easier undertaking – but it will require hard political choices over expenditure.

NOTES AND REFERENCES

1. For a review of the evidence on the redistributional impact of the public sector in Member countries, see Saunders, P. and Klau, F., "The Role of the Public Sector. Causes and Consequences of the Growth of Government", *OECD Economic Studies*, Spring 1985, No. 4, Paris, Chapter VII.

2. The whole topic of public sector growth in Member countries and its implications is discussed in Saunders and Klau, *ibid.*

3. These projections are derived and discussed in Chouraqui, J.-C., Jones, B. and Montador, R., "Public Debt in a Medium-Term Perspective", *OECD Economic Studies*, Autumn 1986, No. 7, Paris.

4. The projection is contained in *OECD Economic Outlook*, May 1986, No. 39, Paris.

5. See for example, Feldstein, M., *Debt and Taxes in the Theory of Public Finance*, NBER Working Paper No. 1433, August 1984, who extends the theory to show that, *inter alia*, if the capital stock is smaller than optimal, even a temporary increase in public spending should be financed through tax increases in many plausible situations. See also Hannson, I. and Stuart, C., "The Welfare Costs of Deficit Finance" (mimeo), August 1985, who find that postponing a tax on labour is advantageous, while postponing a tax on capital is not.

6. See for example, Buiter, W., "A Guide to Public Sector Debt and Deficits", *Economic Policy*, November 1985, No. 1, pp. 13-79; Blanchard, O., Dornbusch, R. and Buiter, W., *Public Debt and Fiscal Responsibility*, CEPS Papers No. 22, Centre for European Policy Studies, Brussels, 1985; Courant, P., "Fiscal Policy and Economic Growth", paper prepared for a *Conference on Impediments to European Economic Growth*, The Brookings Institution, Washington D.C., October 1986.

7. For example, in a plausible case Blanchard, Dornbusch, and Buiter (see Note 6) calculate that a 10 per cent increase in the ratio of debt to income could be serviced equally well by an extra four percentage points of long-run inflation or an extra 0.02 per cent income tax rate.

8. See Note 6 for sample calculations.

9. It is also made more complicated by the fact that "automatic stabilizers" cause budget deficits to increase as private consumption declines. Thus, public sector dissaving offsets private sector saving. This cyclical phenomenon can obscure the longer-run processes that are of interest here, and it is one source of the measurement difficulties mentioned later in the text.

10. Thus, the facts that individual economies are open to trade and capital flows and that exchange rates are not fixed can imply "exchange rate crowding out" as well as "portfolio" or "investment" crowding out. In the former, as real interest rates increase, the domestic currency appreciates, competitiveness weakens, and imports replace domestically produced goods. Foreign saving thereby substitutes for domestic saving. The most recent striking example is, of course, the United States but this is by no means the only one.

11. A good recent summary is provided in Seater, J., "Does Government Debt Matter? A Review", *Journal of Monetary Economics*, July 1985, Vol. 16, No. 1, pp. 121-131.

12. For debt, the difficulties are introduced by the need to separate structural and cyclical components (see Note 9), by the need to value the debt at its current real market value, and by the need to separate existing debt from expectations of future debt. The most important difficulty in measuring real interest rates arises from the fact that they are dependent on unobservable expectations of inflation.

13. See for example, Feldstein, M., *Budget Deficits, Tax Rules, and Real Interest Rates*, NBER Working Paper No. 1970, July 1986, who examines recent evidence from the United States; Barro, R., *Government Spending, Interest Rates, Prices and Budget Deficits in the United Kingdom, 1701-1918*, NBER Working Paper No. 2005, August 1986, who examines evidence for the United Kingdom from 1701 to 1918. For a different view, see Evans, P., "Do Large Deficits Produce High Interest Rates?", *American Economic Review*, March 1985, Vol. 75, No. 1, pp. 68-87; Dwyer, G., "Federal Deficits, Interest Rates, and Monetary Policy", *Journal of Money, Credit and Banking*, November 1986, Vol. XVII, No. 4, Part 2, pp. 655-681.

14. This appears to be the import of Seater's argument (*cf.* Note 11, p. 124, para. 1).

15. See Messere, K. and Owens, J., "International Comparisons of Tax Levels: Pitfalls and Insights", 1985, a revised and updated version of a note provided for the *41st Congress of the International Institute of Public Finance*, June 1985.

16. Australia dropped the indexing provisions in 1982; Denmark and Sweden did so in 1983; and Canada has partially offset the effect of such provisions in recent years.

17. See OECD, *Personal Income Tax Systems Under Changing Economic Conditions*, Paris, 1986.

18. Ballard, C. and Shoven, J., in "The V.A.T.: The Efficiency Cost of Achieving Progressivity by Using Exemptions" (mimeo), April 1985, report that "the average industrial worker in Sweden had a combined (payroll, income and indirect taxes) marginal tax rate of 61 per cent in 1968. By 1978 the average marginal tax rate was 78 per cent." They do not cite the original source of these estimates.

19. See OECD, *The Tax/Benefit Position of Production Workers, 1979-1984*, Paris, 1986, Table E.

20. Martin Feldstein has been one of the most visible exponents of this concern: see for example, Feldstein, M., "Inflation, Income Taxes and the Rate of Interest: A

Theoretical Analysis", *American Economic Review*, December 1976, Vol. 66, pp. 809-820; "Inflation, Tax Rules, and Investment: Some Econometric Evidence", *Econometrica*, July 1982, Vol. 50, pp. 825-862; *Inflation, Tax Rules, and Capital Formation*, University of Chicago Press and NBER, 1983. The hypothesis has been explored in a number of other works: for example, for Germany, Sweden, the United Kingdom and the United States in King, M. and Fullerton, D. (eds.), *The Taxation of Income from Capital; A Comparative Study of the United States, the United Kingdom, Sweden, and West Germany*, University of Chicago Press, 1984. See also Chirinko, R. and King, S., *Hidden Stimuli to Capital Formation: Debt and the Incomplete Adjustment of Financial Returns*, NBER Working Paper No. 1684, August 1985. The last gives several other references.

21. See the discussions in OECD, *Tax Expenditures. A Review of the Issues and Country Practices*, Paris, 1984; United States Government, Congressional Budget Office, *Tax Expenditures: Current Issues and Five-Year Budget Projections for Fiscal Years 1984-1988*, October 1983; Owens, J., "Tax Expenditures and Direct Expenditures as Instruments of Social Policy" in Cnossen, S. (ed.), *Comparative Tax Studies*, North Holland, Amsterdam, 1983, pp. 171-197.

22. The estimates are from United States Government, Office of Management and Budget, "Special Analysis G; Tax Expenditures" in *Special Analyses, Budget of the United States Government, Fiscal Year 1987*, 1986, Tables G-1 and G-2.

23. Because tax expenditures may be analysed equivalently as government spending for which there is no actual outlay, or tax revenues that are not received, their estimation and interpretation presents a number of difficult issues. The two figures cited in the text differ in large part by the amount of the implicit tax receipts that would have been generated by the implicit outlays. The former estimate ($190 billion) does not account for these implicit tax receipts because the figures are meant to be an estimate of equivalent spending; the latter ($120 billion) includes these implicit tax revenues, thus showing the *net* effect of the tax expenditures on total tax receipts and thereby on the budget deficit. In addition, the two estimates differ insofar as the latter figure does not allow for interactions, the magnitude of which would depend upon assumptions concerning the presence or absence of other tax expenditures. Finally, the latter figure, although it is an estimate of "revenue loss", does not represent the revenue gain that could be achieved by eliminating the provision. For example, the estimate includes the loss occasioned by exempting from tax the interest earned on certain bonds used for private purposes. Were this exemption eliminated, it is likely that existing bonds would continue to be exempt, creating both a revenue gain from taxing interest on new bonds and a continuing revenue loss from existing bonds.

24. See United States Government, Office of Management and Budget, *Budget of the United States Government, Fiscal Year 1987* (*cf*. Note 22, p. 4-3).

25. Saunders and Klau take a more favourable view of the earlier evidence and a correspondingly more critical view of newer research in their review (*cf*. Note 1, pp. 164-167).

26. Where tax rates differ among similar activities, the economic costs are, *inter alia*, roughly proportional to the square of the differences among rates.

27. Although not discussed in the text, the "Laffer curve" [see for example, Canto, V., Joines, D. and Laffer, A., "Tax Rates, Factor Employment and Market Production" in Meyer, L. (ed.), *The Supply-Side Effects of Economic Policy*, Proceedings of the 1980 Economic Policy Conference, Federal Reserve Bank of St. Louis, Missouri, May 1981, pp. 3-32] has been the subject of great popular attention in recent years. The curve shows the relationship of tax revenues to tax rates: increasing tax rates lead first to increasing revenues, then to decreasing revenues. There is therefore a tax rate that maximises revenue, and any higher rate is self-defeating. Although much more has been said about such a curve than is known, most economists would not dispute its existence, and its theoretical lineage can be traced at least to Adam Smith (writing in English in 1776, *An Inquiry into the Nature and Causes of the Wealth of Nations*, University of Chicago Press, 1976) and independently to Jules Dupuit [writing in French in 1844, "On the Measurement of the Utility of Public Works" in Arrow, K. and Scitovsky, T. (eds.), *Readings in Welfare Economics*, Richard D. Irwin Inc., Homewood, Illinois, 1969, pp. 281-282]. In practice, such a relationship between tax rates and revenues would depend upon all aspects of the economy, as well as on the relationship of average to marginal tax rates. In this regard, Ballard, C., Fullerton, D., Shoven, J. and Whalley, J., in *A General Equilibrium Model for Tax Policy Evaluation*, University of Chicago Press and NBER, 1985, pp. 188-202, have used their general equilibrium model to produce estimates of Laffer curves for the United States with different assumptions about the responsiveness of labour to taxes. At the value for responsiveness they choose to use in their model (a value selected to be a representative average of a number of studies), they calculate the peak of the Laffer curve to occur at a labour tax rate of about 70 per cent. While it is unlikely that many workers in the United States face rates this high, the tax rates given in Table 6 suggest that computations for Europe may show less comforting results.

28. See for example, Layard, R., Nickell, S. and Jackman, R., *European Unemployment is Keynesian and Classical but not Structural*, comments on the paper by Klau, F., CEPS Working Document No. 13, Centre for European Policy Studies, Brussels, June 1985; Bean, C., Layard, P. and Nickell, S., "The Rise in Unemployment: A Multi-Country Study", *Economica – Unemployment Supplement*, 1986, Vol. 53, No. 210(S), and other articles in the same volume.

29. See Samuelson, P., "A New Theorem on Non-Substitution" in Hegeland, H. (ed.), *Money, Growth and Methodology and Other Essays in Economics in Honor of Johan Akerman*, W.K. Gleerup, Lund, Sweden, March 1961.

30. See Klau and Saunders (*cf*. Note 1) and Godfrey, L., *Theoretical and Empirical Aspects of the Effects of Taxation on the Supply of Labour*, OECD, Paris, 1975, for discussions.

31. Burtless, G. and Haveman, R., "Taxes, Transfers and Labor Supply: The Evolving View of United States Economists", paper prepared for the *41st Congress of the*

International Institute of Public Finance, June 1985, pp. 19-20.

32. See the discussion of results in the review essay by Hausman, J., "Taxes and Labor Supply", *art. cit.* in Table 10.4, pp. 213-263. Hansson, I. and Stuart, C., in "Labour Supply Estimation: A Cross-Country General Equilibrium Study" (mimeo), October 1986, have taken a very different approach: they estimate the responsiveness of labour supply from a cross-section of twenty-two OECD countries within the framework of a general equilibrium model. See also Hausman, J., "Income and Payroll Tax Policy and Labour Supply" in Meyer, L. (ed.), *The Supply-Side Effects of Economic Policy*, *op. cit.* in Note 27, pp. 173-202; "Labor Supply" in Aaron, H. and Pechman, J. (eds.), *How Taxes Affect Economic Activity*, The Brookings Institution, Washington D.C., 1981.

33. See Ashworth, J. and Ulph, D., "Estimating Labour Supply with Piecewise Linear Budget Constraints" in Brown, C. (ed.), *Taxation and Labour Supply*, Allen & Unwin, London, 1981, for the United Kingdom; for Sweden, Blomquist, S., "The Effect of Income Taxation on Male Labor Supply in Sweden", *Journal of Public Economics*, November 1983, Vol. 22, No. 2, pp. 169-198. In Yamada, T. and Chaloupka, F., *A Multinomial Logistic Approach to the Labor Force Behavior of Japanese Married Women*, NBER Working Paper No. 1783, December 1985, some estimates are presented showing that wives in Japan are also quite sensitive to taxation in their decision to enter the labour force. Cloutier, E., "Taxes and the Labour Supply of Married Women in Canada", *Economic Council of Canada*, Working Paper No. 305, May 1986, shows smaller responses for wives in Canada than those from recent estimates for the United States.

34. See Note 30.

35. See the review in Hausman, J., "Taxes and Labor Supply", *art. cit.* in Table 10.4, pp. 249-252.

36. The study, a survey of American business executives, was by Sanders, T., *Effects of Taxation: On Executives*, Harvard University Bureau of Business Research, Boston, 1951. Given the evolution of taxes since that date, it is likely the effects are significantly larger now.

37. Most of the studies reviewed in Hausman, J., *art. cit.* in Table 10.4, pp. 235-260, are analyses of the negative income tax experiments, but he also discusses some work on social security and retirement.

38. See King and Fullerton, *op. cit.* in Note 20, for a complete presentation of sources, methods, and variants. Daly, M., Lastman, G. and Naqib, F., in "The Role of Tax-Deductible Saving in the Transition from a Progressive Income Tax to a Progressive Consumption Tax", *Economic Council of Canada*, Discussion Paper No. 308, June 1986, have prepared estimates for Canada on a basis comparable to those in King and Fullerton. King, M., in "Tax Reform in the UK and US", *Economic Policy*, November 1985, *op. cit.* in Note 6, pp. 220-238, has presented updated results for the United States and the United Kingdom (as well as rates for Japan) in the light of recent discussions of tax reform, as have Fullerton, D. and Henderson, Y., "The Impact of Fundamental Tax Reform on the Allocation of Resources" in Feldstein, M. (ed.), *Taxation and Capital Formation*, University of Chicago Press and NBER (forthcoming), for the United States. Bradford, D. and Stuart, C., in *Issues in the Measurement and Interpretation of Effective Tax Rates*, NBER Working Paper No. 1975, July 1986, discuss some of the shortcomings of the approach.

39. See McKee, M., Visser, J. and Saunders, P., "Marginal Tax Rates on the Use of Labour and Capital in OECD Countries", *OECD Economic Studies*, Autumn 1986, *op. cit.* in Note 3, for sources and methods.

40. King and Fullerton, *op. cit.* in Note 20, refer to this as the "fixed-p" case, for "fixed pre-tax" rates of return. An alternative is to assume the market rate of interest to be fixed – their "fixed-r" case. They write, "The fixed-p calculations are a better guide to the schedule of tax rates levied on different combinations [of project, saver and financing method], and it is this distribution of marginal tax rates that determines the welfare losses resulting from the distortionary nature of the taxation of capital income" (p. 17).

41. See the evidence cited by Sandmo, A., "The Effects of Taxation on Savings and Risk Taking" in Auerbach, A. and Feldstein, M. (eds.), *Handbook of Public Economics*, *op. cit.* in Table 10.4, Chapter 5, p. 283.

42. The estimates are those of Boskin, M., "Taxation, Saving, and the Rate of Interest", *Journal of Political Economy*, April 1978, Vol. 86, No. 2, Part 2, pp. S3-S28.

43. Boskin's estimates have been contested by, *inter alia*, Howrey, P. and Hymans, S., "The Measurement and Determination of Loanable Funds Savings", *Brookings Papers on Economic Activity*, 1978, Vol. 3, pp. 655-685; Friend, I. and Hasbrouck, J., "Saving and After-Tax Rates of Return", *Review of Economics and Statistics*, November 1983, Vol. LXV, No. 4, pp. 537-543. Zietz, J., in "The Interest Elasticity of Savings: An Analysis Based on Explicit Priors", *Oxford Bulletin of Economic and Statistics*, November 1984, Vol. 46, No. 4, pp. 311-327, concludes a more sophisticated statistical analysis with the observation that a wide range of estimates are consistent with the data, so that one's conclusion will necessarily depend upon one's *a priori* belief.

44. The original application appears to be that of Summers, L., "Capital Taxation and Accumulation in a Life Cycle Growth Model", *American Economic Review*, September 1981, Vol. 71, No. 4, pp. 533-544, who presented supporting, though indirect, evidence in *Tax Policy, the Rate of Return, and Savings*, NBER Working Paper No. 995, September 1982, and in "The After-Tax Rate of Return Affects Private Savings", *American Economic Review, Papers and Proceedings*, May 1984, Vol. 74, No. 2, pp. 249-253.

45. The first study to derive empirical evidence using a life-cycle model directly from more microeconomic data appears to be that of Beach, C., Boadway, R. and Bruce, N., "Taxation and Saving", *Economic Council of Canada*, Technical Study (forthcoming).

46. Thus, "...structural tax policies leave the private sector's aggregate income unchanged, but they produce unambiguous substitution effects and, potentially, income effects for specific groups that may, on net, reinforce the substitution effects": Kotlikoff, L., "Taxation and Savings: A Neoclassical Perspective", *Journal of Economic*

Literature, December 1984, Vol. XXII, No. 4, pp. 1576-1629, especially p. 1593.

47. For most countries there is an extensive literature, usually linked to macroeconomic modelling. Two recent examples for the United States are provided by Sinai, A. and Eckstein, O., "Tax Policy and Business Fixed Investment Revisited", *Journal of Economic Behavior and Organisation*, June-September 1983, Vol. 4, Nos. 2-3, pp. 131-162; and Feldstein, M. and Jun, J., *The Effects of Tax Rules on Non-Residential Fixed Investment: Some Preliminary Evidence from the 1980s*, NBER Working Paper No. 1857, March 1985. Some authors, such as Chirinko, R. and Eisner, R., "The Effects of Tax Parameters in the Investment Equations in Macroeconomic Econometric Models" in Blume, M., Crockett, J. and Taubman, P. (eds.), *Economic Activity and Finance*, Ballinger, Cambridge, Mass., 1982, argue that the effects are small, but their results are probably explained by the difficult statistical problems attending work with national aggregates and "expected" yields. Few in the private sector would argue that after-tax returns are unimportant.

48. Gravelle, J., "The Social Cost of Non-Neutral Taxation: Estimates for Non-Residential Capital" in Hulten, C. (ed.), *Depreciation, Inflation, and the Taxation of Income from Capital*, Urban Institute, Washington D.C., 1981, pp. 239-250, reports that an annual gain of 0.1 per cent of GNP could be achieved by levelling the marginal tax rates facing investment projects in the corporate sector in the United States. However, such estimates are highly uncertain, and Jorgenson, D. and Yun, K.-Y., in "Tax Policy and Capital Allocation", *Scandinavian Journal of Economics*, 1986, Vol. 88, No. 2, pp. 355-382, show a gain several times larger using a more elaborate model. For Canada, Daly, M., Jung, J., Mercier, P. and Schweitzer, T., in "The Taxation of Capital Income in Canada: A Comparison with Sweden, the UK, the USA and West Germany", *Economic Council of Canada*, Discussion Paper No. 289, September 1985, show a potential annual gain of 2 per cent of GNP from eliminating such discrimination, even though they calculated Canada to have the smallest dispersion of marginal tax rates on investment of any of the four countries, including the United States, that they examined. Although they used a method similar to Gravelle's for calculating their estimates, their results are more in line with those of Jorgenson and Yun for the United States. They also argue that the "fixed-r" case provides a more appropriate measure of the welfare loss (*cf.* Note 43).

49. This is more a problem for portfolio investment than for direct investment, where the system of treaty-related tax credits eliminates incentives for firms to exploit tax-favoured location. However, it is likely that portfolio investment is the marginal source of funds.

50. See Hartman, D., *On the Optimal Taxation of Capital Income in the Open Economy*, NBER Working Paper No. 1550, January 1985; *The Welfare Effects of a Capital Income Tax in an Open Economy*, NBER Working Paper No. 1551, January 1985.

51. The estimate is from Table III.8 of Fukao, M. and Hanazaki, M., "Internationalisation of Financial Markets: Some Implications for Macroeconomic Policy and for the Allocation of Capital", OECD, Department of Economics and Statistics, Working Paper No. 37, 1986.

See also Boskin, M. and Gale, W., *New Results on the Effect of Tax Policy on the International Location of Investment*, NBER Working Paper No. 1862, March 1986; Summers, L., *Tax Policy and International Competitiveness*, NBER Working Paper No. 2007, August 1986; and Sinn, H.-W., "Die Bedeutung des Accelerated Cost Recovery System für den internationalen Kapitalverkehr", *Kyklos*, 1987, Vol. 37, Fasc. 4, pp. 542-576; "Why Taxes Matter: Reagan's Accelerated Cost Recovery System and the US Trade Deficit", *Economic Policy*, November 1985, *op. cit.* in Note 6, pp. 240-247.

52. For example, Fullerton, D. and Lyon, A., in *Does the Tax System Favor Investment in High Technology or Smoke-Stack Industries?*, NBER Working Paper No. 1600, April 1985, have examined whether the 1983 vintage United States tax system unduly favoured investment in either high technology or "smoke-stack industries". In this particular case they concluded that it favoured neither.

53. See for example, Anderson, F., Beaudreau, B. and Bonsor, N., "Effective Corporate Tax Rates, Inflation and Contestability", *Canadian Journal of Economics*, November 1983, Vol. XVI, No. 4, pp. 686-703, who examine the differences in the Canadian and United States tax system and their implications for "contestability" – the potential for competition – in the pulp and paper industry.

54. See for example, Summers, L., *Tax Policy and International Competitiveness*, NBER Working Paper No. 2007, August 1986.

55. See for example, Auerbach, A. and Hines, J., *Anticipated Tax Changes and the Timing of Investment*, NBER Working Paper No. 1886, April 1986; Skinner, J., *The Welfare Cost of Uncertain Tax Policy*, NBER Working Paper No. 1947, June 1986. Of course, tax-based incentives that are seen to be temporary may occasionally alter the timing of some responses in ways that appear desirable from the point of view of economic stabilization. This creates yet another temptation to change the tax system.

56. For a discussion of current tax reform issues in Member countries, see Messere, K. and Owens, J., "Long-Term Revenue Trends and Current Tax Reform Issues in OECD Countries", paper prepared for the *42nd Congress of the International Institute of Public Finance*, 1986.

57. See Feldstein, M., "Incidence of a Capital Income Tax in a Growing Economy with Variable Saving Rates", *Review of Economic Studies*, 1974, Vol. XLI, No. 2, pp. 505-513. A broad survey of tax incidence is provided by Kotlikoff, L. and Summers, L., "Tax Incidence", in Auerbach, A. and Feldstein, M. (eds.), *Handbook of Public Economics*, Vol. 2, North Holland, Amsterdam (forthcoming).

58. A similar confusion of institutional arrangements with equity and efficiency may occur in the sharing of social security contributions between employers and employees. This sharing is often seen as an important aspect of fairness even though it is likely the distinction has no consequence whatsoever for the ultimate economic impact of the tax, including who pays the tax. It does make a difference during a transition period after the tax is changed.

59. See Gravelle, J., *Assessing Structural Tax Reforms with Macroeconomic Models: The Treasury Tax Proposals and the Allocation of Investment*, United States Congressional Budget Office, 8th April 1985; and *Effects of Business Tax Provisions in the Administration's Tax Proposal: Updated Tables*, United States Congressional Budget Office, 6th June 1985; Fullerton and Henderson, *op. cit.* in Note 38. This last contains estimates of the total marginal tax rate on investment projects by type and industry for 1985 law and for the two Administration proposals that led to the reform, a topic discussed later in this chapter.

60. Though payroll and consumption taxes ultimately have the same long-run effect, there is an extended transition period in which younger people gain at the expense of older generations during a shift towards consumption-based taxation, a point discussed later in the text. As a consequence, saving, investment, and national income may be larger under a consumption tax than under a payroll tax, and rates under the former may be lower.

61. A recent discussion is contained in Boadway, R. and Bruce, N., "A General Proposition on the Design of a Neutral Business Tax", *Journal of Public Economics*, July 1984, Vol. 24, No. 2, pp. 231-239.

62. See Whalley, J., "A General Equilibrium Assesment of the 1973 UK Tax Reform", *Economica*, May 1975, Vol. 42, No. 166, pp. 139-161. General equilibrium models are discussed in the Introduction of the present report.

63. See Borges, A., "Tax Reform in Portugal: A General Equilibrium Analysis of the Introduction of a Value Added Tax", paper presented at the *Second IIASA Task Force Meeting on Applied General Equilibrium Modelling*, June 1984. Hamilton, R. and Whalley, J., in "General Equilibrium Analysis of Taxation in a Small Open Economy: Canadian Sales Taxes" (mimeo), May 1986, analyse a similar set of issues for Canada, examining replacement of existing sales taxes with a comprehensive, uniform sales tax.

64. See the extensive review contained in the papers in Aaron, H. (ed.), *The Value-Added Tax: Lessons from Europe*, The Brookings Institution, Washington D.C., 1981.

65. See Ballard and Shoven, *op. cit.* in Note 18.

66. See for example, Sandmo, A., *art. cit.* in Note 41, p. 272.

67. See Ballard, Fullerton, Shoven, and Whalley, *op. cit.* in Note 27, Chapter 9. This is a revised version of Fullerton, D., Shoven, J. and Whalley, J., "Replacing the United States Income Tax with a Progressive Consumption Tax; A Sequenced General Equilibrium Approach", *Journal of Public Economics*, February 1983, Vol. 20, No. 1, pp. 3-23.

68. Ballard *et al.*, *op. cit.* in Note 27, show gains to be roughly twice as large when they adopt estimates of the saving elasticity commensurate with those proposed by Summers, *art. cit.* in Note 44, using the life-cycle model discussed earlier. See also Auerbach, A. and Kotlikoff, L., "National Savings, Economic Welfare and the Structure of Taxation" in *Behavioral Simulation Methods in Tax Policy Analysis*, University of Chicago Press, 1983; and "The Efficiency Gains from Dynamic Tax Reform", *International Economic Review*, February 1983, Vol. 24, No. 1, pp. 81-100, for explicit, though more hypothetical, computations using a life-cycle model.

69. Ballard *et al.*, *op. cit.* in Note 27, Chapter 11 – a revision of Goulder, L., Shoven, J. and Whalley, J., "Domestic Tax Policy and the Foreign Sector: The Importance of Alternative Foreign Sector Formulations to Results from a General Equilibrium Tax Analysis Model" in Feldstein, M. (ed.), *Behavioral Simulation Methods in Tax Policy Analysis*, University of Chicago Press and NBER, 1983.

70. The Council of Economic Advisers attempted an overall estimate of the "plausible outcomes" of the "President's proposal" in its White Paper of 24th September 1984. The "bottom line" was a "plausible" gain of 2.5 to 3.2 per cent of GNP. However, the estimate is not derived within a systematic framework. See United States Government, *Council of Economic Advisers*, "The Economic Case for Tax Reform" (mimeo), September 1985.

71. According to Fullerton, current Deputy Assistant Secretary for Tax Analysis, the Treasury's chief tax economist. The estimates are from Fullerton and Henderson, *art. cit.* in Note 38.

72. The results are derived using the model in Ballard *et al.*, *op. cit.* in Note 27, but with improvements in the way investment decisions are modelled.

73. See Ballard, C., Shoven, J. and Whalley, J., "General Equilibrium Computations of the Marginal Welfare Costs of Taxes in the United States", *American Economic Review*, March 1985, *op. cit.* in Note 13, pp. 128-138.

74. See Ballard, C., Shoven, J. and Whalley, J., "The Total Welfare Cost of the United States Tax System: A General Equilibrium Approach", *National Tax Journal*, June 1985, Vol. 38, No. 2, pp. 125-140.

75. See Stuart, C., "Welfare Costs per Dollar of Additional Tax Revenue in the United States", *American Economic Review*, June 1984, Vol. 74, No. 3, pp. 352-362.

76. See Hansson, I. and Stuart, C., "Tax Revenue and the Marginal Cost of Public Funds in Sweden", *Journal of Public Economics*, August 1985, Vol. 27, No. 3, pp. 331-353; Hansson, I., "Marginal Cost of Public Funds for Different Tax Instruments and Government Expenditures", *Scandinavian Journal of Economics*, 1984, Vol. 86, No. 2, pp. 115-130.

77. This evaporation of the tax base suggests to Hansson that Sweden is near the peak of the Laffer curve for some taxes (*cf.* Note 27).

Additional references consulted:

Browning, E., "The Marginal Cost of Public Funds", *Journal of Political Economy*, 1976, Volume 84, Number 2, pp. 283-298.

OECD, *Revenue Statistics of OECD Member Countries 1965-1985*, Paris, 1986.

WHERE TO OBTAIN OECD PUBLICATIONS
OÙ OBTENIR LES PUBLICATIONS DE L'OCDE

ARGENTINA - ARGENTINE
Carlos Hirsch S.R.L.,
Florida 165, 4° Piso,
(Galeria Guemes) 1333 Buenos Aires
Tel. 33.1787.2391 y 30.7122

AUSTRALIA - AUSTRALIE
D.A. Book (Aust.) Pty. Ltd.
11-13 Station Street (P.O. Box 163)
Mitcham, Vic. 3132   Tel. (03) 873 4411

AUSTRIA - AUTRICHE
OECD Publications and Information Centre,
4 Simrockstrasse,
5300 Bonn (Germany)   Tel. (0228) 21.60.45
Gerold & Co., Graben 31, Wien 1 Tel. 52.22.35

BELGIUM - BELGIQUE
Jean de Lannoy,
avenue du Roi 202
B-1060 Bruxelles   Tel. (02) 538.51.69

CANADA
Renouf Publishing Company Ltd/
Éditions Renouf Ltée,
1294 Algoma Road, Ottawa, Ont. K1B 3W8
Tel: (613) 741-4333
Toll Free/Sans Frais:
Ontario, Quebec, Maritimes:
1-800-267-1805
Western Canada, Newfoundland:
1-800-267-1826
Stores/Magasins:
61 rue Sparks St., Ottawa, Ont. K1P 5A6
Tel: (613) 238-8985
211 rue Yonge St., Toronto, Ont. M5B 1M4
Tel: (416) 363-3171

DENMARK - DANEMARK
Munksgaard Export and Subscription Service
35, Nørre Søgade, DK-1370 København K
Tel. +45.1.12.85.70

FINLAND - FINLANDE
Akateeminen Kirjakauppa,
Keskuskatu 1, 00100 Helsinki 10   Tel. 0.12141

FRANCE
OCDE/OECD
Mail Orders/Commandes par correspondance :
2, rue André-Pascal,
75775 Paris Cedex 16
Tel. (1) 45.24.82.00
Bookshop/Librairie : 33, rue Octave-Feuillet
75016 Paris
Tel. (1) 45.24.81.67 or/ou (1) 45.24.81.81
Librairie de l'Université,
12a, rue Nazareth,
13602 Aix-en-Provence   Tel. 42.26.18.08

GERMANY - ALLEMAGNE
OECD Publications and Information Centre,
4 Simrockstrasse,
5300 Bonn   Tel. (0228) 21.60.45

GREECE - GRÈCE
Librairie Kauffmann,
28, rue du Stade, 105 64 Athens Tel. 322.21.60

HONG KONG
Government Information Services,
Publications (Sales) Office,
Information Services Department
No. 1, Battery Path, Central

ICELAND - ISLANDE
Snæbjörn Jónsson & Co., h.f.,
Hafnarstræti 4 & 9,
P.O.B. 1131 – Reykjavik
Tel. 13133/14281/11936

INDIA - INDE
Oxford Book and Stationery Co.,
Scindia House, New Delhi 1 Tel. 331.5896/5308
17 Park St., Calcutta 700016   Tel. 240832

INDONESIA - INDONÉSIE
Pdii-Lipi, P.O. Box 3065/JKT.Jakarta
Tel. 583467

IRELAND - IRLANDE
TDC Publishers - Library Suppliers,
12 North Frederick Street, Dublin 1
Tel. 744835-749677

ITALY - ITALIE
Libreria Commissionaria Sansoni,
Via Lamarmora 45, 50121 Firenze
Tel. 579751/584468
Via Bartolini 29, 20155 Milano   Tel. 365083
Editrice e Libreria Herder,
Piazza Montecitorio 120, 00186 Roma
Tel. 6794628
Libreria Hœpli,
Via Hœpli 5, 20121 Milano   Tel. 865446
Libreria Scientifica
Dott. Lucio de Biasio "Aeiou"
Via Meravigli 16, 20123 Milano   Tel. 807679
Libreria Lattes,
Via Garibaldi 3, 10122 Torino   Tel. 519274
La diffusione delle edizioni OCSE è inoltre
assicurata dalle migliori librerie nelle città più
importanti.

JAPAN - JAPON
OECD Publications and Information Centre,
Landic Akasaka Bldg., 2-3-4 Akasaka,
Minato-ku, Tokyo 107   Tel. 586.2016

KOREA - CORÉE
Kyobo Book Centre Co. Ltd.
P.O.Box: Kwang Hwa Moon 1658,
Seoul   Tel. (REP) 730.78.91

LEBANON - LIBAN
Documenta Scientifica/Redico,
Edison Building, Bliss St.,
P.O.B. 5641, Beirut   Tel. 354429-344425

MALAYSIA - MALAISIE
University of Malaya Co-operative Bookshop
Ltd.,
P.O.Box 1127, Jalan Pantai Baru,
Kuala Lumpur   Tel. 577701/577072

NETHERLANDS - PAYS-BAS
Staatsuitgeverij
Chr. Plantijnstraat, 2 Postbus 20014
2500 EA S-Gravenhage   Tel. 070-789911
Voor bestellingen: Tel. 070-789880

NEW ZEALAND - NOUVELLE-ZÉLANDE
Government Printing Office Bookshops:
Auckland: Retail Bookshop, 25 Rutland Stseet,
Mail Orders, 85 Beach Road
Private Bag C.P.O.
Hamilton: Retail: Ward Street,
Mail Orders, P.O. Box 857
Wellington: Retail, Mulgrave Street, (Head
Office)
Cubacade World Trade Centre,
Mail Orders, Private Bag
Christchurch: Retail, 159 Hereford Street,
Mail Orders, Private Bag
Dunedin: Retail, Princes Street,
Mail Orders, P.O. Box 1104

NORWAY - NORVÈGE
Tanum-Karl Johan
Karl Johans gate 43, Oslo 1
PB 1177 Sentrum, 0107 Oslo 1 Tel. (02) 42.93.10

PAKISTAN
Mirza Book Agency
65 Shahrah Quaid-E-Azam, Lahore 3 Tel. 66839

PORTUGAL
Livraria Portugal,
Rua do Carmo 70-74, 1117 Lisboa Codex
Tel. 360582/3

SINGAPORE - SINGAPOUR
Information Publications Pte Ltd
Pei-Fu Industrial Building,
24 New Industrial Road No. 02-06
Singapore 1953   Tel. 2831786, 2831798

SPAIN - ESPAGNE
Mundi-Prensa Libros, S.A.,
Castelló 37, Apartado 1223, Madrid-28001
Tel. 431.33.99
Libreria Bosch, Ronda Universidad 11,
Barcelona 7   Tel. 317.53.08/317.53.58

SWEDEN - SUÈDE
AB CE Fritzes Kungl. Hovbokhandel,
Box 16356, S 103 27 STH,
Regeringsgatan 12,
DS Stockholm   Tel. (08) 23.89.00
Subscription Agency/Abonnements:
Wennergren-Williams AB,
Box 30004, S104 25 Stockholm Tel. (08)54.12.00

SWITZERLAND - SUISSE
OECD Publications and Information Centre,
4 Simrockstrasse,
5300 Bonn (Germany)   Tel. (0228) 21.60.45
Librairie Payot,
6 rue Grenus, 1211 Genève 11
Tel. (022) 31.89.50

United Nations Bookshop/
Librairie des Nations-Unies
Palais des Nations,
1211 – Geneva 10
Tel. 022-34-60-11 (ext. 48 72)

TAIWAN - FORMOSE
Good Faith Worldwide Int'l Co., Ltd.
9th floor, No. 118, Sec.2
Chung Hsiao E. Road
Taipei   Tel. 391.7396/391.7397

THAILAND - THAILANDE
Suksit Siam Co., Ltd.,
1715 Rama IV Rd.,
Samyam Bangkok 5   Tel. 2511630

TURKEY - TURQUIE
Kültur Yayinlari Is-Türk Ltd. Sti.
Atatürk Bulvari No: 191/Kat. 21
Kavaklidere/Ankara   Tel. 25.07.60
Dolmabahce Cad. No: 29
Besiktas/Istanbul   Tel. 160.71.88

UNITED KINGDOM - ROYAUME-UNI
H.M. Stationery Office,
Postal orders only: (01)211-5656
P.O.B. 276, London SW8 5DT
Telephone orders: (01) 622.3316, or
Personal callers:
49 High Holborn, London WC1V 6HB
Branches at: Belfast, Birmingham,
Bristol, Edinburgh, Manchester

UNITED STATES - ÉTATS-UNIS
OECD Publications and Information Centre,
2001 L Street, N.W., Suite 700,
Washington, D.C. 20036 - 4095
Tel. (202) 785.6323

VENEZUELA
Libreria del Este,
Avda F. Miranda 52, Aptdo. 60337,
Edificio Galipan, Caracas 106
Tel. 32.23.01/33.26.04/31.58.38

YUGOSLAVIA - YOUGOSLAVIE
Jugoslovenska Knjiga, Knez Mihajlova 2,
P.O.B. 36, Beograd   Tel. 621.992

Orders and inquiries from countries where
Distributors have not yet been appointed should be
sent to:
OECD, Publications Service, Sales and
Distribution Division, 2, rue André-Pascal, 75775
PARIS CEDEX 16.

Les commandes provenant de pays où l'OCDE n'a
pas encore désigné de distributeur peuvent être
adressées à :
OCDE, Service des Publications. Division des
Ventes et Distribution. 2. rue André-Pascal. 75775
PARIS CEDEX 16.

71055-09-1987

Réseau de bibliothèques Université d'Ottawa Échéance	Library Network University of Ottawa Date Due